THE MARKET FOR LABOR: AN ANALYTICAL TREATMENT

JOHN T. ADDISON
W. STANLEY SIEBERT

Goodyear Publishing Company, Inc. Santa Monica, California

Library of Congress Cataloging in Publication Data

ADDISON, JOHN T
   The market for labor.

   Includes index.
   1. Labor economics. I. Siebert, Stanley, joint
author. II. Title.
HD4901.A35   331.1'2   78-10976
ISBN 0-87620-558-9

Y-5589-0

Current printing (last digit):
10 9 8 7 6 5 4 3 2 1

Production Editor: Linda G. Schreiber
Copy Editor: Al Tommervik
Cover and Text Design: Don McQuiston
Cover photo: IPA/JEREBOAM, INC.

Printed in the United States of America

To our parents and Aleta

CONTENTS

PREFACE

Existing labor economics textbooks are either short on analysis and long on description, or too eclectic. This has been made more apparent by the rapid advance of research findings in the field. In this book, we have sought to remedy these weaknesses by outlining and synthesizing the main theories in each subject area. The results of empirical studies are then used systematically to discriminate among the alternative theories. This more analytical approach provides a firmer basis for policy prescription. Between us, we hope to have covered most of the subject areas, with JTA writing the first drafts of chapters 2, 3, 5, 10, 11, 12, and 13, and WSS the rest.

We extend our thanks to all those who assisted in the preparation of this book. We owe a special debt of gratitude to our reviewers, Michael L. Wachter, Mark R. Killingsworth, and Charles R. Link, who made many helpful comments and suggestions for improving the initial draft. Insightful comments on specific chapters were also received from John Burton, Ray Richardson, Ron Shone, Peter Sloane, and John Vandercamp. None of the above is responsible for any of our subsequent errors and omissions. We are also grateful to our teachers, Sir Henry Phelps Brown, Rodney Crossley, and Sheila van der Horst, and to students on both sides of the Atlantic for stimulating us to write this book in the first place. Finally, we record our sincere thanks to Eleanor Bruce, Freda Rennie, Kathy Mayo, Aileen Fraser, and Margaret McRobb for typing the various drafts of the manuscript.

JOHN T. ADDISON
W. STANLEY SIEBERT

CHAPTER 1
INTRODUCTION

A little over two decades ago, Paul Samuelson suggested that economists horrified by the mathematical and formal directions that much of modern economics was taking might "sublimate their feelings" and "transfer from economic theory" into a safe haven such as labor economics.[1] These words accurately describe the then Cinderella status of labor economics among the various subject areas of economics. As Fisher puts it, "Economic analysis tended to pass it by, either because it seemed to present no demanding intellectual problems or because it was judged to be an area where institutional factors played too dominant a role."[2]

The times, as they say, are changing. Labor economics is beginning to stand on its feet. It is becoming clear that labor economics is an integrated part of the economic system, and its analysts are finding that they are well able to contribute from their specific labor market studies to the general pool of economic ideas. However, the analytical advance in labor economics in the last few years has been so rapid that there has not been time to consolidate, to take a long, dispassionate look at the different elements, and to establish how they all fit together. The present text marks a tentative step in this direction.

1.1 The Economist's Study of Labor

The tools of his trade that an economist applies to labor are in essence the same as those he would bring to any other subject in the field. They consist of micro- and macro-economic theory and a stock of information about institutions and magnitudes. Theory gives the economist a framework within which to arrange his observations and direct his inquiries; it suggests where causes and consequences are to be looked for, and it traces the network of interdependence.

1. P. A. Samuelson, "Some Psychological Aspects of Mathematics and Economics," *Review of Economics and Statistics,* 36 (1954): 380.
2. M. R. Fisher, *The Economic Analysis of Labour* (London: Weidenfeld and Nicolson, 1971), p. ix.

The central core of thought in labor economics, as expressed in the standard texts, can be summarized as follows. The demand for labor is derived from the product, and there is a downward sloping demand curve for labor at the level of the firm, reflecting diminishing returns; this is the marginal productivity theory. Labor demands by firms, when summed, yield total labor demand functions by occupation. Although the individual firm can exercise no significant effect on price in a competitive environment, firms in the aggregate can do so. Accordingly, the aggregate demand curve is supposed to be steeper, with lower product prices associated with lower wage rates. In response to a drop (rise) in factor price, there will be a substitution effect against (toward) other factors and a scale effect through increased (decreased) profit and decreased (increased) cost at a given output. In the normal course of events, both factors work in the same direction to increase (reduce) employment at the level of the firm and the industry.

The supply of labor is comprised of the population and its capacities, together with the hours of effort and intensity of effort provided by that population. The supply of hours offered by the individual is made to depend on the wage adjusted for changes in commodity prices. Movements in this real wage determine the employee's choice between work effort and leisure through two main effects—the substitution and the income effect. It is often maintained that individuals are at best suited for a limited number of occupations, because of either natural or contrived barriers to mobility over a wider range. But it must be recognized that research into the principles governing the distribution of total labor supply is cursory. Formally, the supply functions depicting hours of effort by individuals, when aggregated, yield the backward bending supply curve as a *probable* shape, because of the dominance of income over substitution effects.

Demand and supply are then combined to indicate the equilibrium wage and level of employment, occupation by occupation. In view of the limited opportunity for transference of individual effort between occupations, the more immediate adjustments to facilitate equilibrium mainly proceed through demand, that is, price. The principle of equal net advantage is applied to the choice of occupations by individuals, although emphasis is often placed upon the natural and contrived barriers to mobility arising, respectively, from wide dispersions in natural abilities and unequal access to education.

This basically competitive model has come under attack for a number of reasons. It is argued that wages do not exhibit in practice the degree of flexibility implied by the theory because of imperfections in regular markets. The normal assumptions of imperfect competition theory are invoked to explain the demand for labor. Supply considerations are reformulated in such a way as to draw all potential workers through union organizations, to which are attributed collective goals acceptable to the membership at large. There traditionally follows a consideration of maximizing models of trade union behavior, including elements of downward wage rigidity at the preexisting wage-employment equilibrium. An offshoot—albeit a separate development—of this approach has been the consideration of theories of bargaining.

At this point, it is usual to switch from micro- to macro-economic topics and deal with unemployment and the general level of money wages. Both of these topics can be related with varying degrees of plausibility to the microeconomic foundations discussed above. A natural extension of the point that factors having little impact at the level of the plant can have a sizeable aggregate effect has been used by Keynesian economists to show the weakness of money wage cuts—even if these were practicable—as a cure for unemployment. Whereas wage cuts extend employment along a given demand curve for a firm, economywide cuts, so the argument runs, will merely serve to reduce purchasing power and diminish demand for commodities. The result is a downward shift in the demand curves for both products and factors. Most texts present this Keynesian view either to stress the unpredictable effects of wage cuts on aggregate employment levels or simply to contrast it with the previously held view that wage cuts would propel the economy toward a full employment position. Not analytically far removed from this question is the examination of relative pressures on wages and prices under full employment. If aggregate demand cannot readily be adjusted to ensure full employment conditions, this may lead to demand inflation.

If this is indeed the central core of thought in labor economics, it might justifiably be claimed that the process of consolidation has not progressed far. Most labor economic analysis falls short of a full general equilibrium approach. Yet it is true that the relevant markets considered are often large enough to have important repercussive effects on other prices and quantities, requiring a general equilibrium treatment. Nevertheless, although Hicks has shown how such repercussions can be handled theoretically, his analysis does more to confirm the existence of an equilibrium than to construct a recognizable model of the interrelationships between labor markets.[3] There are formidable difficulties in moving from "existential" to "constructivist" uses of general equilibrium theory.

A more telling criticism of this central core is that most labor texts contain very little that can be identified as *labor economics,* if by that term is meant something more than applied economics in the ordinary sense, which builds upon a neoclassical framework and makes no greater departure from it into such fields as monopoly or institutional behavior than are usually recognized as being necessary in any field of applied economics. As we see it, the need is to develop a labor component within the general framework of neoclassical theory, because the latter remains the best available vehicle for the synthesis of economic thought as a whole. Therefore, while retaining the central core as a descriptive theme, we shall seek to stress the areas within which labor

3. J. R. Hicks, *The Theory of Wages,* 2nd ed. (London: Macmillan, 1963), pp. 323–327.

economics can make, and indeed has made, its greatest impact on the general body of economic thought. Three major developments will be identified.

First, there is the recognition that labor supply is the outcome of household decision making and must consequently be treated integrally with consumption behavior.[4] The work done thus far in this field constitutes little more than a beginning, but already such phenomena as job preferences among workers, and discrimination by employers on what are formally consumption grounds, can now be brought within the ambit of neoclassical theory.

As a second major development, we would point to Becker's theory of investment in human capital. His theory has shown how net or observed pay levels may include elements of current and past outlays on human capital formation in some phases of the life cycle,[5] as compared with the gross pay that would be observed in a simple neoclassical model in which no such investments took place. This analysis has also shed further light on the behavior of human beings (and unions) as economic agents by recognizing that property rights in human capital are vested in them.

A third development in neoclassical theory has introduced uncertainty. What Phelps and others have done in the "new microeconomics" is to demonstrate that the accumulation of knowledge about job opportunities and job offers, and the prices attached to them, takes time and the expenditure of other resources. Consequently, the short run of Marshallian analysis is replaced by a period of search and adjustment toward the long-run equilibrium, which remains essentially intact when full knowledge is achieved.[6] Marshall envisioned most of the short-run adjustments falling on the side of prices rather than quantities, because of an assumed inelasticity of short-run labor supply functions. But the substitution of a search and adjustment process suggests that the time sequencing of price and quantity adjustments may be reversed. Short-period adjustments may take a quantity form if, for example, an employee elects to refuse a relative wage cut in his present job if there is a fall in demand, because he believes he can make a net gain by leaving voluntarily to search for another job at approximately the old wage. Similarly, the employer who has excess demand may choose to use resources to extend his search activity, instead of raising his wage relatively.

Finally, let us turn to the question of the respective roles of market forces versus institutionalist forces in market operation—a question that is a continuing source of controversy in labor economics. Institutionalism in labor economics has come to mean an almost exclusively descriptive approach, often reflecting the personal judgment that labor market facts are interesting in themselves. Sometimes included in the term is the antitheoretical view that

4. G. S. Becker, "A Theory of the Allocation of Time," *Economic Journal* 75 (1965): 493–517.
5. G. S. Becker, *Human Capital,* 2nd ed. (New York: National Bureau of Economic Research, 1975).
6. E. S. Phelps et al., *Microeconomic Foundations of Employment and Inflation Theory* (New York: Norton, 1970).

the facts also speak for themselves. As a practical example, institutionalists assert that wages are not determined by supply and demand; rather, contemporary wage determination can only be understood as the product of social, political, and institutional forces. Institutionalists thus reject abstract general theories and advocate an inductive and interdisciplinary approach to research. Their arguments constituted a serious challenge to the predominance of neoclassical theory in labor economics in the 1940s and 1950s. No less a figure than Hicks was led to concede, with respect to a particular challenge,[7] that, even before the publication date of his own earlier and seminal contribution to the orthodox analysis of wage determination,[8] wages had not been determined by supply and demand but rather "by an interplay between social and economic factors—and crude economic factors at that—alone."[9]

However, despite the prominence of institutionalism in the early postwar economics literature and despite the continued prominence of institutionalist views in many discussions of the contemporary inflation problem, institutionalism has failed to dislodge neoclassical economics as the dominant scientific paradigm in labor economics. The neoclassical retaliation to the institutionalist critique—in the form of human capital theory, labor market search theory, and the new microeconomics—has been developed. These theories have outflanked the institutionalist position by providing neoclassical explanations for many of the empirical phenomena upon which the institutionalist denigration of the explanatory power of orthodox economics has rested.

Nevertheless, the institutionalist analysis of wage determination constitutes a significant research tradition in its own right—one, moreover, that has had a particularly strong impact in political and policymaking circles. Accordingly, the concluding chapter of this book is reserved for a review of the institutionalist literature on wage inflation. Though we are highly critical of these works, the best of the institutionalist literature has yielded powerful insights into the working of labor markets.[10] The fact is that it is useless to deny a role to institutions. The problem with the institutionalist camp is that it has persisted in the notion that institutions in labor economics are somehow "given" from outside the realm of economics. Many labor economists of this persuasion have been curiously reluctant to believe that the genesis of labor market institutions may lie at least partly in economics. The task is, then, to look for a broader framework—a structure that lies behind actual

7. B. Wootton, *The Social Foundations of Wage Policy* (London: Unwin, 1955).

8. J. R. Hicks, *The Theory of Wages* (London: Macmillan, 1932).

9. J. R. Hicks, "The Economic Foundations of Wage Policy," *Economic Journal* 65 (1955): 389–404.

10. See, for example, C. Kerr, "The Balkanisation of Labor Markets," in E. W. Bakke, et al., *Labor Mobility and Economic Opportunity* (Cambridge, Mass.: Technology Press of M.I.T., 1954), pp. 92–110; idem, "Labor Markets: Their Character and Consequences," *American Economic Review*, Papers and Proceedings 40 (1950): 278–291.

market forces—that provides explanations of why the latter take the form they do.

In this context, mention should be made of the so-called new-new micro-economics of idiosyncratic exchange, implicit contracts, and layoffs. Two strains of development can be identified within this literature. The first relies on costly information and worker-job heterogeneity and uses relatively informal analytical tools.[11] The second is an altogether more formal approach. It attempts to rationalize such phenomena as wage rigidity and layoffs without assuming heterogeneity or information costs.[12] Elements of the former approach are discussed in the text, but we have not attempted to introduce the unique uncertainty analysis of the latter. Suffice it to say that, apart from its contribution to unemployment and inflation theory, the introduction of uncertainty per se opens up fascinating possibilities for the theory of the institutions of collective agreements and collective bargaining. These are only now beginning to be explored.

Given the technical progress that has occurred within labor economics, the book combines theory with a larger volume of measurement than is conventional in a text of this nature. Accordingly, the balance of this introductory chapter is devoted to outlining the use of statistics in economics.

1.2   The Use of Econometrics

The distinctive feature of modern social science can be said to be its use of empirical data—summarized by various statistics, such as means, standard deviations, and regression coefficients—to test hypotheses. This is not to say that empirical research is a panacea. There is, unfortunately, much room for individual preference or "art" in econometric analysis in deciding on the empirical counterparts of theoretical variables or in the choice of assumptions (which are not tested) when constructing the hypotheses that are to be scrutinized. Economics is therefore best regarded as a *technique* for analyzing social problems rather than as a science in its own right. Nevertheless, in the employment of this technique, it is always more helpful to present the economic argument in such a way that it can be checked against the available facts. This mode of operation is required even though the principle that there are various ways of selecting and arranging the facts means that we cannot approach the scientific ideal of having empirical results which are completely independent of the investigator and his model.

In this book the relation between theory and empirical findings is emphasized. Moreover, rather than simply presenting a verbal report of the findings, we have in many cases elected to provide the actual numbers

11. See O. E. Williamson, M. L. Wachter, and J. E. Harris, "Understanding the Employment Relation: The Analysis of Idiosyncratic Exchange," *Bell Journal of Economics* 6 (1975): 250–278.
12. See C. Azariadis, "Implicit Contracts and Underemployment Equilibria," *Journal of Political Economy* 83 (1975): 1183–1202; M. N. Baily, "Wages and Employment Under Uncertain Demand," *Review of Economic Studies* 41 (1974): 37–50; D. F. Gordon, "A Neo-Classical Theory of Keynesian Unemployment," *Economic Inquiry* 12 (1974): 431–459.

themselves. For this reason, an acquaintance with the methods of computation and interpretation of statistics commonly used in economics is required. Most readers of this book will have some such acquaintance, although many may have been intimidated by statistical analysis. The purpose of the following paragraphs is to provide a short guide and not rigorously to derive results. Other texts fulfill the latter purpose, and reference will be made to this material where appropriate. We seek to jog the reader's memory and to provide a *structure* on which he or she may hang the various statistical findings.

The discussion is divided into three subsections. The first considers such statistical notions as the normal distribution and its relation to hypothesis testing; the second focuses on problems associated specifically with *regression analysis*. The third subsection considers the issues raised by *systems* of regression equations. The chapter concludes with an appendix that presents a variety of helpful mathematical and statistical results and manipulations.

Hypothesis Testing.   In this book, as in economics generally, the main statistical concepts revolve around the testing of statistical hypotheses— particularly in the context of regression analysis. Before turning to hypothesis testing in general, however, we would stress the importance of using practical working examples as an aid to theoretical understanding.[13] As the tools are used, confidence and the capacity to appreciate the finer points of statistical theory will develop.

In general, economists have to work with data drawn from random samples, that is, where each member of the population has the same chance of inclusion in the sample, and seek to make decisions about the corresponding population on the basis of such data. For example, a sample survey of workers in a particular city might record that vacancies to which men are appointed remain unfilled for a longer period on average than do vacancies to which women are appointed. Such sample data might reveal a vacancy period of 2.7 weeks for men and 2.1 weeks for women. We wish to know whether the vacancy period in the city working population is indeed longer for men than women or whether the difference can be attributed more reliably to chance sampling variation. It is natural—and statistically correct in certain circumstances—to use the sample difference as an estimate of the population difference. It can be seen intuitively that the probability of error in rejecting the *null hypothesis* (that there is no difference in population means) would be smaller as the difference in sample means increases, other things being equal. This problem of incorrectly rejecting the null hypothesis

---

13. A book containing hundreds of worked examples is M. R. Spiegel, *Theory and Problems of Statistics* (New York: Schaum Publishing Company, 1961). If possible, readers should also consult E. S. Pearson and H. O. Hartley, *Biometrika Tables for Statisticians,* 3rd ed. (Cambridge: The University Press, 1970), vol. 1, ibid., 1st ed. (1972), vol. 2. This latter reference tends only to be available in libraries, but has the outstanding virtue that it is very easy to read in its practical sections and gives many worked examples of how to use statistical tables.

is sometimes called the probability of *Type I error*. It is to be distinguished from the probability of incorrectly accepting the null hypothesis, which is known as the probability of *Type II error*.[14]

The probability of Type I error is also lower as the variation among observations in each sample decreases and as the number of observations in each sample increases. In fact, these are the only additional factors we need consider. In seeking to measure sample variability, it is usual to compute the standard deviation, *s*, of observations within each sample.[15] Intuitively, we would expect the probability of Type I error to be lower as *s* for each sample decreases, *ceteris paribus*. This is because it is natural to use the sample *s* to estimate variability within each population. Consequently, a tight clustering of observations within each sample (low *s*) implies a similarly tight clustering in the two populations—in this example, a more precise demarcation between male and female distributions and a smaller degree of overlap.

Turning to the question of the size of the samples, it is to be expected that as the sample size increases, the probability of Type I error decreases, *ceteris paribus*. This statement is most readily appreciated if we consider the case where each sample is so large that it encompasses the entire population. Here, by definition, the difference in sample means equals the difference in population means; so the probability of Type I error must be zero. By an extension of this reasoning, it can be argued that the probability of Type I error will increase as we reduce the size of the sample. However, it should be noted that the important factor is simply the number of sample points and not, as the above demonstration might suggest, the number of sample points as a proportion of the population.

Statistical theory gives us precise formulae corresponding to the above intuitive perceptions. The basic proposition is as follows: If a population is normally distributed with mean μ and standard deviation σ, then an observation randomly drawn from that population will be contained within 1.96 standard deviations either side of μ ninety-five times out of one hundred on average, namely with a 95% probability. It can be shown that the distribution of many sample statistics, such as means, difference in means, or proportions, is normal so long as reasonably large samples are taken. (In effect N must exceed 30—smaller samples are dealt with by a slight modification of procedure, as will be shown.) The mean and standard deviation of these sampling distributions have been calculated. For example, denote the pop-

---

14. Although Type II error does not figure in this text, it is important to avoid confusing it with Type I error. The two *c*s in accepting can be used as a reminder of the II in "Type II," while the *j* in rejection can be used as a reminder of the I in "Type I."

15. The standard deviation, *s*, is defined as

$$s = \sqrt{\frac{1}{N} \sum_{j=1}^{N} (x_j - \bar{x})^2}$$

where N is the size of the sample and $\bar{x}$ is the sample mean. It is simply computed as

$s^2 = \sum_j \dfrac{x_j^2}{N} - \bar{x}^2$ (see appendix 1-A).

ulation mean and standard deviation by μ and σ, respectively; if many samples of size N are drawn, the mean, $\mu_{\bar{x}}$, of this distribution of sample means can be shown to equal μ. Thus,

$$\mu_{\bar{x}} = \mu$$

with a standard deviation, $\sigma_{\bar{x}}$, related to the population σ as follows

$$\sigma_{\bar{x}} = \sigma/\sqrt{N}.$$

It is possible to estimate μ and σ using the mean, $\bar{x}$, and standard deviation, s, from just one sample. Thus, using our basic proposition, we can say that any given randomly drawn sample mean, $\bar{x}$, will fall $1.96s/\sqrt{N}$ either side of the population μ with 95% probability. This is to say, $\bar{x}$ will fall in the interval $\mu - 1.96s/\sqrt{N} < \bar{x} < \mu + 1.96s/\sqrt{N}$ with 95% probability. This interval is known as the 95% *confidence interval.*

Usually we wish to test whether the mean of a given population, μ_R (with standard deviation σ_R) differs from a given value μ_o. We can then use a sample $\bar{x}$ to estimate μ_R and set up a null hypothesis that $\mu_R = \mu_o$. Unfortunately, a complication enters here: it is possible either to test whether μ_R differs from μ_o or whether μ_R is simply larger (or, according to the merits of the case, smaller) than μ_o. In the former case, the alternative hypothesis is $\mu_R - \mu_o \neq 0$ and in the latter, $\mu_R - \mu_o > 0$ (or, alternatively, $\mu_R - \mu_o < 0$). The former example is known as a *two-tailed* test, because the area in both tails of the normal distribution is summed, and the latter is called a *one-tailed* test. For the moment let us concentrate on the more frequently used two-tailed test. Our alternative hypothesis, then, is that $\mu_R - \mu_o \neq 0$ or, in terms of $\bar{x}$, that $\bar{x} - \mu_o \neq 0$. We can rewrite the 95% confidence interval for $\bar{x}$ as a confidence interval for $\bar{x} - \mu_o$, thus

$$-1.96s/\sqrt{n} < \bar{x} - \mu_o < 1.96s/\sqrt{N}$$

or, alternatively,

$$-1.96 < z < 1.96$$

where

$$z = \frac{\bar{x} - \mu_o}{s/\sqrt{N}} \quad \text{is our } test\ statistic.$$

This states that z will fall in the range -1.96 to $+1.96$ in 95% of the cases. If, as is conventional, we wish to have a 5% maximum probability of Type I error (that is, we adopt a 5% *level of significance*) then, if z falls outside the range -1.96 to $+1.96$, we reject the null hypothesis.

For example, we may wish to test whether average unemployment in a given region, μ_R, differs at the 5% level of significance from the national level, μ_o. Suppose that the only information we have about the region is the unemployment rate for fifty towns in the region, with $\bar{x} = 4\%$ and $s = 2\%$. Suppose further that $\mu_o = 5\%$. In this case

$$z = \frac{4 - 5}{2/\sqrt{50}} = -3.57.$$

This z-value is considerably smaller than the lower limit, -1.96, of our 95% confidence interval. In fact, the table of the normal distribution function shows there is a probability of only 0.04%[16] (or 4 times in 10,000) of z falling outside the range -3.57 to $+3.57$ on the basis of chance variation alone. Thus, we would have only a 0.04% probability of making a Type I error (remember, this is to incorrectly reject the null hypothesis) in concluding that, on the given information, unemployment for this region is in fact lower than for the nation as a whole.

It is worth reemphasising that the value of z, ignoring its sign, increases and the probability of Type I error decreases as:

1. The observed difference between sample and population means, $\bar{x} - \mu_o$, increases.
2. The variability, s, in the sample, decreases.
3. N, the number of observations in the sample, increases.

This accords with our earlier discussion.

We have been considering a test for the value of a single sample mean. A more frequently used test in economics, however, is that for the difference between two population means as based on information from two sample means. This test is constructed in analogous fashion to that for the single mean case. The mean of the sampling distribution of difference in means is

$$\mu_{\bar{x}_1} - \mu_{\bar{x}_2} = \mu_1 - \mu_2$$

where $\mu_{\bar{x}_i}$ relates to the sample mean; and
μ_i relates to the population mean ($i = 1, 2$).

Assuming that the sample x_1 is drawn independently of the sample x_2 (otherwise there would be a nonzero *covariance* term—see pages 30–31 of the appendix), the standard deviation is

$$\sigma_{\bar{x}_1 - \bar{x}_2} = \sqrt{\frac{\sigma_1^2}{N_1} + \frac{\sigma_2^2}{N_2}}$$

where σ_i is the population standard deviation; and
N_i is the sample size.

---

16. This is the proportion of the area in the two tails of the normal curve more than 3.57 standard deviations from the mean.

Sample means, $\bar{x}_i$, and standard deviations, s_i, can be used to estimate corresponding population means and standard deviations. The test statistic for the null hypothesis, $\mu_1 - \mu_2 = 0$, becomes

$$z = \frac{\bar{x}_1 - \bar{x}_2 - (\mu_1 - \mu_2)}{\sqrt{\dfrac{s_1^2}{N_1} + \dfrac{s_2^2}{N_2}}} = \frac{\bar{x}_1 - \bar{x}_2 - 0}{\sqrt{\dfrac{s_1^2}{N_1} + \dfrac{s_2^2}{N_2}}}.$$

To demonstrate, take the initial example relating to differences between the vacancy periods of men and women. The data are as follows:

	Men	Women
$\bar{x}$	2.7 weeks	2.1 weeks
s	3.0 weeks	2.5 weeks
N	200	150.

Thus,

$$z = \frac{2.7 - 2.1}{0.295} = 2.03.$$

In this example, z slightly exceeds 1.96, so that, for a 5% level of significance, that is, a 5% probability of Type I error, we would reject the null hypothesis of no difference between the populations. On the other hand, we could not reject the null hypothesis at the 1% level of significance, because, as the normal table shows, this requires a z-value of 2.58. Similar z-statistics can be constructed for other sample statistics (such as proportions) and, most important of all, for regression coefficients. The formulae are listed in appendix 1-A.

Let us conclude this subsection with a consideration of small samples—those cases where $N < 30$. Small samples are often encountered in economics, particularly when dealing with time-series data. As we would intuitively expect, our confidence in the results of our hypothesis testing diminishes as sample size is reduced. To put this in another way, we would require a higher z-value to yield the same chance of Type I error, *ceteris paribus*.

A table, known as the *t-table*, permits such an allowance to be precisely made.[17] Its use depends on the concept of *degrees of freedom*, V, which can be thought of as the size of the sample minus the number of parameters (such as means) measured from the sample. Thus, $V = N - 1$ in the example of a test for the difference between population and sample means. Suppose that V is quite small, say $V = 20$. Then we can say in reference to sample means that any randomly drawn sample mean, $\bar{x}$, will fall $2.09s/\sqrt{N - 1}$ either side of

17. This is the title invented by Gosset, who first calculated these tables. He worked anonymously under the pseudonym "Student," because his employers would not allow him to divulge any information discovered in the course of his employment.

the population mean with 95% probability. The coefficient 2.09 is read from the t-table. Note the slightly different definition of the standard deviation of the sampling distribution of means arising from the small size of the sample (detailed further in appendix 1-A). Test statistics are then constructed exactly as before, but with 2.09 rather than 1.96 becoming the 5% critical value (given $V = 20$).

Regression Analysis. To fix ideas, consider a regression relationship between the rate of change of money wages in period t, $\dot{W}_t$, and the contemporary level, T_t, and rate of change, $\dot{T}_t$, of union membership as estimated by Hines.

$$\dot{W}_t = a + b\dot{T}_t + cT_t \qquad (1.1)$$

where a, b, and c are constants, hypothesized to be positive; and

$$\dot{T}_t \equiv (T_t - T_{t-1})/T_t.$$

Hines collected British data on $\dot{W}_t$, $\dot{T}_t$, and T_t for each of the years 1893–1961, with the goal of estimating a, b, and c. This is known as a *multiple regression of $\dot{W}$ on $\dot{T}$ and T,* indicating that $\dot{W}$ is the dependent, or left-hand-side, variable. A simplified scatter diagram of the relationship between all three variables is given in figure 1.1. This is simplified to the extent that T is assumed to take only two values, namely high (say $T = 1$) and low (say $T = 0$). Each cross represents a value of $\dot{W}$ and $\dot{T}$ for a given year. The effect of T, the third variable, is illustrated as separating the observations into two distinct clouds (ringed). The zero/unity device T is known as a *dummy* or *dichotomous* variable and is often used in economics. Two lines that most accurately approximate the two sets of observations are drawn in dashed form. Notice that these lines have been drawn so as to have the same gradient, b. This particular configuration is required because our model in equation (1.1) makes the assumption that b is constant, whatever the value of T.[18]

18. We could alternatively assume that the slope and not simply the $\dot{W}$ intercept of the fitted lines varied according to the value of T. Suppose we had "specified the model," as the terminology goes, in the following way:

$$\dot{W} = a + b\dot{T} + cT + dT\dot{T}$$

where $T = 1$ for years of high trade union membership, 0 otherwise.
Then we can see that

$$\dot{W} = a + b\dot{T}$$

for years when $T = 0$; and

$$\dot{W} = a + c + d\dot{T}$$

for years when $T = 1$. This is analogous to fitting lines to the two clouds separately.

Figure 1.1 Schematic Relationship between $\dot{W}$ and $\dot{T}$ for Two Values of T

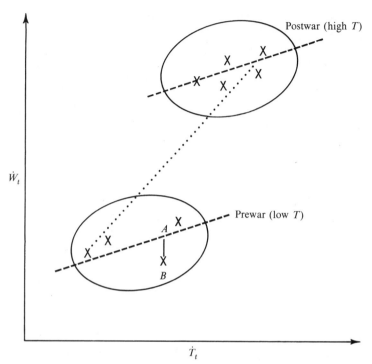

The way the diagram has been drawn indicates that years with high T are also those with high $\dot{T}$. In other words, there is a positive association or correlation between T and $\dot{T}$. Consequently, had we omitted consideration of T when drawing a straight line relating $\dot{W}$ and $\dot{T}$ in the scatter diagram, we would have obtained something like the dotted line of figure 1.1. The latter has a steeper gradient than the dashed lines, but it can be seen that this yields a misleading picture of the effect of $\dot{T}$ on $\dot{W}$. Moreover, increasing sample size would not help. Omitting consideration of T will give a biased estimate of the effect of $\dot{T}$ on $\dot{W}$. In this case, because T and $\dot{T}$ are positively correlated, the bias is positive.[19] If T and $\dot{T}$ were negatively correlated (the upper cloud displaced to the left of the lower), it can be seen that the bias would be negative. In this particular case, the dotted line would have a negative slope while the true (dashed) lines have positive slopes. This possibility underlines the importance of holding other things equal when estimating the effect of one variable on another. A simple relationship between only two variables

---

19. An example of positive bias is given in chapter 8 with respect to the union-nonunion differential, $\bar{R}$, and the level of unionization, U. Here, an omitted variable affecting $\bar{R}$ is positively correlated with U, leading to an overestimate of the strength of the relationship between U and $\bar{R}$.

might thus be meaningless. This in turn explains the popularity of a multiple regression approach.

In practice, curve-fitting, or regression, is not performed by hand, but by a computer using the method of *least squares*. Using this method, the computer finds a line that minimizes the squared vertical deviations from the line (distances such as *AB* squared in figure 1.1). Moreover, many more than two or three right-hand variables are often used. This multiplicity of independent variables makes no difference to the principle of the analysis, which can still be thought of in terms of scatter diagrams. The method of least squares has the advantage of being a mechanical procedure, so that its mathematical properties are known; for example, the way in which our estimate of *b* is biased by neglecting to consider the correlation between T and $\dot{T}$ can be precisely demonstrated. Some of the more useful properties of this method are given in appendix 1-A.

Returning to equation (1.1), we find that the best-fitting line for the observations in question has the following coefficients:

$$\dot{W}_t = -7.357 + 2.922\ \dot{T}_t + 0.317\ T_t \qquad (1.2)$$
$$(16.9) \qquad (7.04)$$
$$R^2 = 0.9069$$
$$DW = 1.57$$

We interpret this equation as follows. First consider the coefficients of $\dot{T}_t$ and T_t. These are both positive, which indicates that, on the basis of the observations used by Hines, an increase in T or $\dot{T}$ is associated on average with an increase in $\dot{W}$. Thus, supposing trade union membership stood at $T = 30\%$, we would have

$$\dot{W}_t = -7.357 + 2.922\ \dot{T}_t + (0.317 \times 30)$$
$$= 2.153 + 2.922\ \dot{T}_t.$$

Consequently, if trade union membership were increasing at $\dot{T} = 1\%$ per year, the rate of increase of wages would be

$$\dot{W}_t = 2.153 + 2.922 \times 1$$
$$= 5.075\% \text{ per year.}$$

Now consider the number given in parentheses beneath each coefficient, C. This is the *t*-value associated with the coefficient, and it provides the basis for a test of the null hypothesis that the population coefficient, P, is zero. This test is constructed in exactly the same way as are the tests of hypotheses concerning means and differences between means considered earlier. The coefficient C is used as an estimator of P and, as before, we have more confidence in the estimate C if the standard deviation of the coefficient, s_C, is small than if it is large.[20] The test statistic that P equals a particular value, $P = A$, is

$$t_C = \frac{C - A}{s_C}.$$

In particular, if the hypothesis is that $P = 0$, we have

$$t_C = \frac{C}{s_C}.$$

This can be shown to be distributed according to the t-distribution with $N - k$ degrees of freedom, where N is the number of observations and k is the number of independent variables including the intercept term a. On this formulation, it can be seen that t_C can take positive or negative values, depending on the sign of C (s_C is always positive). In this book, the practice will be to ignore the sign of t and simply to present its absolute value, $|t|$.

A rule of thumb is to reject the hypothesis that a coefficient is zero if its associated $|t|$ is greater than 2. For $N - k = 30$ or more, this gives us about a 5% probability of Type I error on a two-tailed test. To put this in another way, if t is 2 or more we accept the sign, plus or minus, associated with a particular coefficient. Looking at equation (1.2) on the basis of this rule, it appears that we can be highly confident in accepting the positive signs associated with variables $\dot{T}$ and T. Suppose for a moment, however, that the $|t|$ associated with $\dot{T}$ had been only 1.9 (or, in other words, that $s_C = 1.54$). In this case, we would have accepted the null hypothesis that the true coefficient on $\dot{T}$ was zero. Some economists would then take equation (1.2) to read

$$\dot{W}_t = -7.357 + 0.317\ T_t.$$

Others, however, would reestimate the equation as a relation between $\dot{W}$ and T only, which procedure would yield slightly different coefficients.

However, while it can be seen that the t-test or t-statistic is important as an aid to judging whether or not an independent variable affects the dependent variable, the test procedure is not infallible. This is because of the problem of *multicollinearity*. Multicollinearity arises when any one independent variable is highly correlated with any other independent variable in the equation. In such a case, it is bound to be difficult to isolate the separate contribution of a particular variable to changes in the dependent variable. In our example, suppose that T and $\dot{T}$ were positively correlated so that a high value of T

---

20. The value of s_C is given in the computer printout. It depends not only on the variation in the particular variable associated with C, but also on the goodness of fit of the equation as a whole.

corresponded to a high value of $\dot{T}$, and vice versa. Now the meaning of the coefficient on $\dot{T}$ in equation (1.2) is that it shows the effect on $\dot{W}$ of a change in $\dot{T}$ with T held constant. Yet if T and $\dot{T}$ are highly correlated, we cannot in practice observe many situations in which $\dot{T}$ has changed while T has not. Accordingly, our estimate of the separate contribution of the two variables must suffer.[21] In such a case, the t-statistic associated with each variable will fall. The only way to reduce the multicollinearity problem in practice is to increase the number of observations. At the same time, it should be admitted that the problem is less serious than it might appear at first sight, because multicollinearity always lowers t-values; that is, it serves to make our judgments more conservative. If a variable does yield a significant t-value, it is likely to be important. It is variables with low t-statistics that cause the problem, because their importance may be obscured by multicollinearity.

Next consider the result for the *coefficient of multiple correlation, R^2*; $R^2 = 0.9069$ in equation (1.2). This summary statistic tells us that 90.69% of the variation in wage change ($\dot{W}$) over the period in question is statistically associated with changes in the two independent variables T and $\dot{T}$. This has the corollary that 9.31% of the variation in $\dot{W}$ is not statistically associated with changes in the two independent variables—at least in a linear relationship. A different value for R^2 might be obtained if the function linking $\dot{W}$, T, and $\dot{T}$ were nonlinear. The value of R^2 varies between zero, which means the independent variables have zero explanatory power, and unity, which means the independent variables have perfect explanatory power. A useful way of considering this statistic is in terms of the relative tightness of the cluster of observations around the fitted regression line. A tight clustering indicates a high R^2, and a loose clustering indicates a low R^2. To demonstrate this proposition, suppose that we had ignored T and had simply regressed $\dot{W}$ on $\dot{T}$ alone, that is, fitted the dotted line in figure 1.1. It can be seen that the crosses cluster less tightly around the dotted line than around the two dashed lines. This means that R^2 will be lower—in alternate terminology, the goodness of fit will be lower—if we ignore T than if we include T.

We must not be too mechanical in the pursuit of high R^2 values. The addition of an extra right-hand (independent) variable will always increase R^2, the increase being proportionate to the t-statistic associated with the variable.[22] But a high R^2 is meaningless if we cannot explain why particular variables should affect our dependent variable. In other words, a regression equation is only as good as the theory underlying it. Correlation does not measure causation. Rather, regression equations are an aid to understanding

21. If T and $\dot{T}$ are highly correlated, the least-squares method breaks down, and the computer program will stop. This is because the variables are essentially the same, so it does not make sense to enter them separately in the regression.

22. For this reason, a formula exists for adjusting R^2 to allow for the effect of merely increasing the number of independent variables. The adjusted value, $\bar{R}^2$, is useful if we compare equations which have widely differing numbers of independent variables. In this book, however, we have almost exclusively reported the unadjusted R^2 value.

empirical relationships—and a very powerful aid at that—but they are no substitute for thought.

As a further means of judging the goodness of fit, we have recourse to the *Durbin-Watson statistic*. One such DW-statistic is given under equation (1.2). What is its meaning? The DW value is best understood as measuring whether or not there is any pattern in the deviations of the observations from the fitted line. These deviations are known as *residuals*. If the residuals show a pattern, there is the implication that our equation or model has omitted an important variable, one that is well correlated with an independent variable. We have already noted the ominous consequences for the reliability of our estimates if such a variable is omitted.

To establish this point more clearly, it is necessary to note that our model in equation (1.1) is an exact relationship. But real-world relationships are seldom exact; they are *stochastic* and as such subject to chance factors as well as such deterministic ones as $\dot{T}$. Thus, equation (1.1) should be expressed stochastically in the form

$$\dot{W}_t = a + b\dot{T}_t + cT_t + e_t \qquad (1.3)$$

where e_t is the stochastic term, representing the influence of random or chance factors on $\dot{W}$.

Suppose that e_t was not random, however, but was instead systematically related to one of the independent variables. For example, suppose we had omitted T, which is assumed to be positively correlated with $\dot{T}$, and estimated the function

$$W_t = a + b\dot{T}_t + V_t, \qquad (1.4)$$

When the true relationship is given by equation (1.3). In this case, the residual term V_t would be picking up the effect of T. That is to say,

$$V_t = cT_t + e_t.$$

Because T is assumed to be correlated with $\dot{T}$, the residuals in equation (1.4) are not random but are positively correlated with $\dot{T}$. Consequently, the estimate of b will be biased upward, as already demonstrated in discussion of figure 1.1.

In practice, we do not know the value of e_t and must measure it simply in terms of the residuals from our fitted line. For example, suppose that equation (1.2) had been estimated and had yielded a set of predicted values of wage inflation, $\dot{W}'_t$. The estimated residuals would then be[23]

$$e'_t = \dot{W}_t - \dot{W}'_t.$$

---

23. Note that the average value of e' will be zero. This is a property of the least-squares method of fitting a curve to data and is also what we would expect of a random variable.

If these estimated residuals appear to vary randomly on either side of the regression line, we are more confident that the true residuals are random and, therefore, that the estimates of equation (1.2) are not biased. But if we observe a series of runs of successively positive and negative residuals, our suspicions should be aroused. The *DW*-statistic is a means of transmitting such a danger-signal.

The above discussion may be clarified with the aid of figure 1.2. The observations have been drawn so as to show y parabolically related to x. Inspection of this scatter diagram should suggest to the investigator that he regress y on x and x^2, possibly in the form

$$y = a + bx + cx^2.$$

Suppose that x^2 is ignored, however, and that a simple linear regression is attempted as shown in the figure. Clearly, there is a relationship between y and x, so that the coefficient on x will be highly significant. Moreover, R^2 will be high because the crosses are tightly clustered around the fitted line. The

Figure 1.2   Illustration of a Pattern in Regression Residuals

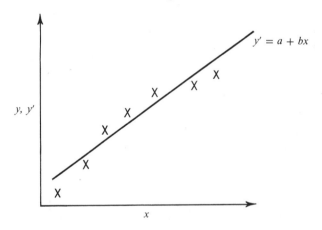

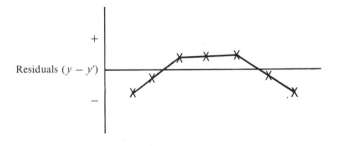

investigator might well be satisfied with this result, although he has obtained a biased estimate of the effect of x on y. However, when he consults the residuals displayed in the bottom panel, he discovers them to have a clear pattern. Specifically, the predicted values (y') are first higher, then lower, and finally higher than the actual values (y).

The Durbin-Watson statistic is based on these residuals. The assigned value that indicates an absence of pattern, or the presence of reliable estimates, is $DW = 2$. If DW is much lower or higher than 2 (how much lower or higher is read from the appropriate table), the indications are that we have a missing variable—that the equation is *misspecified*. The DW value has, in common with other statistics, a sampling variability. Accordingly, low or high values of DW could arise by chance, again raising the possibility of Type I error. Generally speaking, values of DW in the range 1.5 to 2.5 are acceptable at the 5% level of significance.

Thus, it can be seen that the DW test is essentially a test for omitted variables and, as such, very important. Unfortunately, the statistic can only be used if the observations in question are ordered by some characteristic. In all time-series analyses, this condition is met because the observations are ordered by time. If there is no obvious ordering of the observations, however, the DW test is inappropriate. This objection can be understood by considering a situation in which observations are not ordered. In such a case, the observations can be rearranged so as to yield any pattern of residuals, and hence any required DW value. For this reason, inspection of residuals—and calculation of the DW statistic—is only useful in the infrequent cases where cross-section work of an ordering principle suggests itself.[24]

Systems of Equations.   Thus far we have assumed that the relationship between the dependent and independent variables is solely in one direction, namely that the right-hand variables determine the left-hand variable, but not vice-versa. In many cases, this assumption may be invalid. For example, in considering equation (1.1), we might be tempted to argue that increases in the rate of change of wages influence $\dot{T}$, as well as the other way around. Here, we are hypothesizing that a system of simultaneous equations obtains. For example, we could write

$$\dot{W}_t = a_1 + b_1\dot{T}_t + c_1T_t + e_{1t} \tag{1.5}$$
$$\dot{T}_t = a_2 + b_2\dot{W}_t + c_2T_t + e_{2t} \tag{1.6}$$

where e_1 represents random or stochastic effects on $\dot{W}$; and
e_2 stands for stochastic factors influencing $\dot{T}$.

In systems of equations, the jointly determined variables, $\dot{W}$ and $\dot{T}$ in our example, are known as *endogenous* variables. Those variables, T in our

---

24. The DW test also cannot be used in equations where one of the independent variables is a lagged value of the dependent variable.

example, that are specified as not depending on the others are termed *exogenous* variables. Equations which have both endogenous and exogenous variables figuring on their right-hand side, as do equations (1.5) and (1.6), are known as *structural* equations. The equations can be rewritten with only exogenous variables on the right-hand side.[25] Thus, in our example, ignoring the t subscript, we have

$$\dot{W} = \frac{a_1 + a_2 b_1}{1 - b_2 b_1} + \left(\frac{c_1 + c_2 b_1}{1 - b_2 b_1}\right) T + \frac{e_1 + e_2 b_1}{1 - b_2 b_1} \tag{1.7}$$

$$\dot{T} = \frac{a_2 + a_1 b_2}{1 - b_2 b_1} + \left(\frac{c_2 + c_1 b_2}{1 - b_2 b_1}\right) T + \frac{e_2 + e_1 b_2}{1 - b_2 b_1}. \tag{1.8}$$

These are known as *reduced form* equations.

In general, we cannot estimate structural equations such as equation (1.5) using ordinary least squares, because the residuals e_1 in equation (1.5) will not be truly random in such a case, but will be correlated with one of the right-hand variables. The discussion of figure 1.1 showed that this association will generate biased parameter estimates. To understand how the correlation arises, note that, from equation (1.5), e_1 affects $\dot{W}$. However, from equation (1.6), note that $\dot{W}$ *also affects* $\dot{T}$. As a result, e_1 must affect $\dot{T}$, so it follows that e_1 cannot be truly random. Unfortunately, this problem of two-way causation or *simultaneous equation bias,* as when $\dot{T}$ affects $\dot{W}$ but $\dot{W}$ also affects $\dot{T}$, arises often in economics.

The question at issue, then, is whether we can obtain reliable estimates of the coefficients of equation (1.5) in which $\dot{W}$ and $\dot{T}$ are jointly dependent. We will consider two major possible solutions to the problem. The first involves using the reduced form or, as it is sometimes termed, *indirect least squares.* The second uses a simultaneous equation method of estimation called *two-stage least squares.*

Let us first consider using the reduced form equations (1.7) and (1.8). Now suppose $\dot{W}$ were regressed on T as in the reduced form equation (1.7), namely

$$\dot{W}_t = \alpha + \beta T_t + v_t \tag{1.9}$$

where α has the interpretation $\alpha = (a_1 + a_2 b_1)/(1 - b_2 b_1)$;
β has the interpretation $\beta = (c_1 + c_2 b_1)/(1 - b_2 b_1)$;
v has the interpretation $v = (e_1 + e_2 b_1)/(1 - b_2 b_1)$.

This procedure is legitimate because we assume T to be exogenous; that is, T is uncorrelated with the stochastic term (or, as it is sometimes called, the *error*

---

25. This involves solving for $\dot{W}$ and $\dot{T}$ in terms of T. This can be done by substitution or by using Cramer's rule (see appendix 1-A).

term) v. Thus, we can obtain unbiased estimates of α and β. Similarly, we could regress $\dot{T}$ on T, as follows

$$\dot{T}_t = \gamma + \delta T_t + u_t \tag{1.10}$$

and thereby obtain unbiased estimates of γ and δ. It can be seen that α, β, γ, and δ are mixtures of the coefficients in which we are interested, namely the as, bs, and cs. This opens up the possibility of our being able to use the reduced form coefficients to calculate the values of the structural coefficients.

Whether the reduced form coefficients of equations (1.9) and (1.10) can actually be used to calculate the structural coefficients of equation (1.5) hinges on the question of whether the latter equation is *identified*. The concept of identification can be understood intuitively by reference to figure 1.3. Begin with an initial observation given by point C. Now suppose that the exogenous variable, T, changes and shifts the $\dot{W}$ relationship upward, while leaving the $\dot{T}$ relationship unchanged. As a result, point B is generated. Fitting a line through C and B will trace out the $\dot{T}$ relationship, but not the $\dot{W}$ relationship. Because the change in T has not shifted the $\dot{T}$ relationship, that relationship can be identified, although the $\dot{W}$ relationship cannot be iden-

Figure 1.3 The Problem of Identifying a Relationship

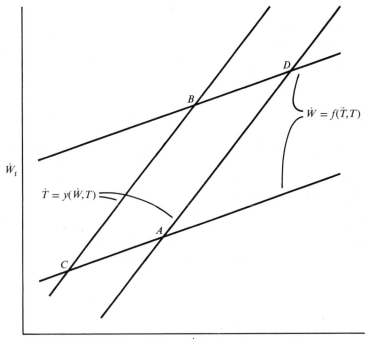

tified. On the other hand, had the change in T shifted the $\dot{T}$ relationship but not the $\dot{W}$ relationship, then observations C and A would have been generated, in which case only the $\dot{W}$ relationship would be identified. Finally, had the change in T shifted both the $\dot{W}$ and $\dot{T}$ relationships, observations C and D would have been generated. In this case, neither relationship would be identified.

In fact, the way in which equations (1.5) and (1.6) have been specified indicates that the exogenous variable T shifts both the $\dot{W}$ and $\dot{T}$ relationships. The result is that neither is identified. Consequently, we cannot use estimates of the reduced form coefficients to calculate the structural coefficients in either equation. If we could argue that T did not shift the $\dot{W}$ relationship—so that T might be excluded from equation (1.5)—then the $\dot{W}$ relationship would be identified. This result can easily be shown algebraically. If T did not enter equation (1.5), c_1 would be zero and the reduced form equations would be as follows:

$$\dot{W} = \frac{a_1 + a_2 b_1}{1 - b_2 b_1} + \left(\frac{c_2 b_1}{1 - b_2 b_1}\right)T + \frac{e_1 + e_2 b_1}{1 - b_2 b_1}$$
$$= \alpha' + \beta' T + v'$$
$$\dot{T} = \frac{a_2 + a_1 b_2}{1 - b_2 b_1} + \left(\frac{c_2}{1 - b_2 b_1}\right)T + \frac{e_2 + e_1 b_2}{1 - b_2 b_1}$$
$$= \gamma' + \delta' T + u'.$$

It can then be seen that

$$b_1 = \beta'/\delta'$$
$$a_1 = \alpha' - b_1 \gamma'.$$

Thus, if T can be excluded from equation (1.5), we can see that the equation is identified and that the reduced form regression coefficients can be used to derive its parameters, even though $\dot{W}$ and $\dot{T}$ are jointly dependent. This result provides an example of the necessary condition for identifiability: a structural equation with G endogenous variables (here, $G = 2$) is properly identified if $G - 1$ of the exogenous variables in the system (in this case, the single variable T) are excluded.

However, problems do arise with this indirect least squares method where the equation in question is overidentified; that is, where the equation excludes more than $G - 1$ exogenous variables. For example, consider the following system

$$\dot{W} = a_1 + b_1 \dot{T} + e_1 \qquad (1.5)'$$
$$\dot{T} = a_2 + b_2 \dot{T} + c_2 T + d_2 Z + e_2 \qquad (1.6)'$$

where $\dot{W}$ and $\dot{T}$ are endogenous variables as before; and
T and Z are supposed to be exogenous variables.

Here it can be seen that equation (1.5)′ excludes not only T but also Z. If the reduced form is computed and if an attempt is then made to use the reduced form coefficients to derive an estimate of b_1, it will be found that two estimates of b_1 can be constructed. And there is no reason to suppose that these should be the same. For this reason, equation (1.5)′ is termed *over-identified*.[26] To deal with this problem, a type of averaging process has been developed, known as two-stage least squares.

Two-stage least squares (TSLS) can be shown to give the same result as indirect least squares in the case of a properly identified structural equation. However, because TSLS can also be applied in the context of overidentified equations, it is more flexible. For this reason, TSLS is the most frequently used method of simultaneous equation estimation and will often be referred to in this book. The bare bones of TSLS are as follows. The first stage involves separating out the endogenous variable of prime interest—say $\dot{W}$ in equation (1.5)′—and then computing the reduced form equations for the other endogenous variables. In our example, this means regressing $\dot{T}$ on T and Z. The second stage is to regress the prime endogenous variable on the calculated values of the other endogenous variables and the exogenous variables. In our example, this involves regressing $\dot{W}$ simply on the values of $\dot{T}$ calculated from the reduced form, because no exogenous variables are specified in equation (1.5)′. In other words, we have the regression

$$\dot{W} = a_1' + b_1'\dot{T}'$$

where $\dot{T}'$ is the value of $\dot{T}$ calculated from the reduced form equation. The estimates a_1' and b_1' are the TSLS estimates of a_1 and b_1. Whether these are free of bias will depend on the validity of our specification of endogenous and exogenous variables in the equations of the system.

---

26. The opposite of overidentification is underidentification. The latter arises when too few exogenous variables are excluded from a structural equation. For example, equation (1.5) is underidentified. All that can be done in this case is to search for a variable which affects $\dot{T}$ but does not at the same time affect $\dot{W}$.

APPENDIX A-1
SOME USEFUL MATHEMATICAL AND STATISTICAL RESULTS[1]

Rules for Taking Sums

The summation notation is

$$\sum_{i=1}^{N} x_i = x_1 + x_2 \cdots + x_N$$

where x_i refers to the ith quantity and i runs from 1 to N.

It then follows that

$$\sum_{i=1}^{N} kx_i = k \sum_{i=1}^{N} x_i$$

where k is a constant.

Also

$$\sum_{i=1}^{N} k = Nk.$$

And

$$\sum_{i=1}^{N} (x_i + y_i) = \sum_{i=1}^{N} x_i + \sum_{i=1}^{N} y_i.$$

Further

$$\sum_{i=1}^{N} i = \frac{1}{2}[N(N + 1)].$$

1. One of the best books available, providing many worked examples and applications to economics, is R. G. D. Allen, *Mathematical Analysis for Economists* (London: Macmillan, 1938). An alternative is T. Yamane, *Mathematics for Economists* (Englewood Cliffs, N.J.: Prentice-Hall, 1968).

The latter result follows from the formula for summing an arithmetic progression, namely

$$\text{Sum (A.P.)} = N\left[A + \frac{d}{2}(N - 1) \right],$$

where N is the number of terms;
   A is the first term; and
   d is the size of step.

The formula for summing a geometric progression is written

$$\text{Sum (G.P.)} = A(1 - h^N)/(1 - h)$$

where N and A are defined as above; and
   h is the common ratio. (For an application, see chapter 4.)

Exponents
The following rules apply

$$x^0 = 1, \, x^1 = x, \, x^{-1} = 1/x$$

where x is any number (e.g., $2^0 = 1$, $2^1 = 2$, $2^{-1} = \frac{1}{2}$).
   Further

$$x^{1/h} = \sqrt[h]{x}.$$

There are also two rules for simplifying exponents. Thus

$$x^z \cdot x^y = x^{z+y}$$

where x, y, and z are any number (e.g., $2^2 \cdot 2^3 = 4 \times 8 = 32 = 2^5$).
And

$$(x^z)^y = x^{z \cdot y}$$

where x, y, and z are any number (e.g., $(2^2)^3 = 4^3 = 64 = 2^6$).

Logarithms
A logarithm is a particular kind of exponent. Its definition is as follows: the logarithm of a number x to a base b is the exponent which has to put on the base to give the number. In other words, if

$$\log_b \ell = x$$

then

$$b^x = \ell.$$

Commonly used bases are 10 and the number $e = 2.7183$. (The number e is often used in mathematics because of its special properties, one of which is $d(e^x)/dx = e^x$). Logs to the base e are written "ln." Thus

$$\log_{10} 100 = 2, \; \log_{10} 0.1 = -1, \; \log_e 100 = \ln 100 = 4.605$$

because

$$10^2 = 100, \; 10^{-1} = 0.1, \; e^{4.605} = 100.$$

A useful property of logs to the base e is that

$$\ln x_2 - \ln x_1 \simeq (x_2 - x_1)/x_1,$$

if the proportionate difference $(x_2 - x_1)/x_1$ is small.
  For example,

$$\begin{aligned}\ln 1010 - \ln 1000 &= 6.9178 - 6.9078\\ &= (1010 - 1000)/1000\\ &= 0.01\end{aligned}$$

A more accurate method of expression is via the use of calculus (see below). Then we can write

$$d \ln x = \frac{dx}{x}$$

which states that small absolute changes in $\ln x$ equal small proportionate changes in x.
  Finally, an often-used approximation is

$$\ln(1 + x) \simeq x$$

where x is small (for example, where $x < 0.2$).

Differentiation and Integration

The following are some useful rules (for an explanation, consult any book on calculus, such as Allen).[2]
  Given $f(x) = x^n$, then

$$\frac{df(x)}{dx} = nx^{n-1}.$$

2. Ibid., chaps. 6–16.

Given $f(x) = g(x) + h(x)$, then

$$\frac{df(x)}{dx} = \frac{dg(x)}{dx} + \frac{dh(x)}{dx}.$$

Given $f(x) = g(x) \cdot h(x)$, then

$$\frac{df(x)}{dx} = g\frac{dh(x)}{dx} + h\frac{dg(x)}{dx}.$$

Given $f(x) = g(x)/h(x)$, then

$$\frac{df(x)}{dx} = \frac{1}{h^2}\left(h\frac{dg(x)}{dx} - g\frac{dh(x)}{dx}\right).$$

Given $f(x) = g[h(x)]$, then

$$\frac{df(x)}{dx} = \frac{dg}{dh} \cdot \frac{dh(x)}{dx}.$$

Given $f(x) = e^{ax}$, then

$$\frac{df(x)}{dx} = ae^{ax}.$$

Given $f(x) = \log_e x$, then

$$\frac{df(x)}{dx} = \frac{1}{x}.$$

Differentiating a function with respect to a given variable enables us to calculate the slope of the function with reference to that variable. Integration, on the other hand, enables us to compute the area under a function for given values of the variable. It is best understood as the reverse of differentiation. Thus, suppose we wished to establish the area under the function $f(x) = x^n$ between $x = 0$ and $x = a$. This is written

$$\int_{x=0}^{x=a} x^n dx = \frac{x^{n+1}}{n+1}\bigg|_{x=a \text{ and } 0}$$

because

$$\frac{d}{dx}\left(\frac{x^{n+1}}{n+1}\right) = x^n.$$

Thus

$$\int_{x=0}^{x=a} x^n dx = \frac{a^{n+1}}{n+1} - 0.$$

A practical example is provided in appendix 10-A.

Simultaneous Equations and Cramer's Rule

Let us take a simple system with only two equations, that is, two jointly dependent variables, x and y,

$$x = a_1 + b_1 y + c_1 z$$
$$y = a_2 + b_2 x + c_2 z$$

where the *as, bs,* and *cs* are constants, and z is exogenous.

Rearrange the equations so that the jointly dependent variables are in columns on the left-hand side:

$$x - b_1 y = a_1 + c_1 z$$
$$-b_2 x + y = a_2 + c_2 z.$$

To solve for x, take the ratio of the two determinants. The determinant in the denominator is made up of the coefficients on the dependent variables, and that in the numerator is the same except that the column of x coefficients is replaced by the column of right-hand-side values. Thus,

$$x = \frac{\begin{vmatrix} a_1 + c_1 z & -b_1 \\ a_2 + c_2 z & 1 \end{vmatrix}}{\begin{vmatrix} 1 & -b_1 \\ -b_2 & 1 \end{vmatrix}} = \frac{(a_1 + c_1 z) - (-b_1)(a_2 + c_2 z)}{1 - (-b_1)(-b_2)}$$

$$= \frac{a_1 + c_1 z + b_1(a_2 + c_2 z)}{1 - b_1 b_2}.$$

To evaluate these determinants, we have made use of the *cross multiplication rule:* take the product of the top left and bottom right elements and subtract the product of the bottom left and top right elements. The solution for y is similar, except that the column of y coefficients in the numerator determinant is replaced by the column of right-hand-side values. The denominator determinant remains unchanged.

Suppose now that we add a third equation to the system; say we assume that z is also jointly dependent, in an equation

$$z = a_3 + b_3 x + c_3 y.$$

Solving for x, we first rearrange the equations

$$x - b_1 y - c_1 z = a_1$$
$$-b_2 x + y - c_2 z = a_2$$
$$-b_3 x - c_3 y + z = a_3$$

and then set up a ratio of determinants according to the same principle as before. Thus,

$$x = \frac{\begin{vmatrix} a_1 & -b_1 & -c_1 \\ a_2 & 1 & -c_2 \\ a_3 & -c_3 & 1 \end{vmatrix}}{\begin{vmatrix} 1 & -b_1 & -c_1 \\ -b_2 & 1 & -c_2 \\ -b_3 & -c_3 & 1 \end{vmatrix}}$$

To evaluate these determinants, we use the following rules: take any column (or row) of coefficients—for example, the first column in the numerator—and proceed element by element along the column attributing a sign to each element, the sign being positive if the sum of the column and row is even (thus, a_1 has a positive sign, since the sum of the first column and first row is even) and negative if that sum is odd. For any given element, construct a minor determinant by deleting the row and column of that element (for example, the first row and column for a_1). Multiply the value of this minor determinant by the given element. Add all three values together. Thus, for the numerator determinant, we have

$$D_x = + a_1(1 - c_2 c_3)$$
$$+ (-a_2)(-b_1 - c_3 c_1)$$
$$+ a_3(b_1 c_2 + c_1).$$

The denominator determinant D is evaluated similarly, and $x = D_x/D$. Similar expressions for y and z can be computed.

The Standard Deviation

The standard deviation of a variable x is defined as

$$s_x = \sqrt{\frac{1}{N} \sum_{j=1}^{N} (x_j - \bar{x})^2}$$

where

$$\bar{x} = \sum_{j \cdot 1}^{N} x_j/N.$$

The squared standard deviation, s_x^2, is known as the *variance* of the variable, var(x). The standard deviation of a sampling distribution is generally known as the *standard error* of that distribution. Thus, we generally speak of the standard error of a regression coefficient. The standard deviation of a variable can easily be calculated once the sum of its squares, Σx_j^2, and its mean, $\bar{x}$, are known. Thus, since

$$s_x^2 = \text{var}(x) = \frac{1}{N} \sum (x_j - \bar{x})^2,$$

it follows that

$$\begin{aligned}
\text{var}(x) &= \frac{1}{N} \sum (x_j^2 - 2x_j\bar{x} + \bar{x}^2) \\
&= \frac{\Sigma x_j^2}{N} - 2\bar{x}\frac{\Sigma x_j}{N} + \frac{\Sigma(\bar{x}^2)}{N} \\
&= \frac{\Sigma x_j^2}{N} - 2\bar{x}^2 + \frac{N\bar{x}^2}{N} \\
&= \frac{\Sigma x_j^2}{N} - \bar{x}^2.
\end{aligned}$$

Here, we have used the rules for taking sums plus the definition of $\bar{x}$.

Rules for Expectation, Variance, and Covariance

A useful way of viewing the mean of a probability distribution of x is as the *expected value* of x, conventionally called $E(x)$. Thus,

$$E(x) = \bar{x}.$$

Similarly, we can view the variance of the distribution as the expected value of the squared deviation of the xs from their mean value, $\bar{x}$. Thus,

$$\begin{aligned}
E(x - \bar{x})^2 &= E[x - E(x)]^2 \\
&= \text{var}(x).
\end{aligned}$$

The *covariance* between two variables, x and y, is defined analogously to the variance, thus

$$\text{cov}(x,y) = \frac{1}{N} \sum_j (x_j - \bar{x})(y_j - \bar{y}) = E(x - \bar{x})(y - \bar{y}).$$

It is simply computed as

$$\text{cov}(x,y) = \frac{\Sigma x_j y_j}{N} - \overline{x}\overline{y}.$$

Their covariance is a measure of the linear dependence between the two variables. Thus the simple correlation coefficient between x and y, r_{xy}, is defined as[3]

$$r_{xy} = \frac{\text{cov}(x,y)}{s_x s_y}.$$

For given s_x and s_y, it can be seen that variables are more highly (positively or negatively) correlated the higher their (positive or negative) covariance.

The following rules should be noted:

$$E(x \pm y) = E(x) \pm E(y);$$
$$E(x \cdot y) = E(x) \cdot E(y) + \text{cov}(x,y)$$
$$= E(x) \cdot E(y),$$

if x and y are linearly independent;

$$\text{var}(x \pm y) = \text{var}(x) + \text{var}(y) + 2 \text{ cov}(x,y)$$
$$= \text{var}(x) + \text{var}(y),$$

if x and y are linearly independent;

$$\text{var}(kx) = k^2 \text{ var}(x),$$

where k is a constant;

$$\text{var}(x \cdot y) = \overline{x}^2 \text{ var}(y) + \overline{y}^2 (\text{var } x) + \text{var}(x) \cdot \text{var}(y),$$

if x and y are linearly independent (for an application, see chapter 10).

---

3. The term r is not to be confused with its square, r^2, or with R^2. Of the latter terms, r^2 is best thought of as the "proportion explained" in a simple two-variable regression equation, and R^2 as the analogous concept in a three or more variable case (a multiple regression).

Means and Variances

Distribution	Mean	Variance
Mean	$\mu_{\bar{x}} = \mu$	$\sigma_{\bar{x}}^2 = \dfrac{\sigma^2}{N}$ for $N \geqslant 30$
		$= \dfrac{\sigma^2}{N-1}$ for $N < 30$
Proportion	$\mu_p = p$	$\sigma_p^2 = \dfrac{p(1-p)}{N}$ for $N \geqslant 30$
		$= \dfrac{p(1-p)}{N-1}$ for $N < 30$
Difference in Means	$\mu_{\bar{x}_1} - \mu_{\bar{x}_2} = \mu_1 - \mu_2$	$\sigma_{\bar{x}_1 - \bar{x}_2}^2 = \dfrac{\sigma_1^2}{N_1} + \dfrac{\sigma_2^2}{N_2}$ for $N > 30$
		$= \left(\dfrac{N_1\sigma_1^2 + N_2\sigma_2^2}{N_1 N_2}\right) \times$
		$\left(\dfrac{N_1 + N_2}{N_1 + N_2 - 2}\right)$
		for $N < 30$
Correlation Coefficient	$r = \rho$ if $\rho = 0$	$\sigma_\rho^2 = \dfrac{1 - \rho^2}{N - 2}$

(*Note:* if the population correlation coefficient, ρ, does not equal 0, Fisher's z transformation must be used. Generally, however, we wish to test the hypothesis that $\rho = 0$.)

Some Properties of Least Squares

Take a regression model of the form

$$y_t = \alpha + \pi x_t + v_t, \; t = 1, 2, \ldots, T.$$

Denote the estimated equation as

$$y_t' = a + Px_t.$$

It can be shown that

$$a = \bar{y} - P\bar{x}.$$

Also

$$P = \frac{\text{cov}(y,x)}{\text{var}(x)}.$$

It therefore follows from the definition of r that

$$r_{xy}^2 = P \operatorname{cov}(y,x)/\operatorname{var}(y)$$
$$= P^2 \operatorname{var}(x)/\operatorname{var}(y).$$

It can further be shown that

$$P = \pi + \frac{\operatorname{cov}(v,x)}{\operatorname{var}(x)}.$$

From this it follows that if $E[\operatorname{cov}(v,x)] = 0$, then $E(P) = \pi$ and P is unbiased. However, if for some reason v is positively (negatively) correlated with x, $E[\operatorname{cov}(v,x)]$ will be greater than (less than) zero, and $E(P) > P(<P)$. This indicates the estimate will be positively (negatively) biased.

CHAPTER 2
THE DEMAND FOR LABOR

2.1 Introduction

The crucial concept underpinning the demand for labor is that of marginal productivity. The concept of marginal productivity can be used to build up a negative relationship between the wage rate and the level of employment offered by a firm. This is basically because employment increases are said eventually to cause labor's marginal product to decrease. Then, because each profit maximizing firm is supposed to attempt to adjust employment so as to equate labor's marginal product with the wage, it follows that increased employment is only compatible with a decreased wage. The firm's demand schedule for labor is thus supposed to be downward sloping. Moreover, because the industry's labor demand curve is derived from those of its constituent firms—though only rarely will it be the sum of the individual firm marginal revenue product schedules—we would also expect the industry curve to be downward sloping. The basic goal of this chapter is to explain these relationships.

According to Clark, whose name is perhaps most associated with this concept, the marginal productivity principle constituted a theory of wages.[1] This is still a popular misconception. It must be stressed that the rule that wages tend to equality with the value of marginal product is only meant to explain the nature of the demand for labor. To explain the wage rate, we must also introduce supply factors. Still applicable is Marshall's famous observation: "Demand and supply exert equally important influences on wages; neither has a claim to predominance any more than has either blade of a scissors. . . ."[2]

From the microeconomic point of view, that is, from the standpoint of a given firm, the marginal productivity principle is best thought of as determining the firm's level of employment rather than contributing to the determination of its wage. This is because, for a given firm, the wage rate can

1. J. B. Clark, *The Distribution of Wealth* (New York: Macmillan, 1900), p. 3.
2. A. Marshall, *Principles of Economics,* 8th ed. (London: Macmillan, 1966), p. 442.

be taken as being determined exogenously by aggregate or nationwide forces, such as government minimum-wage legislation. Employment is then supposed to be adjusted so as to bring labor's marginal product into equality with the wage.

It is really only at the macroeconomic level that the marginal productivity principle can be said to be useful in analyzing the determination of the general wage rate. Here, the supply of labor can be taken as given—determined by demographic or other forces. It might then be argued that the conjunction of the aggregate demand for labor, as derived from some aggregate labor marginal productivity, with the given labor supply will indicate the general wage rate. This particular line of argument is taken up in chapter 8, when the influence of unions on the level of wages is considered. The main focus of this chapter will be on the microeconomic level of analysis. Hence, we will mainly be analyzing the demand for labor of the firm and the industry.

The discussion proceeds as follows. First, the basic theory of the demand for labor under both competitive and noncompetitive market regimes is set out. Then certain criticisms of the theory are presented and evaluated. Finally, we turn our attention to the empirical estimation of demand curves.

2.2 The Firm Demand Curve for Labor

The Case of Labor Being the Sole Variable Input. The proposition we wish to demonstrate here is that the profit maximizing firm will tend to employ labor up to the point at which the value of the marginal product of that labor equals the extra cost of that labor. Generally, the value of labor's marginal product will simply be the output price multiplied by marginal product, and the extra cost of the labor will simply be the wage rate. Qualifications to both statements will be entered subsequently, but the aspect we would emphasize at the outset is that this proposition argues that employment depends on technology (which determines labor's marginal product), on the product market (which determines the price of the product), on the labor market (which determines the wage rate), and on the assumption of profit maximization.

At this point we might ask whether conditions in the capital market affect the firm's employment of labor. This question may initially be sidestepped, because we assume the firm's stock of capital to be given in the short run. Labor is then the sole variable input, and the firm's decision problem is simplified to the extent that it has only to decide on the profit maximizing level of labor input, given capital, and not the profit maximizing level of both types of input simultaneously. In the next section, we shall consider this latter, long-run problem, so labelled because it takes longer to vary the size of a firm's factory and its investment in plant and equipment than to vary its labor input alone. We shall also, for the present, ignore variations in the intensity of labor use—for example, variations in the number of hours worked per man via overtime arrangements—and simply take labor services to be proportional to the number of men hired.

The technological aspect of labor demand and the important distinction between the short run and the long run are illustrated in figure 2.1. Panel (a) of figure 2.1 shows a set of isoquants. Each isoquant is a locus of the various combinations of capital and labor which produce the stipulated output. In the short run, however, we suppose that the capital input is given; this means that all the output possibilities of the isoquant map are not open to the firm. Rather, the firm is free to vary only its labor input. For example, with capital stock $\bar{K}_1$ the firm can expand output only along the straight line parallel to the labor (L) axis. With labor input L_2, the firm would be at point Y, producing 40 units of output; while with labor input L_3 it would be at point Z, producing 60 units. This short-run relationship between output and labor, given capital stock $\bar{K}_1$, is perhaps more easily seen from the total product curve $(L,\bar{K}_1)$ of panel (b) in figure 2.1. In a similar manner, we can also derive a total product curve for a smaller plant, with capital stock $\bar{K}_0$. The assumptions on which the isoquant map has been drawn indicate that smaller plants are more efficient at low levels of labor input—in the engineering sense of producing more output for a given labor input—but are less efficient at higher levels of labor input. This has traditionally been supposed to be the case and accords with common sense.

In the short run, therefore, the production possibilities open to the two plants are illustrated by the total product curves of panel (b). In the long run, however, the firm is assumed to be free to vary its capital stock as well as its labor input. The long-run possibilities can be illustrated by drawing an *expansion path,* given by the dashed line in panel (a). This shows the least-cost factor combinations if both capital and labor are free to vary. At any point on this line the ratio of the marginal products of the factors (the slope of the isoquants) equals the ratio of their prices (the slope of the isocost lines), which is the condition for minimizing cost. If, as both inputs are increased in a given proportion, output increases in the same proportion, we speak of constant returns to scale. If output increases more (less) than proportionately we speak of increasing (decreasing) returns to scale. As drawn, the diagram shows a tendency toward diminishing returns to scale, which seems more plausible.

While in the long run output might increase more or less proportionately with labor input, any given short-run curve is assumed ultimately to be concave to the labor axis. In other words, as the labor input in combination with a *given* capital stock increases, output will eventually increase less than proportionately. Indeed, as the short-run curves of panel (b) of figure 2.1 are drawn, it can be seen that a point is reached where total output fails to increase with increases in labor input (labor's marginal product is zero) and even begins to fall with further additions (labor's marginal product becomes negative). These results can crudely be justified on the grounds that, with a

Figure 2.1 The Production Function Illustrating the Difference between the Long Run and the Short Run

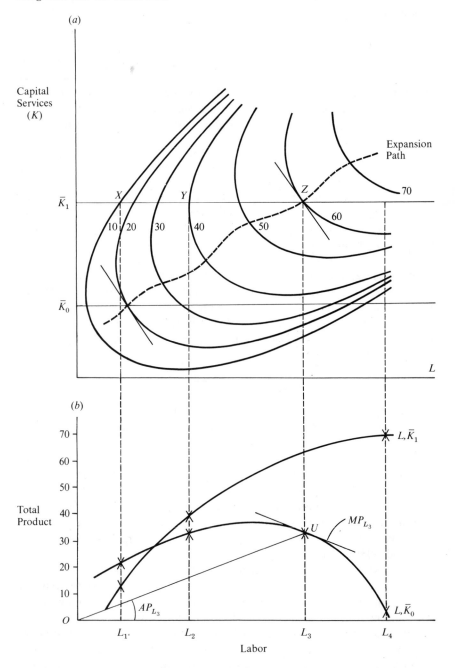

given size factory, as the size of the labor complement is increased, the employees eventually get in one another's way and actually impede the production process.

Thus, it is argued that there will always be eventually diminishing returns to labor in the short run. The economists' statement is that labor's marginal productivity will decline in the short run. This phenomenon is sometimes referred to as the *law of variable proportions*. The short-run total product functions of figure 2.1 have this property. Consider the curve appropriate to plant size $\bar{K}_0$. The marginal product of a given labor input is represented by the slope of the tangent to the total product curve at that point. By definition,

$$MP_{L_i} \equiv \frac{\Delta TP_i}{\Delta L_i} \qquad (2.1)$$

where MP_{L_i} is the marginal product of labor when total labor input is L_i;
$\quad\quad \Delta TP_i$ is the increment in total product consequent upon a small increase in labor input from L_i; and
$\quad\quad \Delta L_i$ is the amount of the small increase in labor input from L_i.

From figure 2.1, it can be seen that, if the labor input is L_3, the marginal product of labor is the slope of the tangent at U, denoted by MP_{L_3}. Because the slope of this tangent is negative, the marginal product of labor at labor input L_3 is negative. It should be noted, however, that the average product of labor is still positive. By definition,

$$AP_{L_i} \equiv \frac{TP_i}{L_i}$$

where AP_{L_i} is the average product of labor input L_i; and
$\quad\quad TP_i$ is the total product associated with labor input L_i.

Figure 2.1 shows that the average product of labor input L_3 is the ratio UL_3/OL_3, which is the slope of the ray from the origin, OU, and is denoted by AP_{L_3}. Observe that AP_{L_3} remains positive. The construction of the curve in panel (b) shows that both the average and the marginal product of labor fall continuously as labor input is increased and also that the average product of labor everywhere exceeds the marginal product of labor. This is a commonly assumed relationship.

The next step is to join the technological component of the theory to the product and labor market components and then apply the profit maximization assumption. This integration is best pursued with the aid of a diagram. Consider figure 2.2, which is somewhat intimidating at first sight but which is useful once understood. Quadrant I shows a short-run production function and indicates the maximum output obtainable from various labor inputs, given $\bar{K}$. In this situation, we are assuming that management is efficient and

Figure 2.2   A Graphical Statement of the Marginal Productivity Theory of the Demand for Labor

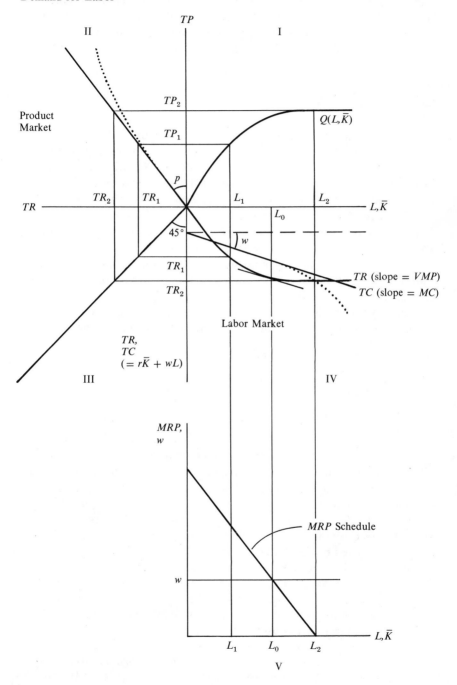

that there are no restrictive/protective labor practices (this latter assumption is taken up in some detail in chapter 9). Quadrant II gives the relationship between physical output, *TP*, and revenue, *TR*. If we assume that the firm is but one of many, so that the price, *p*, of its product does not vary as its output changes, then we have the simple relationship

$$TR = p \cdot TP$$

where *p* is a constant.[3]

Such a function is graphed in quadrant II of figure 2.2. More usually, however, we might assume imperfect competition in the product market, so that the firm must reduce the price of its product as it markets more. In such a case, the total revenue curve of quadrant II would bend inward toward the *TP* axis and would follow a path similar to that described by the dotted line. We shall consider this complication later.

Profits are defined as the difference between total revenue and total costs, *TC*. We assume that the firm wishes to maximize this difference. In our two-factor model, total costs comprise the costs of capital, assumed invariant with respect to output, and labor costs, which vary with output. (Some labor costs are also fixed—for example, expenditures must be incurred in screening new employees whether or not they make much contribution to output—but again we leave this complication for later.) Thus we may write

$$TC = r\bar{K} + wL$$

where *r* is the capital rental rate;
$\bar{K}$ is the fixed quantity of capital; and
w is the wage rate.

The wage rate may or may not vary with labor input and, hence, the firm's output. If the firm is a price-taker in the labor market, we can assume that the wage rate is given and constant. Such a total cost relationship is illustrated in quadrant IV of figure 2.2. More usually, however, we might wish to assume that there are elements of monopsony attaching to the firm's position in the labor market; that is, the firm must pay a higher wage rate as it hires more labor. In this case, the *TC* curve will bend away from the *L* axis and follow the path indicated by the dotted line in quadrant IV. This is another consideration that will be more fully discussed later.

We now have a total revenue curve in quadrant II of figure 2.2 (*TR-TP* space, or product market space) and a total cost curve in quadrant IV (*TC-L* space, or labor market space). It only remains to join them. This is where the 45° line of quadrant III is useful. We can use this construct to trace total

---

3. Think of *p* as the net price, that is, the price of output after subtracting the costs of raw materials going to make up that output. *TR* is thus the sum of factor payments and as such equal to value added.

revenues, as derived in quadrant II, across to quadrant IV. This is useful if we wish to consider labor input explicitly, because L is located on one of the axes. Alternatively, we could trace total costs, as given in quadrant IV, across to quadrant II. It would then be possible to compare total costs and total revenues using output as the explicit variable. The two procedures amount to the same thing, but they must not be confused. It is necessary always to check whether the total cost and total revenue curves are referred to the output axis or to the labor axis.

Let us put figure 2.2 through its paces. Starting in quadrant I, take a particular labor input, L_1. This, in accordance with the short-run production function, is associated with output level TP_1. From quadrant II, it can be seen that output TP_1 is associated with total revenue TR_1. Tracing TR_1 across to quadrant IV gives a point (TR_1, L_1) on the total revenue curve in labor market space. Other points on the (TR, L) curve are drawn up in the same way. Observe that the shape of this curve is closely related to the shape of the production function in quadrant I.

The next step is to compare the TC and TR curves in quadrant IV. If the firm chooses to maximize profits, it will select that labor input for which the difference between the two curves is maximized. In figure 2.2, profit is maximized at labor input L_0. Note that the difference between the two curves is maximized at the point where the slope of the TR schedule equals the slope of the TC curve. The slope of the TR curve gives the value of the marginal product of labor, $p \cdot MP_L$. This is labelled VMP, for value of marginal product.[4] The slope of the TC curve represents the marginal cost of production and here is equal to the wage rate. At maximum profit, the firm that is perfectly competitive in both product and labor markets will select its labor input so as to equate the wage with labor's marginal revenue product. This is the proposition we set out to demonstrate.

Now let us suppose that the wage rate falls. If everything else remains unchanged, the firm will theoretically expand its labor input until the wage rate is once more brought into equality with the new, lower VMP (or MRP) of labor. The firm will always attempt to stay on its VMP (or MRP) of labor schedule, graphed in quadrant V of figure 2.2. In this sense, the VMP (or MRP) schedule can be identified as the demand curve for labor.

At this point, it is useful to interject a brief comment on the *elasticity of substitution*. This concept, measured as the proportionate change in the utilization ratio of two factor inputs divided by the proportionate change in their prices,[5] is indicated by the curvature of production isoquants such as those given in figure 2.1. It is sufficient here to note that the elasticity of substitution will be greater (and the isoquants straighter), the less subject to

4. Sometimes it is worth distinguishing between $p \cdot MP_L$ and $MR \cdot MP_L$, where MR is marginal revenue. Traditionally, the term *value marginal product* (VMP) is assigned to the former while *marginal revenue product* (MRP) is assigned to the latter. Here, because $p = MR$, the distinction is unimportant.

5. For an algebraic formulation, see appendix 8-A.

diminishing returns is the variable factor, labor, and the less steeply sloped is the *VMP* (or *MRP*) schedule. Conversely, right-angled production isoquants imply vertical *VMP* curves.

The Case of Several Variable Inputs. In the long run, the firm uses a number of factors that can be varied in quantity, labor being but one such factor. Given this factor variability, the firm's demand for labor schedule will not be given by the short-run *VMP* curve. This is because a change, say a fall, in the price of labor will not merely imply an increase in the amount of labor associated with a given capital stock, but will also lead to an increase in the amount of capital it is profitable to employ. The latter result may be termed the *scale effect*. The firm supposedly chooses a particular scale so as to maximize profits *on the basis of given factor prices*. If the price of labor falls, it may well be profit maximizing to expand plant size. In these circumstances, the labor force will be expanded because the labor/capital ratio and the amount of capital itself increase.

A method of demonstrating this proposition is given in figure 2.3. Assume that the initial wage is W_H. Given this price and the capital rental rate, we can use the production functions of quadrant I to map out total cost functions in quadrant II. One such function, appropriate to a capital stock of K_0 and a wage of W_H, is illustrated as $TC(W_H K_0)$. A family of such curves can be drawn. The outermost boundary or *envelope* of these curves is shown by $LTC(W_H)$. The firm is supposed to compare this *LTC* curve with the total revenue curve, *TR,* and maximize the difference between them. This point of maximum profit obtains at output TP_0, and the associated short-run total cost curve is $TC(W_H K_0)$. From quadrant I we observe that this curve corresponds to production function $Q(L, K_0)$ and labor input L_0. The total revenue product curve corresponding to $Q(L, K_0)$ is graphed in quadrant V as MRP_0. The intersection of the wage line, W_H, with MRP_0 gives equilibrium at point *A,* with L_0 men employed.

Now assume that the wage decreases to W_L. As a result, costs fall and a new envelope total cost function emerges. This is shown as $LTC(W_L)$ in quadrant II. The output at which there is maximum difference between *LTC* and *TR* is TP_1, and we have illustrated the associated cost curve as $TC(W_L K_1)$. Using the same reasoning as before, this corresponds to a marginal revenue product curve in quadrant V, namely MRP_1. Equilibrium obtains at point *C.* Thus, if the wage falls to W_L, the firm initially moves along its short-run demand curve from *A* to point *B.* In the long run, however, it is profit maximizing also to increase the size of plant, so moving to point *C.*

From figure 2.3, we can also demonstrate the important proposition that the demand for labor will be less elastic as the degree of substitutability between labor and other factor inputs decreases. This is one of Marshall's four *rules for the elasticity of derived demand,* to which we shall have exten-

Figure 2.3   The Derivation of the Long-Run Demand Curve for Labor

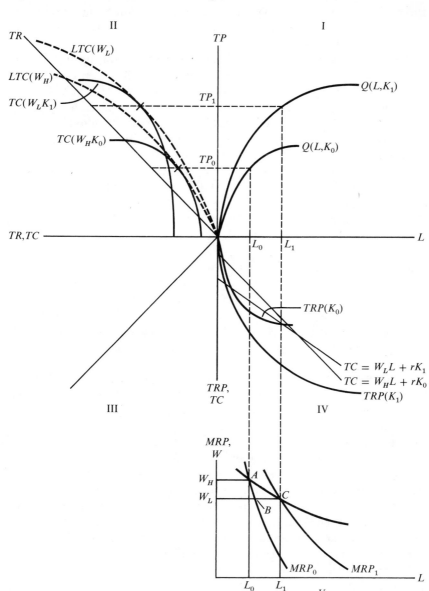

sive recourse when discussing union power and wage setting (chapter 7 and 8). These laws are thought to be relevant to union behavior because the lower the firm's elasticity of demand for labor, the lower the cost, in terms of reduced employment, of high wage settlements. From figure 2.3, it can be seen that, if the elasticity of substitution is high, the firm can more easily move from the inelastic short-run to the more elastic long-run demand curve. If the elasticity of substitution is low, however, only the inelastic short-run curve tends to be relevant. Thus, we can see immediately that low substitutability implies a more inelastic demand curve.

The three other Marshallian rules are also worth introducing at this point. The second rule states that the demand for labor will be less elastic when the demand for the product is less elastic. Up to now, we have been assuming a perfectly elastic demand for the product, that is, a straight line total revenue curve. But this rule can be demonstrated by assuming inelastic product demand; that is, a total revenue curve concave to the output axis. This yields a more steeply declining marginal revenue product curve, which implies a more inelastic demand for labor. The third rule states that demand for labor is less elastic the less elastic is the supply of other factors. The fourth rule is that as the share of labor costs in total costs decreases, demand elasticity decreases. These latter rules are not easily demonstrated using figure 2.3, so our discussion of them is remitted to chapter 7.[6]

2.3   The Derivation of Market Demand for Labor

The market or industry demand curve for labor is the sum of the constituent individual firm demands. However, the industry demand curve is unlikely simply to be the sum of firms' *MRP* (or *VMP*) curves. This is because we took product price and the prices of factors other than labor as given in deriving these curves. When all firms are expanding or contracting simultaneously, these assumptions are scarcely tenable. If the industry were very small in relation to the economy, we could perhaps maintain the assumption of given factor prices; but in the normal course of events, we would expect factor prices to increase with industry expansion—a process attributed to *pecuniary external diseconomies*. In any case, the price of the industry's output is bound to vary as its output changes.

Suppose that the price of labor relative to other input prices falls substantially. This will result in an increased use of labor input by all firms within the industry and in correspondingly increased output. The latter will cause the product price to fall. Unless offset by technical external economies, product price cuts will subsequently shift each firm's value marginal product schedule and hence the individual firm demand curve for labor. By *technical external economies,* we refer to the possibilities of changes in each firm's production function consequent upon an industry expansion that serves to raise the *VMP* curve.

In figure 2.4, the firm demand curve for labor, for the going market price of the commodity, is denoted by $d_0 d_0'$. If the wage rate is W_0, the firm will use l_0 units of labor. Aggregate employment of all firms is L_0 units of labor. Point *A* thus represents one point on the market labor demand schedule. If the

6. See also M. Friedman, *Price Theory,* 2nd ed. (Chicago: Aldine Publishing, 1976), chap. 7.

Figure 2.4   Derivation of the Market Demand for Labor

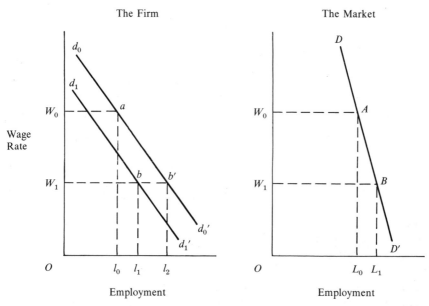

The Firm   The Market

price of labor falls to W_1, we might envision the firm as moving down $d_0 d_0'$ from point a to b'. But, as all firms will increase their utilization of labor, output will expand. The rightward shift in the industry supply curve will cause a fall in product price. The individual firm demand curves will then shift leftward to, say, $d_1 d_1'$. Thus, at wage W_1, b is the equilibrium point and not b'. Aggregate employment then becomes L_2 units of labor, and point B is obtained on the industry demand schedule. DD' represents the locus of such points.

Thus, we would expect the industry labor demand curve to be less elastic than that of the individual constituent firm, unless there are strong forces making for technical external economies. These forces would include factors such as improved information or a better transport infrastructure that tend to be associated with a larger industry. These latter forces presumably are long term in their effect; so we can be reasonably certain that, in the short run, industry demand is less elastic than firm demand.

The question might now be raised: how elastic is the economywide labor demand schedule? This question forces consideration of general equilibrium analysis, or macroeconomics. The issues involved are considered in depth in chapter 12; the following summary is sufficient for present analysis. It is generally assumed by both classical and Keynesian economists that, at the level of the economy, the average real wage rate and the level of employment are inversely correlated. The reasoning is that for an economy in equilibrium, as with the firm in equilibrium,

$$W = P \cdot AMP_L$$

where W is the aggregate average money wage rate;
$\quad P$ is the aggregate average price level; and
AMP_L is the aggregate marginal physical product of labor.

Thus, we can see that

$$W/P = AMP_L.$$

If we also argue that, by analogy with the firm or industry, AMP_L falls as the aggregate employment level rises, it follows that the postulated relationship between the real wage and employment holds.

However, the concept of an aggregate marginal product of labor is much under attack. Moreover, we might well question whether W/P and AMP_L are independent. Thus, following Keynes, it might be argued that a cut in money wages, to the extent that it is successful in lowering real wages, might lead to the expectation of further cuts.[7] The prospect of a slow sag in money wages and prices is unlikely to be conducive to business morale and might itself cause lower AMP_L. These subjects will be taken up in greater detail in subsequent chapters. They are mentioned here to illustrate the difficulties involved in moving from a partial to a general equilibrium framework of analysis. Nevertheless, the much firmer partial equilibrium predictions continue to have important policy implications. This is because many wage movements narrowly affect a particular establishment or industry, as occurs, for example, when government or union action pushes up certain wage rates. In such a case, the partial equilibrium prediction of adverse employment consequences has clear relevance.

2.4 Marginal Productivity Theory and Imperfectly Competitive Markets

Consider the impact of conditions of imperfect competition in the firm's product and/or labor market on the rule that says the wage rate will tend toward equality with the value of labor's marginal product (*VMP*). Let us first look at product market imperfections. These may be introduced into the analysis by assuming that the firm's output price is not given but, rather, varies inversely with the level of output. This condition may be expressed diagrammatically by drawing a total revenue schedule that is not a straight line, but instead curves toward the output axis quadrant II of figure 2.2. It follows that marginal revenue is everywhere lower than average revenue (the price of the product). Consequently, the returns to the firm from employing an additional unit of labor decline, not merely because of diminishing returns

7. J. M. Keynes, *The General Theory of Employment, Interest and Money* (London: Macmillan, 1936), chap. 19.

to the variable input, labor, but also because of the diminishing revenue associated with the output produced by the extra labor input. The total revenue product curve of labor (quadrant IV of figure 2.2) can be seen to bend more strongly toward the L axis under these circumstances than under conditions of perfect competition in the product market. However, it should be stressed that the principle of the firm searching for that labor input at which the slope of the total revenue product curve ($=MRP$) equals the slope of the total cost curve ($=w$) remains the same.

Thus, the labor demand schedule with perfect competition in the product market is the VMP curve, whereas that associated with imperfect competition in the product market is the MRP curve. It can be shown that

$$MRP = MR \cdot MP_L = w \qquad (2.2a)$$
$$VMP = AR \cdot MP_L = w \qquad (2.2b)$$

where MR is the marginal revenue; and
$\quad\ AR$ is the average revenue.

It follows that VMP will exceed MRP for a given labor input, *ceteris paribus,* because MR is always less than AR when the latter is falling. For a straight line demand curve, the output associated with a given MR is exactly half that associated with the same AR.[8]

The relationships given in equation (2.2a) and equation (2.2b) can be derived algebraically. This derivation is worth pursuing, because it provides another vantage point from which to survey marginal productivity theory and will be helpful when we come to consider situations of monopsony.

We begin with the definition of the marginal cost, MC_i, of producing the ith unit of output

$$MC_i \equiv \Delta TC_i / \Delta TP_i$$

8. This can be demonstrated as follows. Take the linear commodity demand curve

$$P = a - bTP.$$

Total revenue is

$$TP \cdot P = aTP - bTP^2.$$

Marginal revenue is

$$MR \equiv \frac{d(TP \cdot P)}{dTP} = a - 2bTP.$$

Thus, we can see that the MR schedule slopes downward twice as steeply as does the price schedule.

where ΔTC_i is the increment in total cost of increasing output by a small
amount from TP_i.

Upon rearrangement, we have

$$MC_i \equiv \left(\frac{\Delta TC_i}{\Delta L_i}\right)\left(\frac{\Delta L_i}{\Delta TP_i}\right). \qquad (2.3)$$

Now $\Delta TC_i/\Delta L_i$ is the change in total cost around output TP_i divided by the
change in labor input associated with this change in cost. Call this the
marginal cost of employing labor, ME_i. If we think of ΔL_i as being an
additional unit of labor, and if competition rules in the labor market, ME_i
will simply be the going wage rate, w. However, if monopsony elements
occur in the labor market, ME_i will exceed the wage rate. From equation
(2.1), we know that $\Delta L_i/\Delta TP_i$ equals $1/MP_{L_i}$. Consequently, equation (2.3)
becomes

$$MC_i \equiv w \cdot 1/MP_{L_i}.$$

The profit maximizing firm will attempt to operate at that output level at
which marginal cost equals marginal revenue. Therefore, in equilibrium,

$$MR_i = w \cdot 1/MP_{L_i} \qquad (2.4)$$

where MR_i is the marginal revenue product associated with output TP_i. By
substituting price (AR) for marginal revenue in this formula, as we are
enabled to do given the assumption of perfect competition in the product
market, we derive the condition for VMP in equation (2.2b) above. If we do
not make the substitution, we have the condition for MRP in equation (2.2a).

It might be thought that, because the MRP schedule will lie below the
VMP schedule, *ceteris paribus,* the amount of employment offered by the
monopolistic firm will be lower than that achieved under perfect competition.
In terms of figure 2.5, faced with a given wage of W_0, the monopolist would
operate at point A (employment L_m units of labor), whereas the competitive
equilibrium for the firm would be at point B (with the associated employment level L_c). Note that this result follows only if other things are equal as
between the monopolistic and competitive situation. Yet it is hard to see
how the two situations can be compared. Presumably, we are comparing the
monopoly with a similar, though competitive, industry. But we have seen that
there is no reason to suppose that the competitive industry's labor demand
curve will have the same elasticity as its constituent firms' VMP curves. The
VMP curve is thus best considered not as a means of comparing monopoly
with competition, but as a special case of the MRP curve that occurs when
price and marginal revenue are equal.

Now let us turn our attention to monopsony. *Monopsony* refers to a
situation in which there is a single buyer in the factor market. A buyer of

Figure 2.5   The Demand for Labor in a Noncompetitive Product Market

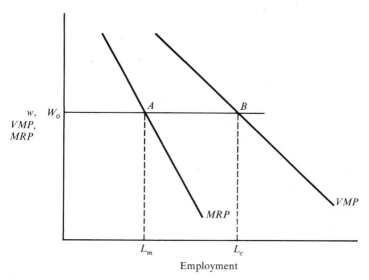

labor in a perfectly competitive input market views the supply curve of labor as a horizontal line with respect to the L axis, because his purchases are so small, relative to the market, that changes on his part do not perceptibly affect market price. A monopsonist, in contrast, being the sole buyer in the market, faces a positively sloped labor supply curve. Changes in his volume of purchases do affect input price, so that input price increases as he expands input usage. The monopsonist has, therefore, to consider the marginal expense or marginal cost of purchasing an additional unit of labor. We can view the labor supply curve to the firm as an average cost of labor curve. The marginal expense or marginal cost of labor input will rise above the supply curve, because all units employed receive the new, higher price. The additional unit of labor increases total cost by more than the price of that additional unit. Suppose the configuration of the supply curve is such that one worker may be hired at a weekly wage of $230 and a second worker for $245. Because both workers must be paid the same amount—in the absence of discriminating monopsony—the price per unit of labor is now $245. The total cost of employment has risen to $490. The marginal expense, or the extra cost, of labor is $260, even though the price of labor is $245 per unit.

The relation between the marginal expense or marginal cost of labor and labor's supply price is charted in panel (b) of figure 2.6. That the marginal cost of hiring labor (ME) will be higher than the wage rate (w') if w' varies directly with L can also be seen using the dashed total cost curve (TC') of panel (a), which is a reproduction of quadrant IV of figure 2.2. The wage rate is measured by the slope of the ray from point A intersecting the TC' curve at the given labor input. For example, at input L_0, this ray is AC, which has

Figure 2.6   Equilibrium Employment of Labor Under Monopsony

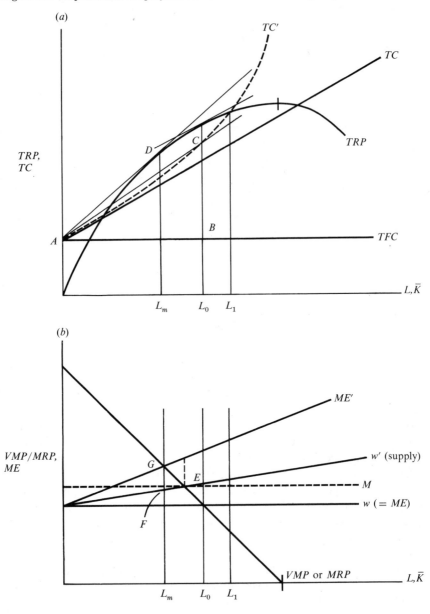

the slope CB/AB. The marginal cost of hiring labor, on the other hand, is measured by the slope of the tangent to the TC' curve at the given labor input. It can be seen that, throughout the range of the TC' function, the slope of this tangent is always greater than the slope of the ray at a given employment level.

Equation (2.2a) states that the condition for profit maximization under perfect competition in the input market is[9]

$$MP_{L_i} \cdot MR_i = w.$$

However, if the firm is a monopsonist, it must set

$$MP_{L_i} \cdot MR_i = ME_i \qquad (2.5)$$

where ME_i is the marginal expenditure associated with changes in labor input around L_i.

The explanation for this substitution can most easily be seen by referring to figure 2.6. Under monopsony, the TC' curve is the appropriate total cost function. The profit maximizing firm is assumed, as before, to seek to employ that quantity of labor for which the distance between the total cost curve and total revenue curve is at a maximum. As before, the profit maximizing labor input is given by the point at which the slopes of the two schedules are equal. This labor input in figure 2.6 is L_m. The slope of the total cost curve, however, is not the wage rate, as it would be were the total cost schedule given by TC, but the marginal cost of employing labor, ME'. Thus, equation (2.5) follows.

The analysis can also be presented in the form depicted in panel (b) of figure 2.6. Indeed, this is the more usual presentation, although it is exactly equivalent to that employed in panel (a). The returns from employing labor are given by the MRP schedule (or the VMP curve—the difference is not material here). The MRP function is the slope of the TRP schedule of panel (a). Note that when the TRP curve reaches a maximum, MRP is zero. Supply conditions facing the monopolist are given by the rising supply curve, w', which measures the changing slope of rays such as AC in the upper panel. If the total cost curve has a constant slope (curve TC), the wage rate is represented by the horizontal line, w, in panel (b). The marginal cost of hiring labor is shown by the curve ME'. It has been drawn so as to have exactly twice the slope of the supply curve, w', as is appropriate if the latter is linear.[10] Equilibrium is given by the intersection of the ME' curve and MRP

---

9. We could also use equation (2.2b) without affecting the argument.

10. Consider the linear supply curve $w' = a + bL$. It follows that total labor costs are

$$w'L = aL + bL^2.$$

The marginal cost of hiring labor is therefore

$$ME \equiv \frac{d(w'L)}{dL}$$

$$= a + 2bL.$$

curve at employment L_m. At this employment level, the wage rate, which is read from the supply curve, will be $L_m F$.[11] Note that $L_m F$ is less than MRP_{L_m}; it is this discrepancy that is termed "exploitation."

Figure 2.6 demonstrates a surprising possibility. In the presence of exploitation, in the technical sense of the word, an increase in the wage rate need not induce a fall off in the level of employment. Thus, the negative relation between wage and employment levels, which demand theory leads us to expect, might be obscured. Consider the imposition of a federal minimum wage at a level given by the dashed curve labelled as M in panel (b) of figure 2.6. Note that the marginal expense of labor input would be coincident with the wage up to point E. Only to the right of point E, which is the intersection of the M curve with the supply or w' function, would the ME' curve diverge from the M curve. The monopsonist could thus be in equilibrium at point E, implying both a higher wage and a higher employment level than at point F. Indeed, the wage could be set even higher than M and labor demanded still exceed L_m. The highest level at which the minimum wage could be set without actually reducing employment below L_m is given by $L_m G$. At this wage, there are no monopsony profits; total costs equal total revenues. The latter point can be better appreciated by considering panel (a) of figure 2.6. The highest minimum wage consistent with employment L_m is represented by the ray AD, implying a total cost schedule just tangential to the total revenue curve at point D (remember that the total cost curve will be rotated to the left by minimum-wage legislation).

The above analysis has an important policy implication: we cannot be dogmatic as to the likely employment effects of minimum-wage legislation. Employment can be either increased or diminished by legislative intervention of this nature. Unfortunately, as will be seen in later chapters, we have no precise information as to the extent of monopsony within the labor market. A favorite textbook example of monopsony is the one-company town. Yet this example must surely be receding in importance with the twentieth century improvement in transportation facilities. A more relevant example could be female employment (further examples will be considered in chapter 5). Women with family responsibilities tend to search for jobs in a more restricted geographical area than do their husbands. On the other hand, it might be argued that because married women are secondary workers (see chapter 3), they find it easier to enter and to exit the labor force—making their labor supply more elastic than that of men. These subjects are considered in more detail in chapter 6, in the context of discrimination. Suffice it to say here that minimum-wage legislation for "women's trades," such as shop assistants, might not have dire employment consequences.

11. Note that point F lies off the MRP curve. This is why the MRP schedule should not strictly be regarded as the monopsonist's demand curve for labor.

2.5 Criticisms of Marginal Productivity Theory

Criticisms of the theory of labor demand have focused on four main issues. The first objection centers on the view that employers cannot make the calculations necessary to equate marginal costs with marginal returns. Second, it is argued that the assumption of profit maximization is invalid over large areas of the economy, particularly in the public sector. Third, the point is made that the smooth production functions employed by the theory give a misleading picture of actual technological possibilities, which are much more likely to be plagued by fixed factor ratios and indivisibilities. Fourth, because labor has certain important fixed costs, it is argued that labor input is best regarded as a quasi-fixed factor and not as a perfectly variable factor. To be sure, the theory has also come under attack from a variety of other directions,[12] but we shall here restrict our attention to these four basic elements.

Marginal Productivity Calculations. A standard criticism of the theory has been that employers are not able to make the kinds of calculation necessary to the setting up of production functions and the equation of marginal revenue product with marginal labor cost. One of the best-known attacks upon marginalism is that of Lester.[13] Employers sampled by Lester indicated that demand for their products was much more important than the level of wages in determining their employment levels. Specifically, in terms of weighted replies, product demand was said to be "twenty-six times as important as wage rates"[14] in determining labor demand. Let us point out at once, however, that this is hardly a criticism of the theory. Product demand is, after all, a basic determinant of marginal revenue product, which depends upon product price as well as workers' physical productivity. This is simply an aspect of the demand side.

A more basic problem is raised by attitude surveys of employers, such as those conducted by Lester.[15] We refer here to the difficulty of interpreting the attitudes displayed by the respondents (see chapter 5). Economists prefer to

---

12. Many have reacted unfavorably to the alleged ethical implications of marginal productivity theory. However, this particular criticism is something of a straw man. Economists need not attribute virtue to a neoclassically determined distribution of factor rewards. Given perfect competition and all the other conditions for a Pareto optimum, the payment of factors according to their marginal contributions to output will be efficient and hence maximize welfare. However, even if all these assumptions hold (and they do not), the normative significance attaching to the factor income distribution thus determined is outside the bounds of economics. For a path-breaking scientific study of justice, see J. R. Rawls, *A Theory of Justice* (Cambridge, Mass.: Harvard University Press, 1971).

13. R. A. Lester, "Shortcomings of Marginal Analysis for Wage Employment Problems," *American Economic Review* 36 (1946): 63–82.

14. Ibid., p. 81

15. See also R. A. Lester, *Hiring Practices and Labor Competition* (Princeton, N.J.: Princeton University Press, 1954).

look at what an individual does rather than what he says. The actions of the individual are then compared with the predictions generated by the economic model in question. Economists continue to work with the model—for example, in making policy recommendations—if its predictions appear to be consistent with the actions of individuals. The actual thought processes of the individual are interesting, but they constitute another research area and as such are the subject of psychological and sociological investigation. In putting forward the marginal productivity theory of labor demand, it is our belief that a firm's employment will respond to wage changes as if the entrepreneur thought in terms of marginal cost and marginal revenue. Discussion over whether he actually conceptualizes the profit maximizing problem in this way serves only to confuse the issue.[16]

The Profit Maximization Assumption.   Next consider the fundamental assumption underlying the model, namely that of profit maximization. It might properly be asked how such an assumption can be applicable to the public sector, in many areas of which there is no product to be sold and hence no profit to be maximized, even if there is the motive. Further, even if there is monetary revenue (for example, in the case of public utilities), there is often no corresponding duty to maximize profits; rather, the financial obligations are often specified in terms of a break-even requirement. Indeed, we might go even further and query whether the organizations of the public sector are stimulated to minimize costs. Alternatively put, public-sector organizations might not achieve the best-practice output for given inputs, as summarized by our short-run production functions. This would reveal itself in a leftward shift of the *MRP* schedule. In the long run, too, we might doubt whether public-sector organizations choose the correct cost minimizing point on the long-run function. These problems arise not so much because of the element of monopoly in the public sector, but because of the difficulty of evaluating the output of many public-sector agencies.

Consider the case of an organization that is constrained only to break even. In this situation, the wage equal to marginal revenue product condition must be violated, as can be seen from panel (a) of figure 2.6. The break-even rule means that total revenue equals total cost. Using the *TC'* curve, break-even occurs at labor input L_1, where the wage exceeds *MRP*. This result can be checked by comparing the w' and *MRP* curves of panel (b). At labor input L_1, the supply curve w' is well above the demand curve *MRP*. The same

16. See F. Machlup, "Theories of the Firm: Marginalist, Behavioral, Managerial," *American Economic Review* 57 (1967): 15. Machlup argues: "The question is not whether the firms of the real world will really maximize money profits, or whether they will even *strive* to maximize their money profits, but rather whether the assumption that this is the objective of the theoretical firms in the artificial world of our construction lead to conclusions—'inferred outcomes'—very different from those claimed from admittedly more realistic assumptions." See also, idem, "Marginal Analysis and Empirical Research," *American Economic Review* 36 (1946): 519–554.

analysis can be applied, with some modification, to the case of the satisficing monopolist. The modification in question would be to assume that such a monopolist aimed to earn a certain minimum profit rather than to maximize profits, thereby employing more labor than is required to maximize profits.[17] Here again the wage would still exceed *MRP*.

No precise rule appears to present itself when we consider the more difficult situation in which output is not marketed. Can we in any sense say that administrators and bureaucrats "economize?" Theories are incomplete in this area, presumably because of the relative unimportance of the public sector during the first half of the present century. However, there has been substantial growth in the public, or nonprofit-making, sector in the postwar interval; for example, by the mid-1960s, United States hospitals employed 1.3 million people—almost twice the employment offered by the automobile industry.[18] Therefore, it is not surprising that research interest in this area has been greatly increased.[19]

The basics of a theory of public-sector employment seem to be crystallizing in the following manner. The fundamental idea is to think of a public-sector agency's labor demand curve as being derived from voter-expressed demands for the services of that agency. The level of services required will be related to some budgetary appropriation. Voter demands can be thought of as one factor underlying the size of the agency's budget.[20] From this viewpoint, the budget can be seen as being a monetary measure of the *community utility* derived from the agency's activities. The budget can be substituted for the total revenue product concept used in the case of revenue-producing firms. Admittedly, objections can be raised to this construct, but it seems a useful first approximation. After all, it is the goal of the democratic political process to register community preferences in areas where the price mechanism fails to do so.[21]

The chief additional influences on the size of agency budgets are supposed to be the lobbying activities of bureau directors, of bureau employees, and of affected employee unions. Bureaucrats, so the argument runs, attempt to maximize the size of their budget.[22] Also, employee groups have more incentive to advance their own interests (they have more to gain) than the

17. W. J. Baumol, "On the Theory of Oligopoly," *Economica* 25 (1958): 190.
18. J. P. Newhouse, "Toward a Theory of Nonprofit Institutions: An Economic Model of a Hospital," *American Economic Review* 60 (1970): 64.
19. For references, see C. M. Lindsay, "A Theory of Government Enterprise," *Journal of Political Economy* 84 (1976): 1061–1077.
20. R. G. Ehrenberg, "The Demand for State and Local Government Employees," *American Economic Review* 63 (1973): 369.
21. The path-breaking analysis here is that of A. Downs, *An Economic Theory of Democracy* (New York: Harper, 1957).
22. W. A. Niskanen, *Bureaucracy and Representative Government* (Chicago: Aldine, 1971), chap. 3.

generality of voters (who must be concerned with many issues) have to cut them back.[23] Thus we would anticipate overproduction of governmental services relative to private services—because government tends to be more strongly unionized than private enterprise—and, by the same token, overproduction of some governmental services relative to others.

Niskanen's model of how the "output" of a government bureau is determined can be used to show how the determination of a bureau's output, and its labor demand, can be analyzed with the usual tools of economic analysis. Consider figure 2.7. We assume that it is somehow possible to measure the output of the bureau, and that a relationship between budgetary expenditures and output can be drawn up. Two such curves, B and B', are illustrated. These curves replace the total revenue curves used in the analysis of the firm. Their curvature summarizes the urgency of voters' demands for the output in question. For the flatter curve, B, we can consider the voters' demands to be elastic; this is, a small fall in the budgetary price per unit of output implies a large expansion in the demand for that output. This is not true of curve B', which represents the inelastic demand case. Line TC is the total cost curve for the agency.

The next step is to argue that the manager of the bureau seeks to maximize the budget of the bureau, subject to the budget at least covering the

23. To quote Downs, *Economic Theory*, p. 254: "Those who stand most to gain from exerting influence in a policy area are the ones who can best afford the expense of becoming expert about it."

Figure 2.7   Output Determination of a Bureaucracy

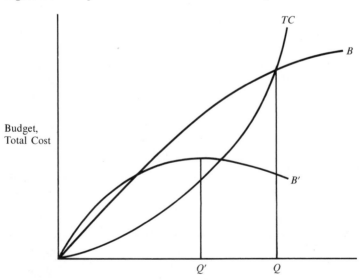

total cost of output. This gives an equilibrium output at point Q' for budget line B', and one at Q for budget line B. We will not pursue this budget maximization postulate beyond observing that it seems plausible. The important point is that the manager of a bureau facing an elastic demand (curve B) has an incentive to produce efficiently, namely to minimize cost (by shifting the TC curve down as far as possible, he can progress further up the B curve and reach a higher budget). However, the bureau in position Q' has no such incentive to economize. As a result, there is a higher probability that an inefficient factor mix will be chosen. This analysis indicates that, in some circumstances, but not others, it is sensible to think of the administrator as attempting to equate the marginal contribution to output of his various factors in the usual cost minimizing way. In both cases, however, more factor inputs will be used than are required for equating factor price with marginal product (here, marginal contribution to the budget). Nevertheless, given this cost minimizing tendency, an increase in the price of a given input should lead to less of it being used, *ceteris paribus*. Thus, we would still expect the demand curve for public employees to be downward sloping. The demand for public employees will, on this reasoning, be a function of the wage rate of the workers in question and the determinants of the agency's budget, such as the fiscal capability of the voters and the level of unionization among the workers in question. This is a testable theory, and we shall consider its empirical performance in the next section.

As for the broader question of whether wages in general approximate to the value of marginal product in general, it is tempting to devise a direct test. We could estimate an aggregate production function for the economy. From this, we could calculate labor's marginal product, which we could then compare with actual wages received. Unfortunately, it is extremely difficult to measure an aggregate production function, although we shall consider the results of some such exercises below.

The Nature of Technology.   The third major area of criticism of the theory concerns its assumptions as to the nature of technology. Factors of production are not perfectly divisible and factor ratios are not perfectly variable in the short run. If factors of production are not perfectly divisible, the demand curves for labor appear not as continuous functions of labor employed but as discontinuous functions. One such function is depicted in figure 2.8. In this case, any level of employment (say L_3) is associated with a range of values for the marginal product of labor (L_3A to L_3B). Alternatively, we may say that specific marginal product values are not related to specific employment levels but to ranges of employment. As a case in point, the marginal product of labor at point C on the wage axis is associated with the employment range L_1L_2. A similar case arises when there are technologically fixed labor requirements. Here, the marginal product schedule rises very rapidly to the point of technical capacity and then falls abruptly. At full capacity, the short-run demand schedule will be completely inelastic, and wage changes

Figure 2.8   The Discontinuous Labor Demand Schedule

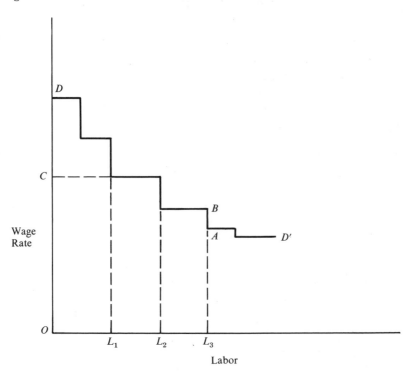

within this zone will leave the employment situation unchanged. The implication is that the smooth marginal revenue product schedule is appropriate
more to the medium term, when enough time has elapsed to change and
reorganize capital equipment in such a way as to give the efficient mix with
different labor inputs.

There is also the possibility that the production function will not be stable
and given. This would arise were output not independent of the wage rate. A
familiar form of this argument is the *economy of high wages* argument. Wage
increases, so the argument runs, raise the efficiency of workers, either by
increasing labor morale or by lifting the standard of living of a worker to a
level where he is more energetic and therefore more productive. An analogous construct is that of the *shock theory*, which hypothesizes that wage
increases serve to improve the efficiency of the enterprise by eliminating
managerial "slack." We should not be surprised to learn that both arguments
are much espoused by union bargainers. More fundamentally, the theories
postulate that there is more than one equilibrium position and that marginal
productivity theory cannot tell us which equilibrium combination of wages
and productivity is the correct one. Instead of a single marginal product
curve, there is a family of such curves, with higher wages corresponding to

higher marginal product schedules. It is possible, however, to construct a demand curve for labor that reflects the nonindependence of productivity: the demand curve simply connects the points at which each wage crosses its own marginal product curve.[24] A question of indeterminancy nonetheless arises, because the demand curve thus derived might be positively sloped over part of its range. In such a case, the demand curve could cut a positively sloped supply function at more than one point or, indeed, at no point— although we would regard this as a theoretical *curiosum*. In severely practical terms, it is unlikely that higher incomes much affect worker efficiency, at least within the developed world. Still, as Perlman observes: "The psychological pressures for higher incomes might affect worker efficiency. The environment of higher consumption standards might be such as to lead to improved attitudes and performances with higher wages."[25] The fact remains that there are limits to the extent to which wages can be raised on this principle, and we should expect a law of diminishing returns to operate.

Labor as a Quasi-fixed Factor.   Finally, let us consider labor as a quasi-fixed factor. Thus far, we have assumed that the only cost of employing labor consists of the wage rate or wage earnings. Yet it is clear that there exist certain fixed costs of employment. The presence of these costs has important implications for the incidence of unemployment by skill and also as regards the employer's choice between changes in the number of workers versus changes in hours of work.

A quasi-fixed factor is defined by Oi as one whose total employment cost is partially variable and partially fixed.[26] While the largest component of total labor costs is the variable wages bill, the firm also incurs fixed costs in hiring a given stock of workers. The fixed costs, comprising hiring costs and training costs,[27] represent an investment by the firm in its labor force. As such, these costs introduce an element of capital into the use of labor. Decisions regarding the labor input cannot now be based exclusively on the current relation between wages and marginal value products, but must also take account of the future course of those quantities. These matters are discussed in more detail in chapter 4, where we consider investment by firms in their workers—human capital formation that is specific to the firm. The essential point is that if a firm incurs investment costs in hiring and training labor, it must realize a return on those costs. The return will consist of the difference between the worker's marginal revenue product and his wage over the period of his employment with the firm. The presence of fixed costs of employment can be expected to drive a wedge between the wage rate and

24. R. Perlman, *Labor Theory* (New York: Wiley, 1969), pp. 50–56.
25. Ibid., p. 55.
26. W. Y. Oi, "Labor as a Quasi-fixed Factor," *Journal of Political Economy* 70 (1962): 538–555.
27. There are other fixed costs that occur throughout the period of employment and that are not related to hours of work. Examples are conventional payroll taxes and flat-rate contributions to private and public pension and welfare schemes.

current *MRP* (see figure 4.1). However, this outcome should not be regarded as damaging to the theory, but as an approach to greater realism.

The existence of fixed costs in the case of labor has interesting empirical implications. These result from the fact that labor in which the employer has invested firm-specific training is less likely to be laid off in the event of a drop in product demand. If such labor is laid off, the firm will lose the opportunity of amortizing the hiring and training costs it has incurred. Thus, identifying higher paid, more skilled individuals with the receipt of higher firm-specific investments, we would expect the demand for their services to fluctuate less over the business cycle than that for their lesser skilled counterparts. If we assume similar elasticities of supply for both these categories, it follows that the more skilled worker will experience greater employment continuity than the less skilled worker.

The notion of fixed costs also has clear implications for labor input utilization in the context of "hoarded" labor (see chapter 11). For the reasons cited above, the onset of a recession is not accompanied by a simultaneous cutback in labor input measured in terms of employees. Thus, the labor utilization rate, which is defined as the intensity with which a stock of labor input is worked, will fall. A revival in the growth of output can likewise be achieved without a simultaneous increase in the number of employees, because the supply of labor services can be increased simply by raising the utilization rate of already employed labor. Only after the labor market has undergone an adjustment to changing demand conditions through a change in the utilization rate of already employed labor will there be a subsequent adjustment in the level of employment in line with the new demand conditions. Thus, we would expect labor productivity to fluctuate procyclically. In the downswing, employers will tend to reduce hours per man rather than lay off workers, so reducing the ratio of output to workers. The converse would be true in the upswing.

2.6   Empirical Results on the Demand for Labor

The major test of marginal productivity theory has taken the form of estimating production functions for particular industry groups. In principle, this procedure permits calculation of the way in which the value of total output changes in response to a change in employment for a given capital stock; stated another way, it measures the actual marginal revenue product of labor averaged over the particular industry group. The *MRP* value thus obtained can be compared directly with the relevant average wage rate. Given the statistical difficulties associated with this approach, much controversy has surrounded production function estimates since Cobb's and Douglas's pioneering study of 1928.[28] Nevertheless, the basic results are

28. C. W. Cobb and P. H. Douglas, "A Theory of Production," *American Economic Review* 18 (1929): 139–165.

interesting and are briefly considered here; more advanced applications are discussed in chapter 8.

Other tests focus on the prediction of a downward sloping demand schedule. We would expect the employment of a particular grade of labor to vary inversely with the grade's wage rate relative to the wage rates of other labor grades and relative to the rental rate of capital, *ceteris paribus*. Results of some such test are also analyzed.

A final test procedure which commends itself is based on the notion that some grades of labor have a greater degree of "fixity" than others. We would expect the demand for such grades of labor to be more stable.

The Production Function Test. Suppose we estimate a relationship between the value of output ($p \cdot TP$), capital (K), and labor (L). The best known form of the relation in question is the Cobb-Douglas production function, which may be written

$$p \cdot TP = AK^{\alpha}L^{\beta}. \tag{2.6}$$

Equation (2.6) gives a relationship that is linear in the logarithms of output, capital, and labor. Thus,

$$\log(p \cdot TP) = \log A + \alpha \log K + \beta \log L.$$

Estimates of the exponents α and β should correspond to the shares of capital and labor in the value of output. This result follows because the *MRP* of labor is given by

$$MRP \equiv \frac{\partial(p \cdot TP)}{\partial L} = \beta AK^{\alpha}L^{\beta-1}$$

$$= \beta(p \cdot TP)/L.$$

According to marginal productivity theory, $w = MRP$. Therefore,

$$w = \beta(P \cdot TP)/L$$

or

$$\frac{wL}{p \cdot TP} = \beta. \tag{2.7}$$

Because wL is the wage bill and $p \cdot TP$ is value added, we can see that $wL/p \cdot TP$ represents labor's share in value added. Thus the test becomes simply: does labor's share equal the estimated value of β?

As we have noted earlier, there are many difficulties in estimating a relationship such as that represented in equation (2.6). These problems will be considered in detail in chapter 8, but we should at least mention the major issues here. The principal difficulty is one of allowing for shifts in the production function over time resulting from technical progress. Alternatively, if the function is estimated from a cross section of industries at a particular point in time, the problem is one of allowing for differences among industries in their production functions. In addition, there are also fundamental problems relating to the measurement of factor inputs in general and of capital services in particular.

The first empirical estimate of a production function for manufacturing industry was obtained by Cobb and Douglas.[29] Their results for United States manufacturing over the period 1899–1922 gave a β value of 0.81. This compared with an actual value for labor's share in manufacturing value added of 0.75, averaged over the period 1909–1918. Results for a cross section of Australian manufacturing industries, as of 1968, gave a β estimate of 0.54, which conforms closely with the calculated share of labor in value added.[30] At first blush, therefore, the model appears to pass the test. But given the difficulties inherent in aggregate production functions, we would not seek to emphasize this result.

However, it is interesting to explore in somewhat greater detail the results of a more recent production function estimate for United States manufacturing industries. Using quarterly data for the period 1949(2) to 1967(4), Craine obtained the following estimate:[31]

$$\ln(p \cdot TP) = -8.20 + 0.68 \ln L + 1.89 \ln H + 0.115 \ln K + 0.009\ T$$
$$(14.4) \quad (20.3) \qquad (13.9) \qquad (1.80) \qquad (17.4)$$

$$R^2 = 0.998$$
$$DW = 1.12$$

where $p \cdot TP$ is the value of the output;
L is the number of production employees;
H is the average number of hours worked per employee;
K is a measure of gross manufacturing capital stock;
T is a time trend; and
$|t|$ is given in parentheses.

Note how a time trend is introduced in this relationship so as crudely to allow for technical progress. Also note that labor input is split into two components, hours and employees. If average hours worked per employee fluctuate

29. Their results are given in full in chapter 8.
30. See P. H. Douglas, "The Cobb Douglas Production Function Once Again: Its History, Its Testing, and Some New Empirical Values," *Journal of Political Economy* 84 (1976): 913. For a criticism of the cross-section approach to estimating the production function, see E. H. Phelps Brown, "The Meaning of the Fitted Cobb Douglas Production Function," *Quarterly Journal of Economics* 71 (1957): 557.
31. R. Craine, "On the Service Flow from Labor," *Review of Economic Studies* 40 (1973): 43.

procyclically—because of the fixed costs of hiring labor—this factor should be allowed for if we are to estimate the marginal product per employee. It can be seen that increasing returns to hours are recorded in the empirical estimate; this is also true in the case of Great Britain.[32] The rationale for this result is that normal hours include training time and coffee breaks, while overtime includes a higher proportion of directly productive time. Hence reductions in average hours due to slack demand tend to reduce output more than proportionately, and vice versa. Note that the coefficient on $\ln L$—the estimate of β—is 0.68. This value accords quite closely to the actual share of labor in net national product, which varied between 0.59 and 0.65 over the period in question.

But a recent study by Thurow, using data for the entire private United States economy over the period 1929-1965, gives results that are inconsistent with the marginal productivity theory.[33] His aggregate production function yields estimates of the marginal value product of labor of \$2,715 in 1938, rising to \$7,236 in 1965, as measured in constant 1958 dollars. Yet actual average labor compensation at the two intervals stood at \$1,537 and \$4,550, respectively. Conversely, Thurow reports estimates of the marginal product of capital that fall considerably below the actual rate of return on capital. But we would repeat the caveat that these results are to be interpreted with more than a degree of caution in view of the aggregation problem, noting that Thurow's production function encompasses the entire private sector. Given the present state of our knowledge of empirical production functions, we would argue that it is dangerous to take sides on the basis of the conflicting evidence.

The Downward Sloping Demand Curve. When we turn to consider the empirical relation between employment and relative pay, it does seem that we can be more positive in our comments. If there were a downward sloping demand curve, we would expect increases in the price of capital relative to that of labor to be followed by a substitution of labor for capital and thus an increased labor input per unit of output. A study of United States time-series data over the period 1929-1965, excluding the war years, suggests that this is indeed the case. The estimated relation is as follows:[34]

$$\ln \frac{(L_t)}{L_{t-1}} = 0.982 + 0.051D + 0.146 \ln \left(\frac{r}{w}\right) + 0.587 \ln Q - 0.012T - 0.777 \ln L_{t-1}$$
$$\quad\quad (4.46)\quad (2.50)\quad (1.83)\quad\quad\quad (11.7)\quad\quad (12.0)\quad (12.9)$$

$$R^2 = 0.889$$

$$DW = 2.11$$

32. M. S. Feldstein, "Specification of the Labor Input in the Aggregate Production Function," *Review of Economic Studies* 34 (1967): 379.
33. L. C. Thurow, "Disequilibrium and the Marginal Productivity of Capital and Labor," *Review of Economics and Statistics* 50 (1968): 25.
34. R. M. Coen and B. G. Hickman, "Constrained Joint Estimation of Factor Demand and Production Functions," *Review of Economics and Statistics* 52 (1970): 293.

where L measures man-hours used in the private sector;

    D is a dummy variable assigned the value of unity in the postwar years and zero otherwise;

    $\left(\dfrac{r}{w}\right)$ is the ratio of the price of capital relative to the real wage rate;

    Q is real gross private nonresidential product;

    T is a time trend; and

    $|t|$ is given in parentheses.

From our viewpoint, the important result demonstrated by this relation is that L_t/L_{t-1} increased in periods when r/w increased, holding output constant.

In a similar vein, it has been indicated that the employment of various categories of employees is negatively related to the wage rate. If we can assume that wage rates are given and that supply is reasonably elastic at these wage rates, this finding can be interpreted as evidence of a downward sloping labor demand curve. Particularly interesting in this context is the study by Ehrenberg. His estimated employment-wage relation for police officers, using interstate data for the period 1958–1969, is as follows:[35]

$$(M/P) = \text{constant} - 0.281 \ln W + 0.795 \ln(B/P) + 0.064 \ln DEN$$
$$\qquad\qquad\quad (5.73) \qquad\quad (16.1) \qquad\qquad (11.4)$$

where M/P is the number of policemen employed per person in a state;

    W is a measure of average police pay;

    B/P is the state budget per head of population;

    DEN is a measure of state population density; and

    $|t|$ is given in parentheses.

We observe an estimate of the wage elasticity of demand for police officers that is both negative and significant. Not surprisingly, the estimated wage elasticity is low. Considerably higher estimates are obtained for education employees (-0.425) and social workers (-1.001). This ranking of wage elasticities of demand conforms to expectations. Ehrenberg also demonstrates that the wage elasticity of demand for a given category of state and local government employee is considerably reduced if all categories push up their wages by the same amount. This also conforms to expectations. Thus, the industry (in this case the government sector taken as a whole) labor demand curve seems to be more inelastic than that for constituent sectors of the industry on the lines suggested in our analysis of figure 2.4.

Fixed Costs and Employment Stability. Consider the implications for labor demand of introducing the notion of fixed costs of hiring and training labor. Earlier analysis indicated these costs are incurred irrespective of the number

35. Ehrenberg, "Demand for Government Employees," p. 372.

of hours worked by the employee. They include screening and training expenses, paid vacations, sick leave, and flat-rate pension and health insurance contributions. The existence of fixed costs serves to stabilize the employment of certain categories of labor, for the simple reason that discharging these workers in the face of a temporary decline in product demand would imply a capital loss. This argument has significant policy implications, for it might well explain a large part of the greater unemployment incidence among blacks and female workers over the cycle. The wage rate of the category of workers in question is one such indicator of the degree of fixity, because it can be argued that the screening process will have to be more thorough and hence more expensive for well paid senior staff than for junior staff.

Oi has performed a test of employment stability on this very assumption. Using observations on wage levels and employment changes by occupation, he presents simple cross tabulations for a variety of industries. An example of his results, taking the men's clothing industry, is contained in table 2.1. On the basis of this admittedly crude test procedure (see chapter 5), we observe that, in men's clothing, those occupations with relatively high wages were much more likely to record a small change in employment than were occupations with relatively low wages. A similar relationship was charted for other industries.

The fact that there are certain fixed costs associated with the employment of labor also has implications for employers' decisions on the length of the workweek. If it is expensive to hire labor, we would expect an increase in labor demand to be first reflected in an increase in the number of hours demanded per worker and only later in an increase in the number of workers.[36] In both the United States and Great Britain, there has been a

36. Thus, a higher-than-average productivity per worker can be interpreted as indicating increased excess demand for labor within the firm, given the level of unemployment in the economy (the usual measure of excess labor demand). This has been used as an argument for including labor productivity in Phillips-type equations explaining the rate of increase of money wages (see chapter 12). In fact, Vanderkamp does find such a variable to be significant— J. Vanderkamp, "Wage and Price Level Determination: An Empirical Model for Canada," *Economica* 33 (1966): 202.

Table 2.1   A Test of the Fixed Costs Model

Occupations with wages that are	Number of occupations with a percentage change in employment that is	
	(a) below median	(b) above median
(a) above median	13	7
(b) below median	7	14

Source:
W. Y. Oi, "Labor as a Quasi-Fixed Factor," *Journal of Political Economy* 70 (1962):548.

tendency for the amount of overtime worked to increase in the postwar period. An economic explanation of this phenomenon would run in terms of the fixed cost of employment becoming larger relative to the overtime premium, the latter having remained more or less constant. Ehrenberg has tested this explanation by correlating the number of overtime hours worked with the ratio of fixed employment costs to the overtime premium.[37] His sample related to production workers in United States manufacturing industries in 1966. There was wide variation among industries in the number of overtime hours worked, ranging from 70 to 270 hours per year. Ehrenberg finds that those industries with higher overtime hours also had higher fixed costs of employment. We can take this finding as supporting the fixed costs model.

2.7 Conclusions

In this chapter, we have considered the basic economic model of the relationship between the quantity of labor demanded by a firm or industry and the wage rate. This model gives rise to the rule that the wage rate tends to equality with the value of labor's marginal product. Given that increased employment lowers marginal product, the basic prediction of the model is, therefore, that increases in employment are compatible only with reduced wages. However, we warned against generalizing this basic prediction to the level of the economy. It is intended to be a valid simplification in only a partial equilibrium sense, that is, when such other things as aggregate demand in the economy are held constant. On this basis, the fundamental implication for policy is that wage increases must be traded off against reduced employment. At the same time, our analysis of this simplified model did make the point that the terms of the trade-off would be more severe (the demand curve would be more shallowly sloped) in the long run than the short run, and would be more severe for the firm than for the industry or group of industries. One important policy implication of the analysis is that unions can be expected to attempt to extend the coverage of a given wage increase so as to mitigate any adverse employment consequences for their members.

These comments stem from the simple model of employment determination. In pursuit of greater realism, we subsequently introduced various complications, the potentially most important of which was monopsony. A monopsonist, being the sole buyer in the market, can be said to face a positively sloped labor supply curve so that changes in his volume of purchases affect input price. In this case, it is possible to show that exploitation, which is technically defined as the payment of a wage less than the value of labor's marginal product, will result. In such a context, appropriate minimum-wage legislation can be shown to increase both the wage *and* the

---

37. R. G. Ehrenberg, *Fringe Benefits and Overtime Behavior* (Lexington, Mass.: Heath, 1971), pp. 65, 90.

level of employment. Thus the trade-off between employment opportunities and wage increases need not hold in labor markets where there are strong elements of monopsony. The difficulty for policy lies in identifying such markets, although this is not impossible in practice. Indeed, in chapter 6, we shall argue that married women are likely to be more subject to monopsonistic influences because of their tendency toward geographical immobility. On this premise, minimum-wage legislation in women's occupations might not lead to adverse employment consequences.

Further movement toward realism can be introduced by examining the public sector, where much production is not for profit. It is also necessary to acknowledge that there are capital costs involved in the employment of labor, which means that labor is a quasi-fixed factor. In looking at the public sector, we found the assumption of profit maximization to be untenable. On the other hand, we examined a model of budget maximization, which, albeit a crude simplification, had the important implication that managers of government agencies would be under some pressure to minimize costs. This pressure was shown to be strongest where the voters' demand for the output of a particular public agency was elastic. Given the incentive to minimize costs, we can still derive the implication of a negative relation between the quantity of input employed and its price, that is, a negatively sloped labor demand curve.

As for the introduction of the concept of fixed costs attaching to the employment of labor, it was noted that this, too, breaks the link between wages and marginal productivity, at least in the short run. It can be shown that employers invest in screening employees for a particular job (the concept of investment in human beings is considered in some detail in chapter 4) and that this provides an incentive to retain such employees in the face of a temporary drop in product demand (and hence marginal revenue product). Once the notion of fixed costs is admitted, it becomes necessary to acknowledge the fact that the labor input to a firm is a function of hours worked per man as well as the number of men employed. The consequence is that the employer will vary hours per worker, possibly by scheduling more or less overtime, rather than the number of workers whenever fixed costs are important. This has several empirical implications. We would expect greater employment continuity among workers with high fixed costs of employment, a procyclical behavior of labor productivity, and more reliance on overtime working in those industries and time periods where fixed costs of employment are relatively high.

In the final section of the chapter, we considered some of the empirical implications of the simplified model, together with those of its extensions. Much of the empirical work on labor demand has centered upon estimation of production functions so as to yield a measure of labor's marginal product, a value which can then be compared with actual earnings levels. The famous Cobb-Douglas production function arose out of just such an attempt. We have examined various empirical production functions, some of which imply a close relation and others a distant relation between the two magnitudes. To this extent, therefore, the empirical evidence is not strongly supportive of the theory. However, some interesting results have been obtained from production functions that distinguish between the hours and employees components of labor input. These support the idea that the two elements should indeed be treated separately on the lines suggested by the fixed costs model.

Turning to the prediction of a negatively sloped demand curve, the empirical results are more clear cut. There does appear to be a negative time-series relation between changes in employment and changes in the cost of labor relative to the cost of capital. There also appears to be a negative relation between the employment of various categories of public employee and their own wage rate. Moreover, this relationship seems to be more pronounced than that obtained when we consider a wage increase for all categories taken together. This lends support to the theoretical suggestion that an industry labor demand curve is more steeply sloped than the demand curve for particular constituent sections of the industry.

CHAPTER 3
THE SUPPLY OF LABOR

3.1 Introduction

Having considered models of the demand for labor, we turn in this chapter and the next to aspects of labor supply. Here we concentrate mainly on the determinants of the individual's participation decision and on the decision as to how many hours the individual will supply given that participation. Although we shall briefly touch upon the longer run aspects of labor supply, the latter question is primarily the concern of chapter 4, in which the determinants of the individual's level of skill or education are analyzed. Nor do we explicitly consider determinants of the size of the population; so the intriguing Malthusian question of whether increases in population are stimulated by increases in real income is ignored.[1] This exclusion reflects our preoccupation with developed rather than developing countries

From the economic point of view, we are interested mainly in supply responses to changes in the wage rate and in nonlabor income. To analyze these responses, it has been conventional to adopt the basic model of consumption demand for goods; the goods in question here taking the form of leisure and money. It is first necessary to outline this model and derive the basic predictions that hours supplied respond positively, or at least nonnegatively, to compensated changes in the wage rate, and negatively to nonlabor income. The analysis can then be applied to such important phenomena as the secular decline in the length of the workweek, the response of participation rates to changes in economic activity (the *discouraged worker* and *added worker* hypotheses), and the marked secular increase in labor force participation of married women. The question of whether the supply curve of working hours is backward bending or forward rising—and over what wage ranges and for which groups—has important implications for income taxation policy and welfare benefit provision. The analysis of past changes in

---

1. But see G. S. Becker, "An Economic Analysis of Fertility," *Demographic and Economic Change in Developed Countries,* National Bureau of Economic Research (Princeton, N.J.: Princeton University Press, 1960).

labor supply should also assist in planning for possible future changes in participation.

There are, however, many econometric and measurement problems associated with the estimation of labor supply responses. These arise partly because the individual's supply decision is not taken alone, but in the context of the decision of other family members. Several individuals must therefore be regarded as making their decisions simultaneously. There is also the difficulty that the participation and hours decisions might be determined together. This problem is compounded by the variety of dimensions of the labor supply decision. In addition to the level of skill and training that workers bring to their jobs, there is also the question of the intensity of work effort that will be offered. Given that the labor supply decision is multidimensional, it must be questioned whether any one dimension can be meaningfully analyzed in isolation of the others. A general equilibrium framework has been proposed, but further development of this model is required before it can be of much practical use.[2]

The analysis proceeds as follows. In section 3.2, we outline the theoretical basis of labor supply. The conventional labor-leisure choice of the individual is first examined, and this framework is next extended to cover the household as the decision unit. A more general analysis of the allocation of time is then introduced and is contrasted with the basic neoclassical model. In the next two sections, empirical estimation of labor supply is considered, beginning with the supply of hours decision. Labor force participation is then examined, taking secular trends and cyclical fluctuations in turn.

3.2   Theoretical Considerations

The Individual.   First consider the elementary neoclassical model of the supply of labor time. This involves an application of the theory of consumer behavior. The representative individual is assumed to devote time both to market work and nonmarketable activities, called leisure. He maximizes his utility, or satisfaction, by choosing combinations of goods (obtained by working) and leisure hours subject to time and price constraints. This formulation of the problem bypasses the possibility that an individual's labor-leisure time allocation is determined by law or collective agreement. To some extent, however, individuals are able to choose between jobs offering varying lengths of working week; and the scope for free choice is widened if we consider hours worked per year, because then the number of weeks worked per year also becomes variable. The theory is still useful if there is some freedom of choice and, as we shall see, institutional limitations can sometimes be allowed for.

The individual's preferences are supposed to be represented by the

2. M. R. Fisher, *The Economic Analysis of Labor* (London: Weidenfeld and Nicolson, 1971).

function $U = U(G,L)$, showing the utility (U) received from various quantities of goods (real income) (G) and leisure (L). The utility function may be depicted as a family of indifference curves, such as those shown in figure 3.1. Each indifference curve represents different combinations of consumer goods and leisure that yield the individual the same level of satisfaction. The most important characteristics of the curves drawn in figure 3.1 are their slope and shape. Their negative slope tells us that it is possible to hold the level of utility or satisfaction constant while substituting leisure for goods in consumption. Their convex shape relative to the origin is a result of the assumption of imperfect substitutability between leisure and goods. Thus, although it is possible to trade goods for leisure and hold utility constant, the greater the ratio of leisure consumed to goods consumed, the greater the marginal amount of leisure required to compensate for giving up a marginal amount of goods, and vice versa. Stated another way, the amount of consumer goods that must be given up per unit of leisure (hours) received to maintain a constant level of satisfaction should fall as the consumption of leisure rises. The marginal rate of substitution of leisure for consumer goods is defined as MU_L/MU_G, namely the ratio of the marginal utility of leisure, MU_L, to the marginal utility of goods, MU_G. This ratio is given by the slope of the indifference curve for any given combination of goods and leisure.[3]

It is assumed that the individual prefers more of both leisure and goods to less, so that indifference curves further away from the origin represent successively higher levels of utility. The individual's objective is to climb onto the highest indifference curve, but his attempt to maximize utility is constrained in two ways. First, he is given the price of a unit of goods, P_G, which he has to earn by working in the market, unless he receives nonlabor (unearned) income, V. Second, because there are only a finite number of hours, T, in any time period, the hours devoted to market work, H, are at the expense of hours devoted to leisure, L, so that the foregone earnings cost of leisure is the wage rate P_L. Assuming that the wage rate is exogenous and

---

3. Taking the total differential of the utility function $U(G,L)$, we obtain

$$\frac{\partial U}{\partial G}dG + \frac{\partial U}{\partial L}dL = dU.$$

For a given indifference curve $dU = 0$, so that

$$\frac{\partial U}{\partial G}dG + \frac{\partial U}{\partial L}dL = 0.$$

Thus, the slope of the indifference curve is

$$-\frac{dG}{dL} = \frac{\partial U}{\partial L} \div \frac{\partial U}{\partial G} = \frac{MU_L}{MU_G}.$$

Figure 3.1   The Utility Function and the Budget Constraint

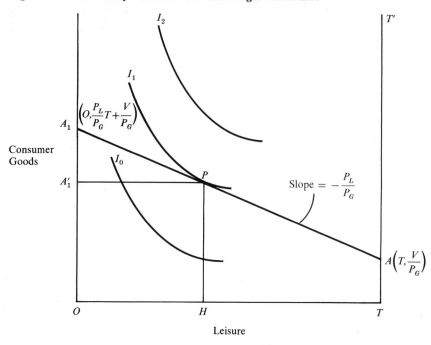

that the individual spends all of his income, we have the following budget constraint:[4]

$$Y = P_G G = P_L(T - L) + V \qquad (3.1)$$

where Y is money income.

Alternatively, in terms of real income,

$$G = \left(\frac{P_L}{P_G} T + \frac{V}{P_G}\right) - \frac{P_L}{P_G} L.$$

The above constraint is represented by the line $A_1 A$ in figure 3.1. Note that $A_1 A$ summarizes the consumption opportunities facing the individual and

4. Equation (3.1) is sometimes written as

$$P_G G + P_L L \equiv P_L T + V \equiv F$$

to emphasize that the individual's full income, $F \equiv P_L T + V$, may be thought of as $P_L L$ dollars spent on leisure and $P_G G$ dollars spent on market goods. It is worth noting that it might well be difficult to separate P_L from V in practice. This is because a high wage rate might well lead, via enhanced saving possibilities, to a high nonlabor income. On the other hand, there is a contrary effect in that people with a low wage rate might have a high V due to transfer payments (see section 3.5).

that its slope gives the exchange rate between the price of leisure and the price of goods—the real wage rate per hour. Note also that A_1A does not intersect the leisure axis at point T. This is because we assume the individual to have an amount of nonlabor income equivalent to $TA(=V/P_G)$.

Maximization of utility subject to the budget constraint involves choosing a particular bundle of goods and leisure that is both on the budget line and also on the highest indifference curve to touch the budget line.[5] The equilibrium condition is shown by point P in figure 3.1, where the marginal rate of substitution of leisure for goods in consumption will equal the slope of the budget line. Thus, at point P,

$$\frac{MU_L}{MU_G} = \frac{P_L}{P_G} \text{ or } \frac{MU_L}{P_L} = \frac{MU_G}{P_G}. \tag{3.2}$$

Equation (3.2) states that the utility to be gained (lost) from spending an extra dollar on consumer goods is equal to the utility that would be lost (gained) from spending one dollar less on leisure. Because no reallocation of time between leisure and work can further increase utility, the individual is said to be in equilibrium.[6]

We are now in a position to investigate the manner in which the chosen equilibrium changes in response to a change in the wage rate, if all other factors, such as the price of goods, are held constant. A wage increase not only raises the price of leisure relative to the price of consumer goods, which induces a substitution of goods for leisure, but also raises the income that can be earned from working any given number of hours, and thus the satisfaction that can be attained at any given level of leisure consumption. So it is useful to split its effect on hours worked into an income and a substitution effect. Consider figure 3.2, in which the initial equilibrium goods-leisure choice is given by point P_0. As a result of the increase in the wage rate, the budget line pivots upward at A, so that the goods intercept increases from OA_0 to OA_1. The new equilibrium is at P_1, at which hours supplied in the market have increased from H_0T to H_1T. To isolate the substitution effect, we notionally decrease the individual's income by imposing a tax, amounting to

---

5. Note that we are assuming that the individual is free to choose his hours at a constant wage per hour. Among other things, we are ignoring the possibility of a fixed workweek and the presence of overtime payments.

6. To solve the individual's maximization problem mathematically, his preference function, $U = U(G,L)$, must be maximized subject to the budget constraint, $P_GG = P_L(T - L) + V$. The procedure is to set up the Lagrangian function,

$$H = U(G,L) - \lambda[P_GG - P_L(T - L) + V]$$

First-order conditions for a maximization of this function are

$$\frac{\partial U/\partial L}{\partial U/\partial G} = \frac{MU_L}{MU_G} = \frac{P_L}{P_G}.$$

Figure 3.2   Income and Substitution Effects

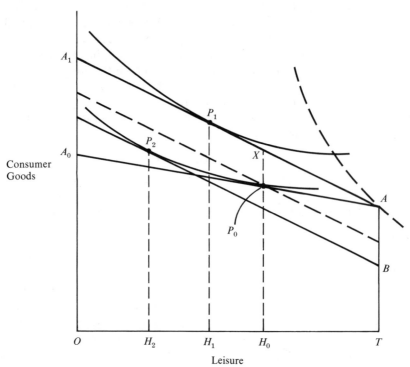

AB, so as to compensate for the improvement in his earning power.[7] The construction of this tax is such that the individual is no better off than before the wage increase; that is, the individual is returned to his original indifference curve. The movement from P_0 to P_2 is the substitution effect; because leisure has become more expensive, the individual substitutes labor for leisure. Having isolated the substitution effect, the income effect is the residual movement H_2T to H_1T.

In figure 3.2, we have shown the income effect to be dominated by the

7. Note that the size of the tax *AB* is not obtainable if we are dealing with an actual worker. We could not see his indifference map and therefore could not know how big a change in his money income is needed to compensate him for the effects on his real income of a particular wage change. It is possible to get around this problem by using an approximation. Instead of defining real income in terms of a particular level of utility, we might define it as the ability to purchase a particular bundle of goods. Thus, instead of treating any budget constraint that is tangent to the original indifference curve as representing a given level of real income, we may treat any budget constraint that allows purchase of the original goods combination (passes through P_0 as does the straight dashed line) as representing constant real income. Thus, *AB* is approximated by P_0X, which is the original level of hours worked (say 40 hours) multiplied by the change in the wage (say $1). Hence $AB \simeq 40.

substitution effect, so that the individual offers more hours of market work in response to an increase in his wage rate. However, the shape of the individual worker's supply curve cannot be determined by a priori analysis. The income effect on work hours may be either positive or negative, according to whether leisure is either an inferior or a normal good, respectively. The substitution effect of a wage increase on work hours is always positive, on the assumption that the indifference curves derived from the utility function are convex to the origin. If leisure is a normal good, defined as a good the consumption of which rises with income, then the total effect cannot be determined a priori but depends on whether the income effect outweighs the substitution effect or vice versa. The net effect of higher wages on labor supply thus depends on the relative strength of two forces operating in opposite directions.

However, the model can be used to say more than this. Income from nonwage sources affects work decisions, but only through the income effect. Income from nonemployment sources, therefore, permits the estimation of an income effect. This income effect estimate can then be used to adjust for the income effect associated with wage rate changes to obtain an estimate of the pure substitution effect.[8] Moreover, although the positively sloped labor supply schedule implied by figure 3.2 need not describe actual labor supply behavior, we can be a little more certain about the supply response to temporary changes in wage rates. Such changes will have only a minor effect

8. The mathematics of income and substitution effects are perhaps set out most clearly by Hicks (J. R. Hicks, *Value and Capital,* Oxford: Clarendon Press, 1946, pp. 303 ff.), who shows that the expression for a change in the demand for good χ consequent upon a change in its price p, with income Y constant, can be written

$$\frac{\partial \chi}{\partial p} = (\bar{\chi} - \chi)\frac{\partial \chi}{\partial Y} + \frac{\partial \chi^c}{\partial p} \tag{1}$$

where χ^c is the compensated demand for χ, so that $\partial \chi^c/\partial p$ is the substitution effect, which, in the case of goods, must be negative;

          $\bar{\chi}$ is the amount of the good initially held; and

$(\bar{\chi} - \chi)\partial \chi/\partial y$ is the income effect.

In the notation of the labor-leisure analysis (remembering T is the amount of leisure initially held), equation (1) can be written

$$\frac{\partial L}{\partial P_L} = (T - L)\frac{\partial L}{\partial V} + \frac{\partial L^c}{\partial P_L}$$

Assuming $\partial L/\partial V = \partial L/\partial Y$, we then derive

$$\frac{\partial L}{\partial P_L} = H\frac{\partial L}{\partial Y} + \frac{\partial L^c}{\partial P_L}. \tag{2}$$

Noting that $\partial L/\partial P_L = -\partial H/\partial P_L$ and $\partial L/\partial Y = -\partial H/\partial Y$, equation (2) may be alternatively written in terms of the demand for hours, thus on income; for this reason, we would expect the income effect to be small and dominated by the substitution effect. For example, a temporary rise in the effective wage rate, resulting from overtime working in an upswing, is likely to elicit an increase in hours supplied, although a permanent wage increase of the same magnitude need not have this effect (see appendix 3-A).

It is worth noting how we would treat the question of participation decisions within the context of this model. The above analysis has been conditional upon participation. The nonparticipator can be visualized as having indifference curves which cause a "corner" solution. One such indifference curve is shown by the dashed curve in figure 3.2. As can be seen, an increase in the wage rate would induce such an individual to participate if it were large enough; that is, he would offer some positive amount of hours on the labor market. Alternatively, a reduction in nonlabor income is likely to encourage participation. Analysis of the participation decision does not, therefore, differ qualitatively from that of the hours decision, although tastes and cultural factors might play a more important part in explaining the former.

In recognition of the role of cultural factors in participation decisions, participation has been related to the phases of economic development. A secular supply curve may be constructed, therefore, along the lines of figure 3.3. Segment *AB* can be described as the Malthusian range, in which each member of the population must work to live. Segment *BC*, on the other hand, a backward rising zone, appears to be typical of countries in the early stages of industrialization, when real incomes have risen but tastes have not much changed. Within this real income range, consumption patterns tend not to change, so that the family sends fewer of its members to the marketplace to achieve customary consumption levels. Segment *CD* corresponds to a widening of expectations following further industrial development. Here, labor participation increases as real income rises. The range *DE* might be thought of as more characteristic of fully industrialized economies. Here, earlier retirement and greater access to full-time education depress participation

$$\frac{\partial H}{\partial P_L} = H \frac{\partial H}{\partial Y} + \frac{\partial H^c}{\partial P_L}. \tag{3}$$

Expressed as an elasticity (multiplying the whole expression by P_L/H and multiplying and dividing the income effect by Y), equation (3) becomes

$$\frac{\partial H}{\partial P_L} \cdot \frac{P_L}{H} = \frac{P_L H}{Y} \frac{\partial H}{\partial Y} \cdot \frac{Y}{H} + \eta_s. \tag{4}$$

Regression of hours on the wage rate and nonwage income, holding other things equal, gives an estimate of $\partial H/\partial P_L$ and $\partial H/\partial Y$. Taking mean values of P_L, H, and Y then enables us to evaluate the uncompensated wage elasticity $(\partial H/\partial P_L) \cdot (P_L/H)$, the income elasticity $(\partial H/\partial Y) \cdot (Y/H)$, and therefore the compensated wage elasticity η_s.

Figure 3.3 The Secular Supply Curve

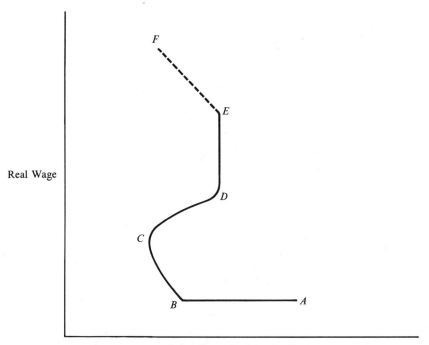

Labor Force Participation Rate

rates, but this is offset by increases in female participation, which reflect a decline in the amount of time it is economical for a wife to devote to the production of home goods. Finally, segment EF is drawn to reflect possible future developments in participation rates attendant upon major technological advances. The latter, which imply increased real income, might be accompanied by a decision not to participate in the labor force for substantial periods of potential working life. Empirical evidence for this pattern of participation behavior is considered below.

The Household. The labor supply decision of the individual cannot strictly be considered in isolation. Rather, that decision has to be seen in the context of decisions taken by other members of the household within which the individual is located. The simpler approach is to assume that the labor supply of at least one family member is independent of that of other family members. Alternatively, we can assume that the labor supply of a given family member is the result of the interaction of labor supply choices of all family members. Under the simpler approach, it is assumed the labor earnings of the husband are regarded by the wife as a form of nonlabor income. But while the husband's earnings will affect the wife's labor supply, the income of the wife is taken to have no effect on the labor supply of the husband.[9] This might be termed the *male chauvinist* model of labor supply.[10]

After Killingsworth, the more difficult interdependence model can be set out as follows. We write the family utility function in the form

$$U = U(G, L_m, L_f) \tag{3.3}$$

where L_m and L_f are the amounts of time spent in nonmarket activity by the
male and female members of the household; and
G is the family's pooled level of consumption.

The decision variables in equation (3.3) must satisfy the family's budget constraint, given by

$$W_m(T - L_m) + W_f(T - L_f) + V = P_G G \tag{3.4}$$

where W_m and W_f are the wage rates confronted by male and female family
members.

In this two-person model, there are two substitution effects relevant to the labor supply of any given family member. First, there is the own-substitution effect, which is the effect on the family member's labor supply of an increase in that individual's own wage. Second, there is the cross-substitution effect on the individual's labor supply of an increase in the wage of the other family member. The structure of the model is such that these cross-substitution effects must always be equal to each other.[11] Thus, the model implies that an income compensated change (figure 3.2) in the husband's wage rate has the same effect on the wife's labor supply as a compensated change in the wife's wage rate has on the husband's labor supply. However, the cross-income effects are not restricted to be equal. Therefore, the total effect of a change in the husband's wage on the wife's labor supply need not be the same as the total effect of a change in the wife's wage on the husband's labor supply, for the cross-income effects might differ.

9. See, for example, W. G. Bowen, and T. A. Finegan, "Labor Force Participation and Unemployment," in A. M. Ross, ed., *Employment Policy and the Labor Market* (Berkeley and Los Angeles: University of California Press, 1965), pp. 115–161; idem, "Educational Attainment and Labor Force Participation," *American Economic Review* 56 (1966): 567–582; idem, *The Economics of Labor Force Participation* (Princeton, N.J.: Princeton University Press, 1969); P. S. Barth, "A Cross-Sectional Analysis of Labor Force Participation Rates in Michigan," *Industrial and Labor Relations Review* 20 (1967): 234–249.

10. M. R. Killingsworth, "Determinants of the Supply of Labor Time at the Micro-Level: A Survey and Critique of Recent Neoclassical Literature," mimeographed (Nashville, Tenn.: Department of Economics, Fisk University, 1972), p. 18; idem, "Must a Negative Income Tax Reduce Labor Supply? A Study of the Family's Allocation of Time," *Journal of Human Resources* 11 (1976): 354–365.

11. See O. Ashenfelter and J. Heckman, "The Estimation of Income and Substitution Effects in a Model of Family Labor Supply," *Econometrica* 42 (1974): 75; Killingsworth, "Determinants of the Supply of Labor Time," pp. 19–22.

For purposes of estimating a family member's labor supply function, Cohen *et al.* note that if cross-substitution terms are assumed to be zero, then the only effect on a family member's labor supply of an increase in another member's wage is a pure income effect.[12] Thus, the income of other family members, rather than their wage rates, should be entered in the family member's supply function. However, it must be remembered that the income of other family members is an endogenous variable in any given family member's supply function. Unlike nonlabor income, its level will be affected by the individual's own labor supply. Hence the labor supply relation must be estimated by simultaneous equation methods.[13]

As Killingsworth reminds us, there is a further problem of interdependence to consider. Individuals are affected not simply by the behavior of persons within the immediate family unit, but also by the activities of other persons in the rest of the economy.[14] Individuals will feel better off as their wages increase relative to others. An increase in the wages of others will, *ceteris paribus,* induce two opposing interdependence effects on the individual's labor supply. In one sense, the implication of a falling relative wage is to reduce the individual's incentive to offer as many hours as hitherto, because work has become less satisfying. In another sense, because others are now paid more for their work, the individual will now wish to supply more hours, or intensify his work-effort if employed on piece-work, to maintain his consumption at its past level of conspicuousness. The net effect on labor supply will depend on which of these two effects is the stronger.[15] But it is likely that the relative wage effects discussed by Hamermesh will largely be confined to the short run, because under competition all earnings tend to grow at the same rate in the long run, *ceteris paribus.*

The General Theory of the Allocation of Time.   The above models assume that all time is allocated either to market work or to leisure. However, there are a range of activities that do not fall easily into this typology. One such activity is the home preparation of food, which does not involve market work nor can it be said to be leisure. Such activities can be termed nonmarket work. The importance of this additional classification is that it suggests that the supply of labor time within the market must be treated as part of a more general analysis of the allocation of time to a number of alternative uses.

Becker has put forward one such general theory.[16] His approach assumes

12. M. S. Cohen, S. A. Rea, and R. I. Lerman, "A Micro Model of Labor Supply," *Bureau of Labor Statistics Staff Paper No. 4,* Bureau of Labor Statistics, U.S. Department of Labor (Washington, D.C.: U.S. Government Printing Office, 1970), p. 186.
13. Killingsworth, "Determinants of the Supply of Labor Time," pp. 23-24.
14. D. S. Hamermesh, "Interdependence in the Labor Market," *Working Paper No. 32* (Princeton, N.J.: Industrial Relations Section, Princeton University, 1971).
15. See Killingsworth, "Determinants of the Supply of Labor Time," pp. 27-29.
16. G. S. Becker, "A Theory of the Allocation of Time," *Economic Journal* 75 (1965): 493-517.

that neither time nor consumer goods are consumed by themselves. Time cannot be enjoyed without goods and all goods require time to be consumed. Accordingly, we may think of consumption decisions as being made among alternative activities that require both goods inputs and time inputs. This means that the total price of any activity should be taken as the sum of its market price plus the value of time required to perform it. An increase in the wage rate thus raises the relative price of time-intensive activities, causes substitution against them, and might thereby induce an increase in hours worked. The individual's supply of labor hours is thereby determined simultaneously with consumption.

The model incorporating the time costs of consumption explicitly has as a utility function

$$U = U(Z_i \ldots Z_m) \tag{3.5}$$

where Z_i are activities which are themselves functions of goods and time inputs.

Households are assumed to combine time and market goods to produce these basic commodities, Z_i. The household production functions may be written

$$Z_i = Z_i(G_i \ldots G_m; t_i \ldots t_m) \qquad i = 1 \ldots m$$

where G_i are goods inputs; and
t_i are time inputs.

It is useful to simplify matters by taking these production functions to be of fixed coefficient type; that is,

$$Z_i = G_i/a_i \text{ and } Z_i = t_i/b_i \tag{3.6}$$

where a_i are the units of goods per unit of activity; and
b_i are the units of time per unit of activity.

Now, because

$$T = \sum_{i=1}^{m} t_i + H$$

and

$$\sum_{i=1}^{m} P_{G_i} G_i = P_L H + V,$$

we have

$$\sum_{i=1}^{m} P_{G_i} G_i + P_L \sum_i t_i = P_L T + V = F \tag{3.7}$$

where F is full income, namely that income that would be realized if $T = H$.

Substituting equation (3.6) into equation (3.7) gives the simplified budget constraint

$$\sum_i P_{G_i} Z_i a_i + P_L \sum_i Z_i b_i = \sum \pi Z_i = F \qquad (3.8)$$

where

$$\pi_i = P_{G_i} a_i + P_L b_i.$$

In this case, π_i is the full cost of activity Z_i, including $P_{G_i} a_i$ as the goods (or earnings) cost component and $P_L b_i$ as the foregone-earnings (or time) component. Maximizing equation (3.5) subject to equation (3.8) gives the equilibrium condition

$$\frac{\partial U/Z_i}{\partial U/Z_1} = \frac{MU_{Z_i}}{MU_{Z_1}} = \frac{\pi_i}{\pi_1} \qquad i = 2 \ldots m \qquad (3.9)$$

The relation between equation (3.9) and equation (3.2) can be seen by assuming first that $m = 2$ and $b_1 = 0$. It then follows that $a_1 = 1$; that is, the cost of commodity 1 depends only upon goods and there is no foregone-earnings component. Second, assume that $b_2 = 1$, so that $a_2 = 0$; the cost of commodity 2 then depends only upon time inputs and is a pure leisure commodity. Under these assumptions, equation (3.9) is identical to equation (3.2), as follows

$$\frac{MU_{Z_2}}{MU_{Z_1}} = \frac{MU_L}{MU_G} = \frac{P_L}{P_G}.$$

The same point can be demonstrated graphically using figure 3.4. The straight lines represent budget constraints. With the goods-intensive Z_1 commodity on the y-axis and the time-intensive Z_2 commodity on the x-axis, the slope of the budget constraint lines is given by

$$-\frac{P_{G_2} \cdot a_2 + P_L \cdot b_2}{P_{G_1} \cdot a_1 + P_L \cdot b_1}.$$

In the limit, a_2 and b_1 drop out, so that we return to the pure goods-intensive axis and the pure time-intensive axis. The slope of the budget line is now given by $-P_L/P_G$. Thus, whereas the traditional analysis distinguishes only between goods and leisure, the more general analysis distinguishes a spectrum of commodities that range from those with a high earnings cost component to those with a high foregone-earnings cost component. Included within the latter would be most forms of leisure and, as we shall see when considering human capital (chapter 4), such activities as studying.

In the context of the general model, consider the effect of a wage increase upon the supply of hours to the market. In the first place, this will have an income effect. The increase in income will cause an increase in the consumption of all normal commodities. Will this cause an increase in the time spent in consumption and a reduction in the time spent working? The answer will be in the negative if time-intensive commodities—those with a large b_i, such as the reading of books—are inferior. Although it is not possible to say a priori which way the income effect will go, it is highly probable that time-intensive commodities are not inferior and that the income effect thus causes less time to be spent on market work.

The wage increase will raise the cost of all commodities, but will raise the cost of those that are time-intensive more. Therefore, we can expect a substitution against these goods in consumption, except in the unusual case of commodities that are highly time-intensive (for example, sailing) yet have low foregone earnings (because the sailing is done at weekends). Subject to this caveat, a shift away from time-intensive commodities will result in a reduction in the total time spent in consumption and a consequent increase in the time spent at work. The income-compensated effect of an increase in the wage rate is shown in figure 3.4. Because Z_2 is the time-intensive

Figure 3.4   The Effect of an Income Compensated Increase in the Wage Rate on Consumption Equilibrium for a Time-Intensive and a Goods-Intensive Commodity

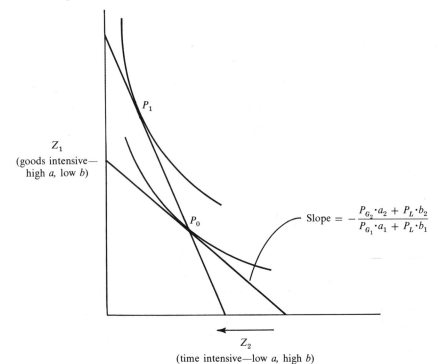

Z_1
(goods intensive—
high a, low b)

P_1

P_0

$$\text{Slope} = -\frac{P_{G_2} \cdot a_2 + P_L \cdot b_2}{P_{G_1} \cdot a_1 + P_L \cdot b_1}$$

Z_2
(time intensive—low a, high b)

commodity, the income-compensated budget curve is rotated clockwise (the individual can consume less Z_2, given his budget, after the change) through the initial equilibrium position, P_0. The new equilibrium, P_1, lies to the left and above P_0. Less Z_2 commodities and more Z_1 commodities are consumed, and more time is devoted to market work.

The secular improvement in capital and technology has increased the productivity of consumption time as well as the level of earnings. An increase in the productivity of consumption time will change relative commodity prices. If all b_i values decline by a common percentage, the relative prices of time-intensive commodities (with large b_i values) will fall, and substitution will be induced toward them and away from other commodities. As a result, hours of work will tend to fall. But there is also an income effect to consider. Because household consumption productivity is up, less time is required to prepare food, travel to work, communicate, and so on; the increase in free time permits households to earn a higher level of full income. Individuals will use this increase in their real income to consume more activities. But an increase in the consumption of activities requires not only more time but also more goods. More goods can only be obtained if one's money income increases—that is, only if one works longer. Thus, the higher real income resulting from an advance in the productivity of consumption time could cause hours of work to increase. Improved household productivity may, then, lead to a reduction in nonmarket work and to an increase in the time devoted to market work and leisure.

An application of this model has been made to the life-cycle pattern of working hours by Ghez and Becker, using data on wage rates and home time of individuals of different ages.[17] Broadly speaking, the age profiles of hourly wage rates and hours per year spent at home by males follow the paths indicated in figure 3.5. The model predicts that an increase in the wage rate causes goods to be substituted for time in the production of commodities, and causes consumption of commodities in the current period to be substituted for consumption in the future, because, according to the wage profile, wages (foregone earnings) eventually fall. This second effect occurs because the increased wage rate raises the foregone-earnings component in the full cost of the commodity. Both effects reduce the demand for consumption of home time and presumably increase the time spent in the labor market.

It will be noted that we have not mentioned income effects resulting from wage rate changes. The argument here is that such effects are not important in the life-cycle context if we assume that individuals know the present value of their lifetime income. Therefore, income effects are unimportant because their present value is given and constant. The latter assumption simplifies matters greatly. We discuss the empirical results of the Ghez and Becker model below; to anticipate our findings, it can be said that the results are

17. G. R. Ghez and G. S. Becker, *The Allocation of Time and Goods over the Life Cycle*, National Bureau of Economic Research (New York: Columbia University Press, 1975), chap. 3.

Figure 3.5   Consumption of Commodities over the Life Cycle

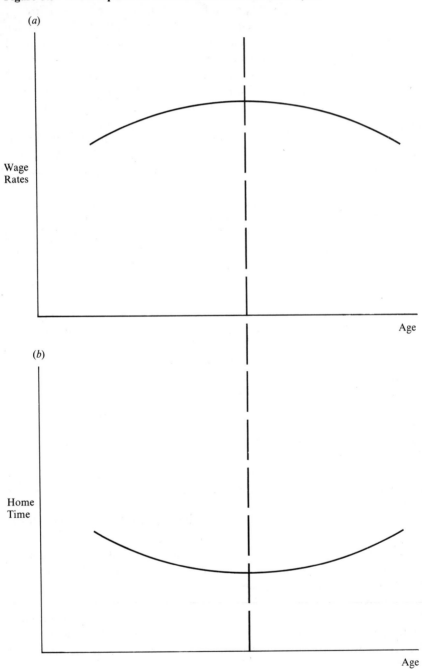

encouraging, and that the approach thus appears to illuminate the life-cycle allocation of time.

In the foregoing discussion, we have also neglected changes over the life cycle in time devoted to human capital accumulation. The pattern of investments in man is analyzed in detail in chapter 4. Briefly, we would expect the time devoted to learning to fall steadily as the individual ages. This is partly because the remaining period in which economic benefit can be obtained from the learning process falls and partly because the foregone-earnings cost of learning rises. As we will show, the typical path described by the age-earning profile of panel (a) of figure 3.4 can be explained in terms of the returns to a varying stock of human capital. The point to be emphasized, however, is that there is a joint allocation of time between consumption, market work, and learning or human capital accumulation.[18] Time is also allocated to other forms of human investment, such as health care. The chief difficulty raised by these new considerations is an empirical one. If we are attempting to explain hours spent consuming, we would not wish to include hours of study or hours spent on personal maintenance. Yet the data available to us often do not permit the distinction to be made, resulting in a biased estimate of consumption hours.[19]

3.3 The Supply of Hours

The earliest estimates of the relation between working hours and hourly earnings were made by Douglas.[20] Using annual time-series data from 1890–1926 for a fifteen-industry sample, he found strong negative correlations ($r < -0.50$ in twelve cases) and only one, low, positive correlation. Interindustry cross sections for 1890, 1914, and 1936 also showed high negative correlations (-0.78, -0.80, and -0.84, respectively). On the basis of this evidence, Douglas concluded that the elasticity of supply with respect to the wage lay between -0.1 and -0.2, implying that an increase of 1% in hourly earnings would tend, *ceteris paribus,* to cause a decrease of from 0.1% to 0.2% in hours normally worked.

Yet we must be cautious in interpreting the observed relationship between hours and wages as revealed by Douglas' study. The problem is one of identifying a supply curve of labor from such observations. Each hours-wage observation may represent the intersection of one particular supply curve and the corresponding demand function—for example, the supply and demand for labor in a particular year, state, industry, or occupation. Thus, the least-squares line that describes the association between hours and wages is not necessarily an estimated supply function.

---

18. See, for example, J. Heckman, "A Life Cycle Model of Earnings, Learning and Consumption," *Journal of Political Economy* 84 (1976): 511–544.

19. Ghez and Becker, *The Allocation of Time,* pp. 94 ff.

20. P. H. Douglas, *The Theory of Wages* (New York: Macmillan, 1934).

Feldstein has argued that there are two methods of tackling this identification problem.[21] The first requires the inclusion of variables additional to wages in the supply equation. For example, in an interindustry study, each observed number of hours worked may reflect not only hourly earnings, but also the percentage of female employees and the percentages of inexperienced workers. The argument here is that if these were the only systematic factors that caused interindustry differences in the supply function, including them within a regression would have the same effect as using a sample of observations which related to a single curve. This leads to Feldstein's second suggestion for overcoming the identification problem, namely to sample observations from a single labor market in which, it is argued, there is likely to be a single supply curve rather than a multiplicity of such curves.[22] This approach was used by Feldstein on United Kingdom data. His results were, on a whole, insignificant—only four out of eleven regression coefficients on hourly earnings were significantly negative. Thus, the tendency toward negative coefficients found by Douglas and others appeared to have been considerably weakened.

Feldstein's first test procedure has found general favor within the American literature, where occupational censuses and the National Longitudinal Survey provide a breakdown of data that cannot be matched in the United Kingdom. Thus, Finegan and Rosen inter al. have incorporated a number of additional variables to reflect the influence of forces other than wage earnings, such as years of school and marital status, that affect hours of work.[23] These inclusions are an attempt both to achieve a relatively unbiased estimate of the effect of wage rates on hours of work and simultaneously to gauge the significance of the forces the variables are thought to represent.

Knowing why the supply curve shifts does not really help up establish a supply curve if the demand curve is shifting at the same time. What is required for identification is that certain variables that do affect demand should not affect supply. The point at issue is that simply including extra variables in the supply equation is less important than ensuring that the variables that do affect demand are excluded from the equation. It may be said, however, that more elaborate studies, such as that by Rosen, which uses a simultaneous model in which supply and demand parameters are jointly estimated, still give rise to a negative coefficient on the wage variable. As the studies summarized in table 3.1 indicate, this tendency toward a negative coefficient is widespread.

It must be remembered, however, that the elasticities reported in table 3.1

21. M. S. Feldstein, "Estimating the Supply Curve of Working Hours," *Oxford Economic Papers* 20 (1968): 74–80.
22. For a criticism of this approach, see A. C. Rayner, "On the Identification of the Supply Curve of Working Hours," *Oxford Economic Papers* 21 (1969): 294–298.
23. T. A. Finegan, "Hours of Work in the United States: A Cross Sectional Analysis," *Journal of Political Economy* 70 (1962): 452–470; S. Rosen, "On the Interindustry Wage and Hours Structure," *Journal of Political Economy* 77 (1969): 249–273.

Table 3.1 Selected Estimates of the Wage Elasticity of Hours Worked

Study	Estimate	Data
Finegan (1962)	−0.25 to −0.35	interoccupational
Harberger (1964)	−0.26	time series
Rosen (1966)	−0.07 to −0.30	interindustry
Winston (1966)	−0.07 to −0.10	intercountry
Owen (1971)	−0.11 to −0.24	time series
Abbot and Ashenfelter (1974)	−0.07 to −0.14	time series

Sources:
T. A. Finegan, "Hours of Work in the United States: A Cross-Sectional Analysis," *Journal of Political Economy* 70 (1962):452–470; A. C. Harberger, "Taxation, Resource Allocation, and Welfare," in J. F. Due, ed., *The Role of Direct and Indirect Taxes in the Federal Revenue System* (Princeton, N.J.: Princeton University Press, 1964); S. Rosen, "On the Interindustry Wage and Hours Structure," *Journal of Political Economy* 77 (1969):249–273; G. C. Winston, "An International Comparison of Income and Hours of Work," *Review of Economics and Statistics* 48 (1966):28–39; J. D. Owen, "The Demand for Leisure," *Journal of Political Economy* 79 (1971):56–76; M. Abbot and O. Ashenfelter, "Labor Supply, Commodity Demand, and the Allocation of Time," *Review of Economic Studies* 43 (1976):389–411.

include both income and substitution effects. Measures of the pure substitution effect can, in principle, be calculated by adjusting the above elasticities according to the formula derived in footnote 8 of this chapter.[24]

A number of studies have separated out the two effects. In an analysis of married males aged 25–64, Ashenfelter and Heckman calculate the substitution elasticity to be +0.12 and the income elasticity to be larger, at −0.27.[25] This evidence again points to a backward bending supply curve, but it gives us the advantage of component magnitudes. Other studies similarly point to a total income elasticity that is usually much larger in absolute value than the substitution elasticity.[26] Such a finding is consistent with the observed long-run decline in the supply of hours worked by males as real wages

24. The substitution effect from equation (3) in footnote 8, is

$$\partial H^c / \partial P_L = \partial H / \partial P_L - (\partial H / \partial Y)(H)$$

where $\partial H / \partial Y$ is the income effect (income $= P_L H + V$);
$\quad$ H is the prechange value of labor supply; and
$\quad$ c distinguishes the compensated wage effect from the uncompensated effect.

The substitution elasticity η_s is obtained from equation (4) of footnote 8 as

$$\eta_s = \eta_w - \eta_y \frac{P_L H}{Y}$$

where η_w and η_y are the wage and income elasticities.
25. O. Ashenfelter and J. Heckman, "Estimating Labor-Supply Functions," in G. G. Cain and H. W. Watts, eds., *Income Maintenance and Labour Supply* (Chicago: Rand McNally, 1973), p. 277.
26. See, for example, G. G. Cain and H. W. Watts, "Toward a Summary and Synthesis of the Evidence," in Cain and Watts, *Income Maintenance*, table 9.1, pp. 332–335.

have increased. If these estimates of a small substitution elasticity are to be believed, the policy implication is that high marginal tax rates might have only a weak disincentive effect on the supply of hours for the largest group in the labor force.

At this point, it is reasonable to ask whether cross-section studies, in particular, can be expected to throw up meaningful estimates of supply elasticities. An initial problem is that the mean hours worked by occupational groups may not represent an approximation to the equilibrium choice of hours by individuals with respect to earning's opportunities, given their other economic circumstances, tastes, and abilities. Rather, weekly hours may be determined by employer preferences, technological constraints, wages and hours legislation, or for that matter union encouragement of standardization. In this context, it is interesting to note that Finegan's data contain a substantial number of occupational listings in which the employees worked exactly 40 hours in the census week. There is thus some suggestion that the above factors exert an influence, in which case some of the observed wage differentials would presumably comprise compensating or equalizing payments to induce workers to make the appropriate alignments. In the extreme case, one might detect zero dispersion in hours accompanied by positive earnings dispersion.

Then there is the issue of simultaneity in labor supply equations. For example, it is likely that the amount of time offered by a worker will partly determine the wage he receives. Thus, full-time workers, for example, may be able to command a higher wage than part-time workers. If this is the case, then both the decision about hours of work and the decision about the wage earned may be simultaneously determined.

Next consider secular changes in hours worked. Data provided by Long suggest that in the United States, for example, the average workweek fell by 4.2 hours (or approximately 8%) per decade over the period 1890–1950.[27] While this outcome is partly to be explained by changes in industry mix—a shift of workers out of high hours industries, such as agriculture, into low hours industries—the standardized fall in weekly hours remains substantial. Can we attribute this decrease in weekly hours to a supply response to rising wages and incomes? The data are consistent with the standard neoclassical model on the assumption that leisure is a normal good and that the income effect outweighs the substitution effect. But the issue is complicated by the impact of legislation and the influence of trade unions. Both factors can be viewed as expressions of a collective decision to take part of rising incomes in the form of leisure. On the other hand, it has been argued that the Fair Labor Standards Act, for example, accelerated the decline of hours worked by reducing employer demand for overtime hours, this effect being only gradually absorbed by the continuing reduction in hours supplied as wage rates

27. C. D. Long, *The Labor Force Under Changing Income and Employment,* National Bureau of Economic Research (Princeton, N.J.: Princeton University Press, 1958), p. 272.

and income rose.[28] As for the impact of unions, it is again possible that union growth has accelerated the trend toward shorter hours by increasing relative wages. In other words, unions have probably caused desired hours to fall more rapidly than they might otherwise have done, leading to a degree of underemployment if the number of union members is held constant. To put things in perspective, however, we should add that unions appear to have won real wage increases that total, at most, only a small fraction of the general rise in real wages since the turn of the century (see chapter 8). So it seems that we can accept the downward trend in hours worked as an indication of the dominance of the income effect over the substitution effect, even though we cannot disentangle in a quantitative way the independent influences of legislation and union growth.

We should also note that average weekly hours have shown no marked tendency to decline in the postwar interval. Are we to assume, therefore, that the historical downward trend of hours ended in the 1940s? To argue in this manner would be to disregard increases in paid holidays and vacations. Official statistics on the length of the workweek measure hours paid for and do not distinguish between paid leave and hours of work. It seems that reductions in the length of the workyear have largely taken the form of increases in paid holidays and vacations during the postwar period.

Finally, it is worth briefly considering some results on the life-cycle pattern of working hours, as estimated by Ghez and Becker. The dependent variable is annual home time, L, of individuals of different ages (measured as 52 weeks $\times$ 7 days $\times$ 24 hours minus hours worked minus 10 hours per day for sleep and personal care). A typical equation relating to white males in 1960 is as follows:[29]

$$\ln L = 7.93 + 0.001A - 0.083 \ln P_L + 0.007 \ln Y + 0.035 \ln Y_f - 0.089 \ln S$$
$$(65.3) \quad (0.13) \quad (1.31) \quad\quad (0.67) \quad\quad (2.79) \quad\quad (1.91)$$
$$R^2 = 0.89$$

where A denotes age;
$\quad$ P_L is hourly earnings;
$\quad$ Y is other income;
$\quad$ Y_f is family income;
$\quad$ S is size of family; and
$\quad$ $|t|$ is given in parentheses.

A key prediction of the theory is that, as P_L increases over the life cycle, L is reduced because of substitution of goods for time in producing activities and because of substitution of consumption in the future for current consumption. The income effect, which in the conventional model would tend to

---

28. See, for example, H. G. Lewis, "Hours of Work and Hours of Leisure," *Proceedings of the Industrial Relations Research Association* (Madison, Wis.: IRRA, 1957), pp. 196–206.
29. Ghez and Becker, *The Allocation of Time*, table 3.1, pp. 98–99.

counteract this process and lead to an increase in L, is supposed to be small in the life-cycle context. As can be seen, the negative sign on the wage variable is consistent with this reasoning, as is the small coefficient on the nonlabor income variable. Admittedly, the negative coefficient on P_L is not significant in this formulation. If the variables are transformed by three-year moving averages, however, the coefficient on P_L becomes -0.275 with a high $|t|$ of 4.1.

3.4 Labor Force Participation

For the population as a whole, or for any section of it by age, sex, or race, the participation rate is defined as the ratio of the economically active, employed or unemployed, population falling within that category to the total population of that category. It may be expressed as

$$LF/(LF + NLF) = (U + E)/(U + E + NLF)$$

where LF is the number in the labor force;
   NLF is the number not in the labor force;[30]
   U is the number unemployed; and
   E is the number employed.

The labor force participation rate can be interpreted as the probability that a person of a certain age, sex, and race will be in the labor force. Analysis of participation can be seen to have important implications for employment policy. Thus, some have attempted to estimate the size of labor reserves within the economy—the so-called manpower gap. The participation rates question has impinged on debates concerning the changing nature of unemployment, such as took place in the United States in the early 1960s and in the United Kingdom in the late 1960s.

Here we shall begin our analysis by investigating the secular supply curve. Especial emphasis will be placed upon the labor force participation of married women and upon the reconciliation of cross-section and time-series findings in respect to this group. Our second major concern is with the relation between labor force participation and hours. Finally, we turn to cyclical fluctuations in labor force participation.

Secular Trends in Labor Force Participation. Combining all labor force groups and standardizing for changing age and sex composition, the labor force participation rate has been remarkably stable in both the United States and Great Britain since the turn of the century. Over the period 1890–1960, the overall labor force participation rate in the United States, for example,

---

30. Those not in the labor force (*NLF*) are classified on the basis of the Current Population Survey as "engaged in own household," "in school," "unable to work because of long-term physical or mental illness," "retirement," "voluntary idle," and a few other special categories. The labor force is now limited to those aged sixteen years and older. Before 1967, the lower age limit for inclusion in the labor force was fourteen.

rose by only three percentage points, from 52% to 55%. This pattern of participation appears to correspond to the range *DE* of figure 3.3, discussed earlier. This broad constancy has been produced by two offsetting trends: first, a fall in the male participation rate because of further schooling and earlier retirement and, second, a substantial rise in married women's participation. Over the period in question, the participation rate of males aged fourteen to nineteen fell from 68% to 31%. At the same time, participation of married women (living with their husbands) rose dramatically, from 4.5% to 31%. The offsetting rise in female participation in both the United States and Great Britain has occurred almost entirely among married women.

The change in married women's participation, therefore, is of special interest. The principal finding from early cross-section analysis by cities was that the higher the earnings of males in a city, the lower the labor force participation of married women.[31] This result is not very meaningful, however, because the influence of the wife's wage on her participation was not controlled. In fact, wives' participation is higher as their own wage rates increase. It is necessary to include both the wage of the husband and that of the wife in explaining the labor force participation of the latter.

One such model has been put forward in a famous study by Mincer.[32] In his model, however, the family income variable is meant to include only permanent income. The argument here is that when family income is low in relation to its normal or permanent level, wives tend in the short run to enter the labor force so as to supplement family income. Consequently, unless income is purged of its transitory elements in the cross section, the short-run negative correlation between wives' participation and family income will obscure long-run behavior. There is the difficulty that permanent income is unobservable. However, if the income of a family is represented by family income averaged over a large number of families (in a given city, for example), the latter can be taken to approximate permanent family income. By the same token, the average family income in a city might also deviate from permanent income as a result of, say, a cyclical high or low in unemployment in that area. For this reason, it is also necessary to allow for the effect of cyclical fluctuations in economic activity on labor force participation. The usual procedure is to include unemployment as a determinant.

Mincer's equation, estimated from data for fifty-seven standard metropolitan areas in 1950, is as follows:[33]

$$LFPR_{mf} = a - 0.62H_p + 1.33P_L + 0.12E - 0.41U - 0.24C$$
$$\quad\quad (2.95) \quad\quad (12.09) \quad (0.44) \quad (0.77) \quad (0.39)$$
$$R^2 = 0.62$$

31. See, for example, Long, *Labor Force,* pp. 54–81.
32. J. Mincer, "Labor Force Participation of Married Women: A Study of Labor Supply," *Aspects of Labor Economics,* National Bureau of Economic Research (Princeton, N.J.: Princeton University Press, 1962), pp. 63–97.
33. Ibid., p. 72.

where $LFPR_{mf}$ is the labor force participation rate of married females
    (husbands present);

H_p is the median income in 1949 (measured in thousands of
    dollars) of male heads, wife present;

P_L is the median income of females (measured in thousands of
    dollars) who worked fifty to fifty-two weeks in 1949;

E is the percent of population aged twenty-five and over with
    completed high school education or better;

U is the percentage male unemployment rate, which serves as a
    proxy for cyclical income fluctuations;

C is the percent of families with children under six years of age;
    and

$|t|$ values are in parentheses.

The effect of a $1,000 increase in husbands' incomes is to reduce the labor
force participation of wives by -0.62 percentage points, *ceteris paribus*. On
the other hand, the effect of a $1,000 increase in the income of wives, holding
constant husbands' incomes and all other variables, is to raise their labor
force participation by a considerably larger amount, 1.33 percentage points.
Several more recent studies have also found the wage response of married
women's participation to be larger absolutely than their income response.[34]
In accounting for this larger wage effect for wives than for males, we could
argue that, in housework, women have a better alternative to market work
than do men. This alternative increases their elasticity of labor supply to the
market, though not necessarily to given firms. In any case, it is worth noting
that the positive coefficient on P_L accords with our earlier analysis of figure
3.2, which indicated that wage increases could only increase participation.
The schooling and preschool children variables (the role of the unemployment variable is considered below) are expected to reflect tastes for work and
to take into account the more important differences in demand for work at
home. These have effects in the expected direction, although in this study
(but not others) statistical significance is lacking.

It is interesting to apply these cross-section results to explain the historical
increase in the labor force participation of married women. Over the postwar
interval, the male-female relative wage ratio has remained roughly constant,
but money wages have risen approximately fourfold. However, when this
increase in money wages is applied to the participation of wives, the use of
the coefficients of participation equations, such as Mincer's, actually under-
predicts the increase in wives' participation. In the British case, for example,
married women's participation actually increased twenty percentage points

34. See G. G. Cain, *Married Women in the Labor Force* (Chicago: University of Chicago Press,
1966), p. 23; Bowen and Finegan, *Labor Force Participation,* p. 789; G. G. Cain and M. D.
Dooley, "Estimation of a Model of Labor Supply, Fertility, and Wages of Married Women,"
Journal of Political Economy 84 (1976): S179–S199; C. Greenhalgh, "A Labour Supply Function
for Married Women in Great Britain," *Economica* 44 (1977): table 2, p. 255.

from 30% in 1951 to 50% in 1971, as against a predicted increase of only twelve percentage points.[35] Clearly, other factors, not captured in cross-section analysis, have been operative over time. An explanation of this phenomenon in a Becker-type framework could run in terms of changes in household technology. This has enabled the increasing substitution of wage goods, such as prepared foods and dishwashers, for wives' time in household production. We must remember, however, that family incomes have been growing, and with them the demand for home production, assuming this to be a normal good. It is necessary, therefore, to argue that the latter effect is small to achieve the result that wives' hours of work at home decrease secularly.

It is also worth considering the labor force participation rates of black wives. The growth in participation for such groups has been at a considerably lower rate than for their white counterparts, although their overall level of participation is higher.[36] In the first place, despite the improvement in the relative wages of black wives, their wage rates remain below those of white wives. This could mean that black wives are less able to afford the cost of substitutes for home work, so that the cost of reducing home work per unit of time is larger for black wives than the wage rate per unit of time. Second, to the extent that black wives already devote less time to home work than do white wives at any wage, there is less scope for greater labor force participation of such groups in response to wage increases. Third, the presence of discrimination, which limits the incentive to attain higher socioeconomic levels, would imply that the negative income effects of higher incomes of family heads upon wives' labor force participation would be stronger for black women than for white women. Cain has provided evidence that income effects are indeed larger relative to wage effects for black married females than for the total married woman sample.[37]

We conclude this section on secular labor force participation with some brief comments on the labor force participation of males at the extreme ends of the age distribution. Secular declines in participation dominate the labor force behavior of older men (aged sixty-five and above) and that of teenagers and young people (aged fourteen [sixteen] to twenty-four). The downward trend in the participation rates of older males has been more or less continuous since the turn of the century; we cannot therefore rely exclusively upon a welfare benefits explanation of this phenomenon. The most intuitively

35. Greenhalgh, "A Labour Supply Function," p. 259.
36. The participation rate of urban black married women aged 15–54 was 47% in 1960, as compared with 35% for white wives. Even after adjustment for the effects of schooling, age, the presence of children, and so on, the participation rate of black married women was still some seven percentage points higher than that of white married women. See Bowen and Finegan, *Labor Force Participation,* pp. 89–94.
37. G. G. Cain, "Unemployment and the Labor-Force Participation of Secondary Workers," *Industrial and Labor Relations Review* 20 (1967): 288–289; see also Cain and Dooley, "Estimation of a Model," table 3, p. S192.

appealing explanation of the downward trend to approximately 1945 is that the movement to earlier retirement was a predictable response to rising per capita income levels. Data provided by Bowen and Finegan, for example, suggest that the labor force participation rates of older males are strongly and negatively related to nonlabor income.[38] Let us assume that the change from 1889 to 1939 in the nonlabor income to which elderly males respond increased by one-half the amount of the change in the full-time earnings of all males.[39] Then the estimated response, using the partial net coefficient on nonlabor income in the older males cross-section labor force participation regression equation, implies a decline in participation between 1890 and 1940 of some twenty-two percentage points. The actual decline is close to this, being twenty-six percentage points. However, it should be noted that the observed association need not necessarily indicate the response of older workers to rising income levels, but, rather, their response to a declining demand for their services relative to younger workers. The argument here is that the educational qualifications of men in the higher age groups have been falling relative to the population as a whole, and relative to younger women in particular, and that employers have increasingly shown a preference for women. Presumably this argument also depends on a degree of wage rigidity, in such forms as minimum-wage legislation, preventing employers from offering older workers lower relative earnings.

As for the postwar period, this has seen a liberalization of the Social Security Act of 1935, which originally made receipt of a pension conditional on cessation of work. The effect of this liberalization was not only to raise potential nonlabor income levels for workers who might quit the labor force, but also to lower real wage rates if monthly earnings exceeded the permitted threshold. Apart from Social Security retirement benefits, there has also occurred a mushrooming of private pension schemes and increases in the accumulated savings of individuals, all of which have served to increase the financial resources at the disposal of older persons. Bowen and Finegan have computed the growth in annual retirement income from Social Security between 1948 and 1965 as $700 (1959 dollars), and the average increase in other forms of nonlabor income at $600.[40] The predicted change in the participation rates of older workers attributable to nonlabor income is −0.75 per $100, which is the calculated coefficient on nonlabor income in the authors' older worker participation regression, multiplied by $1,300. This yields an implied decline in participation of 9.8 percentage points, or 60% of the actual decline, after adjusting for demographic factors. These results suggest that increases in Social Security benefits and coverage, from 14% to 76%, have played an important role in reducing the participation of older males during the postwar years.

38. Bowen and Finegan, "Labor Force Participation," pp. 130–134.
39. The rationale for this is that the share of nonlabor income in national income is roughly half the share of labor income.
40. Bowen and Finegan, *Labor Force Participation,* chap. 11.

Finally, let us turn our attention to the declining labor force participation rates of younger males. It is conventional to regard the historical decline in the participation rate of this group as a response to rising income levels. The argument is that the latter have stimulated greater investment in human capital, particularly in schooling. As we shall see in chapter 4, an individual's schooling is closely related to family income. Given an inverse relation between participation rates and school attendance, the postulated association follows. However, other factors should also be considered. Thus, it has been found that enrollments rise when the labor market is slack—presumably reflecting the decreased opportunity costs of schooling at such times.[41] Moreover, impediments to the employment of younger workers in the form of minimum-wage legislation, union restrictions on entry, and legislation detailing the terms and conditions of employment for younger workers will again serve to reduce their participation.

Labor Force Participation and Hours of Work.   We have treated hours of work and labor force participation as separate topics, although a common set of variables is used to explain them. This approach is that followed within the bulk of the research literature.

A labor supply function, $L = L(P_L, Y)$, can always be written in the form:

$$L = L(P_L, Y) = H(P_L, Y) \cdot LFPR(P_L, Y) \tag{3.10}$$

where $LFPR(P_L, Y)$ is the labor force participation rate for individuals with wage P_L and income Y; and

H is the average hours of work for those who work a positive number of hours.

Studies that are restricted to labor force participants yield estimates of $H(P_L, Y)$, while studies of the entire population provide estimates of $L(P_L, Y)$. Given that our interest must focus upon the overall supply function, it follows that studies restricted to H are incomplete for our purposes because they fail to estimate the participation function. The participation rate is always less than unity, so that H will always exceed $L(P_L, Y)$. Moreover, since $LFPR$ is responsive to P_L and Y, the response of H to a change in P_L and Y will be somewhat different from that of $L(P_L, Y)$ to the same changes.

The problem is to integrate the participation decision and the hours decision. One method is to devise a two-stage procedure that estimates, first, the probability of a potential worker being in the labor force and, second, the expected hours of work conditional upon labor force participation.[42] The full labor supply concept is, therefore, determined by the product of the two separate functions.

41. See, for example, B. Duncan, "Dropouts and the Unemployed," *Journal of Political Economy* 73 (1965): 121–134.
42. See M. J. Boskin, "The Economics of Labor Supply," in Cain and Watts, *Income Maintenance,* pp. 163–181.

A second approach is that followed by Heckman, whose analysis of the supply response of married females rests on two behavior schedules.[43] First, he has a function determining the wage a woman faces in the market, namely the *offered wage*. This wage will be a function of, for example, her education and work experience. Second, he has a function determining the value a woman places on her time, which can be called her *asking wage*. This wage will be determined by factors such as the number of hours she works, her husband's wage, her education, and the number of young children she has. If a woman works, her hours of work adjust to equate the two wages, assuming she has the freedom to set her working hours. On the other hand, if a woman does not work (a corner solution), it follows that no offered wage matches her asking wage. It is possible to estimate both schedules—the market-wage function and asking-wage function—and use the estimated coefficients to determine the probability that a woman works and her actual hours of work given that she works.

Let us next turn to the findings of studies based on these two approches. In table 3.2, we draw on a sample of Boskin's regression results relating to the hours and participation of husbands and wives. Observe that for white husbands of both age groups, prime age and elderly, wages exert virtually no influence upon hours of work once the decision has been made to enter the labor force. For elderly white husbands, however, wages do appear to have some small positive effect on participation. Income exerts practically no influence on participation but has a strong negative influence on hours of work. With respect to wives, the results point to a strong, positive wage effect on either hours of work and participation or both for all four age-race groups. Income effects, however, are either small or absent. But the presence of preschool children reduces the likelihood of labor force participation by around 20%, and this negative effect apparently spills over into hours in the case of black wives. Wives show a tendency, irrespective of race, to withdraw from the labor force as the husband's wage increases.

Boskin also explores income and substitution effects derived from operations on the regression coefficients of table 3.2. Briefly, his findings are that positive wage elasticities of total labor supply ($=LFPR \cdot H$) characterize wives and white husbands at or near retirement age. But for prime-age husbands of either race, there is no evidence of positive substitution effects, so that income effects dominate the total labor supply of these groups.

Heckman's analysis focuses upon married white women. He finds that the effect of the presence of one child under the age of six is to raise the asking wage by roughly 15%, correspondingly reducing the probability of participation for a given offered wage. Also, a one-dollar increase in the husband's wage rate raises the asking wage of the wife by 5%. Table 3.3 shows that increases in the wife's schooling appear to raise the asking wage by less than

43. J. Heckman, "Shadow Prices, Market Wages, and Labor Supply," *Econometrica* 42 (1974): 679–694.

Table 3.2 Estimated Labor Supply Equations for Husbands and Wives, by Age and Race

| | Husbands | | | | Wives | | | |
| | Whites | | Blacks | | Whites | | Blacks | |
Variable	LFP	H	LFP	H	LFP	H	LFP	H
Constant	0.994*	2702.7*	0.984*	2570.4*	0.916*	1747.7*	0.817*	1792.7*
Constant, elderly	−0.069	−578.0*	−0.004	−317.1*	−0.263	−580.4	0.479*	−797.2
Own wage	—	−49.0	0.006	−56.5*	—	48.6*	0.105*	213.9*
Own wage, elderly	0.039*	59.9	0.018	82.4	0.142	360.5*	0.238	371.3
Nonwage income	—	−0.058*	—	−0.029*	—	−0.028*	0.00004	−0.019*
Nonwage income, elderly	—	0.037	—	−0.027	—	−0.059*	−0.000005	−0.030
Number of dependents	0.004*	55.9*	0.003	15.6	−0.042*	90.0*	−0.031*	−14.9
Children under six dummy	0.007*	12.2	−0.003	−53.1	−0.237*	41.1	−0.168*	−180.8*
Other wage	−0.006	−51.0	−0.002	−70.8	−0.031	11.5	−0.142*	96.4*
SSR	247.6	1.29×10^{10}	81.6	1.9×10^{9}	1556.6	1.85×10^{9}	634.8	1.02×10^{9}
SE	0.18	1173.5	0.45	836.4	0.45	816.1	0.47	863.0
v	9	9	9	9	9	9	9	9
n	7571	7303	2820	2733	7590	2789	2801	1379

Notes:

* denotes coefficient is statistically significant at the 5% level.
— signifies that number is too small to be included.
LFP = labour force participation.
H = hours supplied.
SSR = sum of squared residuals.
SE = standard error of regression.
v = number of variables.
n = number of observations.

Source:
M. J. Boskin, "The Economics of Labor Supply," in G. G. Cain and H. M. Watts, eds., *Income Maintenance and Labor Supply* (Chicago: Rand McNally, 1973), table 4.1, pp. 169–170.

Table 3.3   Predicted Probabilities of Working, by Number of Preschool Children and Years of Schooling, Married Females.

Number of Children Under 6 Years of Age	Years of Schooling				
	8	10	12	14	16
0	.30	.38	.47	.56	.66
1	.09	.13	.18	.25	.32
2	.013	.025	.04	.065	.09

Note:
Husband's wage rate is $2.50 per hour, net worth is $5,000, and the woman has four years of labor market experience.

Source:
J. Heckman, "Shadow Prices, Market Wages, and Labor Supply," *Econometrica* 42 (1974): table III, p. 688.

they raise the offered wage. This result implies that more educated women work more frequently and work longer hours than less educated women.[44] This study gives high estimates of substitution elasticities. Specifically, a 10% increase in real wage rates is estimated to increase by 160 the number of hours supplied in the market annually by married women. Comparing these results with those derived from more conventional procedures, which omit data on nonworking wives, suggests that reliance on the latter approach does lead to lower, but not radically different, estimates of labor supply elasticities.

Cyclical Fluctuations in the Labor Force.   Relative to the size of the labor force and the population, net annual fluctuations in the labor force are small. This is particularly evident when the net flows are compared with the gross movements into and out of the labor force.[45] Yet it is the net (nonseasonal) fluctuations that have received the principal focus of attention within the literature. This may be said to reflect the importance of labor force responses to short-run cyclical fluctuations in aggregate demand to an understanding of the problems of inflation and unemployment (chapters 11 and 12).

In explaining cyclical fluctuations of this type, we can again work in terms of income and substitution effects. In the cyclical context, these terms become additional worker and discouraged worker effects respectively. When the level of demand falls it can be argued that:

1. Some workers lose their jobs.
2. Because of variations in the amplitude and timing of wage and price movements, the real wages of people in work fall.
3. Real wages fall in response to reduced opportunities for overtime and incentive payments.
4. The cost of job search rises.

44. Heckman, "Shadow Prices," tables I and II, p. 687.

45. In 1971, for example, the net increase in the United States labor force was approximately 1.4 million. The gross flows into and out of the labor force stood at 11.5 million and 10.1 million respectively.

The first three factors suggest that family real income will fall, the second and third factors indicate that the real wage of the employed will fall, and the last three factors suggest that there will be a drop in the real wage for those seeking work. On the assumption that market work is an inferior good, the implied drop in family income will induce a rise in participation rates, *ceteris paribus*. On the other hand, the drop in the real wage will mean a rise in the cost of market work relative to nonmarket work and to leisure; this relative change in cost will lead to a drop in participation rates, *ceteris paribus*. The added worker hypothesis postulates that of these two opposing forces, the income effect will predominate; that is, labor force movements will be countercyclical. The discouraged worker hypothesis argues to the contrary that the substitution effect will be the stronger and labor force movements will be procyclical. In an attempt to assess the strengths of the opposing influences, let us consider cross-section and time-series studies in turn. We concentrate on the behavior of secondary workers, because the participation rates of primary workers are quite stable in the short run.

Cross-Section Analysis.   The major independent variables in cross-section work are family income and the pay of the individual in the appropriate age/sex/race group. To simplify matters, let $LFPR_i$ be the labor force participation of married women, husband present, in a labor market such as that of a standard metropolitan area. For simplicity, the model can be restricted to the income and earnings variables—Y, husband's income, representing a normal or permanent concept of income, and W_i, the wife's full-time wage earnings. Introducing transitory or cyclical changes in the income and earnings figures as Y_t and W_t, respectively, we have

$$LFPR_i = a + b_1 Y + b_2 W + c_1 Y_t + c_2 W_t \qquad c_1 < 0, c_2 > 0$$

where c_1 is the added worker effect; and
$\quad\quad c_2$ is the discouraged worker effect.

It is reasonable to suppose that the unemployment rate will be a determinant of the transitory changes in income and in addition will capture some of the nonwage adjustments to changes in employment conditions such as the tightening or relaxing of hiring standards. A simple assumption is

$$Y_t = \alpha U$$

where

$$\alpha < 0$$

and

$$W_t = \beta U$$

where

$$\beta < 0.$$

Substituting, we have

$$LFPR_i = a + b_1 Y + b_2 W + b_3 U$$

where $b_3 = (\alpha c_1 + \beta c_2)$ and will be positive or negative as $|\alpha c_1| \gtrless |\beta c_2|$.

This is the basic cross-sectional model, although various studies have also included additional variables, such as schooling, to reflect behavioral differences influencing the supply function.

The United States evidence suggests a strong negative sensitivity of the labor force to unemployment. Bowen and Finegan, for example, obtained for the whole labor force a regression coefficient on unemployment of -0.68, which suggests that a one percentage point increase in the unemployment rate is associated on average with a two-thirds percentage point decrease in the total labor force participation rate.[46] The negative coefficients on unemployment were particularly pronounced in respect of married women (-0.76), young females under nineteen (-0.73), young males (-1.94), and elderly males over sixty-five (-1.62). The participation rates of prime-age males, however, showed little cyclical fluctuation and the general presumption is that such groups make their labor force adjustments in other ways. But the participation stability of the prime-age group probably also points to the greater stability in the demand for their labor. As we have seen in chapter 2, employers will prefer to retain their skilled workers, in whom firm-specific investments have been made, in the event of a cyclical downturn.

Our understanding of the cross-section findings is facilitated by the analysis of Mincer.[47] The dominance of the discouraged worker effect is attributed by Mincer to difference in timing of participation by those not continuously attached to the labor force. The same individuals are sometimes in and sometimes out of the labor force during a period of years. Thus, given some scope for timing of their activities, work in the labor market can be said to be preferred at times when search costs and job conditions are attractive. Then the procyclical behavior of the labor force can be viewed in part as an optimization of the timing of labor force activities, although many other factors will influence that timing.

All this is not to say that all workers are identical in the degree to which they can exercise such choice. During periods of low economic activity, a poor family with limited assets will have no choice except to send secondary workers into the market—here *need* is relatively more important than *price*.

---

46. Bowen and Finegan, "Labor Force Participation," p. 146. See also G. G. Cain, "Unemployment and the Labor Force Participation of Secondary Workers," *Industrial and Labor Relations Review* 20 (1967): 275–297.

47. J. Mincer, "Labor Force Participation and Unemployment: A Review of Recent Evidence," in R. A. and M. S. Gordon, eds., *Prosperity and Unemployment* (New York: Wiley, 1966), pp. 73–112.

Moreover, the ease with which substitution in home production or consumption can be carried out will be an important factor. The lesser the substitutability, the more limited the responsiveness of participation to changes in unemployment. Finally, cases in which taking market jobs involves a corresponding loss in welfare benefits will also impose different constraints on an individual's work decision than is the case for the population as a whole.

Time-Series Analysis. Important initial work in this area was undertaken by Dernburg and Strand, who proposed a model of the form:[48]

$$LFPR_t = a_m + a_1(X/P)_{t+2} + a_2(E/P)_t + a_3(I/P)_t + e$$
$$a_1 > 0, a_2 > 0, a_3 < 0$$

where $(X/P)_{t+2}$ is the ratio of new unemployment-compensation exhaustions to the adult population two months after t;

$(E/P)_t$ is the percentage of the adult population employed at month t; and

$(I/P)_t$ is the reciprocal of the total population in month t.

Variations in (X/P) can be taken to represent short-run variations in income prospects. The presumption is that the prospect of loss of income due to the exhaustion of unemployment compensation causes secondary workers in the family to enter the labor force, albeit some time before the benefits of the unemployed breadwinner actually expire. The term (E/P) is taken to represent variations in employment opportunities. The coefficient of (X/P), which shows the added worker effect, might be expected to be positive; this would also be true of (E/P), which reflects the discouraged worker effect.

The fitted equation was as follows ($|t|$ is given in parentheses):

$$LFPR_t = a_m + 12.347(X/P)_{t+2} + 0.8715(E/P)_t - 3492.2(I/P)_t$$
$$(19.3) \qquad\qquad (28.1) \qquad\qquad (8.33)$$

$$R^2 = 0.8138$$

$$(DW \text{ not provided}).$$

This result appears to be a striking confirmation of the joint presence of discouraged and added worker effects. The net coefficient, which gives the net effects of changes in the employment ratio on the labor force ratio, can be obtained from an auxiliary simultaneous equation relating the exhaustion

48. K. T. Strand and T. F. Dernburg, "Cyclical Variation in Civilian Labor Force Participation," *Review of Economics and Statistics* 46 (1964): 378–391. See also, idem, "Hidden Unemployment 1953–62: A Quantitative Analysis by Age and Sex," *American Economic Review* 56 (1966): 71–95.

ratio to the employment ratio and can be shown to be positive,[49] thus indicating the dominance of the discouraged worker effect. Specifically, over the period 1947–1962, a fall in employment of 100 was associated with a net withdrawal of 38 workers from the labor force.

There exist a number of measurement difficulties and problems of interpretation as regards this procedure. For instance, the coefficient on $(X/P)_{t+2}$ suggests that the prospect of one additional exhaustion of benefits, say by the head of the family, pushes as many as twelve family workers into, or deters them from quitting, the labor market. There is no formal link between $(X/P)_{t+2}$ and $LFPR_t[=(E_t + U_t)/P_t]$, but the former variable, representing unemployment exhaustions, is naturally highly correlated with the unemployment ratio $(U/P)_t$, which is one component of $LFPR$. The other component of $LFPR$ is $(E/P)_t$, which again is an independent variable. Mincer[50] has found a simple correlation of over $+0.9$ between $(U/P)_t$ and $(X/P)_{t+3}$ for the period 1953–1962. This indicates that the model is dangerously close to being tautological.

Because such difficulties exist, others have sought to restrict the equation to (E/P) as a safer, albeit cruder, approach. The regression coefficient of (E/P) will now yield a net outcome of the individual income and substitution effects, but separate identification of each effect is foregone. Such a procedure is followed by Tella in two studies employing a model of the form:[51]

$$LFPR_{it} = \alpha + \alpha_1(E/P)_{i,t-1} + \alpha_2(\log T)_t + e$$

where T is a time trend.

---

49. Because the exhaustions ratio is itself a function of past employment (unemployment), the coefficient 0.872 in the text equation cannot be interpreted as the derivative of labor force participation with respect to employment. It is necessary to add the estimated equation

$$(X/P)_t = b_m + 0.0055(E/P)_{t-1} + 0.863(X/P)_{t-1}.$$

To see what change in *LFPR* follows a change in *E/P*, we have to find a stationary solution; that is, where *E/P* and *X/P* are constant over time. Then

$$(\widehat{X}/P) = \frac{b_m}{1 - 0.863} + \frac{0.0055}{1 - 0.863}(\widehat{E}/P).$$

Substituting this into the text equation for *LFPR* gives a coefficient on steady-state $(\widehat{X}/P)$ of

$$\frac{0.872(1 - 0.86) + 12.35 \times 0.055}{1 - 0.86} > 0.$$

50. Mincer, "Recent Evidence."
51. A. Tella, "The Relation of Labor Force to Employment," *Industrial and Labor Relations Review* 17 (1964): 454–469; idem, "Labour Force Sensitivity to Employment by Age, Sex," *Industrial Relations* 2 (1965): 69–83. See also S. Cooper and D. F. Johnston, "Labor Force Projections 1970–1980," *Monthly Labor Review* 88 (1965): 129–140.

Tella's results, using annual data for males aged fourteen and over for the period 1948–1962, give a coefficient on (E/P) of 0.404 ($|t| = 4.81$). The corresponding coefficient for females is 0.623 (4.55). Again these results point to the dominance of the discouraged worker effect.

Yet Bowen and Finegan have shown that there remain problems with respect to the labor market predictor in studies of this type. Briefly consider $(E/P)_i$. The term E_i represents a very large component of P_i; therefore, autonomous movements in $[(E + U)/P]_i$ that are not caused by changes in labor demand are most likely to be accompanied by similar movements in $(E/P)_i$. The latter will impart a spurious positive association between the two variables. The use of a time trend in the regression will help to reduce this bias, because it can be expected to capture some of the correlated trends in the two variables. However, the fact remains that the time trend cannot impound short-term movements in the variables; so the problem of positive bias still applies. Bowen and Finegan themselves examine the participation rates of some eighteen age-sex groups over the period 1949(2)–1965(3), using as their main independent variable $(U/L)_{t-1}$, which represents the seasonally adjusted overall unemployment rate, lagged by one quarter.[52] The principal finding of this study is that short-period changes in the overall unemployment rate do not appear to have a substantial impact on the labor force participation rate of any population group, with the possible exception of teenagers and males aged sixty-five and older. Moreover, the authors' estimates show the time-series regression coefficients to be very sensitive to changes in the period analyzed.[53]

Given the limitations of time-series analyses, we are perhaps on safest ground in basing our summary comments on cross-section findings. It must be noted that an overstatement of cyclical changes on the basis of cross-sectional tests is likely to occur, because results in the cross section are biased toward situations in equilibrium or full adjustment. This is because different levels of unemployment observed at a particular moment in time among, say, metropolitan areas will have existed for many months longer than the typical business cycle, and participation decisions will have more fully adjusted to labor market conditions. This problem is a standard one in empirical work, namely that of how to use static relations from cross sections to assess dynamic adjustments which involve, in this case, job changes and interarea migrations. On the basis of the evidence, however, we would argue that a positive cycle sensitivity or net discouragement effect is discernible in the behavior of secondary labor force groups. At the same time, we note that the added worker effect seems to be powerful in some of the low-income groups for whom need is relatively more important than price. The overall negative relation between labor force participation and unemployment thus implies

52. Bowen and Finegan, *Labor Force Participation*, pp. 505–515.
53. See J. L. Gastwirth, "Estimating the Number of 'Hidden Unemployed,'" *Monthly Labor Review* 96 (1973): 17–26.

that although some secondary workers enter the labor force when unemployment strikes their household, more depart or more likely delay their entrance until a more favorable market environment appears. This behavior may be interpreted in terms of a wage and/or job opportunity effect dominating the income effect and may be rationalized in terms of the better substitutes for market work among secondary workers. Clearly, different groups of secondary workers will differ in the degree to which they can exercise these choices; so we do not expect to observe uniform income and wage effects across secondary groups.

We should therefore regard the discouraged worker effect as largely reflecting an optimization process. Given that secondary workers have some scope for the timing of their activities, work in the labor market will be preferred at times when search costs are low and job conditions attractive. While there is doubtless some involuntary labor force withdrawal, the regression results give more support to this kind of timing phenomenon than the classic type of the discouraged worker, who, having lost his job, is depicted as having given up hope after fruitless search. For this reason we must be cautious in drawing welfare implications from the analysis.

3.5   Conclusions

Our theoretical analysis has focused on short-run models of labor supply. We began with the elementary short-run neoclassical model of the supply of labor time, which is an application of the theory of consumer behavior. The model assumes that the individual chooses between consumer goods and leisure, hours of work having no impact on utility. It can be shown that the total effect of a change in wages can be separated into income effects and substitution effects, although the direction of the total effect cannot be determined a priori but depends on whether the negative income effect—assuming leisure to be a normal good—outweighs the positive substitution effect.

This simple model can be extended to encompass the household dimension of labor supply. The labor supply of any one member can be analyzed either under the assumption that the labor supply of at least one family member is independent of that of the other family member(s), or on the assumption that the labor supply of any family member is in part the result of an interaction of the labor supply choices of all family members. Under this latter approach, cross-substitution terms are commonly assumed to be zero for all family members, so that the only effect on a family member's labor supply of an increase in another family member's wage is a pure income effect. This formulation implies that the income of other family members' variable is an endogenous variable in any given family member's labor supply function. In other words, it is not nonlabor income as far as the family member in question is concerned, because its level will be in part by his or her own labor supply. It follows that we must treat single-equation estimates of a family member's labor supply with considerable caution.

Up to this point, our analysis was predicated on the assumptions that all time is devoted either to labor or to leisure, that any amount of consumer goods can be accommodated in any amount of leisure time, and that consumer goods are desired in and of themselves. These unrealistic assumptions have been challenged by Becker, who argues that consumption of consumer goods requires not only the goods themselves but also time. Thus, time can be devoted to nonmarket work of various kinds. Becker further argues that consumer goods are demanded because they are necessary to the performance of activities in which one individual wishes to engage. Consumer goods, on this analysis, are simply inputs that together with time inputs produce outputs or activities. It is these activities that appear as arguments in the individual's utility function. The individual chooses not between consumer goods and leisure but between different nonmarket activities, all of which use different combinations of consumer goods and time. The individual is assumed to maximize utility subject to a full income constraint. Utility is found to be maximized subject to this constraint and, as with the sample model, the amount of hours worked emerges out of this equilibrium as a residual, namely as total time available minus total time devoted to activities.

We analyzed the effect of a rise in wage rates in the Becker model. Rising wage rates increase the relative price of time-intensive activities and cause substitution against them, possibly inducing an increase in hours worked. As in the elementary model, the net effect is shown to be dependent upon the strength and direction of the income effect, which will cause less time to be spent in market work if time-intensive commodities are not inferior goods.

While the implications and applications of the Becker model are only now beginning to be worked out and tested, it is clear that the three-way distinction between market work, nonmarket work, and leisure improves our understanding of labor supply. To illustrate this point, we considered the impact of the improved productivity of consumption time resulting from advances in household technology. It was shown how improved household productivity may lead to a reduction in nonmarket work time and to an increase in time devoted to pleasure and to work.

The principal finding of empirical studies of hours of work is that, at or near the mean wage, increases in wage rates are associated with decreases in hours worked. However, there is a relatively wide spread of estimates of the uncompensated wage elasticity of supply. In those studies that have attempted to incorporate nonlabor income, the finding is that the total income elasticity for males tends to be larger in absolute value than the compensated wage elasticity (that is, substitution elasticity). This finding is consistent with the empirically verifiable long-run decline in the labor supply of males. Among females, however, the substitution elasticity tends to be larger than the corresponding elasticity for males, a finding that is also consistent with time-series data. It seems that we can interpret the long-run decline in hours worked as a supply response to rising wages and incomes, although the issue is clouded by the role of unionism and the impact of legislation.

Turning to the question of labor force participation, the empirical literature addresses differences in the strength of attachment to the labor force of
groups differentiated by age, sex, and marital status. Average rates of
participation are much lower for teenagers, the elderly, and married women
than for prime-age males. Such factors as differences in education and
strength of demand induce much larger differences in their participation
rates. The labor force participation of married females has been subjected to
more intensive scrutiny than that of other secondary labor force groups, as is
indeed appropriate given the growing importance of their labor supply
contribution. The labor force participation of wives is strongly and positively
related to their own wages and is negatively related to husbands' income and
nonlabor income, with the positive wage elasticity exceeding, often substantially, the negative income elasticity. This phenomenon can be explained in
terms of the considerably wider substitution possibilities (remember the
three-way choice between leisure, market work, and unpaid home work) for
females than for other population subgroups. However, the labor force
participation rates of married females have risen faster than we would have
predicted on the basis of cross-section regression estimates. This might be
due to an increased substitutability between wives' home production and
wage goods. However, a fuller analysis would integrate the hours and labor
force participation dimension of labor supply. The basic argument here is
that one should include nonparticipants in the estimation of labor supply
sensitivity, because the decision to stay out of the labor force is a major way
in which individuals can affect their labor supply. This is an important area
of current research.

It is also worthwhile considering the effect of cyclical changes in real
income, as proxied by the unemployment rate or employment ratio, upon the
labor force participation of secondary workers. Both time-series and cross-
sectional estimates of cyclical labor force sensitivity point to a procyclical
behavior of the labor force, a fact that indicates the dominance of the
substitution or discouraged worker effect. There are exceptions to this broad
tendency among low-income groups, for whom need is more important than
price; the income or added worker effect appears to be more important in
these cases. The general dominance of the discouraged worker effect can best
be interpreted as reflecting an optimization process associated with the
economical timing of labor force participation decisions and not as describing a class of workers who, upon becoming unemployed, give up hope after
fruitless job search and withdraw from the market. Thus, net discouragement
finds its expression in reduced market inflows rather than increased outflows
(see chapter 11).

There remain very real problems confronting the analyst in the area of
labor supply. The fundamental problem is one of heterogeneity in preferences. The general point about preferences is that personal traits could be
causal to decisions to obtain higher wages and to offer many hours in the
market. The wage variable could then be credited with the positive effect of

ambition. There are methods of obtaining more homogeneity; for example, various categories of persons, such as members of high-income families and members of families on welfare, can be omitted from the regression. But truncation of the sample to eliminate, say, all groups above the poverty line produces its own biases (for an application, see chapter 5). Thus, how does one distinguish, on the basis of current income, the normal or permanent poor from the normally not poor who are having a bad year? In addition, it is generally the case that the more homogenous the group, the lower is the variability in the wage and income variables. Thus, a basic limitation inherent in cross-sectional data is that the variety of demand conditions for equivalent labor suppliers may not provide a sufficient spread of wage levels to permit estimation of a supply response to the large exogenous shifts in net wages consequent upon welfare programs. For example, President Richard Nixon's Family Assistance Plan taxed the income of those eligible for income supplements at 50%.

Similar difficulties apply with respect to the income effect. The question here is also whether there is enough variation in nonlabor income to provide information on what is likely to happen if an income guarantee is introduced that is sufficient for recipients to consider subsisting on. Faced with the difficulties of generating meaningful income and wage elasticities from nonexperimental data, recourse has been made to experimental data. We refer here to the various negative income tax experiments conducted in the United States.[54] Under such experiments, some low-income families are presented with an alternative budget constraint that involves much lower net wages and much higher nonlabor income than their usual budget constraint. Their labor supply responses are documented and are contrasted with the behavior of control families who do not participate in the program. Analysis of this new type of data should prove interesting.

---

54. See, for example, J. A. Peckman and P. M. Timpane, eds., *Work Incentives and Income Guarantees: The New Jersey Income Tax Experiment* (Washington, D.C.: The Brookings Institution, 1975).

APPENDIX 3-A
THE OVERTIME QUESTION

To this point, we have assumed that all hours are paid at the same rate. In the real world, however, we know that hours worked beyond the standard workweek attract an overtime premium, usually 1.5 times the basic rate. Consider figure 3-A.1 and suppose that our representative individual, at the going wage rate on budget line AA_0, was supplying H_0T hours of work. Now suppose that an overtime premium is introduced for all hours worked in excess of H_0T. The effect of this is to kink the budget line at P_0, making it more steeply sloped above and to the left of this point. The new opportunities confronting the worker are shown by the line AP_0A_1. If P_0 was initially an equilibrium point, there must exist a point on a higher indifference curve, such as P_1, which also lies on the more steeply sloped segment of the budget line, movement to which is motivated by a pure (Slutsky) substitution effect.[1]

So we see that the overtime premium is a means to elicit extra hours from the worker. The reasons why employers should prefer to obtain additional hours from their existing work force rather than expanding employment were discussed in chapter 2 and are associated with the fixed costs of hiring and training labor. In the absence of such costs, employers would always prefer to hire additional labor rather than pay penalty rates.

Overtime payment arrangements are a form of price discrimination, in that a different price is paid for different units of the same good. The element of price discrimination involved here clearly reduces the real income of the worker relative to what it would have been had the overtime rate applied to all hours worked and not simply those in excess of H_0T. If the alternatives depicted by the budget line AA_2 were open to the worker, he would choose

---

1. Hitherto, we have isolated the substitution effect of a wage increase by shifting down the new budget line until that line is tangential to the worker's indifferent curve, or initial real income level. This is the Hicks method. Alternatively, we could shift the budget line down until that line passed through the original combination of goods and leisure purchased by the worker (figure 3.2). This latter, Slutsky method is employed in figure 3-A.1. Constant real income under the Hicks method is defined to mean the ability to achieve a given level of satisfaction; under the Slutsky method, it is defined to mean the ability to achieve given real income.

Figure 3-A.1   Overtime and Labor Supply

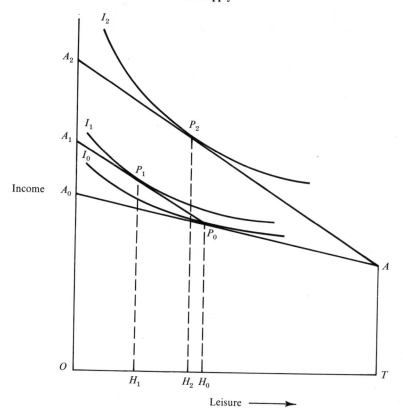

not P_1 but P_2, lying on the higher indifference curve I_2. At P_2, H_2T hours of work would be offered, considerably fewer than at P_1. Thus, an increase in weekly income via the overtime premium will always cause more hours of work to be offered than an equivalent increase in straight-time rates.[2]

2. Note that an increase in the straight-time rate could cause hours of work to fall. Also note that an overtime arrangement need not increase hours offered. Thus, if the indifference curve passing through P_0 in figure 3-A.1 had been drawn to slope more steeply than the section P_0A_1 of the budget line, our individual would have refused to work any overtime. In this case, the individual would have been overemployed at point P_0, though obliged to offer H_0T hours because of a standard workweek requirement.

CHAPTER 4
INVESTMENTS IN MAN

"Ay, ay, a cool hundred a year (for fees)—that's all," said Mr Tulliver, with some pride at his own spirited course. "But then, you know it's an investment. Tom's eddication 'ull be so much capital to him."

George Eliot, *Mill on the Floss*

4.1 Introduction

The analysis of chapter 3, in considering the allocation of time, was largely predicated on the assumption that skills brought to the marketplace, such as schooling and training (and therefore wage rates), were given. Although the simple labor-leisure model was extended to include nonmarket activities, defined as those activities performed by the individual for himself in lieu of being purchased from others in the market, it is clear that our typology of time allocation did not go far enough. When an individual devotes time to studying or acquiring skills, he is certainly not selling this time to someone in the marketplace, nor can he acquire this "human capital" by purchasing it from others. Such training is a form of work. Its essence is that it is not undertaken for present benefit but, rather, for the sake of future pecuniary and nonpecuniary returns. Individuals can thus influence their future time-stream of wages by paying for training in the current period. In this sense, training is to be regarded as an investment.

The present chapter provides the basic explanation of this notion of investment in human capital and explores certain of its implications. We explain what is meant by the concept of a *rate of return to education* and pursue the distinction between *general* and *specific* training. In particular, we show how the shape of the typical lifetime earnings stream can be given an economic explanation. Subsequent chapters, examining such factors as the earnings distribution (chapter 10) and union attitudes toward training (chapter 9), further develop and apply these ideas.

The concept of man investing in himself has a wide application; it covers not only investments in formal schooling and postschool training, but also home investments in the form of family care in the preschool years, the acquisition of improved health, and investments in job search. In the interests of exposition, however, we shall here largely restrict our attention to the issues involved in the acquisition of schooling and on-the-job training (experience). We shall show that schooling can be relatively easily measured and that experience can be identified with time spent in the labor market after schooling. A basic question to be answered is whether the human capital implication that additional schooling yields a return in the form of additional earnings is warranted, holding other relevant factors such as ability constant. This question involves the difficult problem of estimating *earnings functions*.

From a social viewpoint, there are two main policy implications in this area. The first is to ensure that all labor market participants have the opportunity to realize a similar return on given investments. Thus, if it can be shown that favoritism gives certain groups easier access to prestigious occupations, there is a case for policy measures to counter the discriminatory elements involved. The topic of discrimination is the subject of detailed analysis in chapter 6. The empirical results surveyed here will mainly relate to white males, for whom discrimination assumes a secondary importance.

The second implication concerns equality of access to education and training opportunities. Human capital is such an illiquid and lumpy investment for most individuals that there is likely to be a highly unequal distribution of investment, depending upon levels of family financial support. This problem is investigated by considering the determinants of schooling level achieved, via *schooling functions*. Here again there might be a case for state intervention, which in turn raises the question of the appropriate amount of public funds to be devoted to education. In this context, the problem is one of computing a "social" rate of return to education. It is also true that certain training institutions, such as apprenticeship, are intimately bound up with restrictions on entry; and such practices might also require state regulation. For this reason, we analyze the economic constraints within which such policies must operate and touch on such measures as the British Industrial Training Act and the United States Manpower Development and Training Act.

Our treatment proceeds as follows. First, we outline the basic theoretical framework of the human capital model. Then, taking the cost of funds as given, the individual's demand for investments in schooling and postschool training is considered. Finally, the supply of funds, schooling functions, and policy measures required to extend schooling and training opportunities are examined.

4.2 Theoretical Framework

In the interest of clarity, let us begin with a simple model. At the same time let us note that although some of the omitted factors can subsequently be built into the model others will have to be ignored. In particular, we shall not consider the possible political implications of education policy. Radical critics point out that the human capital model, by concentrating on the link between education and production, ignores the role of education in "social production"—that is, in maintaining the established power relations within a country.[1] However, it is possible to work with human capital theory as a framework for economic analysis, while accepting that the education system has a political role. Also, aspects of discrimination and social stratification will be touched upon insofar as they affect access to, or returns from, training (see chapters 5 and 6).

Let us begin by assuming that individuals have a good idea of their earning and training opportunities and also of their abilities. They are then supposed to choose career paths, namely period-by-period combinations of current earning activity and human investment activity so as to maximize their expected lifetime income net of training costs. Constraints on this choice will be the individual's ability, his rate of time preference, and his family's initial financial endowment. For the individual, such human investment activities include all uses of work time that cause current earnings to be lower (than they would be if the investment were not being undertaken) while raising future earnings. Important examples are schooling, postschool training such as apprenticeships, and time spent searching for better jobs or "queuing" to enter jobs where entry is rationed. For example, some people spend an extra year at school so as to improve their chance of entering medical college. This extra year raises the cost of learning medicine and should properly be regarded as an investment.

General and Specific Training. It is conventional to draw a distinction between general and specific training. Completely general training—for example, apprenticeship—increases the marginal product of the trainee by the same amount in the firm providing the training as in other enterprises. By contrast, completely specific training—for example, training in the operation of an individual firm's wage payment system—raises the individual's productivity only with respect to the firm providing that training. Although most training actually falls between these two extremes, it is useful to pursue the distinction.

Specific training can be thought of as mainly an investment by the firm rather than the individual. Assume initially that the firm pays all the costs and receives all the returns to specific training. During the training period, the wage paid the trainee must equal the wage in his best alternative employment, because no rational employee would pay for training that did not benefit him. Given these training costs, it follows that wages will be greater than actual marginal product in the training period and less than marginal product in subsequent periods, so as to enable the firm to recoup its costs. But if the worker were to quit at the end of the training period the

1. See S. Bowles and H. Gintis, "The Problem with Human Capital Theory: A Marxian Critique," *American Economic Review, Papers and Proceedings* 65 (1975): 76.

firm's investment would be wasted. Similarly, if the employee bore all the costs and received all the returns, he would suffer a capital loss were he to be fired on completion of training. In fact, the willingness of workers or firms to pay for specific training will closely depend on the likelihood of turnover. The optimal strategy for the employer is to share some of the costs and benefits of specific training with his employees.

For this reason, we expect to observe a positive relation between specific training and wage rates, though the relationship should be weaker than in the case of general training, according to the precise sharing principle.[2] It should also be noted that factors that tend to lower the potential mobility of workers, such as seniority systems, imply that training will become more specific than otherwise and hence tend to be more employer financed, *ceteris paribus*.

These relationships are illustrated in figure 4.1, which shows simplified age-earnings profiles for trained and untrained workers. Panel (a) indicates the situation when the training is general; panel (b) is indicative of specific training. Consider panel (a): horizontal line W_A gives the wage and marginal product of the untrained worker over his life cycle. The stepped line gives the wage and marginal product of the worker who undergoes training. During the training interval, his wage and marginal product, W_0, can be seen to be lower than it would be if he chose alternative employment. Earnings are thus foregone by the individual, and this represents his investment. Following the training period, however, general skills and marginal product are increased to MP_T; precisely because the skills acquired are general, the wage the trained man can command, W_T, also increases to this level. Over this period, W_T is greater than the untrained wage rate, W_A; this represents the "return" on the investment. The particular relation between costs and returns is detailed later.

Panel (b) represents the case of specific training. As before, the horizontal line marks the wage and marginal product of the untrained individual. The stepped line again marks the marginal product of the worker who undergoes training; however, this line now only refers to his marginal product within the firm in question. His marginal product outside the firm is assumed to be unaffected—it remains at W_A. The wage rate of this individual does not follow the course of the stepped line; instead, his wage rate will be more akin to the horizontal line. Hence, W_A will tend to be close to W_T. In fact, W_T will probably exceed W_A somewhat, because the employer is likely to raise the wage rate of the trained employee so as to reduce the probability of quits. Correspondingly, the wage received during the training interval will be somewhat less than W_A. The dashed line represents the likely course of wage rates for such workers. This means that we would expect the worker to share some proportion of the costs of and returns to specific training. If employers

2. See G. S. Becker, *Human Capital*, 2nd ed. (New York: National Bureau of Economic Research, 1975), p. 30.

Figure 4.1   Age Profiles of Wages and Marginal Product for General and Specific Training Compared

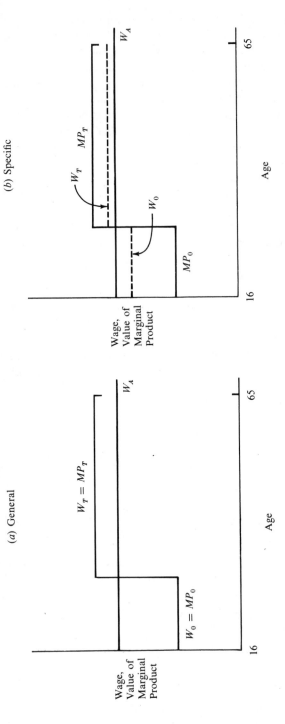

(a) General

(b) Specific

do adopt this sharing strategy, then there is the implication that the quit rate will be higher in firms or industries whose work force requires mainly general rather than specific training, *ceteris paribus*. There are signs that this is the case. Industries with higher proportions of professional workers, whose training tends to be more general, do appear to have higher quit rates than other industries.[3]

General training investments, therefore, can be expected to have a more marked impact on the age profile of wage rates than specific investments. Because the main concern of this chapter is the earnings profile, we will consequently concentrate on general training, such as schooling and home care. However, the concept of specific training will be invoked when policy questions directly involving the employer are considered, such as those involved in the analysis of industrial training programs, where the question of the employer sharing the cost bulks large. In later chapters, where we analyze the internal labor market and problems associated with the presence of trade unions at the place of employment, we shall often have recourse to the specific investment concept.

Investment in Schooling. Concentrating on general training, therefore, let us take the example of a period of schooling. How can we model the factors a person (or his family) would reasonably take into account in deciding whether to invest in a given period of schooling or, for that matter, a shorter or longer period? Let us put forward the rule that, in equilibrium, investment in schooling will be taken to the point at which the present value of expected future earnings exceeds costs by an amount sufficient to yield an acceptable rate of return (see below). Suppose, for example, that an individual is contemplating an extra year at college. If the year is taken, earnings in each succeeding period, t, will be Y_t; if it is not, earnings will be X_t. The cost, C, of the extra year will be the earnings foregone (plus fees and out-of-pocket expenses, which we can assume to be offset by vacation earnings); that is, earnings in the alternative types of job during the initial year, X_0. Thus, we can write

$$C = X_0. \tag{4.1}$$

The return, R, from the extra year is the sum of the differences between Y and X over the remainder of the working life—say, $65 - 20 = 45$, if the proposed course ends at age twenty. This sum can be expressed as

$$R = \sum_{t=1}^{45} (Y_t - X_t).$$

3. See D. O. Parsons, "Specific Human Capital: An Application to Quit Rates and Layoff Rates," *Journal of Political Economy* 80 (1972): 1137.

This sum must then be discounted at some rate, i, to give its present value, PR, so as to be comparable with costs. Thus,

$$PR = \sum_{t=1}^{45}(Y_t - X_t)(1 + i)^{-t}. \tag{4.2}$$

The individual must compare PR and C; the rule is to take the extra year if PR is greater than C. The difficulty here is that PR depends on the value of the discount rate, i, chosen. To get some idea of the impact of i, consider a situation where an investment is expected to yield an income of $1,000 every year for four years (table 4.1). If the discount rate were 5%, PR would equal $3,546; if the discount rate were 10%, PR would be only $3,169. If the appropriate discount rate were 5%, representing the rate at which funds could be borrowed from the bank, then the investment's present value would be $3,546. If the investment cost less than this amount, we would be in favor of proceeding with it. Alternatively, we could compute an internal rate of return, r. The latter is defined as that rate of discount that would equate PR and C. Here the rule would be to proceed with the investment if r were greater than the market interest rate.

In our example, suppose the cost of the investment were $3,169. Then the internal rate of return would be 10%, which would mean that the earnings stream could be discounted by as much as 10% per year before its value equalled the cost of the investment. If the market rate of interest stood at less than 10%, then again the decision would be to undertake the investment.[4]

The analysis is the same in the case of a college investment, even though the prospective stream of returns has a much longer time horizon than four years. Figure 4.2 presents an analysis of the situation, simplified to the extent that the age-earnings profiles are assumed linear. The problem is to decide whether the present value of the returns, area R, is greater than the value of the foregone earnings cost, area C. To ascertain this, we can either discount the stream of returns, R, at the market interest rate and observe whether the resulting present value is greater than C, or we can compute the internal rate of return, r, which equates the present value of R with C, and note whether r exceeds the market rate of interest.

We have been working with the differences, C and R, between the two alternative earnings streams. We could, however, equivalently compare the present value of the two *overall* earnings streams. The goal would be to determine which earnings stream had the higher present value from the

---

4. There is a difficulty in calculating r where the stream of net returns evinces more than one change in sign. This is, however, unusual in the context of human capital. See M. S. Feldstein and J. S. Fleming, "The Problem of Time-Stream Evaluation: Present Value Versus Internal Rate of Return," *Bulletin of the Oxford University Institute of Economics and Statistics* 26 (1964): 80.

Table 4.1 The Present Value of $1,000 per Year Received for 4 Years, Various Discount Rates

Expected Income	5%		10%	
	$1/(1+.05)^t$	Discounted Value	$1/(1.10)^t$	Discounted Value
$1,000 at end of first year, $t = 1$	0.952	$ 952	0.909	$ 909
$1,000 at end of year $t = 2$	0.907	$ 907	0.826	$ 826
$1,000 at end of year $t = 3$	0.864	$ 864	0.751	$ 751
$1,000 at end of year $t = 4$	0.822	$ 822	0.683	$ 683
		$3,546		$3,169

standpoint of the age at which the decision to invest is made. The earnings stream for those who leave college at age nineteen consists of the areas C and D. The alternative stream consists of zero earnings for an extra year to age twenty, plus areas D and R. In comparing these streams, we can use either of the methods previously cited. Thus, the present value at age nineteen of both streams can be evaluated using the market rate of interest, and that option chosen which yields the highest present value. Alternatively, we could find that rate of discount—the internal rate of return—that equated the present values, at age nineteen, of the two earnings streams. The option of an extra

Figure 4.2 Simplified Earnings Streams for the Decision Whether to Undertake an Extra Year of College

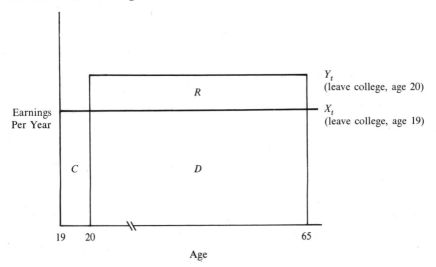

year in college would be accepted or rejected according to whether this internal rate were higher or lower than the market rate of discount. Detailed calculations of an actual rate of return are given in appendix 4-A.

Digressing for a moment, it is worth looking more closely at the internal rate of return concept. By manipulating the definition somewhat, we are able to demonstrate a very simple relationship between r, C (the costs of training), and $Y_t - X_t$ (the prospective annual return from the investment). This relationship is

$$r = \frac{k}{C}, \tag{4.3}$$

where $k = Y_t - X_t$, assumed constant (as in figure 4.2) from year to year.

The derivation is as follows. From equation (4.2), we have

$$PR = \sum_{t=1}^{45}(Y_t - X_t)/(1 + i)^t$$

$$= k \sum_{t} 1/(1 + i)^t$$

assuming $k = Y_t - X_t$ and applying the rule that $\Sigma_i \alpha x_i = \alpha \Sigma_i x_i$, if α is a constant. By definition, r is that rate of discount for which $PR = C$. Therefore

$$C = k \sum_{t} 1/(1 + r)^t. \tag{4.4}$$

This is the sum of a geometric progression. The rule for taking such a sum is to find the first term A [here $A = k/(1 + r)$] and the common ratio L [here $L = 1/(1 + r)$] and substitute into the formula

$$\text{Sum (G.P.)} = A(1 - h^N)/(1 - h)$$

where N is the number of terms (here $N = 45$).[5]

Using this formula to take the sum in equation (4.4), we obtain

$$C = \frac{k}{1 + r}\left(1 - \frac{1}{(1 + r)^{45}}\right)\bigg/\left(1 - \frac{1}{1 + r}\right) \tag{4.5}$$

$$= \frac{k}{r}\left(1 - \frac{1}{(1 + r)^{45}}\right).$$

Because in this case $N = 45$, a large number, the $1/(1 + r)^{45}$ term makes very little difference. For example, if r is 10%, we have $1/(1 + .10)^{45} =$

5. See appendix 1-A.

1/72.9 = .013. Consequently, equation (4.5) can be approximated by equation (4.3) when N is large.

Using equation (4.3), a rough answer to our question of whether to take the extra year of college at age nineteen can be quickly derived. Suppose that the earnings foregone, C, in that year are $3,000. Further suppose that the average differential in pay, k, for the rest of the working life as a result of taking the extra year in college is expected to be $450. Then r is approximately 450/3000 = .15, or 15%. As one would expect, r is higher the larger is k (the annual difference in earnings) and the lower is C (the price of the investment). Moreover, as equation (4.5) demonstrates, r is lower the smaller is N (the period over which the returns are forthcoming). Suppose our potential investors were aged fifty-nine at the time of the decision, so that N were about six. The common factor, if r were .15, would then be large, namely $1/(1.15)^6 = 0.43$. If k were $450, as before, the price of the investment would have to be much lower to yield $r = .15$. Specifically, its value would have to be no greater than $1,710 $\left[= \dfrac{450}{.15}(1 - .43) \right]$.

The previous example serves to indicate that investment in human capital becomes less worthwhile as one ages. There is a good reason, therefore, for expecting such investments to decline over the life cycle. Indeed, from equation (4.5), we see that, at the end of the working life (enter $N = 0$ in the formula), the only terms on which a human investment would be contemplated would be if it were free, that is, if $C = 0$. If time were to be allocated to learning and studying after this point, it could not be given an investment interpretation; rather, it would presumably be allocated for its sheer enjoyment or, to put it more formally, its consumption benefits.

Having estimated the prospective internal rate of return, r, our decision-maker's investment problem is to discover whether r is greater than an acceptable rate of return, i. For simplicity, think of i as being equal to the "market" interest rate. It should be noted, however, that this simplification skates over the fact that i will assume a different value for different people. The rate i will actually be that rate at which the decisionmaker can borrow funds, or, if he already possesses these funds, the rate he could obtain on a comparably risky investment. For those in the former category, however, for whom borrowing is the relevant alternative, the cost of funds will tend to be much higher than for those in the latter category. This is because an individual borrowing to invest in his education cannot, as would be the case if he were investing in a physical asset, offer the asset as collateral. Presumably all he can do is ask the loan authority to trust him. Even for those falling within the latter category, the cost of funds will effectively be lower for the affluent. This is a consequence of another aspect of investment in education, namely its "lumpiness." By this we mean that a small investment tends to be of little use. For the small saver, paying for his own education would be akin to putting all his eggs in one basket. The investment would seem riskier to him than to the big saver, and he would reasonably ask for a higher return before undertaking the project. Government intervention in the form of grants, scholarships, or loans can be seen as tending to make the acceptable rate of return on human capital more uniform for all classes of people.

The above analysis can usefully be summarized in a supply and demand diagram (figure 4.3). On the demand side, we can draw up a schedule of prospective internal rates of return associated with each increment of schooling. This schedule gives the "marginal product" of schooling to the individual, and we would expect it to be downward sloping, as given by curve *D*. Thus, for a person of given abilities, extra education is likely eventually to bring a decreasing return.

The position of the demand curve will, however, vary among individuals. In particular, we would expect a person with greater abilities to be able to secure a more favorable rate of return to a given amount of education. This may be represented by an outward shift, to *D'*, of the demand schedule. Other factors that could also shift the curve would be discrimination and nepotism. For example, black workers probably face a curve that is displaced to the left of that for similar whites. If there is nepotism in the market—the rich making way for their offspring—the demand curve for those from affluent families will tend to be displaced to the right.

On the supply side, we can draw up a schedule showing the cost of funds, which here are the rates of interest that must be paid for differing amounts of investment. The supply schedule is likely to slope upward. The early years of education represent a small investment (foregone earnings being low or zero), the funds for which are likely to be easily forthcoming, partly because of state compulsion and subsidies and partly as a by-product of the custodial

Figure 4.3   Demand and Supply Schedules for Education Investments

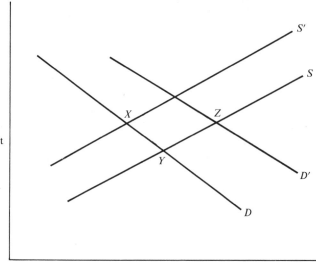

Amount Invested in Education ($)

function of schools. However, funds for larger investments are likely to be less accessible as the individual uses up his own savings and those of his relatives. At the extreme, there might even be the need for recourse to bank funds, which would entail the payment of a high rate of interest. For these reasons, we draw a curve such as *S* in the diagram.

Factors such as the individual's family circumstances and his scholastic ability are likely to shift the supply curve. Low-income family circumstances must imply an earlier recourse to expensive bank funds, thereby displacing the supply curve leftward to *S'*. We might also argue that higher-income parents would demand higher child "quality," assuming child quality is a normal good, implying longer and/or more expensively schooled children. Once more, the individual would find funds for his education more easily forthcoming. Similarly, the offspring of more educated parents might find funds for schooling more easily forthcoming. It might be argued that such parents can more efficiently produce child quality, because they require a lower input of time and goods to obtain a given effect; essentially, the price of child quality is reduced.[6] And if the price of quality is lower, we would expect more of it to be demanded by parents, *ceteris paribus*. As a result, education funds will be made more easily available to the student. Again, more able individuals will receive scholarships, which will have the effect of shifting the supply curve to the right. On the other hand, the pursuit of egalitarian policies by governments—in the form of grants or low-interest loans for education—can be seen as an attempt to make the supply curves more similar for individuals. Indeed, "equality of opportunity" has been defined as being the same supply curve for all,[7] and this seems generally to have been the goal of public policy.

In equilibrium, this analysis assumes that the level of schooling chosen will be that level which brings into equality the supply and demand conditions relevant to the individual. If the relevant curves are *D* and *S*, the combination of schooling and rate of return will be given by point *Y*. A more able individual, however, might have demand curve *D'*; if he faces the same supply conditions, his particular equilibrium schooling/rate of return combination is given by point *Z*, which yields a higher rate of return. Other combinations are possible, point *X*, being one example. Figure 4.3 illustrates the difficulty of identifying a demand or supply curve for education. While it is possible to calculate the rates of return associated with various levels of education—see the estimates contained within appendix 4-A—it is not legitimate to interpret these as points on the demand curve for education unless we can be sure that individuals face similar demand conditions. In particular, we must be able to adjust for ability. Only then can variations in supply conditions be said to trace out points on the demand curve. Figure 4.3

6. See L. N. Edwards, "The Economics of Schooling Decisions: Teenage Enrollment Rates," *Journal of Human Resources* 10 (1975): 153–173.
7. See G. S. Becker and B. R. Chiswick, "Education and the Distribution of Earnings," *American Economic Review* 56 (1966): 362.

also illustrates the possibility that disadvantaged groups might experience *higher* rates of return to education in equilibrium. For example, if female workers face the same demand conditions as males, but more difficult supply conditions, then we can see that they will have higher rates of return to education. At the same time, they will invest less in education.

The above framework enables us to explore the determinants of levels of schooling actually achieved; we are able to calculate schooling functions. Because schooling can be shown to be a major determinant of earnings, this is clearly an important topic. We would expect differences in schooling among individuals to be related to factors such as differences in ability, family background, and opportunity costs of schooling. The empirical relationships in question will be examined later in this chapter. The next step is to extend the model to take account of postschool investments in human capital, such as on-the-job training.

Postschool Investments. To this point, we have presented simplified age-earnings profiles that are horizontal lines stepping up from zero at the age of leaving school, with the size of the step being determined by the quantity of schooling. In fact, the typical postschool age-earnings profile does not conform to this pattern. If we examine the annual earnings of male workers over the life cycle, the pattern is for a steep increase on leaving school, followed by a slower increase until a plateau is reached in the mid-forties, after which point a slow and then a faster descent occurs. Appendix 4-A contains two actual profiles.[8] Similarly, the path described by the hourly earnings of male workers over the life cycle is not horizontal. However, unlike annual earnings, hourly earnings typically appear to increase until the age of sixty or thereabouts before declining.[9] The earlier peak in annual earnings is probably to be explained by the fact that the annual hours worked by males tend to fall off well before hourly wages peak (perhaps because capacity wages peak before observed wages—see below), a tendency that offsets the rise in hourly rates. Be this as it may, the basic question is whether we can use human capital theory to explain the initial increase and subsequent decrease in life-cycle annual or hourly earnings.

One explanation of the earnings profile, based on the concept of school and postschool human capital investments, could run as follows.[10] During the schooling period, all potential earnings are foregone in favor of the

8. We are interested in the path of earnings as a group of given individuals (or cohort) age. However, the earnings data at our disposal is generally cross sectional, giving a point in time observation of the earnings of individuals of different ages. It might be that cross-section data do not accurately represent what would happen to a cohort. For example, if earnings are growing at 2% per year, the earnings of a cohort will not actually decline as that cohort approaches retirement; they will merely reach a plateau. See Becker, *Human Capital,* chart 10.

9. See G. R. Ghez and G. S. Becker, *The Allocation of Time and Goods over the Life Cycle* (New York: National Bureau of Economic Research, 1975), chap. 3.

10. The basic reference here is J. Mincer, *Schooling, Experience and Earnings* (New York: National Bureau of Economic Research, 1974).

production of human capital. Another way of putting this is to say that, during schooling, all potential earnings power or earnings capacity—the earnings that one would make if one entered the market—is directed toward the production of human capital. After leaving school, however, the individual does not simply cease to invest. He is likely still to wish to forego a certain fraction of his earnings capacity, thereby reducing current earnings, so as to accumulate capital and raise his earnings at later stages of his life cycle. The usual analysis applies: training investments will be made until the marginal cost, in terms of foregone earnings, of the training equals the present value of its expected returns. However, the period over which investment costs can be amortized becomes shorter as the individual approaches retirement. Consequently, we would expect a smaller and smaller proportion of earnings capacity to be devoted to investment and the individual's stock of human capital to grow at a slower and slower rate. In turn, this will be reflected in a slower growth of his earnings capacity and also in his observed earnings, which differ from earnings capacity by the ever decreasing amount devoted to human capital accumulation. Eventually, so the argument goes, investment will no longer offset depreciation, and the stock of human capital—and with it earnings capacity—will begin to shrink. For a few years longer, observed earnings will continue to increase as the reduction in earnings foregone to accumulate human capital offsets the shrinkage of earnings capacity. But eventually, observed pay too will decline.

Central to the above explanation is the argument that the amount of an individual's resources or earnings capacity devoted to learning or training will decline as he ages, probably reaching zero on retirement. This argument can be taken to be securely based in models where the individual chooses his investment path so as to maximize his earnings, or his utility, over the life cycle.[11] There is broad agreement that the amount of earnings capacity devoted to human capital will begin to show a steady decline from 100% early in life—perhaps even before the individual finishes schooling. But there is less agreement over the exact form of the curve. Because the principal costs of human capital investments comprise foregone earnings, the question of how much of an individual's earnings capacity will be devoted to training rather than to leisure activities or to wage labor is part of the theory of the allocation of time. All three types of time usage should be analyzed together. Because of the difficulty of such analysis, however, models have generally taken only the labor-leisure choice (as in Ghez and Becker) or the labor-

11. See A. S. Blinder and Y. Weiss, "Human Capital and Labor Supply: A Synthesis," *Journal of Political Economy* 84 (1976): 466; W. J. Haley, "Human Capital: The Choice between Investment and Income," *American Economic Review* 63 (1973): 937; J. J. Heckman, "A Life Cycle Model of Earnings, Learning and Consumption," *Journal of Political Economy* 84 (1976): S16; Y. Ben-Porath, "The Production of Human Capital and the Life Cycle of Earnings," *Journal of Political Economy* 75 (1967): 352–365; T. Johnson, "Returns from Investment in Human Capital," *American Economic Review* 60 (1970): 550; S. Rosen, "A Theory of Life Earnings," *Journal of Political Economy* 84 (1976): S47.

human capital accumulation choice (as in Johnson), and this is the course of the present text. (For a model that considers all three choices together, see Blinder and Weiss.) The difficulty of three-way analysis of time usage explains why there is not full agreement about the optimal life-cycle pattern of human capital accumulation.

Appreciation of the issues involved can be assisted by studying figure 4.4. Consider first panel (b), which depicts a typical earnings profile YY_sY with an assumed step up from zero when the individual leaves school. Our hypothesis is that a certain pattern of school and postschool investments underlies the profile; investments are chosen so as to maximize the earnings stream provided by YY_sY. What is the likely pattern of these investments?

Consider now panel (a) and the curve KK_sK, which depicts the assumed path of the individual's net human capital stock (K). The shape of this path is important, because we derive from it the individual's path of earnings capacity (E) according to the relation: [12]

$$E(t) = rK(t), \tag{4.6}$$

where r is the rate of return per unit of human capital and is assumed to be constant over the life cycle.

Using this relation, a capacity earnings curve EE_sE has been drawn in panel (b), assuming r to be 10%. To justify the capital stock path, we proceed as follows. Assume the child enters school with some human capital—the precise amount depending on how much attention he has been given at home.[13] In this year and succeeding school years, he is assumed to devote all his human capital to the accumulation of further capital, on which he receives a normal rate of return, r. Consequently, we can picture his stock of human capital as growing at a steady proportional rate, r, less the rate of depreciation, δ, on his stock of capital. More specifically, we can write

$$\Delta K(t) = I(t) - \delta K(t),$$

where $I(t)$ is the given output of human capital; and
$\Delta K(t)$ is the change in the net stock of human capital.

The human capital production function can be written

$$I(t) = f[J(t)],$$

where $J(t)$ is the amount of human capital used to produce further capital.

12. See Haley, "Human Capital."
13. See A. Leibowitz, "Home Investments in Children," *Journal of Political Economy* 82 (1974): S115 ff.

Figure 4.4   Life Cycle Patterns of Actual and Capacity Earnings and Human Capital

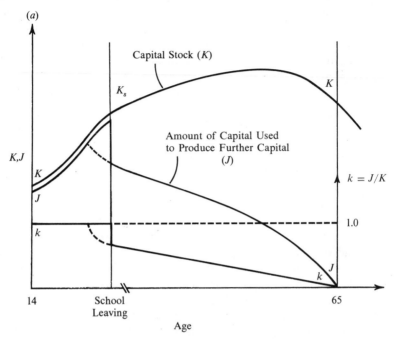

(a)

Capital Stock (*K*)

K_s

K

Amount of Capital Used
to Produce Further Capital
(*J*)

$k = J/K$

1.0

K,J

K

J

k

J

k

14

School
Leaving

65

Age

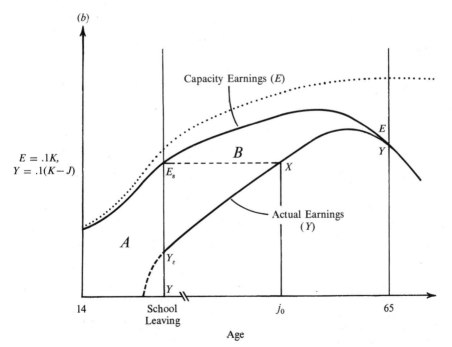

(b)

Capacity Earnings (*E*)

E

$E = .1K,$
$Y = .1(K-J)$

E_s

B

X

Y

Actual Earnings
(*Y*)

A

Y_ε

Y

14

School
Leaving

j_0

65

Age

During the schooling period, $J(t)$ is assumed equal to $K(t)$, as is shown in panel (a) of figure 4.4.[14]

At the end of the schooling period, the figure shows a sudden fall in J, which is the amount of human capital devoted to producing more capital. This decrease occurs because some capital is being devoted to earning money in the market; consequently, the capital stock grows more slowly. This fall has been hypothesized by both Mincer and Johnson, whose estimated value of $k\,(=J/K)$ is 0.5 to 0.6 at age of entry into the labor market.[15] Haley's model, on the other hand, predicts a more gradual transition from complete specialization, with paths for J and K as shown by the dashed lines in panel (a). This would be the case if school children tended to take part-time jobs as they approached completion of their schooling; their actual earnings profile, YY_sY, would commence prior to leaving school and would be represented by the dashed extension in panel (b). Data on the part-time earnings of school children is not yet sufficient for anyone to comment authoritatively on this point.

Continuing beyond the school-leaving age, the JJ curve descends slowly at first and then more rapidly before reaching the zero axis at age sixty-five, which is the assumed age of retirement. This type of path is derived from the models of optimum capital accumulation of Haley and Rosen. The capital stock path follows a similar shape; it increases more slowly as fewer resources are devoted to human capital production, then begins to decline as depreciation on the stock outweighs gross investment by a larger and larger amount. As drawn, the ratio of J to K follows an exact linear downward path on labor market entry. This relation, though a simplification, reflects the basic fact that human capital investment becomes less worthwhile as the individual ages.

Actual earnings, Y, are now calculated from the path for J. Actual earnings are defined as earnings capacity minus returns foregone on capital used to produce further human capital. That is

$$Y(t) = E(t) - rJ(t)$$
$$= r[K(t) - J(t)]. \tag{4.7}$$

In panel (b) of figure 4.4, the actual earnings curve, YY_sY, has thus been

14. Compulsory schooling laws could account for some of this complete specialization, but there is also an interesting human capital hypothesis. The investor attempts to equate the marginal benefit of producing an additional unit of human capital with the marginal cost. However, early in life he has too little human capital to do this. In the case of physical capital, if the marginal revenue product exceeds the capital rental, the firm can borrow capital until the marginal conditions are satisfied. In the case of human capital, however, additions can only be produced by the individual himself, since there is no market in which human capital can be bought. Consequently, there is an incentive for full specialization.

15. J. Mincer, "Progress in Human Capital Analysis of the Distribution of Earnings" (Paper presented to the Royal Economic Society Conference on the Distribution of Income, Lancaster, 1974), p. 17; Johnson, "Investment in Human Capital," p. 559.

drawn as a proportion of the difference between the K and J curves of panel (a). It should also be noted that we can write Y alternatively as

$$Y(t) = rK(t)[1 - J(t)/K(t)]$$
$$= E(t)[1 - k(t)]. \qquad (4.8)$$

To derive earnings capacity, given an observed (actual) earnings profile, we need to possess a form for the foregone-earnings profile, $k(t)$. The difference between actual earnings and capacity earnings may then be used to obtain an estimate of net investment in school and postschool investments. In panel (b) of figure 4.4, area A represents the net investment in schooling, and area B shows the net investment in postschooling. Gross investment would be calculated by adding back depreciation allowances (say $\delta = 2\%$ of capital stock, and hence 0.2% of capacity earnings in our example) so as to derive the dotted curve above EE_sE. Notice that capacity earnings *cannot* fall if we ignore depreciation. This illustrates how essential is the concept of depreciation to the human capital explanation of the earnings profile, for it helps to explain the apparent decrease in actual earnings in later life. Our next task is to show how estimates of r, δ, and the amounts invested in school and postschool training can be derived.

There is the difficulty, referred to above, that our observed age-earnings profiles do not represent the actual pattern of earnings of a cohort of individuals as they age; rather, the data are obtained from a cross section of individuals at a moment in time. If, as a result of technical progress, real earnings are growing secularly at a rate, y, a person aged twenty today need never experience an actual decline in earnings, even as he nears retirement. In terms of figure 4.4, his actual earnings curve YY_sY would look more as though it had been derived from the dotted curve than from the solid capacity earnings curve EE_sE. If we failed to allow for this factor, we might believe that human capital did not depreciate, or that the rate of return to human capital was very high, or both.[16] In practice, an estimate of y can be obtained by comparing the earnings of groups of given age at successive points in time (for example, as between the 1960 census and the 1970 census).

The importance of the postschool investment concept is that it provides a rationale for the curvature of the earnings profile. It should be noted that the term "postschool investment" is not intended to refer exclusively to training. It will also include the efforts made by a worker to improve his stock of knowledge of the labor market, namely his investment in information. Indeed, the worker may have to choose a hierarchy of jobs during his working life, and the necessity of such choices reinforces the importance of information acquisition. This fact also demonstrates why we should not hold occupation constant when working out the returns to a given period of

16. This is demonstrated in T. Johnson and F. J. Hebein, "Investments in Human Capital and Growth in Personal Income 1956–66," *American Economic Review* 64 (1974): 610.

schooling. Workers who do not move in a career progression are likely to have a relatively flat earnings profile.[17] One method by which an individual changes his postschool investments is by moving from jobs that offer more training to those offering less training as he ages. In this model, those who undertake zero postschooling investments will experience a horizontal path of earnings over their working lives that may even bend downward as capital accumulated at school depreciates with the approach of retirement. The beginnings of one such path are shown by the dashed line $E_s X$ of figure 4.4. For such a worker, school investments would be represented by the area A; but postschool investments would be zero, and earnings capacity would equal earnings during working life.

While admitting the usefulness of the concept of worker investments in training and job search, that concept might nevertheless appear irritatingly nebulous. Although we can measure years of schooling and expenditures on schooling, it is not immediately obvious how we might measure the postschool investment catchall. How then do we calculate earnings capacity at the point of entry into the labor market (E_s), and how do we calculate the extent of area B? Moreover, we now see that the rates of return to schooling, estimated by comparing lifetime earnings profiles (as in appendix 4-A), take postschool investment patterns (as exhibited in the earnings profiles) as given. The question therefore arises as to whether we can compute a rate of return to schooling proper and whether this is different from the rate of return to postschooling investments. In fact, Mincer has demonstrated that we can obtain an answer to some of these questions rather simply.[18]

A method of calculating E_s is as follows. Rewrite equation (4.8) as

$$Y_t = E_t - C_t$$

where $C_t = rJ(t)$ and represents net investment costs (earnings foregone less depreciation) during the tth year of work experience.

In particular, in the first year of work experience, we have

$$Y_0 = E_s - C_0$$

where E_s is earnings capacity after s years of schooling.

In the second year,

$$Y_1 = E_s + rC_0 - C_1$$
$$= E_1 - C_1$$

and, in general,

17. See S. Rosen, "Learning and Experience in the Labor Market," *Journal of Human Resources* 7 (1972): 333.
18. Mincer, *Schooling, Experience and Earnings*, pp. 11–18.

$$Y_j = E_s + r \sum_{t=0}^{j-1} C_t - C_j \qquad (4.9)$$

where we assume r is constant from year to year.

We can use equation (4.9) to estimate E_s, which represents earnings capacity on leaving school. As can be seen in figure 4.4, Y grows and eventually equals or overtakes E_s at point X. We have to find that year of work experience, j_0, corresponding to X. Actual earnings in that year will give us an estimate of E_s. During the overtaking year, j_0, we have

$$Y_{j_0} = E_s + r \sum_{t=0}^{j_0-1} C_t - C_{j_0}.$$

In this year, $Y_{j_0} = E_s$; so that $r \sum_{t=0}^{j_0-1} C_t = C_{j_0}$. If $C_t = C$, a constant, during these years, then $rj_0 C = C$ (using the summation rule $\sum_{t=1}^{n} a = na$ if a is a constant), and $j_0 = 1/r$.

Thus, if $r = .15$, then the overtaking year is approximately the seventh year of work experience. According to our model, it will actually be a little sooner than this because the sequence C_t is not constant but declines with experience. Using the data of appendix 4-A, earnings capacity of the man with twelve years schooling would be approximately $4,500. His earnings on leaving school would be about $2,200 (extrapolating back from age twenty-two), which implies that his initial amount of postschooling investment was $2,300, or 50% of earnings capacity.

The concept of the overtaking year is useful because it permits us to estimate E_s and thence, given r and the path of actual earnings, to estimate the path of capacity earnings via equation (4.9). It is also useful in that it identifies the year—say, seven years after school leaving—when an individual's earnings are what they would have been had he not undertaken postschooling investments. In this year, earnings should reflect the influence of schooling investments alone. The empirical implication is that, taking the seven-year experience group and regressing earnings on schooling, schooling should account for a greater proportion of the variance of earnings for this group than for any other group.

Using these formulae, Mincer has also proposed a simple method for estimating the amount of postschool investments for a given schooling group. Once earnings capacity is at its maximum, E_p, net investment reaches zero. The sum of past positive net investments is derived from

$$E_p = E_s + r \sum_{t=0}^{p-1} C_t,$$

so that

$$\sum_{t=0}^{p-1} C_t = (E_p - E_s)/r.$$

Approximating E_p by peak annual earnings Y_p,[19] this formula gives a relatively simple method for estimating postschool investments. These estimates, and those obtained by other methods, will be discussed in detail later.

This, then, is the basic human capital model. There are several objections to the model as an explanation of earnings, the most important of which relate to the role of ability and opportunity (or family background) factors in determining earnings. In particular, we might question whether earnings differentials exclusively reflect the opportunity costs of acquiring different amounts of training; that is, whether the earnings distribution is "equalizing" on opportunity costs of schooling.[20] However, these objections can be better appreciated once some empirical results are in hand.

4.3 Empirical Results

The results in this section are offered with the goal of casting light on the role of human capital in explaining earnings and of highlighting areas where further research is needed. Chapter 10 gives a fuller review of the implications and results of the theory for the earnings distribution—its dispersion and skewness. The plan of this section is first to present some estimates of, and problems connected with, rates of return to schooling, then to turn to postschool investments, and finally to consider the determinants of schooling. Most of the results that we survey relate to the United States because lack of suitable data has much hampered British research in this area. For example, there is no income or earnings question in the British decennial census.[21]

Rates of Return to Schooling. We have seen that the rate of return to schooling can be calculated by comparing the earnings profiles of individuals with different levels of schooling. An alternative method is to regress the natural logarithm of earnings on schooling and then to interpret the resulting coefficient on schooling as the rate of return to each year of schooling, the rate being assumed to be the same for each year.[22] The reasoning underlying this latter procedure is as follows. Let us define the rate of return on the first

19. Ibid., pp. 73–74. This is equivalent to ignoring depreciation, as can be seen from figure 4.4.
20. S. Rosen, "Human Capital: Survey of Empirical Research," mimeographed (Rochester, N.Y.: Department of Economics, University of Rochester, 1976), p. 14.
21. Results based on the United Kingdom General Household Survey are presented by G. Psacharopoulos and R. Layard, "Human Capital and Earnings: British Evidence and a Critique," mimeographed (Centre for the Economics of Education, London School of Economics, February 1976).
22. Using this method for data on individuals by state, Chiswick has been able to calculate rates of return to education within every state of the United States. See B. R. Chiswick, *Income Inequality—Regional Analyses within a Human Capital Framework* (New York: National Bureau of Economic Research, 1974), chap. 4.

year of education, r_1, as

$$r_1 = \frac{Y_1 - X_0}{X_0}$$

where Y_1 denotes earnings after one year's education, assumed constant over the life cycle;

X_0 denotes earnings without education.

Thus,

$$Y_1 = X_0(1 + r_1).$$

Similarly,

$$r_2 = \frac{Y_2 - Y_1}{Y_1},$$

so that

$$Y_2 = Y_1(1 + r_2)$$
$$= X_0(1 + r_1)(1 + r_2).$$

Therefore, after s years schooling,

$$Y_s = X_0(1 + r_1) \cdots (1 + r_s). \tag{4.10}$$

If we assume $r_1 = r_2 = \cdots = r_s = r$, and if we approximate $(1 + r)$ by e^r, as we can if r is small,[23] then equation (4.10) becomes

$$Y_s = X_0 e^{rs}$$

or, in log form,

$$\ln Y_s = \ln X_0 + rs. \tag{4.11}$$

This is a basic form of earnings function. It has to be modified, however, because earnings are not actually constant after leaving school. Earnings follow something like a parabolic path as work experience is gained. Hence equation (4.11) is usually modified by including an individual's years of work experience, t, and their square, t^2. Thus,

$$\ln Y_i = f(s_i, t_i, t_i^2, Z_i) \tag{4.12}$$

where Y_i is observed earnings of the ith individual;

  s_i is schooling measured in years;

  t_i is years of work experience; and

  Z_i is a vector of other variables.

The above quadratic formulation can be rigorously derived on the assumption of a linearly declining fraction of earnings capacity being devoted to

23. Remember $e \simeq 2.718$. Thus $e^{.1} = 1.105$, which is nearly equal to 1.1. The approximation is close if r approximates 10%, as is likely to be the case (see Appendix 1-A).

postschool investments, as illustrated in figure 4.4.[24] For the nonmathematically oriented, however, it is worth noting that the curved path of earnings itself suggests a quadratic formulation—though mathematical analysis is helpful in giving a specific interpretation to the coefficients on t, t^2, and other variables, if included. A derivation of equation (4.12) is given in appendix 4-B.

Thus, rates of return can be computed by either direct comparisons of earnings profiles or the regression method. The latter method is probably to be preferred, because it provides a more flexible method for holding other things constant.[25] British and American estimates of contemporary private rates of return to schooling are shown in table 4.2. The figures have the meaning outlined in the foregoing theoretical section. Thus, for white American males, 14% is the estimate of the internal rate of return to the earnings foregone in completing high school rather than going to work after only eight years schooling.

A number of difficulties arise in interpreting private rates of return such as those shown in table 4.2. Perhaps the foremost problem is one of making an allowance for ability. If ability to earn and the amount of schooling are highly correlated, then we might be attributing to schooling what is really due to ability. Second, there is the problem of measuring schooling. Number of years schooling completed is a very crude measure of educational attainment, given the wide variation in schooling quality as measured by expenditures per pupil. Third, there is the problem of whether the dependent variable, earnings, should be denominated in hourly, weekly, or annual terms. The precise choice of variable is important because the more educated tend to work more hours per year. The return to schooling thus appears larger if we take annual rather than hourly earnings comparisons, as indicated in the final column of table 4.2. Finally, there is the problem of dispersion in rates of return among individuals. If this dispersion is large, it will not be particularly meaningful to base recommendations on the evidence of what happens to the average person.

We might also query the relevance of the data in table 4.2 to the social or political questions of whether to encourage or discourage further investment in education. In other words, what is the social rate of return to education? On the one hand, it is possible to conceive of situations in which education would be useful to the individual but not to society. Here we refer to the question of screening. The possibility exists that education does not raise worker productivity, but simply enables employers better to identify preexisting talents. At the other extreme, education might have benefits to society that cannot be reflected in individuals' earnings profiles. For example, a

24. Mincer, *Schooling, Experience and Earnings,* chaps. 1, 5. And, for an analysis of the assumptions underlying this derivation, see A. S. Blinder, "On Dogmatism in Human Capital Theory," *Journal of Human Resources* 11 (1976): 8–22.
25. Note, however, that earnings profiles can be standardized using regression analysis prior to comparing them. This was the very procedure followed by Hanoch (appendix 4-A).

Table 4.2 Private Rates of Return to Various Increments of Schooling, United States, 1969, and England and Wales, 1967 and 1972

Incremental Schooling Level	United States, 1969			
	Male		Female	
	White	Black	White	Black
High School (12 years compared with 8 years schooling)	14%	20%	15%	19%
College (16 years compared with 12 years schooling)	16%	14%	15%	19%

Incremental Schooling Level	England and Wales, 1967 and 1972		
	1967[a]		1972[b]
	Male	Female	Male
High School plus University (18 years compared with 10 years schooling)	15.0%	20.5%	—
'A' level only [14 years compared with 'O' level (=12 years)]	10.0%	—	11.7% (9.2%)*
University degree (18 years compared with 14 years)	22.5%	—	9.6% (7.7%)

*Figures in parentheses are based on differences in weekly earnings among schooling groups. All other figures in the table relate to annual earnings.

Source:
United States—M. Carnoy and D. Marenbach, "The Return to Schooling in the U.S., 1939–1969," *Journal of Human Resources* 10 (1975):316.
England and Wales—(a) A. Ziderman, "Does it Pay to Take a Degree?," *Oxford Economic Papers* 25 (1973):270–271. (b) G. Psacharopoulos and R. Layard, "Human Capital and Earnings: British Evidence and a Critique." mimeographed (Centre for the Economics of Education, London School of Economics, 1976), table 11, p. 34.

better educated population might well make for a more democratic society. We must consider the pros and cons of this argument too.

First, consider the problem of how to allow for differences in ability. Consideration of figure 4.3 would lead us to expect a positive correlation between the amount of schooling completed and ability. An analysis of the determinants of schooling achieved by individuals is provided in later sections. Suffice it to say here that empirical studies indicate a strong correlation between ability and schooling for males[26] (this might not be true for females).[27] Until Taubman's analysis, which used data on identical twins (who presumably cannot differ in ability), it was not thought that allowance for ability much reduced the rate of return to education.[28] For example, Leibowitz found in her sample of Californians that inclusion of childhood IQ in an earnings function for males did not change the coefficient on schooling at all.[29] Link and Ratledge, in their sample of young men aged sixteen to twenty-six, found that inclusion of an IQ measure lowered the rate of return to education from about 9% to about 7%.[30] Hause's conclusion, after surveying other, broader-based bodies of data, was also that ability made only a modest contribution to explaining differences in earnings.[31]

However, it has long been acknowledged that our measures of ability are poor;[32] the implication is that our control variables might be inadequate. These fears seem to be confirmed by recent results using data from a sample of more than 1,000 pairs of identical twins, aged forty-five to fifty-five in 1973. Because identical twins cannot differ genetically, they cannot differ in ability. Moreover, because they have had the same family background, this latter variable can also be controlled. Relating differences in log earnings between pairs of twins to differences in their schooling gives a coefficient on schooling of only 0.03. Although highly significant,[33] this value stands in marked contrast to the estimates of 0.08 and higher provided in table 4.2. Thus, the results cited in the table could be seriously biased upward—to the tune of 65% or thereabouts. Taubman suggests that measurement errors in the reporting of schooling might reduce this bias to between 40% and 55%. The fact remains that the potential bias is pronounced. At first blush, the low rate of return to education obtained by Taubman suggests that there is either considerable overinvestment in schooling for his sample or that there are considerable consumption benefits attaching to the educational process. Yet

26. See, for example, P. Taubman, *Sources of Inequality in Earnings* (Amsterdam and New York: North Holland and American Elsevier, 1975), p. 175; Becker, *Human Capital,* pp. 158, 162; J. C. Hause, "Earnings Profile: Ability and Schooling," *Journal of Political Economy* 80 (1972): 131; C. R. Link and E. C. Ratledge, "Social Returns to Quantity and Quality of Education: A Further Statement," *Journal of Human Resources* 10 (1975): 85.
27. Leibowitz, "Home Investments in Children," p. S122.
28. P. Taubman, "Earnings, Education, Genetics, and Environment," *Journal of Human Resources* 10 (1976): 447–461.
29. Leibowitz, "Home Investments in Children," p. S127.
30. Link and Ratledge, "Social Returns of Education," pp. 81–83.
31. Hause, "Earnings Profile." See also Z. Griliches and W. M. Mason, "Education, Income and Ability," *Journal of Political Economy* 80 (1972): 587; R. Raymond and M. Sesnowitz, "The Returns to Investments in Higher Education: Some New Evidence," *Journal of Human Resources* 10 (1975): 148; A. Ziderman, "Does It Pay to Take a Degree?" *Oxford Economic Papers* 25 (1973): 270–271.
32. See M. Blaug, "The Empirical Status of Human Capital Theory: A Slightly Jaundiced View," *Journal of Economic Literature* 4 (1976): 843.
33. Taubman, "Earnings, Education, Genetics, and Environment," table 3, p. 453.

doubts must attach to such a low estimate, and further analysis of this intriguing question should prove illuminating.

Consider next the school quality factor. Perhaps the most obvious method of measuring the quality of schooling is to calculate average expenditures per pupil in the individual's school, district, or even state. All three measures have been used.[34] Another method is to insert a dummy for type of school (for example, public/private school) in the earnings function or, alternatively, to construct an index of quality using such external data as the academic rating of an educational institution. The latter procedure has yielded a quality index for colleges, using external data provided by the Gourman Report rating of colleges.[35] Such studies tend to report some direct effect of college and school quality on earnings, *ceteris paribus* (although the main effect seems indirect: higher expenditures per pupil are associated with higher levels of schooling).[36] For example, using the NBER-Thorndike sample of males who had volunteered in 1943 for pilot, bombardier, or navigator training, Wales found that B.A.s in 1969 on average received $340 more per month than did high school graduates, *ceteris paribus*. However, B.A.s from an institution in the top quintile of the Gourman index received on average another $117 on top of this. This incremental earnings factor is quite large, amounting to about 10% of the average monthly earnings of high school graduates. It is interesting to note that omission of the quality index from the regression leads to an overestimate of the effect of education *per se* on earnings. The overestimate is approximately 5% for the B.A. sample, but considerably higher than this for other groups; for example, it is 18% in the case of the Ph.D.[37]

There are diverse interpretations of the quality effect. The quality variable might be measuring the additional skills that a good school imparts. On the other hand, "good" schools might simply be those that attract the more able pupils. In this case, quality might be a proxy for ability, though it should be pointed out that a measure of ability *is* generally included in the regressions. However, there does not appear to be much association between quality— whether measured by the Gourman index or by expenditures per pupil—and ability.[38] As an alternative explanation, Taubman surmises that, on the basis of the correlation between quality and measures of family background, the

---

34. See G. E. Johnson and F. P. Stafford, "Social Returns to Quantity and Quality of Schooling," *Journal of Human Resources* 8 (1963): 139–155; Link and Ratledge, "Social Returns of Education"; T. I. Ribich and J. L. Murphy, "The Economic Returns to Increased Educational Spending," *Journal of Human Resources* 10 (1975): 56–57.

35. This is a report on the quality of undergraduate colleges constructed by J. Gourman. See T. J. Wales, "The Effect of College Quality on Earnings: Results from the NBER–Thorndike Data," *Journal of Human Resources* 8 (1973): 307; Taubman, *Sources of Inequality*, p. 184.

36. Ribich and Murphy, "Returns to Increased Educational Spending," p. 69; Johnson and Stafford, "Social Returns of Schooling," p. 151.

37. Wales, "Effect of College Quality on Earnings," appendix table 1, p. 316.

38. Taubman, *Sources of Inequality*, p. 159; Ribich and Murphy, "Returns to Increased Educational Spending," p. 69.

quality variable is indicative of the effects of nepotism on earnings.[39] The argument here is that good schools provide connections which are useful later in working life. One test that suggests itself is to see how much of the variation in earnings is explained by years of schooling alone. If the fit is good, the implication is that persons with higher levels of schooling receive more pay, and those with lower levels less pay, irrespective of background. We look into these tests in detail later. Suffice it to say here that a simple earnings function, containing only schooling and work experience as independent variables, explains up to 50% of variation in earnings for white males. This result appears to limit the force of the nepotism argument, at least for this group.

There is also the problem of how to treat variations in weeks worked over the year as between more and less well educated individuals. As will be seen when we discuss postschool investments, annual earnings increase as more weeks per year are worked, *ceteris paribus*. Analysis of this issue has stimulated much debate because, as was intimated in section 4.2, our model does not speak directly on the hours of work question,[40] although it does have some implications. For example, Chiswick and Mincer have pointed out that the correlation between the number of weeks worked annually and wages has a human capital interpretation: higher weeks worked for an individual implies higher firm specific, and probably higher general, investments, which in turn imply higher wages.[41] In other words, workers with smaller human capital investments are likely to face more unemployment (see the discussions in chapters 5 and 10). In this case, part of the payoff to schooling takes the form of a larger number of weeks worked per year, so that rates of return calculated on the basis of annual earnings are appropriate. If we make the opposite assumption—namely, that those with fewer weeks worked per year prefer the extra leisure—then the rate of return to schooling falls markedly.[42] This latter presumption seems somewhat unrealistic.

Remaining on the subject of private rates of return, let us turn finally to the question of dispersion in rates of return to schooling. As figure 4.3 indicates, we would not expect all individuals to receive the same rate of return unless there were a perfectly elastic supply curve, indicating complete equality of opportunity. Opportunities to be schooled actually vary widely, as do capacities to benefit from schooling. Some idea of the differences in rates of return among sex and color groups can be gained from table 4.2. The overall impression is one of quite wide variation, though it is worth noting that there is no clear tendency for blacks and females to receive a lower

39. Taubman, *Sources of Inequality*, p. 159.
40. See Blinder, "On Dogmatism in Human Capital Theory," p. 14.
41. B. R. Chiswick and J. Mincer, "Time Series Changes in Personal Income Inequality in the U.S. from 1939, with Projections to 1985," *Journal of Political Economy* 80 (1972): S40.
42. M. Carnoy and D. Marenbach, "The Return to Schooling in the United States, 1939–1969," *Journal of Human Resources* 10 (1975): 323.

return than white males. However, the data in the table refer to rates of return averaged across groups and do not give a full picture of dispersion.

Calculations by both Mincer and Becker indicate that the variation in rates of return is large. For white males, Mincer estimates an upper limit for the standard deviation of r of about five percentage points. Thus, the coefficient of variation of r, the standard deviation divided by the mean, is about one-third.[43] Becker estimates an even higher figure. Using the simplified formula for the rate of return derived in equation (4.3), $r = k/C$, we can derive a formula for the variance in r, var (r), as follows:[44]

$$\text{var } r = \bar{k}^2 \text{ var}\left(\frac{1}{C}\right) + \left(\frac{1}{\bar{C}}\right)^2 \text{ var}(k) + \text{ var}\left(\frac{1}{C}\right) \cdot \text{var}(k).$$

This shows that var (r) will be higher as the variation in returns increases and as the variation in costs increases. Becker estimates the variation in k alone to be very high. Specifically, the coefficient of variation of k for college graduates in 1949 (derived from data on variations in earnings of college and high school graduates) lies between 0.94 and 8.7,[45] depending on the particular assumption made. A coefficient of variation of 2.0 is his preferred estimate. The variation in costs is estimated to be somewhat less than this. However, the outcome is an estimate for the coefficient of variation of r of between 1.0 and 2.0; as such, it is considerably higher than Mincer's estimate. The meaning of these findings is as follows: if r were normally distributed, with $\bar{r}$ equal to 12% and with the coefficient of variation of r equal to 1.0, then one-third of the population would receive an r above 24% or below zero. This is apparently about the same as the coefficient of variation of rates of return to small businesses.[46] At the same time, we should keep in mind that particular individuals will have some knowledge of their abilities and opportunities. This means that their prospective distribution in rates of return will not be so high as the population distribution. Therefore, the Mincer figure might be a better one for the individual to use when appraising his own chances against the backdrop of table 4.2.

One way of allowing for the risks entailed in human capital investment is to estimate the probability of not completing the appropriate course of study, that is, of dropping out. Ziderman presents such estimates for the United Kingdom, although he assumes that those who drop out gain no monetary advantage from their incomplete course.[47] In this case, the rate of return to a university degree is reduced from 20% to 16.5%, and the rate of return to an "A" plus "O" level course from 8.5% to a negative value. However, the

43. Mincer, *Schooling, Experience and Earnings,* p. 56.
44. See appendix 1-A.
45. Becker, *Human Capital,* pp. 185–189.
46. Ibid., p. 189.
47. Ziderman, "Does It Pay to Take a Degree?" p. 271.

assumption of zero economic benefit to noncompletion is surely wrong. From appendix 4-A, we observe positive rates of return to college dropouts (thirteen years to fifteen years of education) and to high-school dropouts (nine years to eleven years of education), although the rate is lower than for those completing the respective courses. The difference in the rates of return between the dropouts and those who complete their courses might be the correct risk adjustment, but we must also allow for the apparently lower ability of dropouts.[48]

We have yet to consider the issue of social rates of return. Social rates will differ from private rates to the extent that the costs of and returns to education for society differ from those of the individual. Social costs are generally higher than private costs because there is usually an element of public subsidy in education. What is free for the individual is not costless for society. However, social returns are more difficult to quantify. One noncontroversial factor is the element of tax. From the point of view of the individual, aftertax values are the appropriate earnings variable; from a public viewpoint, pretax earnings are the relevant yardstick. Making these adjustments will serve to reduce the rates of return shown in table 4.2. The reduction reaches a maximum of 50%,[49] although values within the range 10% to 20% are more usual.[50]

However, in calculating the returns to society from increasing the level of education in the population, we have also to take into account the probability that a better-educated work force makes for an increase in national income. For example, Denison has estimated that, of the annual rate of increase in United States national income per person employed of 1.6% between 1929 and 1957, no less than 0.67 percentage points reflected quality improvements in labor due to education. He attributes a further 0.58 percentage points to the "advance of knowledge," which we might also consider a consequence of the spread of education.[51] Using this information, Becker has calculated that the rate of return to college education might be as high as 25% from a social point of view.[52] To this, we should add all the unquantifiable benefits that flow from a better-educated citizenry, such as more informed consumers and a smoother administration of government.

These arguments carry the policy implication that there is probably an underinvestment in education, but the view has recently been gaining ground that education is less socially useful than it appears. This is the argument that education acts primarily as a filter, or screening device, to identify preexisting

48. Becker, *Human Capital,* pp. 158, 202.
49. Carnoy and Marenbach, "Return to Schooling in the United States," p. 318.
50. Raymond and Sesnowitz, "Returns to Investments in Higher Education," p. 149; Becker, *Human Capital,* p. 195.
51. E. F. Denison, "Education, Economic Growth and Gaps in Information," *Journal of Political Economy* 70 (1962): 128, table 2.
52. Becker, *Human Capital,* p. 197.

talents.[53] Note that this argument relates to higher levels of education and not to the learning of the "3 Rs." According to the filter argument, we can picture a competitive race between individual workers, all eager to impress employers with their "pieces of paper." This race leads to an upward spiral of paper qualifications and time spent in educational establishments. Because, by assumption, these qualifications do not increase output except insofar as they enable employers to identify the more tenacious workers, all would benefit—through the saving of time spent at school—if the race were called off, and there would be no associated drop in national output.

It would take us too far afield fully to debate this issue, which contains the important truth that education has an informational role as well as enhancing productivity. However, the following points have been made in telling criticism of the filter argument.[54] First, if the piece of paper is what counts, why do those without the certificate (the dropouts) experience a rate of return that is but slightly lower than that accruing to those who complete? Second, why do those who possess higher education have higher incomes not only at the beginning of their careers, when the employer will presumably have little to go on but paper qualifications, but also throughout their working lives, when employers have had ample opportunity to assess them? Third, if the educated individual really does not embody higher productivity, but simply costs more, why does the profit maximizing firm not undercut its competitors by employing less well educated, and hence cheaper, labor? The issues raised by these questions should caution us against accepting extreme versions of the screening hypothesis. Consequently, we hold that the social rate of return to education is indeed high.

Postschool Investments. Thus far, we have concentrated on years spent in formal training. However, we must also introduce the notion of postschool investments if we are satisfactorily to explain the shape of the lifetime earnings path. If we assume a linear decline in the fraction of earnings capacity invested, then an appropriate method of allowing for postschool investments in the earnings function is to include years of experience, and their square, as regressors (appendix 4-B). A natural question to ask, therefore, is how successful are these concepts of schooling and postschooling investments—as measured by their empirical counterparts, years of schooling and years of work experience—in accounting for variations in observed earnings among individuals? If the fit (R^2) is good, the implication is that omitted variables such as ability or family background do not exercise much

53. See K. J. Arrow, "Higher Education as a Filter," Institute for Mathematical Studies in the Social Sciences, Technical Report No. 71 (Palo Alto, Calif.: Stanford University, 1972); I. Berg, *Education and Jobs: The Great Training Robbery* (Boston, Mass.: Beacon Press, 1971); R. Layard and G. Psacharopoulos, "The Screening Hypothesis and the Returns to Education," *Journal of Political Economy* 82 (1974): 985.
54. See Layard and Psacharopoulos, "The Screening Hypothesis," p. 985.

influence on returns to human investments. (Still, such factors may be very important in governing the size of investments, a subject considered in the next section on the determinants of schooling and training.) As Mincer puts it: "The coefficient of determination, R^2, is of special interest as an estimate of the fraction of earnings inequality that is associated with the distribution of human capital investments."[55] A further question that arises here concerns the scale of postschool investments. It is also interesting to see if we can infer the rate of depreciation on human capital and whether the rate of return to postschooling investments is similar to the rate of return to schooling investments.

In table 4.3, we present a set of results for earnings functions that include years of schooling, years of experience, and weeks worked per year as regressors. Also, regressions for the experience group that is likely to be near the overtaking year of experience—around ten years for a rate of return of 10%—are shown. Consider first the regressions in columns (1) and (2), where schooling is the only independent variable, experience being uncontrolled. This specification amounts to assuming that the fraction of earnings capacity invested equals unity during the school years and then drops to zero—so that there are no postschool investments. We see that the explanatory power of the specification is poor in both countries, with an R^2 of only 6.7% in the United States and less than this in the British case. These results indicate that people with the same schooling level earn widely different amounts. However, when years and years squared of experience are included [columns (3) and (4)], explanatory power increases markedly, to about 30%. The coefficient on the schooling variable, which is an estimate of the average rate of return to a year of schooling, also increases. This result is to be expected because, with the experience factor controlled, the increased income associated with more schooling is no longer obscured by the negative correlation between schooling and experience.[56]

Let us next consider the effect of controlling for weeks worked per year [columns (5) and (6)]. Weeks worked is clearly a most important variable, the inclusion of which approximately doubles the explanatory power of the equation. The coefficient on weeks worked is an elasticity [$\partial \ln Y / \partial \ln W = (\partial Y / \partial W)/(W/Y)$]; because this elasticity is greater than unity, it follows that annual earnings increase more than proportionately with weeks worked. We have already discussed the difficulty of simply plugging the weeks worked variable into the earnings function; it seems like sleight of hand. For example, weeks worked and weekly earnings jointly influence each other. It would be preferable to have a simultaneous system with an explicit model for the determination of annual weeks worked. This would help answer the question of how much of the variation in weeks worked can be attributed to human

55. Mincer, *Schooling, Experience and Earnings*, pp. 91–92.
56. The correlation between s and t in the British case is high: $r_{s,t} = -0.44$ (see Psacharopoulos and Layard, "Human Capital and Earnings," p. 35).

England and Wales, 1972

Variable	United States (1)	England and Wales (2)	United States (3)	England and Wales (4)	United States (5)	England and Wales (6)	"Overtaking" Experience Group United States[a] (7)	"Overtaking" Experience Group England and Wales[b] (8)
Constant	7.58	6.60	6.20	5.20		0.44	6.36	not reported
s	0.070 (43.8)	0.053 (13.3)	0.107 (72.3)	0.097 (32.3)	D	0.215 (12.6)	0.162 (16.4)	0.068 not reported
s^2						−0.0049 (8.2)		
t			0.081 (75.5)	0.091 (45.5)	0.068 (13.1)	0.068 (68.0)		
t^2			−0.0012 (55.8)	−0.0015 (37.5)	−0.0009 (10.5)	−0.0012 (40.0)		
$\ln W$					1.207 (119.7)	1.115 (85.8)		
R^2	0.067	0.031	0.285	0.316	0.525	0.665	0.306 (0.575)	0.105
var (ln Y)	0.668	0.436	0.668	0.436	0.668	0.436	0.469	0.230

a relates to the eight-year experience group (and the bracketed R^2 value is that obtained when ln W is included in the regression)
b relates to the nine-year to eleven-year experience group

Notes:

D denotes dummies for schooling
|t| appear in parentheses below the appropriate coefficients
s refers to years of schooling completed
t is years of work experience
W is the number of weeks worked during the year
Y represents annual earnings

Sources:

United States—J. Mincer, *Schooling, Experience and Earnings* (New York: National Bureau of Economic Research, 1974), tables 3.3, 5.1.
England and Wales—G. Psacharopoulos and R. Layard, "Human Capital and Earnings: British Evidence and a Critique," mimeographed (Centre for the Economics of Education, London School of Economics, 1976), tables 2, 4, pp. 25, 27.

capital factors; for example, those with more specific human capital tend to work more weeks. If all variations in weeks worked were attributable to human capital factors, then the fraction of earnings explained by human capital would jump to 53% in the United States and to 67% in Great Britain. We do not suggest that this is the only explanation, but doubtless a part of the reason for the increase in R^2 between columns (3) and (4) and columns (5) and (6) can be attributed to human capital factors.

The final two columns of table 4.3 indicate the explanatory power of schooling in the overtaking year of experience. Remember that this year will be somewhat less than $1/r$, where r is the rate of return; for example, it will be about the tenth year if r is equal to 10%. In this year, observed earnings are what they would have been had zero postschool investments been undertaken. In these regressions, it is likely that experience is better controlled than in regressions where t and t^2 are simply added, because the rationale of the latter procedure is that all individuals have the same pattern of decline in the investment fraction k_j. In the overtaking experience group, the dispersion in earnings is supposed to be attributable solely to differences in schooling, thereby avoiding the extra "noise" introduced by different postschool investment patterns. Using data from the United States, we see that schooling alone explains about 30% of the variation in ln Y in the overtaking year. This is actually higher than the explanatory power of schooling alone for other experience groups. For example, in the twenty-two-year to twenty-four-year experience group, schooling alone explains only 13% of earnings variation.[57] This result is explicable within our framework; the argument is that, as individuals gain more experience, their earnings profiles tend to "fan out" due to the influence of different amounts of postschool investments. However, the British evidence is much less clear-cut. There is little evidence of a higher explanatory power of schooling alone in plausible overtaking years. As can be seen from column (8), R^2 is only 10.5% in the nine-year to eleven-year experience group. As such, it is only slightly higher than it has been in other experience groups. This result is frankly puzzling.

However, let us accept that the method of achieving the best estimate of the explanatory power of schooling alone is to take the overtaking experience groups. An estimate of the impact of postschool investments on earnings inequality is obtained by comparing var (ln Y) in the overtaking group (zero postschool investment) with var (ln Y) when there are postschool investments [total var (ln Y)]. The var (ln Y) figures for the United States are 0.469 and 0.668 respectively (table 4.3). Postschool investments can thus be thought of as explaining $(0.668 - 0.469)/0.668 = 30\%$ of total variance. This is probably an overestimate, however, for it attributes all of the greater dispersion in incomes in later years to earlier unrecorded variations in human capital. Yet

---

57. Mincer, *Schooling, Experience and Earnings,* table 3.4.

some of the dispersion is likely to be the result of employers discovering more about their employees as they age and paying them a more individually tailored wage. Be this as it may, if the level and dispersion of postschool investments explain something like 30% of total variance, and school investments explain $(0.30 \times 0.469)/0.668 = 21\%$, all human capital factors can be said to explain 51% of male annual earnings variance in the United States.[58] An even higher figure can be obtained if we also attribute, according to the previously outlined reasoning, the variation in weeks worked to schooling factors. Thus, using data from the United States, R^2 in the overtaking year is 0.575 (table 4.3), which means that school investments explain $(0.575 \times 0.469)/0.668 = 40\%$, and all human capital factors about 70%!

Thus, it is possible to contend that human capital factors explain at least one-third, probably one-half, and, on extreme assumptions, over two-thirds of the variation in log earnings of white males. This raises the question as to what we might ascribe the residual variation. Perhaps the most important factors here would be differences in individuals' abilities and opportunities—in particular, their family background. The latter factor could affect the human capital demand and supply schedules along the lines discussed in connection with figure 4.3. In human capital analysis, these differences in abilities and opportunities would be reflected in the dispersion of rates of return to human investments. Unfortunately, this analysis does not take us far in accounting for such dispersion. Consequently, researchers have introduced measures of ability and family background directly into the earnings regression in an attempt to isolate their contribution.

Studies examining the influence of ability and family background variables upon earnings seem to reach the general conclusion that both variables have an important part to play. However, the explicitly human capital variables, schooling and experience, generally retain a high statistical significance.[59] A possible exception is provided by Taubman's study of twins in which schooling does not seem so important.[60] However, it should be noted that the correlation between (log) incomes of identical twins is only 0.54. In other words, there is still approximately 45% of earnings variance to be explained by factors such as schooling and experience.

At the other extreme, Leibowitz's sample of Californian males shows little

58. A similar value is obtained from analysis of British data, although the component magnitudes differ. Thus schooling alone is estimated to contribute only 6% (taking the overtaking year as nine years to eleven years) and postschool investments no less than 47%. See Psacharopoulos and Layard, "Human Capital and Earnings," table 3, p. 26.

59. See Taubman, "Inequality in Earnings," chapter 3; Leibowitz, "Home Investments in Children," p. S127; Link and Ratledge, "Social Returns of Education," p. S234; D. O. Parsons, "Intergenerational Wealth Transfers and the Educational Decisions of Male Youth," *Quarterly Journal of Economics* 89 (1975): 607; Griliches and Mason, "Education, Income and Ability," p. S87.

60. Taubman, "Earnings, Education, Genetics and Environment." See also S. Bowles, "Schooling and Inequality from Generation to Generation," *Journal of Political Economy* 80 (1972): S234.

association between earnings and measured background or childhood IQ characteristics for those aged thirty-five to forty-five and virtually none ten years later, with the sample aged forty-five to fifty-five. It thus appears that the influence of an individual's upbringing, which might determine his initial job opening and also his schooling, fades with age. This is to be expected in a reasonably competitive market in which employers are stimulated to pay a worker according to his true abilities—which can be better assessed as his time in the labor market lengthens.

Before leaving our discussion of the success of human capital variables in explaining individual earnings differences, it is necessary to consider a recent argument advanced by Becker that family-background-augmented human capital regressions might be "seriously understating the contribution of background to earnings and overstating that of schooling."[61] The argument is as follows.

Suppose, in accordance with the analysis of figure 4.3, that background shifts the supply curve for schooling funds—a richer background shifting that schedule downward. For simplicity, let this be the only cause of shifts. Suppose further that ability shifts the demand curve—greater ability displacing the demand function to the right. Now, let us hold background constant. Persons with the given background but more schooling must, therefore, have more ability. If we then regress earnings on schooling, holding background constant, we will presumably find a positive relation between schooling and earnings; but this is, in reality, a relation between ability and earnings. Similarly, suppose we hold schooling constant. Persons with the given schooling but a poorer home background must, therefore, have more ability. A regression of earnings on background, schooling held constant, will reveal that a poorer background (really higher ability) means higher earnings. This arguments emphasizes the need to standardize for ability as well as background and schooling. Although most of the studies cited in the previous paragraph have attempted so to adjust their estimates, the difficulties involved are such that we must keep Becker's point in mind.

In concluding this section, let us briefly examine estimates of the size of postschool investments, their rate of return, and their rate of depreciation. With respect to the size of postschool investments, there is a wide variation in findings. Mincer has calculated that, as of 1959, the person who moved on to twelve years of schooling from eight years invested about $2,800 more, and later in life accumulated approximately $12,000 of postschool investments. The individual who undertook an additional four years of schooling invested $24,000 and accumulated $23,000 in postschool investments.[62] It can be seen that school and postschool investments rise together—they are complementary—as, indeed, one would expect given the higher parabola described by the earnings path of the better educated. Johnson, on the other hand, has

---

61. Becker, *Human Capital,* p. 118.
62. Mincer, *Schooling, Experience and Earnings,* table 4.2.

obtained considerably higher estimates than these, and he suggests that this outcome is the result of working with gross values.[63] (Mincer presumably used net data.) Nevertheless, Johnson's estimates also retain the feature of complementarity between schooling and postschooling investments.

Johnson and Hebein have also estimated a rate of depreciation, δ, of human capital. This is shown to range from 1% to 3% per year, with an indication of a higher rate for the higher schooling groups.[64] Mincer's estimate of δ, derived in the manner outlined in appendix 4-B, is similar. Mincer also estimates a rate of return to postschooling investments. Depending on the method of estimation, his results yield a range of from 6% to 13%, which is similar to the estimated rate of return to schooling.[65]

4.4   Determinants of Schooling and Training

According to the human capital model, the decision to complete a course of training (high school, college, apprenticeship, inter al.) is fundamentally one of investment, although that decision will also have some consumption aspects.[66] Various facets of the investment decision, including the magnitude of the investment, its rate of return, and its relationship to the age-earnings profile, have been analyzed. We now shift the focus of our analysis to a consideration of the determinants of schooling itself. On the investment model, the amount of schooling a person completes should be determined by the equalization of the present value of expected future returns with present costs. The returns will depend on the structure of market wages and on the individual's ability. The costs will consist of direct outlays and foregone earnings. Family background factors must be considered, because the ability to bear these costs will differ among individuals as their access to parental support—an important factor because loans for human investments are hard to come by—and scholarships differ.

At this point, we might query whether individuals really do make the sorts of calculation implied by the theory. For example, are individuals aware of foregone earnings, are their predictions of posttraining incomes accurate, and do individuals move from low- to high-paying careers? On the basis of Freeman's comprehensive study of college-level manpower, it seems that we can answer these questions in the affirmative.[67] For example, using data on engineers graduating with B.S. degrees during the period 1951 to 1967, Freeman shows that the change in the number of those graduating in any

63. Johnson, "Investment in Human Capital," p. 555.

64. Johnson and Hebein, "Investments in Human Capital," table 1, p. 610. The same pattern is observed by W. J. Haley, "Estimation of the Earnings Profile from Optimal Human Capital Accumulation," *Econometrica* 44 (1976): 1233, table III.

65. Mincer, *Schooling, Experience and Earnings*, p. 94.

66. If the rate of return to schooling is low—Taubman's measurements suggest this possibility—then the consumption aspects of training might be as important as the investment aspects.

67. R. B. Freeman, *The Market for College-Trained Manpower, A Study of the Economics of Career Choice* (Cambridge, Mass.: Harvard University Press, 1971), p. 690.

one year has a significant, positive correlation with the starting salaries of qualified, that is, B.S. certificated, engineers two and three years earlier. Taking observations over fifty-two Ph.D. specializations, he also shows that the increase in the number of Ph.D.s in a given field is well correlated with stipend support in that field.[68] In an analysis of United States time-series data for the period 1919 to 1964, it has also been shown that the proportion of the eighteen to twenty-four age group enrolled as undergraduates increases as the real costs of tuition decrease and as real income per household increases.[69] The latter variable indicates the greater availability of family funds for education, which we would expect to be a significant variable given the self-financing requirement of most educational investments. Unfortunately, a measure of the opportunity costs of education was not included in this particular study. However, there are indications that enrollment does vary inversely with opportunity costs when such a measure is included. For example, enrollment rates tend to be higher in states with higher teenage unemployment rates and in states with a higher fraction of population living in farming areas, where part-time jobs are more easily available and foregone earnings thereby reduced.[70]

Further, on the basis of a questionnaire survey of male students, Freeman has found that students' estimates of their foregone earnings corresponded quite closely to an estimate of actual foregone earnings.[71] Students were also asked to provide estimates of their expected starting salary in their intended occupation. The ranking of these estimates closely paralleled that of the actual salaries of young college graduates in these occupations.[72] It thus seems that persons do calculate in the manner hypothesized and that there are no major informational gaps, at least among the college educated. However, the position could be somewhat different with respect to blue-collar workers, whose more limited human capital investments might perhaps reduce the incentive to be well informed (but see chapter 10).

Accepting that schooling decisions can usefully be analyzed as if they were made in a purposive, rational manner, balancing reasonable estimates of returns against costs, we have yet to consider the degree of influence exerted by family circumstances on the amount of schooling completed. This question has wide policy implications. For if, as is the indication from our study of earnings functions, the distribution of human investments plays a large part in determining the distribution of earnings, we might wish to influence the distribution of human capital. Policies requiring a minimum school-leaving age or providing state financial support to those undertaking particular courses have this very effect. In the absence of such intervention, it is widely

68. Ibid., p. 108.
69. R. Campbell and B. N. Siegel, "The Demand for Higher Education in the United States, 1919–1964," *American Economic Review* 57 (1967): 482–493.
70. Edwards, "The Economics of Schooling Decisions," pp. 164, 165.
71. Freeman, *Market for College-Trained Manpower,* p. 207.
72. Ibid., p. 215.

held that those from affluent families have an advantage in accumulating further capital, thereby promoting the transmission of inequality across generations.

In seeking to ascertain the impact of family background factors on the level of schooling attained, we have also to specify the other likely determinants of that level. However, there is no single, widely accepted model in this area, as there is with respect to the earnings function. Leibowitz, in her illuminating study, specifies schooling to be a function of childhood ability, family income, and home investments. The latter consists of the amounts and quality of time inputs to children, which are expected to be positively related to parents' education and IQ and family income.[73] The education of the mother is thought to be of singular importance, because it is the mother rather than the father who spends most time with the child. This emphasis on the time input of the mother has the implication that children who are the first to be born, or who are born into smaller families, will receive more home investment, because they have the mother's more undivided attention, and will be more receptive to schooling, *ceteris paribus.* An alternative rationale for including measures of parental income and education in the function explaining a child's schooling is to postulate the existence of a good, namely child quality, which is itself a function of schooling. Wealthier parents will then demand more child quality, assuming this to be a normal good, and thus more schooling for their children. This will also be true of better-educated parents, if we assume they can more efficiently produce child quality.[74] A further variable that is sometimes included in schooling functions is a measure of schooling quality. The latter can be measured by taking state or district schooling expenditures per pupil per year. One rationale for including this variable is that good quality schooling in a district might induce the movement into an area of high status parents, whose children will motivate their fellows to achieve.[75]

Results for schooling functions using various American samples are shown in table 4.4. The effects of family characteristics on schooling achieved are in the direction expected and are generally highly significant. The explanatory power of family variables, as revealed by the coefficient of determination, R^2, is not high for the California sample, although it is particularly high in the Detroit and total United States samples, where family variables respectively explain 40% (using a log linear specification) and 51% of the variance in schooling level. It is also interesting to note how powerful is the correlation between IQ and schooling. Although there is undoubtedly a two-way effect operating here, there are indications that children with a high *preschool* IQ achieve more schooling. In the human capital framework, this association can be interpreted as implying that high ability generates greater expected

73. Leibowitz, "Home Investments in Children," p. S112.
74. Freeman, *Market for College-Trained Manpower.*
75. Ribich and Murphy, "Returns to Increased Educational Spending," p. 70.

Table 4.4   Regressions of Number of Years Schooling Completed on Measures of Ability and Family Background

Variable	California, 1940[a]	Detroit, 1966[b]	U.S., 1966[c]
Constant	10.38		8.43
Father's education	0.122 (3.22)	0.116 (4.14)	0.187 (7.55)
Mother's education	0.131 (3.18)		0.153 (5.46)
Father's occupation		0.007 (3.18)	0.005 (1.78)
Family income in 1922	−0.782 (0.58)		
Number of children	−0.123 (2.09)		−0.212 (7.83)
IQ	0.023 (2.29)	0.126 (10.5)	
Religion/ethnic category		0.038 (2.38)	
R^2	0.08	0.51	0.27 (0.40)*

*denotes value for log-linear specification

Note:
|t| appear in parentheses below appropriate coefficients

Sources:
a. A. Leibowitz, "Home Investments in Children," *Journal of Political Economy* 82 (1974): S122.

b. O. D. Duncan and D.L. Featherman, "Psychological and Cultural Factors in the Process of Occupational Achievement," in A. S. Goldberger and O. D. Duncan, eds., *Structural Equation Models in the Social Sciences* (New York: Seminar Press, 1973), p. 231.

c. D. O. Parsons, "Intergenerational Wealth Transfers and the Educational Decisions of Male Youth," *Quarterly Journal of Economics,* 89 (1975): 608.

returns to a given investment—an outward shift of the demand schedule—which we would expect to be reflected in more schooling for a given level of costs.

None of the functions in the table include a proxy for schooling quality, but significant coefficients have been obtained in those studies which have attemped to incorporate this variable. Thus Ribich and Murphy's results for young American males, surveyed in 1968, indicate that, if the authorities increase school expenditures per pupil by $100 per year (average expenditures being approximately $400 per pupil per year), schooling completed would increase by about one-tenth of a year. Alternatively put, one pupil in

Table 4.5 Schooling Completed by Father's Occupational Status, Adult Males, England and Wales, 1949

| | Proportion of the Sample Who Received: | | | |
| | Secondary Education | | University Education | |
Occupation of Father	(a)	(b)	(a)	(b)
White collar (excluding routine nonmanual)	27.0%	38.9%	4.4%	8.5%
Manual and routine nonmanual	4.0%	9.8%	0.9%	1.4%

Note:
(a) refers to those born before 1910, (b) to those born in the period 1910–1929
Source:
J. Floud, "The Educational Experience of the Adult Population of England and Wales as at July 1949," in D. Glass, ed., *Social Mobility in Britain* (London: Routledge and Kegan Paul, 1954), pp. 120–121.

ten would be induced to undertake an extra year of schooling.[76] This suggests an alternative method by which the state could stimulate human capital accumulation. Indeed, it has been argued that increasing the quality of schooling yields a greater increase in earnings than does an increase in the quantity of schooling.[77]

Schooling functions have not been estimated for the United Kingdom, but the impact of family circumstances on schooling attainment would again appear to be strong. Data on those schooled during the interwar period, by the occupational status of father, are shown in table 4.5. A picture of startling inequality emerges. We might note that secondary schools still charged a fee during the period in question, and that access to the limited number of nonfee openings was only available on the basis of a test of ability at the age of eleven.

However, with increasing government intervention and long-term trends toward higher real incomes and smaller families, educational attainment measured in terms of quantity of schooling has both increased and become more equal. The beginnings of this process can be identified in table 4.5. Measures of the current situation in Great Britain and the United States are shown in table 4.6. The picture is one of continuing but—in the light of history—mild inequality. Yet there remains the possibility that schooling opportunities have become less equal as regards quality; and they have become more equal as regards quantity. Attempts to even out quality variations are currently a major political problem in both countries. For

76. Ibid., p. 74. See also Link and Ratledge, "Social Returns of Education"; Johnson and Stafford, "Social Returns of Schooling."
77. Johnson and Stafford, "Social Returns of Schooling," p. 150.

Table 4.6   Male and Female Students by Occupation of Father (Great Britain, 1973) or Income of Family (United States, 1970)

Great Britain, 1973[a]

	Occupation of Father		
	Nonmanual	**Manual and Personal Service**	
Proportion of fathers in sample	39.2%	60.8%	100.0%
Proportion of students aged above 15 years in			
—secondary school	53.4%	46.6%	100.0%
—university/college	57.7%	42.3%	100.0%

United States, 1970[b]

	Family Income		
	Less than $10,000	**$10,000 and above**	
Proportion of family members aged 18–24 years in sample	44.7%	55.3%	100.0%
Proportion of family members in			
—school	37.1%	62.9%	100.0%
—college	30.9%	69.1%	100.0%

Sources:
a. Office of Population Censuses and Surveys, *General Household Survey* (London: Her Majesty's Stationery Office, October 1970), various tables.
b. Department of Commerce, Bureau of the Census, *Current Population Reports,* Series P-20, no. 222 (Washington, D.C.: U.S. Government Printing Office, 1971).

example, one might point to the controversy over the comprehensive school in Great Britain and to the controversy surrounding busing in the United States. Given our results on the importance of quality, such efforts are likely to have an important economic payoff.

Industrial Training.   Within the human capital framework, we are interested not only in schooling but also in investments in on-the-job training. Again, there are a number of problems for public policy in this area. In the case of one important form of industrial training—apprenticeship—we observe craft unions restricting training in their sectional interests. Also, the incentive for the individual to undertake occupational training, as for further schooling, is restricted by the riskiness and illiquidity of such assets. The state need not be so constrained. This problem raises a new question in the context of industrial training: Who should be the beneficiary of subsidization, the trainee or the firm? Even in the case of reasonably general training, the firm's willingness to take on trainees is likely to be reduced by the actions of unions in setting high wage minima for inexperienced workers. This outcome reduces the share of training costs that the learner or trainee can bear. That the bottleneck appears to be unwillingness of firms to train workers, rather than lack of applicants, is illustrated by the grant system favored by the British Industrial Training Act, under which grants are paid to employers for approved schemes of industrial training. The grants are financed by a 2% payroll levy on all firms within a defined industry.

First consider apprenticeship. This is an important source of industrial training in Great Britain and the United States (see chapter 9). Apprenticeship is a method of training for skilled industrial work, but it is also a form of protective practice. Therein lies the obstacle to making it more easily available. Apprenticeship agreements generally set the wage level (currently 45% of the journeyman wage rate for the first year, rising to 90% in the fourth year, for carpenters in the United Kingdom), minimum education standards, duration of training, the apprentice-journeyman ratio (which is 1:4 for the first eighty journeymen and 1:20 thereafter for lithographers in London), and sometimes a maximum age. Because apprenticeship provides general training, it is to be expected that trainees will tend to bear the cost of training. An interesting British study of apprenticeship in the shipbuilding industry indicates that the firm does break even when employing apprentices.[78] This implies that when unions raise apprentices' wages the demand for trainees will be reduced—although more people will wish to train—until value marginal product is sufficiently in excess of the wage to pay for that training. Setting a long duration for apprenticeship will have the opposite effect. The pursuit of both factors, as is the usual case, reduces both applicants and training places.[79] In such a manner, it is possible to set the requirements of apprenticeships so as to restrict the opportunities for people to become skilled or change skills.

Within the human capital framework, we would interpret such union control as being necessary to protect the investment of those who have already served an apprenticeship in a particular trade. Men who have made such an investment cannot easily move should wages in their specialty fall, for they will then suffer a capital loss. Individuals in this position are menaced by "dilutees," who have had a cheaper course of training. Hence, unions are guarded in their welcome of government training programs.[80] Compensation for capital losses is part of the solution (see chapter 9), and a

78. N. Woodward and T. Anderson, "A Profitability Appraisal of Apprenticeship," *British Journal of Industrial Relations* 13 (1975): 245–256.
79. See S. Rottenberg, "The Irrelevance of Apprentice/Journeymen Ratios," *Journal of Business* 34 (1961): 384–386.
80. See K. Hall and I. Miller, "Industrial Attitudes to Skills Dilution," *British Journal of Industrial Relations* 9 (1971): 16.

gradual change causes less loss than a sudden one. However, even setting aside the problem of capital losses for skilled men, there remains the question of how to make apprenticeship more attractive to the employer and the prospective trainee. It has been suggested that grants be paid direct to the trainees on the lines of those paid to students at college.[81] However, it is probably more appropriate to extend grants to the firm. This is because it is the firm that supplies the training place. The high wage of apprentices relative to journeymen, the difficulty of discharging an apprentice, and the trend toward reducing the period of apprenticeship are all likely to reduce the firm's incentive to provide training places.

Turning to the supply of training for what are supposedly less-skilled jobs, we would expect fewer problems to present themselves. This type of training tends to be imparted at the place of work in an informal way and is also of more specific value to the firm. Because it is less formal, interest groups united in defending one form of training rather than another are less likely to form. Because it is more specific, the firm rather than the worker can be expected to bear more of the costs; and problems of finance are correspondingly reduced. Nevertheless, where that training has a general component, and to the extent that a rigid wage structure prevents adequate allowance for inexperience, we would expect the supply of training to be reduced. Furthermore, imperfections inherent in the labor market result in underinvestment in specific training. Because workers cannot sign voluntary indenture contracts, investment in specific training is necessarily more risky than investment in physical capital. The result is a discrepancy between private and social returns to specific training, and government intervention may be required to rectify such a disparity.

4.5   Conclusions

This chapter was divided into three substantive sections. The first set out the theory underlying the human capital model, the second looked at the empirical relationship between earnings and school/postschool investments, and the third examined factors determining the distribution of schooling among individuals. Basic to the theory is the interpretation of earnings as the sum of a return to pure labor power and a return to human capital. Given their access to funds and their abilities and earnings opportunities, individuals are supposed to choose how much to invest and which occupation or series of occupations to enter.

In equilibrium, we expect the rate of return on these human capital investments to be similar to that obtainable on physical investments of equal risk. This is judged by estimating rates of return to various training courses, while attempting to hold other factors—in particular ability—constant. Also, while it is accepted that there will be dispersion in rates of return among

---

81. D. Lees and B. Chiplin, "The Economics of Industrial Training," *Lloyds Bank Review* 96 (1970): 30.

different individuals, it is hypothesized that the main factor accounting for earnings differentials is differences in the opportunity costs of acquiring different amounts of training. This is why the fit of earnings functions is emphasized: differences in measured human capital investments should provide a good explanation of variations in earnings if the hypothesis is correct. Further, it is hypothesized that human investments become less profitable as the individual ages, which has the implication that the increase in earnings with age will slow, and earnings eventually will fall. Finally, on the subject of the distribution of human investments among individuals, it is expected that these will be markedly influenced by family circumstances because human capital is poor collateral for bank loans.

Empirical studies of the private rate of return to particular courses of schooling, or to a year of schooling, estimate returns in the range of 10% to 15%. This return appears comparable with that earned on industrial investments and is, at first sight, supportive of the theory. However, there is an important problem in calculating such rates of return: ability and schooling are likely to be correlated, and this correlation serves to impart an upward bias to the estimated rate of return. Although it is difficult to define or measure ability, experiments with identical twins indicate that the upward bias might be appreciable. On the basis of such studies, the true private rate of return to schooling might be as low as 5%. If this is actually the case, then individuals would appear to be losing money on their education. That they persist in human capital investments in such circumstances would presumably be explained by the consumption benefits that flow from these investments. Yet we note that schooling has a highly significant impact on earnings—even for identical twins. Therefore, we need not abandon our analysis of schooling as an investment, although we should recognize that education probably confers substantial consumption benefits.

It is also true that the presence of a high degree of correlation between ability and schooling casts doubt on the social function of schooling in training people and thereby raising the real national product. Estimates of the social rate of return, which were previously put as high as 25%, might therefore have to be adjusted downward. The fact remains that it is particularly difficult to incorporate the externalities of the educational process (for example, promoting democracy) in quantitative work, necessary though it may be. Consequently, the size of the social rate of return can never be more than an informed guess. On the basis of the available evidence, we would nevertheless be tempted to recommend a policy of further educational expansion geared to improving the quality as well as the quantity of schooling.

Turning to the success or otherwise of human capital related variables in explaining earnings variation among individuals, we are first confronted by the difficulty of defining and measuring the variables in question. Regressions using years of schooling, years of experience, and weeks worked per year explain somewhat in excess of 50% of the variance in log annual earnings for white males in the United States, and about 60% for males in Great Britain. However, we have argued that the weeks worked variable is more equivocal in its identification of human capital factors than are schooling and labor market experience variables. As a result, the success of the model is probably overstated by the R^2 values cited above. On the other hand, Mincer has plausibly argued that there is a bias operating in the other direction. This downward bias arises from the fact that the size of postschool investments is imperfectly measured by the years of labor market experience variable. Even if we accept an estimate of 40% to 50% residual variance, it might yet be argued that this leaves ample room for factors not included in the model—such as discrimination or nepotism—to affect earnings. Indeed, earnings differentials might reflect the impact of power or even class factors as much as they reflect differences in opportunity costs. While the former are undoubtedly of significance—after all, the very purpose of unions and professional associations is to exert power in the market—our prejudice is to reserve for them a secondary role. Certainly the simplicity of the human capital model has an appeal; and, as we shall see, it has some interesting applications to the fields of industrial training (chapter 9) and the earnings distribution (chapter 10).

From explanations of the parabolic form of the age-earnings profile have come the elements that comprise the third major area in which the notions of school and postschool investments have been applied. Models of optimal human capital accumulation describe a path for the fraction of earnings capacity invested that declines toward zero on retirement. This decline in investment is plausibly attributed to the ever shorter period in which the returns may be realized. This type of reasoning permits us to use the path of observed earnings to estimate total schooling and postschooling investments and even to calculate the rate of depreciation on human capital. Competing theories would stress the importance of the learning curve or perhaps argue that capacities first rise, then tend to decline for physical maturation reasons. However, such theories do not yield nearly such specific results.

The concept of human capital is also useful when we come to analyze the distribution of schooling and industrial training. In the context of schooling, if we argue that the main costs represent foregone earnings, the question arises as to how such current sacrifices are to be financed. Outside a system of slavery, property rights in this form of human capital accumulation are not vested in the employer; consequently, there is no market for future earning opportunities. This explains why the individual's own funds, and those of his family, are so important. Further, we can identify one major component of what has been called the "intergenerational transmission of inequality" as unequal access to education. With the twentieth-century trend toward egalitarianism, it becomes clearer why governments have adopted policies aimed at subsidizing education. Such policies have been regarded as necessary so as to equalize earnings opportunities. Our survey of empirical studies of the determinants of schooling has indeed shown that family background factors—together with ability, an acceptable reward criterion in a merito-cratic society—markedly influence schooling.

Questions of schooling apart, we observe that industrial training is also of public concern. Industrial training requires a somewhat different analysis because it is less general and hence more specific than schooling. Specific training raises the trained individual's marginal product mainly within the firm that has provided that training. In these circumstances, the individual will not pay for the training, as he would for general training; rather, the firm must bear at least part of the costs involved. The establishment of high wage rates for trainees, whether by unions or federal minimum-wage legislation, relative to their value marginal product might inhibit the sharing of costs. As a result, firms might be unwilling to provide training, and/or trainees might be reluctant to come forward. Further ramifications of the general/specific training questions are discussed in chapter 9. For the moment it is enough for us to recognize that the distinction is of considerable policy importance.

APPENDIX 4-A
CALCULATION OF THE RATE OF RETURN
TO A GIVEN AMOUNT OF EDUCATION

Consider the two earnings streams in table 4-A.1. These have been estimated by Hanoch and relate to the earnings of white males in the northern states of the United States as of 1959. One stream refers to the earnings of those leaving high school before completing their course of education; that is, with nine to eleven years schooling and a labor market entry at age eighteen or thereabouts. The other stream refers to those completing twelve years schooling and assumes labor market entry at age twenty. We seek to calculate the internal rate of return to the extra two years of schooling achieved by the latter group.

The first step is to calculate the present value of these earnings streams for different rates of discount. For example, take the earnings stream for those entering the labor market at age eighteen and discount back to age fourteen.[1] We can then construct table 4-A.2. This is an approximation with the same

1. The earliest age, because of child labor laws, at which decisions on schooling can be made on an economic basis.

Table 4-A.1 Earnings Streams by Schooling Level

	Annual Earnings ($)	
Age	9-11 Years Schooling (age of entry = 18)	12 Years Schooling (age of entry = 20)
14	0	0
18	1306	0
22	2519	2930
27	3924	4461
37	5398	6052
47	5478	6281
57	5242	6023
67	3079	3897

Source:
G. Hanoch, "An Economic Analysis of Earnings and Schooling," *Journal of Human Resources* 2 (1967):310–329.

Table 4-A.2 Present Value of Future Earnings at Age Fourteen of Those Entering the Labor Market at Age Eighteen

Age	Age Range Assumed	t	Discount Factor		Earnings ($) 9-11 Years Schooling	Present Value at Age Fourteen ($)		
			$1/(1.05)^t$	$1/(1.10)^t$		$i = 0\%$	$i = 5\%$	$i = 10\%$
14	14-16	0	1.0	1.0	0	0	0	0
18	17-19	4	0.822	0.683	1306	1306 × 3	3221	2676
22	20-24	8	0.677	0.467	2519	2519 × 5	8527	5882
27	25-30	13	0.530	0.290	3924	3924 × 6	12478	6828
37	31-40	23	0.326	0.112	5398	5398 × 10	12597	1046
47	41-50	33	0.200	0.043	5478	5478 × 10	10956	2356
57	61-60	43	0.123	0.017	5292	5292 × 10	6509	900
67	61-70	55	0.075	0.006	3079	3079 × 10	2309	185
					Σ	232,527	56,597	24,873

Table 4-A.3   A Comparison of Discounted Future Earnings at Age Fourteen, by Schooling Level

Years of Schooling	Present Value at Age Fourteen ($)			
	$i = 0\%$	$i = 5\%$	$i = 10\%$	$i = 15\%$
9–11 years	232,527	56,597	24,873	13,181
12 years	263,946	66,733	26,260	13,031

earnings figure assumed to hold over the given age range and with the same discount factor applied.

We can make a similar calculation for those who received twelve years schooling. We then effect the comparison shown in table 4-A.3. At low discount rates, it can be seen that the present value of earnings for those entering the labor force at age twenty, with twelve years of schooling, is much higher than for those with about two years less schooling. However, the difference narrows as we increase the discount rate, and the present values of the two earnings streams are roughly equal when $i = 15\%$. This value is an estimate of the internal rate of return to the extra two years of education, Hanoch, using more exact methods, estimates $i = 16\%$. At this rate of discount, a person would tend to be indifferent as to whether he postponed entering the labor force for two years and received higher income subsequently, or entered some two years earlier and received a somewhat lower lifetime income.

We can also calculate internal rates of return to further increments of schooling. This gives a schedule of rates of return associated with each additional year of schooling. Under certain circumstances, this may be interpreted as a marginal product of capital schedule. Again using Hanoch's data, we calculate the following internal rates of return to various schooling levels:

22% for 5–7 to 8 years of schooling,
16% for 8 to 9–11 years of schooling,
16% for 9–11 to 12 years of schooling,
 7% for 12 to 13–15 years of schooling,
12% for 13–15 to 16 years of schooling, and
 7% for 16 to 17 or more years of schooling.

APPENDIX 4-B
THE DERIVATION OF MINCER'S EARNINGS FUNCTION

We have dealt with basic earnings functions of the form

$$\ln Y_t = a + bs + ct + dt^2$$

where Y_t is observed earnings in the tth year of working life;
   s is number of years schooling; and
   t is the number of years of experience.

The purpose of this appendix is to show how such a function is derived. In particular, we wish to show how the assumption of a particular path for the fraction of earnings capacity invested, $k(t)$, over the working life—specifically, a linearly declining path as in figure 4.4—gives the quadratic term in years of experience.

Begin by looking at an individual's working life, including his period of schooling, so that $t = 0$ at age fourteen. Take the following definition

$$E_t \equiv Y_t + C_t \qquad (4\text{-}B.1)$$

where E_t is earnings capacity in the tth year of investment, including the schooling period; and
   C_t is the net cost of that investment.

From this, it follows that $E_0 = Y_0 + C_0, E_1 = Y_1 + C_1, \ldots$. We can think of E_0 as being the earnings capacity resulting solely from preschool and elementary school investments—"raw labor" as it is sometimes called, even though no labor is really raw. The following definitions are also necessary

$$k_t \equiv C_t / E_t \qquad (4\text{-}B.2)$$

where k_t is the net fraction of earnings capacity that is invested. Also,

$$E_t \equiv E_{t-1} + rC_{t-1}. \qquad (4\text{-}B.3)$$

In particular,

$$E_1 = E_0 + r_0 C_0$$
$$E_2 = E_1 + r_1 C_1$$
$$= E_0 + r_0 C_0 + r_1 C_1.$$

Consequently equation (4-B.3) implies

$$E_t = E_0 + \sum_{j=0}^{t-1} r_j C_j.$$

Similarly, we can write equation (4-B.3) in terms of the investment fraction:

$$E_t = E_{t-1} + r_{t-1} k_{t-1} E_{t-1}$$
$$= E_{t-1}(1 + r_{t-1} k_{t-1}).$$

In particular,

$$E_1 = E_0 (1 + r_0 k_0)$$
$$E_2 = E_1 (1 + r_1 k_1)$$
$$= E_0 (1 + r_0 k_0)(1 + r_1 k_1).$$

Consequently,

$$E_t = E_0 (1 + r_0 k_0)(1 + r_1 k_1) \cdots (1 + r_{t-1} k_{t-1})$$

$$= E_0 \prod_{j=0}^{t-1} (1 + r_j k_j)$$

$$= E_0 e^{\sum_{j=0}^{t-1} r_j k_j},$$

because we can use the approximation $1 + r_j k_j \simeq e^{r_j k_j}$ if $r_j k_j$ is small (see appendix 1-A).

In terms of natural logs, and assuming $r_0 = r_1 = r_2 = \cdots = r$, we have:

$$\ln E_t = \ln E_0 + r \sum_{j=0}^{t-1} k_j \qquad (4\text{-B.4})$$

remembering that $\ln e = 1$.

Now split the k_j sequence into the s years of schooling and the T years of net postschool investment, which is supposed to end somewhat before retirement age. Also, let t range only over the years of working life, that is, the period over which earnings are observable.

Then we can write

$$\ln E_t = \ln E_0 + r_s \sum_{i=0}^{s-1} k_i + r_p \sum_{j=0}^{t-1} k_j$$

where, for the sake of conceptual clarity, we distinguish between the rate of return to schooling, r_s, and the rate of return to postschooling investments, r_p.

The next step is to assume an explicit form for k_i and k_j. A simple form, followed in figure 4.4, is to assume:

1. $k_i = 1$, where i ranges over the s years of schooling;
2. $k_j = k_0 - (k_0/T)j$, where j ranges over the working period.

Substituting, we obtain

$$\ln E_t = E_0 + r_s \sum_{i=0}^{s-1} (1) + r_p \sum_{j=0}^{t-1} \left(k_0 - \frac{k_0}{T} \cdot j \right).$$

The sum $\sum_{i=0}^{s-1} (1) = s$, but the next summation requires a little more work. It is an arithmetic progression, and the formula for summing an A.P. is

$$\text{Sum (A.P.)} = N \left[A + \frac{d}{2}(N - 1) \right]$$

where N is the number of terms;
    A is the initial term; and
    d is the size of step.

Thus,

$$\sum_{j=0}^{t-1} k_0 - \sum_{j=0}^{t-1} \frac{k_0}{T} \cdot j = t \cdot k_0 - \frac{k_0}{T} \sum_{j=0}^{t-1} (j)$$

and the sum $\sum_{j=0}^{t-1} (j)$ is

$$\text{Sum (A.P.)} = t \left[0 + \frac{1}{2}(t - 1) \right]$$

$$= \frac{t}{2}(t - 1).$$

Therefore,[1]

$$\sum_{j=0}^{t-1}\left(k_0 - \frac{k_0}{T}\cdot j\right) = k_0 t - \frac{k_0}{2T}\cdot t(t-1).$$

Substituting into the formula for $\ln E_t$, we have

$$\ln E_t = \ln E_0 + r_s s + r_p\left[k_0 t - \frac{k_0}{2T}\cdot t(t-1)\right].$$

The next stage is to substitute observed earnings for capacity earnings in this formula, using the relation

$$Y_t \equiv E_t\,(1-k_t).$$

This gives

$$\ln Y_t = \ln E_0 + r_s s + r_p\left[k_0 t - \frac{k_0}{2T}t(t-1)\right] + \ln(1-k_t). \quad \text{(4-B.5)}$$

It can be seen that we already have our term in s and our terms in t and t^2, but there is the dangling term $\ln(1-k_t)$. One possibility would simply be to substitute $-k_t$ for it, using the approximation $1 - k_t \simeq e^{-k_t}$. However this procedure is only appropriate where k_t is small, and we have here to be prepared for k_t ranging from, say, 0.7 down to zero. The appropriate mathematical procedure here is to expand the function $\ln(1-k_t)$ around a certain value of k_t (say $k_t = 0$) using a Taylor expansion.[2] The formula for such an expansion to the second term is

$$f(x) = (x-a)\frac{f'(x)}{1!} + (x-a)^2\frac{f''(x)}{2!}$$

where the derivatives $f'(x)$ and $f''(x)$ are evaluated at $x = a$.

In our case, $f(k) = \ln(1-k)$, so that $f'(k) = -1/(1-k)$ and $f''(k) = -1/(1-k)^2$. Evaluating these derivatives at $k = a = 0$, and substituting into the formula gives

$$\ln(1-k_t) \simeq -k_t - \frac{k_t^2}{2}.$$

1. An alternative method of evaluating $\sum_{j=0}^{t-1}\left(k_0 - \frac{k_0}{T}\cdot j\right)$ is to express it in integral form, thus:

$$\int_{j=0}^{t}\left(k_0 - \frac{k_0}{T}\cdot j\right)dj = k_0 t - \frac{k_0}{2T}\cdot t^2.$$

2. See R. G. D. Allen, *Mathematical Analysis for Economists* (London: Macmillan, 1938), p. 453.

Table 4-B.1   The Relationship Between ln($I - k$) and $\left(-k - \dfrac{k^2}{2}\right)$ for Different Values of k

k	$\ln(1 - k_t)$	$-k - \dfrac{k^2}{2}$
0	0	0
0.1	-0.1054	-0.1050
0.2	-0.2231	-0.2200
0.6	-0.9163	-0.7800

It is interesting to discover just how close an approximation this is. Consider table 4-B.1. Note that the approximation is very close for the smaller values of k, though it deteriorates a little for the larger values. Using this approximation, therefore, gives

$$\ln(1 - k_t) \simeq -\left(k_t + \frac{k_t^2}{2}\right) = -\left[k_0 - \frac{k_0}{T} \cdot t + \frac{1}{2}\left(k_0 - \frac{k_0}{T} \cdot t\right)^2\right].$$

Substituting this into equation (4-B.5), we arrive at

$$\ln Y_t = \left[\ln E_0 - k_0\left(1 + \frac{k_0}{2}\right)\right] + r_s s$$

$$+ \left[r_p k_0\left(1 + \frac{1}{2T}\right) + \frac{k_0}{T}(1 + k_0)\right]t - \left(r_p \frac{k_0}{2T} + \frac{k_0^2}{2T^2}\right)t^2 \qquad (4\text{-}B.6)$$

or,

$$\ln Y_t = a + bs + ct + dt^2.$$

Thus a regression of $\ln Y_t$ on schooling and years of work experience and their square gives coefficients a, b, c, and d. The coefficients have the interpretation shown in equation (4-B.6).

An alternative specification of the k_j path would suggest a somewhat different interpretation of the coefficients. For example, Mincer[3] also experiments with the formulation $k_j = k_0 e^{-\beta j}$. This formulation has the advantage that it permits estimation of δ, the rate of depreciation. However, the principle is the same as that shown in describing equation (4-B.6)

3. Mincer, *Schooling, Experience and Earnings,* chap. 5; Mincer, "Progress in Human Capital Analysis," pp. 13–15.

CHAPTER 5
MARKET STRUCTURE AND
THE EFFICIENCY OF
LABOR MARKETS

"The whole of the advantages and disadvantages of the different employments of labor and stock must, in the same neighborhood, be either perfectly equal or tending to equality. If, in the same neighborhood, there was any employment evidently more or less advantageous than the rest, so many people would crowd into it in the one case, and so many would desert it in the other, that its advantages would soon return to the level of the other employments. This at least would be the case in a society where things were left to follow their natural course, where there was perfect liberty, and where every man was perfectly free both to choose what occupation he thought proper, and to change it as often as he thought proper. Every man's interest would prompt him to seek the advantageous and to shun the disadvantageous employment."
Adam Smith, *An Inquiry into the Nature and Causes of the Wealth of Nations* (New York: Random House, 1937), p. 99.

5.1 Introduction

This chapter begins with the analysis by Adam Smith so as to establish that the classical model of the labor market has two parts. The first relates to the net advantage maximizing nature of occupational choice. The second relates to the consequences of this behavioral choice system: any disparity in net advantage will cause persons to redistribute themselves. Greater numbers in the relatively more advantageous employment and fewer in the relatively disadvantaged will tend to restore the equality of net advantage in all.

Inequalities may occur in the short run while the process of adjustment works itself out. During this adjustment period, net advantages will be only tending to equality.[1] Otherwise, net advantage in Adam Smith's system will be equal in all employments. In the classical system, there is no reference to wage equality, but only to the equalization of net advantages. According to Smith, wages would vary with the ease or hardship, the cleanliness or

1. See Smith, *Wealth of Nations*, pp. 118 ff.

dirtiness, the honorableness or dishonorableness of the employment, with the ease or low cost or the difficulty and high expense of its learning, with its constancy or inconstancy, with the small or great trust which is reposed in the worker, and with the probability or improbability of success in the employment. Modern theorists elaborate on Smith's second point, expressing the theory of investment in human capital, and on his fifth point, expressing the factor of risk-taking, and generally abandon his fourth point or translate it into a rent concept; otherwise, the modern orthodox theory of the supply of labor is not very much different from Smith's.

Yet this conception of a competitive labor market has been frequently challenged. In this chapter, we shall consider the validity of the competitive model against a backdrop of the barriers to mobility to be observed in real-world labor markets. Although our focus will be upon the impediments to labor mobility, and hence upon the efficiency of the allocative process, the impact of the union will not be emphasized. The role of trade unions will be analyzed in detail in chapters 7, 8, and 9. In this chapter, we restrict our attention mainly to imperfections in markets that may or may not be organized. In section 5.2, the concept of monopsony is considered. In section 5.3, we investigate the controversial subject of labor market information, the imperfections of which are considered by many to be the fundamental barrier to labor market efficiency. A similar controversy surrounds labor mobility, which forms the subject of section 5.4. Here we assess the degree to which labor market flows appear to be in the direction posited by the theory. In section 5.5, we introduce the "internal labor market" construct, which at first blush strikes at the very heart of the competitive model by rejecting the notion of open labor markets and which erects in its place an elaborate system of institutionally determined structured markets based on the plant. Finally, we discuss the possible dichotomization of the labor market into primary and secondary sectors on the lines suggested by proponents of the dual labor market theory.

5.2 Monopsony

Strictly speaking, monopsonistic conditions exist when there is only but one buyer of labor. In such a situation, that buyer confronts an upward sloping aggregate labor supply curve. As a result, his decision to purchase more labor has some effect on the wage level. The monopsonistic employer realizes that the marginal cost and the average cost of an additional worker differ; because of this disparity he hires less labor and pays this labor a lower wage. Widening this analysis, one might hypothesize that the smaller the number of employers within a market, the easier it is to organize and maintain collusive activity. Unfortunately, we possess little information on the degree of employer concentration in local labor markets. If we are to rely on Bunting's study of 1,774 labor markets (as of 1948), then the degree of concentration, as measured by the share of employment accounted for by the largest, four largest, and ten largest firms, appears to be slight.[2] On this basis, monopsony might not be thought to be much of a problem.

However, interesting monopsony effects have been detected in the markets for public school teachers, newspaper printing employees, and construction workers.[3] But perhaps the best example is provided by the market for registered nurses employed by hospitals. Over 70% of the seven thousand hospitals in the United States are the only hospital in the community. Moreover, nursing is a skilled profession, and there are not a great number of professions which are close substitutes. The fact that many nurses are often secondary workers also tends to limit geographical mobility and reduce their elasticity of supply in an area. In a multivariate analysis of wage determination in the United States nursing sector, Link and Landon[4] calculate that a doubling in an index of concentration of hospitals in a city is associated with $400 less in annual starting salaries for nurses with B.S. and other degrees. This result supports the monopsony model and confirms earlier findings.[5]

Monopsony can also arise from collusive activity among employers, where the latter agree not to raise wages unilaterally or to poach one another's labor. Such agreements impart a positive slope to the supply curve. The supply price of employees will vary according to their transfer earnings, which, in the opportunity cost sense, are clearly restricted by collusive activity, and according to the pecuniary and nonpecuniary advantage each worker obtains from remaining in the employ of the firm. Perhaps the best known examples of collusive monopsony occur within the realm of professional sports.

A major difficulty one encounters in describing monopsonistic practices in this area is that institutional and legislative environments constantly change. So it is with major league baseball,[6] which provides our case study of collusive monopsony. Accordingly, the following discussion is only intended

2. R. L. Bunting, *Employer Concentration in Local Labor Markets* (Chapel Hill, N.C.: University of North Carolina Press, 1962), pp. 3–14.

3. See, respectively, J. H. Landon and R. N. Baird, "Monopsony in the Market for Public School Teachers," *American Economic Review* 61 (1971): 966–971; J. H. Landon, "The Effect of Product Market Concentration on Wage Levels: An Intra-Industry Approach," *Industrial and Labor Relations Review* 25 (1971): 237–247; J. H. Landon and W. Peirce, "Discrimination, Monopsony, and Union Power in the Building Trades: A Cross-Section Analysis," *Proceedings of the Industrial and Labor Relations Research Association* (Madison, Wis.: IRRA, 1971), pp. 254–261.

4. C. R. Link and J. H. Landon, "Monopsony and Union Power in the Market for Nurses," *Southern Economic Journal* 41 (1975): 649–659.

5. See R. W. Hurd, "Equilibrium Vacancies in a Labor Market Dominated by Non-Profit Firms: The Shortage of Nurses," *Review of Economics and Statistics* 55 (1973): 234–240.

6. The seminal analysis of which is provided by S. Rottenberg, "The Baseball Players' Labor Market," *Journal of Political Economy* 64 (1956): 242–258. For a wider discussion of such practices in professional sports, see H. G. Demmert, *The Economics of Professional Team Sports* (Lexington, Mass.: Heath, 1973); for examples in industrial labor markets, see R. A. Lester, *Adjustments to Labor Shortages* (Princeton, N.J.: Industrial Relations Section, Princeton University, 1955), pp. 46–49.

to be illustrative of the limitations to mobility and economic opportunity faced by sportsmen. In major league baseball, a player is a free agent until he signs a one-year, renewable, uniform contract with a major league team. The renewable feature of the contract is an option granted to the owner and is known more widely as the reserve clause. The reserve clause restricts the player's freedom of negotiation to the owner of the contract. In effect, the contract grants a license to the owner to dispose of the player's services in the manner he sees fit. He can thus renew, sell, or terminate the contract. If he renews the contract, the player may be relegated to the team roster, transferred to a minor league team on the protected list, or left eligible for the player's draft. In selling the contract to another team, the owner transfers a property right—the exclusive control over the player's services. The player's options, on the other hand, are limited to acceptance of the owner's final offer or withdrawal from organized baseball.

The reserve clause plays a crucial role in the determination of player's salaries. If the labor market in organized baseball were perfectly competitive, player salaries would be equated with player marginal revenue products. The reserve clause prohibits the transfer of player services to teams where their marginal revenue product is higher. Furthermore, the clause restricts player bargaining to one owner, which results in some monopsony power to the owner. The exercise of that power results in a divergence between marginal revenue product and salary. Such divergence is defined as exploitation.

Despite the fact that economic analysis confirms that the reserve clause reduces player economic benefits, it may be difficult for us to accept that a $150,000-a-year baseball player is the victim of exploitation. Yet a study by Scully confirms this very effect and provides crude numerical estimates of the short-fall between wage and marginal revenue product for pitchers and hitters.[7] Scully's findings suggest that, over career length, average players receive salaries equal to about 11% of their gross marginal revenue products and about 20% of their net marginal revenue products. Star players receive about 15% of their net marginal revenue products. Only mediocre players appear to have salaries in excess of their net marginal revenue products!

In this context, we should note the possible existence of a kinked supply curve under conditions of oligopsony. One such curve is shown in figure 5.1. The wage rate W_0 is set in the manner outlined in chapter 2. The supply curve pertinent to this wage is the schedule $S_1 (= AC_1)$, which is the curve facing the oligopsonist on the assumption that none of his competitors react to his actions. Once the wage is set, however, the firm will be aware that changes from the equilibrium will have consequences for its wage/employment situation. If the firm were to reduce wages, then it may reasonably be assumed that other firms will not follow suit. Thus, the relevant supply curve for wage decreases is the portion AB of S_1. If, on the other hand, the firm

7. G. W. Scully, "Pay and Performance in Major League Baseball," *American Economic Review* 64 (1974): 915–930.

Figure 5.1   The Kinked Supply Curve Under Oligopsony

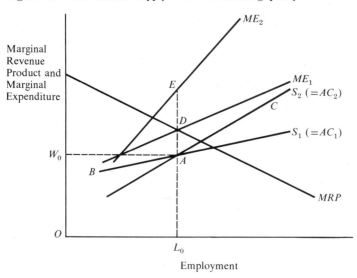

raises wages, it must expect competitors to imitate this action, because they face an outflow of workers. The firm will thus perceive that the curve $S_2(= AC_2)$ exists. The relevant supply curve for increases in wages is segment AC. The firm is, then, faced with a supply curve over the whole range that corresponds to BAC. As a consequence of the kink at A, the marginal expenditure curves ME_1 and ME_2, corresponding to S_1 and S_2, will exhibit a discontinuity at the current wage vertically above the kink in the supply curve. Accordingly, shifts in the MRP curve that fall within the range DE can be accommodated without pressure on the prevailing wage/employment position. When demand increases, the employer may be seen to enjoy an increased surplus; when demand falls, no labor is laid off if the shifts are within the required tolerances.

If a market is subject to monopsony, we would expect long periods of stable wages and employment. But when changes do occur, there might be violent and rapid responses to be followed by another period of stability. Although some sectors of the market for nurses would appear to conform to this pattern,[8] the fact that economic pressures do not bring about the small adjustments to a firm's employment predicted by the traditional theory can, in our view, more convincingly be explained with the aid of a model recognizing firm-financed investments in human capital. The kinked supply curve thus remains something of an analytical curiosity, although it may offer some guidance as to the development of collusive activity among oligopson-

8. See D. Yett, "Causes and Consequences of Salary Differentials in Nursing," *Inquiry* 7 (1970): 90.

ists when faced by organized labor. In such a case, the buyers now act as monopsonists and the kink disappears.[9]

In addition to the cases of single employer and collusive monopsony, there are a number of factors which impart a positive slope to the supply curve facing the individual firm. Such factors as imperfections in information and mobility and the consequences of internal labor market structuring will be discussed in later sections of this chapter. At this point, however, we should qualify our discussion of monopsony by observing that imperfect worker information as to alternative wages will confer on each firm a margin of monopsony power. Thus, each firm will possess a degree of dynamic monopsony power arising from the imperfect information of its employees regarding alternative wages and can therefore administer wages. Recognition that labor market decisions are taken in an environment of imperfect information underpins many of the recent developments in labor economics. However, much of this discussion was anticipated in an early analysis of monopsony by Bronfenbrenner, who argues that monopsony power need not be exercised to the full because firms are likely to set above-equilibrium wages so as to ensure good quality job applicants.[10] Thus, monopoly power may remain more potential than real. To illustrate this point, consider the case of a firm with fixed labor requirements, which are indicated in figure 5.2 as the vertical line labelled AA' between wage rates W_0 and W_2. The supply

9. On this point, see J. Coyne, "Kinked Supply Curves and the Labor Market," *Discussion Paper No. 14* (Department of Industrial Economics, University of Nottingham, 1975).
10. M. Bronfenbrenner, "Potential Monopsony in Labor Markets," *Industrial and Labor Relations Review* 9 (1956): 577–588.

Figure 5.2   Monopsony, Fixed Labor Requirements

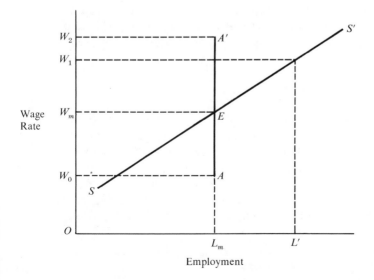

Employment

of labor minimally qualifying for the job description and offering itself is given by some function of the wage rate, SS'. The degree of monopsony is to be gauged by the slope of SS'—the greater its slope, the greater the imperfection of labor mobility. The conventional wage/employment solution is given by point E: the monopsonistic employer will set a wage of W_m and employ L_m units of labor.[11] The implication is that wages will increase whenever the employer's requirements increase, and vice versa. However, it may be more realistic to assume that the monopsonist leaves some portion of his power latent or potential, paying some higher wage, say W_1, within the range $W_m W_2$. Several factors might be expected to condition the actual wage in these circumstances. Bronfenbrenner suggest that the wage selected will be made with reference to what other firms are paying for similar jobs, to what unions may be demanding of employers with less monopsony power, and to the percentage of minimally qualified applicants the firm must employ at the wage rate selected. The latter aspect is of principal interest. The equilibrium wage, W_m, would entail the acceptance of applicants with minimal qualifications, regardless of any special standards of skill which the firm might wish to impose, and regardless also of the employer's prejudice regarding age, sex, race, nationality, religion, and so on. Monopsonists are thus said to set disequilibrium rates somewhat higher, as with W_1, permitting selectivity and eliminating the need to raise wages whenever employment increases. It is interesting to note that this problem of ensuring labor supply is also a factor underpinning the development of the internal labor market, which we shall discuss later.

The question of the prevalence of monopsony is of crucial importance to the allocation of resources in society. Our principal interest is not with monopsony in the strict sense—only one buyer of labor who confronts the positively sloped aggregate supply curve—but with its more general form. That is, we are concerned with those factors that impart a positive slope to the supply curve and the implications raised for the competitive model of wage adjustment and labor mobility. A consideration of such issues follows.

5.3   Information

The competitive theory of the labor market predicts equalization of net advantages through time for homogeneous labor inputs. Yet local labor market studies have consistently reported the existence of a wide dispersion of earnings for a given occupation in a given market (chapter 10). In theory, the equilibrium wage is attained as workers move from relatively low-paying to relatively high-paying activities. Several studies have reported that workers appear neither to possess extensive knowledge of alternative pecuniary and nonpecuniary conditions nor to develop that knowledge via systematic

---

11. As L_m men could have been employed at any wage rate up to W_2, we may treat $W_m W_2$ as a measure of monopsonistic exploitation per unit of labor.

job search activities. From such data, some commentators have reached the conclusion that there is inadequate information for the efficient operation of the labor market and that, accordingly, the competitive model is of dubious validity.

The Extent of Workers' Knowledge: The Questionnaire Approach. Early empirical studies investigating the issues of knowledge and ignorance in job choice were based on respondents' answers to questions designed to test their familiarity with wages and working conditions within the local labor market. At first sight, the results of these studies appear to augur ill for the competitive model. With respect to employed workers, the predominant impression is that the vast majority of production workers are not accustomed to comparing their jobs with alternatives. It appeared unusual for them to be aware of other job opportunities in the locality, and even less usual for them to know about the specific characteristics of these opportunities.[12] Moreover, a worker's attitude toward the relative fairness of his job was seen more as a product of his general feelings of satisfaction or dissatisfaction with his job than of any objective knowledge of the wage pattern in the market.[13]

Studies of the questionnaire type *do* draw a distinction between the employed worker and the worker who has separated from his job, either voluntarily in the form of quits or involuntarily in the form of layoffs. It is conceded that the unemployed worker necessarily learns something about what is available in the process of seeking a job. Yet even here, the studies suggest that the unemployed worker tends to take the first job applied for and that workers do not weigh alternatives.[14] Moreover, the point is often made that there is no real distinction between those who accept the first job offer and those who have one or more offers in addition to the one they eventually accept. All workers are said to take the first suitable job that comes their way. However, suitability is defined in terms of absolute minimum standards rather than by comparison with alternatives.[15]

What is the status of such studies? First, we should note that the extent of workers' knowledge is not readily quantifiable. The evidence in question is based on the supposed attitudes of workers in individual labor market transactions. A better method would be to proceed via an examination of the facts on employee work histories covering extended periods of time.[16]

---

12. See L. G. Reynolds, *The Structure of Labor Markets* (New York: Harper, 1951), pp. 84, 214; L. P. Adams and R. L. Aronson, *Workers and Industrial Change* (Ithaca, N.Y.: New York State School of Industrial and Labor Relations, 1957), p. 156.
13. Reynolds, *The Structure of Labor Markets*, pp. 213–214.
14. C. A. Myers and G. P. Shultz, *The Dynamics of a Labor Market* (New York: Prentice-Hall, 1951), p. 62.
15. Reynolds, *The Structure of Labor Markets*, p. 108.
16. See, for example, G. L. Palmer, "Interpreting Patterns of Labor Mobility," in E. W. Bakke *et al., Labor Mobility and Economic Opportunity* (Cambridge, Mass.: Technology Press of M.I.T., 1954), pp. 62*ff.*

Another possibility, one pursued in the next section, is to consider the process of job changing at a more aggregated level so as to establish whether the outcome of events is in conformity with the predictions of the competitive model.

Second, the real issue is not whether workers are perfectly informed; they are not. Rather, the question is whether this lack of knowledge makes any difference to the propositions derived from simple models of labor supply. It is entirely possible to modify the standard model by allowing for imperfect information; indeed, this has been one of the main areas of research by neoclassical economists during the past decade. For a good many purposes, however, the simple perfect information model is satisfactory; especially as a means of predicting changes in behavior in response to changes in certain economic stimuli.

It seems to be a plausible proposition that even unemployed workers assess alternatives and choose among them. The choice may be said to have two facets. First, the worker will make a comparison between a continued state of unemployment and the job offered. Second, the worker will make a comparison between the net advantages of the job offered and the net advantages of other jobs, which are not offered and known in any specific sense, but which are known in some expectational sense. This merely states that the choice is made in conditions of uncertainty. The worker knows the properties of the job offered to him; he computes the properties of other jobs which he expects to become available; and he compares the two and chooses whether to accept the first or wait for another. The notions that unemployed workers take jobs because they are unemployed and that choice is made by them outside a framework of comparison are unjustified. If the first job offered is taken, it is presumably because the worker, having made an estimate, decides that, all things considered, he is better off with it than without it.

If choices are rational, they are made in terms of the worker's assessment of differences between two situations. It is not the fact that he is badly off in any absolute sense in his present place of employment that causes the worker to move. It is rather that he is badly off relative to what he estimates his position will be after moving. The unemployed worker who sets a minimum standard for jobs that he will find acceptable (*the reservation wage*) is making a choice with respect to the comparative attractiveness of alternatives. Effectively, the worker does not accept a wage of less than $Y because he believes that, if he waits, he will find this price. Even if workers' knowledge of job alternatives is fragmentary and imperfect, movements of workers can equalize earnings in equal employments. Some workers will overestimate the value of a new job and will move more rapidly and frequently than they would if they had full knowledge. Some workers will underestimate the value of a new job and will move less rapidly and frequently than they would if they had perfect knowledge. If both over- and underestimation is randomly distributed among workers, the differences will cancel and movement will tend to be that required to equalize net advantage.[17]

The Economics of Information. In a world of homogeneous commodities, we should normally expect there to be some dispersion in the prices offered by buyers and sellers. Only if the market participants have complete knowledge will there be a single price. Perfect knowledge is seldom possessed once we leave the realm of the obliging and all-knowing neo-Walrasian auctioneer. In the absence of perfect competition, we will observe some dispersion in the price of homogeneous commodities for the simple reason that it costs more to learn about the alternative prices than this information yields at the margin. The analysis is more complicated within the labor market because of the lack of homogeneity of workers and jobs, together with the nonpecuniary conditions of employment. In the following discussion, we will largely ignore the important issue of worker and job heterogeneity for expositional convenience, returning to this topic when we come to consider job search methods.

In trading equilibrium, everyone has equal marginal rates of substitution, but how is that equilibrium equality approached? It is not rational to expect a person to trade with the first person he happens to meet with a different subjective value. It will pay to seek a higher bid or a lower ask. Discovery of the variety of bids and offers and the best path or sequence of exchange prices toward an equilibrium entails costly search over the population.

First, consider the returns to search. At any time, there will exist a frequency distribution of the wage rates offered by employers. If the dispersion of wage rates is at all large relative to the costs of search, it will usually pay to contact several employers. If the wage offers of employers are normally distributed with a mean, $\bar{w}$, and variance σ^2, then the expected maximum wage offer, w_m, at the Nth search can be shown to be approximately

$$w_m = \bar{w} = \sigma\sqrt{2 \log N} \simeq \bar{w} + \sigma \cdot .65 N^{.37} \qquad (5.1)$$

for $3 < N < 20$. The marginal wage gain from one additional search is $\triangle w_m = \partial w_m / \partial N$. The point to note is that, if the standard deviation and mean wage rate are known, the wage gain from additional search can be computed for various numbers of search (N).[18] If the structure of employer wage offers were fixed in perpetuity, and if employees lived forever, only one search would need to be undertaken. Here, the marginal income gain from

---

17. Estimates made under uncertainty may nonetheless lead to some wrong directional movement, and thus there is scope for widening knowledge and diminishing uncertainty. Simply put, the more certain are the conditions within which choice is made, the smaller will be the number of moves required to reach the optimum.
18. See G. J. Stigler, "The Economics of Information," *Journal of Political Economy* 70 (1962): 94–105.

additional search is the capitalized value of the marginal wage rate gain.[19] However, this gain is exaggerated because the distribution changes over time.

Nevertheless, we would expect the gains from search to increase as the prospective duration of employment lengthens. It follows that workers will search longer (and dispersion will be the smaller, *ceteris paribus*) if they intend to stay in jobs longer. Also, the more extensive the search, the smaller will be the dispersion of maximum wage rates; so we can expect diminishing returns to search.

From this analysis, it would be predicted that groups such as women, who generally expect to stay in the labor force for a shorter period than men, should have larger earnings dispersion, *ceteris paribus*. Similarly, we would expect the coefficient of variation of intraoccupational earnings to increase with age, *ceteris paribus,* because younger workers make more extensive search than their older counterparts. But it is difficult to hold other things constant. The age composition of the male labor force and female labor force differs, as does their racial composition. Also, when we come to examine intraoccupational age-earnings distributions, there is the problem of disentangling differing abilities. Older members of the occupational group in question will have different amounts of on-the-job training, which will serve to increase the dispersion of abilities. On the other hand, differences in the ability of members of the occupational group becomes better known to the employer as their length of service increases. The latter effect should reduce the dispersion of earnings of homogeneous workers. Thus, it is difficult to use the above prediction as the basis of a test of the theory.

Let us now consider the costs of search. The cost of search for a worker may be taken as approximately proportional to the number of job offers approached, because the chief cost is time. As with any other productive activity, specialization in information is efficient. It is often assumed that searching is most efficient when the worker is unemployed. In this case, the cost of search is the income that could have been earned during the search period, less any unemployment insurance benefits to which the worker is entitled. These costs represent an investment on which the expected return is the present value of the difference in compensation between the first job offer received and the one finally accepted.[20]

---

19. That is, the marginal income gain will be the value of the annuity,

$$\frac{\triangle w_m}{\gamma} \cdot [1 - (1 + \gamma)^{-t}]$$

where t years constitute the duration of employment; and
γ is the discount rate.

For a derivation of this formula, see equation (4.5).

20. Earlier we gave the marginal income gain from search as

$$\frac{\triangle w_m}{\gamma} \cdot [1 - (1 + \gamma)^{-t}] = \triangle w_m D$$

The larger the costs of search, the less search will be undertaken by a worker at a given level of dispersion of employers' wage offers. One implication here is that the more easily prospective employers can be identified, the lower will be the costs of search, because the worker does not have to waste time on unproductive possibilities. Accordingly, we would expect the dispersion of observed wage rates to be less as the visibility of prospective employers increases, because of the implied reduction in the costs of search.[21]

We might also expect the dispersion of wages to be smaller in periods of expanding employment. This is because the costs of search may be said to be lower as the probability that a given, identified employer is recruiting labor increases. On the other hand, unemployment among a class of workers functions in the opposite manner to reduce the cost of search, because the loss of income during the search period is correspondingly reduced. Working against this, however, is the fact that the higher the level of unemployment in an occupation, the greater the risk that opportunities already discovered may be taken by others if they are not accepted quickly. This likelihood may serve to truncate search. Thus, the effects of the level of economic activity on the variance of wages are difficult to disentangle.

There is direct search by employers, wholly comparable to that of workers, in certain industries. Direct solicitation, such as occurs when employers canvass universities, is most probable when the workers are highly specialized. However, workers can be expected to undertake the main burden of solicitation, because it is cheaper for them than for the employer. Not only is it usually easier for a worker to identify a firm than vice versa, but the probability that a given employer requires additional workers is also much greater than the probability that a given worker will accept a job offer.

There is likely to be a close relationship between the amount of employer search activity within the labor market and the level of activity in that

---

where

$$\triangle w_m = \partial w_m / \partial N = 0.24\sigma N^{-.63}$$

The total income gained is the integral of this expression over the range of search

$$\int_0^N \triangle w_m D \cdot dN$$

$$= \frac{.24\sigma N^{.37}}{.37} \cdot D$$

$$= .65\sigma N^{.37}D = (w_m - \bar{w})D.$$

But note that this income gain from search is both an overestimate and an underestimate. It is an overestimate to the extent that future wage rates paid by various employers are not perfectly correlated with present wage rates. It is an underestimate to the extent that, for periods of employment greater than t, there will be some value to the knowledge presently acquired in the search for alternative employments after t.

21. See D. Metcalf, "Pay Dispersion, Information and Returns to Search in a Professional Labor Market," *Review of Economic Studies* 40 (1973): 491–505.

market, as proxied by unemployment. If there is substantial unemployment in a market, many workers are searching because the marginal cost of search is low compared to the expected marginal return. Quit rates will be low; so employers do not need to hire many workers as replacements. Both supply and demand conditions point to low employer search activity in a loose labor market. But as the labor market tightens, the supply of unemployed workers is reduced. The total amount of search by workers may remain constant or even increase because of a greater amount of search by hitherto employed workers. The net outcome will be determined by worker search costs and by the expected marginal returns from search. In this situation, employers taken together face either a diminished applicant flow, an increased quit rate, or both, depending on the amount of search by hitherto employed workers. The result will be an upward pressure on wage rates (see chapter 12). Employers will respond to this pressure by increased search, because their expected marginal return will have increased, at least to the extent that they view a higher wage as their alternative.

There is considerable empirical support for the negative association between the unemployment rate and the amount of employer search activity in the labor market. This may be seen, for example, in the National Industrial Conference Board series on help-wanted advertising.[22] Studies of local labor markets have also consistently reported the responsiveness of the level of search activity by firms to changes in the unemployment rate.[23]

To sum up the discussion to this point: wage dispersion can be connected to incomplete knowledge or ignorance, and the presence of either can be consistent with labor market efficiency. The facts that information is imperfect and that information has a cost, principally the opportunity cost of a worker's time, may explain wage dispersion among homogeneous labor inputs. The search for information will be of limited duration because of the costs incurred. All offers will not be identified and some wage dispersion will result. Our analysis also provides the basis of a theory of frictional unemployment. The optimal duration of search may be interpreted as the average duration of frictional unemployment. This can perhaps more easily be seen by focusing on the concept of the reservation wage. The *optimal stopping rule* describes the optimal search strategy for the job seeker as being to reject all offers below a single critical value, termed the reservation wage, and to accept any offer above this critical number. The reservation wage can be calculated so that the marginal cost of generating one additional job offer is equal to the expected marginal return of one more offer. In simple job search models, the reservation wage is constant over time and lower costs of search

22. See N. E. Terleckyi, *Help-wanted Advertising as a Business Indicator* (New York: National Industrial Conference Board, 1961).

23. G. P. Schultz, "A Nonunion Market for White Collar Labor," *Aspects of Labor Economics,* National Bureau of Economic Research (Princeton, N.J.: Princeton University Press, 1962), pp. 107–146; R. C. Wilcock and I. Sobel, *Small City Job Markets* (Urbana, Ill.: University of Illinois Institute of Labor and Industrial Relations, 1958), p. 30.

imply higher reservation wages and longer expected periods of search (frictional unemployment).[24] In appendix 5-A, we present a simplified model of the reservation wage construct.

From a social viewpoint, the return from investment in information is the more efficient allocation of labor. The better informed the labor market, the closer each worker's marginal product is to its maximum at any given time. From this viewpoint, the function of information is to prevent lower productivity workers from obtaining higher paid jobs than more productive workers and, correspondingly, to channel workers toward more efficient employers. It should be noted, however, that the social capital of information is not necessarily equal to the sum of private capitals. If some workers search extensively (assuming homogeneous labor), then employers who offer lower wage rates for given productivity will be unable to fill their jobs and will be forced either to terminate their operations or raise wages. The upshot of this is that many workers need not search and yet can profit from the search of others. To this extent, social capital in information is greater than the sum of private capitals.

Job Search Methods. Job search methods have been classified as either formal or informal. Although this division is necessarily imprecise, one can readily see that some methods make more use of established channels of job information than others. For example, workers may register for employment with the state employment service, they may answer advertisements for specific jobs, or they may make use of trade union job-finding networks or private employment agencies. Other methods are usually regarded as informal in nature. They include asking friends and relatives about possible job opportunities, applying to firms on the chance that vacancies exist, or checking gate notices at factories.

Informal methods are widely used both by employers in hiring and by employees looking for work. Thus Parnes, in summarizing the results of six United States local labor market studies, observed that informal sources account for between 50% and 85% of manual worker job finding.[25] Confirmation of these results is found in a more recent study by Rees and Shultz of the Chicago labor market. They estimate that informal sources are responsible for more than 80% of all blue-collar hires within an eight-occupation sample (ignoring rehires).[26] More recent evidence provided by Bradshaw concerning the job-seeking methods of unemployed workers also concludes that informal channels are important, accounting for approximately 55% of

24. For a review of this literature, see S. A. Lippman and J. J. McCall, "The Economics of Job Search: A Survey," *Economic Inquiry* 14 (1976): 155–189.
25. H. S. Parnes, *Research on Labor Mobility–An Appraisal of Research Findings in the United States* (New York: Social Science Research Council, 1954), pp. 162–165.
26. A. Rees and G. P. Shultz, *Workers and Wages in an Urban Labor Market* (Chicago, Ill.: University of Chicago Press, 1970), pp. 201–202. Some of these results are summarized in table 9.2.

all job-search methods.[27] In the British context, MacKay *et al.* find that friends, relatives, and casual applications account for 53% of hires in Glasgow and 66% in Birmingham.[28]

Informal methods are thus much used, but opinion is divided as to how effective they are in achieving a better allocation of labor. For example, in their commentary on manpower policy in the United Kingdom, the Organisation for Economic Co-operation and Development (OECD) observed, "This individualistic approach to job-seeking entails two obvious disadvantages: the period of frictional 'unemployment' tends to be longer than it would otherwise be; and there is little assurance that deployment is carried out with a maximum of efficiency."[29] In contrast, Rees argues that economists have generally undervalued their contribution and that "the effectiveness and advantages of informal networks of information have been too little appreciated."[30]

In accord with Stigler,[31] we may say that search for information in the goods market has both an extensive and an intensive margin.[31] Search at the extensive margin occurs when a buyer seeks an additional price quotation. Search at the intensive margin, on the other hand, occurs when a buyer seeks additional nonprice information, for example, about quality, concerning an offer already received. The essence of this distinction is one of product homogeneity; the more homogeneous the product, the more important search at the extensive margin becomes.

Rees has applied the concept of the intensive and the extensive margins to the employer side of the labor market. He notes that prima facie evidence of worker heterogeneity is provided by the apparent large variance of wages within narrowly defined occupations in particular local labor markets. Rees concludes that the problem facing the employer is not one of making contact with the maximum number of potential applicants. Rather, the problem is one of finding sufficient applicants promising enough to be worth the investment of thorough investigation.[32] Hiring standards of many employers can thus be viewed as devices to narrow the intensive field of search by reducing the number of applicants to manageable proportions. That is to say, employers benefit from use of an extensive preselection screening process before they invest in their own interviewing and testing procedures. The

27. T. F. Bradshaw, "Jobseeking Methods Used by Unemployed Workers," *Monthly Labor Review* 96 (1973): 35–40.

28. D. I. MacKay, D. Boddy, J. Brack, J. A. Diack, and N. Jones, *Labour Markets Under Different Employment Conditions* (London: Allen and Unwin, 1971), p. 357.

29. Organisation for Economic Co-operation and Development, *Manpower Policy in the United Kingdom* (Paris: OECD, 1970), p. 163.

30. A. Rees, "Information Networks in Labor Markets," *American Economic Review,* Papers and Proceedings 56 (1966): 560.

31. G. J. Stigler, "The Economics of Information," *Journal of Political Economy* 69 (1961): 213–225.

32. This point is reinforced by the fact that current seniority arrangements imply that a worker who survives the probationary period is likely to be with the firm for many years.

common practice of referrals by existing employees is one among several such screening processes that provides useful information at low cost. Informal sources also tend to provide applicants from the neighborhood in which the plant is located; this might be particularly important for female employees in reducing turnover and absenteeism. Employee referral can also benefit the applicant, who may thereby obtain more information about the kind of work in which he is interested from a friend who is engaged in such work than from formal information sources.

All this is not to say that extensive search is not important in labor markets or necessarily to denigrate the role of formal sources. The choice of the particular source will presumably depend on the efficiency of the method and also upon the tightness of the labor market. Moreover, although employers may, for the reasons given, prefer informal sources, it does not follow that they will always be able to use them. As Stigler has pointed out, high wages and high search costs are substitutes for an employer. Employers wishing to pay relatively low wages are therefore forced to spend more on search, including the use of high-cost formal information channels, such as advertising and private employment agencies. Empirical support for this hypothesis is provided by Ullman's analysis of the Chicago market for two female clerical occupations—typists and keypunch operators.[33] This study reports significant negative relationships between wages and the proportion of clerical employees hired through newspaper advertising and private agencies.

Let us next examine the allegations of the OECD, drawing upon data from a British study of persons laid off from the engineering and metal-using trades in England over 1966–68.[34] First, are periods of frictional unemployment longer with informal methods of job seeking than with formal methods? In table 5.1, we show unemployment duration of those finding new jobs through the four main channels identified within the study. Chi-square tests reveal that the length of unemployment experienced does not differ significantly according to the method of job finding. The problem in interpreting table 5.1 is that we do not know the length of time that the employee had been searching by that method, so we cannot use it as an indicator of the effectiveness of job-finding methods. For this purpose, we must compare the four methods according to the characteristics of jobs found, for example, the jobs' wage levels. This brings us to the second OECD criticism, which relates to the efficient deployment of workers.

In examining the effectiveness of job-finding methods, the study does not yield any significant differences between job-finding methods in a comparison of take-home pay before and after layoff. The comparison of skill level is similarly inconclusive. However, the study also takes account of the proportion of workers who had left their first postlayoff job and the speed with

33. J. C. Ullman, "Inter-firm Differences in the Cost of Search for Clerical Workers," *Journal of Business* 41 (1968): 153–165.
34. G. L. Reid, "Job Search and the Effectiveness of Job Finding Methods," *Industrial and Labor Relations Review* 25 (1972): 471–495.

Table 5.1   Length of Unemployment Distribution by Method of Job Finding, Terminated Males, West Midlands of England, 1966-68.

Job Search Method	n	Less than 1 Week	1 Week to 4 Weeks	4 Weeks to 16 Weeks	16 Weeks or more
Friends or relatives	196	37.7	17.4	24.5	19.9
Casual callers	127	31.5	15.7	27.5	25.2
Advertisement	122	38.5	14.8	23.8	23.0
Employment service	91	33.0	15.4	23.1	28.5

Note:
n denotes sample size.

Source:
D. I. MacKay, "Manpower Policy and Redundancy in Britain: Some Empirical Evidence on Redeployment," (Paper presented to an expert group on labor market behavior, MS/M/201/396, Paris: OECD, 1972), table 5, p. 8.

which they left. While the proportion quitting their first postlayoff job does not vary systematically according to the method by which the job was found, there are substantial differences in the timing of these quits by method of job finding. The data are shown in table 5.2. There appears to have been more immediate dissatisfaction with jobs found by formal channels. We might ask why, considering there were no significant objective differences between jobs found in different ways, those taking jobs through more formal channels should be more likely to leave quickly? One possibility is that the jobs did not live up to the respondent's expectations, expectations which had been based upon inadequate and imperfect information. The policy implications of the analysis lend support to the view that policymakers should favor the individualistic approach, reserving the public employment service for those who cannot or choose not to find a job on their own.[35] However, until we can say more about the efficiency of job search and the reasons why workers use one strategy rather than another, we cannot be dogmatic about what the role of the public employment service should be.

In much of the theoretical literature on job search, it is assumed that one or more job offers of some kind are produced whenever the searcher looks for a job. Theorists are then able to discuss the optimal decision about which offers to accept or pass up, depending on the probability distribution of offers and search costs. If job-seeking methods differ with respect to their associated costs and also with the likelihood of success associated with the different methods, then an appropriate theory of job seeking should provide for the use of the various methods. To apply such a theory, we would need to know the costs of utilizing various job-search methods and the probability than an offer would be received when a particular method was used. The unsophis-

35. It has been observed by a number of commentators that informal job information networks do not serve the disadvantaged well. See, for example, J. C. Ullman and D. P. Taylor, "The Information System in Changing Labor Markets," *Proceedings of the Industrial Relations Research Association* (Madison, Wis.: IRRA, 1965), pp. 276–289.

Table 5.2   Length of Service of Men in First Job by Method of Job Search, Terminated Males, West Midlands of England, 1966–68.

Job Search Method	*n*	Percentage with Length of Service of:			
		Less than 3 Months	3–6 Months	6–12 Months	More than 12 Months
Friends or relatives	95	14.7	16.8	29.5	38.9
Casual callers	64	20.3	25.0	29.7	25.0
Advertisement	61	47.5	13.1	23.0	16.4
Employment service	44	36.3	20.5	20.5	22.7
Total	279	26.5	19.0	27.6	28.0

Source:
G. L. Reid, "Job Search and the Effectiveness of Job-Finding Methods," *Industrial and Labor Relations Review* 25 (1972): table 7, p. 488.

ticated nature of the above study serves to indicate that we do not possess such estimates, although further analysis of job-search methods might be useful in developing such a theory.

5.4   Labor Mobility

Labor mobility, or more strictly potential mobility, plays a crucial role in the competitive model of the labor market, because workers must move to the most attractive jobs to eliminate wage differentials given the job. Yet an examination of the literature describing the way in which workers move within and between labor markets yields the distinct impression that labor markets do not perform well in allocating labor resources. Such studies have focused on the criteria by which workers evaluate jobs, the reasons for quitting jobs and taking others, the process of finding jobs and the degree of knowledge as to job opportunities and characteristics, and the extent to which employed workers are in the market for better jobs.[36] On the basis of such studies, it has been claimed that most workers make choice decisions with reference to the human relations factors that attach to jobs or for personal reasons; the structure of wages plays a very small role in the choice process. Factors other than price certainly operate to allocate labor. Indeed, in the classical model, workers make choices in terms of comparative total net advantages and not in terms of comparative wages. On the other hand, neoclassical economics does work in terms of price as the instrument for allocating labor among alternative uses subject to the usual *ceteris paribus* assumptions. The fact that the real world is complex and that individuals have diverse motivations does not mean that a particular variable is without influence. For many purposes, it is useful to operate under the *ceteris paribus* assumption and to examine the effect of variations in a single variable, such as price. For that model to be meaningful, however, it must be able to predict

36. For a survey of the material, see Parnes, *Research on Labor Mobility*, pp. 144–190.

behavior. From this standpoint, the best approach seems to be to look at what workers do, rather than at what they say.[37]

Before turning to a consideration of labor mobility by industry, occupation, and region, let us briefly discuss the position of unemployed workers who have been laid off by their employers. How appropriate is the concept of differential economic advantage to them? It is often considered that the job choices of such workers are substantially different from those of voluntary movers. Thus, Parnes has commented that "from the theoretical viewpoint, only the voluntary separations represent choices made by workers and consequently are relevant in the development of theories of motivations of workers."[38] Yet this attempt to distinguish between pushes and pulls to explain worker behavior in the labor market is largely spurious for the reasons advanced in section 5.3. Both the voluntary quit and the involuntarily separated worker will engage in labor market search, although the costs of search and the characteristics of workers will differ as between the two groups.[39] Also, the fact that workers who leave a present job with another specific employment arranged move to a higher gross weekly earnings position more often than do workers who leave without a specific alternative arranged does not imply that the competitive model of labor choice is more consistent with reality in the former case. The only safe conclusion we can draw from this evidence is that choice in a context of less uncertainty is more successful than choice in a context of more uncertainty. We should not infer from differential success patterns of this type that different motivations and behavioral factors characterize the two groups.

Industrial Mobility. Analyses of labor turnover by industry report a consistently negative association between turnover and earnings levels, which suggests that the existing level of earnings is an important influence promoting decisions to leave or not to leave a given job.[40] (This relationship is considered further in chapter 9.) Gallaway, in an interesting analysis of movers and stayers, using Social Security Administration data for 1957 and 1960, has shown that differences in income levels among industries are a strong factor in explaining why people change their industry of major job.[41] However, an interesting theoretical question is whether the negative associ-

---

37. The problem here is similar to that confronted in analyzing the demand for labor. We prefer to analyze employers' actions, rather than their opinions, in evaluating the marginal productivity theory of labor demand.

38. Parnes, *Research on Labor Mobility,* p. 71.

39. For an empirical treatment of the job-choice strategies of the involuntarily separated worker, see D. I. MacKay, "After the 'Shake-Out'," *Oxford Economic Papers* 24 (1972): 89–110.

40. See, for example, OECD, *Wages and Labor Mobility* (Paris: OECD, 1965), pp. 52–53; V. Stoikov and R. L. Raimon, "Determinants of Differences in the Quit Rate among Industries," *American Economic Review* 58 (1968): 1283–1298.

41. L. E. Gallaway, *Interindustry Labor Mobility in the United States, 1957 to 1960,* Social Security Administration, Report No. 28 (Washington, D.C.: U.S. Government Printing Office, 1967); idem, *Manpower Economics* (Homewood, Ill.: Irwin, 1971), chap. 3, pp. 36–42.

ation between quits and earnings levels should be interpreted as a disequilibrium phenomenon, because we associate employment changes with relative wage changes. This interpretation would be correct if net employment changes were explained largely by the industry differences in quit rates, but this is not the case. Industries with high quit rates tend also to have high accession rates and to maintain their position in the turnover ranking for long periods of time. Because high turnover rates and low wages go together, and apparently remain together, the association should probably be interpreted as an equilibrium phenomenon.

It remains to be explained why this association should appear in equilibrium. Recent developments in the theory of human capital have suggested that turnover plays a critical part in the relation between wage rates and on-the-job training. Large investments in firm specific human capital, either by the firm or by the worker, are likely to lead to reduced labor mobility, because the economic cost of worker-job separations is increased (see chapters 4 and 9). Proposing that specific human capital was positively correlated with wages, Oi found that wages in manufacturing industries were negatively related to an aggregate turnover measure and also to quit rates.[42] However, this test of the Becker model is, as Mincer has pointed out,[43] unsatisfactory. The wage differentials used by Oi can be seen to represent returns to two forms of training: school training, which is general, and on-the-job training, which may be general or specific. A higher wage rate could prevail with very little on-the-job training but sufficiently more schooling training. This might serve to obscure the relation which was tested by Oi. Furthermore, the lack of control for age makes for a spurious correlation between the wage rate and turnover, because older workers have lower turnover and higher wages in general.

More recently, however, support for the specific human capital hypothesis has been provided by Parsons, who distinguishes between firm-financed and worker-financed human capital in explaining layoff and quit behavior, respectively.[44] Using cross-section data for 47 three-digit manufacturing industries in 1959 and 1963, Parsons demonstrates that quit rates are negatively related to worker-owned specific capital, while layoff rates are negatively related to firm-owned specific capital.

On the specific human capital model, then, each industry tends to reveal a permanent quit rate associated with the particular characteristics of its labor force (and the share-in-costs principle). Superimposed on this permanent quit rate are transitory movements in quits that result from an industry's net advantage getting out of line with other industries.

42. W. Y. Oi, "Labor as a Quasi-Fixed Factor," *Journal of Political Economy* 70 (1962): 552–553.
43. J. Mincer, "On-the-Job Training: Costs, Returns and Implications," *Journal of Political Economy* 70 (1962): 50–79.
44. D. O. Parsons, "Specific Human Capital: An Application to Quit Rates and Layoff Rates," *Journal of Political Economy* 80 (1972): 1120–1143.

Occupational Mobility. Occupational mobility can be considered either as a movement between occupations during the lifespan of a given worker or as an intergenerational shift, that is, a movement of the offspring of individuals into occupations other than those of the parent. Occupational movement within the lifetime of workers indicates that there is a strong direct relation between the net flow of workers into an occupation and the median income level of that occupation. Aronson found that the rank order correlation across 119 occupations between earnings levels in 1960 and net inward mobility during the period 1950–1960 was +0.598.[45] Similar results were obtained by Gallaway for the same period, using a ten-occupation sample.[46] The pattern shown by the net flows of workers between occupations, however, appears to be different from that exhibited by new entries into occupations. Gallaway found a lack of any relationship between new entries into occupations and the mean income levels attaching to those occupations.[47] He concludes that the choice of entry occupation is significantly affected by job opportunity considerations; but he emphasizes that the entry patterns of those moving into the labor force are not sufficient to vitiate the impact of net mobility on the allocation of resources. However, the former finding must be interpreted with caution because Gallaway fails to control for education and training.

There is also evidence to suggest purposive movement by workers between occupations across generations. One interesting but crude test of the competitive hypothesis in this context is to regress the difference between the proportion of sons and the proportion of fathers employed in an occupation upon the median earnings of that occupation. The hypothesis is that this difference in a given occupation should be positively associated with the income level of that occupation. The results of one such test procedure are reported by Gallaway (t-statistic in parentheses):[48]

$$D_j = -0.0298 + 0.000012w_j \qquad R^2 = 0.73 \qquad (5.2)$$
$$(4.05)$$

where D_j denotes the difference between the proportion of sons and the proportion of fathers employed in the jth occupation as of March 1962;

w_j denotes the median income of the jth occupation in 1960;

$j = 1 \ldots 10$.

It can be seen that sons do appear more likely to have moved into an occupation if its pay is relatively high, which is as we would expect.

45. R. L. Aronson, *Components of Occupational Change in the United States, 1950–1960,* Technical Monograph Series No. 1 (Ithaca, N.Y.: New York State School of Industrial and Labor Relations, 1969).
46. Gallaway, *Manpower Economics,* p. 57.
47. Ibid., pp. 57–60.
48. Ibid., p. 64.

Geographical Mobility. Finally, let us turn to regional or geographical mobility. For the past two decades, many studies have attributed migration flows within a country to economic factors. A widely accepted hypothesis is that net flows among geographical areas increase with increases in earnings differentials. Empirical studies have invariably supported this hypothesis.[49] These studies regress the rate of migration between two locations on the arithmetic difference in median incomes, or some other function of these incomes, because migrants' actual incomes in their origins and destinations are unavailable from the census data which has traditionally served as the primary data source. More elaborate studies have used returns to migration as the explanatory variable. This is computed as the present value of the median income difference between regions. Such studies have been more successful in explaining the observed systematic age-education differences in rates of migration.[50]

While the evidence overwhelmingly favors the differential economic advantage motive in geographical mobility, we might query why migration is not larger than it is in the face of substantial geographic differences in incomes. Gallaway, for example, has calculated that an annual income differential of $1000 is required to offset the impact of having to cross one additional regional boundary for those who are already migrants.[51] Also, results obtained by Sjaastad imply that the typical migrant would be indifferent between two destinations, one of which was 146 miles more distant than the other, if the average annual labor earnings were $106 (1947–49 values) higher in the more distant one.[52] Marginal costs would have to be high indeed to reconcile the negative effect of distance with the present value of the earnings differential, even at very high discount rates.

Clearly, the distance variable is measuring something in addition to the costs of movement. There are two main possibilities. One is that the distance variable may also reflect the subjective costs of moving between regions. The other is that the distance variable may be capturing the impact of barriers to the flow of labor market information between areas. In effect, distance may be considered as a filter through which labor market information must flow; as the distance increases, the filtering effect is greater. There is also a third possibility to consider. If specific training were important, differences in earnings would be a misleading estimate of what migrants could receive. In such cases, it might be perfectly rational not to move.

49. See M. J. Greenwood, "Research on Internal Migration in the U.S., A Survey," *Journal of Economic Literature* 13 (1975): 397–434.
50. S. Bowles, "Migration as Investment: Empirical Tests at the Human Investment Approach to Geographical Mobility," *Review of Economics and Statistics* 52 (1970): 356–362.
51. Gallaway, *Manpower Economics,* p. 48.
52. L. A. Sjaastad, "The Costs and Returns of Human Migration," *Journal of Political Economy* 70 (1962): 84.

5.5   The Internal Labor Market

Under the simplifying assumptions of classical economics, the labor market resembles a bourse, in that it functions as a place where buyers and sellers meet to transact their business and where all vacancies in the economy are continually open to all workers on the same terms and conditions. However, this description of labor market operation has long been challenged. In the view of Kerr, for example, the labor market functions not as an open and competitive bourse, but as a series of distinct markets, each with boundaries determined by geographical, occupational, and, most important of all, institutional factors.[53] While the boundaries of these markets touch or overlap in places, they can largely be regarded as separate entities with respect to labor mobility, according to this view. The existence of such market boundaries creates a segmented or balkanized market system. That is to say, there is a distinction in terms of employment preferences between workers within a particular market and those outside that market.[54]

In the terminology of Kerr, markets may be distinguished according to whether they are "structureless" or "structured." In the structureless or open market "there is no attachment except the wage between the worker and the employer. No worker has any claim on a job and no employer has any hold on any man." The market becomes structured when different treatment is accorded to the "ins" and "outs," that is, when existing employees enjoy favored treatment over potential employees. The structured market is said to possess internal and external components. The internal market is an administrative unit within which the pricing and allocation of labor is governed by a set of administrative rules and procedures. The external market, where pricing and allocating decisions are controlled directly by economic variables, consists of "clusters of workers actively or passively available for new jobs."[55] The two markets are interconnected and movement between them occurs at certain job classifications which constitute *ports of entry* to the internal labor market. The remainder of jobs within the internal market are filled by the promotion or transfer of workers who have already gained entry.

---

53. C. Kerr, "The Balkanization of Labor Markets," in E. W. Bakke et al., *Labor Mobility and Economic Opportunity* (Cambridge, Mass.: Technology Press of M.I.T., 1954), pp. 92–110; idem, "Labor Markets: Their Character and Consequences," *American Economic Review, Papers and Proceedings* 40 (1950): 278–291.

54. Here we detect the influence of the theory of noncompeting groups propounded by Cairnes and Mill, although we should note that labor market segmentation was for them a consequence of differences in education. These differences resulted from the difficulty of financing an investment for which collateral could not be offered. As we have already seen in chapter 4, education data suggest that such imperfections are no longer of crucial importance for whites, though, as will be shown in chapter 6, they are for blacks. See J. E. Cairnes, *Some Leading Principles of Political Economy Newly Expounded* (New York: Harper, 1874), Part 1, Chapter 3, Section 5, pp. 62–65; J. S. Mill, *Principles of Political Economy* (London: Longmans Green, 1909), Vol. 1, Book 2, Chapter 14, pp. 480–481.

55. Kerr, "The Balkanization of Labor Markets," n. 16, p. 101.

Accordingly, such jobs are viewed as being shielded from the direct influence of competitive forces in the labor market.

In this view, institutional rules serve to delineate the boundaries of the internal market and determine its pay structure. The rules themselves are derived from a variety of sources: joint negotiation between labor and management, unilateral imposition, or custom and tradition. Kerr draws a distinction between *horizontal* and *vertical* forms of labor market organization. An example of the first is the market for skilled craftsmen or journeymen who are typically recruited occupationally, that is, direct to the job. The mobility of such workers is traditionally inter-firm. An opposite situation applies to many semiskilled production and process workers, together with those in the middle ranks of business administration, who typically join the enterprise through one of a limited number of ports of entry and then hope to progress upwards through various jobs via promotion, inplant training, and experience. In each of the two cases distinguished by Kerr, the market is then structured by rules that govern such matters as recruitment standards and the recognition of seniority. The main rulemakers are different in the two cases, being the craft union in the horizontal market and the management of the enterprise in the vertical market.

The structured employment relationship of the internal labor market is assumed to have developed partly because of the elaboration of tasks that are specific to a job and hence require specific training, often acquired on the job.[56] Experience with the specific technology in a plant is firm-specific, because the idiosyncrasies of each plant generate training that has value only within the plant. A further reason for the development of internal labor markets is likely to have been union pressures for promotion according to seniority. Management might also prefer the stability conferred by such promotion rules. This subject is covered in more detail in chapter 9.

Institutionalists have claimed that efficiency considerations are not dominant within the structured internal labor market. Specifically, it is alleged that productivity or a high wage adheres to the job rather than to the worker, that the wage structure is dominated not by efficiency considerations but rather by custom and practice, and that good jobs go to people who are already within the firm through promotions that largely reflect institutional arrangements. Thus, the distribution of jobs and income within the structured internal market is not necessarily dictated by ability and human capital.[57]

However, while agreeing with the institutionalist description of internal labor market structuring, it is nevertheless possible to disagree with their interpretation. We may alternatively regard the structured internal labor

56. For a recent exposition of the internal labor market, see P. B. Doeringer and M. J. Piore, *Internal Labor Markets and Manpower Analysis* (Lexington, Mass.: Heath, 1971), chap. 2.
57. Ibid., chap. 3.

market as an efficiency-oriented institutional response to the market forces generated by heterogenous (or idiosyncratic) jobs and the technology of on-the-job training. This efficiency argument has been put forward by Williamson, Wachter, and Harris.[58] The hallmark of their approach is that idiosyncratic jobs requiring specific training present a pervasive problem of bilateral monopoly. An important function of the internal labor market is to neutralize the issue so that it does not absorb the resources of the firm to the detriment of both workers and management. Accomplishing this aim involves minimizing bargaining and turnover costs, encouraging workers to exercise their specific knowledge, and ensuring that investment in idiosyncratic jobs, which constitute a potential source of job monopoly, are undertaken without risk of exploitation by either side. In this view, although firms attach wage rates to individual jobs and not to workers, they do so to reduce bargaining costs and to further the proper functioning of the organizational structure.

Efficiency might be encouraged by the practice of promoting meritorious workers through the organizational structure as they acquire training. With respect to promotions, institutionalists may be said to view promotions as dominated by institutional and social arrangements in general. Yet, promotion ladders fulfill important functions in an efficient internal labor market. Apart from their reward function, promotion ladders have the advantage that workers may acquire not only specific information about their own jobs, but also specific training for higher level jobs in the firm. Simple physical proximity, or the opportunities to observe the job content of those higher on the ladder, facilitates this process. In other words, training for advancement is a joint product with the firm's output as workers perform their jobs. Again, promotion ladders also provide a continuous screening mechanism within the firm; and a structured internal labor market may well be the most efficient apparatus for collecting and analyzing data on individual performance.

5.6   The Dual Labor Market

The dual labor market hypothesis was advanced in the late 1960s to explain the phenomena of urban poverty and unemployment.[59] The theory suggested that a dichotomization of the American labor market had occurred over time, eventuating in the formation of two separate labor markets. The labor market was said to be segmented into a *primary* and a *secondary* sector, within which districts workers and employers operated according to markedly different behavioral rules.

58. O. E. Williamson, M. L. Wachter, and J. E. Harris, "Understanding the Employment Relation: The Analysis of Idiosyncratic Exchange," *Bell Journal of Economics and Management Science* 6 (1975): 250–278.
59. On the evolution of dual labor market theory, see D. M. Gordon, *Theories of Poverty and Unemployment* (Lexington, Mass.: Heath, 1972), chap. 4; G. G. Cain, "The Challenge of Segmented Labor Market Theories to Orthodox Theory: A Survey," *Journal of Economic Literature* 14 (1976): 1215–1257.

A primary labor market has been defined as one composed of jobs in large firms and/or unionized occupations which tend to offer several of the following traits: high wages, good working conditions, employment stability, chances of advancement, and equity and due process in the administration of work rules.[60] The secondary labor market, on the other hand, is said to have jobs which, relative to those in the primary sector, are decidedly less attractive. They tend to involve low wages, poor working conditions, considerable variability in employment, little chance of promotion, and often arbitrary management.

Central to dualist theses seems to be the notion that entry into and confinement of disadvantaged workers within the secondary sector is not attributable to differences in skills, motivation, or demand for labor but to the power of institutional forces such as discrimination by white employers and labor unions. Doeringer and Piore argue that the process of entry into and advancement within the primary sector operates according to an aggregate unemployment queue. Acceptable workers are ranked in relation to their potential productivity and advanced along the queue until employer needs are met. In the secondary market, however, the queueing process is held to be considerably less pronounced, with employers appearing not to draw distinctions between one worker and another. It functions as if employers were hiring from an undifferentiated labor pool.[61] In the market mechanism that matches employer and worker preferences, a discontinuity is hypothesized such that even increases in the aggregate demand for labor will not move workers confined to the secondary labor market upward along the hiring queue and into the vacant jobs in the primary sector. In the extreme version of the dualist hypothesis, there is a complete dichotomy in the labor market. Primary employment will stop expanding when it has absorbed the primary labor force. Thereafter, increases in output will be realized by a shift in demand into the secondary sector without any transfer of the secondary sector labor force into the primary sector.

The dual approach thus rests on four interrelated hypotheses. First, it is useful to dichotomize the economy into a primary and a secondary sector. Second, the wages are determined by different factors in the secondary sector than in the primary sector. Third, economic mobility between the two sectors is sharply limited. Finally, the secondary sector is marked by pervasive underemployment because workers who could be trained for skilled jobs at no more than the usual cost are confined to unskilled jobs. In this sense, the distinction is between "good" versus "bad" jobs rather than between skilled versus unskilled workers.

The policy prescription of creating better jobs or more good jobs is the central conclusion of the dual theory, and this conflicts with standard neoclassical analysis. According to the dualists, the main problem with the

---

60. Doeringer and Piore, *Internal Labor Markets,* chap. 8.
61. Ibid., p. 168.

labor market is a scarcity of good jobs; hence the crucial assignment for public policy is to create such jobs.

By contrast, the most basic form of the neoclassical model argues that labor market success is determined on the basis of marginal productivity and that marginal productivity is a function of an individual's abilities and skills, *ceteris paribus.* Supposedly, these talents are developed by way of various investments in the individual. Thus, abilities and skills comprise one's stock of human capital. It follows from this theory that labor market disadvantage reflects low productivity, which can be seen as deficiencies in human capital. It is implicit within this framework that factors that improve the stock of human capital enhance the probability of labor market success.

In the dual hypothesis, however, the provision of skills by education and training is unnecessary in many cases, because large numbers of workers in the secondary sector already possess the human capital they need; what they need is access to good jobs. Formal training as such possesses little immediate market value. Market value accrues on the job and is vested in the job. Education, so the argument runs, reflects only a screening device or a certificate of the set of attitudes and traits that employers find attractive.[62]

In the light of the above, let us next examine a number of possible tests of the dualist hypothesis. These can be classified into the following groups:

1. The possible existence of bimodality in the distribution of the "goodness" of jobs among individuals.

2. The possibility that schooling might be a more profitable investment for those populating the primary sector relative to those belonging to the secondary sector.

3. The possibility that those in the secondary sector of the labor market may not be able to move to the primary sector.

With respect to individual wages, the dualist's principal hypothesis is that a polarization of the labor market exists. Unfortunately, the theory does not provide an operational definition of good and bad jobs. Empirical dichotomization does not exist without such a definition; so the boundary drawn between primary and secondary sectors is necessarily arbitrary. In addition to the problem of establishing criteria for determining in advance what assigns a worker to either sector, there is also the issue of what degree of bimodality is sufficient to justify the dual label. Wachter has rejected the cross-section bimodality test of the dualist hypothesis by pointing to near-normal shaped distributions of wages and earnings.[63] Having devised alternative methods for weighing the goodness of jobs, Freiman for the United States and

---

62. See, for example, L. Thurow, *Generating Inequality* (New York: Basic Books, 1975), chaps. 4 and 5.
63. M. L. Wachter, "The Primary and Secondary Labor Market Mechanism: A Critique of the Dual Approach," *Brookings Papers on Economic Activity* 3 (1974): 652–653.

Psacharopoulos for the United Kingdom arrive at the same conclusion.[64]

If polarization does exist, are the two sectors governed by distinct processes of wage determination? As we have earlier seen, the dualists argue that human capital is largely irrelevant in the secondary sector. Employers in this sector, anticipating higher turnover, hire workers without much prior screening and provide little subsequent on-the-job training. Hence, individual wages are not a function of the individual characteristics of the worker. Moreover, because promotion is rare and high-wage employment impossible to find, secondary workers exhibit a flat profile of earnings across age groups. The dualist argument is, then, that the two markets have different wage processes because the primary sector rewards human capital, whereas the secondary sector does not—subject to the screening hypothesis mentioned above.

Typically, regression equations have been run for each sector to test the similarity of the wage determination process in the two sectors. In general, it has been found that the wage equation for the secondary sector differs somewhat from the wage equation that describes the primary sector.[65] In particular, human capital, as measured by years of education, seems to be less significant for wages in the secondary sector. This has been taken as evidence of segmentation.

However, in the absence of a better criterion of who belongs to what sector, the usual method of division is according to earnings; the sample is truncated on the values of the dependent variable. Unfortunately, this very procedure ensures that the effect of, say, schooling on earnings is less in the lower segment because the high values of the dependent variable are cut off. This important statistical limitation is shown in figure 5.3, where we observe that truncation of the dependent variable ensures that the regression relation between education and earnings will be lessened. This can be explained if we realize that splitting the sample into two segments amounts to standardizing for occupation. Whatever truncation criterion one adopts, the upper segment is bound to contain the highly paid occupations, and the lower segment will contain the low-paid occupations. Standardizing for occupation in an earnings function understates the return to schooling for the simple reason that it denies the effect of schooling on earnings via changes in occupation (see chapter 4.)

As for the third test of duality, namely the extent of socioeconomic mobility, the evidence is again not favorable to the strict dualist hypothesis.

64. M. P. Freiman, "Empirical Tests of Dual Labor Market Theory and Hedonic Measures of Occupational Attainment" (Ph.D. diss., University of Wisconsin, 1976); G. Psacharopoulos, "Labor Market Duality and Income Distribution: The Case of the U.K." (Centre for the Economics of Education, London School of Economics and Political Science, February 1977).
65. See, for example, B. Harrison, "Education and Underemployment in the Urban Ghetto," *American Economic Review* 62 (1972): 796–812; H. M. Wachtel and C. Betsey, "Employment at Low Wages," *Review of Economics and Statistics* 54 (1972): 121–129; P. Osterman, "An Empirical Study of Labor Market Segmentation," *Industrial and Labor Relations Review* 28 (1975): 508–523.

Figure 5.3   The Regression of Earnings on Schooling, With and Without Truncated Earnings

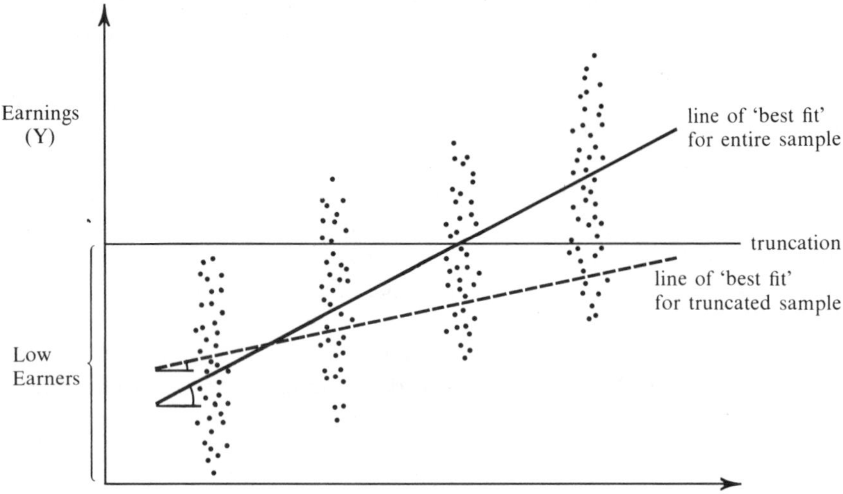

Years of Schooling Completed

We have earlier considered the question of intergenerational mobility (section 5.4) and noted that there exists an appreciable amount of mobility from one generation to the next. With regard to intragenerational mobility, Freiman and Leigh have tested various mobility hypotheses for workers classified by race, previous wage, previous industry and occupation, and other characteristics.[66] They find no support for immobility across variously defined boundaries for low-wage and black workers. Also, Andrisani, using data from the National Longitudinal Survey with respect to the cohort of males aged fourteen to twenty-four in 1966, finds that although a substantial number of white and black youth began their labor market careers in secondary-type jobs—43% of the white youth and 64% of the black youth—only 17% and 36%, respectively, remained in such jobs by 1968.[67] These findings are hardly suggestive of impenetrable boundaries between sectors, although there are substantial racial differences.

There is also the question of how impervious labor market segmentation is to investments in human capital. Andrisani examines the contribution of human capital to improving the chances of beginning a career in a primary-type job and to upward mobility of a career commenced in a secondary-type job. His regression estimates are presented in table 5.3. Among blacks and whites, it can be seen that investments in human capital, as

66. Freiman, "Empirical Tests of Dual Labor Market Theory;" D. E. Leigh, "Occupational Advancement in the Late 1960s: An Indirect Test of the Dual Labor Market Hypothesis," *Journal of Human Resources* 11 (1976): 155–171.
67. P. J. Andrisani, "Discrimination, Segmentation, and Upward Mobility: A Longitudinal Approach to the Dual Labor Market Theory," mimeographed (Philadelphia, Pa.: Department of Economics, Temple University, 1976).

**Table 5.3 The Likelihood of a Primary First Job and the Likelihood
of Secondary-to-Primary Job Mobility, by Race**

Independent Variable	Likelihood of a Primary First Job[a]		Likelihood of Secondary-to-Primary Mobility[b]	
	Whites	Blacks	Whites	Blacks
9–11 years of schooling	14.16 (2.22)*	9.45 (1.77)	36.28 (3.80)*	−11.59 (1.02)
12 years of schooling	35.27 (5.10)*	17.33 (3.06)*	36.99 (3.73)*	7.93 (0.62)
13+ years of schooling	59.95 (8.26)*	24.66 (2.65)*	47.64 (3.75)*	−3.45 (0.17)
I.Q.	3.15 (0.85)	12.43 (1.39)	12.65 (2.13)*	−0.77 (0.05)
Years of work experience (age − years of schooling − 5)	c	c	1.89 (1.78)*	−0.21 (0.15)
Labor market entry post-1964	−1.69 (0.50)	14.41 (3.29)*	c	c
Non-South	1.11 (0.33)	10.59 (2.48)*	1.93 (0.37)	37.11 (4.30)*
Constant	11.26 (1.72)*	0.94 (0.16)	19.55 (1.46)	40.15 (2.19)*
$\bar{R}^2$	0.123	0.121	0.083	0.183

Notes:

$|t|$ is given in parentheses

a dependent variable = 1 if respondent has first job in primary sector, 0 otherwise

b dependent variable = 1 if respondent shifted from secondary to primary sector from time of first job, 0 if respondent started and remained in secondary sector

c explanatory variable not included in regression

* significant at 5% level

Source:

P. J. Andrisani, "Discrimination, Segmentation, and Upward Mobility: A Longitudinal Approach to the Dual Labor Market," mimeographed (Philadelphia, Pa.: Department of Economics, Temple University, 1976), Table 3, p. 22.

embodied in the first five variables, increase the likelihood that young men will be in primary rather than secondary jobs. Among both race groups, years of schooling, for example, has a strong, positive, and monotonic effect upon entry into the primary sector at the time of initial entry into the labor market. In addition, the access of black youth to the primary sector at the time of initial entry into the labor market also appears strongly affected by the overall level of demand for labor (picked up by the dummy variable "labor market entry post-1964"). Those black youth whose first jobs occurred when the labor market was tightening were thus over 14 percentage points more likely to find a primary-type job than a secondary one.[68]

It is true that while initial access to the primary sector is linked to the schooling of black workers, the link is less close for black youth than for white youth. Completing high school raises the probability that a black youth will enter in a primary sector job by about 8 percentage points. Completing high school raises the likelihood of entering the labor market in a primary job by better than 18 percentage points among white youths. Moreover, racial discrimination is strongly in evidence when we consider secondary-to-primary mobility. The upward mobility of blacks appears unrelated to their levels of human capital, in sharp contrast to the close association for whites. Also, vestiges of labor market discrimination against blacks appear to remain deeply entrenched in the South, where a black youth is estimated to be about 11 percentage points less likely to find a primary job first and 37 percentage points less likely to be upwardly mobile out of a secondary first job than his non-South counterpart. These results point unequivocally to the presence of discrimination against blacks. This subject will be considered in more detail in chapter 6. However, we would stress that dualism is not to be taken as synonymous with discrimination. It is also interesting to note that investments in human capital appear to be important in penetrating labor market boundaries even for black workers, for whom the burden of discrimination is clearest.

Alternative test procedures can be devised,[69] but on the balance of the evidence it is difficult to accept an extreme hypothesis of labor market segmentation. It can be said that dualist explanations for the lack of competitive response have added very little to our knowledge of labor market imperfections that were already treated by a series of sub-theories peripheral to the neoclassical core. The dualist analyses emerge as mainly descriptive in content, rather than analytical on the causes of the phenomenon of good and bad jobs and therefore do not qualify as alternative labor market theories. On the positive side, the dualist challenge can be said to have provoked extension of orthodox economic analysis to consideration of new problems.

5.7   Conclusions

Central to the theory of the competitive labor market are numerous well-informed buyers and sellers in the market, ease of entry and exit, free mobility of resources, and lack of collusion. Yet the concept of a competitive labor market has frequently been challenged because these assumptions do

---

68. Respondents whose first job was taken during 1965 or 1966, a tight labor market, were assigned the value of unity, while those with first jobs taken prior to 1965, a looser labor market, were assigned the value of zero.

69. See Wachtel and Betsey, "Employment at Low Wages"; Thurow, *Generating Inequality*, pp. 119 ff.

not appear to be sufficiently realistic. We have attempted to assess the competitive model against the backdrop of observed barriers.

Our discussion began with monopsony. We were able to detect elements of monopsony in the market for nurses and evidence of collusive monopsony in the area of professional sports. At the same time, it was noted that monopsony power may be more potential than real in the sense that it is not exercised actively, and this point was taken up in the analysis of internal labor market structure.

Our interest in monopsony, however, is considerably broader than this, because we are concerned with all factors which impart a positive slope to the supply curve. One such factor is the absence of costless information. Early empirical studies of the questionnaire type appeared to suggest that workers neither possess extensive knowledge of alternative pecuniary and nonpecuniary conditions of employment nor develop that knowledge by systematic job-search activities. However, interpretation of attitudes uncovered by questionnaires is fraught with difficulty. In any case, it is necessary to recognize that information has a cost, principally the opportunity cost of a worker's time. This means the search for information will be of limited duration, that not all wage offers will be identified, and that some wage dispersion will result. Modifying the competitive model by dropping the assumption of perfect information thus enables us to extend the predictive reach of the model.

It is also necessary to consider job changing at a more aggregated level, so as to establish whether the evidence in the form of the outcome of events is in conformity with the predictions of the competitive model. Analysis of labor mobility by industry, occupation, and region points to the importance of differential economic advantage in job changing. Further, analyses of labor turnover by industry report a consistently negative association between turnover and wage level, which suggests that the existing level of earnings has an important influence on decisions to leave or not to leave a job.

The above considerations led us also to a consideration of the internal labor market. It is generally agreed that the internal labor market consists of a set of structured employment relationships within a firm. The structure embodies a set of rules, either formal or informal, that govern each job and job interrelationships. Many jobs in a given firm will be unique and thus lack an external market. New workers are used to fill entry jobs, while most higher-level positions are filled by promotion from within. Ports of entry— the immediate contact points between internal and external markets—are most likely to be open to the unskilled and to those who have craft-oriented skills. On the basis of the above description, some have claimed that the wage and employment structure of the internal labor market is dominated not by efficiency considerations but by custom and practice. It is possible to argue, however, that the internal labor market is an efficiency-oriented institutional response to the basic market imperfections arising from specific training and the costs of information. Idiosyncratic jobs requiring specific training imply a potential monopsony situation, yet the worker's power is enhanced because the employer faces the prospect of capital loss if specifically trained workers move. This brings about a situation more akin to bilateral monopoly. One important role of the internal labor market could be to neutralize the resultant bargaining. There is also the point that the internal labor market provides a continuous screening mechanism. Credentials acquired elsewhere are evaluated at the hiring point; thereafter, an internal market is likely to be an efficient apparatus for collecting and analyzing data on individual performance in technologies that require specific training.

The concept of the internal labor market is closely related to the dualist thesis of labor market dualism. In the secondary sector, it is argued, jobs are sufficiently plentiful to employ all available workers, but they are low paying, unstable, and generally unattractive. Workers are barred from the primary sector not so much by their lack of human capital as by the institutional restraints on the demand side and by a basic dearth of good jobs. The lack of good jobs results from the primary sector consisting of a series of highly structured internal labor markets. However, the empirical evidence does not support a strict dualist division between primary and secondary sectors. Mobility between the two sectors exists, and the wage structure shows no evidence of bipolarization. Nor is there evidence that the underlying process determining wages and employment behavior in the two sectors differs. Positive elements in the dualist thesis, however, include the stress that has been put on the institutional factors impeding mobility, especially those falling under the heading of internal labor markets, and on the presence of feedback effects, whereby workers in the secondary market adopt unstable work patterns.

APPENDIX 5-A
THE RESERVATION WAGE

Consider the case of a worker who has been dismissed or laid off from his present employment. He is now in a position to search for job information—it being assumed that he can always find a job if he is willing to accept anything, *ceteris paribus*. The rational worker will logically formulate a reservation wage, below which he will reject all job offers. To estimate the magnitude of the reservation wage, we will make the following simplifying assumptions:[1]

1. The worker has full knowledge of the probability distribution of wage offers.
2. The worker is risk-neutral, and thus seeks to maximize the mathematical expectation of his wealth position.
3. The worker receives total unemployment compensation of U_b per period.
4. The wage distribution is time invariant.

It follows from item 2 that the reservation wage should be set so as to maximize the expected wealth position of the worker. Thus, the reservation wage must be such that the expected wage position to be realized by remaining unemployed as long as wage offers are below the reservation wage is equal to the present value of accepting the reservation wage.

The present value of accepting the reservation wage, W_r, is:

$$\sum_{t=0}^{\infty} \frac{W_r}{(1+i)^t} = \frac{W_r(1+i)}{i}. \tag{5-A.1}$$

The expected net worth of remaining unemployed until receiving a wage offer equal to or better than W_r is:

---

1. For an analysis that relaxes the restrictive assumptions of the present model, see Lippman and McCall, "The Economics of Job Search."

$$U_b + \sum_{t=1}^{\infty} \frac{H(\widehat{W})}{(1 + i)^t}$$

$$+ (1 - \pi)\left(\frac{U_b}{1 + i}\right) + (1 - \pi) \sum_{t=2}^{\infty} \frac{H(\widehat{W})}{(1 + i)^t}$$

$$+ (1 - \pi)^2 \left(\frac{U_b}{1 + i} + \frac{U_b}{(1 + i)^2}\right) + (1 - \pi)^2 \sum_{t=3}^{\infty} \frac{H(\widehat{W})}{(1 + i)^t}$$

$$+ (1 - \pi)^3 \left[\frac{U_b}{1 + i} + \frac{U_b}{(1 + i)^2} + \frac{U_b}{(1 + i)^3}\right]$$

$$+ (1 - \pi)^3 \sum_{t=4}^{\infty} \frac{H(\widehat{W})}{(1 + i)^t} + \cdots \qquad (5\text{-}A.2)$$

where i = the rate of discount;

π = the probability of accepting a job offer in any one period—that is,
$\pi = \int_{W_r}^{\infty} f(\widehat{W})\, d\widehat{W}$, where $f(\widehat{W})$ is the probability distribution of wage offers;

$H(\widehat{W}) = \int_{W_r}^{\infty} \widehat{W} f(\widehat{W}) d\widehat{W}$—that is, the expected wage conditional on W_r.

With a known distribution of wage offers, the probability of a wage offer equal to or better than W_r is easily obtained, as can be seen in figure 5-A.1. Equation (5-A.2) simplifies to:

$$\frac{U_b(1 + i)}{i + \pi} + \frac{H(\widehat{W})(1 + i)}{i(i + \pi)}. \qquad (5\text{-}A.3)$$

Thus, the optimal reservation wage has the following property:

$$\frac{W_r(1 + i)}{i} = \frac{U_b(1 + i)}{i + \pi} + \frac{H(\widehat{W})(1 + i)}{i(i + \pi)}. \qquad (5\text{-}A.4)$$

Multiplying through by $i/(1 + i)$ gives:

$$W_r = \frac{i U_b + H(\widehat{W})}{i + \pi}. \qquad (5\text{-}A.5)$$

Note that the optimum reservation wage will be higher as unemployment compensation is higher and as the mean of the probability distribution of wage offers is higher. It can also be seen that unemployment in this model has the nature of an investment decision, making it negatively related to the real rate of discount.

Figure 5-A.1 The Probability of Accepting a Job Offer

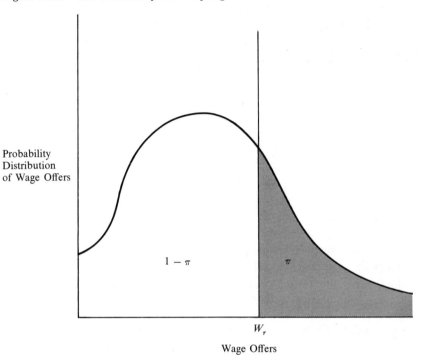

Probability
Distribution
of Wage Offers

$1 - \pi$

π

W_r

Wage Offers

CHAPTER 6
DISCRIMINATION IN
LABOR MARKETS

6.1 Introduction

Certain aspects of discrimination, as it related to investment in human capital, were considered in chapter 4. We found evidence of unequal opportunity in the acquisition of schooling, though there seemed broad similarity in the rate of return to schooling once such schooling had been acquired. In chapter 5, moving on to black workers, we pointed to elements of racial discrimination in limiting the access of black youth to primary sector jobs at the start of their careers and in reducing the probability of secondary-to-primary sector mobility once in the market. Here, we shall attempt a more thorough-going analysis of discrimination as it operates against blacks and female workers. Our emphasis will again be upon differences in earnings and occupations, leaving discussion of the effects of discrimination upon unemployment to chapter 11.

In seeking to establish why one group, say blacks, has lower earnings than another, say whites, it is useful to keep the following schema in mind. Average earnings differ as between the two groups because:

1. Blacks have less access than do whites to productivity augmenting opportunities such as schooling.

2. Blacks occupy less favorable jobs than do whites, for a given set of qualifications such as education and experience. In this case, if tastes for jobs do not differ and if differences in qualifications have been properly allowed for, we observe *employment discrimination*.

3. Blacks receive lower pay given the job. This reflects *wage discrimination* if similar jobs are in fact being compared.

These categories are useful in analyzing antidiscrimination policy. The lower education of blacks is mainly a result of conditions facing them prior to labor market entry. Higher education funding for blacks—or different syllabuses, in the case of women—would be the most important policy instrument here and as such would be the responsibility of government. Measures to counter discrimination in the market would be of limited effect, although we do not seek to deny that anticipated market discrimination deters individuals from investing in education. On the other hand, the final two categories specifically relate to postentry discrimination. They point to a need for measures to open up job opportunities for blacks, or enforcing equal pay, or both. Nevertheless, the first problem is to reach a judgment as to the reasons and importance of preentry discrimination. Using conclusions reached in such an investigation, we can then proceed to assess the importance of labor market discrimination.

It seems certain that market discrimination has in the past operated against women in both the United States and Great Britain and, in particular, against blacks in the former country. For discrimination to occur within a competitive market, it is sufficient that certain groups in society exhibit a taste for discrimination. A theory predicated on tastes has been developed by Becker.[1] However, Becker's approach begs the question of what determines these tastes and, moreover, ignores noncompetitive supply-side elements associated with the exercise of power by trade unions and professional associations. Thus, an alternative theoretical position would be to argue that certain types of discrimination occur because the discriminators profit from such practices. The important case in question is collusion, whereby trade union members combine to raise their pay by barring entry to certain groups. However, even where collusion is absent, it can be income maximizing to discriminate for informational reasons. Thus, if employers cannot readily assess job applicants' qualifications, they might use sex or color as a supplementary, inexpensive text. Accordingly, to the extent that some members of the lower productivity group do not possess the characteristics of the stereotype, they will be discriminated against. This source of discrimination becomes more important if the stereotype is actually incorrect, as is likely when the motivations and labor force participation rates of certain groups, such as married women, are rapidly changing.

Such theories are considered in more detail in section 6.2. In section 6.3, we examine empirical findings concerning the magnitude of discrimination and its possible contributory factors. An analysis of antidiscrimination policies is presented in section 6.4.

6.2 Theory of Economic Discrimination

Becker's pioneering treatment of discrimination focuses on wage discrimination. It can be shown that a wage difference can arise in competitive circumstances between blacks and whites in a given job if whites have a distaste for working alongside or associating with blacks. This, like any other taste, determines market behavior in conjunction with relative prices, given utility maximization.

1. G. S. Becker, *The Economics of Discrimination,* 2nd ed. (Chicago: University of Chicago Press, 1971).

In noncompetitive circumstances, where power can be exerted, the taste for discrimination concept is inappropriate. In such circumstances, one group can collude in discriminating against others and thereby raise the income of its membership. In this case, the taste to discriminate cannot be taken as an independent determinant of rational economic behavior. Rather, it is a consequence of such behavior and is thus endogenously determined. For example, it is likely to be to the pecuniary advantage of Southern whites (or males in trade unions) to restrict access of blacks to education (or females to apprenticeships). In so doing, whites (or males) are improving their job opportunities and thus their incomes. Such behavior follows from economic motives, not dislike or prejudice.

Inferior provision of schooling and formal training for blacks, together with discrimination in access to jobs, are not based primarily on action by individuals. They are to a great extent the result of governmental and trade union actions. Consequently, in these areas, a power theory of discrimination would be relevant. Nevertheless, some discriminatory practices in hiring are likely to be the result of a lack of information on the part of both employers and workers and are not the result of collusion. Thus, an informational theory of discrimination has a part to play. As for enduring wage differentials, given the job, a tastes theory might also be relevant if it can be shown that there are competitive pressures acting on employers. In these circumstances, if the least costly labor for a given job is not employed, it is plausible to hypothesize that this is because of nonpecuniary disadvantages, as reflected in tastes, associated with this labor.

Unequal Schooling.   Different groups can have unequal levels of schooling for two reasons. On the supply side, there might be discrimination in the provision of public funds. On the demand side, a group might face a lower return to given amounts of schooling and so decide to invest less. Among the reasons here could be expectations of future discrimination once in the market and, for females, expectations of future family commitments.[2]

In the context of discrimination in the provision of funds, experience in the United States would suggest that there has been and continues to be inferior public provision for schooling blacks.[3] There is to some degree a taste element here, because white teachers apparently prefer to teach white children. Given that these teachers are on the average more experienced and therefore better paid than their black counterparts, greater expenditure per white pupil results.[4] However, teacher/pupil ratios and physical plant are

2. In equilibrium, these demand-side factors will only cause differences in the amount of schooling among groups and not differences in the rate of return to schooling. The latter should be determined mainly by the cost of funds for the relevant group (chapter 4).

3. For the earlier period, see G. Myrdal, *The American Dilemma* (New York: Harper and Row, 1962), p. 1271; for the later period, see J. D. Owen, "The Distribution of Educational Resources in Large American Cities," *Journal of Human Resources* 7 (1972): 30.

4. Owen, "The Distribution of Educational Resources," p. 36.

also relatively unfavorable in black schools, and this points to an overall lack of concern for black schooling.

Researchers have often pointed to the connection between this lack of concern for the education of black Americans and the fact that blacks have historically been unable to exercise their voting rights.[5] It should be remembered that even today blacks are greatly underrepresented in most state legislatures.[6] If a group cannot vote, we would not generally expect its interests to be much taken into account in the formulation of public policy. Whites have therefore had more power than blacks and would appear to have exercised that power to limit black schooling expenditures.

It is tempting to conclude that such collusion by whites has in fact been income maximizing for the white group. Certainly Myrdal had no doubts; he wrote of blacks being "robbed."[7] However, there is at least the possibility that education discrimination against blacks, by associating capital with whites at the lower end of the ability distribution, actually lowers the absolute income level of the white group even as it raises it relative to blacks. In other words, elimination of discrimination in education funding would cause an increase in total wealth that would more than compensate those whites whose income was thereby reduced. That discrimination has persisted, however, could be explained in terms of its benefits being certain for some groups of whites, although its compensation is uncertain. However, opportunities for this particular form of discrimination are likely to be narrowing as blacks take up their votes, helped by legislation such as the 1965 Voting Rights Act.

Combining the supply and demand sides, we would expect much lower investment in education by blacks than whites. However, there seems little reason to expect much difference in the respective rates of return to education, because supply restrictions are likely to be offset by the lower productivity of black schooling. Females, on the other hand, would appear to enjoy much the same access to schooling as males. This is to be expected given that they have long possessed equal voting rights.[8] However, because the productivity of their schooling is likely to be lower than that of males, we would expect to observe in equilibrium a lower female investment in schooling and thus a lower rate of return, *ceteris paribus*. An important implication of the power model is that augmented political power for black Americans should,

---

5. See, for example, R. B. Freeman, "Decline of Labor Market Discrimination and Economic Analysis," *American Economic Review,* Papers and Proceedings 63 (1973): 286.
6. See H. Walton, *Black Politics—A Theoretical and Structural Analysis* (Philadelphia, Pa.: Lippincott, 1972), p. 199.
7. Myrdal, *American Dilemma,* p. 341.
8. Differences in syllabuses there certainly are, but it is hard to see how this may be construed as a consequence of male power as Madden would have us believe. See J. F. Madden, "Discrimination—A Manifestation of Male Market Power?" in C. B. Lloyd, ed., *Sex Discrimination and the Division of Labor* (New York and London: Columbia University Press, 1975), p. 159. Women could, if they wished, presumably use their voting power to bring about identical courses for both sexes, as is the case in Sweden.

both by causing more equal funding of schooling and by increasing its productivity via lower employment discrimination, increase their schooling level relative to that of whites. However, no such implication follows in the case of women.

Factors Affecting Employment, Given Schooling. Differences in the pattern of employment among groups are explained in part by differences in the amount of education. For a variety of reasons, the better schooled are likely to be employed in the higher grade jobs. It might be because of the skills imparted by education, or because of education's socializing effects (for example, in improving perseverance), or even perhaps because some employers can afford to indulge a taste for educated employees. Whatever the reason, a positive correlation between schooling and earnings must exist if education is to pay its way as an investment and if people are to continue to come forward to be trained. However, the pattern of employment is clearly affected by other forces. The most important of these can be said to be power factors, as when unions enforce direct barriers to entering certain occupations, supply-side differences in motivation and/or job preferences, particularly between men and women, informational factors or role stereotyping, and crowding effects which result from disadvantaged groups moving from occupations where job barriers and wage discrimination are relatively high to those occupations where such factors are low.

First, consider the question of direct barriers, leaving aside for the moment the matter of their identification. The important issue is whether such barriers can be said to arise from a taste or from collusive action based on economic incentives. In the latter case, it is necessary to determine who gains, who loses, and who might thus require compensation, or careful policing, in the event of discrimination being outlawed. The points can be illustrated using Becker's well-known trade model of discrimination.[9] In this model, a labor-rich black sector and a capital-rich white sector are envisaged as trading capital. Discrimination takes the form of a reduction in white capital "exports." White unions, for example, could be interpreted as limiting, via restrictions on training and promotion, the amount of capital invested in blacks by firms.

The model assumes that both sectors have similar production functions, that there is only one commodity, and that only white capital is traded. It is also assumed that whites collect the return on capital exported to the black sector, that is, all capital is privately owned. Becker supposes that whites are interested not in the money but in the *net* return on capital, defined as the money return minus the disbenefits felt from associating white capital with blacks. Capitalists will then demand that the net (=money) return on domestic capital equal the net return on exported capital. Note, however, that both returns will be lower than the money return on exported capital by

---

9. Becker, *Economics of Discrimination,* chap. 2.

the amount needed to offset the taste for discrimination. The white sector's net income, $Y(W)$, will therefore be

$$Y(W) = (c + c_t)\frac{\partial f}{\partial K}(K = c, L_W) + L_W\frac{\partial f}{\partial L_W}(K = c, L_W)$$

where c_W is total white owned capital;
  c is capital retained in the white sector;
  c_t is capital exported to the black sector, $c_W = c + c_t$; and
  L_W is white labor.

There is a similar expression for total black net ($=$money) income. However, white money income, $Y'(W)$, is derived by supposing that domestic (exported) capital receives the marginal product of capital in the white (black) sector. That is,

$$Y'(W) = c\frac{\partial f}{\partial K}(K = c, L_W) + c_t\frac{\partial f}{\partial K}(K = c_t + c_n, L_n)$$

$$+ L_W\frac{\partial f}{\partial L_W}(K = c, L_W) \qquad (6.2)$$

where c_n is black-owned capital; and
  L_n is black labor.

  Discrimination in this model is expressed by reducing white capital exports. It can be shown that (1) white workers' money ($=$ net) income is reduced by a decrease in discrimination, (2) white capitalists' net income increases steadily with decreases in discrimination, and (3) white capitalists' money income will eventually fall off with decreases in discrimination, reaching a maximum when there is no discrimination (that is, when the marginal product of capital is equal in both societies). To establish these points the reader should consult appendix 6-A. Consequently, while total white *net* income is reduced by an increase in discrimination (implying that the burden falls on whites),[10] total *money* income can actually be increased up to a point by discriminating against blacks. This implies that there is a motive for collusion. These relationships are shown in figure 6.1, where B denotes the zero discrimination point and A gives the white money income maximizing point.

  In line with the tastes hypothesis of discrimination, if capital exports were restricted so that point A were attained, then presumably capitalists would be paying for this discriminatory behavior. Alternatively, it may be argued that white workers force capitalists to lower exports of capital, thereby raising the incomes of white workers. The latter argument appears the more plausible.[11]

10. This is the point made by Becker, ibid., p. 34.
11. Given that whites have dominated government and given that white workers are in the majority, it is probable that their interests would prevail in formulation of legislation.

Figure 6.1   Effects of White Capital Exports on White Sector Income

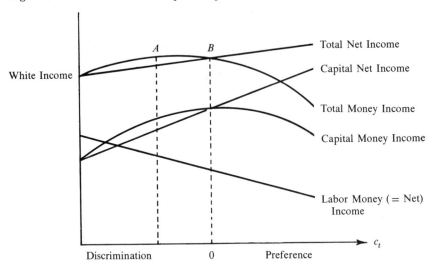

Moreover, it appears that the gains of white workers would exceed the losses of capitalists, so that there would be scope for trading. Also, craft unions and professional associations are likely to have provided an institution supplementary to the voting system for colluding against blacks and putting pressure upon employers.[12] The power hypothesis has clear empirical implications. We would expect employment and education discrimination against black Americans to have declined over time as black political power has increased. And we would expect craft unions and professional associations to be major sources of discrimination in employment, for the simple reason that they have a strong economic motivation for so acting.[13]

The applicability of the trade model as regards employment discrimination against women is more questionable on the face of it.[14] We would not normally regard females and males as forming separate societies. Consequently, there is much less likelihood of an overall discriminatory system operating against females; they do, after all, possess equal political power. Nevertheless, unions and professional associations do provide an institutional framework for collusion against women, as against blacks, and for the same economic reasons.

12. The same cannot be said of industrial unions, which rely on extensive organization and the strike threat rather than restriction of entry.
13. To the extent that the benefits of discrimination to union or association members have been capitalized (in the form of entry fees and income foregone while waiting to join the occupation), we should note that a sudden removal of discrimination would cause genuine hardship. On the other hand, to the extent that entry has depended upon nepotism, the removal of discrimination would simply involve the elimination of monopoly gains.
14. For a criticism, see J. F. Madden, *The Economics of Sex Discrimination* (Lexington, Mass.: Heath, 1973), chap. 4.

The problem of assessing employment discrimination against women is not so much one of estimating the benefit obtained by men from its application, but one of judging the impact of supply-side differences in motivation and/or job preference. Without knowledge of the latter, we can only loosely assess the extent of employment discrimination. The problem is of major importance with respect to married women, whose labor force participation differs markedly from that of men over the life cycle.

Research in human capital theory is currently developing hypotheses which assist our understanding of the impact of supply-side differences. One such hypothesis is that withdrawal from the labor force for extended periods results in an accelerated depreciation of schooling and postschooling investments. Support for the hypothesis is indicated by earnings functions that are segmented to take account of discontinuities in labor force participation.[15] An implication of this analysis is that women who expect to be absent from the labor force for either long or frequent intervals will elect to invest less than males in on-the-job training. They will present themselves for occupations in which training is less important or, looked at from another perspective, in which the penalty for intermittent participation is lowest.[16] This human capital oriented reasoning leads to the expectation that women will be less well represented in professional and managerial jobs for reasons of income maximizing choice—quite apart from possible discrimination in hiring or promotion practices. Another implication of this hypothesis is that the job opportunities of single women, while similar to those of men, will differ markedly from those of married women, because the root of the supply-side difference is assumed to be the differential family care commitment of married women.

Informational theories of employment discrimination similarly interpret discrimination to be an income maximizing behavioral activity. Unlike the power theories, however, they apply also in competitive circumstances in which power cannot be exerted. The theories derive from the fact that employers have very imperfect information about the potential productivity of job applicants.[17] They will nevertheless have some idea, from past experience, of the probability distribution of productivity across individuals with given characteristics such as education, color, sex, and marital status. Employers must therefore act as statisticians and develop decision-rules, which

15. See J. Mincer and S. W. Polachek, "Family Investments in Human Capital: Earnings of Women," *Journal of Political Economy* 82 (1974): S76–S108.

16. S. W. Polachek, "Occupational Segregation Against Women: A Human Capital Approach," mimeographed (Toronto, Ontario: Third World Conference of the Econometrics Society, 1975), p. 7.

17. G. J. Stigler, "Information in the Labor Market," *Journal of Political Economy* 70 (1962): 102; J. J. McCall, "Racial Discrimination in the Labor Market—The Role of Information and Job Search," *RM 6162* (Santa Monica, Calif.: The Rand Corporation, 1970), p. 15; M. A. Spence, "Job Market Signalling," *Quarterly Journal of Economics* 87 (1973): 356; D. J. Aigner and G. G. Cain, "Statistical Theories of Discrimination in Labor Markets," *Industrial and Labor Relations Review* 30 (1977): 175–187.

we have earlier termed stereotypes, in an attempt to predict applicants' performance on the basis of easily observable characteristics. If color or sex is well enough correlated with attributes that have a direct bearing on production, such as absenteeism, it will pay the employer to screen job applicants on this basis. This practice will necessarily involve some unjustified discrimination (or favoritism) to particular individuals who are atypical of their group. But it need not entail discrimination on average. This procedure is, indeed, the rational one for the employer to follow.

The stereotypes developed by employers and workers need continual updating in the light of changes in the labor market. Because information about these changes is costly to obtain, the process of updating will never be complete. Consequently, it is quite likely that the empirical rules developed will be outdated and that incorrect or biased decisions will tend on average to be made. This tendency will be exaggerated during periods of rapid change. Nevertheless, we would expect the actors to learn. It has been said that tight labor markets favor minorities via the induced experimentation and revision of stereotypes.[18] The empirical implication of the informational theory is, then, that hiring and promotion policies are likely to be suboptimal over a much wider area than unionized and/or monopolistic firms, particularly with respect to married women whose labor market participation has greatly increased over time. The importance of a general antidiscriminatory policy is correspondingly underlined.[19]

A final factor to consider in the context of occupational composition relates to the labor flows which result from wage and employment discrimination. In the next section, we show how one group will be paid less than another for equal work in certain circumstances. Such discrimination will not be uniform across occupations and industries—it is likely to be lower in competitive industries—and this will set up equilibrating responses in the labor force. Disadvantaged groups will avoid high wage discrimination jobs and those jobs with high entry barriers, and will crowd into occupations where discrimination is less intense. As a result, better qualified blacks (and females) will be channeled into a given range of jobs. In turn, some of the less qualified blacks, who are thereby excluded from those jobs, will be "bumped down" to the next rung of the occupational ladder, and so on. Many workers will thus tend to be crowded on the bottom rungs.

Differences in Pay, Given the Job.   Wage differences in a given job are likely to be interestablishment rather than intraestablishment, with disadvantaged

18. McCall, "Racial Discrimination," p. 19.
19. There is currently much interest in determining the extent to which hiring practices are suboptimal. Additional interest in this area might also be occasioned by the possibility that stereotypes, once established, are difficult to change because they tend to be self-confirming. This leads to the labor market segmentation hypotheses of radical theorists (see M. Reich, D. M. Gordon, and R. C. Edwards, "A Theory of Labor Market Segmentation," *American Economic Review* 63 (1973): 359).

groups tending to be confined to the lower-paying firms. Nevertheless, we must consider this topic, which has traditionally been the focus of discrimination studies and which has seemed to evoke most lay discussion. It is worth noting that some areas in which discrimination is most intense, such as the craft occupations, ban all differentiation in pay because this would lead to undercutting. This is one reason why minorities are poorly represented in such areas: if a wage differential is required in equilibrium, measures to eliminate that differential will result in the minority losing employment. Craft insistence upon a common rate will have this very effect.

However, consider the situation in which one worker receives less pay than another for performing a given job. The question now arises: what prevents individual employers hiring the relatively inexpensive labor, thereby bidding up its pay and eliminating the differential? We can look for the answer on the demand side by considering in turn the actions of employers, fellow workers, and consumers. It is also necessary to consider the supply side—in particular, the likely lower supply elasticity of women than men.

In the first place, an employer might prefer to hire whites. This will raise his costs but, if he has a nontransferable monopoly, other employers with a lower taste for discrimination will be unable to undersell him or buy him out. Accordingly, wage discrimination will not be progressively eliminated in this circumstance. Even if there is competition in the product market, however, discrimination might still be an equilibrium phenomenon. This would be the case were nondiscriminatory firms unable to hire all of the available black labor; that is, if diminishing returns to scale prevented the nondiscriminatory firms from expanding indefinitely, leaving a residual of blacks to be hired by discriminatory firms. Central to this model is the implication that the greater is the number of blacks, the greater will be the wage discrimination. Also, it is predicted that wage discrimination will be higher in monopolistic industries than in competitive industries, because employers in the former sector will have most leeway to indulge or gratify their tastes.[20] Discrimination should be lowest for the self-employed, *ceteris paribus*.

Let us now turn to the employee taste for discrimination model. Although we might consider this to be a rather more plausible approach, there is the initial objection to be entered that such discrimination is more likely to be income maximizing than resulting from taste factors. In any event, let us suppose that a group of employees have, for some reason, an objection to blacks (or women) being employed either alongside them or alongside them and in complementary grades. In this situation, mixed-employment will be more costly to the employer because of consequent work discontinuities within the plant. In terms of the former, the cost minimizing employer would presumably respond by segregating blacks and whites and the end result would be zero wage discrimination. In terms of the latter, however, segrega-

20. See A. A. Alchian and R. S. Kessel, "Competition, Monopoly and the Pursuit of Money," *Aspects of Labor Economics* (Princeton, N.J.: Princeton University Press, 1962), p. 162.

tion will be impossible because, if blacks are underrepresented in the skilled grades and whites are underrepresented in the unskilled grades, as is indeed likely, the two groups will be complementary. The end result will be that blacks are employed alongside whites and will have to discount the extra trouble they cause the employer by accepting lower wages for a given job.[21] If the objections of whites become more strident as a greater number of blacks are employed, this model will lead to a direct relation between wage discrimination and the proportion of blacks employed, as in the model involving an employer taste for discrimination. It is also likely that discrimination will be pronounced in monopolistic firms, because white workers are less likely to jeopardize their jobs by pressuring management not to employ blacks. But there is a further implication of this model, one which does not arise with the employer taste model. This relates to *inequality* in the earnings distribution of white workers, given the job. If white workers do indeed discriminate, the variance of white earnings for given levels of education and experience should increase with the proportion of blacks in the labor force. Simply put, the higher that proportion, the more likely are whites to be working with blacks and thus the higher the wage premium.[22]

The third proposition is that white consumers are willing to pay more for goods sold—or, in the extreme, made—by whites. This directly lowers the marginal revenue product curve of nonwhites in the same way as would lower motivation, such as might be induced by a lack of promotion possibilities. Discrimination of this type is more likely to prevail in service jobs, which will consequently tend to be populated by individuals who possess the same color characteristics as their clients. A wage differential will result, given that whites can afford to pay more for services than blacks. Unfortunately, many of the jobs offering opportunities for self-employment—which we have earlier argued permit incumbents to evade employer (or worker) discrimination—are located within the service trades and are thus likely to experience consumer discrimination. This confounds empirical attempts to distinguish between the two hypotheses in this area.

Finally, there is an additional factor for women, unconnected with tastes for discrimination, which could give rise to wage differentials within a given job. Women are likely to be more inelastic in supply to a given firm than are males. The principal reason for this is that women tend to search for jobs in closer proximity to the home because of their differential family care commitment.[23] The relevance of greater inelasticity of supply is that women will

21. For a model, see K. J. Arrow, "Some Mathematical Models of Race in the Labor Market," in A. H. Pascal, ed., *Racial Discrimination in Economic Life* (Lexington, Mass.: Heath, 1972), pp. 188 ff.; Becker, *Economics of Discrimination,* p. 59.
22. See B. R. Chiswick, "Racial Discrimination in the Labor Market—A Test of Alternative Hypotheses," in G. M. von Furstenberg et al., *Patterns of Racial Discrimination* (Lexington, Mass.: Heath, 1974), p. 113.
23. A contributory factor could also be that women in a given occupation are less subject to negotiated wage minima than are men; again, this is less true of blacks, who are as highly unionized as whites in the United States.

be more subject to monopsony than men and, accordingly, will receive lower wages in equilibrium.[24] This line of argument also permits a distinction to be made between married and single women, because the latter are likely to be more elastic in supply than the former.

Thus far, we have been comparing workers in the "same" job, that is, assuming full adjustment for differences in qualifications and motivation. In practice, however, we can rarely adjust for differences in absenteeism or quit behavior. We next show that such differences are unlikely to explain much of measured wage discrimination. According to human capital theory, the employer will attempt in equilibrium to adjust employment (and thus marginal product) and/or wage rates so as to earn a market rate of return on hiring and training costs, C. Thus, for each employee, we may write

$$C = \sum_{t=0}^{T} (MP - W)\left(\frac{1-s}{1+r}\right)^t \qquad (6.3)$$

where T is the employer's time horizon;
MP is the marginal product;
W is the wage rate;
r is the market rate of discount; and
s is the probability of separation.

If T is large, equation (6.3) becomes

$$C = (MP - W)(1 + r)/(r + s) \qquad (6.3a)$$

Writing corresponding expressions for men and women and equating marginal products, we find[25]

$$W_M - W_F = \frac{C}{1 + r}(s_F - s_M) \qquad (6.4)$$

where subscripts M and F refer to males and females respectively.

We see that the wage differential varies directly with specific investment costs in the job and with the difference in the probability of separation. High absenteeism among women can also be shown to increase the differential. Yet, given plausible values for C and r (say, \$1,000 and 0.06 respectively), differences in separation rates and absenteeism in the range of observed

---

24. See B. Reagan, "Two Supply Curves for Economists?" *American Economic Review* 65 (1975): 100–107; N. M. Gordon and T. E. Morton, "A Low Mobility Model of Wage Discrimination with Special Reference to Sex Differentials," *Journal of Economic Theory* 7 (1974): 241–253.
25. See R. S. Goldfarb and J. Hosek, "Explaining Male-Female Wage Differentials for the 'Same' Job," *Journal of Human Resources* 11 (1976): 99.

values could not account for much more than a difference of about $8.00 in weekly rates of pay, given the job.[26] This value may be compared with differences in the order of $15.00 to $25.00 to be observed in the United States in 1971 for various clerical grades in establishments employing both men and women.[27] For this reason, incomplete standardization is unlikely to be the major factor explaining pay differences within a given job.

6.3   Empirical Analysis of Discrimination

In this section we first consider the entry barriers confronting blacks. Next, we examine evidence relating to the household division of labor, which we have earlier argued to be a factor in female earnings differentials. Finally, we review a number of intra-firm studies in the hope of shedding some light on the rationale behind the hiring and promotion practices of firms and thus on the role of monopsony and informational factors in discrimination.

Evidence Bearing on Entry Barriers Against Blacks.   Black Americans are known to have a much less favorable occupational distribution than their white counterparts. One method of demonstrating this disparity is to compute an index number by weighting the proportion of black workers in each occupational category by a given measure of pay in that category and comparing the result with the corresponding figures for whites.[28] Using 1939 white income weights by category, Becker found that the index number obtained for blacks in Northern states was 77% of that for whites in 1949. The corresponding value in Southern states stood at 65%.[29] This result implies that even if there had been no difference in pay by occupation, blacks would have received only 77% of the income of whites solely because of their relatively unfavorable occupational distribution.

26. Ibid., pp. 100, 103. Note this value is obtained on the maximum assumption that the annual female separation rate is 60% (males, 25%) and that females work 95% of the days worked by males. However, it is possible that the higher average separation rates evinced by females are mainly a consequence of their being employed in the less skilled occupations. In this case, there may be very little difference between the sexes in their separation rates.
27. See J. E. Buckley, "Pay Differences Between Men and Women in the Same Job," *Monthly Labor Review* 94 (1971): table 1, p. 37.
28. That is, we compute

$$\sum_{i=1}^{P} \frac{L_{ni}}{L_n} \cdot W_{wi} \text{ and } \sum_{i=1}^{P} \frac{L_{wi}}{L_w} \cdot W_{wi}$$

where L_i refers to the number working in the ith category ($i = 1, \ldots, P$);
W_{wi} refers to white pay in the ith category; and
n and w are subscripts denoting blacks and whites respectively.

An alternative measure using black pay can also be constructed.
29. Becker, *Economics of Discrimination*, p. 140.

Table 6.1   Percentage of Sons in the Labor Force with a White Collar Occupation, by Father's Occupation, United States, 1962

| | Father's Occupation | | | | | |
| Race | White Collar | | Manual | | Farm | Not Reported |
	Higher	Lower	Higher	Lower		
Non-Negro	69.9	59.4	39.1	37.8	23.5	36.3
Negro	20.1	23.6	15.6	15.0	6.1	8.9

Source:
J. S. Coleman, *Resources for Social Change* (New York: Wiley Interscience, 1971), p. 111.

One important question concerns the extent to which this relatively unfavorable distribution is justified in terms of differences in education and to what extent it is a result of entry barriers in employment. There is clear evidence of widespread entry barriers. Consider, for example, table 6.1. This shows that in the early 1960s, whatever the occupation of the father, blacks had far less chance than did whites of advancing into white-collar jobs. Education appears to help advancement in that the sons of white-collar fathers, who were thus likely to have been better educated, had a significantly better chance than others. Nevertheless, that the chance was so much less for blacks than for whites provides striking evidence of entry barriers operating against the former.

Evidence of employment discrimination against blacks is also available in the United Kingdom context. Experiments have been conducted in which letters of job application were sent out for various white-collar vacancies. The applications purported to come from persons with the same education and experience, but who differed in origin. In the 1969 experiment, it was found that 78% of applicants purporting to be British-born were invited for interview. Corresponding figures for Australian, West Indian and Cypriot, and Asian applicants were 78%, 69%, and 35%, respectively. More recent results conform to a similar pattern, although the position of Asians appears to have been strengthened.[30]

It is more satisfactory, however, to look at all occupations and to provide a numerical measure of the effects of productivity characteristics on relative occupational distributions. Attempts have been made to do this by standardizing for education, which is one of the main characteristics. Standardization takes the form of calculating a hypothetical occupational distribution for the black labor force, on the assumption that blacks have the same chance of entering the various occupations, given education, as do whites with a

30. See, respectively, R. Jowell and P. Prescott-Clark, "Racial Discrimination and White Collar Workers in Britain," *Race* 11 (1970): 467; N. McIntosh and D. J. Smith, *The Extent of Racial Discrimination,* P.E.P. Broadsheet No. 547 (London: Political and Economic Planning, 1975), p. 31.

corresponding education.[31] Some such calculations are presented in table 6.2. It can be seen that urban black males in 1960 were greatly underrepresented, even after adjusting for education, in the managerial, craft, and sales categories, but overrepresented in the service and laborer classifications. Attempts have been made to refine this standardization procedure by allowing for the probability that blacks lag behind whites at school—perhaps requiring twelve years to reach the level of scholastic achievement attained by whites in nine years.[32] The effect of this procedure is shown in the last column of table 6.2, and we observe that most of the ratios move closer to unity. Standardization along these lines clearly leaves much to be desired. However, the marked variation between occupations does lend support to the view that special barriers exist for managerial jobs, where specific training is important, and for craft and sales jobs, indicating union entry barriers and consumer discrimination. Perhaps the poorly paid service and laborer categories absorb blacks bumped down from higher rungs of the occupational ladder.

With respect to the role played by trade unions in this process, we would expect the craft rather than the industrial union to be the more discriminatory. For the former, the ability to raise wages depends more on restriction of entry than on the strike threat, which may be said to require wide organization. Moreover, once a policy of exclusion is adopted, there is an incentive for it to be maintained; otherwise, a capital loss would be sustained by members who had entered the occupation on the expectation of high relative wages.[33]

31. We assume that the proportion of each education group represented in the various occupations will be the same across color groups; that is,

$$L'_{ijk}/L_{jk} = L_{ij}/L_j$$

where L'_{ijk} is the hypothetical number in the ith occupation,
jth education level, and kth color group.

Summing across education level gives

$$\sum_j L'_{ijk} = L'_{ik} = \sum_j \frac{L_{ij}}{L_j} \cdot L_{jk}$$

where L'_{ik} is the hypothetical number in each occupation by color group.

The groups can be seen to differ only in educational distribution, L_{jk}, when L'_{ik} is calculated.
32. Using the notation of footnote 31, this standardization procedure involves the calculation of a new L_{jk} for blacks in terms of white equivalent years of education. Effectively this means the allocation of a greater proportion of the black population to the lower education cells. In this way, we allow for the fact that blacks have been given less education than they appear to have. See J. D. Gwartney and K. M. McCaffree, "Variance in Discrimination Among Occupations," *Southern Economic Journal* 38 (1971): 141–155.
33. For a concrete expression of the economic fears expressed by white craft members over the training of nonwhites, see Department of Employment, *Report of the Committee of Enquiry into a Dispute Between Employees of the Mansfield Hosiery Mill Ltd. and their Employer* (London: Her Majesty's Stationery Office, 1972), pp. 12, 14. See also "A Unique Competence," A Report by *EEOC* into Discrimination at Bell Telephone, *Congressional Record* 118, no. 4 (1972): 4513–4524.

Table 6.2 Occupational Representation, Actual and Standardized for Education and Scholastic Achievement, Negro Males, United States, 1960

| | Urban, 35-44 Age Group[a] | | | | Urban and Rural, 25 years and over | |
| | North | | South | | Total United States[b] | |
Occupation	Actual (%)	Actual ÷ Standardized for Education	Actual (%)	Actual ÷ Standardized for Education	Actual ÷ Standardized for Education	Actual ÷ Standardized for Education and Achievement*
Professional	3.8	0.65	4.0	0.80	0.69	1.72
Managerial	2.3	1.24	1.9	0.18	0.26	0.33
Clerical	7.9	1.39	5.0	1.15	0.85	1.34
Sales	1.4	0.27	0.8	0.16	0.23	0.33
Craft	13.3	0.50	12.5	0.43	0.53	0.49
Operative	30.2	1.06	27.3	0.93	1.14	0.99
Laborer	16.8	2.00	25.5	3.03	3.01	2.24
Service	13.2	2.38	15.4	4.00	2.63	2.21

*The adjustment for scholastic achievement was calculated assuming blacks lagged behind whites 0 years when both groups had 0 years education, rising linearly to 3 years when blacks had 12 years education—with constancy thereafter.

Sources:

(a) W. Fogel, "The Effects of Low Educational Attainment and Discrimination on the Occupational Status of Minorities," *Conference on the Education and Training of Racial Minorities* (Madison, Wis.: University of Wisconsin, 1968). table 4.

(b) J. D. Gwartney and K. M. McCaffree, "Variance in Discrimination Among Occupations," *Southern Economic Journal* 38 (1971):145, table 1.

Accordingly, we would anticipate that criteria for exclusion, whether practiced against blacks or women, will persist through time. Such a conclusion is supported by the evidence.[34] In craft-dominated industries, increased unionization actually seems to widen the black/white wage differential, because blacks tend to be excluded from the union and thus from craft jobs.[35] Outside the craft sector, however, unionization appears to narrow that differential.[36]

Let us next turn to estimates of the overall impact of discrimination. The method here is to compute the relation between earnings and various productivity factors for each color group, that is, to compute earnings functions. Differences in the coefficients—for example, a smaller increase in black earnings than white earnings with age—indicate differences in treatment within the labor market and can be taken to show the immediate or cumulative effects of discrimination.[37] The total effect of discrimination on earnings is evaluated by using the index number method. We calculate black average earnings using black characteristics but white coefficients and compare the resulting value with actual white earnings. The difference represents all the standardizing factors left out of the equation plus discrimination. The method is best considered with the aid of figure 6.2, which shows two simplified earnings functions depending only on experience. Inserting the average black level of experience into the white function gives a hypothetical average black earnings value of $\bar{W}'_B$, assuming that blacks differ from whites only in experience. Of the actual difference in earnings (given by $\bar{W}_W - \bar{W}_B$), $\bar{W}_W - \bar{W}'_B$ is attributable to experience and the remainder to other factors, including discrimination. An alternative measure can be obtained by using the black equation. However, this procedure is probably less meaningful because in the event of discrimination being eliminated it is more likely that the black earnings function would come to resemble that of the white than vice versa.

Earnings functions for black males and white males have been calculated by Blinder.[38] He stardardizes for education, occupation, current job tenure, and union membership, together with a variety of exogenous variables including age, health, residence, and local labor market conditions. On this

34. See O. Ashenfelter, "Racial Discrimination and Trade Unionism," *Journal of Political Economy* 80 (1972): 450, table 5.

35. Table 6.2 indicates the proportion of blacks in craft occupations to be about 12% in the United States, that is, approximately one-half the expected value. In fact, the position is worse than it appears because high black representation in some crafts (plasterers) conceals very low representation in others (toolmakers).

36. Ashenfelter, "Racial Discrimination," p. 452.

37. This is not necessarily the case in a comparison between males and females. Here, it is to be expected that married, and to some extent single, women's earnings functions will differ from those of men for the familiar life cycle reasons. For example, married women who anticipate dropping out of the labor force will invest less in training and hence their earnings will rise less with age than is the case for men.

38. A. S. Blinder, "Wage Discrimination: Reduced Form and Structural Estimates," *Journal of Human Resources* 8 (1973): 451–453, table A.1.

Figure 6.2   Actual and Hypothetical Earnings Levels, Given Experience, by Color

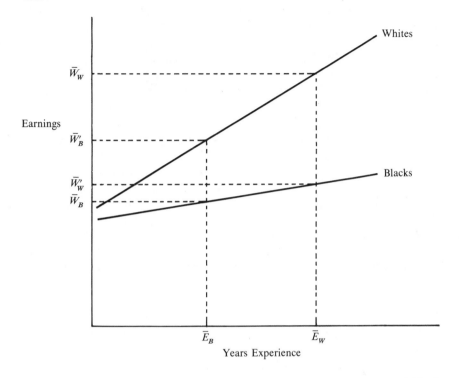

Years Experience

basis, it is calculated that differences between white characteristics and black characteristics, evaluated using white coefficients, are responsible for 60% of the differential in average earnings.[39] The residual 40% is presumably due to wage discrimination, because we are holding occupation, education, tenure, union membership, and the exogenous variables constant between groups. We can go somewhat further and ask whether the poorer education and occupational distribution of nonwhites is attributable to family background or whether there is something extra holding them back. In the absence of the latter, using family background variables instead of education, occupation, and so on in the earnings equation and evaluating according to given coefficients should result in differences in background characteristics being able to explain 60% of the earnings differential, as before. Such variables actually explain only 30%, which would indicate that whites receive more favorable treatment in the labor market, given background, than do nonwhites. This simply confirms what we know from table 6.1, but with the advantage that we now possess numerical estimates. Thus, 40% of the average male white/nonwhite earnings differential is indicated as being due to differences in pay for a given job, 30% to differences in educational attainment, occupation, job tenure, and union membership for a given family background, and 30% to differences in background.[40]

However, the wage discrimination contribution of 40% is also likely to reflect differences in job opportunities. Similar very high estimates of wage discrimination have been obtained using British data in the case of women. It has been calculated that female full-time employees in 1974 would have earned 83% of male earnings on average if the two groups differed in occupational composition alone.[41] The ratio of actual earnings was 55%, so it might be concluded that differences in pay contributed 62% $[=(0.83 - 0.55)/(1 - 0.55)]$ to the differential and differences in occupational composition only 38%. But estimates in both cases suffer from the fact that job categories are so broad that the same job is not actually being compared. Research in the case of women would indicate that wage discrimination within a firm appears to be small.[42] The same is likely to be true of blacks, though employers or unions are able to veil direct comparison to some extent by job title differentiation. Further, holding the type of firm constant—that is, confining comparisons to firms in which both men and women are employed in the given occupation—also gives a lower estimate of wage discrimination.[43] The predominant reason for minorities apparently earning less than white males doing similar work thus seems to be that minorities are, for some reason, employed within low-wage firms; earnings differences largely reflect different job opportunities.

Therefore the trail returns to employment opportunities. Union entry restrictions are likely to provide one explanation for the location of blacks in low-wage firms. However, there is reason to believe that the low-wage firms are generally not only nonunion but also small and/or in areas of low population density.[44] One reason why smallness may be associated with lower wages for a given job concerns imperfections of information: small firms may be more adroit in judging the quality of job applicants and may thus be able to pay a lower wage for a given quality of labor.[45] Because the small firm is better able to select out the promising black or female candidates, these are the more likely to be hired. However, we would expect this factor to be more important with respect to females, whose labor market

40. Ibid., p. 447.
41. B. Chiplin and P. J. Sloane, "Male Female Earnings Differences: A Further Analysis," *British Journal of Industrial Relations* 14 (1976): 78, table 1.
42. J. E. Buckley, "Equal Pay: Progress and Problems (America)," *International Journal of Social Economics* 1 (1974): 89, table 2.
43. Buckley, "Pay Differences," table 1, p. 37.
44. See, for example, L. W. Weiss, "Concentration and Labor Earnings," *American Economic Review* 56 (1966): 96; P. Nelson, "The Elasticity of Labor Supply to the Individual Firm," *Econometrica* 41 (1973): 855.
45. Stigler, "Information in the Labor Market," p. 103. There is some evidence to suggest that large firms put more weight on formal requirements than do the small. In this context, see G. S. Hamilton and J. D. Roesner, "How Employers Screen Disadvantaged Job Applicants," *Monthly Labor Review* 95 (1972): 27.

behavior has changed so fundamentally over the postwar period. The isolation of a firm can also lead to lower wages, *ceteris paribus,* because workers' alternatives will be fewer. This will increase the possibility of exploitation. We would consider this locational factor to be more important in the case of females, who tend to search for jobs within a restricted area.[46]

Firm size, being positively correlated with monopoly in the product market, might be connected with wage or, if wage differentiation is restricted, employment discrimination for taste as well as informational reasons. Standardizing for occupation, Becker has found some evidence of fewer blacks being employed relative to whites in monopolistic industries than competitive industries.[47] Such a relation does not appear to apply when government (generally a monopoly) and private industry are compared.[48] On the other hand, some support for Becker's finding is reported in an analysis of black representation in managerial and professional occupations for the 200 largest United States firms compared with the manufacturing industry as a whole. As of 1966, the appropriate black/white employment ratio for the former approximated only two-thirds that of the latter. By 1970, the relationship had been reversed, with the ratio in large firms being some 10% better than the average.[49] Such flexibility would indicate the scope for influences such as tastes and public pressures to alter the factor mix.

Let us now turn to the employee taste for discrimination model. Chiswick has tested the implications of the model with respect to white earnings *inequality,* given the job. White earnings inequality can be expected to increase if whites have an aversion to working alongside blacks, and the number of blacks in the work force is such as to cause some of them so to associate. Chiswick does demonstrate a positive relationship between white earnings inequality and the proportion of the state labor force that is black, holding a limited number of variables, including education, experience, and their variances, constant.[50] Power factors could also account for this relationship; unions might be more exclusive, even at the expense of whites, in states with large numbers of blacks. Chiswick does not include power or informational variables (such as unionization or company size, respectively) in his analysis; hence, his findings must be treated with some caution.

Finally, what changes in discrimination may be discerned through time as a result of civil rights legislation and the new-found political power of black Americans? As regards changes in relative occupation position, indices

---

46. But it would be interesting to conduct a hiring study of the response-to-application type (see Jowell and Prescott-Clarke, "Racial Discrimination and White Collar Workers") to discover whether blacks were more likely to be hired, given the job, in the nonunion, small, and relatively isolated firm.

47. Becker, *Economics of Discrimination,* table 2, p. 48.

48. J. E. Long, "Public-Private Differences in Employment Discrimination," *Southern Economic Journal* 42 (1975): 92, 94, tables 1, 3.

49. W. G. Shepherd and S. G. Levin, "Managerial Discrimination in Large Firms," *Review of Economics and Statistics* 55 (1973): 415, table 2.

50. Chiswick, "Racial Discrimination in the Labor Market," pp. 108 ff.

provided by Freeman enable us to chart the progress of black males over the period since 1890.[51] Using 1959 income weights and an eleven-occupation sample, Freeman obtains the following black/white ratios:

1890	1900	1910	1920	1930	1940	1950	1960	1970
.68	.69	.68	.71	.72	.68	.76	.79	.87

It would appear that entry barriers gave way during World War II and the sixties, precisely the period when the laws and attitudes affecting employment of black labor changed most. The findings support the notion that past discrimination against blacks has been of an organized form and not the result of individualistic behavior.

That there has been a decline in market discrimination against blacks in the sixties can also be shown by comparing earnings functions at different points in time. The results of one such study are summarized in table 6.3. It can be seen that the actual black/white earnings ratio improved markedly, from 57.7% in 1959 to 66% in 1969. This improvement is partly due to a favorable relative shift in nonwhite characteristics, for example, education, whether evaluated using the white or the nonwhite equation.[52] But the main source of improvement is to be attributed to changes in the coefficients, as can be seen if characteristics are held constant.[53] Because differences in the coefficients between the two groups are indicative of discrimination, this improvement is evidence of a reduction in the intensity of labor market discrimination in the sixties.

The Household Division of Labor as a Factor in Female Earnings Differentials. There are direct barriers to women entering certain craft and professional occupations, just as there are for other minorities. But we would expect these barriers to have been of lesser overall significance for women than black workers, mainly because of the more favorable legislative infrastruc-

---

51. Freeman, "Decline of Labor Market Discrimination," p. 282. The relative quality of black schooling has also improved over time, although it still remains substantially inferior; see F. Welch, "Black-White Differences in Returns to Schooling," *American Economic Review* 63 (1973): 900–902.

52. See the final two entries of table 6.3.

53. The following relationship holds among the ratios.

The actual ratio, R, is defined as $R = \dfrac{\Sigma_i X_{Bi}\alpha_{Bi}}{\Sigma_i X_{Wi}\alpha_{Wi}}$;

that taking white X_i is given by $D_W = \dfrac{\Sigma_i X_{Wi}\alpha_{Bi}}{\Sigma_i X_{Wi}\alpha_{Wi}}$;

that taking black α_i is given by $I_B = \dfrac{\Sigma_i X_{Bi}\alpha_{Bi}}{\Sigma_i X_{Wi}\alpha_{Bi}}$.

where X = characteristics, α = coefficients, and subscripts, W and B refer to whites and blacks respectively.

Thus it can be seen that $R = D_W \cdot I_B$ and, similarly, $R = D_B \cdot I_W$.

Table 6.3   The Standardized Ratio of Nonwhite/White Earnings Under Various
Assumptions as to the Effect of Productivity Characteristics on Earnings, Males,
United States, 1959-1969

	Earnings Ratio	
	1959	1969
Actual ratio (R)	57.7	66.0
Ratio assuming groups have their own earnings function,* but given:		
(D_W) white characteristics	70.8	79.0
(D_B) nonwhite characteristics	70.9	76.9
Ratio assuming groups have their own characteristics, but given:		
(I_W) white earnings function*	81.3	86.0
(I_B) nonwhite earnings function*	81.5	83.5

*Included in the function are age, schooling, annual hours worked, and marital status.
Source:
J. G. Haworth, J. Gwartney, and C. Haworth, "Earnings, Productivity, and Changes in Employment Discrimination During the 1960's," *American Economic Review* 65 (1975): 162.

ture confronting the former. It is difficult to believe that women did not join men in support of, for example, the British Factory Act stipulation that women may not work two shifts in immediate succession. Consequently, it is probable that this type of act is what it purports to be, namely a humane provision, rather than a concealed means of preventing women from entering certain operative jobs as some writers would have us believe.[54]

When we turn our attention away from such obvious barriers, a major difficulty in comparing men with women is to ascertain what weight to put on differences in male and female employment preferences and ways of life. It does seem reasonable to suppose that preferences will differ, although clearly these differences will not be static. For example, even single women have been estimated to spend much more time on household work (twenty hours per week) than single men (seven hours).[55] An associated difficulty presents itself: if preferences and consequently expectations of lifetime labor market experience differ, then so too will the jobs for which women offer themselves. Thus, we would expect married women to occupy very different jobs from men, although single women should exhibit more similar preferences. This is quite dramatically confirmed when we compare female to male pay ratios among marital status groups. In the United States, adjustments for differences in age, education, and hours worked bring the expected ratio for single

54. See, for example, Madden, "Discrimination—A Manifestation," p. 156. At this point we should note that the guidelines established by the Equal Opportunities Commission in the United States rule that such laws are now discriminatory.
55. See J. Gwartney and A. Stroup, "Measurement of Employment Discrimination According to Sex," *Southern Economic Journal* 39 (1973): 578.

Table 6.4   Median Income Ratios, by Sex and Marital Status, United States, 1959

	Single, Never Married	Married, Spouse Present
Actual	0.98	0.33
Adjusted using:		
female earnings function	0.91	0.51
male earnings function	0.96	0.50

Source:
J. Gwartney and A. Stroup, "Measurement of Employment Discrimination According to Sex," *Southern Economic Journal* 39 (1973): 580

persons into close agreement with the actual ratio. For married persons, however, there is still a large unexplained difference in wage ratios after adjustment, as shown in table 6.4. However, the unexplained difference cannot simply be interpreted as reflecting discrimination against women, for there is little evidence of discrimination against single women. It is difficult to distinguish elements of discrimination operating against women from those factors which underpin their very different role in society.

One of the major advances in analyzing women's earnings has been the development of the segmented earnings function, which permits adjustment for the fact that some people spend a considerable part of their potential working life out of the labor force. During such intervals, they invest less in market skills; perhaps their investment is not enough to prevent the skills they already possess from becoming rusty. For example, a United States study of a sample of women aged 30–44, conducted in 1967, showed white married women with children to have spent 6.4 years in the labor force since school and 10.4 years out of it; this compared with 14.5 years in the labor force and 1.5 years out of it for never-married women.[56] Consequently, instead of assuming a monotonic decline in postschool investment functions, Mincer has proposed a segmented postschool investment function. Let us assume there to be three segments: the first ending with the birth of the first child, the second comprising a broad nonparticipation interval in which children are reared, and the third defining the period of reentry to continuous work. There is likely to be little training undertaken during the first segment and even disinvestment in the second segment. There will be a certain amount of new investment, taking such forms as refresher courses, within the third segment. Some results of the segmentation approach are given in table 6.5.

The principal finding for white married women is that the coefficient on current job tenure is higher than in other segments and the home time coefficient is actually negative. This bears out the hypothesis that, for women,

56. Mincer and Polachek, "Family Investments in Human Capital," p. S88. The figures for black married women were 9.1 years in and 10.3 years out of the labor force and, for single women, 13.4 and 4.7 years, respectively.

Table 6.5   Regression of Log Female Earnings on Schooling, Segmented Work Experience and Other Variables, United States, 1967

Variable	White			Black	
	Married with Children (a)	Never Married (a)	(b)	Married with Children (a)	Never Married (a)
Constant	0.09	0.55	1.48	−0.02	−0.48
Schooling	0.064*	0.077*	0.054*	0.095*	0.100*
Work before first child	0.008*			0.005	
Work after first child	0.001			0.001	
Current job tenure	0.012*	0.009		0.006	0.001
Total years worked		0.026	0.036*		0.004
Square of total years worked		−0.0007	−0.0005*		−0.0003
Home time after first child	−0.012*			−0.006	
Other home time	−0.003			−0.005	
Total home time		−0.009			−0.02
ln hours per week on current job	−0.11*	−0.43*		−0.30*	−0.13
ln hours per year on current job	0.03	0.21	0.666*	0.08*	0.03
R^2	0.28**	0.41**	0.67	0.39**	0.46**

Notes:
(a) hourly earnings
(b) annual earnings
* indicates significance at the 5% level
** indicates inclusion of other variables in the regression (for example, illness and years resident in state)

Sources:
(a) J. Mincer and S. W. Polachek, "Family Investments in Human Capital: Earnings of Women," *Journal of Political Economy* 82 (1974): 588 ff.
(b) S. W. Polachek, "Potential Biases in Measuring Male-Female Discrimination." *Journal of Human Resources* 10 (1975): 215.

investment and earnings depend strongly on family commitments. Investment in the current job, because it takes place for most women when children have grown up, is higher than in the early jobs, when there is anticipation of dropping out of the labor force. The negative coefficient on home time indicates a net depreciation of earning power of about 1.2% per annum, although this can be shown to be much higher for women with higher levels of education. It is interesting to note that the home time coefficient for never-married women is not significantly negative; this might be explained by their periods of nonparticipation being search oriented. For black women, the experience coefficients are smaller and there is less variation between segments, although differences are in the same direction as for whites. The greater family responsibilities of black women vis-a-vis white women might partially explain their investing less on the job, as the coefficients would indicate. However, there are other factors at work, such as discrimination. This is indicated by black *single* women also having lower coefficients than their white counterparts.

The estimated equations also indicate that for women as for men the human capital framework is quite successful in explaining the distribution of earnings. It is even better at explaining annual earnings dispersion, as the third column of table 6.5 indicates. Moreover, as would be expected given optimizing behavior, the rate of return on education appears to be slightly higher for blacks than for whites.[57] This may be taken as indicating the likely higher marginal cost of funds for blacks.

Attempts are also currently being made to incorporate the intermittent labor force participation of women directly into analysis of their occupational composition. Clearly, intermittent participation will count against women from the employer's point of view in jobs requiring considerable specific training. This would probably account for women's low representation as managers, where much training is needed.[58] But we should not ignore supply-side influences. It might be that the extra deterioration of earnings capability caused by extended periods of nonparticipation is more pronounced in managerial and professional occupations than others. This could be because such occupations require that knowledge be continually updated. In these occupations, continual postschooling investments are required in addition to schooling. The implications would be that a woman who expects to absent herself from the labor force for some time, and who wishes to minimize loss of human capital, will opt against entering these very occupations. Preliminary research on this hypothesis does indicate that it lessens the imbalance in male to female representation in the cited occupations.[59] However, it does not appear to explain the extremely low representation of females in the craft occupations. Fewer than 1% of white females in the 1967 United States sample were in this category; this compares with 26% of males. There seems little reason to expect skills gained in an apprenticeship to depreciate particularly quickly as a result of nonparticipation. This serves to emphasize the possibility of union-imposed barriers to entry.

57. This is also true of males, as we have seen in table 4.2.
58. See R. B. Mancke, "Lower Pay for Women: A Case of Economic Discrimination?" *Industrial Relations* 10 (1971): 320.
59. Polachek, "Occupational Segregation Among Women," table 4, p. 19.

Further Factors in Female Earnings Differentials—Monopsony and Imperfect Information. Women are more likely to be subject to monopsonistic influences than men. Because monopsony applies more to married women than to single women, there is also reason to expect pay differentiation within the ranks of the female labor force. The monopsony model also leads us to expect a higher female/male earnings ratio where employers are bunched, as for example in the urban areas, because the more geographically limited job search of females will here be of less consequence.

If monopsony is an important factor in the lower pay of women, this has far reaching policy implications. In particular, the implementation of equal pay laws is less likely to cause female unemployment. Unfortunately, there is little direct evidence on the monopsony question, although the United States market for nurses would appear to conform to the monopsonistic model because of the tendency toward concentration of nursing employment among a few hospitals in a given area.[60] But this is hardly comprehensive evidence of monopsony influence. One American study does find that male wages increase less than female wages as size of town increases, *ceteris paribus*, which is to be expected given that males have more mobility. Holding regions, education, and labor force experience constant, women in towns of under 250,000 population earned 35% less than those in towns of over 750,000. The corresponding figure for males was 20%.[61] A British study of female earnings differentials in the teaching profession found that the differentials betweeen single women and men could be explained on the basis of measured differences in education and experience. No such satisfactory explanation existed in the case of married women. This latter result was interpreted in terms of the lower supply price of married female teachers either because of their lower ambition or because of their lower geographical mobility.[62]

An attractive possibility would be to attempt a direct test of the monopsony hypothesis by estimating sex differences in the elasticity of supply to firms and relating this to earnings differences, having standardized for skill. One study has followed this test procedure, although its estimates relate to the metropolitan area rather than to the firm.[63] Unfortunately, this approach founders because the elasticity of labor supply to the metropolitan area will not be related to that of the firm. Thus, males might be quite inelastic in

60. R. Hurd, "Equilibrium Vacancies in a Labor Market Dominated by Non-Profit Firms: The 'Shortage' of Nurses," *Review of Economics and Statistics* 55 (1973): 237.
61. R. H. Frank, "Sources of Male-Female Wage Differential—The Theory and Estimation of Differential Over-Qualification," *Discussion Paper No. 133* (Ithaca, N.Y.: Department of Economics, Cornell University, 1976), table 7.
62. R. Turnbull and G. Williams, "Sex Differentials in Teachers' Pay," *Journal of Royal Statistical Society,* Series A 137 (1974): 255.
63. L. Cardwell and M. Rosenzweig, "Monopsonistic Discrimination and Sex Differences in Wages," *Discussion Paper No. 222* (New Haven, Conn.: Economic Growth Center, Yale University, 1975).

supply to the market and yet highly elastic in supply to the firm for such reasons as union-imposed minimum wages. It is to be hoped that further tests of this important hypothesis will be forthcoming.

In considering the role of employer hiring standards, imperfect information, and discrimination, two problems must be distinguished at the outset. The first is that the employer's *a priori* beliefs about the various labor force groups might be false in the sense that discrimination against certain groups is no longer profit maximizing. The distribution of such productivity characteristics as education and experience across labor force groups might have changed over time without employers being fully aware of these developments. Here, we observe the problem of unequal treatment: workers who on objective grounds may be expected to exhibit the same productivity as others who do not enjoy the same probability of being hired. The second problem relates to the justification of the productivity criteria themselves. An employer might stipulate a high level of experience as a requirement for a given job. This could have the effect of screening out women. On the other hand, the electorate might decide that women should be employed in this particular job classification even though they possess lower levels of experience; this has occurred to some extent. The bankruptcies and/or higher costs and reduced output that ensue from such electoral decisions are to be seen as the purchase price of this method of increasing female employment opportunities. However, the "price" might be lower if the burden were shifted from the firm to society via the payment of subsidies to the firm. But the general problem is one of differences in treatment. Women are not simply to be treated *equally* with men; rather, they are to be treated in the *same* way as men. Unlike the first problem, which arises from imperfections in information, this second problem reflects an issue of social welfare. The two problems are related to this extent: if the employer can be shown to labor under large information imperfections, so that his hiring standards are in any case rather arbitrary, the price of enforcing a similar hiring standard for all labor force groups is correspondingly reduced.

Because of the policy importance of the optimality or otherwise of employer stereotypes, there is a growing amount of research effort devoted to this question. There would seem to be a good *a priori* reason for expecting such stereotypes to be somewhat out of line. Here, we would again point to the pronounced upward movement in the labor force participation of married women.

However, investigation of hiring standards is no easy matter because they are not immutable. As Reder observed long ago in his classic study of wage differentials, the profit-maximizing employer can trade off hiring standards against wage offers and the speed of filling a vacancy.[64] Accordingly, hiring

64. M. W. Reder, "The Theory of Occupational Wage Differentials," *American Economic Review* 45 (1955): 834–840.

standards will vary over the cycle (between regions), being higher in periods (areas) of high unemployment than low.[65] Indeed, it is this very process that causes the employer to modify his beliefs. When the labor market is tight, the employer is perhaps more likely to indulge in experimentation. It might be for this reason that, in periods of expansion, the lower tail of the nonwhite income distribution improves relative to that of the white distribution.[66] Thus, variability of hiring standards among time periods or firms for a given job is not necessarily evidence of any degree of arbitrariness.

This problem dogs attempts to study hiring practices. The United States Department of Labor has prepared lists of the "general education development" and "specific vocational preparation" required for 4,000 different jobs.[67] However, these listed requirements can only provide a rough guide, because actual requirements will vary over time. Consequently, attempts to assess actual employer requirements against the theoretical in the hope of determining whether an educational standard is set "too high" are likely to be subject to a very wide margin of error.[68] In another Department of Labor–sponsored study, hiring standards between firms in New York and St. Louis were compared and much made of the variability in standards between regions.[69] But only if excess demand were held constant could such a study prove informative. More suggestive is the investigation by Hamilton and Roesner. They found higher entry requirements for service and some white-collar occupational categories that employers defined as "dead end" jobs than for jobs from which promotion was possible.[70] In the blue-collar and laborer categories, however, the relationship was more as expected and so the results would seem to be inconclusive. Clearly, this is a difficult field in which more research is required.

It is probable that public concern does not focus upon the optimality of employer hiring practices. Rather, that concern seems to arise from the fact that hiring practices are seen as a link in the "cycle of deprivation." People with poor work habits (for example, a tendency to higher absenteeism) are not hired into jobs requiring stable attendance—usually the primary sector jobs. Instead, they are relegated to more menial jobs that serve to ingrain these habits. Moreover, the latter areas offer little training, so it becomes more difficult to escape from such activities with the passage of time. One

65. Evidence strongly supporting this contention is shown in R. J. Gaston, "Labor Market Conditions and Employer Hiring Standards," *Industrial Relations* 11 (1972): 273.
66. McCall, "Racial Discrimination in the Labor Market," p. 19.
67. These are described in J. C. Scoville, "Education and Training Requirements for Occupations," *Review of Economics and Statistics* 48 (1966): 387–394.
68. For one such attempt, see I. Berg, *Education and Jobs: The Great Training Robbery* (Boston, Mass.: Beacon Press, 1971), p. 46.
69. U.S. Department of Labor, "Hiring Standards and Job Performance," *Manpower Research Monograph No. 18* (Washington, D.C.: U.S. Government Printing Office, 1970).
70. Hamilton and Roesner, "How Employers Screen Disadvantaged Job Applicants," table 4, p. 19.

mode of attack is to change housing and education policies so as to eliminate productivity and motivational differences at their root. But clearly this is a long-term strategy and its success may depend crucially upon assistance in the form of "positive" discrimination, another term for favoritism, in the labor market. Consequently, there is emphasis on more immediate measures that operate directly on the firm. Such measures have the additional advantage that they challenge those barriers that are unrelated to informational imperfection, such as those erected by unions. However, in the areas in which union barriers have not much distorted hiring policy, there is no reason to expect, given present research results, that modification of employer hiring requirements will be costless.

6.4   Policy Measures

Broadly speaking, three different types of policy have been proposed to help groups at the lower tail of the earnings distribution: measures to improve education and formal training opportunities, proposals to operate the economy with a lesser degree of labor market slack, and instruments to counter directly wage and employment discrimination by imposing fair employment practice laws.

Radical theorists have tended to interpret the first policy measure as a mere palliative or as inculcating a servile mentality.[71] While such issues as the content of curricula and the manner in which education improves job opportunities merit closer attention, the analysis presented here and in chapter 4 has sought to stress the importance of equality of educational opportunity as regards both quantity and quality. This is undoubtedly a vital basic step.

The fact remains that education programs are long term in their effect and by no means provide a complete solution. We have noted the existence of a potential for discriminating against women even though they possess educational opportunities similar to those of men. One measure which might improve the labor market position of disadvantaged workers in the short term is the pursuance of a tight labor market policy.[72] It is argued that the tighter the labor market, the more expensive it is for the employer to indulge his white (or male) workers' desire to discriminate. The desire to discriminate might itself diminish at such times to the extent that the allocation of jobs is less likely to be seen as a zero-sum game. In a tight labor market, too, experimentation is more likely to occur, thereby diminishing employer misconceptions about minority workers. American and British evidence would suggest that black workers tend to be at the bottom of the waiting list

71. See, for example, S. Bowles and H. Gintis, "The Problem With Human Capital Theory—A Marxian Critique," *American Economic Review* 65 (1975): 77.
72. See J. Tobin, "On Improving the Economic Status of the Negro," *Daedalus* (Fall 1965): 78–98.

for vacancies.[73] For this reason, many would advocate a tighter labor market. But we should be aware of the inflationary consequences of expanding the level of aggregate demand. The controversial issues involved here will be explored in greater detail in chapters 11 and 12.

Turning to direct intervention, both the United States and Great Britain now have laws enforcing equal pay for similar work. Under the British legislation, wage rate comparisons among different groups are restricted to a given firm. The Americans interpretation is somewhat broader. Under Title VII of the Civil Rights Act of 1964, wages for a given job in a plant can be compared with wages in other plants within the industry. This opens up the possibility of narrowing the wage gap between plants within an industry—equal pay within an industry clearly means more than equal pay within a plant—although it is difficult to see how this could be enforced. Both countries have also outlawed discrimination in hiring and with similar intentions: the emphasis is to be on the same rather than equal treatment for the various groups. Hiring procedures that have the effect of screening out more of one group than another, even if this is justified in terms of productivity, will come under increasing pressure, if only because it is difficult to test hiring standards.[74]

Equal pay laws can be expected to increase the unemployment of minority groups, given that the workers affected are already receiving a wage equal to the value of their marginal product. But to the extent that there is monopsony power over women—which we have reason to believe is the case, although the evidence is not clear-cut—equal pay could even create employment. Equal pay could nevertheless lead to increased unemployment among blacks (for whom there is less likelihood of exploitation), if not accompanied by measures to improve productivity and also to compensate whites for dropping entry barriers. On our analysis, it should be remembered, discriminatory attitudes are in large part determined by fear of capital loss attendant upon a derestriction of entry. This points to the need for "buying the book."

What impact has this type of legislation had upon the market position of minorities? With respect to black Americans, the effects are doubtless intermeshed with the outcome of a variety of other legislative and educational changes, all of which must have contributed to the observed improvement in

73. See, respectively, L. C. Thurow, "The Changing Structure of Unemployment: An Econometric Study," *Review of Economics and Statistics* 47 (1965): 142ff; D. J. Smyth and P. D. Lowe, "The Vestibule to the Occupational Ladder and Unemployment," *Industrial and Labor Relations Review* 23 (1970): 561–565.

74. Thus in Griggs v. Duke Power Co., 1971, the Supreme Court ruled against educational requirements that had the effect of screening out a greater proportion of blacks than whites and that, in the opinion of the judges, bore "no relation to the jobs in question." See H. C. Jain, "The American Anti-Discrimination Legislation and its Impact on the Utilisation of Blacks and Women," *International Journal of Social Economics* 3 (1976): 113.

the black/white earnings ratio (table 6.3). However, it is possible in principle to distinguish the effects of fair employment practice laws on a state-by-state basis following the methodology of Landes. His calculations show that the nonwhite/white wage ratio averages 68% in states without fair employment laws as compared with 71% in states with such laws.[75] Because there was no corresponding difference in 1949, prior to the passing of most fair employment laws, the inference is that the laws were responsible for this favorable change. On the other hand, Landes' results also reveal that nonwhite unemployment varies directly with the wage ratio; however, this result might reflect the fact that states with fair employment laws attracted a larger share of migrants from the South.

It is difficult to discern whether it is the fair employment laws themselves that have improved black economic opportunities or the generally more favorable political climate facing black Americans in those states possessing fair employment laws. In other words, the laws could be an effect and not a cause of lower discrimination. That there is a generally more favorable climate is shown by the fact that blacks currently have much fairer political representation in those states which passed fair employment laws in the 1940s and 1950s than in other states, both in the South and non-South. (See table 6.6.) There is the possibility that blacks were more militant in those states that were in the vanguard of fair employment law adoption—states which tended to be the most industrialized and presumably contained black proletariats. Accompanying this militancy, we would anticipate better black political representation, a higher incidence of fair employment laws, and fewer possibilities for market discrimination.

The effects of fair employment laws on the labor market position of women should be easier to discern because there have not been recent changes in their political position. In Great Britain, the Equal Pay and Sex

---

75. Standardizing for interstate differences in the proportion of nonwhites, nonwhite/white education, and urbanization. See W. M. Landes, "The Economics of Fair Employment Laws," *Journal of Political Economy* 76 (1968): 517.

Table 6.6   Black Political Representation and Fair Employment Laws, 1970

State	Proportion of Blacks in	
	State Legislature	Population
States with fair employment laws as of 1963	3.4%	4.6%
Other states	1.2%	4.2%
Southern states	1.9%	24.1%

Sources:
H. Walton, *Black Politics—A Theoretical and Structural Analysis* (Philadelphia, Pa.: Lippincot, 1972), p. 199; W. M. Landes, "The Economics of Fair Employment Laws," *Journal of Political Economy* 76 (1968): 507.

Discrimination Acts only became enforceable in 1976, and so it is too early yet to be positive as to its effects. Nevertheless, there is evidence of a 3 to 4 percentage point upward movement in the female/male earnings ratio from a long-term position of stability at around 60%. This outcome is probably attributable in part to the effects of equal pay, although it is also likely to include the effects of a compression of skill margins under successive pay restraint policies. Doubtless more pronounced effects will become apparent once the Equal Opportunities Commission begins its work.

Public concern in the United States over sex discrimination has lagged behind that expressed for other minority groups. Of the states with fair employment laws, only two had prohibitions on discrimination based on sex prior to the Civil Rights Act of 1964. However, with the out-of-court settlement by American Telephone and Telegraph in 1973 of $15 million in compensation to groups such as female telephone operators, who claimed to have been injured by company employment practices that kept them out of the craft grades, it is apparent that attitudes have rapidly hardened.[76] The Act may have had some influence in promoting the generally favorable female occupational shift in the decade up to 1974, although the improved labor market position of these years must also have been a factor. Whether women would retain these gains in a sustained downswing is another question, because seniority rules operate against them. Such rules suggest one area in which minority groups are at a disadvantage, and they will be discussed in some detail in chapter 9. Suffice it to say here that remedial action on seniority rules implies a large capital loss for the group with seniority were such practices much altered.

6.5 Conclusions

In this chapter, we have considered discrimination under three headings: discrimination in the public provision of education, discrimination in the sense of inferior job openings for given levels of schooling, and discrimination in the sense of lower pay for a given job. The first factor mainly affects black Americans, whose poor schooling attainments and low scholastic achievement can be related to discrimination in the allocation of public funds for schooling. This in turn can be related to exclusion of blacks from the franchise, a factor which is now in the process of being corrected. It is probable that discrimination in this area is income maximizing, at least for white groups of lower ability, and has little to do with a taste for discrimination in the sense of determinant of behavior independent of income.

As for discrimination in the market, its extent cannot accurately be measured because of the difficulty of standardizing for intergroup differences in productivity. Yet there is unequivocal evidence of hiring discrimination against blacks in more responsible white-collar occupations such as accountants. Postal experiments in Great Britain show that whites are more

76. See Jain, "The American Anti-Discrimination Legislation," pp. 118–119.

likely to be invited for employment interviews than similarly qualified blacks. It is also evident that blacks, even allowing for their lower education and scholastic achievement, are poorly represented in skilled manual occupations and overrepresented in laboring jobs. For women, there are the additional problems of allowing for the possibility of different occupational preferences and, especially for married women, of different motivations caused by family care commitments. The very low representation of women in managerial and craft jobs, and their high representation in clerical jobs, will to some degree be explained by such supply-side differences rather than discrimination in hiring. Thus, earnings functions for married women indicate little investment in training prior to or during the period when the family is growing up. While this is unlikely to explain the very low representation of women in the crafts, it will be a factor in their low representation in managerial categories where much specific training is required. Strong evidence that supply-side differences do have a large impact on women's relative earnings emerges from a comparison of married women with single women. In the United States, for example, the earnings ratio for the former, adjusted for productivity differences, stood at 50% in 1959; but for the latter, for whom supply-side differences vis-a-vis men are less important, it was 96%.

When we come to consider differences in pay within a common job classification, the disparities are often quite marked. In Great Britain, for example, it has been estimated that pay inequalities, rather than women's unfavorable occupational distribution, account for 62% of the female/male earnings differential. The corresponding figure for blacks in the United States has been estimated at 40%. To a large extent, however, such differences arise because minorities are probably overrepresented in the low-paying firms. In other words, the problem is still one of different employment opportunities, arising from factors such as union exclusion in the larger firms and, for women, a tendency to search over a smaller area. In the case of women, American findings would indicate that wage discrimination within a firm is small. Indeed, such discrimination is prohibited within craft occupations because of fears of undercutting. The fact remains that certain groups might be less productive (have lower motivation) or be more costly to employ (have a higher quit rate or be subject to objections from fellow employees) than other employees, given the job. In this case, a wage differential is required *in equilibrium* if both are to be employed.

Three types of explanation for market discrimination can usefully be distinguished. The first concerns that discrimination resulting from one group being able to benefit economically at the expense of another; this is the power explanation. This would seem the best way to account for direct barriers to entering the crafts and various professional associations. The members of these organizations can be shown to obtain a clear economic gain from entry restriction and, moreover, to possess the means to bring about such restriction. It would also seem to be the most important general factor influencing employment discrimination against black Americans. Not only has there been discrimination by the government (and hence by whites acting in collusion) in education funding, but also in state employment. This explanation gains support from the finding that the large increases in the male black/white earnings ratio, from 58% in 1959 to 66% a decade later, is not associated with a corresponding movement in black productivity characteristics. The improvement must presumably reflect a different treatment of blacks in the market; for this, one can look to the civil rights legislation of the period. This finding is emphasized by the sudden improvement in the relative occupational position of blacks during the period in question.

A second explanation for discrimination rests on the famous Becker hypothesis that members of one group act as if they prefer not to be associated with members of another. Gratification of this taste, whether on the part of male (or white) employees or employers, raises costs. Thus, an implication of this theory is that wage discrimination or, if this is ruled out, employment discrimination will be higher in monopolistic industries than in competitive industries. We have some evidence, albeit weak, to this effect. Another implication follows with respect to occupations in close contact with the public. Consumer preference for the ambience of stores with a predominantly white staffing could be the explanation of low black representation in service occupations. Because consumers rarely collude, the power explanation cannot be brought forward here. On the whole, however, we would conclude that the tastes explanation is subsidiary to the former explanation, particularly in the important area of discrimination by fellow employees.

The third explanation for discrimination rests on informational imperfections. Every hiring decision requires an element of judgment as to the quality of the applicant. This decision will be based on past experience with similar employees. If perceptions of the distribution of productivity characteristics according to such factors as color, sex, and education are correct, this will not result in discrimination on average—though there will be some discrimination to the extent that members of a group who do not share its typical characteristics are passed over. However, if the distribution of characteristics is incorrectly perceived, there will be discrimination or bias against certain groups on average. In the case of married women, whose labor force status has changed markedly, the hiring rules or stereotypes could well be out of date, thereby giving rise to bias. Bias of this informational nature has yet to be firmly established, because research within this area is in its infancy. A major empirical difficulty is that the hiring or promotion requirements for a job are likely to vary through time or between regions according to the tightness of the respective labor markets. In any case, the requirements will very much depend on the judgment of the employer. The employer who makes appropriate hiring decisions will prosper, but this proposition offers no easy handle for testing particular hiring requirements, as, indeed, courts of law must increasingly do in enforcing the new equal opportunities legislation.

APPENDIX 6-A
THE TRADE MODEL OF DISCRIMINATION

It is assumed that the production functions in equation (6.1) and equation (6.2) are the same in both sectors and exhibit constant returns to scale. Differentiating equation (6.1) with respect to c_t gives

$$\frac{\partial Y}{\partial c_t} = -c_t \frac{\partial^2 f}{\partial c_t^2}(K = c,L_w) \geqslant 0$$

showing that net income decreases with decreases in capital exports.

However, differentiating equation (6.2) with respect to c_t shows that, for some values of c_t, money income increases with decreases in capital exports (that is, $\partial Y'/\partial c_t \leqslant 0$), as follows

$$\frac{\partial Y'}{\partial c_t} = c \frac{\partial^2 f}{\partial c_t \partial K}(K = c,L_w) + \frac{\partial f}{\partial K}(K = c,L_w) + L_w \frac{\partial^2 f}{\partial c_t \partial L}(K = c,L_w)$$

$$+ \frac{\partial f}{\partial K}(K = c_t + c_n,L_n) + c_t \frac{\partial^2 f}{\partial c_t \partial K}(K = c_t + c_n,L_n).$$

But

$$\frac{\partial f}{\partial c_t} \equiv \frac{\partial f}{\partial K} \cdot \frac{\partial K}{\partial c_t} \equiv \frac{\partial f}{\partial K} \cdot \frac{\partial(c_w - c_t)}{\partial c_t} \equiv -\frac{\partial f}{\partial K}$$

when $K = c_w - c_t$.
   Similarly,

$$\frac{\partial f}{\partial c_t} \equiv \frac{\partial f}{\partial K}$$

when $K = c_t + c_n$.
   By Euler's Theorem,

$$K \frac{\partial^2 f}{\partial K^2} \equiv -L \frac{\partial^2 f}{\partial K \partial L}$$

so that

$$c\frac{\partial^2 f}{\partial c_t{}^2} \equiv L_w \frac{\partial^2 f}{\partial c_t \partial L_w}$$

when $K = c$.
  Consequently,

$$\frac{\partial Y'}{\partial c_t} = c_t \frac{\partial^2 f}{\partial c_t{}^2}(K = c_t + c_n, L_n)$$

$$-\frac{\partial f}{\partial c_t}(K = c, L_w) + \frac{\partial f}{\partial c_t}(K = c_t + c_n, L_n).$$

From this it can be seen $\partial Y'/\partial c_t \leqslant 0$ so long as

$$e + \frac{\partial f}{\partial c_t}(K = c_t + c_n, L_n) \leqslant \frac{\partial f}{\partial c_t}(K = c, L_w)$$

where e (<0) is the first term on the R.H.S.

  Thus, at maximum Y', the marginal product of capital in the white sector will be lower than in the black sector by the amount e, which implies discrimination. This can also be seen from the results of Kreuger.[1]
  We might note in parenthesis that the analysis of this appendix differs from that employed by Madden,[2] whose equation (A.6) exhibits the wrong signs due to a failure to recognize that $\dfrac{\partial f}{\partial c_t} \equiv \dfrac{\partial f}{\partial K}$ when $K = c_t + c_n$.

1. A. O. Kreuger, "The Economics of Discrimination," *Journal of Political Economy* 71 (1963): 486.
2. J. F. Madden, *The Economics of Sex Discrimination* (Lexington, Mass.: Heath, 1973), Appendix A.

CHAPTER 7
NEGOTIATION AND CONFLICT

7.1 Introduction

The central concern of this chapter is the use of power by unions and management in the negotiation of the employment contract. In the last chapter, we considered power as a factor contributing to the explanation of discrimination. In the present chapter, we examine another facet of the exertion of power in the labor market which is associated with the periodic meetings of employer and union representatives to negotiate new agreements and of the strikes and lockouts that sometimes accompany this process. What determines the power of a union[1] in relation to an employer? Are some unions more powerful than others? Why are there strikes? These are the questions we shall consider. Our aim is to analyze the bargaining process and its breakdown. The analysis assists in the formulation of appropriate dispute management procedures. More generally, the approach adopted here will lay the basis for our subsequent analysis of the effects of unions on relative pay (chapter 8), job regulation (chapter 9), and wage inflation (chapters 12 and 13).

But before proceeding with an analysis of bargaining strategies, it is first necessary to investigate the circumstances in which bargaining arises. The conventional economic approach centers on the bilateral monopoly model. Yet there are real difficulties in applying such a model. Thus, in what sense may a trade union be likened to a monopoly? There are no obvious, single-value goals for which a union can be said to aim. Accordingly, it will be necessary to clarify the issue of union bargaining goals.

Given a bargaining situation, we next investigate the determinants of union power. Again there is a traditional approach to this question, centering on Marshall's four laws of derived demand. Conditions that are propitious for the exertion of power by a union can also be said to be conducive to

---

1. When we speak of "unions," the term is intended to encompass all organizations that exercise some degree of control over labor supply to an occupation or industry. Professional associations, such as the American Medical Association, are thus included under the term.

union growth. Therefore, this will be an appropriate point to raise some questions concerning the factors influencing that growth.

We can then turn to bargaining theory proper. Models of the bargaining process are useful in two main areas. First, they can be used to provide an insight into the causes of stoppages. Are strikes, to use Hicks' famous phrase, "the result of faulty negotiations"?[2] We contrast the reasoning behind this dictum with that of other, superficially more appealing, explanations of strikes. Proceeding from this, bargaining theories can assist in evaluating union impact on wage inflation. For example, if strikes are the result of bargaining mistakes by either side, it does not seem appropriate to consider strikes as a systematic determinant of union pressure on wages. Second, models of the bargaining process can provide qualitative pointers that are of use from a policy viewpoint, namely with respect to the management of industrial conflict. For example, one model yields the depressing result that the faster one party concedes, the more will the other demand.[3] This result, if correct—although empirical tests suggest that it might not be—points to the special value of having an intermediary in the bargaining process so as to prevent the parties becoming trapped into intransigent positions.

The theoretical issues will be considered first. We will then examine some empirical results with a bearing on the determinants of strikes and union growth. Finally, we consider the policy implications of the analysis for dispute settlement.

7.2 Bilateral Monopoly, Power, and Theories of Bargaining

Bilateral Monopoly. First consider the concept of a *bargaining zone*. For the moment, let us assume the union to be analogous to a single, utility maximizing individual—temporarily sidestepping the problem of determining in what sense a union is a monopoly. Under this assumption, it is possible to show why the outcome of bargaining is indeterminate and to depict a bargaining zone.

Consider the Edgeworth Box construction of figure 7.1. Any point within the box represents a certain "share of the cake," defined in terms of the potential labor time possessed by the union's members and of the capital possessed by the firm. It can be seen that we have simplified matters by assuming that the size of the cake, given by the length of the sides of the box, is unaffected by the particular share-out principle. Points O and O' refer respectively to the origins of the union and firm axes. Curves I_u and I_f denote union and firm indifference curves, respectively.

Suppose that the initial share is given by the point (M_o, L_o), measuring labor traded and the wage bill from A. It is evident that both parties could

2. J. R. Hicks, *The Theory of Wages*, 2nd ed. (London: Macmillan, 1963), p. 146.
3. J. G. Cross, "A Theory of the Bargaining Process," *American Economic Review* 55 (1965): 67–94.

Figure 7.1   The Contract Curve Representing Union-Employer Bargaining

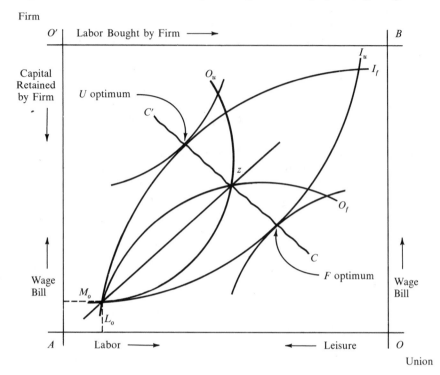

move to a higher indifference curve by negotiating a different share, whereby union members sell more of their time to the firm and the firm exchanges some of its capital for labor.

The minimum share acceptable to each party is dictated by the indifference curve upon which each is presently located. This serves to define the bargaining zone. The *contract curve, CC'*, is the locus of tangencies of the parties' indifference curves. The parties will always move to a position on the contract curve; the union would like the highest wage bill possible (there being no involuntary unemployment in the model) and the employer the lowest. Such points are indicated by arrows in figure 7.1 and are designated *U* optimum and *F* optimum, respectively. Either of these points is Pareto optimal, as is any other point along *CC'*, because neither party can be made better off without making the other party worse off—no further gain from trade is possible. The difficulty is one of knowing at which point along *CC'* the parties will conclude a contract. If there were a Walrasian auctioneer and both parties were price takers (and we make the heroic assumption that the curves do not then shift), the only wage rate that would clear the market would be that which brought the parties to point *z*, where their offer curves, O_f and O_u, intersect. This solution is represented by the ray through *z* of slope $-w$, where the slope is measured with reference to the *O'B* axis. In this case, it can be seen that we would have a determinate outcome. However, the parties to a collective bargaining process are not price takers, and so this solution is not open to us. The outcome is indeterminate, and an explicit bargaining model is required if we are to proceed further.

Before examining such theories, it is first necessary to clarify the issue of the bargaining goals of a union. Previously, we depicted the union as preferring a higher wage bill for its members, given employment, to a lower. Although this assumption is helpful in illustrating the concept of a bargaining zone, it begs some important questions. In the first place, there is the question of union politics. Ross has contended that there is likely to be a divergence between the goals of the membership and those of the union leadership. For example, union leaders might prefer to enter a lower wage claim than the members in the interests of an easier relationship with the employers and perhaps a faster growing union.[4] As we shall see, this idea of tension between members and leaders has a contribution to make in constructing a political model of industrial conflict.

Second, the assumption of a given level of employment rules out the likely divergence of goals between employed and unemployed members. In analyzing this question, Dunlop has proposed that unions be considered as aiming to set a wage at which the wage bill for workers in the relevant industry is maximized or a wage at which only union members are employed, if this is the higher.[5] Ignoring the theoretical curiosum that maximization of the wage bill might entail a lower wage than would prevail in the absence of a union,[6] the principal difficulty with this approach is that many members might be unemployed at such a wage and can be expected to voice their discontent. It is true that, if wage policy were determined by majority vote, such members could be overruled. In fact, if members were selfish and if the order of layoff were known, a wage could be chosen at which just under half the members were unemployed. This policy could be pushed through the union council because the votes of the 51% of employed members pushing up their own wages could overrule the 49% unemployed members. However, there is no reason why the wage so determined should correspond to that at which the wage bill is maximized. It would do so only by fluke.[7]

The important question of the weight unions might give to the employment effects of their wage claims most likely cannot be answered by using a simple maximizing rule. For one thing, increased levels of unemployment benefits might cause modern unions to place less weight on employment effects. Nevertheless, the main cost of a high wage settlement, from a

---

4. A. M. Ross, *Trade Union Wage Policy* (Berkeley and Los Angeles: University of California Press, 1948), chap. 2.
5. J. T. Dunlop, *Wage Determination under Trade Unions* (New York: Kelley, 1944), chap. 3.
6. This is the case where the demand for union labor is of unit elasticity at less than the nonunion wage.
7. See W. N. Atherton, *Theory of Union Bargaining Goals* (Princeton, N.J.: Princeton University Press, 1973), p. 20.

microeconomic point of view, is the possibility of the members becoming unemployed. This effect is the basis of the Marshallian rules that relate union power to demand elasticity. Consequently, we could not agree with Ross that unions hardly consider these employment effects,[8] though we can agree that lack of information might cause unions to put too little weight on them.[9] Concern over the employment effect is also likely to depend on the voice or status of unemployed members within the union and on the level of union democracy. In some unions, unemployed members might drift away or fail to make their voices heard; this would lead to underemphasis on employment effects. The issue requires investigation on a case-by-case basis.

Finally, there are likely to be asymmetries in union wage behavior.[10] Money wages are likely to be maintained in recessions for political reasons, even if such a stance entails pronounced and unfavorable employment consequences. This result reflects the fact that a money wage cut agreed to by a particular union might not be followed by other unions, causing that union's members to make invidious comparisons unfavorable to the leadership.[11] A real wage cut, caused by inflation, is less likely to be resisted, because it does not disturb interunion relativities. In expansionary times, the employment effect is less compelling than in normal times and the wage claim is likely to be formulated without much consideration being paid to it.

Power and the Marshallian Rules. Accepting the general importance of the employment effect in union bargaining, and leaving aside for the moment the possibility of tension between leaders and members, let us inquire more closely into the determinants of this employment effect. For this inquiry the Marshallian rules for the elasticity of derived demand, which were briefly described in chapter 2, are an essential starting point.[12] It is plain that a union need have less fear for the employment consequences of a given wage claim if the elasticity of demand for union labor is low, *ceteris paribus*. In this case we could say the union has more power. It was Marshall who first categorized the determinants of this elasticity.[13]

The four Marshallian rules state that a trade union is likely to be better placed vis-a-vis the employer in obtaining higher wage rates for a given grade:

1. The less elastic is final demand for the product (low η).
2. The less easy it is to substitute other inputs for the grade in question (low σ).

8. Ross, *Trade Union Wage Policy*, chap. 4.
9. See also Hicks, *Theory of Wages*, p. 184.
10. See A. M. Cartter, *Theory of Wages and Employment* (Homewood, Ill.: Irwin, 1959), p. 91.
11. See Ross, *Trade Union Wage Policy*, pp. 71, 111.
12. A. Marshall, *Principles of Economics*, 8th ed. (London: Macmillan, 1948), pp. 384–386, 852–853.
13. For a mathematical analysis, see Hicks, *Theory of Wages*, pp. 235 ff.

3. The smaller is the grade's share in total expenses of production (low κ). This is the so-called "importance of being unimportant" rule.

4. The lower is the elasticity of supply of cooperant (substitute or complementary) factors (low ϵ).

Some comments on these rules are necessary, although both rules 1 and 2 are plain enough. For example, there has been much controversy over rule 3.[14] This is because Hicks has demonstrated that sometimes it is "important to be important," rather than the converse, when negotiating. The occasion in question appears to be where the elasticity of substitution is high relative to the elasticity of final demand ($\sigma > \eta$). It is possible to make sense of this proposition in the following way. Consider two labor groups, both of which face the same η, but for one of which it is much easier to substitute other inputs. The group for which substitution is relatively easy will be in the weaker position unless it is at the same time economically important to the firm (as indexed by κ). If κ is large, much dislocation to the firm would be caused by the very scale of the required substitution.

As for rule 4, take first the case where the labor grade organized by the union is competing with other factors, that is, where σ is high. A wage increase for the unionized grade will be reflected in an increased demand for other factors. If the supply of the competing factors is elastic, it follows that the unionized group can be inexpensively replaced. Thus, the latter's bargaining power is low. Second, take the case where the other factors are complementary, that is, where σ is low. A wage increase for any one group would now cause a reduction in demand for all. And if the supply of complementary factors is elastic, then these factors will leave if offered a slightly lower remuneration. This outcome also bodes ill for the unionized group.

To these rules it would seem worthwhile to add a fifth, relating to the effectiveness of union control over alternative supplies of labor to the grade in question. This effectiveness is a function of union density. It is true that if conditions 1 and 2 are favorable to the union a high union density is automatically implied. Thus, if the grade were not well organized, there would be substitution in production against union firms in the event of a wage increase; that is, product-demand facing union labor would be elastic. Similarly, because we may classify nonunion labor as an alternative, easily substitutable input, union labor could be undermined and thus condition 2 would not be favorable. But it is also true that union growth, by improving union density, could alter the conditions described by rules 1 and 2 in a manner advantageous to the union. The implication is that union growth, which is sometimes represented as being more in the interests of union leaders than the membership, will also confer benefits upon the members. It

14. See S. C. Maurice, "On the Importance of Being Unimportant: An Analysis of the Paradox in Marshall's Third Rule of Derived Demand," *Economica* 42 (1975): 385–393.

will do so by increasing union bargaining power and thus the equilibrium wage.[15]

In addition to providing a framework for analyzing union wage policy, therefore, the Marshallian rules also help us to understand union growth or, more specifically, the incidence of unionism across occupations and industries. It is likely soon to become apparent that a particular occupation or industry is favorably placed for the exertion of monopoly power, and an organization will be formed to exploit this power. It is no coincidence that airline pilots, for example, are strongly organized on both sides of the Atlantic. This is what we would expect, given the benefits to organization in this particular occupation. It is scarcely possible to replace pilots by other inputs (low σ), and the salaries of pilots constitute a very small component of total flight operator costs (low κ).

But the Marshallian rules apply only to the benefits derivable from organization. A full theory of union incidence would also have to take into account the costs of organization. It has been argued that these costs are likely to be higher in sectors with small and/or dispersed establishments, or in sectors characterized by high worker mobility.[16] A further factor influencing the costs of organization is governmental policy towards recognition: official encouragement lowers such costs. During the New Deal period, for example, workers received leaflets proclaiming, "The President wants you to organize,"[17] and membership rose markedly. In Great Britain, the important nationalized industry sector has had a duty to recognize unions; it is estimated that this recognition factor has been partly responsible for the substantial postwar growth in white-collar unionization.[18]

Finally, a certain simultaneity is evident in all of this. We have seen that strong organization is likely to shift the Marshallian conditions in a manner favorable to the union, thereby raising the equilibrium wage. But this higher wage is, of itself, likely to increase the returns to unionization and thus stimulate further organization. We shall consider a model that recognizes the simultaneity between wages and unionization in section 7.3.

In the foregoing, we have dealt exclusively with the wage aspects of collective bargaining. Yet clearly, collective bargaining is concerned with a variety of nonwage issues, including disciplinary and grievance procedures

15. S. Rosen, "Trade Union Power, Threat Effects, and the Extent of Organisation," *Review of Economic Studies* 39 (1969): 185–196, finds evidence consistent with the hypothesis of a positive relation between union density and the wage rate. See also Hicks, *Theory of Wages*, p. 161, who points out that, if the bulk of the employers in the industry are organized, they will be more willing to concede, for they can thereby more easily pass on wage increases in the form of higher prices (see also chap. 2).

16. See J. H. Pencavel, "The Demand for Union Services: An Exercise," *Industrial and Labor Relations Review* 24 (1971): 180–190.

17. H. B. Davis, "The Theory of Union Growth," *Quarterly Journal of Economics* 55 (1941): 631.

18. See G. S. Bain, *The Growth of White Collar Unionism* (Oxford: Clarendon Press, 1970), p. 183.

and seniority rules. However, for the problems tackled in this chapter, the distinction does not appear vital. We would argue that the circumstances under which a union has power to raise wages will also provide the conditions for improving nonwage elements of the contract of employment.

Thus, the Marshallian rules are useful in explaining both union power and union growth. We have therefore gone some distance towards answering, in a general way, one of the initial questions raised in the introduction: why some unions appear more powerful than others. We now return to a consideration of the process of negotiation and the problem of explaining strikes.

Bargaining Theories.   Having categorized the determinants of union power, let us turn to a consideration of how that power is exerted in the bargaining process. Zeuthen's bargaining model is taken as our foundation because it gives a relatively simple appreciation of the factors involved in the bargaining process and its failures.[19] The parties are treated symmetrically, so we can remain open-minded as to which side might make an error. A basic assumption of the model is that each party is pessimistic about the outcome of a wage settlement achieved via a strike: the union believes it will be a low wage, the employer a high wage. Thus, although there are possible benefits to be gained by disagreeing with the other side, there are definite potential costs as well, because the other side might fail to agree and precipitate a strike. Given this possibility, each party is supposed to edge toward the other because each believes concession will lower the other party's benefits from disagreement relative to its costs from disagreement. A party is supposed to stop conceding when a concession would raise its own benefit/cost ratio above the ratio it believes the other party faces; that is, give it a smaller relative gain than it believes the other is securing. The possibility of final failure to agree, and therefore of a strike, arises because either party's beliefs about the *other's* relative benefits and costs from disagreement might well be wrong. Although miscalculation need not be taken to be the sole factor explaining strikes, the proposition nonetheless provides a baseline from which to judge other theories of strikes, such as the *isolated mass* theory,[20] and also facilitates analysis of the relation between strike activity and the business cycle.[21]

Zeuthen's model can be outlined in the following manner.[22] Refer first to figure 7.2. Line *A* of the figure shows a possible path for union utility

19. F. Zeuthen, *Problems of Monopoly and Economic Warfare* (London: Routledge and Kegan Paul, 1930), chap. 4. Though the model of Hicks, *Theory of Wages*, chap. 7, is the more famous, it fails to incorporate the essential element of risk captured in the Zeuthen model.
20. C. Kerr and A. Siegel, "The Interindustry Prospensity to Strike—An International Comparison," in A. Kornhauser et al., *Industrial Conflict* (New York, Toronto, and London: McGraw-Hill, 1954), pp. 189–212.
21. See A. Rees, "Industrial Conflict and Business Fluctuations," *Journal of Political Economy* 60 (1952): 371–382.
22. For an alternative statement, see E. Saraydar, "Zeuthen's Theory of Bargaining: A Note," *Econometrica* 33 (1965): 802–813.

Figure 7.2   Representation of Union Utility from Wage Claims with and without Conflict

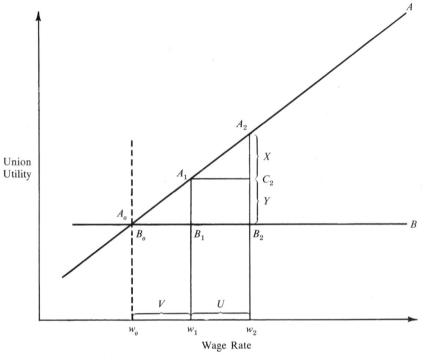

associated with various wage settlements, assuming the latter are obtained without a strike. Line B, on the other hand, indicates the utility expected by the union from a wage settlement after a strike. It can be seen that B is drawn so as to pass below A for all wage rates above a certain minimum, w_o. This is a consequence of the assumption that any wage settlement above w_o obtained without a strike is preferable to a settlement after a strike. In other words, a strike is supposed to be costly to the union.

From the construction of figure 7.2, it can be seen that the cost of a strike to the union declines the closer is the wage settlement to w_o. More formally, suppose that the employer had offered w_1 in the face of a union claim of w_2. The employer could then calculate that the union stands to gain $A_2 - C_2$ by risking conflict, although if there is conflict, and assuming C_2 was certain, the utility level falls back to B_2, causing a loss of $C_2 - B_2$. If the employer offers w_1 instead of the union claim of w_2, then there is a risk of a strike. This risk will presumably be such that the union's expectation of gain from rejecting w_1 in favor of w_2 equals the expectation of loss if w_2 is not conceded and a strike occurs. That is,

$$(1 - r_2{}^u)(A_2 - C_2) = r_2{}^u(C_2 - B_2) \tag{7.1}$$

where r_2^u is the risk of a strike that the union is willing to face in pressing for w_2 rather than accepting w_1.

From equation (7.1), we see that r_2^u has the value

$$r_2^u = \frac{A_2 - C_2}{A_2 - B_2}.$$

From figure 7.2, we see that

$$r_2^u = \frac{X}{X + Y},$$

or, in money terms,

$$r_2^u = \frac{U}{U + V}$$

because we have assumed A and B to be straight lines. r_2^u can also be interpreted as

$$\frac{\text{the benefits of disagreeing with offer } w_1 \text{ in favor of } w_2}{\text{the costs of disagreeing with offer } w_1}$$

Note that this ratio is always less than 100% within the contract zone.

It is apparent that the risk of conflict the rational union would be willing to face (and which its opponent would expect it to face) in pursuing wage w_2 if wage w_1 is offered—an index of its "determination" or "bargaining power" at that wage claim and offer—is somewhat less than 100%. By similar reasoning, we can show that as the employer lowers his wage offer toward w_o the risk of conflict the union should be willing to face in pursuing a wage claim will increase toward 100%. Thus, w_o may be said to delineate the lower limit of the "range of practicable bargains" (to use Professor Pigou's graphic term) or contract zone.

Let us now turn to the employer. The analysis can be brief because the same line of reasoning applies as in the union case. Thus, suppose that, from figure 7.3, the union claims w_{N-1}. Under what circumstances should the employer push for w_{N-2}? If he pushes without incurring conflict, he gains $A_{N-2} - C_{N-2}$. If, on the other hand, conflict results, the employer might expect pessimistically to drop back to utility level B_{N-2} (associated with a high wage w_N), thus losing $C_{N-2} - B_{N-2}$. These two options are equivalent when $(1 - r_{N-2}^m)(A_{N-2} - C_{N-2}) = r_{N-2}^m(C_{N-2} - B_{N-2})$, so that

$$r_{N-2}^m = \frac{A_{N-2} - C_{N-2}}{A_{N-2} - B_{N-2}}.$$

We see that w_N marks the upper point of the range of practicable bargains, because the risk of conflict the employer is willing to face becomes 100%

Figure 7.3   Representation of Employer Utility from Wage Offers with and without Conflict

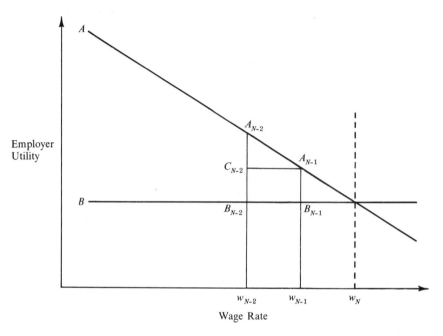

when the union advances this claim. Table 7.1 provides a numerical example of how the willingness to fight of the employer and the union varies for different claim/offer combinations within the contract zone. Assuming the union expects a $10 wage after conflict, it can be seen that the risk of conflict it would be willing to face falls from 100% to 16.6% as the management's offer rises from $10 to $60 (schedule r^u). However, if the union expected a $20 wage after conflict, the risk of conflict would be 100% at a management offer of $20 and would fall to 20% for an offer of $60 (schedule $r^{u'}$). Similarly, the risk of conflict management would be willing to face rises from 16.6% to 100% as the union claim escalates from $10 to $60 (schedule r^m). A diagram of these schedules is presented in figure 7.4.

The next step is to argue that, if the r^m and, say, the r^u schedules are the true schedules, and if there is complete information about them on the part of both parties, the wage settlement will tend to be where $r^u = r^m$. Here, the benefits of disagreement relative to the costs are the same for both parties. A possible sequence of offer and counter-offer is illustrated in table 7.2. The parties are shown as beginning their negotiations at either end of the contract zone, with each on the verge of fighting (situation 1). Management, however, by making a concession (situation 2) undermines the union's bargaining power and thereby lowers the benefit to be obtained by union members from strike action. We can then visualize the union as conceding (situation 3). The process continues until a wage approximating $40 is reached. That such a

Table 7.1 Hypothetical Acceptable Risks of Conflict for Management and Union at Various Wage Claims/Offers

	Union					
Union wage claim (A)	$20	$30	$40	$50	$60	$70
Management offer (C)	10	20	30	40	50	60
Expected wage after conflict:						
(B_u)	10	10	10	10	10	10
(B'_u)	20	20	20	20	20	20
$r^u = \dfrac{A - C}{A - B_u}$	100%	50%	33.3%	25%	20%	16.6%
$r^{u'} = \dfrac{A - C}{A - B'_u}$	–	100	50	33.3	25	20
	Management					
Management offer (A)	$10	$20	$30	$40	$50	$60
Union claim (C)	20	30	40	50	60	70
Expected wage after conflict (B_m)	70	70	70	70	70	70
$r^m = \dfrac{A - C}{A - B_m}$	16.6%	20%	25%	33.3%	50%	100%

Note: m and *u* denote management and union, respectively.

Figure 7.4   The Derivation of Bargaining Equilibrium

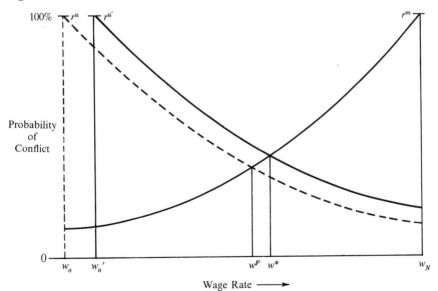

Table 7.2   Hypothetical Sequence of Offer and Counter-Offer Leading to a Determinate Wage

Situation	Offer/Claim	Estimated Risk of Conflict
1	m offers \$10, u claims \$70	$r^u = \dfrac{70 - 10}{70 - 10} = 100\%;$
		$r^m = \dfrac{10 - 70}{10 - 70} = 100\%$
2	m offers \$20, u claims \$70	$r^u = \dfrac{70 - 20}{70 - 10} = 83.3\%;$
		$r^m = \dfrac{20 - 70}{20 - 70} = 100\%$
3	m offers \$20, u claims \$60	$r^u = \dfrac{60 - 20}{60 - 10} = 80\%;$
		$r^m = \dfrac{30 - 60}{20 - 70} = 80\%$
4	m offers \$30, u claims \$60	$r^u = \dfrac{60 - 30}{60 - 10} = 60\%;$
		$r^m = \dfrac{30 - 60}{30 - 70} = 75\%$
5	m offers \$30, u claims \$50	$r^u = \dfrac{50 - 30}{50 - 10} = 50\%;$
		$r^m = \dfrac{30 - 50}{30 - 70} = 50\%$
6	Final wage equals \$40	

Note: m and *u* denote management and union, respectively.

wage would eventuate is also apparent from table 7.1, from which it can be seen that the risk schedules of union and employer, r^u and r^m, respectively, cross at a wage of \$40 or thereabouts.

The working of the model can be further clarified with the aid of figure 7.4. Let us assume that the curves labelled r^u and r^m show the risks that union and management are respectively willing to incur in advancing the given wage claim or offer. Each party will attempt to advance a claim/offer that lowers the benefit-cost ratio (probability of profitable conflict) that it believes the other side faces.[23] Suppose r^u and r^m to be the true curves and as such correctly estimated by the opposing parties, with respective strike points of w_o and w_N for union and management. Then the point of equal risk of conflict for both parties is given by wage w^F.

This model thus illustrates how an economic measure of bargaining power, relating gains to losses from settlement on given terms, may be formulated and how a point on the contract curve may be reached by each

23. For a discussion, see J. C. Harsanyi, "Approaches to the Bargaining Problem Before and After the Theory of Games: A Critical Discussion of Zeuthen's, Hicks' and Nash's Theories," *Econometrica* 24 (1956): 144–157.

party rationally exerting power. This point has also been derived using an alternative, axiomatic approach by Nash and is thus also referred to as the *Nash point*.[24] Each party is equally satisfied (or dissatisfied!) and thus, in a sense, the point corresponds to that obtained by splitting the difference between the union's minimum claim (the wage at which $B_u = C$) and management's maximum offer (where $B_m = C$).

Once the assumption of complete information is abandoned, the possibility of a strike arises. Thus, one party could underestimate the other's costs of agreement. For example, due to a tightening of the labor market, the union's estimate of its wage after conflict could be $20 rather than, say, the $10 assumed by the other side. As shown in table 7.1 this would give rise to the $r^{u\prime}$ rather than the r^u schedule. Since the union believes it has less to lose from conflict, the equilibrium wage should be higher (around $50 in the table). The point can be illustrated from figure 7.4. r^u is the curve management has in mind for the union, with strike point w_o. However, the union's true decision curve is $r^{u\prime}$, with strike point w_o'. Then the employer would stick at offer w^F, while the union would stick at w^*. Such misestimation is quite possible because negotiation does not always improve the parties' perception of each other's willingness to fight—it is in each party's interest to exaggerate this willingness. A strike might then result despite the fact that a settlement anywhere in the range $w_o' w_N$ would, by definition, be more advantageous than conflict to either party. Within this framework, a strike would be the result of the overoptimism of one party or the other; it would be an accident.

While miscalculation need not be taken to be a full explanation of strikes, it is perhaps not as unlikely as it may sound. In the first place, it should be remembered that the number of strikes is quite modest in relation to the many thousands of bargains that are struck both at factory floor and national level in a given time period. Thus, there would not have to be many miscalculations. Moreover, this maintained hypothesis of misinformation simplifies the explanation of strikes. The explanation of strikes over working conditions can be seen to boil down mainly to an explanation of the factors that increase the difficulty of the parties in assessing each other's bargaining power. For example, inflationary surprises or unexpected changes in the unemployment level can be expected to upset established bargaining relationships and increase the possibility of strikes.

Further, if strikes are to some extent the result of mismatched expectations, and because changes in business activity or technical progress or alterations in payment systems can make forecasting more difficult, we would expect industries or periods affected by such changes to be characterized by increased strike activity. More importantly, if employers and unions formulate their expectations according to different criteria, strikes should be more prevalent when and where these criteria are divergent. Rees has obtained some suggestive findings in this respect. He found that the trough of the cycle

24. J. E. Nash, "The Bargaining Problem," *Econometrica* 18 (1950): 155–162.

of the number of strikes beginning monthly tended to lag the business cycle trough and to lead the business cycle peak.[25] This result can be plausibly explained in terms of each party emphasizing its own criteria at the expense of the other's in formulating bargaining strategy. To explain the lead at the peak, for example, employers can be thought of as looking at indicators, such as investment intentions, which tend to fall off before (that is, lead) the peak; and the unions at indicators, such as current levels of unemployment, which tend to lag the peak. A similar line of reasoning can explain the lag at the trough.

The effect of certain government policies on strikes can also be analyzed within this framework. Statutory incomes restraint or minimum-wage legislation, by defining more precisely the possible alternatives open to the parties, is likely to decrease strikes.[26] (This is akin to a reduction in the length and a more precise determination of the ends of the range $w'_o w_N$ in figure 7.4.) At the same time, the number of bargaining pairs, and thus the opportunities for miscalculation, would be decreased with the same effect. The lifting of incomes policy, on the other hand, is likely to bring about the opposite result. This is a testable implication. Furthermore, the application of social policy in depressions, by ruling out wage cuts, might diminish bargaining uncertainty and so diminish strikes.[27] This gives further cause to expect strike activity and the business cycle to be correlated.

Emphasizing the element of miscalculation in strikes also enables us to dispose of some alternative explanations for strikes. It is sometimes argued that increased welfare benefits, by lowering the costs of stoppages to the workers involved, are likely to increase the number or length of stoppages, or both.[28] However, this result would follow only if the increase in union bargaining power were not foreseen by employers. Otherwise, the outcome would seem simply to be higher equilibrium wage settlements, not more stoppages, as may be demonstrated by displacing the r^u curve of figure 7.4 rightwards. Similarly, rising employment prospects and improving business conditions leading to greater union bargaining power[29] are not enough *of themselves* to account for the apparent tendency for strikes to increase at these times. The explanation must be couched in terms of the failure of employers to perceive these power-augmenting developments. Equally, on

25. Rees, "Industrial Conflict," pp. 374–378. For similar findings, using more up to date American data, see A. R. Weintraub, "Prosperity Versus Strikes: An Empirical Approach," *Industrial and Labor Relations Review* 19 (1966): 231–238.
26. See J. Vanderkamp, "Economic Activity and Strikes in Canada," *Industrial Relations* 9 (1970): 219.
27. Ibid.
28. See, for example, J. W. Durcan and W. E. J. McCarthy, "The State Subsidy Theory of Strikes: An Examination of Statistical Data for the Period 1956–70," *British Journal of Industrial Relations* 12 (1974): 26–44.
29. Rees, "Industrial Conflict," p. 81, appears to argue along these lines.

this model, we could not accept that strikes are in any sense revolts against oppression.[30] The oppressed are much more likely to have low wages.

Perhaps the most important alternative theory of strikes is the *political* theory. This rests on the notion, mainly associated with Ross, that there is likely to be a divergence of goals and/or knowledge between the union members and the union leadership. Ashenfelter and Johnson, for example, build their important theory of strikes on the assumption that members are systematically less well-informed about the likely outcome of a strike than is the leadership, which nonetheless plays along so as not to appear to be selling out. A strike is thus seen as having the effect of lowering the rank and file's expectations, because of the shock effect of the firm's resistance and the resulting loss of normal income. As the authors put it, "The basic function of a strike is as an equilibrating mechanism to square up the union membership's wage expectations with what the firm can be expected to pay."[31] Union members thus repeatedly make unrealistic wage claims. The model, therefore, rests upon an assumption of systematic miscalculation. It also assumes asymmetric behavior as between union and employer sides; it being the union side which, in a sense, causes the strike.

Also in the tradition of political theories is the isolated mass theory propounded by Kerr and Siegel to account for the especially high strike proneness of industries such as coal mining.[32] Yet we would observe here that the reward system in coal mining has traditionally been payment by results—the "checkweighman" being in many countries the mine workers' shop steward.[33] This particular method of wage payment increases bargaining opportunities, and perhaps uncertainty, and is likely therefore to increase the possibility of miscalculation. For example, Scott's study of industrial relations in a British colliery points to "wildly fluctuating conditions" caused by the piecework system.[34] Factors such as this reduce the need for a special explanation.

Ross and Hartman also point to the broader aspect of the industrial relations sytem as a determinant of strikes. A young union movement, rival unionism, and decentralized bargaining systems are all thought to increase strike activity.[35] But even this view, which emphasizes the maturity of the

30. See S. Hyman, *Strikes* (London: Fontana, 1972), p. 121.
31. O. Ashenfelter and G. E. Johnson, "Bargaining Theory, Trade Unions and Industrial Strike Activity," *American Economic Review* 65 (1969): 39.
32. Kerr and Siegel, "Interindustry Propensity to Strike." And for a catalog of theories, see Hyman, *Strikes,* pp. 56–73.
33. See J. T. Dunlop, *Industrial Relations Systems* (New York: Holt, 1958; reprint ed., Carbondale, Ill.: Southern Illinois University Press, 1970), p. 179.
34. W. H. Scott, E. Mumford, I. S. McGivering, and J. M. Kirkby, *Coal and Conflict* (Liverpool: Liverpool University Press, 1963), p. 150.
35. A. M. Ross and P. Hartman, *Changing Patterns of Industrial Conflict* (New York: Wiley, 1960), p. 79.

relations between employers and employees, can be analyzed in terms of the uncertainty theory of strikes. A mature bargaining relation can be thought of as one in which the parties are likely to have built up a good knowledge of each other's bargaining power and strike point.[36]

A final explanation for some strikes must be entered at this point. Contrary to the assumptions of our uncertainty model, some strikes might not be part of a bargaining situation. In plants with an endemic strike situation, for example, it is possible that the parties, while ostensibly bargaining with each other, are actually seeking to provoke government intervention, which they believe will be favorable to themselves.[37] The work force might wish to see nationalization, as in Great Britain, or the establishment of a beneficial product marketing arrangement—the setting up of the Bituminous Coal Commission in the United States was at the instigation of the mine workers. For their part, employers might believe they can be bought out or assisted on favorable terms by the government. In these circumstances, a strike need not be the result of a divergence of opinion as to the outcome. The fight itself brings a return to both parties.

In this discussion, the psychology of bargaining has not been emphasized. We have assumed that the parties are good bargainers, as would seem appropriate in an economics text; a contrary assumption might be appropriate in a manual for arbitrators or in a work of sociology.[38] Nor for that matter have we touched upon the theory of games. For the severely practical objectives of the present chapter, this theory does not yet seem sufficiently developed.[39]

However, the knife edge that bargainers must walk can be nicely illustrated using the "prisoner's dilemma" model of game theory.[40] Table 7.3 gives a possible matrix of payoffs to various strategies. Let us suppose the union is persuaded to concede by management's promise of a similar concession. Further suppose that this promise is not then fulfilled. In this case, the union is forced into a disadvantageous position (upper right corner). It now appears that the union will be motivated in turn not to concede, as a result of which strategy the members' losses can be assumed to be smaller. But with both parties pursuing a no-concession strategy, there will be a strike in which both lose (lower right corner). Management might then wish to obtain the reasonable wage/no strike payoff (upper left corner), but this payoff is only available if the union can be persuaded to switch to the

36. See M. W. Reder, "The Theory of Union Wage Policy," *Review of Economics and Statistics* 34 (1952): 40.

37. See Ross, *Trade Union Wage Policy*, p. 105.

38. See R. E. Walton and R. B. McKersie, *A Behavioral Theory of Labor Negotiations* (New York: McGraw-Hill, 1965), chaps. 6–7.

39. For references see A. Coddington, *Theories of the Bargaining Process* (London: Allen and Unwin, 1968), chap. 5.

40. For an analysis of this dilemma, see A. Rapoport and A. M. Chammah, *Prisoner's Dilemma* (Ann Arbor: University of Michigan Press, 1965).

Table 7.3   Hypothetical Payoff Matrix for Employer and Union

		Management Strategy	
		Concede	Not Concede
Union Strategy	Concede	No strike, reasonable wage	*m* enforces a low wage, profit share rises
	Not Concede	*u* enforces a high wage, *m*'s profits cut	strike, both lose (but less than if unilateral concession had been made)

cooperative strategy at the same time. Parties might thus become locked into a strike situation even though both lose thereby.

According to the Zeuthen model, therefore, strikes are associated with uncertainty. Periods of unexpected inflation/deflation, technical change, fluctuations in earnings, such as might be caused by the operation of piece-work systems, or new bargaining relations, such as occurs when unions are not recognized or have only recently been recognized, are likely to be characterized by increased levels of strike activity. Apart from Rees' early findings, such hypotheses have not been systematically tested. However, using simplified bargaining models in which the parties miscalculate each other's readiness to fight, a relation may be predicted between strike activity and various economic variables. It is to a consideration of such relationships that we now turn.

7.3   Empirical Analysis of Bargaining

The following discussion considers time-series and, to a lesser extent, cross-section models of strike propensity. Discussion of other major aspects of collective bargaining, such as its effect on job security and relative wages, is remitted to later chapters. Our concern is with strike functions, which tend increasingly to be used in analysis of union pressure on wage rates.[41] Such functions might also shed some light on the issue of whether strikes can usefully be depicted as the consequence of miscalculation.

However, collective bargaining and strikes presuppose some degree of organization. Indeed, early attempts to incorporate union pressure into models of pay determination did not use strikes but, rather, indices of union membership growth.[42] Thus, it is appropriate first to consider some results on the growth of unions.

Union Density.   Why does the density of unionization vary so widely across industries and over time? To take the example of production workers in

41. See, for example, J. Johnston and M. C. Timbrell, "Empirical Tests of a Bargaining Model of Wage Rate Determination," *Manchester School* 41 (1973): 141–167.
42. A. G. Hines, "Trade Unions and Wage Inflation in the United Kingdom, 1893–1961," *Review of Economic Studies* 31 (1964): 221–252.

American manufacturing, we discover that no less than 90% of such employees in petroleum refining are in establishments where the majority of workers are covered by collective bargaining, whereas the proportion is only 30% in textile mills.[43] Large movements are also apparent over time. In Great Britain, for example, though total work force unionization has remained fairly static since World War II, this constancy emerges as the result of a decline in traditionally well-organized industries, such as coal mining, being counterbalanced by a rapid increase in white-collar unionization.

As yet, there has been no systematic inquiry into the growth of unions within the theoretical framework of the costs of and benefits to organization on the lines outlined above. Nonetheless, certain empirical findings can be interpreted within this framework. Let us first consider the variation of union membership across time. A major study is that of Hines,[44] which links the rate of growth of total union membership to the level of membership, retail price changes, and the level of industrial profits. The rationale for the first variable is that, after a certain level of organization has been reached, further membership advances become increasingly difficult to attain. This can be seen as a component of the costs side, reflecting diminishing returns to the production of union services. The rationale for the price change variable is that an increased rate of inflation breeds militancy and hence increased membership. Firmer reasoning might be that unions are credited with the wage increases that ensue in times of inflation, and their membership consequently increases.[45] Profits are included on the reasoning that the higher are profits the more likely are unions to claim, and employers to concede, higher wages. Both variables can be seen as entering on the benefits side of organization.

One formulation of the Hines model gives the following results for British union growth over the period 1921–61 (excluding war years):

$$\dot{T} = 4.115 - 0.0881 T_{t-1} + 0.324 \dot{P}_{t-\frac{1}{2}} - 0.0161 D_{t-\frac{1}{2}}$$
$$\quad\quad\quad\quad (2.45) \quad\quad\quad (7.90) \quad\quad\quad (0.77)$$

$$R^2 = 0.668$$
$$DW = 1.57$$

where $\dot{T}$ is the yearly rate of change of total union membership;
$\dot{P}$ is the yearly rate of change of consumer prices;
D is the level of profits; and
$|t|$ are given in parentheses.

---

43. G. Pierson, "The Effect of Union Strength on the U.S. 'Phillips Curve,'" *American Economic Review* 58 (1968): 457.

44. Hines, "Trade Unions," pp. 233 ff.

45. See M. Friedman, "Some Comments on the Significance of Labor Unions for Economic Policy," in D. M. Wright, *The Impact of the Union* (New York: Harcourt-Brace, 1951), p. 231.

It can be seen that the model is quite successful, explaining nearly 70% of the variation in union growth.

A similar type of model has been developed by Ashenfelter and Pencavel for American trade union growth. Their chief additional variable is a party political one, which seeks to allow for changes in political influences on trade union growth. The political climate has at times been favorable to union growth (for example, the National Labor Relations Act of 1935 encouraged unions), and at other times unfavorable (witness the constraints on picketing and sympathy strikes imposed by the Taft-Hartley Act of 1947). The proxy the authors use is the proportion of the House of Representatives affiliated to the Democratic Party. The authors find, as does Hines, that $\dot{T}$ is significantly positively related to P and negatively to T. Unlike Hines, however, they have to include the political variable, which is highly significant, to achieve a 70% explanatory power.[46] Still, the performance of the basic economic model of union growth seems impressive. In the American case, a rise of 1 percentage point in the inflation rate causes a 0.65 percentage point increase in union growth, other things being equal. This is a larger coefficient than that obtained in the British case. The authors interpret this result as indicating that American trade unions are primarily "defensive" organizations,[47] in the sense that they strive to defend real living standards.

An economic model also performs well when we come to consider variations in the density of unionization among industries. Bain has found that nearly 50% of the interindustry variation in density of organization of British white-collar workers in 1964 can be explained by a single variable—average establishment size in the industry. For some occupations, the association is even stronger. The following zero-order correlation coefficients between the proportion of white-collar workers unionized by industry and the average number of white-collar employees per establishment were obtained: 0.911 for draftsmen, 0.756 for clerks, 0.636 for scientists and technologists, and 0.597 for foremen.[48]

The above results might be explained in terms of the fact that concentrated industries, with a few large visible plants, are less costly to organize. Moreover, concentration could also be correlated with monopoly in the product market, thereby implying a less elastic derived demand curve for labor. This would bring greater returns to organization. A study separating out these different effects has yet to be performed.

Ashenfelter and Johnson, in their American cross-section study of wages and unions, include the industry wage rate in addition to a measure of concentration to explain unionization. This might be rationalized on the ground that higher wages indicate greater benefits to organizing the industry.

46. O. Ashenfelter and J. M. Pencavel, "American Trade Union Growth 1900–1960," *Quarterly Journal of Economics* 83 (1969): table 1, pp. 442–443.
47. Ibid., p. 444.
48. Bain, *White Collar Unionism,* p. 79.

One specification of their model, which accounts for a large proportion of the variance in the incidence of unionization, gives the following result for nineteen manufacturing industries as of 1960:[49]

$$T_i = 0.175 + 0.481 W_i + 0.304 CON_i$$
$$(1.63) \quad (3.64) \quad (2.10)$$

$$R^2 = 0.667$$

where W_i and CON_i respectively measure the wage rate and degree of concentration of the ith industry;
$|t|$ are given in parentheses.

Here, as in the time-series case, the success of economic variables in explaining unionization might indicate that the emphasis usually accorded government intervention in promoting unionization is overplayed. The results might even be regarded as providing support for the view that pro-union legislative measures tend to be an effect, rather than a cause, of increased unionization,[50] though more research is needed.

Industrial Disputes. Our theoretical schema relates industrial disputes to miscalculation. Factors raising the number of bargaining pairs, or widening the bargaining range ($w_o' w_N$ in figure 7.4), may be said to increase the likelihood of such failure. In a time-series context, there are a number of factors that might then explain the observed association between the number of strikes and the business cycle. First, negotiations about employment conditions are likely to be reopened at longer intervals in the trough, so that there are fewer bargaining pairs. Second, there are increased constraints at such times, such as the inadmissibility of money wage cuts, which reduce bargaining alternatives, and thereby lessen the possibility of miscalculation. Government incomes control, by narrowing the bargaining zone, should have a similar effect during periods of "policy on." If there were fewer strikes in depressions, the interpretation would be that there was a lower probability of accidents occurring at such times, because fewer and more limited negotiations were in progress.

Dropping the assumption that the parties gain knowledge of each other's changes in bargaining power—the political theory—opens up other possibilities. Reduced union bargaining power at times of recession could then be a sufficient condition for fewer strikes. For example, an increase in unemployment, a decrease in price inflation, or a decrease in union membership

49. O. Ashenfelter and G. E. Johnson, "Unionism, Relative Wages and Labor Quality in U.S. Manufacturing Industries," *International Economic Review* 13 (1972): 500. The equation was estimated by two-stage least squares to reduce bias arising from the simultaneity of the relation between unionization and wage rates (see section 1.2).
50. Davis, "Union Growth," p. 632.

could reduce strikes by lowering union militancy, given that the employers do not take advantage of such developments. An increase in profits might have a similar effect by making employers more willing to concede, given that the union members, if not the leadership, are unaware of the change. But, as we have observed, the assumption of systematic miscalculation seems implausible.

The main results of time-series analyses of strike frequency are shown in table 7.4. Other measures of strike activity, such as working days lost, are treated later. Interpretation is difficult. It can be seen that for Great Britain, the United States, and Canada, there is certainly evidence of an association between strike frequency and business activity. Decreases in unemployment are, *ceteris paribus,* significantly associated with an increase in strike fre-

Table 7.4 Postwar Strike Functions for the United States, United Kingdom, and Canada

(Dependent variable: the number of strikes beginning per unit time interval)

Variable	U.S.[a]	U.K.[b] Excluding Coal	Coal	Canada[c]
Constant	1579.8*	−147.9	909.8*	45.1*
Q_1	213.6*	74.9*	33.2	
Q_2	594.8*	38.0*	48.2*	
Q_3	457.9*	7.0*	−20.4	
Trend	−2.2*	5.50*	−10.1†	2.39*
Profit share	1.6	1.87*		
Total unemployment rate	−123.0*	−41.3*	−13.2†	−5.17*
Past real wage increases	−62.2*	−42.5*	−44.1*	−1.80*
Industry unemployment rate			−13.1†	
R^2	.938	.869	.943	0.638
DW	1.44	1.36	1.48	not reported

Notes:
[a] quarterly observations, 1952(I)–1967(II).
[b] quarterly observations, 1950(I)–1967(II).
[c] yearly observations, 1946–1966.
* indicates significance at the 5% level.
† the trend and unemployment variables taken together are significant.
Q_1, Q_2 and Q_3 are dummies for the first three quarters.
Sources:
[a] O. Ashenfelter and G. E. Johnson, "Bargaining Theory, Trade Unions and Industrial Strike Activity," *American Economic Review* 59 (1969): table 1, p. 44.
[b] J. H. Pencavel, "An Investigation into Industrial Strike Activity in Britain," *Economica* 37 (1970): tables 1 and 3, pp. 245, 252.
[c] J. Vandercamp, "Economic Activity and Strikes in Canada," *Industrial Relations* 9 (1970): 227.

quency in all three countries.[51] This is consistent with both the political and accident theories. The profit share variable, however, does not appear to have much impact on strike frequency. On the political model, this might be explained in terms of an increase in profits making the employer more willing to concede and the union more ambitious in its claims, with consequent ambiguous results for strike frequency.[52] But the question then arises as to why the same sort of argument should not render the sign of the unemployment coefficient uncertain as well. The accident theory here seems easier to defend, because there is in this model no presumption that profits and strikes are related. Backing for this theory is also to be found in studies investigating the impact of government incomes regulatory policies, which have in all cases concluded that such policies appear to reduce strike frequency.[53] Again, studies indicate that increases in union membership increase strike frequency.[54] This seems most naturally explained in terms of denser organization increasing the frequency and/or range of negotiations.

For all three countries, table 7.4 also shows that the higher the past rate of increase in real wages, the lower tends to be the frequency of strikes. This result appears to hold whether the real wage increase comes about via higher nominal wages or lower price inflation. This accords well with the political model; if real wages have been rising, union members are less militant and provoke fewer strikes. In the accident theory, however, we would expect a positive association on the basis that change breeds uncertainty. High past wage increases seem just as likely to widen the bargaining zone as the reverse. Nevertheless, that the specifications contained in table 7.4 indicate a negative association does not close the matter. This is because cross-section findings, to which we now turn, give precisely the opposite sign for the wage variable. This discrepancy has still to be explained.

Modern analysis of strike frequency on a cross-section basis is sparse.[55] Suggestive work using British data has, however, been undertaken by Shorey. One of his results for a sample of thirty-three manufacturing industries is as follows:[56]

$$S_i = -710.3 - 2.3F_i + 2.7PBR_i + 115.1\dot{W}_i + 8.9RW_i$$
$$(5.5) \quad (6.7) \quad (8.2) \quad (6.0) \quad (5.6)$$

51. There is some evidence, however, that for the United Kingdom, in the period since 1967, a measure of unfilled vacancies performs better than unemployment. See L. C. Hunter, "The Economic Determination of Strike Activity: A Reconsideration," *Discussion Paper No. 1* (Glasgow: Department of Social and Economic Research, University of Glasgow, 1973), table 3.
52. This is the reasoning of Ashenfelter and Johnson, "Bargaining Theory," p. 41.
53. Pencavel, "Union Services," p. 245; Hunter, "Strike Activity," p. 17; Vanderkamp, "Strikes in Canada," p. 226.
54. See Hunter, "Strike Activity," table 3; Vanderkamp, "Strikes in Canada," p. 227.
55. For a descriptive investigation, see K. G. J. C. Knowles, *Strikes—A Study in Industrial Conflict* (Oxford: Basil Blackwell, 1952), pp. 161–209.
56. J. Shorey, "A Cross Section Analysis of Strike Activity," mimeographed (Cardiff: Department of Economics, University College, 1975), app. 2. Some of these results are replicated in idem, "The Size of the Work Unit and Strike Incidence," *Journal of Industrial Economics* 23 (1975): 175–188.

$$-0.04FS_i + 5.9\dot{K}_i - 7.3\dot{Q}_i - 0.04CON_i$$
$$(2.2) \quad\quad (3.8) \quad\quad (3.0) \quad\quad\quad (0.01)$$
$$R^2 = 0.899$$

where S_i is the number of strikes divided by the number of employees in the ith industry;

F is the proportion of women workers;

PBR is the proportion of workers on payment by results schemes;

$\dot{W}$ is the rate of change of manual worker earnings;

RW is the reference wage—each industry is allocated to one of eight groups, the reference wage for any member of that group being the highest in the group;

FS is the average number of workers per firm;

$\dot{K}$ is the rate of change of capital per year;

$\dot{Q}$ is the rate of change of productivity per year;

CON is a measure of concentration in the industry; and

$|t|$ are in parentheses.

The coefficients in question are again open to a variety of interpretations. The positive coefficients for PBR and $\dot{K}$, and perhaps RW, seem to be consistent with the accident hypothesis; this is because piecework payment systems, faster technical change, and changes in wage differentials all give rise to additional bargaining opportunities and to increased uncertainty. On this argument, however, one might also expect $\dot{Q}$ to have a positive coefficient rather than a negative one, because changes in productivity upset established relationships and thus cause uncertainty. But the author's interpretation of both the negative coefficient for $\dot{Q}$ and the positive coefficient for $\dot{W}$ seems to favor the political theory. Because higher labor productivity is associated with higher profits, this is supposed to bring about a greater propensity to concede by the employers (presumably the union members are not informed of this development by their leaders, otherwise strike frequency need not diminish). In the same vein, the $\dot{W}$ variable is taken to indicate the effect of "the level of productive activity in the industry."[57] As this level increases, workers are thought to feel they are contributing more, causing them to raise their minimum claims and so precipitating more strikes. Yet it can be seen that the coefficient on the wage variable is opposite in sign to that obtained in time-series analyses. This difference casts a shadow on this explanation. A further difficulty, if we accept that wage changes affect strike frequency, is that there is then a problem of simultaneity; strikes are usually considered likely to affect wages positively.

The coefficient on the firm size variable indicates that large firms have fewer strikes,[58] though strike length might be longer. This is surprising,

57. Shorey, "Strike Incidence," p. 183.
58. This accords also with the impression of H. A. Turner, G. Clack, and G. Roberts, *Labor Relations in the Motor Industry* (London: George Allen and Unwin, 1967), pp. 230 ff.

because most research indicates that industrial morale is lower in large establishments.[59] We might expect lower morale to be reflected in greater opportunities for misunderstanding. Moreover, given the fact that large firms are more likely to be monopolists, and as such shielded from competition, their managements would be better placed to indulge any taste they might have for conflict (chapter 6). However, recent research indicates that the relationship between size and conflict might not be either uniformly increasing or decreasing. It seems that there might be ranges toward the bottom and the top ends of the plant size scale, within which plant size is positively associated with strikes. But within the medium-sized plant range, say 500 to 1,000 employees, there is a zero or even a negative relation.[60] It might be that medium-sized firms can afford to introduce well-developed personnel policies that minimize the likelihood of strikes, but that as firm size increases such beneficial results are swamped by the pure size effect.

We have been concentrating on strike frequency. There are also the problems of analyzing what will happen once a strike begins: questions of strike periodicity, the number of men involved, and the eventual wage outcome. Unfortunately, our knowledge of strike severity, measured in working days lost, is even more rudimentary than our knowledge of strike frequency. Canadian experience would suggest that strike severity also follows a procyclical movement.[61] On the other hand, there is evidence from the British automobile industry that strikes become more protracted in (short) recessions, perhaps because strikes are a form of work spreading for the industry at such times.[62]

As for the outcome of strikes, it does not seem very useful to approach the question from the viewpoint of which side wins.[63] This is because of the difficulty of deciding a time horizon over which to make the calculation; a defeat now might lay the basis for victory in the future. Nevertheless, Zeuthen's model does imply that the parties will gradually compromise until, under certain conditions, they split the difference. The conditions are that the parties be equally proficient at bargaining, possess the same type of utility function, and be able to discount bluffing.

There have been interesting exploratory studies of the process of yielding and of splitting of the difference. Taking eight American strikes, Comay and his associates have looked at the course of employer offers and union claims

59. The classic statement is in A. W. Revans, "Industrial Morale and Size of Unit," *Political Quarterly* 27 (1956): 303–311.
60. C. F. Eisele, "Organisation Size, Technology, and Frequency of Strikes," *Industrial and Labor Relations Review* 27 (1974): 560–571. For a similar result, see H. A. Turner, G. Roberts, and D. Roberts, *Management Characteristics and Labor Conflict* (Cambridge: Cambridge University Press, 1977), p. 42.
61. Vanderkamp, "Strikes in Canada," p. 224.
62. Turner et al., *Labor Relations,* p. 118.
63. The United Kingdom Ministry of Labour once attempted such a classification of the outcome of strikes. See Knowles, *Industrial Conflict,* p. 242.

over time.[64] A finding with important implications is that the higher the management side's rate of concession over time, the higher tended to be the union's. This runs counter to a prediction of Cross's model. Thus, a conciliatory attitude by one side tends to cause concessions to be made by the other and leads to shorter stoppages. In its policy implications, this finding would seem to provide support for the National Labor Relations Board's 1960 decision to disallow *Boulwarism,* the policy then practiced by the General Electric Company of making a single offer and not deviating from it thereafter.

On the question of splitting the difference, Hamermesh has investigated the initial difference in wage claims between the parties for a sample of forty-three negotiations between 1968 and 1970 and compared this to the final wage outcome.[65] On average, the unions wanted a 23% wage increase, management was prepared to concede 8%, and the final outcome was a 12% increase. In fact, in eleven cases out of the forty-three, the employer side made no concession at all, which would indicate that Boulwarism is by no means extinct. On this evidence it is interesting to note that management and union sides do proceed differently when negotiating. This finding is, then, supportive of the asymmetry assumed in the political model and goes against the even-handed treatment implicit in the accident theory.

7.4 Policy Issues

We have considered the determinants of union power over wage rates and the exercise of that power. The former can be related to the theory of union growth, and the latter to problems of industrial disputes. We have seen that the growth of unions can be related to economic factors. Indeed, it is possible that the legislative element in union growth has been exaggerated; legislative support of unions might tend to follow, rather than precede, union membership increases. On the matter of the determinants of strikes, we seem to be on firmest ground in associating strikes with bargaining mistakes. There are signs in the cross-section analysis that this view is correct; for example, strike-prone industries tend to be those with high technical change and/or extensive use of payment by results. The procyclical movement of strike frequency over time can also be interpreted in this framework: fewer strikes occur in recessions because of the smaller number and more limited range of negotiations during such intervals.

The current atmosphere would seem to be one of encouraging collective bargaining and favoring unionization. Under the Kennedy administration, for example, Executive Order 10988 encouraged collective organization among public sector employees. There are various arguments in favor of this

64. Y. Comay, A. Melnik, and A. Subotnik, "Bargaining, Yield Curves and Wage Settlements: An Empirical Analysis," *Journal of Political Economy* 82 (1974): 303–313.
65. D. S. Hamermesh, "Who 'Wins' in Wage Bargaining?" *Industrial and Labor Relations Review* 26 (1973): 1146–1149. See also M. F. Bognanno and J. B. Dworkin, "Comment," *Industrial and Labor Relations Review* 28 (1975): 570–572.

approach. Collectively negotiated wages are said to be more equitable, as are agreed layoff and discharge procedures. In addition, unions are said to remedy a deficiency in the democratic system. This view holds that, because it is more difficult to organize financial contributions among many than few people, the more affluent might be able to lobby more effectively than the poor in the absence of unions.[66] However, unionization is likely to bring strikes in its train, if only because of the larger number of bargaining opportunities. We have surveyed a number of empirical studies that point to this very connection. A major policy issue thus becomes how to obtain the benefits of collective bargaining with less of the strike disbenefit.

In the light of our analysis, let us consider some of the proposals put forward to lower strike propensity. Most in accord with our analysis is the advocacy of detailed written agreements. It has been said that an agreement with detailed procedures for layoffs or transfers means that "workers and their representatives *know what to expect* when specific problems arise,"[67] and so too, it might be added, does management. There is thus less need for negotiations just at the time when emotions are high. Under the written agreement of specified periodicity, strike frequency, but not necessarily severity, is likely to be reduced. Moreover, because strikes tend to occur at fixed renegotiating intervals, they are therefore predictable. Even if these strikes are just as long as strikes at other times, they are less damaging because the expected is always less damaging than the unexpected.

Arbitration is sometimes also put forward as a means of reconciling collective bargaining with a limitation on strikes. This is not the place to consider arbitration in detail. However, the development of *final offer arbitration* since 1971 in the United States is particularly interesting from the theoretical point of view. As we have seen, for there to be a contract zone, the costs of disagreement must be greater than the benefits from disagreement for both parties within some wage range. The threat of a strike, by forming a large part of these costs of disagreement, thus generates a bargaining zone. But what will generate that zone if the strike threat is removed?

The answer is that arbitration can also impose a cost of disagreement—the possibility that the arbitral award will be less favorable than a freely negotiated agreement. There will be prearbitration negotiations if both parties have different expectations as to the arbitral award, each fearing the arbitrator will favor the other. A way of stimulating prearbitration negotiations, therefore, is to have a scheme whereby the arbitrator has to choose between one party or the other's final offer. Both parties, fearing the worst, are then expected to be stimulated to reach a free agreement, or at least to moderate and simplify their positions in the hope that the arbitrator will choose their claim or offer

66. See M. W. Reder, "Job Security and the Nature of Union Power," *Industrial and Labor Relations Review* 13 (1960): 361–362.
67. J. Stieber, "Unauthorised Strikes under the British and American Industrial Relations Systems," *British Journal of Industrial Relations* 6 (1968): 236 (emphasis added).

in preference to the other side's.[68] This method can be likened to "sudden death" in contrast to the split the difference tendency of conventional arbitration. Conventional arbitration is likely to provoke wide prearbitration differences between the parties who, moreover, will feel it advantageous to keep the number of issues in dispute as formidable as possible. Preliminary research results indicate that final offer arbitration does indeed have the described advantage over conventional arbitration.[69]

Other measures put forward to mitigate strikes are conciliation or mediation procedures, fact-finding commissions, and the institution of "cooling off" periods. All can be seen to accord to some extent with the view of industrial disputes as resulting from miscalculation. In Great Britain and the United States, there have long been official conciliation services—dating from 1896 with the Conciliation Act in the former country, and from 1913 in the latter when the predecessor of the Federal Mediation and Conciliation Service was set up. A form of permanent mediation also exists over the substantial area of British industry governed by wage councils (15% of the work force). Here, wage rates are set jointly by employer and union representatives, but an important role is reserved for an independent chairman.

The very role of the conciliator has been said to be to "clear up misunderstandings," "get around personal animosities," and "bring out the real issues."[70] This can be seen as supportive of the accident theory of strikes. A fact-finding body performs a similar role, though it has the extra sanction of public opinion, of informing the parties by laying out the facts in a considered, impartial way.

As for cooling off, the Taft-Hartley Act makes a postponement of up to eighty days possible for a strike judged likely to threaten national health and safety. Also, strikes require sixty days notice if contemplated during the currency of a collective agreement. The ill-fated Industrial Relations Act, since repealed, attempted to institute similar measures for Great Britain. The term "cooling off period" would indicate that the root of the measure is in the uncertainties associated with collective bargaining. The difficulty with this particular measure, however, is that in many disputes, particularly in regard to dismissals, delay is more favorable to the employer's claim. Ordering delay does not simply allow more time for calculation, but in some cases can represent, perhaps by intention, a loss of bargaining power for the unions that we can naturally expect them to reject. In this case, enforced delay would be a "heating up" period rather than the reverse! Nevertheless, it should be possible to separate out those issues in which delay is not more

68. An early suggestion for the use of final offer arbitration is to be found in C. M. Stevens, "Is Compulsory Arbitration Compatible with Bargaining?" *Industrial Relations* 5 (1966): 38–52.
69. See P. Feuille, "Final Offer Arbitration and the Chilling Effect," *Industrial Relations* 14 (1975): 302, 310.
70. See C. W. Guillebaud, *The Role of the Arbitrator in Industrial Wage Disputes* (Welwyn: Nisbet, 1970), p. 2.

favorable to one side than the other and use the cooling off device with benefit.

Finally, it is worth pointing out that certain policy measures, such as the payment of welfare benefits to striker's families, need not, as is often alleged,[71] have any effect on the number or severity of industrial disputes. Their most sure effect is to increase union bargaining power, resulting in an increased wage share. In a somewhat similar category comes the increasing trend among American firms to insure each other against strike losses.[72] This need have no effect one way or the other on strikes. However, strike insurance is likely, as union indignation would imply, to represent an increase in the employer side's bargaining power, presumably resulting in a lower equilibrium wage share in the industries concerned.

7.5 Conclusions

The view we offer here of strikes builds up from the concept of a bargaining zone. Only if there is some possible gain from trade can there be bargaining, and, when both parties are organized, the strike threat becomes a necessary part of bargaining. Indeed, on Zeuthen's model, it is this very threat that brings about a determinate wage outcome. The important point to note is that, in this view, strikes will be accidents, because the costs of disagreement exceed the benefits for any settlement within the bargaining zone. This suggests that strike functions should be specified in terms of first and second differentials of economic variables—indicating the difficulty of adapting to change—rather than their levels, as has been the tendency. Moreover, the interpretation of strikes as accidents, rather than the result of calculation, also suggests that attempts to specify union pressure on wage rates in terms of strike frequency, rather than in such terms as changes in union membership, are mistaken.

It also follows from this view that strikes are "discommodities"—they are to be avoided and are not "bought" with the objective of a future stream of benefits. This view might well be too narrow for some strikes. There are likely to be circumstances in which a strike will create opportunities for bargaining where none existed before. To this extent, we should modify our interpretation of strikes as simply a threat to exploit existing opportunities. However, these circumstances are probably rare. It is also difficult to give empirical content to the theories designed to deal with them.[73]

Because strikes are bound up with collective bargaining in our theoretical framework, it can be seen that the connection between strikes and unionization is a close one. Therefore, it is likely that measures to increase unioniza-

71. See, for example, G. F. Bloom and H. R. Northrup, *Economics of Labor Relations* (Homewood, Ill.: Irwin, 1973), p. 677. See also n. 28 of this chapter.
72. See J. S. Hirsch, "Strike Insurance and Collective Bargaining," *Industrial and Labor Relations Review* 22 (1969): 399–415.
73. For a first attempt, see J. Johnston, "A Model of Wage Determination Under Bilateral Monopoly," *Economic Journal* 82 (1972): 837–852.

tion will increase strikes, *ceteris paribus*. The analysis does, however, suggest ways of mitigating the problem. Broadly speaking, the attack on strikes should take the form of an attempt to bring certainty into the relations between labor and management. Unexpected changes from any source, prices, money wages, or technology, are likely to bring about miscalculation and tip the process of bargaining into a strike situation.

Some forms of uncertainty, such as that connected with payment by results systems, where piecework rates have frequently to be renegotiated, are thus certainly contraindicated. It is true that uncertainties brought about by various forms of change, such as technical progress, can never be ruled out. However, uncertainties of this nature can be diminished by having detailed, jointly negotiated procedures to deal with the contingencies in advance. Encouraging possibilities are also opened up by the new form of final offer arbitration. The latter appears to provide a means of shaping the arbitration institution in such a way as to give the parties an incentive to agree, rather than to disagree as under conventional arbitration. If arbitration can be made a viable alternative, as now seems possible, resort to strike threats could be diminished.

CHAPTER 8
COLLECTIVE BARGAINING AND THE STRUCTURE OF PAY

8.1 Introduction

In this chapter, we take up the question of the effects of collective bargaining on levels of pay within the economy. There are several aspects of the pay structure to which we might look for a union effect. Perhaps the most obvious area concerns the influence of collective bargaining on the pay of covered workers relative to similar workers who are not covered. We refer here to the question of the *union-nonunion differential*. It is useful to form some judgment as to the average size of this differential within the economy as a whole and to its variations among industries or occupations. The issue of the union-nonunion differential raises important policy implications: if it is established that unions have succeeded in greatly raising the pay of unionized grades of labor, it follows that income in the nonunion sectors of the economy will tend to be depressed, or that sectoral profits will fall, or that sectoral unemployment will rise, or, indeed, all three occurrences. In actuality, the union-nonunion differential does not appear to be pronounced in most industries. Unionized employers appear to adjust upwards their hiring standards when applying union rates, so that wages per efficiency unit need not be much higher than in the nonunion case. However, this result is by no means firmly established because of the difficult problems of measurement that confront the analyst in this area. It might be the case that wage levels in both organized and unorganized sectors have been raised at the expense of profits.

This latter observation brings us to two further aspects of the pay structure. Worker organization might have succeeded in raising the pay of both organized and unorganized groups via the *threat effect*. Thus, the nonunion employer might pay the union rate, or one approximating it, so as to forestall the unionization of his labor force. Also, if the morale of nonunion employees were adversely affected by declining relative wages, or if the more able employees left to join unionized firms, there are grounds for expecting compensatory wage adjustments in the nonunion sector. In any case, this possibility requires that we consider the effect of collective bargaining on the *average* level of real pay and not merely focus our attention upon the structure of pay. It is also necessary to examine labor's share in the national income: if the pay of both union and nonunion workers has been increased, there is the possibility that this will be reflected in a larger share of labor income in the national income. It is only a possibility, because rising levels of factor productivity could reconcile higher wage rates with a lower wage share if most of the increased productivity were appropriated in the form of profits.

There are thus three areas with which we will be concerned: the determinants of the average real wage rate, the dispersion in pay around this average, with particular reference to differences in the pay of union and nonunion pay levels, is remitted for discussion to chapters 12 and 13. income. A fourth major area, concerning the effect of unions on aggregate nominal pay levels, is remitted for discussion to chapters 12 and 13.

8.2   Theoretical Considerations

The Level of Real Pay.   In brief, the basic building block of the real pay structure can be said to be the socially determined subsistence level at which the least skilled worker is remunerated. Given this level, we suppose there will be an equilibrium pattern of wage differentials across occupations corresponding to the income foregone in training (itself a function of the subsistence level of pay) for the particular skill. On this theory, wage differentials correspond to the costs of production of each skill.

But what determines the social minimum? It has been suggested that the crucial determinant is the pressure of population. Convincing evidence of the force of this factor has been provided by Phelps Brown and Hopkins in their survey of the association between real wage movements and changes in population growth in England and certain parts of Europe in past centuries.[1] If this view is correct, then custom, unions, government wage minima, and controls imposed by other wage-setting agencies have little to do with the real wage; or, if they do exercise some influence, then the wage is set with the specter of unemployment in the near background. In this view, the supply of labor is the overriding factor. Given the supply of unskilled labor and given the marginal product of such labor (derived from the *aggregate production function*), the subsistence wage will be determined by the equality of labor supply and demand. An outward shifting labor demand schedule will, then, presumably mean a higher real wage. Thus, there is scope in this model for higher labor productivity to cause higher wages, although such an association is ruled out at the microeconomic level. In fact, for both the United States

1. E. H. Phelps Brown and S. V. Hopkins, "Seven Centuries of the Price of Consumables, Compared with Builders' Wage Rates," *Economica* 23 (1956): 306; idem, "Wage-Rates and Prices: Evidence for Population Pressure in the 16th Century," *Economica* 24 (1957): 289–305; idem, "Builders' Wage-Rates, Prices and Population: Some Further Evidence," *Economica* 26 (1959): 25.

and Great Britain over the past century, periods of high labor productivity increase have tended also to be periods of high real wage increase.[2]

However, the latter observation does not prove that higher productivity causes higher real wage levels. A reverse direction of causality might equally apply and, indeed, is more likely to have been the case over the course of the present century, when the minimum-wage setting agencies, such as unions, appear to have been more creative. However, this creativity is only possible when there is not a flood of new labor onto the market. Accordingly, a slow rate of labor force growth can be seen as the basic factor without which higher wage minima are not viable. The conclusion is that unions can only raise the social minimum, without creating unemployment, when the underlying growth rates of population and productivity are favorable. Because unemployment has generally constituted but a small proportion of the labor force, the role of unions must have been secondary. Unions might yet have played an important role by raising worker aspirations, thereby encouraging a reduction in family size and so permitting productivity to edge ahead of population pressure and allowing the social minimum to be raised without creating unemployment. However, this is mere speculation. The process of value formation and of the development of norms and aspirations is generally taken to fall outside the province of economics, which takes these factors, like tastes, as given. Until a method measuring the impact of unions upon aspirations becomes available, the orthodox approach must continue to be followed.

The main point to emphasize here is that if the average level of real pay has risen over time, union wage setting activity cannot continuously have reduced the pay of nonunion workers. Any redistributive effect between union and nonunion workers, although not necessarily between wage earners and capitalists, must be once-for-all, after which point the wages of nonunion workers will continue to rise at about the same rate as union workers.[3] This can be shown with the aid of figure 8.1. Here, it is assumed that labor in the union and nonunion sector is similar, so that one demand curve may be drawn for both, with $D_U = D_N$. The total demand curve is depicted as D_T. With a given supply of labor, SS', the ruling wage rate would be W_0. Assuming that pay within the union sector is raised to W_U, employment in that sector would fall to OD. The released workers, DE, would exert a downward influence on the nonunion sector wage rate. Equilibrium in this sector would eventually be reached at a wage W_N and employment OF. The

2. See E. H. Phelps Brown and M. H. Browne, *A Century of Pay—The Course of Pay and Production in France, Germany, Sweden, the United Kingdom and the United States of America 1860–1960* (London: Macmillan, 1968), table 30, p. 312.

3. As Milton Friedman has pointed out, the wages of domestic servants have risen as fast over time as have the wages of workers in other sectors, such as automobiles and coal mining, where the workers are heavily unionized. See M. Friedman, "Some Comments on the Significance of Labor Unions for Economic Policy," in D. M. Wright, ed., *The Impact of the Union* (New York: Harcourt Brace, 1951), pp. 222 ff.

Figure 8.1   The Effect of an Increase in Union Pay on Nonunion Pay and Employment

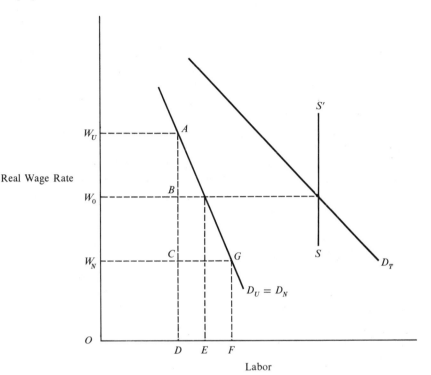

new average wage over both sectors would tend to be lower than W_0.[4] We have been observing a continuous rise in the real world analog of W_0 over time. This can be seen to be compatible with either a continuous widening in the difference between W_U and W_N or with an upward movement in both. Because there has not been much widening in the union-nonunion differential over time,[5] the latter interpretation is to be favored. This would imply that the real wages of unionized workers have responded to the same forces as the wages of nonunionized workers and, therefore, that unionism itself cannot be responsible—except in the indirect sense referred to above, namely

4. Take the average wage as a weighted average of union and nonunion wage rates, the weights being given by compensation levels within the respective sectors. Then the new average wage, $\bar{W}$, will be the same as W_0 if the elasticity of demand for labor, η, equals unity. $\bar{W}$ will be greater (less) than W_0 as η is less (greater) than unity. Using employment weights, however, $\bar{W} < W_0$ except in the unlikely circumstance that $\eta = 0$.
5. Lewis has calculated average annual full-time compensation in a set of union industries (principally mining, manufacturing, construction, and transport) and nonunion industries (the rest). The ratio of union to nonunion compensation averaged 1.19 over 1919–28, and 1.36 over 1949–58. See H. G. Lewis, *Unionism and Relative Wages in the United States* (Chicago: Ill.: University of Chicago Press, 1963), table 54, p. 204.

by raising aspirations and reducing population pressure—for the increase in average real wages.

The Union-Nonunion Differential. Taking up the question of the degree to which, and under what circumstances, unions have raised the pay of their membership relative to equivalent nonunion labor, we encounter a number of interesting theoretical and econometric issues. The modern attack upon the question whether unions have had significant positive effects on union relative wages can perhaps be traced back to Milton Friedman, who surmised that unions had had little effect on the structure of wage rates. He argued that 90% of the American work force had its wages little affected by unionism and that wages were raised by as much as 15% for only 10% of the work force.[6] Since then, a variety of attempts have been made to arrive at more precise estimates; in the process of empirical testing, the theoretical issues have become clearer. Indeed, it now seems likely that unions have exercised very little influence upon the wage structure. Two reasons for this might be cited. First, when wages are raised for a certain group, firms have an incentive to screen job applicants more carefully and to take on only the better qualified. In principle, this adjustment could be carried far enough to iron out most differences in terms of efficiency units. Second, wages and union membership might be jointly determined. Once we take into account the fact that much of the measured impact of unions in causing higher wages might in reality be the effect of higher wages encouraging unionization, the union-nonunion differential is further diminished.

These problems can be better considered by stating the underlying relationships somewhat more formally. Let W_{Ui} and W_{Ni} represent the wage rates of union and nonunion workers in the ith group, respectively. Let W_{Ci} be the wage rate that would prevail if there were no unions within the economy. Define relative wage effects as

$$R_{Ui} \equiv (W_{Ui} - W_{Ci})/W_{Ci}$$
$$R_{Ni} \equiv (W_{Ni} - W_{Ci})/W_{Ci},$$

which values, however, are unobservable, and the observable effect

$$R_{Oi} \equiv (W_{Ui} - W_{Ni})/W_{Ni}.$$

The average observed wage, $\bar{W}_i$, can be taken to be a geometric mean of union and nonunion wages, thus

$$\ln \bar{W}_i \equiv U_i \ln W_{Ui} + (1 - U_i)\ln W_{Ni}$$
$$\equiv \ln W_{Ni} + U_i \ln(1 + R_{Oi}),$$

6. Friedman, *Impact of the Union*, p. 216.

where U_i is the proportion unionized in the ith group.[7]
Now

$$\ln W_{Ni} \equiv \ln W_{Ci} + \ln(1 + R_{Ni})$$
$$\equiv f(X_i) + \ln(1 + R_{Ni}) + \epsilon_i$$

where X is a set of determinants of the competitive wage, such as age,
education, and sex; and
ϵ_i is an error term used in the empirical formulation.

Also,

$$\ln(1 + R_{Oi}) \equiv \ln(1 + \bar{R}_0) + \ln\left(\frac{1 + R_{Oi}}{1 + \bar{R}_0}\right)$$

where $\bar{R}_0 \equiv (\bar{W}_U - \bar{W}_N)/\bar{W}_N$ is the average union-nonunion wage differential.
Thus,

$$\ln \bar{W}_i = f(X_i) + U_i \ln(1 + \bar{R}_0)$$
$$+ \left[\ln(1 + R_{Ni}) + U_i \ln\left(\frac{1 + R_{Oi}}{1 + \bar{R}_0}\right) + \epsilon_i\right]$$
$$= f(X_i) + U_i\lambda + \epsilon_i' \tag{8.1}$$

where $\lambda \equiv \ln(1 + \bar{R}_0) \simeq \bar{R}_0$, the estimated average differential; and
ϵ_i' is the term in square brackets and is treated as a residual for
estimation purposes.[8]

There are two main problems here. First, there are the implicit restrictions
on λ, the average union wage effect. We would wish to allow λ to vary with
U_i, so as to establish whether the extent of unionism does affect the differential. The analysis of the Marshallian rules of derived demand leads to the
expectation of a positive association (chapter 7). This modification can be
accomplished simply by including a nonlinear term in U, such as U^2.
Alternatively, we can partition U into various size categories and estimate λ
for each category, that is,

$$\ln \bar{W}_i = f(X_i) + \sum_j U_i D_{ij}\lambda_j + \epsilon_i'' \tag{8.2}$$

7. Compensation weights would be preferable to U_i, because they have the advantage of not
varying so much with changes in the union relative wage effect. Unfortunately, such data are
seldom available. On this problem see n. 5 of this chapter, and also Lewis, *Unionism and
Relative Wages*, p. 15, n. 8.
8. This will give rise to biases because $\text{cov}[U_i, \ln(1 + R_{Oi})]$ is probably greater than zero, that
is, better unionized groups have higher wage differentials. This misspecification will cause us
to overestimate λ. See Appendix 1-a.

where D_j are a set of dummy variables defining the various size categories.[9] Again, it is necessary to determine whether λ varies, for given U, with some of the elements in X_i. For example, we would wish to test whether a union had a more marked effect on relative pay in monopolistic product markets. This is accomplished by including interaction terms,

$$\ln \bar{W}_i = f(X_i) + \sum_j U_i Y_{ij} \lambda_j + U_i \lambda + \epsilon_i''' \qquad (8.3)$$

where Y_j are the various factors, such as concentration in the industry or the share of labor in total costs, that are expected to influence union bargaining power, and thus the size of λ.

If one of the elements of Y_j were, say, industrial concentration, CON_i, then the sign of the coefficient on $CON_i \cdot U_i$ would indicate the direction of association between union relative wage effect and concentration.[10] The coefficient turns out, rather surprisingly, to be negative, which would indicate that unions create a smaller wage differential when there is monopoly power in the product market.

The second problem is that U_i is not exogenous or predetermined as is required if ordinary least squares is to be applied to estimate equation (8.1) or its variants. Union density within an industry or occupation is itself likely to be determined by the wage in that industry or occupation. This is the sense behind Dunlop's union membership function,[11] which postulates a direct relation between union membership and the wage rate. In fact, most of the empirical membership functions already considered (chapter 7) have included the wage rate as a determinant of union organization. This misspecification will lead to an overestimate of λ. The remedy is to consider U and W as jointly determined and to use a simultaneous equation method of estimation, such as two-stage least squares (chapter 1).

However, the problem of simultaneous equations bias has further ramifications, for some of the elements in the set X will be determined by W as well as determining W. For example, one important element of X will be education, because we would expect the level of education in a given group to be closely related to its competitive wage level. Another important element will be the specific training investments made in the group. It is true that specific training will not be so fully reflected in the wage rate as will general training (chapter 4); nevertheless, it must be remembered that, in industries whose technology requires high specific training, employers will raise wage rates so as to lower the losses associated with high turnover. Indeed, the wage rate (given education) has been used as an index of specific training in one

9. See S. Rosen, "Trade Union Power, Threat Effects, and the Extent of Organization," *Review of Economic Studies* 36 (1969): 187.
10. See, for example, L. W. Weiss, "Concentration and Labor Earnings," *American Economic Review* 56 (1966): 98.
11. J. T. Dunlop, *Wage Determination Under Trade Unions* (New York: Kelley, 1944), p. 32.

important study of turnover.[12] Further, we would expect increases in the wage rate, however caused, to affect employer hiring requirements and specific training decisions. For example, if a high wage has to be paid, employers are likely to adjust by demanding better-educated workers.[13] Thus, it seems that we would need to include a third dependent variable in the system, the level of education, if we are to meaningfully interpret the results.[14] The empirical section considers the results of this course of action.

Labor's Share. It is possible that the real pay of both union and nonunion workers has been increased over time at such a rate as to increase the share of *wages* in the national income relative to that of profits. This is the next aspect of the structure of income that we must consider. In particular, we are interested in establishing the effect of unions on labor's share. It has often been asserted that unions wish to raise this share quite as much as they wish to improve the real wage rates of their members.[15] However, it is quite possible for unions to have been successful in raising real wage rates relative to profit rates and yet to have diminished labor's share, because of the induced substitution of capital for labor. This is the core of the neoclassical analysis of the problem, based on marginal productivity theory. Unfortunately, a cloud hangs over this theory at the macroeconomic level, because of its reliance upon an aggregate production function. It is not certain how one should interpret such a function, or even whether it is measurable.[16] Consequently, other theories have been developed, the chief of which is the *Keynesian* theory of distribution. This relates the distribution of income to the amount of savings required to bring savings into equality with exogenously determined investment. It is assumed that workers save less than do capitalists, so that the larger is the wage share the smaller will be the amount of savings.[17] This theory has the advantage that less controversy surrounds its

12. See J. H. Pencavel, "Wages, Specific Training and Labor Turnover in U.S. Manufacturing Industries," *International Economic Review* 13 (1972): 58.

13. See M. W. Reder, "Unions and Wages: The Problems of Measurement," *Journal of Political Economy* 73 (1965): 188–196. He surmises that "as a result (of changes in relative labor quality), it is doubtful that on the evidence available we could reject the null hypothesis that the relative wage effect of unionism has been zero for 'most' of the period since 1920." (p. 195.)

14. The only study encompassing this full system is O. Ashenfelter and G. E. Johnson, "Unionism, Relative Wages, and Labor Quality in U.S. Manufacturing Industries," *International Economic Review* 13 (1972): 488–508.

15. See C. Kerr, "Labor's Income Share and the Labor Movement," in G. W. Taylor and F. C. Pierson, eds., *New Concepts in Wage Determination* (New York: McGraw-Hill, 1957), p. 260; E. H. Phelps Brown, "Pay and Profits—The Theory of Distribution Reviewed in the Light of the Behavior of Some Western Economies over the Last Hundred Years," mimeographed (Department of Economics, London School of Economics, 1968), p. 14.

16. In particular, is aggregate capital measurable? This issue has given rise to the "Cambridge Capital Controversy." See H. G. Johnson, *The Theory of Income Distribution* (London: Grey-Mills, 1973), pp. 42, 96.

17. See N. Kaldor, "Alternative Theories of Distribution," *Review of Economic Studies* 23 (1955–56): 83–100.

empirical content. On the other hand, great controversy attaches to its microeconomic underpinnings.

Logically prior to both theories, however, is the question of whether the share of income accruing to labor has actually changed. In turn, this raises difficult problems of measurement. For example, the change in labor's share over time could be a chimera. The illusion could be simply the result of an expanding public sector that appears to be more labor intensive than it is because government capital assets tend to be undervalued, or even ignored, in national income accounts.[18] Moreover, even if labor's share in national income has increased, this might simply result from a growth of more labor intensive industries, such as the services, relative to capital intensive industries, such as rail transportation. Thus, an increase in the overall share could be compatible with unchanged factor shares at the industry level. It is first necessary to net out changes consequent on these interindustry shifts,[19] for they presumably require a different explanation than do changes in the share within given sectors.

Let us for the moment sidestep the difficulties involved in measuring labor's share and consider instead the contribution of orthodox theory to its explanation. The basic proposition here is that, given full employment, factor shares are determined by the amounts of factors employed in conjunction with their marginal productivities. Given competition, an increase in the relative price of a factor will tend to lead to its substitution by a less expensive factor. Whether or not the relative quantity decrease outweighs the relative price increase will depend upon the elasticity of substitution, σ. It can

18. For a discussion of this issue, see D. C. Johnson, "The Functional Distribution of Income in the U.S., 1850-1952," *Review of Economics and Statistics* 36 (1954): 179.

19. The normal procedure is as follows: Write

$$\Delta\left(\frac{W}{Q}\right) \equiv \left(\frac{W}{Q}\right)_2 - \left(\frac{W}{Q}\right)_1$$

where W and Q are measures of labor income and total income, respectively, and the subscripts refer to different periods.

Then

$$\Delta\left(\frac{W}{Q}\right) \equiv \sum_i \left(\frac{W_i}{Q_i}\right)_2 \cdot \left(\frac{Q_i}{Q_i}\right)_2 - \sum_i \left(\frac{W_i}{Q_i}\right)_1 \cdot \left(\frac{Q_i}{Q_i}\right)_1$$

$$\equiv \sum \left(\frac{Q_i}{Q}\right)_2 \left[\left(\frac{W_i}{Q_i}\right)_2 - \left(\frac{W_i}{Q_i}\right)_1\right] + \sum \left(\frac{W_i}{Q_i}\right)_2 \left[\left(\frac{Q_i}{Q}\right)_2 - \left(\frac{Q_i}{Q}\right)_1\right]$$

$$+ \sum \left(\frac{Q_i}{Q}\right)_2 \left[\left(\frac{W_i}{Q_i}\right)_2 - \left(\frac{W_i}{Q_i}\right)_1\right] - \sum \left(\frac{Q_i}{Q}\right)_1 \left[\left(\frac{W_i}{Q_i}\right)_2 - \left(\frac{W_i}{Q_i}\right)_1\right]$$

gives a base weighted system. Ignoring the last two terms, the first term is the change in labor's share due to changes in the share within industries and the second term gives the change in share due to interindustry shifts. A similar index can be constructed using current year weights. See A. P. Thirlwall, "Changes in Industrial Composition in the U.K. and U.S. and Labor's Share of National Income," *Bulletin of the Oxford University Institute of Economics and Statistics* 34 (1972): 375.

be shown that, where substitution against the more expensive factor is easy ($\sigma > 1$), the quantity effect will predominate and the factor's share will decrease. The converse holds if it is difficult to substitute for the factor ($\sigma < 1$). Detailed construction of this reasoning is contained in appendix 8-A. The expression for the elasticity of capital's share, π, with respect to changes in the capital/labor ratio, k, is given by

$$\frac{d\pi}{dk} \cdot \frac{k}{\pi} = (1 - \pi)\left(1 - \frac{1}{\sigma}\right), \tag{8.4}$$

which indicates that a rise in the price of capital relative to the wage rate and the consequent fall in the equilibrium capital/labor ratio will only increase capital's share (that is, equation (8.4) will be negative) when $\sigma < 1$. Similarly, a rise in the capital/labor ratio will only increase labor's share if $\sigma < 1$.

In principle, several empirical implications follow from the theory. But such implications rely on our being able to estimate an aggregate production function, which raises a number of difficult problems. The fundamental issue here concerns the measurement of the stock of capital. To aggregate different types of capital equipment, it is necessary to express capital in money terms. To arrive at this money quantity, an interest rate has to be chosen. Yet the interest rate is precisely that which is meant to be determined by the production function. According to one authority, the problem can be solved in most cases "with enough general equilibrium mathematics."[20] Somewhat more heuristically, we might also argue that, because those who estimate production functions have generally taken other investigators' estimates of capital stock,[21] the two interest rates—the one used in estimating capital, the other derived from the production function—are to some extent independent. Even if we accept this line of argument, other major difficulties present themselves. For example, how are we to allow for technical progress? How are we to make intertemporal comparisons of capital and labor? How are we to proceed from data on capital and labor stocks to the more relevant consideration of capital and labor services? Although a number of attempts have been made to answer such questions, it is prudent for us to adopt a skeptical position. At the same time, it should be emphasized that empirical studies are of vital importance in this area and that there are always difficulties of interpretation and measurement attaching to such estimates. Hence, it is most constructive to suspend judgment until the evidence has been considered.[22]

20. Johnson, *Theory of Income Distribution*, p. 37. See also the comments of M. Bronfenbrenner, *Income Distribution Theory* (Chicago, Ill.: Aldine, 1971), pp. 397–398.
21. For example, Thurow's recent attempt to estimate an aggregate production function uses independent estimates of the capital stock. See L. C. Thurow, "Disequilibrium and the Marginal Productivity of Capital and Labor," *Review of Economics and Statistics* 50 (1968): 23–31.
22. See M. W. Reder, "Alternative Theories of Labor's Share," in M. Abromowitz et al., *The Allocation of Economic Resources* (Stanford, Calif.: Stanford University Press, 1959), p. 193.

The first and most famous estimated form of the aggregate production function was that of Cobb and Douglas.[23] They chose the following functional form:

$$Q = AK^{\alpha}L^{\beta} \qquad (8.5)$$

where Q is an index of the physical volume of production;
    L is man-hours;
    K is a measure of the capital stock; and
A, α, β are parameters.

It can be seen that this form restricts σ to a value of unity, which implies constant factor shares. This provides the first testable implication. The second implication is that the estimated parameters α and β should be similar to the actual factor shares. In the case of capital, for example, that share is defined as

$$\pi = r \cdot K/Q,$$

where r denotes the return on capital in terms of product price.
In competitive equilibrium,

$$r = \partial Q/\partial K,$$

so that the share, according to the estimated function, is

$$\widehat{\pi} = \frac{\partial Q}{\partial K} \cdot \frac{K}{Q}$$

$$= \alpha A K^{\alpha-1} L^{\beta} \cdot \frac{K}{Q}$$

$$= \alpha.$$

Initially, estimates of α and β closely approximated actual factor shares. More recently, diverging values have been reported. And of late, there is also evidence to suggest a rising share of labor, which would imply that σ is less than unity and/or that technical progress has not been neutral (appendix 8-A). These issues can be dealt with by appropriate modification of the functional form. For example, a constant elasticity of substitution function has been developed of the form:[24]

$$Q = A[\theta K^{-\psi} + (1 - \theta)L^{-\psi}]^{-(1/\psi)}, \qquad (8.6)$$

23. C. W. Cobb and P. H. Douglas, "A Theory of Production," *American Economic Review* 18 (1928): 139–165.
24. K. J. Arrow, H. B. Chenery, B. S. Minhas, and R. M. Solow, "Capital-Labor Substitution and Economic Efficiency," *Review of Economics and Statistics* 43 (1961): 225–250.

where $\psi = (1 - \sigma)/\sigma$; and
   A and θ are parameters.

This formulation provides a method of estimating σ directly. Yet we would in any case expect σ to be considerably less than unity in the short run. Thus, a further implication of the theory would be that a given increase in, say, labor relative to capital earnings should be matched by a short-term increase in labor's share.

Let us now turn to the main alternative interpretation of labor's share—the Keynesian theory. This is built up in the following manner. First, it is assumed that there is full employment, so that total income, Y, can be taken as given and is defined as

$$Y \equiv W + P,$$

where W is the wage bill; and
   P denotes the amount of profits.

In equilibrium,

$$I = S$$

where I is investment; and
   S denotes savings.

If

$$S = s_w W + s_p P$$

where s_w and s_p are the propensities to save out of wages and profits, respectively, and $s_p > s_w$,

then

$$I = (s_p - s_w)P + s_w Y$$

and

$$P/Y = \frac{I/Y}{s_p - s_w} - \frac{s_w}{s_p - s_w}. \tag{8.7}$$

Equation (8.7) indicates that the share of profits depends upon the investment/income ratio, assuming the propensities to save out of wages and profits are constant. However, Kaldor would take the view that this dependency applies only within a certain range of profits shares—the upper boundary being delineated by the lowest tolerable real wage and the lower boundary by the minimum acceptable profit rate.[25] The workings of the model are

25. Kaldor, "Theories of Distribution," pp. 97–98.

illustrated in figure 8.2, which demonstrates the assumption of given investment plans. On the assumptions about savings behavior, these plans are
consistent only with one income distribution, P^*/Y.

The principal difficulty with this approach is its apparent incompatibility
with microeconomic considerations. At the microeconomic level, we would
expect investment to be closely related to the rate of profit and, consequently,
to the profit share. Once this is conceded, then an increase in interest rates,
perhaps occasioned by an increase in investment demand, will simultaneously choke off that demand while increasing savings. Equilibrium will have
been brought about with no change in income distribution.[26] Another
problem with the theory is whether the savings propensities—assuming these
are measurable, which some would doubt[27]—can possibly remain constant
over time. It has also been pointed out that, in this model, any income
recipient group could, by choosing the appropriate savings ratio, absorb the
entire national income. In the case of labor, for example, the appropriate s_w

26. Phelps Brown, "Pay and Profits," p. 32.
27. See I. B. Kravis, "Relative Income Shares in Fact and Theory," *American Economic Review*
49 (1959): 939.

**Figure 8.2   The Determination of the Share of Profits by the Equality of
Savings and Investment**

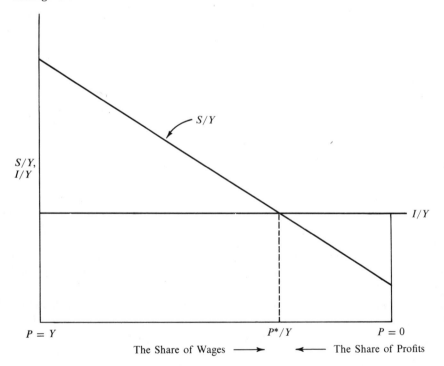

would be $s_w = I/Y$, which is only compatible with the relation $I = s_w W + s_p P$ if $P = 0$.[28]

The main empirical implication of the theory would appear to be the existence of a positive association between I/Y and P/Y through time. Yet, even if the postulated relation were to hold, there remain problems of interpretation. For example, it could be that in periods of inflation (when I/Y tends to be high) profit margins tend to increase before wages (so that P/Y rises), and conversely when I/Y is low. This might point to the influence of institutional factors, such as union bargaining inertia, rather than a macroeconomic income redistribution mechanism. It is to a consideration of such problems that we now turn.

8.3 Empirical Analysis

Union Relative Wage Effects. Let us first consider the issue of the relative wage effects of unionism. There are a number of worthwhile questions in this area. The main factual questions relate to the current size of the union-nonunion differential among those workers towards whom unions direct their principal efforts, namely manual workers within manufacturing, mining, and construction. We would also seek to ascertain whether this differential varies over time and between unions. This leads to the main theoretical question: on what does the differential depend? Here we enter the testing ground for the predictions derived from the Marshallian rules of derived demand, for example, that concentration or extent of unionization affects the differential. Moreover, there is the point that, although unions might succeed in establishing a wage differential in favor of their membership, employer hiring standards might be adjusted thereupon. The question is, then, does the differential represent a higher wage per efficiency unit, or are the hiring policies in unionized firms so adjusted that union workers are effectively of higher quality than their nonunion counterparts?

Estimates of the current magnitude of the manual worker union-nonunion differential are presented in table 8.1. These estimates have, with the exception of rows 5, 6, and 7, where the dependent variable is entered in absolute rather than logarithmic form, been derived by the regression methods earlier outlined in equations (8.1), (8.2), and (8.3) and are thus estimates of the average union-nonunion wage differential for the group in question. The standardizing variables used (which are intended to be the determinants of the competitive wage) are indicated in the third column, in which it is also noted whether union membership is included as an exogenous variable.

It is apparent that a wide range of estimates of the wage effects of unions have been obtained, depending upon the specification of exogenous variables and the restrictions placed on the unionism coefficient. Lewis, in his standard

28. Johnson, *Theory of Income Distribution,* p. 204.

Table 8.1   Estimates of the Average Differential in Pay between Union and Nonunion Workers, Manual Workers, U.S. and U.K.

Group and Year	Estimated Differential	Standardizing Variables Selected
1 Production workers, U.S. manufacturing, 1960[a]	40%—OLS	Indexes for industry education and concentration, industry proportion female, proportion unionized.
2 As above	4%*—simultaneous methods	Indexes for industry skill and concentration; industry proportion female, proportion urban.
3 All blue-collar males, U.S., 1966[b]	30%	Individual's education, age, unionism, region, urban/rural location.
4 Production workers, U.S. industries, 1958[c]	35% in industries where unionization > 80%; 10% in industries where unionization ≤ 80%.	Indexes for industry education, concentration and age; industry proportions male, nonwhite, urban, production workers, unionized; industry man-hours worked in South and size of establishment.
5 All full-time workers, U.S., 1967[d]	10%—OLS	Individual's education, experience, race, sex, region, union membership.
6 As above.	7%*—simultaneous methods	As above, but excluding union membership.
7 Male operatives in manufacturing, construction, and mining, U.S., 1959[e]	18% (low concentration) 8% (high concentration)	Indexes for industry skill, concentration and change in employment; industry proportion female and unionized; size of establishment.
8 As above	12%* (low concentration) 16%* (high concentration)	As above and, in addition, 31 personal characteristics to include schooling, color, age, family size, residence, and weeks worked per year.

Table 8.1 (*Cont.*)

Group and Year	Estimated Differential	Standardizing Variables Selected
9 Manual males, U.K. manufacturing, 1973[f]	25%	Indexes for industry skill, concentration, and change in employment; output per man, plant size, and coverage by collective agreement.
10 Manual workers, U.K. industries, 1964[g]	10%	Index for industry skill; industry proportion of female workers, young workers, and union members.

*indicates not significant at the 10% level or better.

Sources:

[a] O. Ashenfelter and G. E. Johnson, "Unionism, Relative Wages and Labor Quality in U.S. Manufacturing Industries," *International Economic Review* 13 (1972): table 1, p. 500.

[b] G. E. Johnson and K. C. Youmans, "Union Relative Wage Effects by Age and Education," *Industrial and Labor Relations Review* 24 (1970): table 1, p. 174.

[c] S. Rosen, "Trade Union Power, Threat Effects, and the Extent of Organization," *Review of Economic Studies* 36 (1969): 190.

[d] P. Schmidt and R. P. Strauss, "The Effect of Unions on Earnings and Earnings on Unions: A Mixed Logit Approach," *International Economic Review* 17 (1976): 207.

[e] L. W. Weiss, "Concentration and Labor Earnings," *American Economic Review* 56 (1966): 105, 108.

[f] C. Mulvey, "Collective Agreements and Relative Earnings in U.K. Manufacturing in 1973," *Economica* 43 (1976): table 1, p. 422.

[g] J. H. Pencavel, "Relative Wages and Trade Unions in the U.K.," *Economica* 40 (1974): 202. (The union differential here refers only to those industries with considerable domestic bargaining activity.)

work, has set the "normal" wage effect of unionism at 10%, outside those periods of rapid inflation when the differential is said to be lower.[29] However, there is little evidence of a central tendency in the modern estimates, which, in the case of the United States, range from 30% to 40% (rows 1 and 3) down to insignificant (rows 2 and 6). Similarly, we observe a wide range in the two British estimates; from 10%, and barely significant, up to 25% (rows 9 and 10). In the British case, it is true that the discrepancy can probably be attributed to the different collective bargaining variable employed in the two studies. In the one study (row 10) the variable selected is union membership by industry, while in the other it is an estimate of the fraction of employers, be they union or nonunion, applying a collective agreement (row 9). Use of the latter variable has the advantage that the estimate of the nonunion wage is less likely to be contaminated by observations of firms which, although nonunion, are in fact paying the union rate for a variety of reasons—for

29. Lewis, *Unionism and Relative Wages,* p. 190.

example, to preempt the unionization of the work force. However, there is no published study in Great Britain that allows for the simultaneity between wages and unionization. In the American studies, recognition of the simultaneity problem appears dramatically to reduce the wage effect of unions (compare rows 1 and 2 and also rows 5 and 6).

What factors might be expected to explain the differences in the estimates shown in table 8.1? There are two main lines of explanation that might usefully be pursued here. The first relates to the simultaneity problem, to which we have already referred. While research is only now being undertaken on any scale within the area, the results of the two simultaneous equation studies quoted in table 8.1 provide cause for concern. They indicate that failure to allow for simultaneity causes a large overestimate to be made of the union wage effect. It is as though unions flourish among those work force groups in which the climate is right—presumably as determined by the Marshallian rules and indexed by the wage rate—but do not of themselves much affect this climate.[30] Allowing for simultaneity reduces our estimate of the differential, partly because the estimated coefficient is reduced in size, but also because its standard error is increased.[31] It might be thought that the presence of larger standard errors—greater uncertainty of estimation—is an inevitable concomitant of the application of more intricate econometric methods, so that they can be discounted to some extent. However, it should be pointed out that this need not be the case. The other equation in the system—union membership as a function of the wage rate—is little changed, whether estimated by ordinary least squares or by simultaneous methods.[32] Thus, it would seem that the wage rate as a function of union membership is the weaker relation.

The other main reason why estimates of the wage effects of unions differ is that specifications of the union effect in the estimating equation vary. Table 8.1 indicates that the more densely organized industries appear to have a higher differential than the less organized (row 4). Again, it is possible that unions are less powerful in more concentrated industries (row 7). There are also differences in the standardizing variables included within the regressions. Inclusion of many *personal characteristic* variables might be enough to reduce the union effect to insignificance, indicating that union labor tends to be of higher quality than the nonunion. There are signs that this is, in fact, the case (compare rows 7 and 8). It would thus appear that employers, when confronted by higher wages, do adjust their hiring policies in the direction marginal productivity theory would lead us to expect. It is first necessary to establish the extent of this adjustment before we can measure the degree to

30. However, unions might have important nonwage and political effects, which would not be picked up by the type of study considered here.
31. See P. Schmidt and R. P. Strauss, "The Effect of Unions on Earnings and Earnings on Unions: A Mixed Logit Approach," *International Economic Review* 17 (1976): 209.
32. See Ashenfelter and Johnson, "U.S. Manufacturing," table 1, p. 500.

which unionized firms have to pay higher wages for given job categories.[33]
The question therefore arises as to the correct method of specifying the union effect. The answer here depends upon our theory as to the causation of the union-nonunion differential. In chapter 7, we argued for an approach that relates the benefits derivable from organization to the determinants of the elasticity of derived demand, given the costs of organization and of maintaining organization. On this basis, the union effect would depend upon the degree of monopoly in the relevant product markets, the ease with which union labor could be replaced by other factors, the extent of unionization itself, and, perhaps, the union group's share in total costs. If this framework is accepted, then it is not very meaningful to look for an average union effect over a large group. Rather, we would seek to discover how this effect varies according to our theoretical determinants. For example, it can be seen from table 8.1 (row 4) that the union-nonunion differential does indeed appear to be larger in industries that are more extensively organized.[34] This implies that we should specify the level of unionization when comparing estimates of the union differential.[35]

When we come to consider the other determinants of union power, it can also be seen from table 8.1 that the union differential appears to vary according to the degree of concentration of output by industry, although the direction of variation is uncertain (rows 7 and 8). There are good reasons for expecting market structure to influence union power.[36] However, the empirical results of table 8.1 point to an insignificant or even a negative correlation between market concentration and the union differential, *ceteris paribus*.[37] Such results might nonetheless reflect deficiencies in the concentration measure as an index of monopoly market structure. For example, it is

33. Weiss, "Labor Earnings," pp. 97, 135, emphasizes this distinction in the context of concentrated and nonconcentrated industries.

34. This effect must taper off after some high degree of organization is attained, reflecting the fact that, once 100% organization is achieved, the union-nonunion differential must be zero. For this reason, Phelps Brown believes that the average union differential is likely to be smaller in Great Britain than the United States, given the higher degree of unionization in the former country. But we would question whether unionization is yet high enough to actually compress the differential. See Royal Commission on Trade Unions and Employers' Associations *Minutes of Evidence No. 38* (London: Her Majesty's Stationery Office, 1967), pp. 1615–1616; reprinted in W. E. J. McCarthy, ed., *Trade Unions* (Harmondsworth, England: Penguin, 1972), pp. 313–341.

35. See S. Rosen, "Unionism and the Occupational Wage Structure in the United States," *International Economic Review* 11 (1970): p. 283.

36. Market structure effects which favor unions could arise both from the point of view of costs, (easier maintenance of jurisdiction, once established) and benefits (lower elasticity of derived demand). The arguments are well put in M. Segal, "The Relation between Union Wage Impact and Market Structure," *Quarterly Journal of Economics* 78 (1964): 96–114.

37. See, for example, Rosen, "Trade Union Power," p. 190; Rosen, "Unionism and . . . Wage Structure," table 1, p. 278; Weiss, "Labor Earnings," pp. 104–106; Lewis, *Unionism and Relative Wages*, pp. 159–161, 178.

possible for an industry to be competitive on a national basis and yet possess strong local monopoly power. We might cite the construction and road haulage industries as cases in point.[38] The question of the relation between concentration and the union differential is by no means closed, therefore, and experimentation with alternative measures of market structure should continue. In this context, it is worth noting that industries characterized by large plants (which can be seen to be related to product monopoly) appear to experience the stronger union effect.[39]

As for the effect of the elasticity of substitution on union power, there is some evidence to suggest that a low elasticity is associated with a higher union wage effect. For example, workers in certain craft-type occupations—commercial airline pilots, medical practitioners, and lawyers—appear to have earnings much higher than can be explained on the basis of competition. Such earnings differentials are presumably maintained because it is difficult to substitute other factors of production for these groups. Again, if we surmise, as seems plausible, that capital is more easily substitutable for unskilled labor than for skilled labor, then we would expect a smaller union-nonunion differential for the former than the latter. This does appear to be the case—at least when a comparison is drawn between skilled and semiskilled labor. At the same time, there is evidence that unionism has a more favorable wage effect for the very low skilled groups, who are numerically unimportant, than for craft groups.[40] This latter result might be an instance of the "importance of being unimportant" condition. However, where we have craftsmen, operatives, and laborers organized within the same union, as is the case in an industrial union, it could also be a consequence of the solidaristic goals of trade unions. But most plausible is the argument that laborers in union firms, given the widespread operation of seniority systems in the United States, will be hired with an eye to promotion. Much of the union differential might, therefore, reflect a quality difference that the standardizing variables fail to pick up.[41]

The elasticity of substitution parameter also has important implications for union wage effects over time. Because the elasticity of substitution is always higher in the long run than the short run, we can be sure that union wage effects will be less marked in the long run than in the short run. For this reason the estimates of the union-nonunion differential presented in table 8.1, constructed as they are on the basis of long-term, cross-section data, will underestimate the possible *impact* or short-term wage effects of unions.

There remain two further questions to consider: first, the course of the

38. See H. M. Levinson, "Unionism, Concentration and Wage Changes: Toward a Unified Theory," *Industrial and Labor Relations Review* 20 (1967): 198–205.
39. Rosen, "Unionism and . . . Wage Structure," table 1, p. 278.
40. *Ibid.*; Weiss, "Labor Earnings," p. 115; M. J. Boskin, "Unions and Relative Real Wages," *American Economic Review* 62 (1972): table 2, p. 469.
41. See G. E. Johnson and K. C. Youmans, "Union Relative Wage Effects by Age and Education," *Industrial and Labor Relations Review* 24 (1970): 176–177.

union-nonunion differential over time and, second, the effect of unionism on overall earnings dispersion. In the former context, it is generally agreed that union relative wage effects will be least pronounced in times of unexpected inflation and most pronounced during intervals of depression, *ceteris paribus*.[42] The most plausible line of reasoning here is that unionized workers are able to escape money wage cuts. This could account for a lag in union wage increases at the beginning of the upturn, because employers will be reluctant to concede wage increases, which are difficult to revoke, until they are sure that the expansion phase is well under way. It could also account for a widening of the differential in recession, because at such times nonunion labor will be in a position to accept a wage cut whereas union labor will not. Lewis has estimated that, in the depression years 1930–32, unions raised the wages of their members more than 23% above the average wage for the whole work force and caused the average wage of the nonunionized to drop about 2%.[43] In the postwar inflation, on the other hand, Lewis estimated that unions increased the relative wage of their membership by no more than 5%. Though these estimates have come under criticism for failing to make allowances for changes in quality over time as between union and nonunion labor,[44] they are at least in the direction we would expect.

As for the effects of unions on the dispersion of earnings, the consensus seems to be that their role has been minor.[45] This is because unions tend not only to raise the pay of unionized groups relative to nonunionized groups, but also to equalize pay levels within the area of their jurisdiction. Certainly, it is clear from the British evidence that the manual worker earnings distribution has hardly altered during the course of the present century, from which we would conclude that the effect of unions must wash out (chapter 10). However, when we come to consider the entire earnings structure (wages and salaries together), it is a fact that the lesser unionized groups tend to be white-collar workers,[46] who constitute the higher-paid categories. Thus, unions might have been partially responsible for the observed shrinkage of the manual-nonmanual differential, so as to reduce the overall dispersion of earnings (but see chapter 10).

The Distribution of Income. It is possible that unions have not so much affected the pay of union members relative to nonunion groups as they have

---

42. Friedman, *Impact of the Union*, p. 222; Lewis, *Unionism and Relative Wages*, p. 219; Royal Commission on Trade Unions and Employers' Associations, *Minutes*, p. 1616.
43. This follows from the relationship $\ln \bar{W} \equiv U \ln W_U + (1 - U)\ln W_N$, where W refers to economywide aggregates and U is the proportion unionized. Because $U \simeq 7\%$ in the United States in 1931–32, and given $W_U/\bar{W} \simeq 1.23$, it follows that $W_N/\bar{W} \simeq 0.98$.
44. See n. 13 of this chapter.
45. Royal Commission on Trade Unions and Employers' Associations, *Minutes*, pp. 1612 ff; Lewis, *Unionism and Relative Wages*, p. 295.
46. It also appears that white-collar unions are less effective than their blue-collar equivalents in raising their members' pay. See D. S. Hamermesh, "White-Collar Unions, Blue-Collar Unions, and Wages in Manufacturing," *Industrial and Labor Relations Review* 24 (1971): 168.

Table 8.2 Measures of Labor's Share in Gross Domestic Product, Britain and America, Selected Intervals 1900-1969

	Wages Plus Salaries (%)	Wages Plus Salaries Plus Imputed Earnings of Self-employed (%)
United States		
1900–1909[a]	55	63–76
1949–1957[a]	67	74–80
1948[b]	63	
1969[b]	73	
United Kingdom		
1910–1914[c]	47	60
1950–1954[c]	65	74
1960–1963[c]	67	75
1969[b]	69	

Sources:
[a] I. B. Kravis, "Relative Income Shares in Fact and Theory," *American Economic Review* 49 (1959): 919.
[b] A. P. Thirlwall, "Changes in Industrial Composition in the U.K. and the U.S. and Labor's Share of National Income," *Bulletin of the Oxford University Institute of Economics and Statistics* 34 (1972): 377–379.
[c] C. H. Feinstein, "Changes in the Distribution of the National Income in the U.K. since 1860," in J. Marchal and B. Ducros, eds., *The Distribution of National Income* (New York: St. Martin's Press, 1968), pp. 117, 126.

affected the remuneration of all wage and salary earners relative to the return on capital. In other words, it is possible that the unions' effect in raising the absolute wage of both unionized and nonunionized groups is more important than their relative wage effect.[47] An interesting question then arises: have the owners of labor been made better off, in terms of their share in national income, as a result of these efforts? Keynes himself computed the relative share of manual labor in national income for Great Britain and the United States over the earlier years of this century and found a stability that he termed "a bit of a miracle."[48] Since then, controversy has continued to rage

47. The two are independent; see Lewis, *Unionism and Relative Wages*, p. 16. In an interesting general equilibrium analysis, using a two-sector model and assuming that unions *do* create a wage differential (union labor being paid 15% more than nonunion), it has been suggested that the principal gains of union labor have been achieved at the expense of nonunion groups and not of capital. See H. G. Johnson and P. Mieszkowski, "The Effects of Unionisation on the Distribution of Income: A General Equilibrium Approach," *Quarterly Journal of Economics* 84 (1970): 547, 560. If unions simply raise wages without creating a differential, then the analytical problem is similar to that posed by minimum-wage legislation. The two-sector model again gives pessimistic results; upholding, for example, the traditional conclusion that minimum-wage legislation tends to cause unemployment. See H. G. Johnson, "Minimum Wage Laws: General Equilibrium Analysis," *Canadian Journal of Economics* 2 (1969): 599–604.
48. J. M. Keynes, "Relative Movements of Real Wages and Output," *Economic Journal* 49 (1939): 48.

over the stability or otherwise of labor's share and the reasons for any observed movements in that share.

A pressing problem concerns the constituents of labor's share. It might be thought that the appropriate division is between wage earners (the hourly or weekly paid) and the rest, which is to group salary earners with capitalists. This delineation would have its rationale in a class division. In fact, the share of wages alone appears to have been decreasing steadily with the growth of salaried employment. Given this structural shift, and given that unions are increasingly organizing the salaried groups, it would seem more appropriate to include salaried workers when computing the share of labor. A further, more intractable problem is how to impute a value to the labor of the self-employed. Because part of the income of the self-employed represents a return to their labor, it is desirable for some purposes also to include these imputed earnings within labor's share. The imputation can be made by assuming that the self-employed earn as much as the average employee; the residual income would then be their return on capital. Measures of labor's share, with and without the imputed earnings of the self-employed, are shown in table 8.2. It can be seen that, for both Great Britain and the United States, the share, regardless of the definition adopted, has increased considerably over the past fifty to sixty years.[49]

In part, this increasing share is explicable in terms of measurement biases, of which the most important comprise the underevaluation of government capital income and farm labor income. The consequence of both biases is to increase labor's measured income share over time, because over time the weight of government has been increasing and that of agriculture decreasing. However, such influences are unlikely to cancel out the increase. In the case of the United States, for example, Kravis estimates that such biases could account for only one percentage point of the overall increase of about eight percentage points over the first half of this century.[50]

In part, the increasing share is also likely to reflect structural changes within the economy, namely a shift towards high labor share industries within such sectors as education, health, and services. This shift, unless

49. Estimates for the longer period are provided by Phelps Brown and Browne, *A Century of Pay*, p. 335. Lowest and highest values of seven-year moving averages of a measure of labor's share are as follows (measurements in percent):

U.K.			U.S.		
1870–1913	¯1924–1938	1950–1960	1889–1919	1924–1938	1950–1960
63–73	68–71	76–82	59–71	68–80	71–76

This again indicates an upward trend, comparing end-points. On these figures, most of the increase in the United States, unlike Great Britain, appears to have occurred prior to World War II. However, this is contrary to Thirlwall's estimates in table 8.2. It thus seems safer to confine ourselves to judgments about long-term trends only.
50. Kravis, "Relative Income Shares," p. 927.

counteracted by changes in labor's share within industries, could account for the observed change in labor's aggregate share. In fact, this factor does not seem very important. For the postwar period, taking the share of wages and salaries alone, it has been calculated that changes in industry weights contribute not at all to the observed change in the British overall share. In the case of the United States, changes in industry weights appear to have had more effect, but their influence remains modest, accounting for about three percentage points in the overall postwar change of some ten percentage points.[51] Thus, there seems to have occurred a definite improvement in labor's share within industries, if not in the interwar period, then certainly in the postwar interval.[52] Looking only at manufacturing industries, the sector for which aggregate production functions are usually estimated, the signs are that here, too, there has been a genuine increase in labor's share. Again, the evidence would suggest that most of the observed increase has taken place in the postwar period, with constancy in the interwar years.[53]

Materials useful in constructing an explanation of changes in the distribution of income are assembled in table 8.3. Over the past sixty years, the real wage rate has tripled within the United States and doubled in the United Kingdom. Because the return on capital appears to have remained constant, perhaps declining somewhat in the United Kingdom, this has meant a large increase over time in the wage-to-capital rental ratio. Accompanying these changes has been a doubling of the capital-to-labor ratio in both countries, a development that is at least in the direction predicted by neoclassical theory! At the same time, we observe a sizable increase in labor's share, from which it follows that the historical elasticity of substitution, σ, must have been considerably less than unity. In fact, the historical σ turns out to be 0.69 for the United States and even lower, at 0.48, for Great Britain.[54] The latter values do not provide a true, that is, technological, elasticity of substitution, because they include the effect of technical change. However, other estimates indicate σ to be less than unity,[55] in which case marginal productivity theory would predict an increase in the share of labor consequent upon an increase

51. Thirlwall, "Industrial Composition," pp. 379–380.
52. See Kerr, "Labor's Income Share," pp. 280, 288–289.
53. See Reder, "Alternative Theories," table 2, p. 198.
54. These values are computed according to the arc elasticity formula:

$$\sigma = \frac{(\Delta K/L)/(K/L)}{(\Delta w/r)/(w/r)}.$$

Thus, in the case of the United Kingdom,

$$\sigma = \frac{(3711 - 2227)/\tfrac{1}{2}(3711 + 2227)}{(1.09 - 0.337)/\tfrac{1}{2}(1.09 + 0.337)}$$

$$= 0.48.$$

55. See Arrow et al., "Capital-Labor Substitution," pp. 228, 244.

Table 8.3 · Variables Related to Labor's Share, Great Britain and the United States, Selected Intervals 1900–1963

United States[a] (1929 dollars)

	Capital/Output (per $ of output)	Capital/Labor (per man-hour)	Wage, w (per hour)	Return to Reproducible Capital, r	$\dfrac{w}{r}$	National Income ($ billion)	Total Labor Share
1900–1909	$3.2	$1.26	$0.284	8.8%	3.24	$39.1	0.72
1949–1957	$2.2	$2.60	$0.964	8.9%	10.87	$167.7	0.80

United Kingdom[b] (1958 pounds)

	Capital/Output (per £ of output)	Capital/Labor (per worker)	Wage, w (per annum)	Return to Reproducible Capital, r	$\dfrac{w}{r}$	National Income (£ billion)	Total Labor Share
1910–1914	£4.0	£2,227	£338	10.0%	0.337	£10.5	0.60
1960–1963	£4.1	£3,711	£673	6.2%	1.09	£22.5	0.75

Sources:

[a] I. B. Kravis, "Relative Income Shares in Fact and Theory," *American Economic Review* 49 (1959): 936–940.

[b] C. H. Feinstein, "Changes in the Distribution of the National Income in the U.K. since 1960," in J. Marchal and B. Ducros, eds., *The Distribution of National Income* (New York: St. Martin's Press, 1968), pp. 131–134.

in its relative price. If we ascribe to unions a role in raising the relative wage, as it seems we might, it therefore follows that unions have played a role in increasing labor income relative to capital income.

The difficulty with the above interpretation is that it depends upon the concept of the elasticity of substitution and consequently upon that of an aggregate production function. But one of the principal arguments favoring the empirical estimates of such a function, namely that the estimates implied constant factor shares and that this corresponded to the facts, no longer holds. It is now clear that factor shares are not constant, although they once tended to be (at least for the private nonfarm sector earlier in the century).[56] One response could be to await the development of improved production functions.[57] The alternative would be to deny this approach in its entirety and instead to adopt a macroeconomic theory of distribution. This is the course followed by Kaldor, whose theory leads to a direct relationship between the investment/income ratio and the profit share. In fact, there does seem to be a tolerably good association between the two variables. Correlating changes in the investment/income ratio with changes in the American wage share over the period 1921–60 gives a simple correlation coefficient $r = -0.78$, which is highly significant.[58] In Great Britain, there does not seem to be such a close relationship; perhaps because of shifts in savings propensities, which the theory assumes constant.[59] Supportive of the theory, however, is the fact that in the long run both the investment/income ratio and the profit share have tended to be stable.

Attempts have been made to reconcile the marginal productivity and Kaldorian theories of distribution. For example, it has been suggested that the division between total labor income, including the imputed earnings of the self-employed, and other income might be determined by marginal

---

56. Full results from Douglas' data (although not reported by him) are interesting. The equation given is for the period 1899–1922,

$$\ln Q = -0.1773 + 0.233 \ln K + 0.807 \ln L$$
$$(0.40) \quad (3.67) \quad (5.57)$$
$$R^2 = 0.957$$
$$DW = 1.52$$

where Q, K, and L are measures of output capital and labor;
$|t|$ are given in parentheses.

The fit is very good and the estimated parameters roughly equal factor shares in the sectors covered. Not surprisingly, this was the precursor of many other attempts to estimate aggregate production functions.

57. One attempt to fit a production function to a particular industry, namely the British electrical engineering industry, finds that estimated marginal products correspond quite closely to actual earnings. See P. R. G. Layard, J. D. Sargan, M. E. Ager, and D. J. Jones, *Qualified Manpower and Economic Performance* (London: Allen Lane, 1971), p. 147.

58. L. E. Gallaway, "The Theory of Relative Shares," *Quarterly Journal of Economics* 78 (1964): 589.

59. Phelps Brown, "Pay and Profits," pp. 36–38.

productivity factors. On the other hand, so the argument runs, within the ranks of labor, the distinction between self-employed and other labor might tend to be determined along Kaldorian lines. In this case, labor would tend to shift from employee into self-employed status (thus saving more, given income) if higher equilibrium savings are required to be consistent with given investment plans.[60] However, this line of argument cannot be said to be other than speculative. The prudent course of action would be to focus upon improving the well-proven tools of marginal analysis. The latter extends to unions a limited role in influencing the distribution of income. Were income distribution to be determined according to Kaldor's theory, however, then unions would appear to exercise no influence whatever. Distribution will simply be determined by effective demand in conjunction with given consumption propensities.

8.4   Conclusions

Examination of the effects of collective bargaining on the various facets of the structure of income has taken us to the boundary of economics. Here the tools of economic analysis have to be employed in conjunction with those of other disciplines, such as demography, history, and sociology, and the whole blended into a general equilibrium framework within which everything depends on everything else. This is particularly true when analyzing the determinants of the real wage rate and the share of national income among the productive factors. Given this, it is perhaps pardonable to be sympathetic to the view that the issues in question, though fascinating in themselves, are hardly yet susceptible to scientific economic analysis. We are thus confined at the moment mainly to speculation. However, the third area with which this chapter has been concerned, the size of the differential between union and nonunion labor and its determinants, is rather more tractable. We have uncovered several promising lines of inquiry.

Looking at the determinants of the general level of real pay, economic theory suggests that the basic factor will be the level of subsistence. In equilibrium, and given competition, a set of earnings differentials will be established above this basic level so as to secure the requisite supply of workers with various periods of training. Yet the determinants of the subsistence level itself remain somewhat obscure. Population pressure is likely to play a part, rising levels of labor productivity a part, and aspirations and cultural norms a further part. Trade unions may exert an influence via this last factor. We have found enormous increases in average real wage levels over the past fifty years—a tripling in the United States and a doubling in Great Britain. That this has occurred with the demand for labor keeping pace with the supply encourages us to think that direct intervention has played but a small part. Factors limiting the size of families in the face of ever-growing

60. See Reder, "Alternative Theories" pp. 201–202; Gallaway, "Relative Shares," pp. 588 ff.

real income levels will be the dominant influences, but we are a long way from uncovering these factors.

As for the question of labor's share in the national income, there are again competing explanations. On the one hand, there is the marginal productivity theory, with its emphasis upon relative factor prices, factor quantities, and technology—in particular, the elasticity of substitution. And on the other, we have the Keynesian theory, stressing aggregate demand and differences in savings propensities between the classes. Both theories have their associated advantages and difficulties. It seems that the share of labor in the national income has increased over the course of the present century, even allowing for structural shifts, such as the increase in the weight of the more labor-intensive industries. Is this because, the relative wage having risen, the elasticity of substitution of labor for capital is less than unity? Or is it because, the investment/income ratio having declined, this has forced a change in income distribution in favor of wage earners, who have lower savings propensities?

The difficulty with any marginal productivity explanation is that marginal productivity is a microeconomic concept. We are not sure of its existence at the macroeconomic level; and we note the controversy surrounding the measurement of capital at the macro level. But there is the hope that these difficulties can be overcome, in which case we will be able to retain the strengths of the well-tried traditional analysis. The Keynesian theory does not have microeconomic underpinnings and is therefore difficult to interpret in the context of orthodox analysis. Why, for example, has the invest-ment/income ratio declined? In this light, we would therefore pin our hopes upon improvements in the techniques of aggregate production function analysis and in general equilibrium models. Within this framework, dimly deciphered though it may be, it is possible that trade unions have been responsible for some of the increase in labor's share over time. This is because we can probably credit them some of the increase in real wage rates over time.

Turning to the firmer ground of union relative wage effects, there is a basic issue to be raised. Are unions the cause of higher wages for unionized groups, or is it more the case that higher wages attract union members? If we are to allow unions a creative role in seeking out and exploiting pockets of mo-nopoly power, as it seems we must, then the causation runs from unions to wages. At the same time, however, we must recognize that the pockets of monopoly power are to some extent determined by the product and by the technology (as is shown by the Marshallian rules), and thus cannot be brought about by the union. To this extent, therefore, the causation would run from wages to unionism. Whatever our judgment on this question, we have found that allowing for simultaneity greatly reduces the size of the estimated differential. Ignoring simultaneity, the differential, with respect to manual workers in industry, can be set at 20% to 30% on both sides of the

Atlantic. Perhaps a middle-of-the-road position and a differential in the range preferred by Lewis, 10% to 15%, is the most surely defended position.

There are also some additional topics of interest in this area. For example, there is the research that has been undertaken into the determinants of the differential. We have shown that the differential increases with the extent of unionization, which is expected, but does not appear to be higher in monopolistic industries, which is contrary to expectation. A fruitful field for further research will be to ascertain whether different measures of monopoly in the product market, such as establishment size, provide the theoretically expected relationship. There is also the question of whether quality differences between union and nonunion labor tend to cancel out the differential measured in efficiency units. There are signs that such is the case.

Broadly speaking, then, this survey of the influence of collective bargaining on the structure of income and earnings has not uncovered firm evidence of pronounced union effects. This result might be due in part to the inadequacy of our theoretical framework and, consequently, of our measurements. Here, we would point in particular to the analysis of the effect of collective bargaining on labor's share. Nevertheless, the signs at the moment are that the main effects of collective bargaining are in the areas of discrimination, job regulation, and featherbedding, rather than in determining the level and structure of real pay.

APPENDIX 8-A
FACTOR SHARES AND THE ELASTICITY OF SUBSTITUTION

Consider a production function of the form

$$Q = F(K,L) \qquad F_K > 0, F_L > 0, F_{KK} < 0, F_{LL} < 0$$

where Q, K, and L are quantities of output, capital, and labor, respectively.

The marginal rate of substitution of labor for capital (R) is given by

$$R \equiv -dK/dL = F_L/F_K,$$

where $dR/d(K/L) > 0$.

The elasticity of substitution, σ, is defined as[1]

$$\sigma \equiv - \frac{dK/L}{dR} \cdot \frac{R}{K/L}.$$

Assuming $F(K,L)$ is constant returns to scale, or, less stringently, constant returns to scale over the relevant range, we can write

$$q \equiv Q/L = F(K/L,1) = f(k),$$

where $k \equiv K/L, f' > 0, f'' < 0$.

Then

$$F_K = \frac{\partial}{\partial K}[Lf(k)] = f'(k)$$

and

$$F_L = f(k) - f'(k) \cdot k.$$

1. See J. R. Hicks, *The Theory of Wages,* 2nd ed. (London: Macmillan, 1964), pp. 235 ff.

Thus,

$$\sigma = \frac{dk}{d\left(\dfrac{f - f'k}{f'}\right)} \cdot \frac{(f - f'k)/f'}{k}$$

$$= -\frac{f'(f - f'k)}{fkf''}.$$

For this expression to have any practical value, we have further to assume that there is perfect competition and profit maximization, so that there is a link between R and factor prices. The relation is given by

$$R = w/r,$$

where w and r are respectively the wage and capital rental rates measured in terms of the price of the product.

It is now possible to derive an expression for the behavior of factor shares as k changes, in terms of $f(k)$ and σ. Thus the profit share π is

$$\pi = r \cdot k/q = kf'/f,$$

so that

$$\frac{d\pi}{dk} = \frac{fkf''}{f^2}\left(\frac{f'(f - f'k)}{fkf''} + 1\right)$$

$$= -\frac{kf''}{f}(\sigma - 1).$$

Because $(-kf''/f)$ is positive by assumption, the expression shows

$$d\pi/dk \gtrless 0 \text{ as } \sigma \gtrless 1.$$

The above expression can alternatively be written in terms of an elasticity:

$$\frac{d\pi}{dk} \cdot \frac{k}{\pi} = (1 - \pi)\left(1 - \frac{1}{\sigma}\right).$$

This tells us that the profit share will be the more sensitive to changes in k the lower is π or the higher is $1 - \pi$, labor's share, for given σ.

It is also helpful to view the above relationships graphically. Consider figure 8-A.1, in which it is assumed as before that production is constant returns to scale. The value of output is measured in terms of the total quantity of either factor that the output could buy. At the initial equilibrium position, α, because $-w/r = AB/CF$, labor's income is

$$CF \cdot \frac{AB}{CF} \cdot r = AB \cdot r.$$

Figure 8-A.1   Factor Shares with Differing Elasticity of Substitution

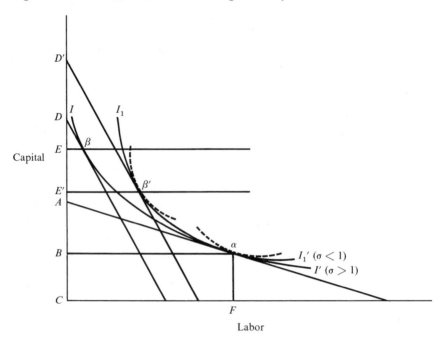

Capital income is given by $BC \cdot r$, and the income of capital relative to that of labor is BC/AB.

If now there is an increase in the relative price of labor, the consequence for labor's share will depend crucially upon the factor quantities used at the new equilibrium position, which will in turn depend on σ. Two possibilities are shown in the diagram. The flatter of the two indifference curves, II', corresponds to a high σ ($\sigma > 1$), and its more sharply curved companion, I_1I_1', to a low σ ($\sigma < 1$). The shares associated with the two different equilibrium positions (β, β') can be read off the diagram, as before. The income of capital relative to that of labor is EC/DE and $E'C/D'E'$, respectively. It can be seen that labor's share, almost 50% at α, falls markedly at position β ($\sigma > 1$), but is increased at position β' ($\sigma < 1$).

The diagram can also be used in a negative vein to show that it is improper to infer the size of σ from K/L, w/r, and factor shares taken at two points in time. This is because the two observations might encompass different technologies. In the diagram, the broken curves indicate two isoquants where $\sigma \simeq 0$. The possibility of capital-using technical change, in combination with $\sigma = 0$, could thus give rise to the same equilibria, α and β', as would zero technical change and $0 < \sigma < 1$.

CHAPTER 9
JOB REGULATION

9.1 Introduction

In this chapter, we consider union influences on patterns of labor utilization. These influences include the emphasis on seniority as a criterion for promotion and layoff, control of entry to the occupation, control of discharge, establishment of manning levels (which may entail featherbedding), reservation of work for particular work groups or unions (demarcation and jurisdiction), and also limitations on plant closures, subcontracting, or mergers. Our goal is to show why these protective practices develop and to discuss their advantages and disadvantages for the economy as a whole. We then analyze some of the policy measures put forward to ameliorate the unfavorable consequences of such practices.

In explaining the development of protective practices, we shall have recourse to the human capital model introduced in chapter 4. In this regard, an individual investing in entering an occupation can be said to guard against capital loss by ensuring that the occupation does not become obsolete or taken over by other work groups; hence the emphasis on the jurisdiction of a particular trade and on controlling labor intake. Human capital theoretic considerations will also provide a stimulus for individuals to restrict management's power to discharge, the collective agreement providing the means for such restriction. Indeed, it has been said that, in the United States, the typical worker covered by a collective agreement is so unlikely to be dismissed that he has "a kind of life tenure in his job so long as it continues to exist."[1] It follows that our inquiry will take us into the field of job ownership.

Further strands in the explanation of some aspects of job regulation, in particular the stress on protecting the senior employee at the expense of the junior, have a basis in political theories. Given the presence of a union, methods of labor adjustment are likely to favor senior workers. This is because senior workers are said to develop the most weight in influencing the

---

1. F. Meyers, *Ownership of Jobs: A Comparative Study* (Los Angeles, Calif.: Institute of Industrial Relations, University of California, 1964), p. 7.

union attitude or *voice* with respect to management. In the absence of a union, the preferences of the marginal worker have more influence upon the employer, because the *exit* mechanism, chiefly taking the form of quits but also including reductions in work effort,[2] is dominant. Other political elements in job regulation are reflected in the perceived objectivity of promotion and layoff according to seniority. This means that the union concerned can more easily take a potentially unpopular decision. There might also be gains for management resulting from the increased certainty and hence smoother industrial relations consequent upon having an agreed seniority rule. Human capital factors will also be important here. Both employers and workers will gain to the extent that flexible seniority rules lower quits and safeguard investments in specific training.

Precise measurements of the impact of inefficiencies in labor utilization on output are not possible, but the importance of the problem has been increasingly recognized since Leibenstein's work on "X-efficiency."[3] Economists have been prone to assume that firms can effectively minimize costs, so that society moves out onto its production possibility frontier. Here, the main problem is viewed as one of ensuring that price distortions, reflecting monopoly elements and subsidies, do not cause a nonoptimal point on the frontier to be chosen. On the other hand, Leibenstein's analysis of the many cases where unit costs could be substantially reduced without changing the scale of production indicates that society is likely to be well within the production frontier. The most commonly cited reason for this organizational slack is absence of competitive product market pressures. The contributory role of organized labor might not have received enough emphasis because of an identification problem: the well-organized firms tend also to be the larger firms that are likely to be less subject to competition. In any case, the subject matter of this chapter should be seen in the context of a wider debate as to the causes of lapses from X-efficiency.

The problem appears to be more serious in some industries, such as printing, than others and is widely acknowledged to be more serious in Great Britain than the United States.[4] In both countries, attempts have been made to cushion the impact of labor market change on the work force and thereby alleviate the need for certain protective practices. Attempts have also been made directly to outlaw certain practices, such as the closed shop or featherbedding. It will be necessary to consider these policies.

The plan of the chapter is as follows. First, we consider the theoretical basis of the various forms of job regulation and investigate certain aspects of their impact on output and price. Second, we analyze a number of studies of

---

2. The basic discussion of voice and exit mechanisms is to be found in A. O. Hirschman, *Exit, Voice and Loyalty* (Cambridge, Mass.: Harvard University Press, 1970), chap. 1.
3. H. Leibenstein, "Allocative Efficiency versus 'X-Efficiency,'" *American Economic Review* 56 (1966): 392–415.
4. See L. Ulman, "Collective Bargaining and Industrial Efficiency," in R. E. Caves, ed., *Britain's Economic Prospects* (Washington, D.C.: The Brookings Institution, 1968), p. 328.

job regulation. Finally, we turn to policy questions and discuss buy-out approaches to the problem as well as more general measures, such as severance and redundancy (or termination) pay, designed to make job protection less necessary for the workers concerned.

9.2 Theory of Job Regulation

It is useful to break down job regulation into three principal categories. First, we may identify those practices that control entry into an occupation or job. We refer here to the various forms of closed shop, restrictions upon apprenticeship, and controls over job assignment. These practices have a long history, perhaps as long as unionism itself, and are predominantly union initiated. They apply in the main to craft rather than industrial unions. Second, there are make-work practices, which encompass overmanning and/or the rejection of modern machinery. This second category sometimes shades into the first, but the distinction is worth preserving because of the glaring inefficiency of make-work practices. Third, there are the practices associated with the use of seniority to assign priority in such matters as promotion, demotion, and layoff. Seniority practices are associated mainly with industrial unionism. They merit separate identification because they are much more a joint creation of management and unions than are the former two categories. Training and screening investments can be shown to create a natural precedence for senior workers, which would imply that seniority practices need not be cost increasing.

Let us examine each category in turn. Having done this, we will then consider the principle of compensation as a means of adapting protective practices to labor market change.

Licensing and Job Assignment Rules. Consider the behavior of the union or professional association as a monopoly supplier of labor. Union members are expected to be more willing to collude to raise their average level of pay the lower are the costs of such action in the form of reduced job opportunities for members, *ceteris paribus*. The circumstances under which these costs can be expected to be low are determined according to the Marshallian rules for the elasticity of derived demand (chapter 7). In its simplest form the theory argues that, if such monopoly power exists, its exertion in raising wages will yield a once-for-all gain. Moreover, that gain will be restricted to the current membership.[5] It is a once-for-all change because the union is supposed to move quickly to exploit its monopoly power once this has been recognized. Its benefits accrue to existing members alone because the resulting improvement in relative pay over occupations requiring similar training is presumed to attract new entrants. Thus, places will have to be rationed. In equilibrium and assuming no favoritism is extended to particular classes of applicants,

---

5. M. R. Fisher, *The Economic Analysis of Labor* (London: Weidenfeld and Nicolson, 1971), p. 147.

new entrants are likely to pay to enter to the point where, at the margin, there is no advantage to entering the unionized occupation over any other. However, if there is favoritism, those so favored will be able to enter the profession at lower cost, and they will consequently receive a higher rate of return on capital invested than is available in alternative occupations.[6]

On this view, union members are held to have a capital investment in their occupation, for which they hope to obtain a competitive return. The erection of higher licensing standards has the effect of bringing a windfall capital gain to incumbents,[7] providing the existing membership is exempted by a "grandfather clause." Accordingly, there is an incentive to follow this course of action. A corollary of this is that any influx of qualified applicants, possibly occasioned by a change in immigration patterns or in work assignment rules, will tend to bring about a capital loss for incumbents. Thus, those who seek to enter the occupation will be regulated via the closed shop or work permit. Also, the definition of the occupation itself will be continually policed by enforcing work assignment or demarcation rules. Finally, there is an obvious incentive to discriminate in favor of members' relatives when considering applications for entry. Such a policy is consistent with the goal of *family* income maximization. Indeed, there is evidence to suggest that self-recruitment is pervasive in professional occupations and craft unions.[8]

Human capital theoretic considerations thus provide a common thread linking the closed shop, high occupational entry standards, favoritism, careful job definition via work assignment rules, and opposition to technical change. This is not to say that human capital theory requires that such practices develop; rather, it posits that they will prove difficult to remove once established. This is because individuals invest in an occupation on the expectation that income flows, buttressed by the rules, will be maintained. In a very real sense, they can thus be seen to have "property rights in the form of inherited protective practices."[9] The major factor in the development of these rules is likely to be work force organization.

Featherbedding.   Make-work practices, or featherbedding, can similarly be interpreted as an attempt to protect, or enhance, a human capital investment. Indeed, in a number of cases, the connection between the rules described above and featherbedding will be a close one. For example, the British practice of forbidding the craftsman's mate to perform skilled tasks, or the prohibition on foremen doing the work of bargaining unit (union) employ-

6. W. S. Siebert, "Occupational Licensing: The Merrison Report on the Regulation of the Medical Profession," *British Journal of Industrial Relations* 15 (1977): 30.

7. S. Rottenberg, "The Economics of Occupational Licensing," *Aspects of Labor Economics,* A Conference of the Universities, National Bureau of Economic Research (Princeton, N.J.: Princeton University Press, 1962), p. 15.

8. See, for example, G. S. Becker, "Union Restrictions on Entry," in P. Bradley, ed., *The Public Stake in Union Power* (Charlottesville, Va.: University of Virginia Press, 1959), p. 73.

9. A. Flanders, *The Fawley Productivity Agreements* (London: Faber and Faber, 1964), p. 10.

ees, can sometimes give rise to featherbedding. However, it is more usual to regard featherbedding not as a preconceived strategy, but as resulting from attempts to balk technological change—"the carrying forward of a set of practices appropriate for one technology to another where it is alien."[10] An American example is the rule, since modified, in West Coast longshoring prohibiting the lifting of loads heavier than 2,100 pounds.[11] Once a safety measure, this became a make-work practice. As in the case of licensing rules, featherbedding tends to be more a problem with craft than industrial unions. This is because industrial unions generally comprise a number of diverse groups, some of which will be helped and others harmed by a given technological change. Accordingly, concerted opposition is less easily practiced.

A diagrammatic exposition of the evolution of featherbedding rules consequent upon changing technology is given in figure 9.1. Assume a situation of Hicks-neutral technical change that, at the existing capital/labor ratio, raises the marginal productivities of both capital and labor in the same proportion. In this case, if relative factor input prices remain unchanged, less capital and less labor will be used, but the factor input ratio will be unchanged. Technical change is depicted as an inward shift of the production isoquant Q_o' to Q_o (quadrant II). If the number of efficiency units per unit of

10. P. Weinstein, "The Featherbedding Problem," *American Economic Review* 54 (1964): 147.
11. See C. C. Killingsworth, "The Modernization of West Coast Longshore Work Rules," *Industrial and Labor Relations Review* 15 (1962): 298.

Figure 9.1 The Origins of Featherbedding

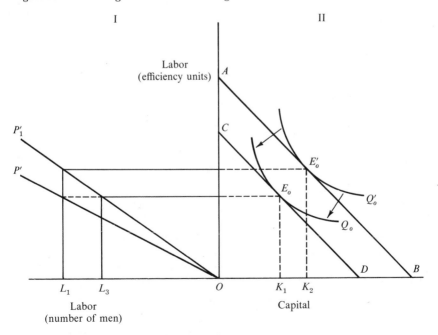

labor are maintained at their old level, given by the slope of OP'_1, then it follows that the labor force will be reduced from OL_1 to OL_3. However, the work force may actively resist this depletion of its numbers and press for maintenance of the employment status quo. If this strategy is successful, the efficiency of the labor force will fall off and workers will presumably enjoy increased leisure on the job. Thus, OP'_1 will shift downward to OP' and OL_1 units of labor will continue in employment.

Featherbedding, contrary to what one might expect, need not always reduce an industry's output and raise the price of its product. To establish this point, we distinguish between *level* and *ratio* featherbedding. The former relates to a featherbedding rule that specifies a minimum level to the labor force—the negotiation of a work force stabilization or "no terminations" clause. The latter specifies that labor shall be employed in a given ratio to some other factor, for example, a fixed number of men per machine.[12] The importance of the distinction is that, in the case of level featherbedding, the marginal cost of labor is zero and consequently the marginal costs of production are lower, but average costs are higher, than in the no-restriction example, up to the stipulated minimum labor force. Ratio featherbedding, on the other hand, causes marginal costs of production to be higher than they would otherwise be at all levels of output. If it is possible to increase average costs without driving the firm out of business, that is, if the industry is monopolistic, it follows that level featherbedding increases output while the ratio variety reduces output. Within a competitive scenario, the imposition of either variant will drive some firms out of business.[13]

This argument can be made clearer with the aid of figure 9.2. Consider first a monopoly situation, so that TC and TR are total cost and revenue curves applicable to the industry as a whole. L' is that output level corresponding to some specified minimum labor force. In the absence of featherbedding, the TC curve takes the form $ACTC$, whereas with level featherbedding it follows $ECTC$ and with ratio featherbedding it follows ATC'. Corresponding maximum profit output levels are L, L', and L''. Level featherbedding has the effect of bargaining away monopoly profits, thereby benefiting workers and consumers at the expense of the owners of capital. At L', the average cost of labor will be higher than marginal revenue product, that is, the employer will be pushed rightward to a position off his labor demand curve. The intersection of the TC and TR schedules marks the limit to which he can be forced.

Assuming perfect competition (dashed line TR'), where the diagram is now taken to apply to a representative firm, imposition of level featherbedding would require the TR' curve to shift upward to bring tangency at C. This will result in a price increase. While some firms would be able to maintain the

12. P. Weinstein, "Featherbedding: A Theoretical Analysis," *Journal of Political Economy* 68 (1960): 379–381.

13. See N. J. Simler, "The Economics of Featherbedding," *Industrial and Labor Relations Review* 16 (1962): 111–121.

Figure 9.2   The Effect of Featherbedding on Output

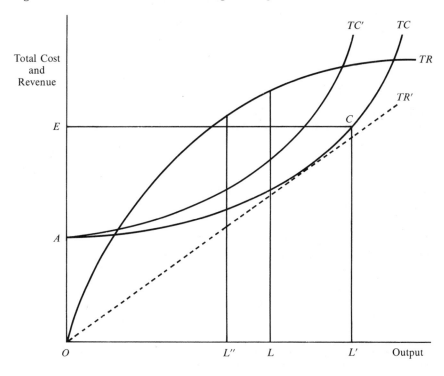

stipulated employment level, employment in the industry as a whole would contract. The price increase consequent on industry contraction can be seen to be even more pronounced for ratio featherbedding.

The implication of this analysis is that featherbedding will certainly increase unit costs. It will generally increase prices too, except in the case of a monopoly where featherbedding takes the form of a minimum labor force requirement. Because of its likely smaller impact on prices (and thus employment) in monopolistic industries, we would expect featherbedding to be more prevalent in precisely such industries. However, it is possible to over-emphasize the distinction between market structures. Political theory would suggest that union policies tend to reflect the demands of some average of workers—the median voter model—who will be relatively less mobile and have greater specific training than the marginal worker (who is most likely to lose employment). To this extent, the long-term unemployment consequences of protective practices are less of a deterrent, and they can be expected to affect the more competitive as well as the monopolistic sectors.

The point here is that an important strand in the explanation of X-inefficiency, that is, higher than best practice costs, would be protective labor practices. Academics have tended to stress the role of lack of knowl-edge or imperfect markets for managerial labor in accounting for this phenomenon.[14] Lay opinion, on the other hand, would regard union-imposed manning standards as the more important factor.[15] But labor productivity varies for many reasons other than union action, for example, scale and technology, and investigation of this issue is difficult. A recent comparative study of British and American plants found that output per man was on average some 50% higher in the latter. Of this difference, thirty-five percentage points were tentatively attributed to factors such as scale, technology, and product mix, and fifteen points to behavioral factors such as strikes, restrictive practices, and overmanning.[16] Because there is evidence of wide interindustry variation in labor productivity within, and not merely between, countries, it is to be hoped that this type of study will be extended. But, on the basis of the above study, it is clear that a strong case can be made for arguing that labor practices are of importance in determining lapses from X-efficiency. At the same time, it is necessary to avoid the connotation of blame for the development of such practices. Rather, the economic point that we are making here is that most protective practices are to be viewed as a rational response to potential job loss. The goal should be to alleviate or remove this fear. Management action that ignores the welfare of workers,[17] or ineffectual government policy in dealing with displaced workers, could well be the root cause of the problem. We shall investigate these issues in section 9.4.

Promotion, Demotion, Layoff, and Other Forms of Labor Force Adjustment. Unions are likely to affect the entire pattern of labor force adjustment. The basic reason for this is to be found in the development of seniority practices. The origins of the seniority principle appear partly to be the result of union political processes and partly the consequence of such economic forces as firm size and internal labor market structuring. But whatever the reasons for its development, the application of the seniority principle means that longer service workers are the last to be laid off. Given that senior members exercise a disproportionate influence in union councils, this implies that layoffs will be the preferred method of labor force adjustment. The alternative methods of adjustment available to the firm are attrition (quits, discharges for cause, and retirements), hours reduction, which is a form of work sharing, and wage rate shading. However, the alternatives facing the union firm are limited. For example, where seniority is applied, the quit rate will be reduced because

---

14. See Hirschman, *Exit, Voice and Loyalty,* p. 10; Leibenstein, "X-Efficiency," p. 407.

15. Thus, in an editorial within the London *Times,* we read: "Britain is not competitive with other major industrial powers in the production of a range of manufactured goods which are particularly important for our export trade, largely because of overmanning. This is where we should be most concerned about the record of trade unions, because overmanning is very largely a trade union phenomenon." (*The Times,* 27 October 1976.)

16. C. F. Pratten, *Labor Productivity Differentials Within International Companies* (Cambridge: Cambridge University Press, 1976), p. 61.

17. For a forceful statement of this problem, see Flanders, *Fawley Productivity Agreements,* p. 235.

separating from the firm will entail the loss of substantial privileges. Furthermore, the relative wage option is not generally available to the union firm. In consequence, the layoff becomes the dominant form of adjustment.

Methods of regulating promotion within a unit—department, plant, or division—of a firm may be classified under the heading of seniority practices. Here, we will focus only upon the general aspects of seniority; its intricacies are to be found elsewhere.[18] A basic point to be made at the outset is that seniority, unlike the job regulation practices considered above, is to some extent employer initiated. In other words, seniority practices need not be cost increasing. But once seniority systems are widely implemented, it becomes costly for individuals to enter the more skilled jobs. Thus, human capital analysis once more becomes applicable to problems of capital loss consequent upon technological change or plant closure. At the same time, a system of seniority allied to bumping rights confers job security. This protects workers and makes them less likely to block technological changes to the extent that it is the younger and more easily reemployable of their number who tend to bear the burden of work force reduction.

The main force making for job regulation by seniority is likely to be a union desire to avoid the arbitrary exercise of authority by management.[19] This factor is reinforced by arbitrators' concepts of equity—the "ethics of the queue."[20] The influence of the arbitrator deserves note. In British firms, there seems to be less of a seniority system than in their American counterparts. In part, this might reflect the wider coverage of craft labor markets in Great Britain, which require interfirm mobility. In part, however, it would seem to point to the greater development of arbitration within the United States. In part, it probably also reflects the different philosophy of the American and British trade union movements: the former attempt to control job loss via seniority at plant level; the latter seek national policies to ensure full employment and severance pay.[21]

There are also forces promoting seniority on the side of the employer. A seniority system ties workers to the firm and this outcome is in accord with the interests of the employer in situations where specific training investments have been made. To some extent, specific investments must accumulate in workers as they serve with the firm and come to know its methods and/or clientele. The firm in a recession will thus attempt to postpone the layoff of experienced workers. To this extent, there is a natural seniority system built on profit maximization. However, this aspect should not be overemphasized, because we would expect the firm to have a wide capacity for adjustment to

18. See, for example, S. H. Slichter, J. J. Healy, and E. R. Livernash, *The Impact of Collective Bargaining on Management* (Washington, D.C.: The Brookings Institution, 1960), chaps. 5–7.
19. For an analysis that emphasizes the role of the union, see A. M. Ross, "Do We Have a New Industrial Feudalism?" *American Economic Review* 48 (1958): 903.
20. See Slichter et al., *Impact of Collective Bargaining*, p. 104; M. W. Reder, "Job Scarcity and the Nature of Union Power," *Industrial and Labor Relations Review* 13 (1960): 358.
21. See Meyers, *Ownership of Jobs*, pp. 10, 31, 111.

different degrees of emphasis on seniority. A system without seniority rules and, consequently, with more interfirm mobility would simply mean that, in equilibrium, workers would finance more of their own training; that is, training would tend to be less specific. Conversely, in a system with seniority rules, specific investments will increase in relation to general ones. Training that would ordinarily be general has to be financed by the firm, and screening expenses are also greater, because workers at the bottom of the ladder must be of suitable material eventually to fill the spaces at the top. Firms or industries emphasizing seniority are thus likely more carefully to screen their job applicants. Also, because screening is so important, employers might prefer current employees to bring along relatives to fill vacancies. This gives rise to the possibility of nepotism in industrial as well as craft occupations. In sum, therefore, we would expect the main impetus to seniority systems to be provided by unions. However, because screening and training costs can be suitably adjusted, and perhaps also because of the certainty introduced into industrial relations by an objective decision rule, management may be expected to accept such provisions.

Turning to the impact of unions on labor force adjustment, the possibilities are as follows. Unionization can affect the hiring policy of firms together with their promotion, demotion, layoff, discharge, and overtime/hours reduction policies. Unions can also affect employee quit rates. It might well be argued that these effects are far more significant than union relative wage effects, which, as we have seen in chapter 8, are disputable. Flanders has argued:

The rules in collective agreements may also regulate such matters as dismissals, discipline, promotion or training, which cannot by any stretch of the imagination be included under price. . . . Thus one great accomplishment of collective bargaining has been its promotion of the "rule of law" in employment relationships.[22]

Reder goes further and points to "the adjustment of worker grievances" as the main function of union power.[23] In practice, however, it is difficult to separate out union influences from the effects of increased government intervention, which presumably will reflect collective preferences. (For example, why has the average workweek fallen?) But certain avenues of union influence can be suggested, and these may be tested in cross section by comparison with nonunion firms.

The first point to be made is that the greater rigidity of wages under unionism should mean that more weight in the adjustment process is given to varying hours worked per employee and/or the number of workers employed

---

22. A. Flanders, "Collective Bargaining: A Theoretical Analysis," *British Journal of Industrial Relations* 6 (1968): 14.
23. Reder, "Job Scarcity," p. 361.

in union than nonunion firms. However, seniority practices have an important effect in both of these areas. In the case of hours per employee, unions have typically been thought of as seeking to reduce hours of work in times of recession and to increase them in expansion.[24] To the extent that discharging workers is more costly in union firms, we would also expect the employer to exhibit much the same preference for variations in hours. This is because greater care will need to be exercised in selecting new employees and these higher specific capital investments will lead employers to attempt to reduce turnover. Yet in the United States, there are signs that the advent of seniority practices, together with increases in unemployment benefits, have reduced the union preference for work sharing.[25] The favored alternative is for layoffs, because the senior worker usually retains seniority while on layoff and enjoys compensation levels that are greater than those provided under state unemployment insurance schemes (as in the case of the auto workers, where a supplementary unemployment benefit scheme has been negotiated), and can avoid being bumped down to a lower-paying, less-skilled job. This would imply that cyclical differences in intensity of labor use between union and nonunion firms are probably not very important. At any rate, during the economic downturn of 1973–75, the number of hours worked by production workers in manufacturing declined by much the same amount in both union and nonunion sectors.[26]

As for adjustments in the number of workers, union firms might differ from the nonunion because of their lower quit rate and discharge rate, *ceteris paribus*. With respect to quit rates, one line of reasoning might be that the higher specific capital investments in workers in union firms tend to reduce quits. However, it should be noted that union workers probably also have more general capital and thus a greater propensity to quit, *ceteris paribus,* that nonunion workers.[27] In fact, there is evidence to suggest that unions do reduce quits,[28] presumably because the specific capital effect is the more powerful influence. This result is to be expected if union workers have

24. See, for example, Organisation for Economic Cooperation and Development, *Manpower Policy and Programmes in the United States* (Paris: O.E.C.D., 1964), para. 74; A. I. Marsh, *Industrial Relations in Engineering* (Oxford: Pergamon Press, 1965), p. 336.
25. See Slichter et al., *Impact of Collective Bargaining*, p. 142 ff.
26. At the time of the May 1973 Current Population Survey, hourly-rated production workers in manufacturing who were union members worked 42.4 hours per week and comparable nonmembers worked 41.2 hours. At the time of the May 1975 survey, the corresponding figures were 40.5 and 39.9 hours, respectively. See J. L. Medoff, "Layoff and Alternatives under Trade Unions in United States Manufacturing," *Discussion Paper No. 525,* (Cambridge, Mass.: Harvard Institute of Economic Research, Harvard University, 1976), p. 24.
27. See D. O. Parsons, "Specific Human Capital: An Application to Quit Rates and Layoff Rates," *Journal of Political Economy* 80 (1972): 1132–1134, whose model yields an ambiguous prediction for the relation between quit rates and unionization.
28. See J. F. Burton and J. E. Parker, "Interindustry Variations in Voluntary Labor Mobility," *Industrial and Labor Relations Review* 22 (1969): 199–216; V. Stoikov and R. L. Raimon, "Determinants of Differences in Quit Rates Among Industries," *American Economic Review* 58 (1968): 1283–1298.

accumulated seniority rights. Nevertheless, a reverse direction of causality might also apply. If quitting is difficult, workers will be more prone to unionization. Blinder has shown, for example, that older workers and those with family responsibilities are more likely to be union members.[29]

Looking at dismissals, we might have expected unions to make their greatest impact within this area. Slichter et al. attribute the origins of a union in many plants to a belief on the part of employees that management exercised "arbitrary, discriminatory, or capricious" dismissal procedures.[30] Meyers has pointed to the fact that, in the United States, those covered by collective agreements can only be dismissed for improper conduct and must generally be reinstated if the employer's decision is reversed on appeal. No such protection is, however, extended to those not covered by collective agreements.[31] In Great Britain, there are fewer grounds for expecting such a marked contrast between union and nonunion workers, because discharge is regulated by statute—the Trade Union and Labour Relations Act, which lays down grounds for fair dismissal—rather than collective agreement.[32] Nevertheless, we might expect trade union members to be better informed of their rights. For all these reasons, unions are likely to lower the discharge rate for their members. Working against this, however, is the possibility that union members will be more subject to disciplinary proceedings because the cost of an offense is reduced. There is also the possibility that the need for a more rigorous screening process, in the presence of seniority rules, will result in more dismissals of junior (that is, probationary) workers in union firms, ceteris paribus. The end result will thus be the outcome of these two opposing forces. In fact, the only firm evidence that we have—relating to United States manufacturing—indicates no significant relation between discharge rates and unionization after standardizing for all other important influences.[33]

There remain the areas of layoff and termination policy. We would expect layoffs to be higher in unionized firms, which expectation is confirmed by the facts. Indeed, given that alternative methods of adjustment, such as variations in hours, do not appear to vary much according to unionization, there seems little other way in which union firms can adjust their labor input costs given their greater wage inflexibility. The basic question is then perhaps one of why unionization should give rise to layoffs rather than wage flexibility as the mode of adjustment. Apart from the fact that wage bargaining is a decentralized process in which a decision by one particular group to accept a money wage cut will probably not be followed by similar wage cuts by other groups, two main reasons may be advanced for this preference. The first is that the senior workers, who tend to control the union, prefer layoff. Given a

29. Quoted in R. B. Freeman, "Individual Mobility and Union Voice in the Labor Market," American Economic Review, Papers and Proceedings 66 (1976): 367.
30. Slichter et al., Impact of Collective Bargaining, p. 624.
31. Meyers, Ownership of Jobs, pp. 5, 18.
32. See Incomes Data Services Ltd., Unfair Dismissal (London: I.D.S., 1976), chap. 6.
33. Medoff, "Layoff and Alternatives," p. 30.

system of seniority, the burden of adjustment thus tends to be pushed on to the junior workers. The second reason hinges on the higher specific training of union workers. This will act to cause the employer to prefer layoff to relative wage reductions and the subsequent possibility of quits. Higher general training of union workers, by making them more likely to quit in the face of wage declines, can be seen to reinforce this reaction.

Let us turn finally to the question of permanent reductions in the size of a firm's work force, whether these be caused by diminished commodity demand or technological displacement. Once unions begin to emphasize the seniority principle, we observe the building up of capital in the job. This building up of capital is similar to that observed in the case of occupations regulated by licensing rules, with the difference that here it is capital tied to a particular firm. One advantage of this specificity is that it is likely to inculcate more responsible[34] attitudes toward the firm and to manning demands. On the other hand, there is the concomitant danger that large industrial changes—plant closure, merger, or subcontracting—will tend to be impeded because of the workers' fear of having to start again at the bottom of the occupational ladder. At the same time, resistance to smaller technological changes, which do not menace the survival of the relevant seniority unit, will be lessened when job security guaranteed by seniority is operative. Indeed, an important policy question is whether a general system of severance payments, such as that provided by the British Redundancy Payments Act, is as effective in providing security as the American system of collective agreements detailing seniority rights in layoff. But we should note that a major disadvantage attaches to seniority provisions with respect to minority workers. Such groups are disproportionately represented among the ranks of junior workers and are thus the first to suffer in recession, thereby undoing the good done by affirmative action programs. Here, compensation plans accompanying inverse seniority seem necessary if senior workers are to be persuaded to accept layoff before the junior.

Severance Pay. We have seen that licensing in the craft occupations and seniority provisions in the general industrial occupations both associate certain costs with entry to a job. Changes in the size of a plant's work force, or in technology, or in craft practices, that lower the expected income from the job—or job progression in the case of a ladder—threaten the amortization of these costs and are therefore resisted. To secure these changes, therefore, it might be argued that compensation be paid. The difficulty with this line of argument is that we do not ordinarily compensate those individuals who make bad investments. For example, on this reasoning it might be

---

34. Thus, in a careful comparison of British and American firms in the chemicals sector, the British Chemical Economic Development Council (hereafter referred to as Chemical E.D.C.), *Manpower in the Chemical Industry*, (London: Her Majesty's Stationery Office, 1967), p. 9, came to the conclusion that American firms had "jobs wider in scope" and "greater job interest" than their British counterparts.

said that the owners of factories producing obsolete goods should also be compensated, because their capital plant has been rendered worthless by product innovation.[35]

In equilibrium, if we assume that labor market participants are well informed, the wage—or, more accurately, the present value of the earnings stream of the job taken over its expected duration—can be expected to reflect the risks of entering an occupation. If the occupation is one in which there is a high risk of obsolescence due to technological advance, then we would reason that wages will be higher in that occupation, *ceteris paribus*. Now let us suppose there is a plan to compensate for the risks of the job becoming obsolete. If this plan is not imposed on the employers before the workers are hired, but only afterward, then that compensation will contribute a capital gain for the workers involved. However, a more normal situation would be where the plan is known about in advance. In this case, we would expect the wage rate attaching to the job to fall, for the occupation is now insured against the risk of obsolescence. Here, it appears that severance pay will simply reflect deferred earnings.[36] Severance pay, if expected, is seen on this argument as a form of insurance against job loss. It is a form of insurance that alters the time pattern of remuneration from a job, but not the present value of its eventual earnings stream, plus eventual compensation, relative to other jobs.

We might therefore ask whether there are any social grounds for encouraging this kind of insurance or compulsory saving. Two comments can be made with respect to the argument that questions the need for severance pay schemes. It might well be true that the risk of an occupation becoming obsolete are already reflected in a relatively high wage. Equally, the union can be expected to press for the retention of the labor and thereby realize a windfall gain for the workers involved. This is a bargaining situation. On second best grounds, there might thus be scope for the use of severance pay as a bargaining counter facilitating the process of change. That is to say, change that might otherwise be indefinitely blocked can be introduced so long as the innovation yields the owners a profit as well as compensating those affected by the change for job loss. Second, the public benefit from a relatively smooth adaptation to technological change could be greater than that accruing to the immediate parties. In this case, there is likely to be underproduction of severance pay insurance if there is not public encouragement. Thus, a case may be made for the encouragement of such policies and productivity bargaining. However, the latter should be considered in association with other manpower measures, for example, a better counseling service, that reduce the costs of adapting to labor market change.

35. To quote S. Rottenberg, "Property in Work," *Industrial and Labor Relations Review* 15 (1962): 403, "Shall proprietors of buggy-whip factories be compensated by automobile manufacturers for the damage done to them by the motor car?"
36. Ibid., p. 404.

9.3 Empirical Studies of Job Regulation

Let us consider licensing and jurisdiction rules, featherbedding, and regulation of labor force adjustment in turn.

Licensing and Jurisdiction. Problems within this area apply in the main to industries employing members of craft or professional associations. A substantial minority of the British and American labor forces are organized in such associations. It has been estimated that American industries involving the craft system represent about 10% of total employment, whereas the figure approximates 25% in Great Britain.[37] To this must be added the professional associations, which account for a further 10% of the work force in both countries.

In our earlier discussion of craft-type unions, we found it would be income maximizing for unions to attempt to raise entry standards over time and to guard or even extend the areas of work restricted to union members, that is, the union's jurisdiction. Exogenous increases in the supply of qualified labor, for instance via immigration, would also tend to be opposed. We would also expect a tendency to confine entry opportunities to members' relatives (nepotism). Yet higher entry standards and tighter demarcation of union boundaries can be defended on the grounds of increasing safety or standards of service for the public. Indeed, this will inevitably be the argument advanced by union leaders. Increased training of doctors (possibly accompanied by a widening area of drugs that are available only on prescription) or teachers will raise standards as well as improving the earnings of incumbents. Thus, evidence of pressure for additional training does not of itself support the hypothesis that craft-type organizations manipulate entry rules so as to maximize earnings. However, the public interest can hardly be invoked to defend other protective practices, such as nepotism or the closed shop, which involve the rejection of qualified applicants.

In looking at the evidence on craft union behavior, let us first consider those policies that regulate entry to the union. We observe a tendency toward rising entry requirements in a number of associations. This is true of the medical profession on both sides of the Atlantic,[38] and also of a number of other occupations such as the barbers.[39] It is true that it is also possible to discern a contrary tendency in that periods of apprenticeship have been shortened. However, this move has been accompanied by a rising appren-

---

37. Using 2.5 or more percent apprentices employed in an industry as an indication of a substantial craft element. See A. L. Stinchcombe, "Social Structure and Organization," in J. B. March, ed., *Handbook of Organizations* (Chicago: Rand McNally, 1965), p. 166.
38. M. Friedman, "Some Comments on the Significance of Labor Unions for Economic Policy," in D. M. Wright, ed., *The Impact of the Union* (New York: Harcourt-Brace, 1951), p. 157; Siebert, "Occupational Licensing," p. 33.
39. Rottenberg, "Economics of Occupational Licensing," p. 15.

tice-journeyman wage ratio,[40] making it less possible for apprentices to bear the cost of their own training. As such training is general, the rising ratio may be seen as an attempt to shift the costs of apprenticeship onto the employer, who has responded by reducing the number of training places available (chapter 4). Indeed, it would appear that much of the "crisis in apprenticeship" stems from employer reluctance to make training places available.

Further, the closed shop has been maintained despite periodic legislative attacks upon it. The prohibition of the closed shop under the Taft-Hartley Act appears simply to have "driven it underground."[41] Similarly, the curb placed on closed shops by the British Industrial Relations Act of 1971 has had to be lifted. This lack of success is to be expected on human capital grounds. Neither measure has included any attempt to compensate the interest groups for the undoubtedly large capital loss that they would suffer through an influx of new entrants were the closed shop actually to collapse. For example, the British National Union of Seamen has claimed, probably with justification, that its organization would "completely disintegrate within a period of approximately three months" without the closed shop, because employers would take on low-cost foreign seamen.[42] There is also the "free rider" problem to be considered. If workers in unionized industries can benefit from union negotiated wage and nonwage benefits without paying union dues, there will be little incentive to pay them and the union will be weakened. For this reason, and that of controlling supply, unions need to enforce membership. Unions actively resist denial of this power in the form of state right-to-work laws. Regression results for 1970 show that a state is significantly less likely to possess a right-to-work law if the proportion of the work force unionized in that state is high, *ceteris paribus*.[43] The problem of the closed shop is indeed an intractable one, and the only course seems to be one of ensuring the right of independent appeal against union action and of guarding against further restriction of entry.

The jurisdiction of the craft is also carefully guarded against competition. Thus, in the United States, dentists and lawyers tend not to have arrangements that recognize qualifications granted in another jurisdiction—Illinois barbers also oppose reciprocity.[44] In addition, the states in which practitioners have high incomes are also those with high failure rates for applicants, indicating a successful attempt by incumbents to preserve their high in-

40. See, for example, Slichter et al., *Impact of Collective Bargaining*, p. 84.

41. R. L. Miller, "Right-to-Work Laws and Compulsory Union Membership in the United States," *British Journal of Industrial Relations* 14 (1976): 187.

42. See Trade Union Congress, *Report of the 104th Annual Congress* (London: T. U. C., 1972), pp. 43 ff.

43. W. J. Moore, R. J. Newman, and R. W. Thomas, "Determinants of the Passing of Right-to-Work Laws: An Alternative Interpretation," *Journal of Law and Economics* 17 (1974): 197–211.

44. See Rottenberg, "Economics of Occupational Licensing," p. 19.

comes.[45] And in Great Britain, there is evidence that doctors are currently pressing for an arrangement whereby they, and not the hospital administrators, can set the standards for specialists in addition to their long-standing licensing of junior doctors.[46]

An indication of the effect of occupational entry restrictions may be gained by comparing the present value of lifetime earnings for occupational categories where there is restriction with those for which there is none. The results of one such exercise, using British data, are shown in table 9.1. This compares lawyers and general practitioners with the generality of first-degree university graduates. It appears that the internal rate of return for lawyers and general practitioners is much higher than we would expect if a competitive return were being earned on their extra investment in training. An American comparison of general practitioners' lifetime earnings with those of college graduates also yields a high internal rate of return—24.1%.[47] Aftertax values are also cited in table 9.1, so as to show the redistributive effect of direct taxation. But it should be remembered that, because we are evaluating market power, our concern is with the pretax level of relative pay and not the posttax level; the latter is only the relevant criterion when analyzing occupational choice. We cannot be certain, however, that higher rates of return

45. A. S. Holen, "Effects of Professional Licensing Arrangements on Interstate Labor Mobility and Resource Allocation," *Journal of Political Economy* 73 (1965): 492–498.
46. *Report on the Committee of Inquiry into the Regulation of the Medical Profession* (London: Her Majesty's Stationery Office, Cmnd. 6018, 1975), para. 151.
47. F. Sloan, "Lifetime Earnings and Physicians' Choice of Specialty," *Industrial and Labor Relations Review* 24 (1970): 49. See also idem, "Real Returns to Medical Education—A Comment," *Journal of Human Resources* 11 (1976): 118–126.

Table 9.1 The Present Value of Earnings for Different Professions at Age 21, Males, England and Wales, 1966/67

	All First Degree	Legal Services	General Medical
Discount Rate			
5%	£40,100	£58,000	£56,700
10%	£20,500	£26,900	£26,400
Internal Rate*	—	23%	18%
		(18%)	(12%)

* equates the present value of earnings in the given occupation with that in the 'All First Degree' column. Figures in parentheses refer to corresponding posttax values.

Note:
Earnings relate to taxable personal incomes excluding dividends and capital gains. Age of entry is assumed to be 24 for medical graduates, followed by four years hospital internship, 21 for others.

Source:
W. S. Siebert, "Occupational Licensing: The Merrison Report on the Regulation of the Medical Profession," *British Journal of Industrial Relations* 15 (1977): 35, table 1.

are actually captured by entrants to the professions in question. The considerably higher relative earnings of such groups might simply reflect the higher ability and/or effort input required of medical/law students; in such a case, the increment would represent an equilibrium differential. The answer to this particular question will depend on the extent of favoritism in medical or law school entry procedures. There are grounds for believing that nepotism is indeed pervasive in these areas.

Jurisdictional issues have also been of importance within the manual crafts. Although there might be greater flexibility in the United States than in Great Britain, it remains the case that jurisdictional agreements are the subject of hard bargaining in both countries. In the chemical industry, for example, jurisdictional questions form the main subject of grievance committee meetings.[48] Flexibility could be a less important issue for the American craftsman because of his stronger internal labor market orientation, meaning that it is the employer who tends to finance training. For example, one study of American construction craftsmen estimated that only 20% of the sample had experienced an apprenticeship, the rest had learned the trade informally.[49] By way of contrast, a British study of various craft groups showed that 58% of craftsmen had served an apprenticeship.[50] In both countries, however, the bilateral monopoly situation of management and union can be expected to result in bargaining over job assignment. In British shipbuilding, a formal arrangement for settling such issues has existed since 1912. This procedure involves a joint Demarcation Court to decide the issue, although management is permitted to make a temporary decision while the machinery is in process.[51] The American construction industry has since 1948 had a National Joint Board to settle jurisdictional disputes referred to it, although it is again the employer who makes the interim assignment pending the board's decision.[52] In some areas of the British printing industry, however, although job assignments are decided jointly, grievance procedures are significantly different. In the event of disagreement, machines are operated on alternate weeks according to union, then management, standards and so on until agreement is reached![53]

A final point to be covered is the propensity toward nepotism on the part of professional associations and craft unions. There is widespread evidence of this practice within American construction and other unions, and its presence

48. Chemical E.D.C., *Manpower*, p. 10.
49. G. Strauss, "Apprenticeship: An Evaluation of the Need," in A. M. Ross, ed., *Employment Policy and the Labor Market* (Berkeley and Los Angeles: University of California Press, 1965), p. 300.
50. D. Robinson, "External and Internal Labor Markets," in D. Robinson, ed., *Local Labor Markets and Wage Structures* (London: Gower Press, 1970), table 2.6, pp. 58–59.
51. See Court of Enquiry into a Dispute at Vickers Ltd., *Report* (London: Her Majesty's Stationery Office, Cmnd. 3984, 1969).
52. See Slichter et al., *Impact of Collective Bargaining*, p. 260.
53. See L. C. Hunter, G. L. Reid, and D. Boddy, *Labor Problems of Technological Change* (London: George Allen and Unwin, 1970), p. 49.

has been well documented in the case of the British medical profession.[54] Nepotism is to be seen as a way of inheriting favorable job opportunities and for this reason must be reduced if minority groups, including women, are to have their employment prospects improved.

Featherbedding. There are many examples of featherbedding, principally in such areas as printing, rail transportation, and harbor work.[55] Because the latter tend to be monopolistic industries, this would tend to bear out the theoretical implication that featherbedding occurs in those circumstances where a sharing of monopoly gains is possible. An important gap in the case studies relates to the investigation of overmanning in government service. The growth in collective power of government workers, allied with the monopoly nature of government, would appear to provide an ideal environment for the growth of featherbedding practices.

The circumstances in which featherbedding has resulted in an increase of output to the consumer—for example, newspapers with fewer typographical errors or more pages—have not been investigated. It seems possible that the short-run effect of featherbedding in rail transportation has been to improve services for the consumer. Over the long run, however, the resulting increase in average costs has permitted undercutting by other forms of transport. In these circumstances, it might appear as if the rail unions had overestimated the degree of monopoly possessed by the industry—featherbedding causing a perverse effect on employment. Such apparently suboptimal decisionmaking would be explicable if union democracy were such that marginal members, those most likely to become unemployed, had less voice in union councils (chapter 7).

A novel alternative explanation has, however, been advanced by Hirschman. His argument runs in terms of the lack of stimulus to good management in industries such as railroads, which are neither completely monopolistic, because of competition from trucking, nor competitive.[56] In such industries, poor management is penalized neither by the exit of dissatisfied customers nor by their complaints (or voice). This is because, even if customers switch loyalties, the government usually stands ready to make up the loss. In such

54. Strauss, "Apprenticeship," p. 260; Slichter et al., *Impact of Collective Bargaining*, p. 73; Royal Commission on Medical Education, *Report* (London: Her Majesty's Stationery Office, Cmnd. 3568, 1968), chap. 5.

55. W. Gomberg, "Featherbedding: An Assertion of Property Rights," in R. L. Rowan, ed., *Readings in Labor Economics and Labor Relations* (Homewood, Ill.: Irwin, 1972), pp. 350–359; Royal Commission on Trade Unions and Employers' Associations, *Evidence of the International Printing Corporation,* Selected Evidence no. 59 (London: Her Majesty's Stationery Office, 1966); G. H. Hildebrand, "Comment," *American Economic Review* 54 (1964): 55 ff; Court of Inquiry into a Dispute between British Railways and the National Union of Railwaymen, *Report* (London: Her Majesty's Stationery Office, Cmnd. 3426, 1967); Killingsworth, "Longshore Work Rules"; Court of Inquiry into Certain Matters Concerning the Port Transport Industry, *Final Report* (London: Her Majesty's Stationery Office, Cmnd. 2734, 1965), pp. 11–16.

56. Hirschman, *Exit, Voice and Loyalty*, pp. 44–46.

circumstances, the making of a loss is little deterrent, particularly in view of the likely political costs of, say, rooting out overmanning. Moreover, because it is perhaps the most concerned customers—those who would "raise hell" if there were a poor service—who leave first, the voice channel to management is correspondingly muted. This line of argument serves to emphasize that featherbedding requires management complicity.

Although featherbedding is outlawed under Taft-Hartley, the provision appears to have been singularly ineffective.[57] Given the power of the union to oppose and their interest in so doing, this outcome is less than surprising. On the other hand, dockworkers on both sides of the Atlantic have been able to receive compensation for work rule changes, and here real progress has been made.[58] The compensation principle has either taken the form of a direct cash payment, as in the case of the Pacific Coast Longshoring Mechanization and Modernization Agreement, or indirect remuneration through the provision of job security via "decasualization," as in the East Coast and British dock industry cases. The main point is that, to enable technical change to proceed, it seems to be necessary to provide job security or its equivalent, and it is to job security that we now turn.

Labor Force Adjustment.   Thus far, we have largely focused our attention upon craft labor markets that are structured horizontally by occupational licensing, so that the main form of mobility is between firms rather than occupations. But we may also identify "enterprise" markets.[59] The latter are characterized by promotion ladders within the firm, generally according to seniority, and imply little interfirm mobility. There is also a third market form—that of the unstructured or open competitive market. This latter market form does not much concern us here for the simple reason that there is little associated job regulation, apart from that relating to shiftworking and maximum hours as laid down by statute and thus applicable to all firms. Here we shall mainly consider the second labor market form, which is generally insulated from the external market except at its ports of entry— those jobs at which entry to the enterprise market occurs.

We have considered several ways in which unions, mainly by developing seniority rules, but also by causing wage rigidity, might affect labor force adjustment. Let us summarize. By increasing a worker's stake in the firm, seniority rules mean that the employer will pay for a greater proportion of training; that is, training will be more specific. Also, because workers must eventually be promoted as they age, initial screening is likely to be more carefully undertaken. This implies a further increase in specific capital.

57. See Gomberg, "Featherbedding," p. 356.
58. See J. P. Goldberg, "Longshoremen and the Modernization of Cargo Handling in the United States," *International Labor Review* 107 (1973): 272; F. Mellish, *The Docks After Devlin* (London: Heinemann, 1970), pp. 79–84.
59. Using the terminology of P. B. Doeringer and M. J. Piore, *Internal Labor Markets and Manpower Analysis* (Lexington, Mass.: Heath, 1971), chap. 1.

Union grievance procedures, to the extent that they reduce employers' powers of discharge, will also intensify screening.

What implications flow from this greater specificity of unionized labor? First, union firms should place greater reliance than comparable nonunion establishments on varying hours per worker, as opposed to varying the number of workers employed, as a form of adjusting labor input. Second, greater specificity will be accompanied by reduced quit rates, a trend that will further be encouraged by the failure of wages to drop during the downturn. Third, there is likely to be an increase in layoff rates. Finally, there might be a more favorable attitude toward work force reductions to the extent that these fall mainly upon younger workers who can more easily find alternative work.

Before turning to the empirical evidence, it is worth noting that enterprise markets appear to be quite extensive. The proportion of the American labor force within internal labor markets is perhaps 30%.[60] Internal labor market structuring is probably less extensive in Great Britain, apart from such conspicuous areas as process workers in steelmaking[61] and government service. In British engineering, there is little evidence of widespread application of the seniority principle,[62] and this probably holds true for the rest of manufacturing. We have already touched upon the reasons for this difference. Its relevance here is that we would expect a more marked contrast in patterns of labor force adjustment between union and nonunion firms in the United States than in Great Britain.

Let us first examine the effect of unionization on a firm's screening practices. This is an area in which research is just beginning, but there are some pieces of evidence that would suggest that unions have the expected effect, causing employers to vet job applicants more carefully. For example, Slichter has pointed out a case where even the cleaners in a steel plant had to be carefully selected, because once inducted they were on the promotion ladder.[63] Other observers have pointed to the high educational standards demanded of new hires in American industry,[64] and the problem of *credentialism,* formal hiring standards that appear higher than necessary for a given job (chapter 6), has received much attention. More attention appears to be given to screening in the United States than Great Britain, which is to be expected given the stronger seniority system prevailing in the former country. This is illustrated in table 9.2, which compares engagements by methods of

60. Doeringer and Piore, *Internal Labor Markets,* p. 42, cite a value of 54%, but their figure includes the 27% of the work force employed in small enterprises. Here, low unionization is likely to mean that internal labor markets are less well developed in practice than the authors suggest.
61. See Hunter et al., *Labor Problems,* p. 125.
62. See D. I. MacKay, D. Boddy, J. Brack, J. A. Diack, and N. Jones, *Labor Markets Under Different Employment Conditions* (London: George Allen and Unwin, 1971), p. 320.
63. Slichter et al., *Impact of Collective Bargaining,* p. 195.
64. Chemical E.D.C., *Manpower,* p. 26.

Table 9.2 Percentage of Engagements by Methods of Job Search, Chicago, Birmingham, and Glasgow

Method of Job Search	Chicago[a] (1963)			Birmingham (U.K.)[b] (1967/68)			Glasgow (U.K.)[b] (1967/68)		
	Skilled	Semiskilled	Unskilled	Skilled	Semiskilled	Unskilled	Skilled	Semiskilled	Unskilled
Employee Referral	47.0	52.1	58.2	20.6	25.5	24.9	14.1	22.2	25.9
Gate Application	15.1	7.9	8.0	29.4	39.0	48.8	25.4	39.2	32.7
State Employment Service	1.0	1.8	2.7	13.2	12.6	20.2	29.6	18.4	39.5
Advertisement	10.0	6.6	4.3	20.6	7.4	1.4	25.4	17.8	0.9
Other*	26.9	26.8	26.8	16.2	15.5	4.7	5.4	2.5	0.9

* "Other" includes a large proportion of rehires in the Chicago case.

Sources:
[a] derived from A. Rees and G. P. Shultz, Workers and Wages in an Urban Labor Market (Chicago: University of Chicago Press, 1970), table 13.1, pp. 201–202.
[b] D. I. MacKay, D. Boddy, J. Brack, J. A. Diack, and N. Jones, Labor Markets under Different Employment Conditions (London: George Allen and Unwin, 1971), table 13.3, p. 357.

job search in a sample of firms drawn from the Chicago (U.S.), Birmingham (U.K.), and Glasgow (U.K.) labor markets. It can be seen that employee referrals constitute a much more important job source in Chicago than in the two British cities. Also, gate applications appear a much less successful method of finding employment in the United States than in the United Kingdom, which again would seem to point to greater precision in hiring practices. These findings are suggestive rather than definitive, but they point in the predicted direction.

Unions also appear to affect quit rates, layoff rates, and also perhaps the intensity of labor use (that is, hours worked per employee). The evidence is most clear-cut with respect to quits. For American manufacturing data, both Pencavel and Medoff[65] report a significantly negative relation between the proportion covered by collective bargaining in an industry[66] and the industry quit rate. This is a relationship that holds given the wage, showing that unions do not simply lower quits by raising wages. An example of one such relationship, for forty-seven American manufacturing industries in 1959, is as follows:[67]

$$QUIT = 2.55 - 0.195^*W - 0.069SIZE - 0.007^*UN$$
$$- 0.011^*CON + 0.135^*ACC$$
$$\bar{R}^2 = 0.780$$

where $QUIT$ is the monthly quit rate per 100 workers;
$\quad SIZE$ is a measure of industry plant size;
$\quad\quad W$ is a measure of industry wage rate;
$\quad\quad UN$ is the collective bargaining coverage variable;
$\quad CON$ is a measure of concentration of output;
$\quad ACC$ is a measure of the industry accessions rate in 1958; and
$\quad$ * denotes significance at the 5% level or better.

In 1959, the monthly average industry quit rate was approximately 1.4 workers per 100 employed. It can be seen that a fully unionized industry would have had a corresponding quit rate of 0.7 ($= 100 \times 0.007$), that is, approximately one-half of the average. Yet it must be admitted that other investigators have failed to find a significant relationship.[68] The fact remains that no one can be said to have found that unions actually raise quits, and the balance of evidence at the moment can be taken to favor our hypothesis.

65. J. H. Pencavel, "Interindustry Variations in Voluntary Labor Mobility: Comment," *Industrial and Labor Relations Review* 23 (1969): 81; Medoff, "Layoff and Alternatives," p. 21.
66. Specifically, the fraction of an industry's work force in plants within which the majority of workers are covered by collective agreements.
67. Pencavel, "Labor Mobility," p. 81.
68. Burton and Parker, "Interindustry Variations," pp. 199–216; Parsons, "Specific Human Capital," p. 1136.

There is a more marked divergence of finding with respect to the influence of unions on the layoff rate. Data provided by Medoff, for example, imply that in a typical year during the 1965 to 1969 period, unionized firms laid off about twenty-one more workers per hundred than did comparable firms that were not organized—the predicted layoff values being twenty-seven and six workers per hundred respectively. On the other hand, Parson's measurements, in a very different model, indicate no significant relationship.[69] The effect of collective bargaining on layoffs cannot, therefore, be said to be clearly established on the basis of current research. The same can be said of the influence of unions on adjustments of labor hours per man over the course of the cycle. However, there does indeed seem to be more reliance placed by modern firms on overtime working in boom and short-time working in recession.[70] This result could follow from increased unionization as well as from the more usually advanced reason of higher fixed costs per worker, although the two variables are related. However, these impressions have yet to be systematized, and this will undoubtedly constitute an interesting area of research in the future.

Seniority rules might also have beneficial effects for the economy. This would be the case, given that training is more specific, were the firm rather than the craft to mark the jurisdictional boundary. In such circumstances, manning would be more flexible. Adjustments to technological change might also be more easily accomplished, partly because of this increased flexibility and partly because the burden of labor market change is likely to be borne by low seniority workers who tend to be younger. Older workers can be shown to suffer most in the event of becoming unemployed. This may be shown by the regression equations of table 9.3, in which the dependent variable is weeks unemployed following employment termination. It can be seen that, in both the United States and Great Britain, the age variable has a large positive coefficient. Moreover, a recent American study shows that the earnings of older employees, even three years after termination, remained lower than those of their younger counterparts, *ceteris paribus*.[71] Therefore, the old can be expected to be particularly hostile to labor market adjustment, unless compensated.

One authority has given the goal of unions in widening the seniority unit and negotiating relocation allowances as being "to moderate the impact of displacement through contract clauses which seek to ease the period of transition."[72] Against this interpretation, however, we might point to the American rail transportation industry, where the enforcement of seniority

69. Medoff, "Layoff and Alternatives," p. 12; Parsons, "Specific Human Capital," p. 1136.
70. R. G. Ehrenberg, *Fringe Benefits and Overtime Behavior* (Lexington, Mass.: Heath, 1971).
71. J. L. Stern, "Consequences of Plant Closure," *Journal of Human Resources* 7 (1972): 90.
72. J. Barbash, "The Impact of Technology on Labor-Management Relations," in G. G. Somers, E. L. Cushman, and N. Weinberg, eds., *Adjusting to Technological Change* (New York: Harper and Row, 1963), p. 47.

Table 9.3   Determinants of Weeks Unemployed After Employment Termination

Variable	General Foods Corporation[a] (1962)	Birmingham (U.K.) Engineering[b] (1966–68)
Constant	7.247	20.46
Age	0.274	
(continuous)	(2.95)	
Age		17.19
(55 = 1)		(6.38)
Age		3.35
(30–54 = 1)		(1.64)
No. of Dependents	−1.230	
	(2.08)	
Marital status		−5.37
(Married = 1)		(2.40)
Other Weekly Income	0.0376	
	(1.73)	
Unemployment Benefit		0.42
(£)		(2.00)
R^2	0.174	0.245*

*equation includes other variables: staff status, skill category, percentage vacancies, job search strategy.

Note:

$|t|$ are given in parentheses.

Source:

[a]D. B. Lipsky, "Interplant Transfers and Terminated Workers," *Industrial and Labor Relations Review* 23 (1970): 204.

[b]D. I. MacKay and G. L. Reid, "Redundance, Unemployment and Manpower Policy," *Economic Journal* 82 (1972): 1264.

has not been accompanied by any marked acceptance of technological change. Indeed, the evidence is quite the reverse. But perhaps this industry is atypical in that its monopoly position, together with its political sensitivity, make it easier to provide government subventions than to reduce overmanning. The interpretation that seniority systems reduce the impact of dislocation caused by labor force reductions nevertheless appears to be a generally valid one. Perhaps because of this, severance pay schemes appear more fully developed in Great Britain, where seniority is less prevalent, than in the United States.[73]

Finally, seniority systems have the serious disadvantage that they perpetuate past unfavorable minority employment patterns. Thus, if women or black workers are among the last hired in an expansionary phase of the cycle, they will tend to be the first fired at the approach of a downturn. This

73. See Meyers, *Ownership of Jobs,* p. 112.

problem is distinct from that of discriminatory seniority lines, whereby blacks are placed on different and less favorable seniority rosters than whites.[74] The latter is not necessarily a part of the functioning of seniority rules and is amenable to legal correction. But the principle of "last hired, first fired" is the very definition of seniority, and so resolving its retrograde impact on minorities is a more intractable problem. Gilman's investigation into unemployment differentials by color (chapter 11) did in fact reach the conclusion that the higher propensity of blacks to be laid off—due, for example, to the operation of seniority—must account for some of their higher unemployment.[75] This result follows from the fact that only one-half of the unemployment differential could be explained by measured labor market factors, such as the lower skills of blacks relative to whites. The impact of seniority rules in causing substantial layoffs of minority groups has been well illustrated in a study of a large aerospace manufacturer, which had to lay workers off because of a contraction in orders between 1970 and 1971. The proportion of salaried blacks—those not covered by seniority rules—remained constant at 1.3% of the work force, although total employment dropped from 4,400 to 2,700. However, the proportion of nonsalaried blacks fell from 14.3% to 9.5%.[76]

There are various ways of attempting to reduce the cyclical hiring and layoff experience of minorities. One method is to encourage plantwide seniority rather than restricting employees to departments or narrower lines of progression. This can facilitate the movement of the more junior workers into jobs that are less sensitive to layoff. An additional method is to provide payment schemes that encourage senior employees to accept layoff before the junior; these are the *inverse seniority* or optional *leave* (for senior employees) plans.[77] Such schemes provide greater security for junior workers and also more incentive for the firm to train them. One advantage, from the company's point of view, might be that there is less disruption associated with downward bumping—in one factory, every layoff is reported to have resulted in no less than 3.5 bumps, which is an unacceptable amount of reshuffling.[78] Yet costs attach to such schemes, because the senior workers have to be paid to accept temporary layoff. Nevertheless, in view of the public benefits to be associated with a more favorable minority group occupational representation, there would seem to be a clear case for government assistance.

74. See F. R. Marshall, *The Negro and Organized Labor* (New York: Wiley, 1965), chap. 7.
75. H. Gilman, "Economic Discrimination and Unemployment," *American Economic Review* 55 (1965): 1077–1096.
76. A. V. Adams, J. Krislov, and D. R. Lairson, "Plantwide Seniority, Black Employment, and Employer Affirmative Action," *Industrial and Labor Relations Review* 26 (1973): 686–690.
77. For an example of one such plan, see R. T. Lund, D. C. Bumstead, and S. Freidman, "Inverse Seniority: Timely Answer to the Layoff Dilemma?" *Harvard Business Review* 53 (1975): 69–70.
78. Ibid., p. 68.

9.4 Conclusions for Policy

Job regulation rules on our interpretation have the basic rationale of maintaining existing earnings opportunities. Policies designed to amend these rules, for example, the amelioration of entry restrictions or feather-bedding, must therefore offer compensation as a quid pro quo. These are the buy-out or *productivity bargaining* policies. To some extent, however, job regulation rules are socially useful. Seniority rules, for example, by increasing job security reduce fears of employment termination consequent upon economic change, allowing such change to proceed more quickly. The questions here are whether such rules can be improved and the extent to which they are a substitute for a generalized system of severance payments. Let us separately consider the buy-out and severance pay policies before bringing together our observations on other nonwage effects of unionism.

Buy-out Policies. These policies take the form of an agreement in which advantages of one kind or another, such as higher wages or increased leisure, are given to workers in exchange for changes in working practice or in methods or in organization of work that will lead to more efficient working. An important example of such policies is what has come to be known as productivity bargaining.

The best known productivity bargaining agreement in Great Britain was that concluded in 1960 at the Fawley refinery of Esso Petroleum, a subsidiary of Standard Oil, New Jersey. The agreement itself was largely a response to the discovery that the Fawley refinery had considerably higher unit costs than its American counterparts using similar technology. Thus, we may here identify a clear lapse from X-efficiency. The agreement yielded increases of about 40% in hourly rates of pay, spread over two years, in return for relaxation of job demarcations, withdrawal of craftsmen's mates and their redeployment on other work, additional temporary and permanent shift working, and greater freedom in the use of supervision. In addition, the company undertook to cut overtime working drastically over the life of the agreement, from the average of 18% of total hours worked at which it stood in 1959. These interrelated changes were to be achieved without layoffs.[79] The agreement does seem to have been successful. Output per man-hour rose by approximately 50%, and the refinerywide overtime average was reduced to 7.5% as average working time declined by $5\frac{1}{4}$ hours. However, less progress was achieved on intercraft flexibility: only 5% of craftsmen's time after the agreement was found to be spent working outside the craft.[80] On the other hand, craftsmen's mates were eliminated, and substantial flexibility was achieved among process workers.

79. For a detailed analysis of the Fawley agreement(s), see Flanders, *Fawley Productivity Agreements*.
80. Royal Commission on Trade Unions and Employers Associations, *Research Paper No. 4* (London: Her Majesty's Stationery Office, Cmnd. 3623, 1967), p. 66.

In the United States, a well-known agreement is that concluded in the docks industry on the West Coast. In 1960, the Pacific Maritime Association and the International Longshoremen's and Warehousemen's Union concluded the Mechanization and Modernization Agreement.[81] The agreement was basically a buy-out of protective practices in cargo handling, achieved through annual payments. Reduction in gang size and increased flexibility in the use of labor was permitted, with a guarantee that no regular employee be laid off. Early voluntary retirement was encouraged with the payment of $7,920 to fully registered longshoremen with twenty-five years of service who retired between the ages of sixty-two and sixty-five. A fund was established guaranteeing a minimum of thirty-five hours of work per week, provided the loss of work was occasioned by the introduction of labor-saving devices and changed work practices, and not by economic conditions. In fact, average hours never fell below thirty-five on average; so the guarantee was discontinued and the fund dispersed by paying $1,223 to each fully registered longshoreman. A similar buy-out policy was negotiated for the Port of New York. In both cases, there appear to have been dramatic increases in labor productivity. For example, on the West Coast between 1960 and 1970, the number of tons moved per man-hour increased by 124%, thereby achieving a saving of $1 billion. And in New York between 1964–65 and 1970–71, labor productivity increased by 58%, yielding a saving of $400 million.[82]

Other American productivity agreements over the past decade have involved construction, printing, railroads, and air transportation.[83] These are industries with a reputation for a heavy incidence of restrictive work practices. They are also industries with large complements of craft employees. Much less has been seen of such agreements in industries dominated by industrial unions, which appears to bear out the prediction, made above, that make-work rules tend to be less important where there are industrial unions. This is because technical change, which is generally the forcing ground for such rules, affects the various groups within such unions differently, thereby discouraging concerted opposition.[84]

From these experiences, therefore, it seems that there are often large inefficiencies in production, but that it is possible to buy these out. However, there is the difficulty that such agreements are likely to become less popular

81. See Killingsworth, "Longshore Work Rules," pp. 295–306; Goldberg, "Cargo Handling," pp. 253–279.
82. Goldberg, "Cargo Handling," p. 264.
83. See J. P. Goldberg, "Bargaining and Productivity in the Private Sector," in Industrial Relations Research Association, *Collective Bargaining and Productivity* (Madison, Wis.: I.R.R.A., 1975), pp. 15–62.
84. By the same token, the greater experimentation with productivity bargaining in British manufacturing industries would appear to reflect the strongly prevailing craft system in many manufacturing sectors within that economy. Also, and more generally, the pronounced differences in collective bargaining structure as between Great Britain and the United States have a major part to play in explaining the differential experience of the two countries. See L. C. Hunter, "Productivity Bargaining Abroad: An Evaluation," ibid., pp. 170–175.

with the work force in periods of rising unemployment, thus requiring much heavier compensation. An indication of this difficulty might be the apparent waning popularity of productivity agreements in recent years, particularly within the United Kingdom.[85] This points to the need for severance pay policies at the firm level and perhaps also at the government level to cushion the impact of necessary involuntary job changes.

Job Security Policy. In any economy, firms and industries will expand or contract so that jobs are created or destroyed continually. These changes benefit society as a whole, although the burden in terms of unemployment tends to fall far less on some groups, such as government workers, than others, such as the unskilled. Yet in equilibrium, as we have seen, earnings levels in the various occupations should reflect such differences in security of tenure. Consequently, the argument that it is equitable to compensate[86] is not watertight. Nevertheless, given the bilateral monopoly aspect of collective bargaining, compensation techniques can be justified on pragmatic grounds as necessary if the workers' side is to accept economic and technological change.

The interesting feature of the American and British industrial relations systems, from the job regulation point of view, is the quite different compensation techniques adopted in industrial labor markets. In the United States, job security is underwritten by seniority and bumping rules within a company, backed up where necessary by agreements on severance pay and interplant transfer payments. The main advantage here of seniority rules is that the burden of labor market adjustment is shifted from the old to the young. Therefore, worker losses consequent upon termination are lower. This is because the younger worker has accumulated less experience specific to the industry than his older counterpart and is likely also to have more flexibility in job search. Because the younger worker has less at stake, we would expect the compensation necessary to secure a given change to be reduced.

A disadvantage of seniority rules is that they exacerbate the plight of the senior employee should the eventuality arise that he must be laid off. This reflects the fact that his skills are effectively nontransferable and, accordingly, he has to start again not only at the bottom of the seniority list, but also at the bottom of the skill ladder in a port of entry job. Far reaching economic change is thus likely to raise more fundamental problems of compensation than would otherwise be the case. As we have seen, an additional disadvantage of this technique is that minorities tend to suffer most in the event of a downswing. A new compensation principle making temporary layoff more attractive to the senior employee, namely optional leave, has been required here.

85. See J. T. Addison, "Whatever Happened to Productivity Bargaining?" *Management Decision* 13 (1975): 337–347.
86. See P. Taft, "Organised Labor and Technological Change: A Backward Look," in Somers et al., *Technological Change*, p. 38.

We have earlier noted that seniority rules seem much less pervasive under the British system. As a result, the older worker appears to be more at risk. This could provide an explanation for the more cautious British attitude toward technological change and also for the attempts of organized labor to ensure job security by demanding that the industry be taken into public ownership. Against this background, an interesting measure is the Redundancy Payments Act of 1965. This provides a termination or redundancy fund which is financed by a levy on all employers. Workers with more than two years' service with a firm become eligible for a lump sum payment from the fund in the event of being terminated; the employer is reimbursed 50% of this amount. The amount of payment increases with age and service[87] up to a maximum determined by twenty years service. According to an official survey conducted in 1968, the average payment made was £260, although those with more than ten years' service received £400.[88] Compensation on this scale can be seen to be reasonably generous when compared with, for example, average annual earnings in manufacturing at this time of around £1,100. Even so, it has been estimated that contributions to the fund amount to only 0.1% of employers' total wage and salary costs.[89]

The British approach has been said to be "aimed at securing a greater acceptance by workers of the need for economic and technological change."[90] And it does indeed appear to be the case that workers with longer posttermination spells of unemployment—generally the older workers—receive greater compensation, although one study has suggested that the correlation between the size of lump sum payment and the economic cost of redundancy, though positive, is weak.[91] However, some have pointed to the possibility that the older employee's job security is eroded by the enactment to the extent that employers have fewer scruples about laying them off.[92] The data are inadequate to test this hypothesis, but the claim seems unlikely at face value because the immediate financial cost of termination has been increased, which should serve to make the employer less willing to cause terminations, *ceteris paribus*. It is thus probable that the underlying resistance to technological change has been somewhat modified by the Act, although we would not put it more strongly than that.

Other Policies.   Apart from their effects upon entry and job security, we must also consider the impact of unions on processes of labor adjustment.

87. For each year of service over age forty-one (between ages twenty-one and forty), 1.5 (1.0) weeks' pay is received. The upper limit of weekly earnings eligible for compensation currently stands at £80.
88. S. R. Parker, C. G. Thomas, N. D. Ellis, and W. E. J. McCarthy, *Effects of the Redundancy Payments Act* (London: Her Majesty's Stationery Office, 1971), p. 81.
89. S. Mukherjee, *Through No Fault of Their Own* (London: Political and Economic Planning, 1973), p. 88.
90. Parker et al., *Redundancy Payments Act,* p. 4.
91. MacKay and Reid, "Redundancy," table 4, p. 1270.
92. MacKay et al., *Labor Markets,* p. 379; Mukherjee, *Through No Fault,* p. 109.

Undoubtedly, unions have played an important role in protecting their memberships from the arbitrary actions of management. They have also obtained changes in the legislative structure that are of benefit to employees. But we must attempt to balance these advantages against the disadvantages attendant upon reduced flexibility within the economy. Although we cannot make a formal assessment, we can at least be certain that practices making it more difficult to discharge employees and prescribing objective criteria for promotion have a disadvantage that we ignore at our peril. The disadvantage is that employers must thereby exercise greater care in their selection of employees. Thus, these very rules tend to make more difficult the position of the less qualified workers—the marginal men and women. Recognition of this fact requires that we advance policies, such as a widening of the seniority unit, antidiscrimination legislation, and a measure of subsidization, specifically designed to help minorities.

CHAPTER 10
THE DISTRIBUTION OF INCOME

10.1 Introduction

In this chapter, we provide an account of the main characteristics of the pay structure, namely of the differences in pay between groups possessing different skills or employed in different industries or firms or regions. Differences in pay between persons occur because of such economic factors as differences in ability, information, human capital, attitudes toward risk, nonpecuniary differences in jobs, and short-run forces reflecting the state of the market for the good or service produced by the individual. Differences in pay are also said to reflect institutional or class influences associated with unions, discrimination, and nepotism (the influence of a rich parent) and hence with the exertion of power within the market. One of the basic questions with which income distribution analysis has been concerned is the relative importance of economic versus power factors. On the assumption that the distribution of human abilities is normal, many have questioned whether there can possibly be an exclusively economic rationale for the very skewed distribution of incomes and wealth.[1] Our answer to this type of question has important implications for policy, as well as for assessing the "justice" of labor market operation. This is because administration of the earnings distribution, which involves such issues as narrowing the skill margin via the imposition of flat-rate pay increases, or equal pay for female workers, is an important facet of government activity today. A theory of why there are differences in pay between persons is necessary if we are able to alter the distribution, for example, by equalizing educational opportunities, and also to predict the consequences of particular policy instruments.

In the following discussion, the emphasis is upon incomes from employ-

---

1. To quote A. C. Pigou, *The Economics of Welfare* (London: Macmillan, 1932), p. 650: "When, for instance, a curve is plotted out for the heights of any large group of men, the resulting picture will not, as with incomes, have a humped and lop-sided appearance, but it will be a symmetrical curve shaped like a cocked hat. . . . Now, on the face of things, we should expect that, if, as there is reason to think, people's capacities are distributed on a plan of this kind, their incomes will be distributed in the same way."

ment and self-employment—that is, earned income. But we will also consider income from investments and transfer incomes, such as welfare payments. These latter forms of income are determined outside the labor market by inheritance customs and the tax/transfer policies of governments. Thus, the extremely unequal distribution of property tends to be maintained by customs whereby inheritances are not equally apportioned among family members and by the rich marrying the rich (assortative mating). Although analysis of such factors would take us too far afield,[2] we will briefly consider the evidence with respect to the total income and wealth distributions and chart their changes through time. This provides a useful backdrop to our analysis of the earnings distribution and its determinants, because the distribution of wealth need not be independent of that of labor earnings. Thus, if there is nepotism in the market, it is quite possible that a wealthy, well-connected individual will have a better job and higher earnings than his poorer counterpart, *ceteris paribus*. American results do indeed point to a strong positive association between wealth and earnings.[3] If this relationship holds, it follows that a diminution of wealth inequality would entail a reduction in earnings inequality.

It remains the case, however, that income from employment and self-employment provides by far the most important source of income. In the United States, for example, the fraction of total income of families and unrelated individuals accounted for by employment income stood at 89% in 1959.[4] The corresponding figure for Great Britain, as of 1973, was 80%.[5] It is unlikely that employment income has always been this important. For Great Britain in 1938, it would appear that the fraction of total income made up of employment income was as low as 70%, because rent and dividend income was then more important.[6] But even at this time, it can be seen that earnings from employment contributed the major source of income.

The earnings distribution is influenced by the dispersion of pay both within and among jobs. Competitive theory suggests that, for any given job category, differences in "full" pay—that is, including nonpecuniary factors—among firms and industries will tend to be eliminated in the long run. Clearly, this is one contention that we must examine. On this reasoning, most of the dispersion in the distribution should result from differences in full pay between jobs requiring different degrees of skill and ability. Skilled work, as

---

2. For models of this process, see J. E. Stiglitz, "Distribution of Income and Wealth Among Individuals," *Econometrica* 37 (1969): 382–397; A. S. Blinder, "A Model of Inherited Wealth," *Quarterly Journal of Economics* 87 (1973): 608–626.

3. See P. Taubman, *Sources of Inequality in Earnings* (New York and Amsterdam: American Elsevier and North Holland, 1975), pp. 39, 193 ff.

4. H. P. Miller, *Income Distribution in the United States,* Bureau of the Census (Washington, D.C.: U.S. Government Printing Office, 1966), pp. 43–46.

5. Royal Commission on the Distribution of Income and Wealth, *Report No. 1* (London: H.M.S.O., Cmnd. 6171, 1975), table 8, p. 32.

6. H. F. Lydall, "The Long Term Trend in the Size Distribution of Income," *Journal of the Royal Statistical Society,* Series A, 122 (1959): 17.

we have seen in chapter 4, is supposed to require a positive pay differential so as to elicit from workers the investment in training required to become skilled. The dispersion of earnings is thus dominated by such factors as the dispersion of education and ability among the population and the dispersion of rates of return.[7] It is necessary to examine these relationships. Finally, there are also differences in the average level of pay among industries or among regions. These might be thought of as mainly reflecting differences in skill composition. But there are undoubtedly other factors, such as the rate of expansion of an industry, that require investigation.

The plan of this chapter is as follows. In section 10.2, we consider interfirm differences in pay so as to establish whether differences in pay for a given job category do tend eventually to iron out and whether such differences as remain can be reconciled with competitive theory. The next set of problems concern the factors explaining differences in pay between different job categories. These issues are addressed in section 10.3. Questions that arise when firms and occupations are aggregated by region and industry are next analyzed in sections 10.4 and 10.5. Finally, having considered these components of earnings distribution, we turn to an examination of the distribution as a whole, contrasting it with income and wealth distributions and considering observed changes through time.

10.2 Interfirm Wage Dispersion

Competitive labor market theory predicts that, within a local labor market, there will be a tendency for labor of the same quality to obtain parity of net advantages irrespective of place of employment. Yet empirical studies have consistently reported evidence of a wide spread in observed occupational earnings values between plants operating within the same labor market.[8]

A *range theory of indeterminacy* has been postulated by Lester on the basis of the wide starting rate and average hourly earnings dispersion he observed in a sample of manufacturing plants in Trenton, New Jersey, in 1951.[9]

---

7. See G. S. Becker and B. R. Chiswick, "Education and the Distribution of Earnings," *American Economic Review* 56 (1966): 366; B. R. Chiswick, *Income Inequality—Regional Analyses within a Human Capital Framework* (New York: National Bureau of Economic Research, 1974), chap. 8; B. R. Chiswick and J. Mincer, "Time-Series Changes in Personal Income Inequality in the United States from 1939, with Projections to 1985," *Journal of Political Economy* 80 (1972): S34–S66.

8. Unfortunately, little attention has been paid to the definition of a local labor market, and generally the requirements of statistical convenience have taken priority. On the issues involved in labor market delineation, see W. Goldner, "Spatial and Location Aspects of Metropolitan Labor Markets," *American Economic Review* 45 (1955): 113–128; J. F. B. Goodman, "The Definition and Analysis of Local Labour Markets," *British Journal of Industrial Relations* 8 (1970): 179–196.

9. R. A. Lester, "A Range Theory of Wage Differentials," *Industrial and Labor Relations Review* 5 (1952): 483–500. See also, idem, *Hiring Practices and Labor Competition,* Research Report Series 88 (Princeton, N.J.: Industrial Relations Section, Princeton University, 1954); *Adjustments to Labor Shortages,* Research Report Series 91 (Princeton, N.J.: Industrial Relations Section, Princeton University, 1955).

Starting rates and average hourly earnings within the lowest wage establishments emerged as only half those prevailing within the highest wage plants. Lester also found wide diversity in pay for the same occupation in two middle-sized cities, drawing on data published by the Bureau of Labor Statistics. In table 10.1, we summarize these data, using the three most common measures of earnings dispersion. More recent data for a wider sample of metropolitan areas is supplied in table 10.2. Lester interpreted such dispersion of intraoccupational earnings as reflecting the outcome of institutional rules. These included collusive activity between employers in the form of antipirating agreements, the use of stereotypes in hiring, the application of seniority rules in filling job vacancies, the use of informal sources of information concerning potential recruits, and the nontransferability of benefit plans following termination of the contract of employment. Such rules acted to impede the free operation of the market and were reinforced by what was seen as a random and impulsive mobility process (chapter 5). Consequently, individual plants were depicted as having substantial discretion in fixing wage rates within a generous range—the range of indeterminacy—according to their internal promotion, hiring, and associated labor management practices. A wage rate selected within this range would be compatible with a position of long-run stability.

Table 10.1 Dispersion of Straight-Time Average Hourly Earnings in Manufacturing for Selected Occupations in Denver, Colorado, and Atlanta, Georgia, 1951

	Range* (%)		Interquartile Range (%)		Coefficient of Variation (%)	
· Occupation	Denver	Atlanta	Denver	Atlanta	Denver	Atlanta
Order fillers	175.5	222.6	15.3	42.4	10.9	23.9
Stock handlers and hand truckers	172.7	216.1	9.8	52.2	10.9	31.0
Truck drivers, light	158.5	—	13.7	—	10.7	—
Truck drivers, medium	221.2	203.2	16.7	24.5	12.4	18.3
Truckers, power (forklift)	—	222.6	—	41.7	—	24.4
Watchmen	183.9	171.0	19.3	30.2	15.3	19.2
Stationary engineers	132.7	—	9.1	—	5.9	—
Machinists, maintenance	132.8	165.3	5.0	13.7	5.4	11.3
Mechanics, maintenance	147.3	180.0	13.9	27.5	9.6	16.5

*highest earnings value as a percentage of lowest

Source:
Computed from R. A. Lester, "A Range Theory of Wage Differentials," *Industrial and Labor Relations Review* 5 (1952): 486.

Table 10.2 Dispersion of Straight-Time Average Hourly Earnings, Selected Occupations in Manufacturing and Nonmanufacturing Selected Metropolitan Areas, 1967–68

Sector/Occupation	Boston	New Haven	Philadelphia	Atlanta	Dallas	Chicago	Des Moines	Denver	Portland	S.F.-Oakland
Manufacturing										
Electricians	12	18	13	21	24	15	9	7	14	17
Machinists	10	14	15	14	11	11	13	6	14	9
Mechanics	25	16	18	28	18	15	15	10	17	11
Tool and die makers	10	8	9	18	13	14	24	9	10	5
Janitors, porters, and cleaners	18	25	17	62	27	21	24	26	22	12
Laborers, material handling	21	24	22	25	35	21	17	29	16	10
Truckers, power (forklift)	37	17	23	53	25	21	10	7	14	11
Nonmanufacturing										
Mechanics, automotive	5	11	11	12	33	2	3	7	8	13
Janitors, porters, and cleaners	26	22	11	8	15	33	25	15	13	14
Laborers, material handling	35	53	18	72	67	29	63	31	14	14

Interquartile Range (%)

Source:
J. E. Buckley, "Intraoccupational Wage Dispersion in Metropolitan Areas, 1967–68." *Monthly Labor Review* 92 (1969): 27, table 2.

Similar evidence of local labor market wage dispersion has been reported by Robinson in a series of studies relating to the British engineering industry.[10] A set of typical findings of observed earnings disparity for British local labor markets is presented in table 10.3. It can be seen that there is indeed considerable dispersion. On the basis of such results, Robinson has argued that the "going rate" is an almost mythical construct. His interpretation of these findings is that economic forces do not in fact exert inescapable influences to which firms must yield or perish.

What, one might ask, is the status of this institutionalist interpretation? There can be little doubt that it has been influential in the formulation of policy. It might be argued that the British use of productivity bargaining (chapter 9) as an instrument of incomes policy rested on the assumption that the benefits of an exercise often involving substantial straight-time earnings advance would not be dissipated by either spillover or market-induced pressures on other plants, because the "evidence" of wide earnings dispersion within the local labor market discounted the links between pay in different plants.[11] However, even when viewed in the most flexible way, that is, assuming an accurate identification of discrete labor markets and the existence of a positive correlation between nonpecuniary benefits and earnings levels, the various studies tell us surprisingly little about labor market operation. In the first place, they make no real attempt to allow for differences in worker efficiency. What is the effect of differences in ability or experience on earnings for a given job? Second, they do not consider whether acknowledged institutional factors, such as those associated with the operation of the internal labor market, have an economic origin and justification (chapter 5). Third, they do not erect a theory capable of being generalized and amenable to empirical testing. Meanwhile, it is the case that recent theoretical and empirical developments have yielded more than a measure of support for the competitive model.

Human capital theory has shown that, where there is specific training, employers and employees will normally share both the costs of and returns to that training. From the point of view of the worker, part of the costs of specific training are paid for by a reduction in wages during the training period (chapter 4). However, as Becker has pointed out, the shares of each will vary considerably among firms and will depend on the relationship between quit rates and wages, layoff rates and profits, the cost of funds, attitudes toward risk, and desires for liquidity.[12] This has clear implications

10. D. Robinson, "Myths of the Local Labor Market," *Personnel* 1 (1967): 36–39; *Wage Drift, Fringe Benefits and Manpower Distribution* (Paris: Organization for Economic Cooperation and Development, 1968), pp. 73–74, 76–82; "External and Internal Labour Markets," in D. Robinson, ed., *Local Labor Markets and Wage Structures* (London: Gower Press, 1970), pp. 36–51.

11. See J. T. Addison, "Productivity Bargaining: The Externalities Question," *Scottish Journal of Political Economy* 21 (1974): 123–142.

12. G. S. Becker, *Human Capital,* 2nd ed. (New York: Columbia University Press, 1975), pp. 29–30.

Table 10.3   Interplant Earnings Differentials, Selected Occupations, Males, United Kingdom, 1966-67

Labor Market/Occupation	Range* (%)	Interquartile Range (%)	Coefficient of Variation (%)
Glasgow, 1966[a]			
Fitters	167.7	—	14.4
Turners	169.2	—	14.2
Unskilled	165.4	—	15.4
All workers	168.1	—	14.6
Birmingham, 1966[a]			
Toolroom	223.4	—	22.7
Semiskilled	177.6	—	19.9
Unskilled	175.8	—	16.0
All workers	170.2	—	17.5
"Engineering," 1967[b]			
Fitters	124.2	18.3	—
Turners	79.0	19.3	—
Welders	60.3	20.7	—
Machine tool fitters, maintenance	55.5	9.1	—
Millwrights/maintenance fitters	87.9	18.8	—
Electricians	113.7	46.6	—
Toolroom operators	59.7	2.8	—

* highest earnings value as a percentage of lowest

[a] standard weekly earnings

[b] standard hourly earnings

Sources:

a. D. I. MacKay et al., *Labor Markets Under Different Employment Conditions* (London: Allen and Unwin, 1971), tables 4.1 and 4.2, pp. 71-72.

b. D. Robinson, "External and Internal Labor Markets," in D. Robinson, ed., *Local Labor Markets and Wage Structures* (London: Gower Press, 1970), table 2.3, p. 45.

for wage level diversity within the labor market and seems to be particularly relevant with respect to semiskilled workers because of the considerable technical differences among firms in the need and scope for specific training. Moreover, we would expect starting rates to differ systematically according to the expected duration of employment and the potential for vertical mobility within the organization. Again, because the theory postulates an equalization of efficiency unit earnings, there is an obligation to assess the contribution of labor quality differences to differential wage levels. Weiss has indicated that quality differences are important in explaining personal wage differentials, for he finds that the familiar positive association between product market concentration and earnings appears insignificant once personal characteristics are introduced (section 8.3).[13] Rees and Shultz also find positive association between wage levels for a given job and various proxies for worker efficiency, such as previous work experience, seniority, and schooling;[14] and Metcalf reports that wage dispersion within the British academic labor market is substantially reduced after correction for labor heterogeneity.[15]

The critics of competitive theory have made no real attempt to evaluate the costs of search associated with the employment contract. We would expect wage costs and search costs to be substitutes. As Stigler has observed, "Wage rates and skilled search are substitutes for the employer: the more efficiently he detects workers of superior quality, the less he need pay for such quality."[16] Shultz provides some direct evidence that employers in the Boston area increased their "buying effort" by advertising and more careful employment interviewing as a partial substitute for increases in wage rates.[17] The extent of search/wage substitutability may, then, be said to reflect the efficiency of the labor market information system. The more closely differences in search costs offset differences in wage costs, the more perfect the market information system. If workers had no knowledge about wages, the highest paying firm would have to search as much as would low-wage employers. Implicitly, search and quality become substitutes if wages are held constant. Ullman[18] tests the relationships between wages and search costs, together with training costs, for a random sample of Chicago employers employing key-punch operators and typists.[19] His results indicate that high-wage employers search less, and have less recourse to market intermediaries, than do lower-wage plants, *ceteris paribus*.

Thus far we have largely ignored the question of earnings dispersion across occupations. We might plausibly argue that skilled earnings will exhibit a wider dispersion than those of the unskilled. There is unlikely to be much variation in the human capital content of unskilled labor. Moreover, those individuals who remain as laborers, even with four years high school for example, are precisely those who have failed to capture returns on their

13. L. W. Weiss, "Concentration and Labor Earnings," *American Economic Review* 56 (1966): 96–117.
14. A. Rees and G. P. Shultz, *Workers and Wages in an Urban Labor Market* (Chicago: University of Chicago Press, 1970), chap. 11.
15. D. Metcalf, "Pay Dispersion, Information and Returns to Search in a Professional Labor Market," *Review of Economic Studies* 40 (1973): 491–505.
16. G. J. Stigler, "Information in the Labor Market," *Journal of Political Economy* 70 (1962): 102.
17. G. P. Shultz, "A Nonunion Market for White Collar Labor," *Aspects of Labor Economics,* National Bureau of Economic Research (Princeton, N.J.: Princeton University Press, 1962), pp. 107–146.
18. J. C. Ullman, "Interfirm Differences in the Cost of Search for Clerical Workers," *Journal of Business* 41 (1968): 153–165.
19. Search costs were proxied by the percentage of key-punch or typist positions filled through want ads and, in addition, the percentage of positions filled through private employment agencies. Both variables represent high cost recruitment channels and are expected to be negatively related to wage level.

investment in education. Moving upward on the occupational ladder is one of the principal means of realizing this return. Thus, it is likely that unskilled labor will have less experience and less ability and a smaller dispersion of both than will skilled groups. An additional factor that we should also consider here is the greater risk of failure apparently to be associated with entering the higher income occupations. For example, there seems to be a strong positive relation between mean earnings and the standard deviation of earnings by occupation (section 10.3). This would suggest that part of the return to skill is a return to risk. Yet the data of table 10.2 indicate that earnings dispersion is less for the higher skilled (maintenance) occupations. Although this finding is not replicated in table 10.3, evidence has been provided by Douty that the dispersion of earnings within any one area tended to be less for skilled maintenance occupations than for clerical jobs and substantially less than for unskilled classifications.[20] The argument is sometimes made that the higher human capital content of skilled work tends to reduce the dispersion within any one occupation to the extent that the capital market, having fewer imperfections than the labor market, introduces, in the rate of return to capital, a less dispersed component in the total return to labor. But we are seeking to explain earnings dispersion in terms of differences in human capital investments, abilities, and risk. One possible explanation for the relatively low earnings dispersion of the skilled maintenance occupations shown in table 10.2 relates to the homogeneity of the skill group. The skill acquired by such workers is usually obtained through a formal apprenticeship. Once this has been acquired, the maintenance trades are unlikely to represent career occupations and the emphasis upon seniority is thereby reduced. Moreover, these groups are usually employed in large establishments, where the volume of maintenance work is sufficient to warrant the employment of such specialists. In turn, labor-management agreement coverage is more extensive in large than in small establishments, and this may serve to centralize wages. We thus return to our original point, that we would normally expect earnings dispersion to increase with the level of skill.

Local labor market earnings dispersion would seem mainly to depend upon establishment characteristics; that is, the major force in occupational wage dispersion within labor markets is, in fact, differences in wage levels among establishments. Evidence to this effect for the United States is provided by Douty[21] and for the United Kingdom by MacKay et al.[22] Interestingly, Douty finds that interestablishment differences contribute relatively least for clerical occupations as compared with skilled and un-

20. H. M. Douty, "Sources of Occupational Wage and Salary Rate Dispersion Within Labor Markets," *Industrial and Labor Relations Review* 15 (1961): 70, table 1.
21. Ibid.
22. D. I. MacKay, D. Boddy, J. Brack, J. A. Diack, and N. Jones, *Labor Markets Under Different Employment Conditions* (London: Allen and Unwin, 1971), pp. 124–125.

skilled manual classifications.[23] This result might reflect, on the demand side, a better organized external labor market for clerks[24] and, on the supply side, a better informed labor force. But these possibilities remain conjectures; so the implication that employers have a wider set of alternatives in the hiring and retention of manual workers than clerical groups must be resisted pending further analysis of quality differences and job ladders.

Most of the explanations of wage dispersion discussed above can be classed under the heading of the labor management policy of the establishment. They are less a refutation of Lester's range theory than a recognition that his institutional and historical factors often have an economic origin and rationale. It remains the case that our theory of the firm as a purchaser of labor services should take these studies into account, even if our interest focuses upon market rather than establishment phenomena (chapter 5).

In this light, it can be argued that much of the interestablishment dispersion of wages in a local labor market can be given an equilibrium interpretation—an interpretation favored by the empirical finding that there is greater uniformity in rates of change of wages through time than in wage levels at a point in time. Nevertheless, it is unlikely that this is the entire explanation. In particular, if product markets can be assumed competitive, it seems possible that another factor may be differences in the efficiency of the establishment as a whole, rather than the labor force taken by itself. No direct tests of this hypothesis are available, but efficiency is likely to be an increasing function of scale up to a certain size of firm. There is certainly a positive association between earnings level and plant size,[25] such that employers may be sharing the benefits of increased efficiency with their labor forces, *ceteris paribus*. There is also the possibility, as yet insufficiently researched, that large plants pay more because they must draw workers from a wider catchment area than small plants.[26] Firms can be expected to minimize this effect by locating in urban areas if large, and rural areas if small, but doubtless cannot overcome it altogether.

In conclusion, it is apparent that a plant may not set wages without regard to the actions of its competitors in the labor market. We do not argue that the firm is a passive price taker or that it has little freedom of maneuver in the context of wage strategy.[27] Equally, it is clear that costs attach to the selection

23. Douty, "Salary Rate Dispersion," table 3, p. 71.

24. See G. P. Shultz, "A Nonunion Market for White Collar Labor," *Aspects of Labor Economics,* National Bureau of Economic Research (Princeton, N.J.: Princeton University Press, 1962), pp. 107–146.

25. See, for example, R. A. Lester, "Pay Differentials by Size of Establishment," *Industrial Relations* 7 (1968): 57–67.

26. See P. Nelson, "The Elasticity of Labor Supply to the Individual Firm," *Econometrica* 41 (1973): 853–865.

27. Thus, a firm that operates a highly structured internal labor market may have considerable flexibility in setting its relative wage structure, subject to the constraints imposed by the external market at port-of-entry jobs, so long as the average wage is sufficiently high to attract the necessary labor supply.

of any particular wage strategy. We have illustrated this point by referring to the substitutability of search costs, turnover costs, and wage costs. Therefore, the notion of a competitive labor market appears reasonably realistic.

10.3   Dispersion in Pay Among Jobs

We now turn to factors explaining the spread in pay between different job categories. We first consider long-run equilibrium and then turn our attention to secular and cyclical influences.

The Long Run.   In explaining differences in pay among different occupations, the main factors looked to are differences in education and training. The ideas underlying the human capital explanation of earnings differentials have been outlined in chapter 4, but may usefully be recapitulated here. Some jobs require longer periods of schooling, university, and other types of training, such as apprenticeship, than do others. Because training is expensive (mainly in terms of earnings foregone during the training period), it follows that earnings once training is completed must be higher than if no training costs had been incurred. Just how much higher will depend on the costs of production of the skill, that is, on factors such as the length of the training period and the rate of return available on alternative investments. To some extent, however, if tastes for performing the occupation differ, earnings differentials will also depend on demand side factors—even in the long run. For if tastes differ, supply curves for the occupation slope upward in the long run as well as the short run. A similar result follows where there are differences in abilities.

According to this reasoning, occupational earnings differentials are required to motivate labor force participants to enter jobs that have a high training requirement. Too low a differential will be manifested in a long-term decrease in the supply of labor with the given skills. It will also be associated with a windfall capital loss to those who have already invested in learning these skills. The analysis of chapter 4 has shown that extra education and training do have an economic payoff and that the payoff is worthwhile in terms of the investment alternatives open to the individual. At the same time, incomes for the educated/trained individual do not in general seem too high relative to his less educated/trained counterpart as is the drift in some areas of popular social criticism.

The goal of the present analysis will be to estimate the contribution that differences in education and training make to the dispersion of income. Considerable research has been undertaken in this area, using American data. A basic earnings function, dependent only upon schooling, can be written[28]

$$\ln Y_i = \ln X_{oi} + r_i s_i + u_i \qquad (10.1)$$

28. See chap. 4, p. 131.

where Y is a measure of income for the ith individual;
X_o is income in the absence of schooling;
r is the rate of return to schooling;
s is the number of years schooling; and
u is an error term.

Taking the variance of ln Y, which is a measure of income dispersion, we derive

$$\text{var}(\ln Y) = \bar{r}^2\text{var}(s) + \bar{s}^2\text{var}(r) + \text{var}(s) \cdot \text{var}(r) + \text{var}(u). \quad (10.2)$$

Here we have assumed $\text{var}(\ln X) = 0$ and have used the Goodman result that $\text{var}(xy) = \bar{x}^2\text{var}(y) + \bar{y}^2\text{var}(x) + \text{var}(x) \cdot \text{var}(y)$, where x and y are independently distributed.[29] The assumption that r and s are independently distributed seems reasonable enough. Because the cost of borrowing increases with s—as presumably does its productivity—the sign of the correlation between r and s, while probably positive, is in fact ambiguous a priori.[30] But the equation does lead us to expect dispersion in earnings to be greater (1) the greater the average rate of return to schooling, (2) the greater the dispersion in schooling, (3) the greater the level of schooling, and (4) the greater the variation in rates of return to schooling. Extending the model by including experience, which is measured as age minus schooling minus five, we can perform similar manipulations using the Goodman result. These show that earnings dispersion can be expected to be greater (1) the greater the level and variance of age, and (2) the greater the level and variance in rates of return to experience.

It can be shown empirically that earnings dispersion, as measured by $\text{var}(\ln Y)$, is positively related to the level and dispersion of schooling. Using states as his unit of observation, Chiswick has reported that a regression of $\text{var}(\ln Y)$ by state on state $\bar{r}$, $\bar{s}$, and $\text{var}(s)$ gives the following results for white males in 1960:[31]

	$\bar{r}$	$\bar{s}$	var(s)
coefficient	6.945	0.033	0.012
t-value	10.96	2.73	3.82

29. This very useful result is proved in L. A. Goodman, "On the Exact Variance of Products," *Journal of the American Statistical Association* 55 (1960): 708–713. See also appendix 1-A.
30. See figure 4.3.
31. For each state, $\bar{r}$ was computed by regressing log income on schooling, using individual data for each state and interpreting the coefficient on schooling as the rate of return, according to the usual human capital reasoning. Note that this method does not permit calculation of the dispersion of r within each state. See B. R. Chiswick, "The Average Level of Schooling and the Intra-Regional Inequality of Income: A Clarification," *American Economic Review* 58 (1968): 495–500. See also Chiswick, *Income Inequality*, pp. 59 ff.

We observe that the coefficients have the expected signs. However, the level and dispersion of schooling appear much less important than the level of returns to schooling in explaining earnings dispersion. This finding is replicated in a study by Chiswick and Mincer using the extended model that includes experience and the rate of return to experience. The authors calculate that reducing both the return to schooling and that to experience by 30%, from their assumed values of 11% and 4%, respectively, would reduce income inequality by no less than 24% of its 1959 level.[32] A drastic change in the distribution of schooling, resulting in zero dispersion, would be required to reduce income inequality by a similar amount (assuming that the mean schooling level remained unchanged; if the mean rose, then the reduction in dispersion would be less). The policy implication would appear to be that, if the aim is to reduce earnings dispersion, there should be measures both to reduce schooling dispersion and to reduce returns to schooling. The former variable is presumably more easy to influence than is the latter (which will depend, in equilibrium, upon the market rate of interest)[33] and hence should be of more significance from the practical point of view.

The association between schooling dispersion and earnings dispersion has been confirmed in a number of countries. Lydall presents data on earnings inequality and schooling inequality for several countries and finds a rough positive correlation. In particular, the United Kingdom has a somewhat more equal earnings distribution than the United States, and this result is consistent with what appears to be a more equal distribution of schooling in the United Kingdom.[34] Chiswick, in an analysis covering the United States, Canada, Puerto Rico, and Mexico, demonstrated that those countries with greater earnings inequality also have greater dispersion in schooling and higher returns to schooling. Schooling *inequalities* thus seem an important determinant of earnings dispersion. It is a depressing fact, however, that schooling *levels* also appear to determine dispersion, so that raising average schooling levels actually increases earnings dispersion, *ceteris paribus*.

Thus far, we have stressed differences in education and training as underlying long-run occupational earnings dispersion. Yet it is also necessary

---

32. Chiswick and Mincer, "Time-Series Changes," p. 547.

33. That is, we would expect individuals to adjust the amount of their education investments so as to yield a rate of return similar to that at which funds could be borrowed (chapter 4). Lack of information or the presence of discrimination might, however, greatly slow down this process. That this possibility is a very real one is shown by the long-term difference in estimated rates of return between southern and northern states in the United States—estimates are 5% to 8% (7% to 9%) in the non-South (South) (Becker and Chiswick, "Education and Earnings," p. 366). This continuing difference has been explained in terms of the immobility of uneducated workers, who earn less in the South than the North, coupled with a national market, which equalizes rates of pay, for educated workers. See Chiswick, *Income Inequality*, pp. 8, 59. On the other hand, the difference might simply reflect an undervaluation of the income in kind received by unskilled workers in the South, who tend to be rural.

34. H. F. Lydall, *The Structure of Earnings* (Oxford: Clarendon Press, 1968), pp. 211–212.

to consider the contributions of ability, tastes (in particular, attitudes toward risk), the congeniality or otherwise of jobs, and the influences of nepotism and discrimination. Measures of mathematical ability in Taubman's comprehensive study are found to have a substantial direct effect on earnings.[35] And ability also exercises a large indirect influence in that those with higher I.Q. are schooled for longer intervals (chapter 4).[36] This positive correlation between ability and human capital investment is one good explanation for the skewed nature of the earnings distribution. For even if the ability and investment distributions were symmetrical, the product of two positively correlated distributions must be skewed.[37] Because earnings are a function, inter alia, of the product of the rate of return on human capital and the amount invested, then, if the more able have higher rates of return and invest more, we will observe a skewed distribution of earnings.

In point of fact, it is quite probable that ability is not symmetrically distributed,[38] but is itself positively skewed. This would be the case if environment were to play a large part in determining ability, because we can be reasonably sure that the distribution of favorable learning environments is highly skewed. Results obtained by Sir Cyril Burt, using intelligence and reading test scores from identical twins reared apart, and unrelated children reared together, indicate that environment explains about 25% of the variance in intelligence test scores and 55% in the case of reading scores.[39] Regression results explaining ability for the quite different samples employed by Leibowitz and Taubman show that the mother's education is an important determinant but not that of the father.[40] This again points to the influence of home environment, as does the finding that firstborn and children from small families score higher in intelligence tests. Environment thus appears to be an important factor in determining ability, which is therefore probably highly skewed in its distribution, contributing in turn to the skewness of the earnings distribution. From the standpoint of policy, ability is unlikely to be important, because its distribution is presumably highly stable over time. Yet, it is worth noting that efforts to reduce education inequality might, by improving home environments, also reduce the dispersion of ability.

35. Taubman, *Sources of Inequality,* p. 38.
36. See A. Leibowitz, "Home Investments in Children," *Journal of Political Economy* 82 (1974): S116 ff.
37. See Becker, *Human Capital,* p. 87; Lydall, *Structure of Earnings,* p. 36.
38. Note that we cannot settle this question simply by examining the I.Q. frequency distribution across a population, for such tests are constructed so as to evince a normal distribution. On this, see T. Mayer, "The Distribution of Ability and Earnings," *Review of Economics and Statistics* 42 (1960): app.
39. These results are reported in Lydall, *Structure of Earnings,* pp. 74 ff. Burt's statistical methods are unfortunately under a cloud at this time. See for example, H. Eysenk, "The Case of Sir Cyril Burt," *Encounter,* January 1977, p. 24. Burt's experimental procedures are, however, a valuable contribution in this murky area, and the results themselves perhaps give the orders of magnitude involved.
40. Leibowitz, "Home Investments," p. S116; Taubman, *Sources of Inequality,* p. 172.

Let us now consider the influence of differences in tastes, particularly with respect to risk taking, upon earnings dispersion. Friedman has argued that a society embracing a large number of individuals who like risk will have a more unequal distribution of income than a society where most are risk averse.[41] Further, attitudes toward risk could explain the skewness of the earnings distribution. Thus, a few successful risk-lovers would constitute the long right-hand tail, but the unsuccessful risk-lovers would be prevented from making up a similar left-hand tail because of their inability to raise enough capital to sustain substantial losses. Neither of these propositions is easily amenable to testing. Nevertheless, we would expect that if most people were risk averse, risky jobs would carry a premium, *ceteris paribus*. This results from net advantages of jobs tending toward equality. As evidence, there is an impressively strong relation between the mean and the variance of earnings by occupation in Taubman's sample: the higher the variance of the distribution, and thus presumably the risks, the higher the mean pay.[42] From this sample, we also find that persons with a self-expressed taste for helping others, having job security, working independently, or doing unchallenging work all earn less, *ceteris paribus*. This demonstrates the influence of tastes and of nonpecuniary differences in jobs on personal earnings differences. Again, such factors are likely to be quite difficult to alter and are thus not particularly significant from the policy viewpoint. Still, it is reassuring to note that nonpecuniary differences among jobs, for example, one job's greater security of tenure than another's, are apparently compensatory.

The main alternative explanation of occupational differentials hinges on restriction of entry into higher grade occupations. This is the idea that Cairnes made famous with his concept of noncompeting industrial groups.[43] Certainly, entry into many occupations is governed by factors that need not be related to an applicant's training or other qualifications. In the case of the British medical profession, for example, there has been much criticism of the role of nepotism in medical school admission procedures, and similar charges have been laid at the door of the American Medical Association.[44] The extended earnings functions computed by Taubman can also be interpreted as indicating some degree of nepotism. For example, there is the finding that possession of business assets, as an explanatory variable for a person's earnings, explains 10% of earnings variance—more than any other variable. This could be rationalized on the grounds that those who have acquired

41. M. Friedman, "Choice, Chance and the Personal Distribution of Income," *Journal of Political Economy* 61 (1953): 277–290.
42. Taubman, *Sources of Inequality,* pp. 90–92.
43. J. E. Cairnes, *Some Leading Principles of Political Economy Newly Expounded* (New York: Harper, 1874), pp. 64–68.
44. See M. Friedman, "Some Comments on the Significance of Labor Unions for Economic Policy," in D. M. Wright, ed., *The Impact of the Union* (New York: Harcourt-Brace, 1951); W. S. Siebert, "Occupational Licensing," *British Journal of Industrial Relations* 15 (1977): 18–27.

assets are the more able. (Marshall, for example, argued that business ability and ownership of physical capital are positively correlated.) It could also point to favoritism for the rich. Perhaps more convincing is the finding of a relationship between an individual's earnings and his father-in-law's education, *ceteris paribus*. The presence of a positive relation between earnings and private high school attendance might also indicate nepotism, because measurements do not indicate that private high school increases ability.[45]

In many cases, including those cited above, training has still to be acquired; consequently, the burden of criticism falls upon the procedures by which applicants are selected for training. The schooling functions of chapter 4 indicate that poorer groups in society are broadly destined to be unable to acquire much general training. This arises most fundamentally because human capital is not good collateral for a loan. Accordingly, wealthier families can invest, whereas the poor cannot. In this sense, the children of wealthier parents inherit the opportunity to have a good education, just as doctors' sons appear to inherit the right to enter training courses for the profession. At this point, it can be seen that the theory of inheritance and the theory of earnings distribution meet. However, our observations constitute a criticism of the organization of the capital market rather than an alternative theory of the earnings structure.

Secular Movement.   Much of the evidence on long-run changes in the occupational wage structure relates to the ratio between the wages of skilled and unskilled manual workers in the same industry. For the United States, studies by Ober and Kanninen show a narrowing of the skill differential from 2.05 in 1907 to 1.55 in 1945–47[46] and to 1.45 in 1952–53.[47] Similarly, Keat estimated the corresponding ratio to be 2.01 in 1903 and 1.42 in 1956.[48] For the United Kingdom, Knowles and Robertson show that the skill ratio declined substantially over the period 1880 to 1950. At the end of the period, the premium for skill, as measured in terms of negotiated rates, within a sample of thirty-four industries stood at 1.24.[49] Using an average annual earnings definition, Routh estimated the skill ratio at 1.57 in 1913–14 and

45. See Taubman, *Sources of Inequality*, pp. 194, 45, 159. Marshall's observations on the likely correlation between business ability and possession of physical capital are cited in Becker, *Human Capital*, p. 85.
46. H. Ober, "Occupational Wage Differentials, 1907–1947," *Monthly Labor Review* 71 (1948): 127–143.
47. T. Kanninen, "Occupational Wage Relationships in Manufacturing," *Monthly Labor Review* 76 (1953): 1171–1178.
48. P. G. Keat, "Long Run Changes in the Occupational Wage Structure, 1900–1956," *Journal of Political Economy* 68 (1960): 584–600.
49. K. G. J. C. Knowles and D. J. Robertson, "Differences Between the Wages of Skilled and Unskilled Workers, 1850–1950," *Bulletin of the Oxford University Institute of Economics and Statistics* 13 (1951): 109–127.

1.49 in 1960.[50] The narrowing process in both countries has tended not to be a steady one from year to year but, rather, has occurred through quite drastic changes within the two war periods with some reversal thereafter and a broad stability in normal peacetime years.

The reduction in the skilled manual worker's margin appears to have been paralleled by a decline in the dispersion of the earnings structure as a whole. Measures of manual worker and all-worker earnings distributions over most of this century are summarized in table 10.4. With regard to male manual workers, we observe a definite contraction in earnings dispersion over the course of the present century; most of this contraction occurred prior to 1939 in the case of Great Britain, but continued strongly during World War II in the case of the United States, after which time there has been stability. This picture appears broadly true of the male all-worker distribution as well. Thus, there has been a decline in the differential for skill in its widest sense, at least for males. Females seem to present a somewhat different pattern. There is a tendency in both countries for the female dispersion to widen through time, which development is possibly to be attributed to the increased participation rates of unskilled and semiskilled females—the modern counterpart to the flow of immigrants and former agricultural workers that earlier prevented the male skill differential from contracting.

A number of rival hypotheses have been advanced to explain the secular decline in the skill differential and in earnings dispersion. For example, it is usually argued that the supply and demand curves for skill shift in a systematic way over a period of time encompassing the entire process of industrialization. Thus, so the argument runs, the demand for skills is high at the early stages of growth, when there is a sharp increase in the specialization of labor, the range of skills, and the need for coordinating ability.[51] The supply of labor of the required type is very limited, however, and a developing country faced with an inability to transfer skills from old to new technology may need to employ skilled immigrants at high rates of pay. The latter are then reflected in the domestic wage structure. The high rate of return to education, and the wide dispersion of education, should also imply higher earnings dispersion. According to some observers, the demand for skill is also proportionate to the rate of growth;[52] and for this reason skill differentials are said to be wider in economies in the take-off stage of growth than in both less developed and more developed economies.

50. G. Routh, *Occupation and Pay in Great Britain, 1906–1960* (Cambridge: Cambridge University Press, 1965), table 47, p. 104.

51. See A. Lewis, *The Theory of Economic Growth* (London: Allen and Unwin, 1955), pp. 180–181.

52. See, for example, C. Kerr, "Wage Relationships—The Comparative Impact of Market and Power Forces," in J. T. Dunlop, ed., *The Theory of Wage Determination* (New York: St. Martin's Press, 1957), p. 187.

Table 10.4 Distribution of Earnings, Manual and Nonmanual Workers, United States and Great Britain, Selected Years

| Country | Classification | Year | Earnings as a Proportion of Median (%) | | |
			top 10%	top 20%	bottom 25%
G.B.	Manual, male[a]	1906	157		80
	Manual, male[a]	1938	140		82
	Manual, male[a]	1960	145		83
	Manual, female[b]	1959	138		85
	Manual, male[a]	1966	143		82
	All workers, male[b]	1911–12		153	72
	All workers, female[b]	1911–12		125	73
	All workers, male[b]	1961–62		137	82
	All workers, female[b]	1961–62		142	76
U.S.	Manual, male[b]	1897		144	79
	Manual, female[b]	1897		130	81
	Manual, male[b]	1939(1949)		140(130)	72(76)
	Manual, female[b]	1939		133	83
	Manual, male[b]	1959	149	131	74
	Manual, female[b]	1959	162	140	72

| | | | Proportion of Wage and Salary Income Received by: | |
			top 25%	bottom 25%
U.S.	All workers, male[c]	1939	48.7	3.5
	All workers, female[c]	1939	46.5	3.0
	All workers, male[c]	1949	40.1	3.6
	All workers, female[c]	1949	42.9	2.2
	All workers, male[c]	1960	42.5	2.5
	All workers, female[c]	1960	47.3	2.4

Sources:
a. A. R. Thatcher, "The Distribution of Earnings of Employees in G.B.," *Journal of the Royal Statistical Society* 131 (1968): 163.

b. H. F. Lydall, *The Structure of Earnings* (Oxford: Clarendon Press, 1968), app. tables 1–5 (G.B.), 16–23 (U.S.).

c. H. P. Miller, *Income Distribution in the United States,* Bureau of the Census (Washington, D.C.: U.S. Government Printing Office, 1968), p. 77.

With the spread of compulsory education and the raising of the school leaving age, the process goes into reverse. With the state subsidizing first elementary, then secondary, and now tertiary education, the private costs of education have diminished over time. This will reduce the equilibrium earnings differentials required to bring a given rate of return on human capital investments. The process can be strikingly illustrated for manual workers, using some roughly realistic values put forward by Keat, which are here summarized:

	1903	1956
Actual skilled/unskilled wage ratio $\left(\dfrac{a^*}{b^*}\right)$	2.01	1.42
Extra schooling of craftsmen vis-a-vis the unskilled worker (d_1)	1.5 yrs	1.0 yrs
Extra training of craftsmen $(d_2 - d_1)$	4.5 yrs	3.5 yrs
Apprentice/unskilled wage ratio $\left(\dfrac{c}{b}\right)$		
(a measure of expenses during training)	60.0%	95.0%
Rate of discount	14.0%	14.0%
Predicted skilled/unskilled wage ratio $\left(\dfrac{a}{b}\right)$	1.70	1.28

It can be seen that the extra period of training and schooling of the skilled man is assumed to have shortened between 1903 and 1956, and the foregone earnings while training to have been reduced. To provide a rate of return of 14%, therefore, the equilibrium skilled/unskilled wage ratio need only be 1.28 instead of 1.70.[53] This illustrates that changes in the cost and period of training could conceivably account for much of the long-term decline in the skill differential.

Further, for both Great Britain and the United States, there appears to have been a reduction in education dispersion. This would be consistent with a more equal earnings distribution. Lydall has provided the following values for the Gini coefficient of the American education distribution:[54]

Year	1910	1920	1930	1940	1950	1960
Coefficient	0.390	0.373	0.358	0.335	0.317	0.303

Although we observe a large reduction in education dispersion, it should also be remembered that an increase in the level of schooling acts to increase dispersion—equation (10.2). These two effects have been working in opposite directions. Their net outcome is presumably an empirical matter. Using 1959 census data to estimate the magnitude of the relation between earnings dispersion and schooling dispersion and that between earnings dispersion and schooling level for the postwar period, it appears that the two effects have cancelled out one another—at least for white males. The actual reduction in schooling dispersion between 1949 and 1970—the standard deviation was 3.7 years in 1949 and 3.0 years in 1970—implies a reduction in earnings dispersion over the same period that happens to be nearly the same as the

53. See Keat, "Long Run Changes," p. 599. Details of the calculation involved are presented in appendix 10-A.
54. Lydall, *Structure of Earnings*, p. 221. For a definition and description of this statistic, see appendix 10-B.

increase in dispersion implied by the large rise in schooling level, namely from 9.7 years in 1949 to 11.7 years in 1970.[55] These pessimistic findings relate only to white males. Moreover, they relate only to the postwar period when earnings dispersion appears to have been static (table 10.4). Nevertheless, the results cast a cloud on the effectiveness of past educational programs in reducing earnings inequality. If earnings equality remains the goal, then future programs should be geared to providing similar levels of education for all, rather than generally increasing levels of education.

Additional factors that might be brought forward to account for the secular decline in earnings dispersion and skill margins are immigration policy and rural-urban migration. The introduction of immigration laws curtailing the entry of largely unskilled immigrants is thought by Keat to have had a substantial effect in the American case, although this effect is not quantified.[56] We note that the proportion of foreign-born workers in the American labor force was 20% in 1920, but only 12% by 1940 and 7% by 1960.[57] Rural-urban migration might be thought to affect the differential because rural workers are likely to be at a disadvantage in finding skilled jobs in urban areas. Unskilled rates will thereby be depressed. A change in the structure of the economy, whereby rural skills become less useful, can be seen as analogous to an increase in the dispersion of relevant, that is, urban, skills. As the flow to urban areas lessened, so this skill dispersion would lessen, implying a reduction in earnings dispersion, *ceteris paribus*. If we can accept that after a point the percentage of males in agriculture has little further effect on the degree of dispersion, and if we consider this watershed to be 25%, then it would appear that somewhere around 1930 the United States entered a phase in which the proportion of workers in agriculture was no longer an important influence on the dispersion of nonfarm earnings.[58]

Having considered competitive explanations of the narrowing process, let us turn to certain institutional explanations. Such explanations are necessary, if only to account for the timing of the narrowing process, which has not been continuous but concentrated during periods of war and postwar boom. Knowles and Robertson emphasize the role played by flat rate increases to all workers to meet cost-of-living increases in eroding differentials. They claim that narrowing has taken place "in a fit of absence of mind."[59] But it

---

55. See Chiswick and Mincer, "Time-Series Changes," p. S44. The calculations are based on the assumption that the 1959 relations between schooling level/dispersion and earnings dispersion remain constant over the entire period 1949–70. This assumption is probably reasonable enough with respect to the period in question, but we would not wish to apply the coefficients to periods further away in time, such as the interwar period.

56. Keat, "Long Run Changes," p. 543.

57. Lydall, *Structure of Earnings*, p. 221.

58. Ibid., pp. 217, 222.

59. Knowles and Robertson, "Difference Between Wages," p. 121. The explanation could also run in terms of partial money illusion (partial, because the scale of the reduction in the absolute differential falls well below the rise in the general money wage level). However, over the longer term, it seems logical to regard price expectations as adjusting fully to experience.

is surely implausible to attribute to inadvertence a causal role in the narrowing process, at least in the context of year-to-year developments under normal peacetime conditions. The other factors at work have their effects mainly on percentage rather than absolute differentials; a mechanism that gave equal cash increases would only be tolerated under certain economic conditions. One such condition would be because supply and demand conditions were shifting in such a way as to require a reduction in the percentage differentials anyway. For example, cheaper, more widely available education would narrow the percentage differential. In this case, the equal cash increase hypothesis describes only the mechanism through which the more fundamental influences work themselves out.

The equal cash increase mechanism does not in any case appear to characterize normal peacetime conditions of money wage inflation. The narrowing process has occurred principally during periods of inflation in wartime or shortly thereafter. Such periods have more often than not been associated with an actual decline in real wages. It seems that a policy of equal cash increases has been deliberately engineered under such conditions as a means of mitigating the effects where they were felt most keenly—namely among low-paid workers. The consensus that price inflation should have a progressive incidence on money income thus appears only under the special hardships of war conditions. Nevertheless, the fact remains that differentials have not rebounded back to their previous levels with the recovery of prewar real income levels. In addition to fulfilling the function identified above, therefore, the wartime disruptions of the skill margin may have served as a catalyst permitting the underlying changes in demand and supply conditions to break through the inhibitions of social conventions.[60] A major change in working practices, such as is brought about by war, will alter traditional attitudes and bring them more into line with underlying economic pressures.

Another group of institutional theories has been concerned with the effects of trade unionism and collective bargaining on the skill differential over the long run, although there has been no rigorous attempt to measure the effects on skill differentials comparable with that of Lewis for the industrial wage structure.[61] A basic problem confronting us in this area is one of discovering what trade union policy has been. Moreover, even if trade unions can be demonstrated to have sought a long-run reduction in the skill differential on grounds of equity, how is their success to be measured? The competitive model would suggest that economic influences have been operating in the same direction, implying trade unions may have been pushing on an open door.

60. To some extent, the reservation prices of workers or union negotiating teams, or the concessions that employers will make, are governed by attitudes based on what has happened in the past. On the role of "custom," see E. H. Phelps Brown and S. V. Hopkins, "Seven Centuries of Building Wages," *Economica* 21 (1955): 195–206.
61. H. G. Lewis, *Unionism and Relative Wages in the United States* (Chicago: University of Chicago Press, 1963).

It is useful at this point to consider Turner's influential analysis of British trade union wage policy.[62] As trade union leaders sought, for political reasons, to extend their membership downward from the skilled to the semiskilled and unskilled, Turner argues that they found it necessary to offer the unskilled a relative wage gain in those industries where they could not anticipate becoming skilled workers themselves. Turner notes that in career-oriented industries where, exceptionally for Great Britain, the recruitment of skilled workers is by progression from unskilled and semiskilled jobs, the narrowing process has failed to occur.

By emphasizing the political motives of skilled workers in extending trade union organization, while at the same time attempting to retain control, Turner leaves largely unexplored the question of whether their actions have had important economic effects and, if so, whether these have figured in the formulation of policy. Interestingly, the downward extension of trade union organization in several major British industries coincided with the large-scale introduction of mass production techniques in the years following World War I. Thus, the operation of the labor market would eventually have bid up the price of unskilled labor relative to skilled labor to a point where it was no longer profitable to substitute the unskilled for the skilled even in the absence of trade union pressure on the lines suggested by Turner. However, it is possible that the fear of being undercut encouraged skilled worker unions to extend their organization downward and, at the same time, anticipate the equilibrium wage outcome, thereby forestalling much of the substitution.

Cyclical Changes. It is generally agreed that, in the short run, skill differentials change relatively little during normal periods but contract sharply during periods of very full employment. It is also possible that they widen during major depressions, although the evidence is ambiguous on this point.[63] It has further been argued that the overall earnings dispersion will widen in depression, and there is some evidence of this phenomena.[64]

Over the cycle, variations in demand for skilled workers are likely to be smaller than for the unskilled, because of the higher investments in hiring and training the former.[65] Thus, during a business contraction, employers

62. H. A. Turner, "Trade Unions, Differentials and the Levelling of Wages," *Manchester School* 20 (1952): 227–282.
63. During the Great Depression of 1929–33, for example, Keat, "Long Run Changes," finds evidence of a narrowing process, as for the depression of 1920–21. On the other hand, P. W. Bell, "Cyclical Variations and Trends in Occupational Wage Differentials in American Industry Since 1914," *Review of Economics and Statistics* 33 (1951): 332–333, notes the stability of the differential over this period. And for Great Britain, Knowles and Robertson, "Difference Between Wages," p. 111, found that skill differentials failed to widen over 1929–32, although narrowing did occur in the early 1920s.
64. See, for example, M. W. Reder, "A Partial Survey of the Theory of Income Distribution," in L. Soltow, ed., *Six Papers on the Size Distribution of Wealth and Income* (New York: National Bureau of Economic Research, 1969), pp. 238–239.
65. See W. Y. Oi, "Labor as a Quasi-Fixed Factor," *Journal of Political Economy* 70 (1962): 538–555.

will tend to lay off the unskilled but attempt to hoard skilled workers, perhaps by downgrading them to unskilled work or putting them on short-time, so as to be able to recoup these investment costs when their order books are again full. If the supply curves of both grades of worker were similarly inelastic, this differential movement in demand would give rise to a contraction in the skilled/unskilled wage ratio in the upswing and a widening in the downswing. However, it is more likely that the short-run supply of labor to skilled jobs is less elastic than to unskilled jobs, if only because skilled men can turn their hands to unskilled jobs if necessary, whereas the unskilled cannot quickly enter skilled jobs.[66] On this reasoning, therefore, the skill margin will not contract in the upswing unless the latter movement is very strong, as in wartime. For then, as Reder has argued,[67] the supply of unskilled workers is likely to be much attenuated. A reasonable explanation for this is that secondary workers (chapter 3), who often fill unskilled jobs, are less geographically mobile, so that the limit of their supply is reached before that of the skilled. At the same time, hiring standards for the skilled grades will tend to be relaxed, thereby reducing pressures to raise pay in these grades. We should note that this downward adjustment of hiring standards is likely relatively to increase the supply of skilled labor for some period extending beyond the initial interval of labor market tightness and its subsequent relaxation. In turn, this will have the effect of prolonging any contraction in skill margins.

It can be seen that cyclical movement in skill differentials will not be automatic but will depend on the intensity of the cycle and other imponderables. But we can certainly accept that the unskilled will experience larger fluctuations in employment and unemployment over the cycle than the skilled. We would therefore expect the *annual* earnings of skilled workers relative to unskilled workers to increase in contraction and decrease in expansion, even if the hourly wage ratio remains constant. This is because the number of weeks worked per year by the unskilled decline in a contraction on average more than those worked by the skilled (chapter 11).

The consequence of the differential impact of unemployment on unskilled vis-a-vis skilled workers is that we would expect earnings dispersion to widen in periods of economic contraction. This tendency would be strengthened were unskilled wage rates to decline relative to skilled rates at such times, although we do not need to assume this. In the functions advanced in chapter 4 to explain annual earnings, we found that weeks worked per year was an important independent variable. To explain the variance of earnings—that is, the dispersion of earnings—it therefore follows that the dispersion of weeks worked should also be included. The reasoning is analogous to that em-

66. See R. Perlman, "Forces Widening Occupational Differentials," *Review of Economics and Statistics* 40 (1958): 107–109.

67. M. W. Reder, "The Wage Structure and Structural Unemployment," *Review of Economic Studies* 31 (1964): 309–322. See also idem, "The Theory of Occupational Wage Differentials," *American Economic Review* 45 (1955): 833–852.

ployed in including the dispersion of schooling in the function explaining earnings dispersion. For the human capital reasons outlined above, unemployment rises relatively more among the unskilled in a contraction and so the dispersion of the distribution of weeks worked will widen in a contraction. This will lead to an increase in the dispersion of annual earnings.

There is evidence of an association between unemployment and earnings dispersion and also between dispersion of weeks worked and the earnings dispersion. Using American time-series data for the period 1944–65, Schultz has regressed the Gini coefficient of income concentration on unemployment, standardizing for the rate of price increase and the rate of real national output increase and using a time trend. The coefficient on the unemployment term has the expected positive sign, and that on the price increase term a negative sign. Although neither coefficient is separately significant, it would be interesting to discover if they were jointly significant.[68] A similar analysis for the Netherlands yields highly significant coefficients. For the United States, going further back in time, it does appear to be the case that the period of the Great Depression was also the interval of greatest income inequality. (Unfortunately there is no parallel study of earnings inequality.) In 1930, the share of total income received by the top 5% of the population has been estimated at 26%, compared with 22% a decade earlier and 23% in 1940.[69] Alternative estimates are 30% in 1929, 21% in 1944, and 20% in 1962,[70] which again indicate the depression years to have the greatest inequality. Most interesting, however, is the study by Chiswick and Mincer, because this enables a judgment to be made of the relative importance of differential unemployment, compared with such other factors as schooling dispersion, on earnings inequality. The earnings function for the census year 1959 gives the standardized relation between the dispersion of log earnings and log weeks worked. In 1964–65, years of relatively full employment, the standard deviation of the weeks worked distribution for white males was about 1.4 weeks; in 1958, a low activity year, the corresponding figure was approximately 1.7 weeks. If these values are substituted into the 1959 earnings function, it emerges that earnings dispersion would have been 18% lower had the 1964–65 value rather than that of 1958 prevailed.[71] If we attribute the difference between 1964–65 and 1958 to cyclical unemployment, then the conclusion is that cyclical unemployment widened earnings dispersion by as much as 17%. This is a considerably larger value than that to be associated with plausible changes in either the schooling or experience distributions.

68. Because the rate of price change and the level of unemployment are likely to be highly correlated, it might not be possible to disentangle their separate contributions to earnings dispersion. But this need not imply that they do not jointly contribute. See T. P. Schultz, "Secular Trends and Cyclical Behavior of Income Distribution in the United States: 1944–1964," in Soltow, *Six Papers*, p. 87.
69. Miller, *Income Distribution*, p. 19, with adjustment for comparability.
70. Ibid., p. 3. See also section 10.6.
71. Chiswick and Mincer, "Time-Series Changes," p. S46.

For future research, it would be interesting to extend the analysis beyond a sample of white males. There are indications that the dispersion of weeks worked is much larger among the nonwhite than the white population.[72] It is also likely that the dispersion of weeks worked by nonwhites varies more over the cycle. Allowing for this, unemployment effects might emerge as even more important a factor in earnings inequality than are the indications at present.

10.4 Interindustry Differentials

We now consider differences in pay by industry. In the long-run equilibrium of the competitive model, interindustry wage differentials for a given occupation are supposed not to exist, except where they are needed to compensate for differential nonpecuniary advantages between one industry and another. However, it can be accepted that the tendency toward equilibrium takes a long time to work itself out and that the wage differential requirements of past structural changes in labor force distribution are mingled with those of more recent structural changes. Also there is the influence of institutions, including collective bargaining and custom, which may be expected to impinge upon competitive forces. Again, short-run variations in industrial wage differentials, associated with cyclical changes in the economy, are superimposed on the wage structure in a manner such as to divert it from the long-run equilibrium of the competitive model.

In this section, we first consider the long-run behavior of industrial wage differentials and the stability of the industrial wage structure. We then proceed to examine the association between that structure and the operation of the labor market. Finally, cyclical changes in the dispersion of industry wage levels are investigated.

The Industrial Structure in the Long Run. Strictly defined, industry differentials are wage comparisons between workers who differ only with respect to the product they make, and ideally this comparison should be restricted to common occupations within a single labor market. The general procedure usually followed, however, has been to compare broad industrywide earnings values. Yet such averages will reflect the influence of differences in skill mix and regional composition among industries, as well as true differentials. Nevertheless, it does seem to be the case that some industries are high-wage while others are low-wage, *ceteris paribus,* and it is necessary to account for this.

Reynolds and Taft have offered the general hypothesis that interindustry wage dispersion tends to reach a maximum during the early stages of industrialization and to diminish gradually after that point.[73] Consider an

---

72. Chiswick, *Income Inequality,* pp. 116, 170.

73. L. G. Reynolds and C. H. Taft, *The Evolution of Wage Structure* (New Haven, Conn.: Yale University Press, 1956), p. 356.

economy that is at the start of its economic development. Here, a substantial differential first appears between subsistence farm income and the new industry, which needs to attract labor out of agriculture. With the passing of time, this first industry will experience less need to offer a relatively high wage. Meanwhile, however, new industries will have appeared to go through a similar *life cycle*. They will tend to sink in the wage hierarchy in their turn with the appearance of yet newer industries. Provided that new industries appear uniformly over time, the process will leave the dispersion more or less unchanged in percentage terms. Also, we would expect the ranking of industries in the wage structure to be inversely related to the date of their appearance.

There is some evidence in favor of this simple life-cycle hypothesis. It has been estimated that, for a sample of eighty-four American manufacturing industries, the dispersion of earnings, as measured by the interquartile range, fluctuated within narrow limits around the 25% mark throughout most of the 1899–1950 period.[74] There appears to have been no narrowing tendency, although there were cyclical changes. Data provided by Reynolds and Taft for France, Sweden, Great Britain, Canada, and the United States also indicate that the older industries, such as clothing manufacture, boots and shoes, food processing, and textiles, lie near the bottom of the wage structure. Industries such as automobile production, electrical equipment, and petroleum refining stand near the top.[75]

It is likely, however, that factors other than the age of an industry determine its position in the wage hierarchy. Two such factors are the rate of technical progress and the degree of concentration. Looking at the former, increases in labor productivity (a crude proxy for technical progress) permit firms within an industry to raise wages while maintaining profit levels. This might lead to successful short-run pressure from workers to raise wages, although we would expect a tendency in the long run toward equality of net advantages among industries. In fact, over the long run, the rate of change of wages by industry does not appear to be correlated with rates of change of physical output per man. American data for the period 1899–1953 yield an insignificant correlation of 0.28 between changes in average hourly earnings and output per man-hour, and the corresponding British coefficient is actually negative.[76] This factor thus seems unimportant.

As to the effect of monopoly on the industrial wage structure, a number of studies have found evidence of a positive association between concentration

74. D. E. Cullen, "The Interindustry Wage Structure, 1899–1950," *American Economic Review* 46 (1956): table 3, p. 361.
75. Reynolds and Taft, *Evolution of Wage Structure,* chaps. 8–12.
76. See S. Fabricant, *Basic Facts on Productivity Changes,* National Bureau of Economic Research, Occasional Paper no. 63 (New York: Columbia University Press, 1959), pp. 45–46; W. E. G. Salter, *Productivity and Technical Change* (Cambridge: Cambridge University Press, 1960), pp. 114–115.

and the rate of change of wages.[77] There are, however, difficulties in measuring monopoly power. Some have sought to proxy monopoly power by value productivity changes on the logic that, if increases in product demand and rates of technical change are not correlated, industries that raise prices, presumably given product demand increases, will be the monopolistic ones. The association between value productivity changes and wage movements, though often close in the short run, is weak over the long run.[78] It seems, therefore, that the association between wage changes and degree of monopoly power cannot be taken as firmly established. Thus, there is some evidence to favor an interpretation of the industrial wage structure as behaving in the manner of the competitive model working itself out slowly in the life-cycle process.

Stability of the Industrial Wage Structure.   The stability of the industrial wage structure can be shown by ranking industries by average wage at one date and comparing this with the ranking of industries by wage at another date. Comparing 1899 and 1947 in this manner, Cullen calculated a rank correlation coefficient of 0.73 for his sample of eighty-four American manufacturing industries.[79] More recent estimates for Great Britain and the United States are given in table 10.5. The rank correlation coefficients can generally be seen to be very high, although the case of Great Britain over the more recent period is anomalous.

The stability of the wage structure over the long run has occasioned a lively debate as to the respective roles of market and institutional forces in the determination of wages. A detailed review of this debate is conducted in chapter 13. Let it suffice to say here that the stability can be given a competitive long-run supply price explanation. If differences in industry average wages mainly reflect differences in skill mix and nonpecuniary advantages and disadvantages, and if these do not change much over time, then neither will the wage structure. The competitive hypothesis would predict greater variability in the short run than in the long run, however, given the maintained hypotheses that supply curves are less elastic in the short run and that demand rather than supply curves do most of the shifting. There is evidence to support this interpretation: wage movements among industries are more uniform over five- or ten-year periods than over shorter intervals.[80] On the other hand, the difference is not marked. This has led to

77. See, for example, W. G. Bowen, *Wage Behavior in the Postwar Period: An Empirical Analysis* (Princeton, N.J.: Princeton University Press, 1960), pp. 74–81; H. M. Levinson, "Postwar Movements in Prices and Wages in Manufacturing Industries," *Study of Employment, Growth, and Price Levels,* Study Paper No. 21, Joint Economic Committee, U.S. Congress (Washington, D.C.: U.S. Government Printing Office, 1960), pp. 2–5, 21.
78. R. Perlman, "Value Productivity and the Interindustry Wage Structure," *Industrial and Labor Relations Review* 10 (1956): 35–37; idem, *Labor Theory* (New York: Wiley, 1969), p. 113.
79. Cullen, "Interindustry Wage Structure," table 2, p. 359.
80. See Organisation for Economic Cooperation and Development, *Wages and Labor Mobility* (Paris: O.E.C.D., 1965), pp. 29–31, 152–171.

Table 10.5   The Stability of the Industrial Wage Structure, Great Britain and the United States

Study	No. of Industries Sampled	Definition of Industry	Time Period	Type of Worker	Type of Earnings	Rank Correlation Coefficient U.S.	U.K.
Haddy and Tolles, 1957	28	3-digit	1939–51	All production workers	Average weekly earnings	.823	
	28	3-digit	1938–51	All production workers	Average weekly earnings		.879
	16	2-digit	1938–51	Male production workers	Average weekly earnings		.4964
OECD, 1965	21	2-digit	1948–61	Wage earners, both sexes	Average hourly earnings	.92	
	21	2-digit	1948–60	Wage earners, both sexes	Average yearly earnings	.95	
	11	2-digit*	1948–61	Wage earners, both sexes	Average hourly earnings	.98	
	31	2-digit*	1948–61	Wage earners, both sexes	Average hourly earnings	.93	
	21	2-digit	1948–60	Salaried employees, both sexes	Average yearly earnings	.61	
	79	3-digit	1954–58	Men	Average hourly earnings		.94
Turner and Jackson, 1969	n.s.**	n.s.**	1956–65	Men	Average hourly earnings	.98	.95
Papola and Bharadwaj, 1970	n.s.**	2-digit	1948–55	Men	Average gross money earnings	.9789	.8879
		2-digit	1955–60	Men	Average gross money earnings	.9759	.9636
		2-digit	1960–65	Men	Average gross money earnings	.9197	.4909
		2-digit	1948–65	Men	Average gross money earnings	.9756	.3243

* includes nonmanufacturing

** not stated.

Sources:

P. Haddy and N. A. Tolles, "British and American Changes in Interindustry Wage Structure under Full Employment," *Review of Economics and Statistics* 33 (1957): 409, 411; Organisation for Economic Cooperation and Development, *Wages and Labor Mobility* (Paris: O.E.C.D., 1965), table 2, p. 26; H. A. Turner and D. Jackson, "On the Stability of Wage Differences and Productivity—Based Wage Policies: An International Analysis," *British Journal of Industrial Relations* 17 (1969): 3; T. S. Papola and V. P. Bharadwaj, "Dynamics of Industrial Wage Structure: An Inter-Country Analysis," *Economic Journal* 80 (1970): 83, table 3.

the plausible argument that it is trade unions that "damp down" short-run changes in wages and, moreover, that this process is efficient because it reduces labor market uncertainty.[81]

The Relation Between Industrial Wage and Employment Structures.   The association between relative changes in industry wages and employment is well researched, but it remains a controversial area. This is because almost any development in the wage structure can be explained in terms of appropriate shifts of supply and demand schedules. However, making the usual assumption that supply curves are likely to be less elastic in the short run than in the long run, we would expect to observe a positive relation between industry wage and employment changes in the short run though not in the long run.

A number of industry-level studies have revealed evidence of small but usually significant positive correlations between relative changes in wages and employment in the short run.[82] This association is most pronounced among those industries experiencing the greatest and least changes in employment.[83] The long-run association between relative wage and employment changes is somewhat more difficult to test because of the problem of obtaining uninterrupted data series covering sufficiently long periods of more or less full employment. Nevertheless, British evidence points to a statistically insignificant association over 1924-50. For the United States, the data cited by Kendrick for the period 1899-1953 again show no statistically significant association.[84]

It has been argued, however, that this evidence is, on the face of it, equally consistent with the view that movements of labor are predominantly wage insensitive. The Organization for Economic Cooperation and Development (OECD), for example, considers that changes in the allocation of labor are often brought about by mechanisms other than changes in the wage structure and that changes in the wage structure are often brought about by forces other than those that allocate labor. Indeed, the OECD interpretation of the evidence favors the *prosperity thesis*.[85] According to this view, there is no

---

81. See J. R. Crossley, "Collective Bargaining, Wage Structure and the Labour Market in the United Kingdom," in E. M. Hugh-Jones, *Wage Structure in Theory and Practice* (Amsterdam: North Holland, 1966), pp. 226-229.

82. See for example, L. Ulman, "Labor Mobility and the Industrial Wage Structure in the Postwar United States," *Quarterly Journal of Economics* 79 (1965): 73-79; W. B. Reddaway, "Wage Flexibility and the Distribution of Labor," *Lloyds Bank Review*, no. 54 (1959): 32-48; O.E.C.D., *Wages and Labor Mobility*, pp. 95-96; Crossley, "Collective Bargaining," pp. 216-220.

83. See O.E.C.D., *Wage and Labor Mobility*, pp. 101-104; E. H. Phelps Brown and M. H. Browne, "Earnings in Industries of the United Kingdom: 1948-59," *Economic Journal* 62 (1962): 535-536.

84. See, respectively, Crossley, "Collective Bargaining," p. 220; M. W. Reder, "Wage Differentials: Theory and Measurement," *Aspects of Labor Economics*, National Bureau of Economic Research (Princeton, N.J.: Princeton University Press, 1962), p. 278.

85. OECD, *Wages and Labor Mobility*, pp. 104 ff.

causal link between wage and employment changes: the association is fortuitous and arises because both variables are related to a third factor—the prosperity of an industry. When demand rises in a particular sector, so the argument goes, employment will increase at the same time as conditions are created that encourage unions to demand, and employers to yield, above average wage increases. Job vacancies are, meanwhile, sufficient to attract labor at the going rate.

The multicountry OECD analysis established the existence of a strong positive association between percentage changes in profits and contemporaneous percentage changes in earnings. Similarly, when changes in total output were correlated with changes in relative employment, most correlation coefficients were positive and significant and generally remained so even when the influence of changes in earnings was held constant. However, this study does not provide us with a basis for discriminating between the competitive labor market hypothesis and the prosperity thesis. This is because, under the former hypothesis, we should also expect an association between the profit rate, wage change, and employment change within industries where final demand has been rising and where the adjustment to high levels of output has not fully been realized. Moreover, despite the weakening in association between wage and employment changes, with profits held constant, that association does not disappear. Indeed, in the case of the United Kingdom, we observe a substantial decline in the degree of association between profits change and wage change when the influence of employment change is held constant.[86] In summary, there appears little or no evidence to favor that formulation of the prosperity thesis that asserts that there is no need for differential wage changes on labor market grounds, although we would not seek to deny the allocative role of the existing wage structure (chapter 5).

Cyclical Changes in Interindustry Wage Dispersion. A number of commentators have noticed a tendency for the overall dispersion of the industry wage structure to narrow under full employment and inflationary conditions and to widen again in the depression phase of the cycle.[87] However, unlike other types of differential, the dispersion of the industry wage structure has reasserted itself; over the long run, there is no evidence of a significant narrowing influence. One explanation of this phenomenon follows from the suggestion that there are some industries, toward the top of the wage hierarchy, the firms of which for reasons of union pressure or because of taste factors pay wages higher than are required on allocative grounds. Such

86. Ibid., p. 111.
87. See, for example, P. Haddy and N. A. Tolles, "British and American Changes in Interindustry Wage Structure under Full Employment," *Review of Economics and Statistics* 33 (1957): 410 ff; Reynolds and Taft, *Evolution of Wage Structure,* p. 364.

industries will, in the terminology of Reder, be in a situation of "labor slack,"[88] in that there will be more applicants than jobs currently available in the industry concerned. The disappointed applicants have to search for jobs elsewhere in the economy, thereby increasing the supply of labor to lower-paying industries. The surplus is then envisioned ultimately to reach the low-wage, nonunionized service trades at the bottom of the industrial wage structure, where wages are flexible enough to permit absorption of the excess labor. Consider a cyclic expansion of demand under these conditions. If all labor demand curves shift equally in all sectors, the industries with labor slack will be able to expand their employment without raising their relative wage. The low-wage sector(s), on the other hand, will be losing labor rapidly. Such industries will be forced to raise wages, tending in this way to cause a narrowing of the industry wage structure as the general level of unemployment falls. The argument is reversed for the depression phase of the cycle.

A more formal model along these lines is presented by Wachter.[89] In Galbraithian fashion, the economy is visualized as being divided into two sectors: a competitive, or price taking, sector, in which wages respond rapidly to market forces, and an administered sector of high-wage, capital-intensive, oligopolistic industries of high union density. In the administered sector, prices change only infrequently due to the need to minimize the risk of breakdown of implicit price collusion agreements. In turn, this requires that cost conditions are stable over the horizon of the prices-planning period, so that there is an incentive to settle for long-term contracts and also to offer a wage-premium over the competitive sector wage, resulting in the large firms being insulated from fluctuations in the aggregate demand for labor by the formation of a worker queue for jobs in the administered sector. Consequently, this model predicts that an increase/fall in aggregate demand, as proxied by a fall/rise in unemployment, should lead to a decline/increase in the dispersion of the interindustry wage structure as the competitive sector responds more quickly to changed marked conditions.

In practice, however, the above process is likely to be modified by a variety of other influences. In the Reder model, the low wage alternative to unemployment may not be available when there exists a statutory minimum wage or a high level of unemployment benefits. Moreover, the compression phase of the argument should allow for contingents of the reserve of secondary workers. In the Wachter model, more work is required with respect to the determinants of the planning periods in the administered sectors of the economy.

88. Reder, "Occupational Wage Differentials," p. 837.
89. M. L. Wachter, "Cyclical Variations in the Interindustry Wage Structure," *American Economic Review* 60 (1970): 75–84. See also S. A. Ross and M. L. Wachter, "Wage Determination, Inflation, and the Industrial Wage Structure," *American Economic Review* 63 (1973): 675–692.

10.5 Regional Differentials

There is evidence of sizable geographic variation in wages. Fuchs, using census data for 1959, estimated southern average hourly earnings to be 80% of the non-south level ($2.12 compared with $2.65).[90] In gauging such regional differentials, we must proceed with caution. What is the proper definition of a regional differential? Is it appropriate to compare the average hourly wage paid to all workers in a particular region with that in other regions, as in the case of the above example, or should a standardization procedure be adopted to show what the regional differentials would have been had all regions the same labor and industry mix? Empirical investigation has favored standardization, so as to focus on whether there are differences in pay among regions, which would reflect on the allocative efficiency of labor markets. Nevertheless, the removal of the industry-mix effect leaves open the question as to why regions differ in their industrial structure. From the point of view of economic welfare comparisons between regions, it is perhaps the total effect that is relevant.

Figures cited by Fuchs and Perlman for the United States in 1954 show that the unadjusted annual wage level in the South Atlantic and East South Central regions stood at 77.1% and 79.1%, respectively, of the national average.[91] Had every southern worker been paid at the national rate for his industry, this ratio would have been 86.0% and 90.5% respectively. This hypothetical relative wage level indicates that southern wage levels would have been ten to fourteen percentage points lower than northern levels, simply because of the relative preponderance of low-wage industries in the South. Because actual wage levels were more like twenty-two percentage points lower in the South, it is evident that southern manufacturing workers show annual earnings considerably below the national average, even allowing for industry mix. However, there are many factors other than industry mix that might affect the average wage of one region relative to another, and it is necessary to make allowances for these as well.

Before turning to these factors, it is worth noting that regional differences have persisted for long periods of time. To be sure, the wage differential has narrowed since the turn of the century. According to Bloch, the difference in pay between northern and southern workers in 1907 was about 100%. By 1946, the wage differential had narrowed to about 25%.[92] But the narrowing process has not been uniform. The period 1919–29 evidenced a relative stability of regional wage differentials, while the period 1929–47 witnessed an

90. V. R. Fuchs, *Differentials in Hourly Earnings by Regions and City Size, 1959,* National Bureau of Economic Research, Occasional Paper no. 101 (New York: Columbia University Press, 1967), p. 7.
91. V. R. Fuchs and R. Perlman, "Recent Trends in Southern Wage Differentials," *Review of Economics and Statistics* 42 (1960): 293.
92. See J. W. Bloch, "Regional Wage Differentials, 1907–1946," *Monthly Labor Review* 66 (1948): 371–377.

improvement in the southern wage position.[93] Evidence for the period 1947–54 is conflicting.[94] Most observers would agree that the overall differential in manufacturing for 1954 was in the order of 20%, and there had evidently been little change in the differential by 1963.[95] The lack of any uniform narrowing tendency is true even of Great Britain, where the effect of a strongly unionized labor force, together with a centralized collective bargaining framework, might have been expected to eliminate regional differentials. Thus, although we can discern a very substantial reduction in minimum rate differentials over the course of the present century in Great Britain, this seems to have had considerably less impact upon the structure of regional earnings.[96]

The persistence of regional wage differentials has often been explained as a disequilibrium phenomenon, in which the adjustment mechanism of labor (and capital) mobility from labor surplus to labor shortage regions is seen as working only very slowly. However, it must be said that we do not yet have enough data to hold "other things equal," so as to establish whether there are in fact differences in pay for the same type of job among regions. Ideally, we would wish to standardize thoroughly for differences in labor quality between the regions, including variables representing skill, education, experience, age, motivation, and ability. We should also seek to standardize for other factors that can be expected on competitive grounds to yield equilibrium wage differentials in a given job; in particular, firm size, tastes, and size of town.[97] In fact, we can do little of this and are thus not really in a position yet to form a judgment as to the spatial allocative efficiency of labor markets.

The most thorough study is by Scully, who has been able to standardize for industry, color, sex, and capital intensity. He also attempts a partial standardization for education by forming an index of the amount of expenditure on education for the average worker, by industry. Data on unionization by industry and state were not available, however, which shows graphically the empirical problems to be encountered in this area. Instead, he included a variable based on the proportion of the industry work force

93. See G. H. Borts, "The Equalization of Returns and Regional Economic Growth," *American Economic Review* 50 (1960): 319–347; Fuchs and Perlman, "Southern Wage Differentials," p. 293.
94. Thus, M. Segal, "Regional Wage Differentials in Manufacturing in the Post-War Period," *Review of Economics and Statistics* 43 (1961): 248–255. has noted some narrowing for a majority of manufacturing industries, whereas Fuchs and Perlman, "Southern Wage Differentials," p. 293, discern a relative stability.
95. See H. M. Douty, "Wage Differentials: Forces and Counter-forces," *Monthly Labor Review* 91 (1968): 74–81.
96. See C. E. V. Leser, "Earnings in British Regions," *Scottish Journal of Political Economy* 1 (1954): 268–272.
97. As we have seen in earlier chapters, smaller firms are likely to pay less for labor of given quality for informational reasons—they are better at judging applicants. People might also prefer to work in small firms, in which case lower pay given the job would represent compensation for nonpecuniary benefits. As for the size of town, those working in smaller communities are more likely to be subject to monopsony and thus to be paid less.

involved in strikes, which should be roughly correlated with unionization (chapter 7). The results for a regression of the 1958 average hourly wage rates of production workers (across seventeen manufacturing industries within seventeen southern and nine northern states) on the above independent variables are as follows:[98]

for northern states,
$$W = 2.02 + 0.0293^*K/L + 1.466^*N/L + 0.319^*H/L + 0.759^*S/L$$
$$-0.760^*F/L + \text{industry dummies}$$
$$\overline{R}^2 = 0.943, n = 92$$

for southern states,
$$W = 2.18 + 0.0327^*K/L - 0.499^*N/L + 0.385^*H/L + 0.483^*S/L$$
$$-0.766^*F/L + \text{industry dummies}$$
$$\overline{R}^2 = 0.895, n = 164$$

where K/L is the capital-labor ratio;
N/L (F/L) is the fraction of industry labor force nonwhite (female);
$\quad H/L$ is average educational expenditure per worker;
$\quad S/L$ is the faction of industry labor force involved in strikes on
$\qquad$ average over 1956–60; and
$\quad$ * denotes significance at the 1% level or better.

The equations can be seen to be quite similar, and the variables have the signs we might expect, apart from the large positive coefficient on N/L in the northern equation. Thus, there is apparently little wage discrimination against nonwhites in manufacturing in the North, but considerable discrimination in the South. This, together with the larger utilization of nonwhite labor in the South, is one important reason why relative wage levels are lower on average in the South.

The other important reason for lower wages in the South appears to be the higher average quality of northern labor. The equations show wages to vary positively with the education expenditures, which are a proxy for human capital embodied in the labor force. Here, as was observed earlier,[99] there is an indication that the rate of return to capital is somewhat higher in the South. Because the amount of human capital embodied in manufacturing workers is much higher in the North than in the South—twice as high according to Scully[100]—this disparity is a major factor accounting for the wage differential. The other variables are not so important. We see that in both regions wages are higher, and by about the same amount, in the more capital-intensive industries. This is presumably because capital intensity

98. G. W. Scully, "Interstate Wage Differentials: A Cross-Section Analysis," *American Economic Review* 59 (1969): 768.
99. See footnote 33 of this chapter.
100. Scully, "Interstate Wage Differentials," p. 769.

makes for higher labor productivity, *ceteris paribus*. Because capital/labor ratios apparently tend to be somewhat higher in the South than the North,[101] this is a factor working to diminish the North-South differential. Wages vary negatively, and by the same amount, according to the proportion of women in the labor force. Still, whatever might be our explanation of this negative coefficient (chapter 6), sex differences do not contribute to the differential. This is because there are similar levels of utilization of female labor in both regions. The industry dummies and overall constant pick up the differences in industrial composition between the two regions and omitted variables. The greater prominence of low-wage industries in the South can be shown also to contribute to the differential. Finally, there is the strikes variable, which has a higher coefficient in the North. However, too many difficulties of interpretation surround this particular variable for us to make much of the observed difference. In any case, the number of strikes is too low, in both regions, to much affect the differential.

These findings indicate that pursuit of regional wage uniformity depends heavily on elimination of human capital differences and discrimination. However, it should be pointed out that lack of data causes the standardizing procedure to be crude. To some extent, therefore, we would expect the proportion nonwhite variable to pick up differences in labor quality, because nonwhites are more poorly educated and trained, as well as discrimination factors. The likely extent to which there are differences in pay given the job between North and South is, therefore, further diminished.

We should not close this discussion of regional wage differentials without mentioning the possibility of an alternative explanation of persistent wage differentiation. It could be argued that, if labor and capital are indeed interregionally immobile, we should abandon the notion of unified markets in which rates of return tend to equality through factor mobility and work instead in terms of trade theory. This puts factor movement in a secondary role and stresses a different primary adjustment process. If labor were the only factor of production, and if regions differed in their labor input ratios within each industry, there would be specialization and trade between regions according to comparative advantage in the usual way. The existence of national and international product markets with uniform prices for traded goods would impose on a region with a low absolute advantage the choice between unemployment or a reduction in the wage level, relative to other regions. Wage differentiation would then be an equilibrium phenomenon, related to the spatial distribution of comparative advantage, which changes only slowly through time. If this interpretation is correct, then the simple Ricardian trade model has important policy implications. If the adjustment mechanism focuses primarily upon the general money wage level of a region,

101. Ibid. It has sometimes been thought that capital-labor ratios were lower in the South than in the North. See L. E. Galloway, "The North-South Wage Differential," *Review of Economics and Statistics* 45 (1963): 270.

rather than upon factor mobility, then regional wage disparity may be more amenable to correction by such means as discriminatory fiscal measures. Despite its important policy implications, the trade model has been surprisingly underinvestigated, and we must await its further development.

10.6 The Income and Wealth Distributions

Let us now consider the wealth and income distributions. Although personal income from wealth is not the major part of total income, it represents a highly unequally distributed component of that income. This makes for greater dispersion of total income than of total earnings. But we should note that the wealth distribution also affects the earnings distribution in its own right. Its most important effect here concerns the distribution of schooling (and the quality of schooling), because the more affluent achieve more schooling, *ceteris paribus*. There are also indications that the possession of physical capital itself improves earnings opportunities, irrespective of relevant personal characteristics such as ability and schooling. Thus, we may identify favoritism for the rich. For these reasons, the distribution of earnings should not be studied in isolation from the distribution of wealth.

Aspects of the distributions of wealth and income are presented in table 10.6 for Great Britain and the United States, covering most of the present century. Table 10.6 should be read in conjunction with table 10.4, which relates to earnings. It appears that wealth is most unequally distributed, followed by incomes and then earnings. In both countries, all three distributions have become less dispersed over time, although the narrowing process seems to have been halted in the postwar interval. Table 10.6 also indicates the British wealth distribution to be markedly more unequal than the American, at all times. This has been ascribed chiefly to the more unequal distribution of land in Great Britain, which is the consequence of land scarcity and that country's feudal past.[102] The British earnings distribution is rather less dispersed than the American, however, which is consistent with the less dispersed education distribution in Great Britain. That the two countries have similar income distributions presumably will reflect in part the net outcome of these two opposing forces. However, other factors will be at work widening the dispersion of American incomes relative to the British. These will include the lower coverage of state welfare payments, the larger number of subsistence farmers, and the greater significance of racial discrimination.[103]

Perhaps most significant of all are the changes over time in the respective distributions. Let us first consider the wealth distribution. The continued contraction of this distribution, apparently even in Great Britain, naturally raises the question of whether we are observing a trend to a more egali-

---

102. H. F. Lydall and J. B. Lancing, "A Comparison of the Distribution of Personal Income and Wealth in the U.S. and G.B.," *American Economic Review* 49 (1959): 65.
103. Ibid., p. 60; Chiswick, *Income Inequality,* p. 103.

Table 10.6   Measures of the Distribution of Wealth and Income, United States and Great Britain, Selected Years

| Measure/Country/Year | Proportion held by top: | | | Gini Coefficient |
	1%	5%	20%	
Personal Wealth*				
U.S. 1860	43%[a]			.924[a]
1922	32[b]			
1953	28[d], 24[b]		65[c]	
1969	25[d]			
G.B. 1911–13	66[e]	86[e]		
1951–56	42[e]	68[e]	89[e]	
1954	43[e]		88[c]	.98[e]
1968	32–40[f]	54–64[f]		.68[f]
Household Income**				
U.S. 1929		30[g]	54	
1944		21[g]	46	
1962		20[g], 15[h]	46[g], 49[h]	.44(.44)[h]
1970		16[h]	51[h]	.45(.45)[h]
G.B. 1913				.47–.59[j]
1938		29(24)[k]	51(46)[k]	
1957		18(14)[k]	41(38)[k]	.33(.29)[l]
1972–73			39[l]	.31(.27)[l]

* total net capital excluding pensions and trusts.

** bracketed figures are post direct tax.

Sources:

a. L. Soltow, "The Wealth, Income and Social Class of Men in Large Northern Cities of the U.S. in 1960," in J. D. Smith, ed., *The Personal Distribution of Income and Wealth* (New York: National Bureau of Economic Research, 1975), p. 238. (Data relate to 10 cities only.)

b. R. J. Lampman, "Changes in the Share of Wealth Held by Top Wealth Holders 1922–1956," *Review of Economics and Statistics* 41 (1956): 391.

c. H. F. Lydall and J. B. Lansing, "A Comparison of the Distribution of Personal Income and Wealth in the U.S. and G.B.," *American Economic Review* 49 (1959): 60. (Interpolated from table 8.)

d. J. D. Smith and J. D. Franklin, "The Concentration of Personal Wealth 1922–1969," *American Economic Review* 66 (1976): 164. (This figure includes trusts.)

e. H. F. Lydall and S. G. Tipping, "The Distribution of Personal Wealth in Britain," *Bulletin of the Oxford University Institute of Economics and Statistics* 23 (1961): 91–92.

f. A. B. Atkinson, "The Distribution of Wealth in Britain in the 1960s—The Estate Duty Method Re-examined," in Smith, *Personal Distribution of Income*, pp. 278, 308.

g. H. P. Miller, *Income Distribution in the United States*, Bureau of the Census (Washington, D.C.: U.S. Government Printing Office, 1966), pp. 3, 24.

h. M. Reynolds and E. Smolensky, "Post-Fisc Distributions of Income in 1950, 1961 and 1970," *Public Finance Quarterly* 5 (1977): 428, 430.

j. L. Soltow, "Long-Run Changes in British Income Inequality," *Economic History Review* 21 (1968): 22.

k. H. F. Lydall, "The Long-Term Trend in the Size Distribution of Income," *Journal of the Royal Statistical Society,* Series A, 122 (1959): 14.

l. Royal Commission on the Distribution of Income and Wealth, *Report No. 1* (London: H.M.S.O., Cmnd. 6171, 1975), p. 36.

tarian society via progressive tax laws. This latter possibility would be particularly important in Great Britain, where until recently the sharing out of property during the life of the donor served to reduce the liability of his estate to death duty. The proposed replacement of death duty (or estate duty) by a tax on large gifts inter vivos—a capital transfer tax—was indeed designed to close this particular loophole. We observe that there has been a reduction in the wealth shares not only of the top 1% but also of the top 10% of the population. Here, there would seem to be grounds for qualified optimism, because the latter group is less likely to be affected by the tactics of sharing out. Also, work performed by Harbury on the role of inheritance in building up wealth suggests that in Great Britain—there are no equivalent studies for the United States—this factor has become less important in the postwar period. Whereas in 1956/57, some 68% of sons leaving estates valued at over £100,000 had fathers who had bequeathed them more than £25,000, that proportion had fallen to 58% in 1973. In case this figure still seems very high, a bright side to the analysis should be pointed out: no less than 21% of sons leaving estates valued at £100,000 or more in 1973 had fathers who had bequeathed them less than £1,000. The corresponding figure was 15% in 1956/57.[104] We might conclude that there remains hope for most of us!

With respect to the household income distribution, it is as well to mention one factor that often tends to be overlooked: the tendency for families to split up and no longer pool their incomes, thereby constituting separate households. Because it is the young and the old, and hence low-income recipients, who tend to act in this manner, it can be seen that the dispersion of the distribution will thereby be widened even though no individual is worse off than before. Some idea of the effect of including these one- or two-person households on the distribution of income can be gauged by comparing the Gini coefficient for the family income distribution with that for family-plus-unrelated-individuals. In the United States, as of 1965, the coefficient for the former was 0.37. The coefficient for the latter group was higher, at 0.41.[105] In practice, however, this factor does not seem to have had much effect on observed movements in income dispersion.[106] In particular, it cannot be said that a genuine reduction in dispersion has been obscured by changes in household composition.

Other factors likely to influence the income distribution are the relative increase in income from employment, the increasing tendency for women to work, taxation policy, and the state of the labor market. A favorable combination of these circumstances is probably responsible for the marked long-term narrowing of the income distribution. In particular, modern industrial society appears to allow much more scope for the use of human capital, which tends to be more equally distributed, than did preindustrial society,

104. C. D. Harbury and D. M. Hitchens, "The Inheritance of Top Wealth Leavers: Some Further Evidence," *Economic Journal* 86 (1976): 324, table 2.
105. Schultz, "Secular Trends," p. 79.
106. Miller, *Income Distribution*, p. 20.

where the predominant type of capital was physical.[107] The importance of this factor is indicated by the fact that the dispersion of income has been much more reduced over time than that of physical wealth. However, it is perhaps the tendency toward a secular rise in unemployment since the 1950s that is mainly responsible for the absence of further narrowing in income dispersion. A rise in unemployment is to be associated with a relative increase in the number of low-income recipients. Indeed, if labor earnings continue to form a larger and larger component of total income, we would expect the total income distribution to become more sensitive to the level of business activity. Taxation does appear to have somewhat narrowed the income distribution in Great Britain but not in the United States.[108] However, the redistributional effects of taxation (and benefits) require further investigation. From the viewpoint of economic policy, therefore, maintenance of stable economic conditions together with programs to equalize educational opportunities emerge as the main instruments for promoting a more egalitarian income distribution.

107. See L. Soltow, "Long-run Changes in British Income Inequality," *Economic History Review* 21 (1968): 29.

108. See, respectively, Lydall, "Long Term Trend," p. 34; M. Reynolds and E. Smolensky, "Post-Fisc Distributions of Income in 1950, 1961 and 1970," *Public Finance Quarterly* 5 (1977): 428, 430.

APPENDIX 10-A
ILLUSTRATIVE CALCULATION OF THE EFFECT
OF LOWER TRAINING REQUIREMENTS ON
THE EQUILIBRIUM SKILLED/UNSKILLED
WAGE DIFFERENTIAL

Figure 10-A.1 presents hypothetical simplified earnings profiles for skilled and unskilled workers in 1903 and 1956, earnings flows in the latter year being represented by broken lines. Unskilled workers are assumed to enter the labor market at the age of sixteen and to work until sixty-five. They receive a wage rate of b throughout their working life. Skilled workers, on the other hand, are assumed to require d_2 years additional training: d_1 of these extra years represent a schooling interval, during which time no pay is received, and $d_2 - d_1$ represent an on-the-job training interval during which the apprentice wage c is received. Thereafter, the skilled worker obtains wage a throughout his working life.

Figure 10-A.1 Skilled and Unskilled Worker Earnings Flows, Reductions in Schooling and Training Costs

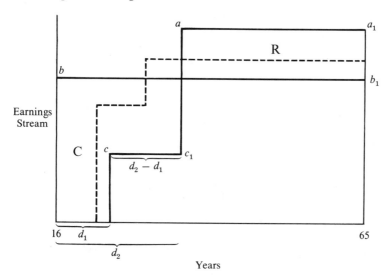

In equilibrium, for a given rate of discount, the present value of the costs of skilled training (area C) must equal the present value of returns to that training (area R). If, over time, area C becomes smaller, as indeed seems to have been the case, and if the rate of discount does not change,[1] this is compatible with a smaller R and, consequently, a reduced skilled/unskilled wage ratio, $\frac{a}{b}$. Alternatively, we can say that, in equilibrium, the present values of earnings over the age range from sixteen to sixty-five must be equal in both occupations: if they are not, then individuals will move between occupations, so changing a and b, and perhaps c, until the present values of the alternative earnings streams are equated. Thus, for skilled workers, the present value of the area(s) under the discontinuous curve(s)—either the solid or broken line discontinuous curves—must equal the present value of the area under the continuous curve representing the unskilled worker earnings stream, here designated as bb_1. Formally, we may write

$$\int_{t=0}^{t=T} be^{-it}dt = \int_{t=d_1}^{t=d_2} ce^{-it}dt + \int_{t=d_2}^{t=T} ae^{-it}dt$$

where T is the length of working life (forty-nine years in this example); and e^{-it} is the continuous discounting factor, analogous to $(1+i)^{-t}$ used in the discrete discounting procedure employed in chapter 4.

Thus, the present value of the unskilled wage for life, $T - 0$, is equal to the present value of the apprentice wage for period $d_2 - d_1$ plus the present value of the skilled wage for the period $T - d_2$.

The integral of xe^{-it} can be shown to be $-\frac{x}{i}e^{-it}$, so that the above expression becomes

$$-\frac{b}{i}e^{-it}\Big|_{t=T\,\text{and}\,0} = -\frac{c}{i}e^{-it}\Big|_{t=d_2\,\text{and}\,d_1} + -\frac{a}{i}e^{-it}\Big|_{t=T\,\text{and}\,d_2}$$

or

$$b(e^{-iT} - 1) = c(e^{-id_2} - e^{-id_1}) + a(e^{-iT} - e^{-id_2}).$$

Solving for $\frac{a}{b}$, we derive

$$\frac{a}{b} = \frac{e^{id_2} - e^{i(d_2-d_1)} + \left(\dfrac{b-c}{b}\right)(e^{i(d_2-d_1)} - 1)}{1 - e^{i(d_2-T)}} + 1.$$

1. Or, to put this in another way, if the rate of return to training and schooling is unaltered.

Putting the values shown in the text for i, d_1, d_2, T, and $(b - c)/b$ into this formula, and assuming the denominator approximates unity, we derive

$$\frac{a}{b} \simeq 1.70, \text{ using 1903 assumed values,}$$

$$\frac{a}{b} \simeq 1.28, \text{ using 1956 assumed values.}$$

APPENDIX 10-B
THE GINI COEFFICIENT

The Gini coefficient is best considered with the aid of figure 10-B.1. For any distribution, say the income distribution, we may draw up a Lorenz curve, which depicts the percentage of total income obtained by a percentage of income recipients, cumulated from the smallest. Data representing one such Lorenz curve for Great Britain as of 1964 are as follows:

Percentage of population	10	20	50	80	90
Cumulative share of income (%)	2.0	5.1	22.8	55.8	70.7

The diagonal line in figure 10-B.1 is the line of complete equality and is in fact the configuration assumed by the Lorenz curve if all income recipients

Figure 10-B.1 The Lorenz Curve and the Gini Coefficient

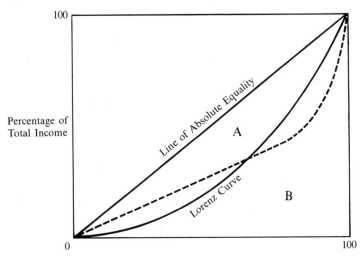

Percentage of Population
(rising from smallest to highest income recipients)

have equal shares—that is, where 10% of the population have a 10% share of total income, 20% have a 20% share, and so on. The extent to which the Lorenz curve deviates from this line indicates the degree of inequality within the population.

A summary measure of the amount of inequality indicated by the Lorenz curve is provided by the Gini coefficient. The latter is defined as area A divided by areas $A + B$. The more equal the distribution, that is, the lower the dispersion, the smaller area A and the lower the coefficient. The coefficient is thus an alternative to the variance of the distribution as a measure of dispersion. However, one distribution can be more equal than another over one range, less equal over a succeeding range, and yet both might record the same coefficient.[1] Such a situation is represented by the broken Lorenz curve of figure 10-B.1, which can be seen to intersect its solid counterpart. To decide whether, in such a case, one distribution is more equal than the other requires us to make a judgment as to whether we are more concerned with equality among the rich as opposed to equality among the poor. There might thus be no unambiguous way to rank distributions according to their dispersion.

---

1. See A. B. Atkinson, "On the Measurement of Inequality," *Journal of Economic Theory* 2 (1970): 244–263.

CHAPTER 11
UNEMPLOYMENT

11.1 Introduction

Our concern with unemployment stems from three main sources. These are (1) a wish to minimize the economic waste that arises because of the underutilization of a factor of production, in this case labor, (2) a desire to have some measure of the social waste that arises from inadequate employment opportunities, and (3) the need to provide an indicator of excess capacity in the economy as a guide to economic policy.

The cost of the 1969-70 recession, as compared with an alternative policy that would have maintained unemployment at a steady 4%, has been estimated at $100 billion in lost output.[1] This estimate is based on the _Okun's Law_ loss in aggregate output that is statistically associated with a given short-run increase in the unemployment rate.[2] In crude terms, this procedure says that the cost of a temporary increase of one percentage point in the unemployment rate is 3% of final output. However, measurement of the economic loss induced by a downturn is difficult. In the first place, any estimate must impute a value to nonmarket activity, which includes such home activities as time devoted to consumption, household production, including child care, and sleep in addition to hours spent by unemployed individuals searching for new jobs. We should stress that the search time of unemployed individuals is productive in raising future income, although the magnitude has to be determined. Secondly, we must pay regard to the question of inflation: a reduction in unemployment may be accompanied by an acceleration in the rate of inflation.

Already we begin to see that unemployment is a multifaceted concept. As in the depressed years of the 1930s, much still depends on one's view of the

---

1. See R. J. Gordon, "Inflation in Recession and Recovery," _Brookings Papers on Economic Activity_ 1 (1971): 142.
2. A. M. Okun, "Potential GNP: Its Measurement and Significance," in American Statistical Association, _Proceedings of the Business and Economic Statistics Section_ 1962, pp. 98–104; reprinted in A. M. Okun, _The Political Economy of Prosperity_ (Washington, D.C.: The Brookings Institution, 1970), pp. 132–145.

unemployment problem. Friedman, for example, in analyzing the effects of an increase in the aggregate unemployment rate from 3.5% to 4.5%, ignores the question of output loss and tends to minimize the welfare cost of extra unemployment, observing, "In fact, the number who each week start to look for work would be raised very little—from 530,000 to perhaps 560,000. But these job seekers would spend on average an extra week or so finding an acceptable job. . . . The most serious effect would be to raise the number of persons unemployed at any one time for more than six months from 180,000 to perhaps 300,000."[3] Between the output loss interpretation and that of Friedman there lies a very different attitude to the causes of unemployment and its cures. The principal task of this chapter will be to state the opposing positions taken on unemployment and to consider their ramifications.

The plan of the chapter is as follows. In section 11.2, we introduce an analysis of unemployment in terms of a simplified flow analysis, so as to establish at the outset that unemployment is not a residual state resulting in a surplus after all vacancies have been filled. In section 11.3, the conventional breakdown of unemployment by type is assessed, before turning, in section 11.4, to an alternative theoretical approach based on the distinction between voluntary and involuntary unemployment. In the light of this discussion, we next consider in section 11.5 the status of official unemployment statistics. Here, the analysis deals with questions such as the impact of unemployment insurance schemes and wider labor reserve issues associated with the concepts of hidden unemployment and labor hoarding. In section 11.6, we consider the issues raised by the uneven incidence of unemployment in the economy.

11.2 Labor Market Flows

The labor market is in continuous internal motion with workers moving rapidly between jobs, unemployment, and nonparticipation, even during periods of stable economic activity. Holt has described the facts about unemployment and the flow of workers into the unemployed category in 1969 in the following way:

In the United States currently there are about 80 million employed workers, 3 million unemployed workers and probably a considerable number of vacancies, but data on this are inadequate. Employment durations for all accessions average roughly 2.7 years. Unemployed workers and vacancies wait roughly a month on average before finding work or employees. The total flow of quits and layoffs amounts to 30 million per year. Some workers even travel the quit or layoff loop several times in a year. Turnover rates of the order of 3 or 4 percent a month account for this tremendous flow of accessions. The stock of unemployed workers is replaced every month on average. Offsetting this flow from the stock of employed workers is a roughly equal flow of accessions. Employers

3. M. Friedman, *An Economist's Protest* (Glen Ridge, N.J.: Horton, 1972), pp. 5–6.

have to recruit continually in order to hold a constant workforce. The proba-
bility that an unemployed worker will find a job is roughly 20 percent per week
and gives a long-tailed exponential distribution of unemployment duration.[4]

The level of unemployment has changed substantially since 1969, but again
we note that heavy flows of workers are absorbed with only small month-
to-month net changes in the unemployment rate. For example, between
October 1973 and June 1975, the unemployment rate in the United States
rose from 4.2% to 9.2%, and unemployment rose by an average of some
321,000 workers each month. Yet over that same interval, no less than 2.7
million workers became unemployed on average each month. Thus, in considering unemployment, we must consider the nature of labor market flows.

The main flows into and out of the labor market are illustrated in figure
11.1, where the blocks contain stocks of vacancies and workers and the
arrowed lines represent corresponding flows.

At the base of figure 11.1, we depict the production apparatus of the
economy. Firms will wish to maintain a current stock of vacancies at a level
determined by the gap between the desired and the actual labor force, and by
the anticipated quits, retirements, and terminations that will occur during the
average lead time required for hiring and training new workers and for
recalling former employees. On the supply side, we see that workers flow into
the market as they leave the family, graduate from schools, quit previous
employment, and are laid off. They leave the market as new hires, recalls, or
they return to family or school. The stock of unemployed workers in the labor
market is thus regulated by the flow of quits (though we observe that some
workers will quit to take new jobs without ever becoming unemployed),
layoffs plus terminations, recalls, hires, and also the difference between
entries into the unemployed work force from households and the corresponding withdrawals.

Three points should be made concerning this simplified scheme. First,
unemployed persons and unfilled vacancies coexist—normally in large
numbers. Unemployment is not then a residual state resulting in a surplus
after all vacancies have been filled. Rather, it is more accurate to view
unemployment as a state through which most workers pass and not as a
description of certain kinds of people. It is true, however, that some categories of worker face more frequent and longer spells of unemployment than
others (section 11.6). Second, the flows through the market are not independent of one another. The system is said to exhibit negative feedback,
which occurs for example when a decrease in a stock leads to an increase in
one of the flows that determines the stock, thereby tending to restore the
stock to its initial level. For example, an increase in vacancies tends to

4. C. C. Holt, "Improving the Labor Market Trade-Off between Inflation and Unemployment,"
American Economic Review, Papers and Proceedings 59 (1969): 137.

Figure 11.1   Labor Market Flows and Stocks

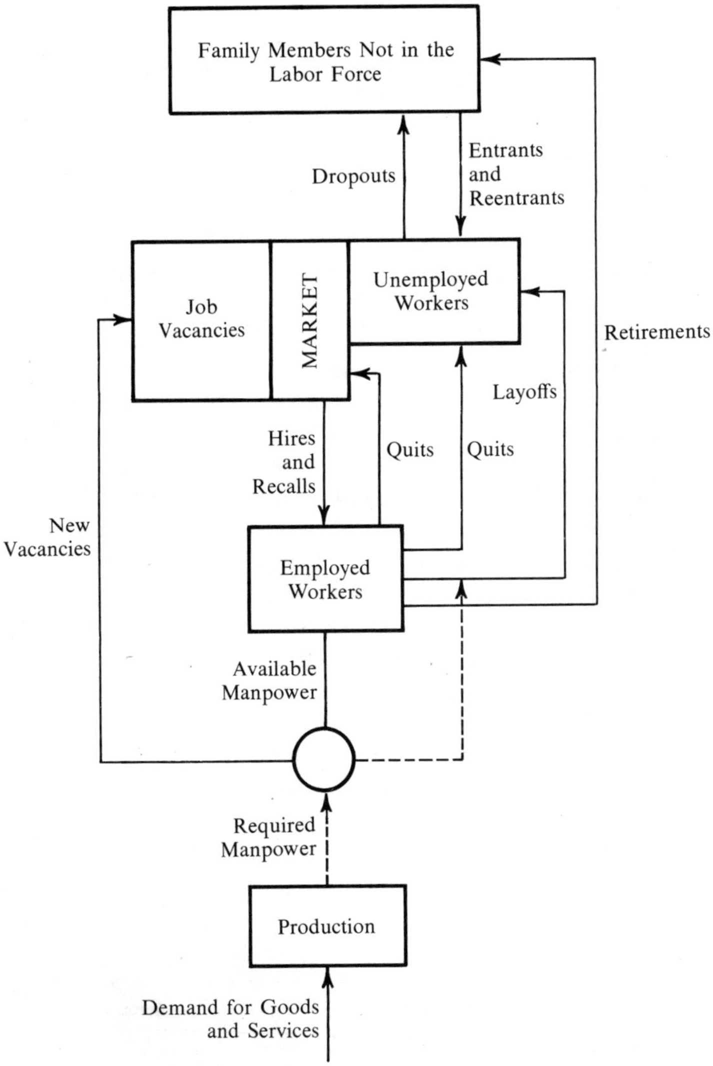

increase both the quit rate and the flow of new workers into the labor force. In this way, the unemployment pool is replenished. Third, turnover flows do not vary much over the cycle. The total turnover flow is the sum of quit and layoff flows. During the downswing, the layoff rate rises and the quit rate falls; during the upswing, the converse is the case. These opposing fluctuations in quits and involuntary separations roughly offset one another, so that the total flow through the market fluctuates by relatively small percentages over the cycle.

Alternatively, we may think of the flows through the labor market in the following Markovian way:

Labor Force Status in Previous Period	Current Labor Force Status		
	E_t	U_t	O_t
E_{t-1}	EE	EU	EO
U_{t-1}	UE	UU	UO
O_{t-1}	OE	OU	OO

where E, U, O respectively denote employed, unemployed, and out of the labor force.

The elements of this 3×3 matrix indicate the absolute number of workers moving from the designated state in the previous period to a given state in the current period. The probability of making such a transition is obtained by dividing the number of persons in the flow by the number of persons in the origin state. Thus, the probability that an unemployed worker will become employed is given by UE/U. The flow probabilities are often termed "flow rates" or "transition" rates, and they determine the relative number of persons in each labor market state.[5] Because the unemployment rate is the number of unemployed workers expressed as a fraction of the labor force, flow probabilities also determine the unemployment rate.[6]

11.3   The Classification of Unemployment

It has often been taken as useful to classify unemployment into two basic categories: unemployment that results from a deficiency in the aggregate effective demand for labor, and all other unemployment due to frictions and labor market adjustments. Each form of unemployment, thus described, can be said to possess its short- and long-run variants, giving the following four-way classification:

	Short Term	Long Term
Deficient demand	Cyclical unemployment	Growth-gap unemployment
Labor market (mal)adjustment	Frictional unemployment	Structural unemployment

The above classification omits seasonal and hard-core unemployment, which are sometimes grouped under structural and normal unemployment

5. Note we only require information on six of the nine flows. This is because the fraction of people remaining in any one state is equal to unity minus the fraction that leaves to enter the two other states. Thus, only two probabilities in each row are necessary.
6. See S. T. Marston, "Employment Instability and High Unemployment Rates," *Brookings Papers on Economic Activity* 1 (1976): 170–178.

rubrics, respectively. Seasonal unemployment is the more obvious category and occurs in such activities as construction and the tourist trade, in which weather or the calendar determine when production can be carried on or govern the level of demand. Seasonal unemployment is much less pronounced today than it was, say, thirty years ago because of the regularization of production and also because of the introduction of centralized hiring procedures in the casual trades. Unemployment statistics are usually provided on a seasonally adjusted basis, whereby unemployment is averaged or smoothed over the year. Hard-core unemployment is sometimes considered to be the long-term variant of normal unemployment—frictional unemployment being the short-term variant. Hard-core unemployment is said to arise because any society encompasses a number of workers who, because of their mental and physical condition, their attitude toward work, and their age, form an irreducible minimum value of unemployment. United Kingdom Department of Employment estimates as of 1964 put this unemployment at 0.8% of the labor force. The definition of such workers is, however, more elusive than it at first appears. First, the total does after all appear to be sensitive to the overall level of demand within the economy. Second, the characteristics of unemployables are not necessarily independent of the duration of unemployment, so that the term hard-core may include structural elements.

Returning to our four-way classification, however, we have seen in section 11.2 that unemployment and unfilled vacancies exist side by side, because it takes time to match jobs and men appropriately. The unemployment that is often said to accompany this matching process is termed *frictional unemployment* and is normally viewed as that amount of unemployment that corresponds to unfilled vacancies in the same occupation and the same place. Thus, frictional or search unemployment arises simply because it takes time and resources for workers to change jobs, either voluntarily or involuntarily, even though suitable job vacancies exist and can be found without the worker having to adjust his broad occupational status or his reservation wage.

More stubborn frictions are said to occur when the unemployed are mismatched with job vacancies because they do not possess the right skills or live in the right places—the result being *structural unemployment*. Finding jobs for the structurally unemployed requires more than search in local labor markets, for workers must be retrained or change location. Structural unemployment can, however, be said to result from a mismatching of demand and supply at the current level of wages. Theoretically, if relative wages adjusted to underlying shifts in demand, whether caused by shifts in product demand or changes in productive methods, then structural unemployment per se could largely disappear. Frictional and structural unemployment thus have a fine dividing line. The point at which a worker decides to lower his reservation wage, change his criterion of an acceptable job, or, for that matter, give up looking entirely can be said to vary across individuals depending upon financial resources and attitudes. The dividing line is often drawn at some arbitrarily selected unemployment duration interval, say 10 weeks.[7]

We might ask why the economic system fails to adjust sufficiently to eliminate structural unemployment. First, all adjustments, such as training and relocation, are costly and the changes must be considered permanent enough to justify incurring such expenses. Second, the psychological costs of adjustment may be a serious deterrent to a migration solution to the problem. Third, there are problems arising from the interdependence of supply and demand. For example, an adjustment involving the migration of labor from a declining area to an expanding one may further reduce the demand for labor in the declining region. Fourth, and most significant, certain wage rigidities may hinder or prevent adjustments of the wage structure from doing its part to bring about a reasonable equality between the amounts of labor supplied and demanded. A minimum wage, for example, may result in structural unemployment because the value of a worker's services is less than the wage the firm must pay him. Alternatively, the market clearing wage may not be acceptable to portions of the labor force, in which case there may be a shortage of acceptable jobs. The presence of unions may also serve to impart rigidity. These issues will be examined in more detail in sections 11.4 and 11.6.

Deficient demand unemployment is said to occur when there is not enough aggregate demand to provide work for the whole labor force no matter how it is trained or deployed. The assumption here is that the unemployed outnumber job vacancies at the current money wage rates demanded. The long-term variant of deficient demand unemployment involves growth theory, and a much simplified model is presented in appendix 11-A. The short-run variant of deficient demand unemployment, namely *cyclical unemployment,* is traditionally associated with the trade cycle. The question of why fluctuations in aggregate demand appear inevitably to cause similar fluctuations in labor demand without a decline in labor supplied has no simple answer. As we shall see in section 11.4, the answer depends on whether one follows a Keynesian or new microeconomic approach. The result is either to be associated with clear-cut money wage rigidity or a sluggish response of wage offers and reservation wages to unexpected changes in demand.

Attempts have been made to divide total unemployment (U) into its frictional (U_F), structural (U_S), and demand deficient (U_{DD}) components.[8]

7. See, for example, A. Rees "The Meaning and Measurement of Full Employment," in *The Measurement and Behavior of Unemployment* (Princeton, N.J.: Princeton University Press, 1957), p. 27.
8. J. C. R. Dow and L. A. Dicks-Mireaux, "The Excess Demand for Labor: A Study of Conditions in Great Britain, 1945–56," *Oxford Economic Papers* 10 (1958): 1–33; R. Perlman, *Labor Theory* (New York: Wiley, 1969), chap. 8.

The starting point is a simple definition of excess supply. The total supply of labor (S_L) is given by the sum of those employed (E) and those seeking work, the unemployed (U). The total demand for labor (D_L) is equal to employment (E) plus unfilled vacancies (V). Thus, excess supply can be written as

$$S_L - D_L = (E + U) - (E + V) = U - V, \qquad (11.1)$$

which is equivalent to demand deficient unemployment, U_{DD}. Because U_{DD} cannot meaningfully be negative when there is excess demand for labor, all unemployment, as seasonally adjusted, is either frictional or structural:

$$U_{DD} = S_L - D_L = U - V \geqslant 0$$
$$U_{DD} = 0 \text{ for } U - V \leqslant 0.$$

Because by assumption $U = U_{DD} + U_S + U_F$, it follows that

$$U = U_S + U_F \text{ when } U - V \leqslant 0.$$

Unemployment is frictional when there are vacancies for the unemployed to fill (V_R), and structural if the vacancies are not suitable (V_W). Thus,

$$U_F = V - V_W = V_R$$
$$U_S = V - V_R = V_W.$$

How then do we measure frictional and structural unemployment when $U > V$? Vacancies of the right type consist of the total sum of vacancies in occupations where unemployment in an occupation exceeds vacancies plus the total sum of unemployment in occupations where unemployment in an occupation is less than the level of vacancies.[9] Thus,

$$U_F = V_R = \sum_{i=1}^{n} V_i + \sum_{i=n+1}^{T} U_i \qquad (11.2)$$

where n is the number of occupations for which $U_i > V_i$;
   $T - n$ is the number of occupations for which $V_i > U_i$; and
      T is the total number of occupations.

Vacancies of the wrong type consist of the excess of vacancies over unemployment in occupations where $V_i > U_i$ at a time when, in other parts of the labor market, $U_i > V_i$. That is to say, unemployment is structural if the unemployed in occupations where $U_i > V_i$ do not have the characteristics of

9. This relationship depends on the assumption that all workers attached to a particular occupation i are qualified to fill the vacancies within i.

the labor in occupations where $V_i > U_i$.[10] The absolute size of structural unemployment will depend upon the size of the gap between vacancies and unemployment in shortage occupations. Thus,

$$U_S = V_W = \sum_{i=n+1}^{T} (V_i - U_i).$$

When aggregate vacancies exceed aggregate unemployment, there is no deficient demand, or cyclical, unemployment and all unemployment is by definition either frictional or structural:

$$U = U_F + U_S.$$

Frictional unemployment is measured as before, namely

$$U_F = \sum_{i=1}^{n} V_i + \sum_{i=n+1}^{T} U_i. \qquad (11.3)$$

Clearly, all unemployment, other than the excess of unemployment over vacancies in the occupations where $U_i > V_i$, is accounted for in equation (11.3), and so structural employment is given by

$$U_S = \sum_{i=1}^{n} (U_i - V_i). \qquad (11.4)$$

Typically, structural unemployment is first isolated and frictional unemployment is obtained as a residual. When $U > V$, structural unemployment is measured as $\Sigma(V_i - U_i)$ in occupations where $V_i > U_i$. Frictional unemployment is then total vacancies minus structural unemployment. When $V > U$, structural unemployment is measured as $\Sigma(U_i - V_i)$ in occupations where $U_i > V_i$. Frictional unemployment is now $U_F = U - U_S$.

Apart from difficulties attaching to vacancy statistics,[11] there are a number of problems with this analysis. It is based on the supposition that vacancies in

10. If $U_i > V_i$ for occupation i, then all the vacancies are matched by frictionally unemployed workers, and the excess of unemployed to vacancies measures the contribution of the occupation to overall cyclical and structural unemployment. If the excess is to contribute to structural unemployment, there must be occupations for which $V_i > U_i$. Thus, for an occupation to contribute to structural unemployment, the number of vacancies must exceed the volume of unemployed workers attached to the job.

11. Such data are available only quite recently for Great Britain and to all intents and purposes not at all for the United States. In the former country, because the reporting of vacancies is not compulsory and because agencies other than the public placement agencies are used by firms hiring labor, reported and true vacancy data may diverge. Accordingly, for the United Kingdom, we have at best an ordinal index giving rough orders of magnitudes of changes in the level of vacancies rather than an accurate cardinal indicator.

sectors where $V_i > U_i$ cannot be converted into vacancies in sectors where $U_i > V_i$. Given a sufficiently large wage differential, employers will have an incentive to substitute, say, unskilled labor for skilled workers, or to reduce the differential by training. Moreover, it can still be argued that unemployment can be increased and given structural undertones because of wage and price rigidities. Thus, unrealistic wage increases negotiated for lowly skilled workers because of minimum-wage legislation may cause additional unemployment of precisely this type, whereas this analysis argues that increased structural imbalance cannot of itself cause structural unemployment.

Furthermore, the sensitivity of the measures should be apparent. The logic of a situation in which $U > V$ and where there are not occupations for which $V_i > U_i$ is that an expansion in aggregate demand is called for. Yet in the extreme, if demand is increased and extra jobs become available only in those occupations for which $V_i = U_i$, then overall unemployment will remain unchanged and demand deficient unemployment will be converted into structural unemployment.

In this light, are there alternative routes of classifying unemployment by component? The approach traditionally used within the United States has been to classify unemployment according to the possible means of reducing it, assuming certain constraints on action. Let us assume that there is a general consensus that a 5% annual rate of price inflation is just tolerable. Given this constraint, deficient demand unemployment emerges as the difference between the actual amount of unemployment and that associated with price increases of 5%. This is shown diagramatically in figure 11.2, where, given the actual empirical association between the percentage rate of unemployment and the rate of inflation, as represented by the PP' curve or Phillips curve (chapter 12), the share of demand deficient unemployment in

Figure 11.2   Unemployment Classification by Cure

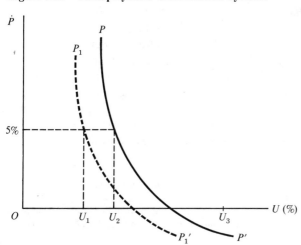

a total unemployment rate of OU_3 is $OU_3 - OU_2$. This amount of unemployment could be removed without unacceptable policy conflicts.

Within this framework, structural unemployment is a residual after the amount of demand deficient unemployment has been determined. Not surprisingly, structural unemployment has been defined in several ways. Some have chosen to regard it as all unemployment that cannot be eliminated by expanding demand without violating the price constraint—that is, OU_2. It is in this sense that writers have tended to use the terms "structural" and "frictional" synonymously; but the term "frictional" is borrowed from the causal classification of unemployment, because in a cure classification, frictional unemployment must clearly be part of what is defined as structural. Others have considered structural unemployment to be less than OU_2. Bergman and Kaun define it as "that amount of unemployment less minimum frictional and seasonal which cannot be removed by monetary and fiscal policy without creating substantial continuing inflation"[12] (or violating a specified price constraint). Alternatively, we might envision structural unemployment as that which can be removed through labor market policies that permit the economy to operate at a low level of unemployment without violating the price constraint. Thus, if such policies were to displace the PP' curve of figure 11.2 to $P_1 P_1'$, unemployment measured by $OU_2 - OU_1$ could be regarded as structural and presumably unemployment represented by OU_1 as frictional.

But perhaps the best known ex-post definition of structural unemployment is that of Lipsey. He terms it as that which can be removed by structural measures, such as retraining, "some of which pay for themselves on an analysis of the money costs and money benefits and some of which are justified because the nonpecuniary social benefits are judged to justify the net cost of the scheme."[13] For Lipsey, the residual item of frictional unemployment is to be equated with the full employment level of unemployment. Lipsey used a preference curve in his analysis as a substitute for the absolute price constraint we have used in figure 11.2. The amount of structural unemployment then depends on a new point of tangency between the PP' curve, shifted to the left by a specified amount after a benefit-cost appraisal of structural cures, and the policymaker's concave preference curve between the discommodities of inflation and unemployment (chapter 12). However, we should note that Lipsey's approach is not easily testable because rightward shifts of the PP' curve, a necessary condition for a rise in structural unemployment in his model, can arise from a variety of causes. Increased union power, for example, could displace the curve outward.

12. B. R. Bergman, and D. E. Kaun, *Structural Unemployment in the United States* (Washington, D.C.: The Brookings Institution, 1966), p. 1.
13. R. G. Lipsey, "Structural and Demand-Deficient Unemployment Reconsidered," in A. M. Ross, ed., *Employment Policy and the Labor Market* (Berkeley and Los Angeles: University of California Press, 1965), p. 214.

To be useful, a classification of unemployment needs to satisfy two main conditions. First, it should lend itself to measurement. Second, it should be based on clearly defined, objective criteria to avoid arbitrariness and inconsistency in the process of measurement. Neither of the above bases of classification performs well in these respects.

11.4 Unemployment Theory

The Classical Analysis. To the classical economists, the equilibrium real wage was determined by the interaction of labor demand and supply. The classical labor demand function, in terms of real wages in accordance with marginal productivity theory, is simply the downward-sloping marginal physical productivity schedule (chapter 2). The intersection of this demand schedule and the forward rising labor supply function—in real wage-employment space—determines the equilibrium level of employment and the associated real wage. In figure 11.3, for example, OL^* is the equilibrium or full employment level of employment at the equilibrium real wage OW^*. OL^* is the full employment level of employment, because if it were possible to increase employment beyond this level the real wage would have to fall to, say, OW_o and at this real wage, L_oL^* less labor would willingly be supplied. There would develop excess demand in the labor market, which would raise money wages, commodity prices remaining constant, until the real wage had risen to the original equilibrium, OW^*. Conversely, if there were an excess

Figure 11.3 The Classical Labor Market

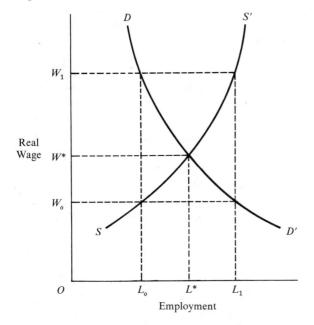

supply of labor, say L_oL_1, implying a real wage greater than the equilibrium value, namely OW_1, then this excess supply would lead to cuts in money wages. These would culminate in a restoration of OW^*. Thus, on this classical view, there can be no involuntary unemployment—in the sense of workers being willing but unable to find work for a real wage below the current level—except of the transitional form while money wages are being cut (in the excess supply case) to restore the full employment equilibrium real wage. Any unemployment existing at OW^* must therefore be voluntary in form.

The Keynesian Approach. Keynes countered this classical view by arguing in part that money wages were sticky downward and that, even if they did fall, this would not necessarily produce a cut in real wages.[14] In this view, if aggregate demand fell proportionately with any decline in money wages, real wages would be unchanged and the effect could be wholly neutral on employment. Moreover, a decline in money wages could result in an expectation of further declines in wages and prices, which would serve to aggravate the unemployment situation.

Let us take the money wage rigidity issue first. While holding that money wages were downwardly rigid, Keynes argued that workers are in fact willing to accept a decline in real wages brought about by a rise in prices relative to wages. Money illusion is probably not the issue here, and the phenomenon may plausibly be explained in terms of supply functions that display a high degree of interdependence.[15] Real wage declines engineered by an increase in prices relative to wages will not disturb relativities (chapter 7) and will not give rise to "political" problems, because price increases affect all groups equally. However, money wage cuts accepted by one particular group in the decentralized wage bargaining process will probably not be followed by similar wage cuts for other groups; hence, they will be resisted.

This analysis implies that unemployment can be permanently cured, and is therefore involuntary, by forcing up prices sufficiently, through monetary and fiscal action, to reduce the real wage to the equilibrium level. In terms of figure 11.3, if money wages are inflexible downward at the real wage OW_1, the only way to raise the level of employment from OL_o to OL^* is via a price increase. The implication arising from Keynes' denial of the classical position is that whenever an increase in effective demand is successful in reducing unemployment, the unemployment must have been involuntary. This is clearly the spirit of Keynes' observation that, "More labor would, as a rule, be forthcoming at the existing money wage if it were demanded."[16] But Keynes' formal definition of involuntary unemployment ran as follows:

14. J. M. Keynes, *The General Theory of Employment, Interest and Money* (New York: Harcourt-Brace, 1936), chap. 19.
15. See J. A. Trevithick, "Money Wage Inflexibility and the Keynesian Supply Function," *Economic Journal* 86 (1976): 327–332.
16. Keynes, *General Theory*, p. 7.

Men are involuntary unemployed if, in the event of a small rise in prices of wage goods relative to the money wage, both the aggregate supply of labor willing to work for the current money wage and the aggregate demand for it at that wage would be greater than the existing volume of employment.[17]

This definition, which many would consider to be unnecessarily convoluted,[18] can be explained by reference to figure 11.3. Consider real wage OW_1, corresponding to which there is a certain rigid money wage. Now assume an increase in the price level such that the real wage falls to a position between OW_1 and OW^*. Clearly the demand for labor at the fixed money wage, but reduced real wage, will exceed the existing volume of employment, OL_0. Assuming, as did Keynes, that the supply curve again conforms to SS', we observe that the supply of labor will also exceed OL_0. Note that we do not argue that the supply of labor will *increase* when real wages fall, merely that the supply of labor in the real wage range $OW^* - OW_1$ will exceed OL_0.

For Keynes, the level of employment and the real wage were jointly determined by the level of aggregate demand. Money wage cuts need not necessarily confer beneficial effects on employment; in such cases, wage OW_1 and employment level OL_0 could be equilibrium values despite the excess supply of labor. Employment could be increased by expanding aggregate demand. But the latter will require that more workers be employed at a real wage lower than OW_1 because of the downward drift along the marginal product schedule. In a sense, then, the distinction between voluntary and involuntary unemployment is an unreal one until aggregate demand is raised. If the situation described by points OL_0 and OW_1 is an equilibrium one, the fact that some workers refuse to offer their services below real wage OW_1 is purely academic, because wage reductions of themselves are not the key. The distinction becomes appropriate only when a move has been made to raise aggregate demand. If workers refuse to accept the decline in real wages, then the potential increase in aggregate demand will be thwarted and unemployment of $L_0 L_1$ will be both permanent and voluntary.

The notion of underemployment equilibrium is perhaps best considered with the aid of figure 11.4, which demonstrates the main elements of the Keynesian system. In figure 11.4, the demand for and supply of labor appear as a function of the effective demand for goods. Looking at panel (i), when aggregate demand is D_0 $(= C + I)$, the equilibrium level of output is y_0. Output y_0 requires, as is indicated by reading from the short-run production function $y(n)$, a labor input of n_0. This combination is plotted as point b in the fourth quadrant of panel (i). Other points may be derived in similar fashion to construct a curve, DD', relating effective demand and the demand

---

17. Ibid., p. 15.
18. See, for example, R. Kahn, "Unemployment as seen by the Keynesians," in G. D. M. Worswick, ed., *The Concept and Measurement of Involuntary Unemployment* (London: Allen and Unwin, 1976), p. 21.

Figure 11.4   The Keynesian Model: Labor Demand and Supply as a Function of Aggregate Demand

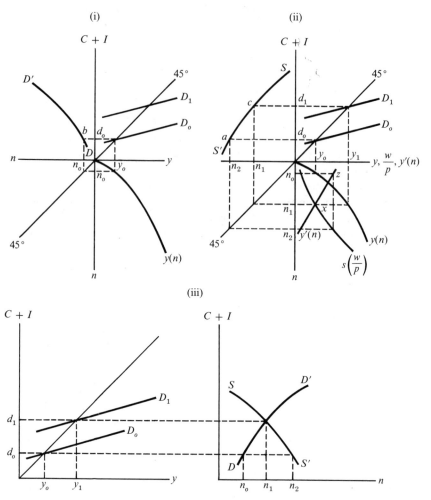

for labor. Thus, *DD'* tells us what the demand for labor will be at different levels of aggregate demand for goods.

In panel (ii), we relate the supply of labor to the level of effective demand. Before proceeding with the construction of this particular supply curve, we must introduce two new functions and an extension of axis. Dealing with the latter first, note that the horizontal axis of the first quadrant of panel (ii) now measures real output, y, real wage, w/p, and marginal physical product, $y'(n)$. All three variables are measured along the same axis, using different units. Corresponding to this, we introduce two new functions in the second quadrant. First, a traditional labor supply function is shown as $s(w/p)$, relating the amount of labor supplied to the real wage. Second, the function $y'(n)$ is the first derivative of the short-run production function with respect to labor, it being assumed that $\partial y/\partial n > 0$, $\partial^2 y/\partial n^2 < 0$. Having defined these two schedules, we may proceed. Let us begin with the aggregate demand function, D_0, which gives an equilibrium output level of y_0. To produce an output of y_0, n_0 units of labor are required. With employment at n_0, the associated marginal physical product of labor is $n_0 z$. Assuming producers to be in competitive equilibrium, the real wage will be equated with the marginal physical product of labor. Thus, when effective demand is at d_0, the amount of labor willingly supplied will be n_2 at a real wage of $n_0 z$. This particular combination of effective demand and the supply of labor is shown as point a in the fourth quadrant of panel (ii). Other points, such as c, may be derived in similar fashion to construct the curve SS', which shows the amount of labor willingly supplied at each level of effective demand.

Panel (iii) of figure 11.4 combines schedules DD' and SS'. Demand for labor varies directly and supply of labor negatively with effective demand. SS' is inversely related to effective demand because an increase in the latter leads to a decline in the marginal physical product of labor, which must equal the real wage if producers are to be in equilibrium. Consequently, because the equilibrium real wage rate falls, so does the amount of labor supplied.

Inadequate effective demand can now be shown to result in involuntary unemployment. Given our aggregate demand function, D_0, effective demand is d_0. When real output is at y_0, we have equilibrium in the goods market but not in the labor market, where there is involuntary unemployment equaling $n_0 n_2$. Only at the equilibrium real output level of y_1, as shown in panel (ii), is the labor market also in equilibrium. That is, only at n_1 employment is there no involuntary unemployment. We may thus term n_1 as the full employment level of employment. The limiting volume of Keynesian involuntary unemployment at effective demand level d_0 is $n_0 n_2$, because a slightly smaller excess supply of labor would exist given the smallest decline in real wages. The volume of involuntary unemployment shrinks with the fall in the real wage, implied by a growth of effective demand, until it is eliminated at d_1. Again, note that in the current sense, with effective demand d_0, all $n_0 n_2$ units of labor may be considered to be involuntarily unemployed because aggregate demand has not risen to require real wages to fall to $n_1 x$ to attain full employment.

Corresponding to his view that real wages must fall when aggregate demand increases, which is why the supply of labor falls as D increases, as shown in figure 11.4, Keynes speculated that the data would show real wages fell when money wages rose with output and employment.[19] Yet Keynes' prediction that the real wage will vary countercyclically has been shown to be

19. Keynes, *General Theory*, p. 10.

false.[20] The real wage does not appear to fall, or fall relative to trend, during the cyclical upturn. Nor, for that matter, does the real wage seem to have any other pronounced pattern in the course of short-run economic fluctuations.[21]

However, the countercyclical behavior of the real wage is not essential to the Keynesian model. For example, let us assume that there are constant marginal returns to labor. In this case, the production function $y(n)$ will be linear and $y'(n)$ a constant. It follows that the supply curve of labor will be invariant with respect to the effective demand for goods, because marginal product and the real wage do not change. Thus, SS' is vertical while DD' maintains a given positive slope, and we may still observe Keynesian underemployment equilibrium.

Damaging to the Keynesian argument against money wage cuts, however, is the possibility that reductions in money wages and prices will indirectly generate an increase in real spending, output, and employment. How might this come about? According to Keynes' own analysis, the very process of deflation may produce a new set of relationships favorable to employment. Wage cuts will cause money incomes to fall, and falling incomes will reduce money sales volume and hence the transactions demand for money. Because more money would be available for the speculative motive, we would move down the liquidity preference schedule and the rate of interest would tend to fall. A lower rate of interest could be favorable to investment. But it will be remembered that the resulting increase in output will be subject to the limiting influence of the Keynesian liquidity trap and also to a likely interest-inelastic investment demand schedule during depressions. In the extreme Keynesian model, the demand for money is highly interest-elastic and aggregate demand is unresponsive to interest rates.

Modern macroeconomic models, such as the MIT-Pennsylvania-Social Science Research Council (MPS) model, permit investigation of these issues.[22] Hall, for example, has claimed that the MPS model constitutes an empirical refutation of Keynes' recommendation against wage cuts as a cure for depression.[23] The evidence Hall refers to is a simulation in the MPS model of the effects of a change in money supply and not the wage per se. However, the homogeneity of the model makes an increase in the money supply

20. J. T. Dunlop, "Movement of Real and Money Wage Rates," *Economic Journal* 48 (1938): 413–434; L. Tarshis, "Changes in Real and Money Wages," *Economic Journal* 49 (1939): 150–154; E. Kuh, "Unemployment, Production Functions, and Effective Demand," *Journal of Political Economy* 74 (1966): 238–249.

21. See, for example, R. M. Solow and J. E. Stiglitz, "Output, Employment and Wages in the Short Run," *Quarterly Journal of Economics* 82 (1968): 537–560.

22. See "Equations in the MIT-Penn-SSRC Econometric Model of the United States," mimeographed (Boston, Mass.: Department of Economics, Massachusetts Institute of Technology, 1975).

23. R. E. Hall, "The Rigidity of Wages and the Persistence of Unemployment," *Brookings Paper on Economic Activity* 2 (1975): 307–310.

equivalent to a reduction in wages and prices, so that a 1% increase in the money supply will have the same effect on output as a 1% reduction in all wages and prices, under the assumption that the wage and price cut does not feed back through the expectations equations of the model. Hall notes that a one-time reduction of 1% in all prices and wages, money stock held constant, raises gross national product by about 0.1% after a full year and achieves its peak of approximately a 1.5%·increase after two years. Hall thus concludes that money wage reductions would quickly stimulate employment because of their sharp effect on interest rates. But Hall ignores the effect of wage cuts on expectations. Wage reductions might create political and social unrest, thereby causing unfavorable business expectations. In response to the latter, one might expect to observe a downward shift of the investment-demand schedule and an upward shift of the liquidity preference schedule. There is also the possibility of a deleterious effect on investment of a greater burden of debt, both private and public. Sims has contended that Hall's evidence cannot be taken seriously, mainly for the reason that the MPS model was fitted to a period when money wages were not flexible.[24] Had they been, the coefficients might have been quite different because the expectations equations of the model would surely have changed substantially. For this reason, the increase in money supply is perhaps best regarded as not equivalent to a reduction in wages and prices.

A second attack on the Keynesian position rests on the Pigou "real balance" effect, which Keynes overlooked in his analysis of possible effects of wage reductions on employment. The argument here is that wage cuts will indirectly cause an upward shift in the consumption function and thus increase output and employment.[25] Wage cuts, by reducing incomes, will raise the value of liquid assets in relation to income. An increase in the real value of accumulated savings will raise consumption in relation to any given level of income. Thus, having gone through a process of deflation, an improved ratio is reached between liquid assets and income that is favorable to employment. If a rising real value of wealth stimulates consumption, there is always some decline in prices that will be adequate to stimulate consumption sufficiently to eliminate any deficiency of aggregate demand. Theoretically, then, flexible prices are an almost infallible cure for deficient aggregate demand.[26] But in practice, we have to question the precise magnitude of the required decline in prices, the time dimension of change, and, implicitly, the effect on the general health of society.

---

24. C. Sims, "Comments and Discussion," ibid., p. 337.
25. A. C. Pigou, "The Classical Stationary State," *Economic Journal* 53 (1943): 343–351. See also G. Ackley, *Macroeconomic Theory* (New York: Macmillan, 1961), pp. 269–273.
26. We say "almost" because of the complications introduced by the notion of the elasticity of price expectations. See D. Patinkin, *Money, Interest and Prices,* 2nd ed. (New York, Evanston, and London: Harper and Row, 1965).

The Monetarist and New Microeconomic Approach.   The analyses of Friedman and Phelps[27] have challenged the Keynesian position that unemployment is involuntary whenever it can be reduced by raising aggregate demand. They argue that there is a *natural rate* of unemployment due to frictional and structural forces. This natural rate is supposed not be reducible in the long run by raising aggregate demand without an accelerating increase in the price level. In this view, the reduction in unemployment below the natural rate achieved by an expansion of demand is purely a temporary phenomenon based on faulty expectations, because it is not sustainable in the long run when workers adjust their expectations in the light of experience (chapter 12). In such a situation, there are three types of nonemployment. The first arises from the labor-leisure choice of households, the second from job search, and the third from labor market imperfections.

The basic elements of this model are given in figure 11.5. In panel (i), we reproduce the demand and supply curves of the classical model. In panel (ii), these curves have been multiplied by the initial price level (P_1). Let us now trace out the short-run effects of an increase in aggregate demand. Prices will rise to, say, P_3 and the increased demand for labor induces a rise in money wages from W_1 to W_2 and in employment from n_1 to n_2. At this stage, then, workers have not realized that prices have risen and, accordingly, supply advances along $SS' \times P_1$. But, in the longer term, the increase in consumer prices will be fully reflected in the supply curve, which, as we see from panel (iii), will shift inward to $SS' \times P_3$. The effect of this shift will be to put further pressure on the money wage level, causing it to rise to W_3. Thus, the upward shift in the demand schedule is offset by an equal upward displacement of the supply curve, with the end result that the real wage and the level of employment remain unchanged.

27. M. Friedman, "The Role of Monetary Policy," *American Economic Review* 58 (1968): 1–17; E. S. Phelps, "Money Wage Dynamics and Labor Market Equilibrium," *Journal of Political Economy* 76 (1968): 678–711.

Figure 11.5   The Supply of Labor and Short-Run Money Illusion

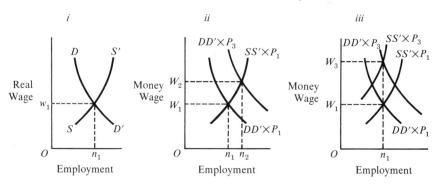

In this model, the equilibrium rate of inflation is said to be determined by the rate of growth of the money supply, but the natural rate of unemployment is determined by real factors independently of the equilibrium rate of inflation. To quote Friedman:

At any moment of time, there is some level of unemployment which has the property that it is consistent with equilibrium in the structure of real wage rates. . . . The "natural rate of employment," in other words, is the level that would be ground out by the Walrasian system of general equilibrium equations, provided there is imbedded in them the actual structural characteristics of labor and commodity markets, including market imperfections, stochastic variability in demands and supplies, the cost of gathering information about job vacancies and labor availabilities, the costs of mobility, and so on.[28]

In what circumstances will unemployment differ from its natural rate? The answer to this question involves the process of job search and forecasting errors arising from divergencies between actual and anticipated price changes. In chapter 5, we assumed that the unemployed worker knew the probability density function of wage offers (appendix 5-A). Assume now that the individual worker has full knowledge of the relevant real wage offer distribution, but not of the nominal wage rates corresponding to appropriate real wages. If the worker predicts correctly, he will invest the optimal amount of time in search unemployment. However, if his estimate of the nominal wage rate is too high, he will set his reservation wage too high and will invest too much time in search unemployment. The average duration of unemployment will lengthen and the probability of accepting a job offer will be reduced. Alternatively, when his estimate of the nominal wage rate is too low, he will set his reservation wage below the optimal level and therefore invest a suboptimal amount of time in search unemployment. In this case, the average duration of unemployment will be too short.

Aggregating across individuals, any unanticipated increase in the rate of inflation, and hence wage offers, will produce a reduction in the average duration of employment. Yet this reduction in duration, and in the unemployment rate, too, if the flow of workers into unemployment pool is constant, does not imply an improvement in economic welfare. In the long run, labor can only increase its real wages by increasing its marginal productivity. One important source of productivity improvement arises from the purposive mobility of labor from low-wage (low marginal product) to high-wage (high marginal product) sectors. In situations where the actual mean of wage offers exceeds its expected value, that is, in periods of unanticipated inflation, workers will underinvest in their search for job offers. The additional employment and production thereby created will be worth less than the job-seeking time displaced.

28. Friedman, "Monetary Policy," p. 8.

Thus, forecasting errors in estimating the mean of the distribution of nominal wage offers are supposed to cause fluctuations in the average duration of unemployment. Whenever the expected mean of nominal wage offers is greater than the actual mean, workers will set their reservation wage rates too high and the average duration of unemployment will be too long. Alternatively, when the expected mean of job offers is less than the actual mean, the reverse will be true.[29]

In addition to search unemployment, there are two other forms of informational unemployment noted in the new microeconomics approach—*speculative* and *precautionary* unemployment. These additional types, together with search unemployment proper, are termed by Phelps to be frictional in nature; as such, they would presumably include structural unemployment in the language of section 11.3.[30] Speculative unemployment, more accurately called speculative underemployment, refers to the withholding by the family unit of a full-time or part-time worker from paid employment on the speculation that money wage rates currently available are temporarily depressed in terms of their prospective over-life purchasing power. Assume, from an initial position of equilibrium, a decline in aggregate demand that causes a decline in the market clearing levels of the various money wage rates. The new, unaccustomed wage rates will probably be regarded as abnormal and temporary. Accordingly, many families may respond by reducing the number of hours offered; this outcome may be no more than a change in the timing of an unaltered number of man-hours that the family plans to supply over its lifetime.

Precautionary or wait unemployment hinges on the necessity of some workers choosing between taking a job at the present time and getting a different job in the near future. It characterizes those individuals who face a stochastically fluctuating demand for their services. Thus an individual, say a house painter, who finds his services not in demand at his normal wage may indeed choose to reduce his wage so as to hasten the expected arrival of the next job offer. But by so doing, he increases the risk that he will have to reject an offer of employment at his normal wage during the course of that new job. This form of unemployment is again dependent upon the level of aggregate demand. A decline in demand reduces the frequency of demands for the services of the workers in question at their previous fees—or, equivalently, a reduction in clients' offering prices. Perfect knowledge would lead such workers to set a new fee structure that would enable them to obtain the desired frequency of employment over time. More realistically, they may be expected to mistake the systematic decline in the demand for their services for a transient disturbance and maintain their existing fee structure. In this

29. This argument was first proposed by A. A. Alchian, "Information Costs, Pricing, and Resource Unemployment," in E. S. Phelps et al., *Microeconomic Foundations of Employment and Inflation Theory* (New York: Norton, 1970), pp. 27–52. For a more formal statement, see D. T. Mortensen, "A Theory of Wage and Unemployment Dynamics," ibid., pp. 167–211.
30. E. S. Phelps, *Inflation Policy and Unemployment Theory* (New York: Norton, 1972), chap. 1.

situation, the typical worker is in disequilibrium in the sense that he has incorrectly predicted the mean demands for his services.[31] We may similarly describe a position of disequilibrium overemployment. In both cases, as they accumulate experience of a systematic change in the frequency of demands, workers will gradually revise, as appropriate, their estimate of the mean of the probability of demands and will adjust their fee structures.

Search theory has come under sustained attack from dual labor market theorists, who have argued that most of the observed search by unemployed workers within the United States is concentrated in the secondary labor market, which is made up of disadvantaged groups (chapter 5). Search by the unemployed in such markets is said to be the unproductive consequence of dissatisfaction rather than a rational quest for self-improvement. We shall examine this contention in section 11.6.

The modern theory of unemployment has also been attacked for its alleged failure to explain the persistence of unemployment at levels either above or below the equilibrium or natural rate value. Yet it must be said that search theory does contain an explanation for unemployment persistence in terms of delays in the flow of information. Unfortunately, the delay is not generated endogenously by the model and its length is a matter of judgment. Accordingly, it is difficult to test just how much of the observed variance in unemployment can be attributed to inflationary/deflationary surprises.

More recently, the search literature has been criticized on the grounds that the models in question strain reality by forcing all entry to unemployment through the mold of voluntary quit decisions with no explanation for the real world phenomena of firings and layoffs. This criticism has found expression in the form of the "new-new" microeconomics, which shifts the focus of attention from model building exercises in which output and employment changes are caused by price surprises to those that attempt to explain wage and price contracts, and hence sluggish price adjustments, as the result of microeconomic optimizing behavior.[32] Suffice it to say here that the new-new microeconomics supplements rather than supplants search theory by incorporating the real life features of job rationing and what we might term as everyday involuntary unemployment. Basically, the idea is that certain sectors of the labor market respond to uncertainty—stochastically fluctuating demands and supplies—with the devices of job rationing and quasi-contracts, the latter being defined as unwritten job tenure rules which promise tenured workers a pecuniary premium over the labor services supplied by temporary workers. As a result, the onset of a deficiency in aggregate demand tends, at least temporarily, to produce a recession with decreased employment. But there is no underemployment equilibrium in the Keynesian

31. See D. F. Gordon and A. Hynes, "On the Theory of Price Dynamics," in Phelps et al., *Microeconomic Foundations,* pp. 369–393.
32. For a useful and mercifully brief summary of the new-new microeconomics, see R. J. Gordon, "Recent Developments in the Theory of Inflation and Unemployment," *Journal of Monetary Economics* 2 (1976): 205–210.

sense, because the market responds to changing conditions via a revision of quasi-contracts. The interesting question raised by the new-new microeconomics is, rather, whether job rationing and quasi-contracts stimulate an excess of search unemployment in stochastic general equilibrium.

11.5   Estimating Unemployment, Hidden Unemployment, and Hoarded Labor

Unemployment can be measured in a variety of ways. Unemployment ". . . may describe a 'condition'—that of not being at work; an 'activity'— that of seeking work; an 'attitude'—that of desiring a job under certain conditions; and a 'need'—that of needing a job."[33] The first is the least interesting, because it makes unemployment and employment exclusive categories, so that participation rates are always 100%. The notion of need has ambiguities—for example, can those incapable of work need a job?—and is probably more appropriate for studies of poverty rather than labor supply. The choice, then, is that between unemployment as an activity and unemployment as an attitude. In fact, the desire for a job can only be measured for a specific vector of prices of labor. In determining attitudes toward work, for example, by household survey, the vector of prices is never specified, so that a count of those volunteering information that they desire work cannot constitute a measure of the supply of labor. Hence, activity measures of unemployment are usually preferred.

Early attempts to measure unemployment in the United States involved asking a representative group of individuals whether they were working and, if not, whether they thought they were unemployed. Doubts about this procedure led to the use of a more behavioral definition. The Gordon Committee laid down as its first general rule that "each concept should correspond to objectively measurable phenomena and should depend as little as possible on personal opinion or subjective attitudes."[34] The objectively measurable phenomenon underlying the measure of unemployment currently in use in the United States is specific job-seeking activity within the past four weeks. An attempt is also made to identify discouraged workers—those who want work but have stopped looking for work because of a belief that their search would be in vain. Although such workers are not included in the unemployment count, we see here evidence of an attitude approach.

There has long been criticism of official unemployment statistics, much of which focuses on the allegation that they distort the extent of involuntary unemployment by including in the unemployment count those who only have a tenuous attachment to the labor market and who are only vaguely

33. L. Levine, "Unemployment by Locality and Industry," in National Bureau of Economic Research, *The Measurement and Behavior of Unemployment* (Princeton, N.J.: Princeton University Press, 1957), p. 323.

34. President's Committee to Appraise Employment and Unemployment Statistics, *Measuring Employment and Unemployment* (Washington, D.C.: U.S. Government Printing Office, 1962) p. 43.

seeking work. As we have seen in section 11.4, the issue of involuntary unemployment is a highly contentious one. However, even accepting that the unemployment count may include many whom we would not consider as actively seeking employment, we might ask whether changes in the unemployment rate nevertheless provide a useful indicator of changes in welfare or changes in labor market slack. This involves consideration of the impact of unemployment insurance on the duration of search, the availability of potentially more sensitive indicators of the labor market slack, such as labor hoarding, and the role of hidden unemployment.

In both the United Kingdom and the United States, it has been claimed that legislative changes have led to increases in voluntary unemployment. Let us first consider the evidence for the United Kingdom. Here, Gujarati has interpreted the positive shift in unemployment against vacancies as purely artificial.[35] In his view, the Redundancy Payments Act (1965) and the National Insurance Act (1966), by lowering the costs of voluntary unemployment, generated a jump in registered unemployment. The former enactment required employers to make lump-sum compensation payments to employees dismissed on grounds of redundancy. The latter introduced earnings-related benefits and contributions, replacing the previous flat-rate system. If this interpretation is correct, it might be argued that all that is needed to obtain the true level of unemployment is an application of the pre-1966 relation between vacancies and unemployment to the post-1966 vacancy levels—the latter series thus remaining a better measure of the true level of demand pressure in the economy. Supporting this argument is the finding that an increase in unemployment benefit of £1 per week tended to increase the length of unemployment by almost one-half of a week.[36] On the assumption that earnings-related benefits added an average of £3 per week to flat-rate benefits, these results suggest that their introduction in 1966 could have increased the average duration of unemployment for redundant males by some 1.26 weeks (table 9.3).

Unemployment insurance provision was introduced in the United States in 1935. It pays benefits to between 40% and 60% of the unemployed—the proportion varies cyclically.[37] Most studies have examined the impact of unemployment insurance on unemployment duration. Because the amount and coverage of unemployment insurance benefits vary widely among states, interstate comparisons provide a natural testing ground.[38] Thus, Chapin, for

35. D. Gujarati, "The Behaviour of Unemployment and Unfilled Vacancies: Great Britain, 1958–1971," *Economic Journal* 82 (1972): 195–202.

36. D. I. Mackay and G. L. Reid, "Redundancy, Unemployment and Manpower Policy," *Economic Journal* 82 (1972): 1256–1272.

37. See P. Green, "Measuring Total and State Insured Unemployment," *Monthly Labor Review* 94 (1971): 37–48.

38. In most states, benefits are based on the worker's highest quarterly earnings, although some states have benefit schedules based on annual earnings and others use average weekly wages. Duration of benefits depends on previous earnings and length of time worked. Rules for determining eligibility also vary among states.

example, regresses the actual duration of unemployment claims, D, on the insured unemployment rate, U, the average benefit payment divided by the average wage of the insured unemployed on their last job, B/W, and the maximum duration of unemployment claims, M.[39] Also included in the analysis are the percentage of nonwhites in each state—nonwhites, being subject to discrimination, might face a lower expected alternative wage—N, the degree of urbanization—more urbanized areas might be less likely to apply welfare eligibility requirements with severity—Z, and regional dummies picking up variations in workers' tastes for leisure and the social stigma attached to receipt of unemployment benefits by region. Using pooled data over 1962–67, his results are as follows ($|t|$ are given in parentheses):

$$D = 0.268 + 0.861U + 0.046B/W + 0.116M + 0.006N$$
$$ (14.698) \quad (2.602) \qquad (4.169) \quad (2.129)$$

$$+ 0.015 + \text{dummies.} \qquad\qquad\qquad R^2 = 0.636$$
$$(2.456)$$

It can be seen that an increase in the level of benefits relative to wages of one percentage point is associated with an increase of about one-twentieth of a week in the average duration of benefits. Similarly, an increase in the maximum benefit period of one week leads to an increase in the average duration of benefits of one-tenth of a week. In terms of elasticities, increasing the level of benefits relative to wages by 10% appears to increase average unemployment duration by about 1.3%, which is the equivalent of one day. A recent study by Holen also finds a positive relation between compensation and duration.[40] Her estimate is that an increase of about \$12 in weekly benefit payments would lead to an increase of almost one week in unemployment duration. Holen's calculations controlled for the base-period wage, the number of quarters of previous earnings, which represent a measure of earnings stability, and a number of labor market variables, including city dummies and unemployment rates at the time the claim began. A difficulty with both studies, however, is that the dependent variable relates only to claimants and not to the aggregate unemployed, which would include those who are not insured. Nonetheless, the indications are that the more liberal unemployment benefits of recent years do explain some of the tendency toward higher unemployment rates.

Another approach is to compare the job-search activity of insured workers with that of the uninsured. On the face of it, we might attribute the difference between the average of 14.2 weeks of unemployment benefits drawn per

39. G. Chapin, "Unemployment Insurance, Job Search and the Demand for Leisure," *Western Economic Journal* 9 (1971): 102–107.

40. A. Holen, "Effects of Unemployment Insurance Entitlement on Duration and Job Search Outcome," *Industrial and Labor Relations Review* 30 (1977): 445–450. See also K. P. Classen, "The Effect of Unemployment Insurance on the Duration of Unemployment and Subsequent Earnings," *Industrial and Labor Relations Review* 30 (1977): 438–444.

beneficiary in fiscal 1971 and an average estimated unemployment duration of 8 weeks for the uninsured to the disincentive effects of unemployment insurance.[41] However, such a crude comparison could mask important demographic differences between the two groups. Holding age-sex characteristics constant, Marston has concluded that the average insured job seeker is likely to experience a spell of unemployment that is some 16% to 31% longer than that of his uninsured counterpart.[42] The lengthened duration is said to reflect the "less intensive efforts" and "more selective behavior" of those searching for jobs when they have the cushion of unemployment insurance. At the same time, Marston notes without quantification that duration might also tend to be extended because the insurance system requires beneficiaries to keep looking for work. Hence, insured workers might tend to stay in the labor force and thus in the pool of unemployed until they take another job, rather than dropping out of the labor force as discouraged job seekers.

It is important not to lose sight of the benefit of unemployment insurance to be associated with a better matching of workers and jobs—namely, a greater efficiency in the job search process. To the extent that we observe fewer square pegs in round holes, there should be clear production gains. Moreover, if unemployment insurance inhibits withdrawal from the labor market, there will be an increase in unemployment that is not associated with lost production. This increase in participation may eventuate in more output and thus be a positive factor. Again, it might be claimed that there are important social benefits resulting from labor mobility, which is inevitably associated with unemployment. Thus, unemployment insurance might be thought of as compensation to the unemployed for providing this service.[43] On the other hand, unemployment insurance may provide an incentive to organize production in a way that increases unemployment by aggravating seasonal and cyclical variations and by making casual and temporary jobs too common. As we shall see, it may do so by raising the net wage to the employee relative to the cost to the employer.

One method of estimating social benefits involves an assessment of the potential impact of unemployment payments on the postunemployment wage. Provided wages reflect productivity, so the argument runs, social benefits can be obtained by discounting the value of the additional earnings

41. M. S. Feldstein, "Policies to Lower the Permanent Rate of Unemployment," in *Reducing Unemployment to 2 Percent,* Hearing before the Joint Economic Committee, 92nd Congress, 2nd Session (Washington, D.C.: U.S. Government Printing Office, 1972).
42. S. T. Marston, "The Impact of Unemployment Insurance on Job Search," *Brookings Papers on Economic Activity* 1 (1975): 13–48. Note that Marston's relatively conservative estimates have attracted criticism on the grounds that his analysis shows that, immediately following exhaustion of benefits, the rate of leaving unemployment shoots up rapidly. Thus, if every insured worker were delaying his exit from the labor force to the same degree as apparently do those who have exhausted their benefits, unemployment insurance could be lengthening unemployment duration substantially.
43. R. E. Hall, "Comment and Discussion," *Brookings Papers on Economic Activity* 1 (1975): 50.

made possible by longer search. Ehrenberg and Oaxaca,[44] using National Longitudinal Survey data covering noninsured and insured workers alike, have fitted equations of the form:

$$\ln(W_{67}/W_{66}) = b_0 + b_1 F + \sum_{j=2}^{k} b_j x_j$$

where W_{67}/W_{66} is the individual's wage at the 1967/66 survey date;

F is the replacement ratio (the ratio of an individual's weekly unemployment insurance benefits to his preunemployment wage); and

x_j are the vector of variables other than F that are likely to influence an individual's postunemployment wage.

The authors' findings are summarized in table 11.1. We note that an increase in unemployment insurance benefits appears to produce additional productive job search for both older males and females,[45] with more pronounced positive effects for the male sample. In contrast, an increase in benefits for both the younger male and female samples has no effect on their postunemployment wages. This may be because younger recipients of unemployment insurance benefits search for jobs that offer better opportunities for on-the-job training, in which case we would expect their postunemployment wages to be relatively low because of worker investment in such training. On the other hand, this result could be interpreted as implying that the job search of such groups is unproductive; for example, young workers may use their benefits to subsidize nonmarket activities rather than job search.

We should not close our discussion of unemployment insurance without mentioning that an unintended consequence of such schemes in the United States may have been to encourage unstable employment. In the United States, employers contribute to their state unemployment insurance fund by experience rating—that is, on the basis of the unemployment experience of their own previous employees.[46] Due to imperfections in the experience rating system, however, many firms with high layoff rates have negative balances in their accounts; they have paid less in taxes than their employees have received in benefits. Such firms with high turnover rates pay the maximum tax rate, and an increase in layoffs causes no increase in tax payments. Feldstein has argued that the current inadequate experience

44. R. G. Ehrenberg and R. L. Oaxaca, "Unemployment Insurance, Duration of Unemployment and Subsequent Wage Gain," *American Economic Review* 66 (1976): 745–766.

45. See also Holen, "Job Search Outcome," pp. 448–450. She calculates that a $10 increase in weekly benefits would increase earnings by approximately $90 a quarter. On the other hand, Classen, "Subsequent Earnings," p. 441, has found that, at least for the Pennsylvania and Arizona labor markets, there is no such relation.

46. For a description of experience rating, see J. Becker, *Experience Rating in Unemployment Insurance* (Baltimore, Md.: Johns Hopkins University Press, 1972).

Table 11.1 Estimated Impact of Unemployment Insurance Benefit Changes on Postunemployment Wages

	Effect of Current Benefit Levels to the Absence of Benefits				Effect of Increasing the Replacement Ratio[a] from 0.4 to 0.5				Effect of Increasing the Replacement Ratio[a] from 0.0 to 1.0			
	M	F	B	G	M	F	B	G	M	F	B	G
Annual percentage wage change	9.0	2.5	*	*	7.0	1.5	*	*	97.3	16.1	*	*

*—regression coefficient statistically insignificant.
M—males aged 45–59 years
F—females aged 30–44 years
B—younger males, 14–24 years
G—younger females, 14–24 years
a. Denotes the ratio of an individual's weekly unemployment benefit to his preunemployment wage.

Source:
R. G. Ehrenberg and R. L. Oaxaca, "Unemployment Insurance, Duration of Unemployment and Subsequent Wage Gain," *American Economic Review* 66 (1976): table 5, p. 765.

rating system and the tax-free status of unemployment compensation have induced employers and employees to organize production and work rules in ways that create excessive unemployment.[47]

Let us next turn to the concepts of labor hoarding and hidden unemployment. Labor hoarding can be defined as the underutilization of employed labor[48] and arises because labor is a quasi-fixed factor of production. Thus, at the onset of a recession, the input of labor measured in terms of employees is not simultaneously cut back with output, and the labor utilization rate falls accordingly. With the upturn, increased output can similarly be achieved without a simultaneous increase in labor input, again measured in terms of employees, because the supply of labor services is increased simply by raising the utilization rate of already employed labor. In both cases, there will be a lagged adjustment of employment to changes in output. In these instances, it seems that rates of measured unemployment will be lagged indicators of excess supply in the labor market.

One method of estimating labor hoarding is to examine the time-series data of output per unit of employed labor and seek out the peak observations. At such peaks, it is assumed that the utilization rate of employed labor is 100%. The peaks may then be joined by fitting linear segments to estimate the full employment output/labor ratio for other points in time. The amount of hoarded labor is then determined by the ratio of actual to full employment output per employee.

47. M. Feldstein, "The Importance of Temporary Layoffs: An Empirical Analysis," *Brookings Papers on Economic Activity* 3 (1975): 725–745; idem, "Temporary Layoffs in the Theory of Unemployment," *Journal of Political Economy* 84 (1976): 937–958.
48. See J. Taylor, "Hidden Unemployment, Hoarded Labor, and the Phillips Curve," *Southern Economic Journal* 37 (1970): 1–16.

The main drawback to this trend-through-peaks technique of estimating labor utilization is that the actual employed labor utilization rates may not be identical at each of the peaks. In this case, the procedure of fixing the labor utilization rate at 100% at each of the peaks will lead to inaccuracies in estimating labor utilization rates for the interpeak periods. Pending the resolution of this difficulty, we may be obliged to continue using the unemployment rate as a cyclical indicator, in conjunction with a variety of other measures.[49]

Finally, let us consider the vexing question of hidden or disguised unemployment. Many have argued that the official unemployment rate considerably understates the volume of true unemployment in society, because it excludes from the unemployment count those who would like to work but have become so discouraged about finding jobs that they cease active search. Calculation of this deficit utilizes regression equations that relate labor force participation ratios to a variable reflecting the cyclical variability in the demand for labor plus a time trend (chapter 3). A full employment level of the demand variable, traditionally measured by the unemployment rate or the employment-to-population ratio, is then selected and fed into the regression equation to generate a full employment labor force participation rate for any point in time encompassed by the equation. The difference between this estimate and the recorded labor force represents the estimate of hidden unemployment—the manpower gap.

However, estimates of hidden unemployment obtained in this way vary considerably according to the demand variable employed, the specification of the trend variable, and the full employment assumption. For example, estimates of hidden unemployment in the United States in 1960 ranged from 380,000 through 780,000 to 1.2 million.[50] Moreover, we might question whether it is appropriate to add the hidden unemployed to the recorded unemployed when the motivations and productivities of the two groups might differ widely. The disguised unemployed are principally to be found with the secondary labor force. It follows from the estimation procedure that the importance of hidden unemployment in any population group is a direct function of the degree of labor force responsiveness to short-run variations in employment conditions. It is no accident that the hidden unemployed are found mainly in the secondary labor force, where there is greater scope for substitution between market and nonmarket activities. Presumably, disguised unemployment indicates potential availability at higher than currently

49. See J. Shiskin, "Employment and Unemployment: The Doughnut or the Hole?" *Monthly Labor Review* 99 (1976): 3–10.

50. See respectively, W. G. Bowen and T. A. Finegan, "Labor Force Participation and Unemployment," in A. M. Ross, ed., *Employment Policy and the Labor Market* (Berkeley and Los Angeles: University of California Press, 1965), pp. 115–161; A. Tella, "Labor Force Sensitivity to Employment by Age, Sex," *Industrial Relations* 4 (1965): 69–83; T. F. Dernburg and K. T. Strand, "Hidden Unemployment 1953–1962: A Quantitative Analysis by Age and Sex," *American Economic Review* 56 (1966): 71–95.

prevailing wage conditions. Recorded unemployment, on the other hand, is implicitly defined in terms of currently prevailing wage conditions.

Whether fluctuations in the labor force are regarded as evidence of labor reserves depends in the final analysis upon one's theory as to why they occur. If one accepts Mincer's permanent income explanation of cyclical fluctuations, it can be questioned whether the hidden unemployed constitute a labor reserve at all (chapter 3). If variations in participation are purely a matter of timing, then increased participation now is at the expense of participation in the future. On the other hand, secondary workers are not always in a position to synchronize their active participation in the labor force with swings in the business cycle. Thus, there is likely to be some involuntary labor force withdrawal. The difficulty is one of estimating the magnitude of this effect, having allowed for quality differences. Preliminary analysis of Bureau of Labor Statistics data on the hidden unemployed suggests that true discouragement is only a small component of the labor force reserve estimated by econometric studies—amounting to perhaps less than 10% of recorded unemployment over 1967–71.[51] The slowdown of labor force growth, or its actual decline, in the cyclical downswing appears predominantly the result of reductions in labor force *entries* rather than increases in labor force *withdrawals* resulting from futile search by the unemployed. This would indicate that econometric estimates apparently do capture the timing phenomenon of labor force activities.

11.6 The Differential Impact of Unemployment

Unemployment rates vary widely among different groups in the population. The unskilled experience higher unemployment than the semiskilled, who in turn have higher rates than craft groups. In 1974, for example, the unemployment rate of nonfarm laborers, operatives, and craftsmen stood at 10.1%, 7.5%, and 4.4%, respectively. Similarly, white-collar groups had lower employment rates (3.7%) than blue-collar workers (6.7%).

Nonwhites experience more unemployment than whites—partly, but not entirely, because they frequent the lower occupational classifications. Teenagers have higher rates than older workers, and females experience higher unemployment than males. Unemployment differentials by demographic groups are provided in table 11.2.

We might ask whether those groups that bear a disproportionate share of unemployment actually experience more frequent unemployment, or unemployment of longer duration, or both. Unfortunately, the answer to such questions cannot directly be found in official unemployment statistics, for the latter are static in nature. Published statistics provide information on the total number of unemployed at a moment in time, together with the length of each unemployment spell up to that moment, even though that spell is not

51. See J. Mincer, "Determining Who Are the 'Hidden Unemployed,'" *Monthly Labor Review* 96 (1973): 27–30.

Table 11.2   Unemployment in the United States by Sex, Color, and Broad Age Group, 1970–75.

| | Percentages (Annual Average) | | | | | |
| | Whites | | | Nonwhites | | |
Year	Male 20+	Female 20+	Male & Female 16–19	Male 20+	Female 20+	Male & Female 16–19
1970	3.2	4.4	13.5	5.9	5.3	29.1
1971	4.0	5.3	15.1	7.2	8.7	31.7
1972	3.6	4.9	14.2	6.8	9.0	32.8
1973	3.2	4.8	14.5	5.7	8.2	30.2
1974	3.8	5.5	16.0	6.8	8.4	32.9
1975	6.2	7.5	17.9	11.7	11.5	36.9

Source:
U.S. Department of Labor, Bureau of Labor Statistics, *Monthly Labor Review* (Washington, D.C.: U.S. Government Printing Office, various issues).

yet complete. Thus, the duration statistics do not pick up completed spells, measure only part of any spell of unemployment, and at the same time oversample long spells.

Methods have been derived for estimating the mean length of completed unemployment spells, based on the probabilities that govern the flow of workers into and out of employment, from which the frequency and duration of unemployment spells can be calculated for any unemployment rate. Perhaps the best known model is that of Perry,[52] which compares the frequency and duration of unemployment spells for eight age-sex groups at different equilibrium or steady-state levels of unemployment for the 1972 economy.[53] His findings can be summarized as follows. At a steady-state level of unemployment of 5%, teenagers of either sex apparently experience an average of nearly two unemployment spells a year, while men over forty-five have an average of only one spell every four to five years.[54] Between these two extremes, the frequency of unemployment spells declines steadily as the

52. G. L. Perry, "Unemployment Flows in the U.S. Labor Market," *Brookings Papers on Economic Activity* 2 (1972): 254–278.
53. A steady-state level of unemployment is one in which the flows into and out of unemployment are equal and where the mean duration of unemployment is constant. In such a situation, the unemployment rate is a product of the number of spells of unemployment and the expected duration of unemployment.
54. Estimates by R. E. Hall, "Turnover in the Labor Force," *Brookings Papers on Economic Activity* 3 (1972): 709–756, indicate that blacks have longer spells of unemployment than comparable white workers—about one-third longer in the case of black males, almost 50% in the case of black females. But again, the biggest difference is in the number of unemployment spells per year; black males become unemployed almost twice as frequently as white men, and black females more than twice as often as white women.

age of workers of either sex increases. The average duration of spells, on the other hand, varies in the opposite direction.

Much has been made of such differences in the frequency and duration of unemployment. The fact that women, teenagers, and blacks suffer higher unemployment rates primarily because of more frequent spells, rather than longer spells, does not necessarily mean that these groups find jobs nearly as easily as do mature white males. It could reflect their tendency to give up job search and exit from the labor force. Full investigation of this question requires that we examine not only data on the flows of workers into and out of unemployment, but also movements into and out of the labor force. As we have noted in section 11.2, there are six flows that require investigation. Marston has calculated the significance of the flow rates to the average unemployment experience of female, black, and teenage groups over 1967 to 1973.[55] His findings suggest that it is the high rate at which employed women enter and leave the labor force that is the main factor in the higher unemployment rates they experience vis-a-vis males. The explanation is that labor force entry involves a high probability of becoming unemployed. For teenagers, the same argument—participation instability—appears to hold. However, an important additional cause is the relatively high rate of their quits and layoffs that result directly in unemployment; this might be related to shopping around for jobs. Finally, the higher unemployment rates experienced by nonwhites reflect their high probability of becoming unemployed as a result of quits and layoffs and their relatively low probability of finding employment when entering or reentering the labor force or when unemployed. Thus, with the exception of nonwhites, there does not appear to be any special difficulty in finding jobs among groups recording above-average unemployment rates.

Informational theories of wage and job decisions predict a disproportionate incidence of unemployment among groups relatively high in new entrants, hence the young, and relatively high in reentrants, hence adult women. The obsolescence of labor market information means that the reentrant will be forced to engage in labor market search. Also, the young entrant having left school will have limited information and may fumble his way to a satisfactory job on a trial-and-error basis. If there is a substantial random element in the process of job search, then job choosers are more likely to locate jobs in higher turnover industries because these will have higher vacancies. There is also the point that, because the gains from search are larger the longer the prospective period of employment, young workers can be expected to make more extensive search than older workers and for this reason record higher unemployment rates on optimizing grounds.

On the demand side, the heterogeneity of workers makes it uneconomical for any firm to find out all the information about a job applicant that would be relevant to it. An attribute that will help to make one worker a better

55. Marston, "Employment Instability," pp. 178–184.

candidate for a job than another is experience—especially experience in the very firm itself. As a consequence, the firm will often rehire an ex-employee with whom it has actual experience in preference to an unknown worker. This consideration works to the disadvantage of those members of the labor force who are seeking their first job. As for the choice between two workers with whom there is equal inexperience, the expected cost minimizing decision here can only be based on readily available data that the firm believes to be operational in predicting worker performance. We refer here to the concept of statistical discrimination (chapter 6). The firm will likely fasten onto such data as age, sex, color, and years of schooling. Some amount of statistical prejudice is economical for the firm in a range of decisions for the simple reason that it is too costly to get all the facts. However, the application of such rules is likely to operate to the disadvantage of the young, women, and blacks.

Discrimination against a given group can be shown in certain circumstances (chapter 6) to require a wage differential in equilibrium if the group is to be employed. Under complete wage flexibility, the presence of economic discrimination against, say, nonwhites need not therefore lead to higher unemployment among members of this group. In practice, however, wage flexibility is constrained and nonwhites often have to be paid the same rate for the job as whites. This is particularly likely where the firm or industry is well unionized. Accordingly, we might view differences in nonwhite-white unemployment rates as due in part to differential wage rigidity in the presence of discrimination. Such a case has been persuasively argued by Gilman.[56] One strand of evidence favoring this interpretation is the fact that the nonwhite-white unemployment difference is most marked in skilled blue-collar jobs, where the pressure for wage standardization is strongest, and tends to be lower at the bottom and top ends of the occupational hierarchy, where this pressure is lacking. Another strand of evidence pointing in the same direction is that standardizing for occupational composition apparently reduces the nonwhite-white unemployment differential by more in the South than the non-South. Gilman's results for the period 1960-61 indicate that standardization reduces that differential by 68% in the South but by only 43% in the non-South. This result might be related to the lower federal minimum wage coverage and lower unionization of the South.

Where blacks and women succeed in being hired, it may often be the case that they find themselves the first to be fired and the last to be hired. This is because they tend to be in the less skilled jobs, in which the employer has made a smaller investment in hiring and training. When a firm is subject to a hierarchical structure of tasks, a decline in demand for its products may precipitate a domino effect in which some of those holding the most skill-demanding jobs are downgraded—formally or not—to less skill-intensive

56. H. Gilman, "Economic Discrimination and Unemployment," *American Economic Review* 45 (1965): 1077–1096.

assignments, some of the workers in those jobs are downgraded to assignments in the next level, and so on. The end result is the layoff of the least skilled workers. The reason for this is that the firm has typically its largest investments in the most skilled workers. Human capital theory would lead us to expect that the worker in whom the firm has invested specific training will be less subject to layoff, and also less prone to quit, than one for whom no such firm-specific investment has been undertaken. Research findings do indeed suggest that, in response to a decline in the demand for labor, unemployment rates of the least skilled rise, instead of wage rates declining, and the opposite occurs when demand rises.[57] The increase in unemployment makes it less attractive for some of the marginal workers to remain in the labor force when demand declines, so they leave; when demand rises, similar workers enter the labor force. Reder's model has the further implication that the unemployment rate of the less skilled workers should be greater than that of the higher skilled at any given time. Thus, in the presence of a wage structure that does not adjust rapidly in the short run to changes in demand and supply conditions, and with a social minimum wage that adjusts only under extreme conditions of excess demand or supply, the lowest skilled workers not only have higher unemployment rates than others, on average, but they also bear the brunt of increases in unemployment when aggregate demand falls.

Mention should be made of the dualist interpretation of unemployment in the secondary sector (chapter 5). Dualists argue that in spite of high unemployment rates within the secondary market, anyone who desires a typical secondary sector job can find such work because vacancies are abundant at the prevailing wage for such jobs. The problem is that as a consequence of low wages, poor promotion prospects, and "bad" jobs, individuals choose not to work steadily at any one job and drift in a random fashion between jobs. The theoretical underpinnings of the dualist position may be given a neoclassical interpretation, with workers viewed as maximizing utility. Family utility may be said to depend upon the wages offered, upon hours worked by family members, and upon transfer payments that establish a floor on the standard of living. The higher this floor vis-a-vis the wage rate, the more likely family members will choose not to work the full year. The unemployment that results does not fit a traditional job-search model, in which periods of unemployment are spent searching for another job. Workers appear to move from one bad job to another. But the findings are consistent with what Phelps has termed speculative unemployment and with the timing phenomenon suggested by Mincer.[58] If benefits are normally received and if labor is

57. M. W. Reder, "Wage Structure and Structural Unemployment," *Review of Economic Studies* 31 (1964): 309–322.
58. See, respectively, Phelps, *Inflation Policy,* pp. 4–9; J. Mincer, "Labor Force Participation of Married Women: A Study of Labor Supply," in National Bureau Committee for Economic Research, *Aspects of Labor Economics* (Princeton, N.J.: Princeton University Press, 1962), pp. 63–97.

less onerous when the individual works only part of the year, the instability pattern noted by the dualists emerges. Rather than work at random, however, individuals will attempt to participate when jobs are easiest to find and wages are relatively high. Also, although upward mobility to the high-paying sector may be constrained, searching for a higher paying and better secondary job may be worthwhile, especially when the opportunity cost is relatively low.[59]

Dual labor market theorists argue that disadvantaged groups become trapped in bad jobs and that they therefore have higher turnover and resulting high unemployment rates. It is incontrovertible that the high unemployment rate of blacks, teenagers, and women are the result of high flows out of employment. But the question at issue is whether it is bad jobs that lead to these flows out of employment or a process more closely connected to personal characteristics; the dualist position is that good workers are trapped in bad jobs. Marston has attempted a preliminary test of this argument by regressing the flows into unemployment from employment on a variety of personal and job characteristics.[60] He finds that personal characteristics, such as age, sex, educational attainment, and marital status, are more important than job characteristics, such as industry in which employed, occupation, wage, and whether the job is full time, in explaining the flows out of employment. Marston's findings thus challenge the dualist thesis that attributes the high unemployment of blacks, teenagers, and women to the bad jobs in which they become trapped. If jobs determined labor turnover, and these groups experienced higher rates of unemployment only because of their bad jobs, all of the personal variables would have insignificant coefficients. And if jobs and personal variables were very highly correlated, so that problem groups had only bad jobs while mature whites always had good jobs, both sets of variables would be insignificant. Unfortunately, the problem with Marston's analysis is that his industry and occupational groupings (fourteen industries, twelve occupations) may be too broad to capture the bad job characteristics that matter. Thus, within the same industry, occupation, wage, and workweek there may exist both good and bad jobs, and problem groups may have a disproportionate share of the latter. In this case the regression equations would incorrectly attribute to personal variables that which is due to job variables. Further analysis of this intriguing question is necessary, therefore, before we can make hard and fast conclusions.

There is, as we have seen, considerable controversy as to the causes of unemployment, but a number of policy implications may be drawn from our analyses. A case can be made for the view that teenagers receive too little

---

59. For a fuller analysis of this model, see M. L. Wachter, "Primary and Secondary Markets: A Critique of the Dual Approach," *Brookings Papers on Economic Activity* 3 (1974): 665–667; S. A. Ross and M. L. Wachter, "Wage Determination, Inflation and the Industrial Structure," *American Economic Review* 63 (1973): 675–692.

60. Marston, "Employment Instability," pp. 188–200.

preparation in school for work and inadequate information about the sorts of job available when they leave school. As a result, they tend to move from one job to another, finding out in a rather expensive way what kind of work they like. Therefore, there is scope for encouraging students in the final school years to participate in state-funded work study programs to facilitate the transition from school to work. There is also scope for a margin of subsidization to firms to permit employers to offer students work experience. However, we should recognize that much of teenage unemployment might essentially be a voluntary response associated with a greater choosiness among jobs due to the general increase in family income levels. This choosiness is a necessary means of exploring personal capabilities as yet unrevealed in the young worker.

Institutional barriers in the labor market, based on discrimination, occupational licensing, and union membership, inhibit the response of labor to production requirements and exacerbate unemployment and skill shortages. The issues involved and the questions of costs associated with attempts to dissolve such barriers to employment were discussed in chapters 6 and 9.

Minimum-wage laws are likely to have had some tendency to reduce the frequency of employment. Workers who are full-time and affected by the legislation will presumably be drawn to employment activities less well liked than those made difficult to enter by high wage minima. In many cases, they will have to accept infrequent and temporary work at various jobs paying the minimum wage or better. In this context, there might be room for a two-tier system, whereby young people in particular may be hired at a rate below the general minimum for a limited period of time, during which they can be screened, trained, and raised to normal productivity levels.

Turning to dualist notions, intervention to encourage firms to undertake specific training or to reduce labor turnover can, in our view, be justified in certain circumstances. This is because of the external effects associated with specific training—such investments being undersupplied because of the risks of a trained worker leaving the firm—and the social costs of high turnover. The measures that might be called for, therefore, are those that encourage human capital formation and discourage turnover in low-wage industries. They include manpower training in the form of government-run training programs and an expansion of private sector on-the-job training achieved through subsidies or taxes.

11.7 Conclusions

It is conventional to break down unemployment by cause into its frictional, structural, and demand deficient components. On the face of it, the conceptual boxes are appealing—the more so because they indicate that different remedies might be required according to the box in which the unemployment is located. Unfortunately, there are problems with this causal or ex-ante classification system. For example, is there more than a difference of degree between frictional unemployment and structural unemployment (that which is due to changes in relative supplies and demands at a given level of aggregate demand)? Moreover, is not the observed level of frictional-structural unemployment in part dependent upon the level of aggregate demand? Similar problems are encountered in respect of the cure or ex-post classification.

There is also the distinction between voluntary and involuntary unemployment. According to the classical model, the rapid clearing of the labor market means that unemployment scarcely deviates from its equilibrium or voluntary value. The Keynesian model, on the other hand, specifically tackles the question of deviations from the full employment level of employment, as defined in classical real wage-employment space. Such deviations are explained in terms of downwardly rigid money wage rates. The key to full employment in Keynes' view lay in the expansion of aggregate demand, which would have the effect of raising prices relative to wages (real wage declines engineered in this way are supposed to be acquiesced in by labor because relativities are maintained). In its most basic formulation, the Keynesian model implies that any unemployment that can be permanently reduced by raising aggregate demand without affecting the level of money wages is involuntary in form.

Modern theories of unemployment have challenged the Keynesian position that unemployment is involuntary wherever it can be reduced by raising aggregate demand by arguing that there is a natural rate of unemployment due to frictional and structural forces. This natural rate is based on the search theory of unemployment, which emphasizes that it is not rational for the individual to take the first job that is offered him. But note that the natural rate will also include nonemployment stemming from imperfections such as the minimum wage, information externalities in the labor market, union monopoly power, and firm monopsony power; it will even reflect the distortion of the labor-leisure choice caused by the progressive personal income tax. The modern theories of unemployment explain divergencies between the actual jobless rate and the natural rate in terms of inflationary and deflationary surprises. Wages do not react instantly to excess supply or demand because of the time it takes for information to spread. Employers do not take immediate advantage of a slackening in demand by reducing wage offers because they become aware only gradually that workers have become more readily available. Similarly, workers continue to hold out for the kind of job they would have been able to get under normal conditions. The initial impact of a reduction in demand is an increase in unemployment. Subsequently, wages will fall, merely stimulating demand for labor and reducing unemployment to its natural level. While information is diffusing slowly through the market, nonclassical quantity adjustments take place, but the market behaves classically in the longer run.

Natural rate theories have been criticized on the grounds that they are unable to explain the persistence of unemployment at levels either above or below the natural value. Yet, we would argue that the new theories do contain an explanation of unemployment persistence—namely, delays in the flow of information. Unfortunately, the delay is not generated endogenously by these theories and its length is a matter of judgment.

In fact, the theoretical distinction between voluntary and involuntary unemployment is something of a red herring once we move away from the crude notion of underemployment equilibrium, as it seems we must. Thus, much of the disequilibrium unemployment admitted to by search theory could be termed Keynesian involuntary. Moreover, the terms are often inappropriately used as a signal for government policy. Thus, "voluntary" tends to be a code word denying the desirability of government action and "involuntary" tends to be a code word supporting government action. Voluntary unemployment is the hallmark of search theory, but search theorists would not maintain that all voluntary unemployment is socially beneficial. A person who is involuntarily unemployed, on the other hand, is generally termed to be one who would like a job but has looked for work without success. Yet that person may have applied inappropriately for jobs, been searching in the wrong area, or operated with too high a reservation wage. However, we should not disregard the possibility of efficiency gains from policies designed to change the nature of unemployment. The crucial point for us to recognize is that, once we label unemployment as a problem, we must show that it implies an inefficiency. In this sense, there is nothing sacrosanct about a particular equilibrium unemployment rate: efficiency considerations might imply a greater or a lesser natural rate.

The postwar acceptance by governments of some fairly low target levels of unemployment has come under increasing attack. The main line of criticism has centered on the view that unemployment statistics distort the extent of involuntary unemployment within the market so that pursuit of the target has had unacceptable inflationary consequences. It has been suggested that there has been a structural change in both the United States and the United Kingdom leading to an increase in the amount of normal or frictional unemployment, or, in terms of modern theories, in the natural rate of unemployment. One commonly cited reason for this increase is more generous and liberalized unemployment insurance benefits, which, by lowering the foregone earnings cost of search, increase the mean duration of unemployment spells and hence the jobless rate. Other reasons will be considered in chapter 12. The empirical studies of the relation between unemployment benefit and duration reviewed in this chapter point to a lengthening of duration consequent upon improved benefits. Although it is difficult to extrapolate these results to the national economy, we can be reasonably sure that at least part of the increased unemployment in both countries is attributable to the subsidization process.

At the same time, we should not lose sight of the possible benefits of unemployment insurance associated with a better matching of workers and jobs—namely, a greater efficiency in the job search process. There are two main questions to consider. First, how much of the lengthened duration of unemployment is spent in productive search, as opposed to waiting? Second, why should one subsidize the job searcher if the returns to search are private? On the former question, there is some evidence to suggest that the post-unemployment wage is increased by subsidization. However, more work remains to be undertaken in this area, particularly with respect to the job-search activity of younger workers. As regards the second question, the search argument for unemployment insurance must rest on the divergence between the private and social returns to employment or on the inability of individuals to borrow based on their human capital. We can be certain that the debate on unemployment insurance will increasingly capture the center of the stage in unemployment research because of the very tentative evidence we have on the above issues.

Concern over the use of official unemployment statistics as a labor market indicator has led to the argument that estimates of hoarded labor should be subtracted from the employment total and estimates of hidden unemployment added to recorded unemployment. Statistical difficulties attach to the estimation of labor hoarding, although it appears to offer a potentially more sensitive measure of labor slack than the unemployment rate alone. Hidden unemployment, on the other hand, is an altogether more ambiguous concept. We have argued that little is to be gained by adding this total to the recorded unemployed. The hidden unemployed are concentrated among labor force groups who exercise considerable discretion in the timing of their labor force participation.

As for the uneven incidence of unemployment across the labor market, informational theories of wage and job decisions lead us to expect that the incidence of unemployment will fall disproportionately upon groups relatively high in new entrants, the young, and relatively high in reentrants, adult women. Moreover, these economic notions suggest that disadvantaged workers and victims of statistical discrimination will also suffer above-average unemployment rates insofar as the inferior jobs to which they are consigned tend to offer less steady work. The question at issue is whether this body of theory is a tolerably accurate description of unemployment determination given the scale of unemployment differences in the present economy. We have seen that certain groups in society have rates of unemployment well in excess of those to be associated with a normal transition from one job to another. Some workers exhibit a chronic instability in holding jobs, moving from one low-paying, unpleasant job to another, often several times a year. This pattern can hardly be said to be the outcome of a normal process of career advancement. Dualists argue that, as a consequence of low wages, poor promotion prospects, and bad jobs, individuals choose not to work steadily and instead move in a random fashion. Yet, we have argued that the theoretical underpinnings of the dualist position can after all be reconstructed in a neoclassical form, with workers viewed as maximizing utility. On the other hand, we should recognize the possibility of feedback effects, whereby workers who hold bad jobs may tend to become bad workers—that is, accept bad work habits—and thus in some sense justify their labor market disadvantage.

The general point to be emphasized is that problem groups should be able to obtain analogous options to other groups, for whom brief periods of employment are not correlated with low earnings. In principle, wages can be traded off against employment continuity. That some groups regularly experience higher unemployment rates implies either that, given the terms of tradeoff that confront them, they prefer more unemployment than other grades, or that they face some special difficulty in altering the terms of tradeoff. Given the relative importance of intermittent job seekers, the role of employee preferences should not be overlooked, although once again we note that acceptance of the notion that unemployment is voluntary is not an excuse for inactivity in the area of policy. Our quantitative knowledge of factors impeding the alteration of the tradeoff is rudimentary, but it is possible that the operation of minimum wage laws, internal labor market structuring, and trade unions may play a more important role in limiting wage flexibility and thereby causing differential employment stability than is generally supposed.

APPENDIX 11-A
GROWTH-GAP UNEMPLOYMENT

Given the rapid growth of population during the last 200 years, the question arises: is there a dichotomy between this enhanced labor supply and the number of jobs on offer? The Keynesian analysis is not helpful in this area because it deals only with a permanent and fixed labor force. Accordingly, we turn to the classical economists, who believed in the existence of automatic adjustment mechanisms. The classicals claimed that there would be a decline in the real wage if the rate of growth of labor demand were too slow to absorb labor coming onto the market, and vice versa. This claim amounts to no more than a simple application of the concept of factor substitution in a dynamic setting. Consider a situation in which labor and capital output ratios are constant through time, so that labor, capital, and output are growing at the same rate. How are the rates of growth of capital and output brought into equilibrium with the rate of growth of population, n? The rate of growth of the capital stock will depend on net investment, I, and the latter, divided by the capital stock, K, gives the proportionate rate of growth of the capital stock, I/K. In equilibrium, the rate of growth of the capital stock must equal the ratio of savings, S, to the capital stock, Thus,

$$\frac{I}{K} = \frac{S}{K}. \tag{11-A.1}$$

If total savings are some constant value, s, of the level of income/output, Y, then the equilibrium condition may be written

$$\frac{I}{K} = \frac{S}{K} = s\frac{Y}{K}. \tag{11-A.2}$$

Replacing K/Y—the capital-output ratio, or accelerator coefficient—by v gives

$$\frac{I}{K} = \frac{s}{v}. \tag{11-A.3}$$

If the capital stock is growing at this rate, then so too will Y, given v. Dynamic equilibrium requires that the two rates of growth be brought into line with the exogenous growth in population, n, so as to maintain a constant labor/capital ratio. Thus,

$$n = \frac{s}{v}. \tag{11-A.4}$$

If the savings function is a constant, then the burden of adjustment has to fall upon the capital output ratio in the movement toward equilibrium. Thus,

$$v = \frac{s}{n},$$

and v must be at one particular level, corresponding to a particular factor-price ratio.

Let us now ask what will happen if, say, the birth rate rises. An increase in n, s being constant, will reduce the fraction on the right-hand side. The implication is that the wage rate will have to fall relative to the profit rate so as to reduce K/Y. Then, because less capital is used per unit of output, presumably more labor will be used.

There remain a number of obstacles to full employment in a setting of long-run growth, ignoring those arising out of the nature of technical progress. Thus, where there is complementarity, or fixed inputs, the capital-output ratio is no longer a variable. Indeed, the possibilities of limited substitutability imply that, beyond a point, a progressive lowering of the real wage level—even to zero—will not serve to decrease the capital output ratio. Somewhat more realistic is the potential for inflexibility resulting from a social minimum wage that is greater than the equilibrium real wage required by the economic system. In the light of this analysis, we might seek to vary s in the face of a rapidly growing population. And, as the Irish experience of the 1850s all too graphically reminds us, an alternative (Malthusian) solution is to vary n.

CHAPTER 12
WAGE INFLATION

12.1 Introduction

Labor economists today are much concerned with the topic of money wage changes. This emphasis on money wage behavior can be ascribed to Keynes, who argued that the money wage level could not be taken as passively adapting to the full employment level indicated by the model of perfect competition. The modern aim has been to extend the Keynesian framework for dealing with macroeconomic issues. That framework, embodied in the IS-LM model,[1] treated the money wage rate as exogenous. The goal, beginning with the famous Phillips curve, is now to explain changes in money wages either in terms of the excess demand for labor, or in terms of institutional factors, or both. In this chapter, we shall review these approaches to the question of wage inflation, concentrating mainly on excess demand theories. In chapter 13, institutional theories are investigated in greater detail.

The analysis begins with an examination of the various macro models of the inflationary process. Then we review the Phillips curve and show how more realistic models can also point to a relation between money wage changes and excess demand. We also consider a number of alternative routes to the inflation question, including a brief analysis of the effect of collective bargaining and trade unions, before turning to recent empirical developments more truly within the excess demand tradition. The chapter concludes with a policy section that focuses upon the role of wage restraint in limiting inflation and also briefly considers manpower policy.

12.2 Theoretical Aspects of Inflation

An important question for labor economics is the possible role of labor market forces in causing inflation. The Phillips curve—considered in its most general form as a relation between money wage increases and such factors as

---

1. See J. R. Hicks, "Mr. Keynes and the 'Classics': A Suggested Interpretation," *Econometrica* 5 (1937): 147–159; A. H. Hansen, *A Guide to Keynes* (New York: McGraw-Hill, 1953).

unemployment, price increases, and/or measures of trade union *pushful-ness*—provides a central framework for analyzing this question. It appears to offer a way of looking at the impact of labor market forces on wage increases and thus, at one remove, on price increases. It also points to a tradeoff between wage increases and unemployment, in which case it is suggested that measures to reduce inflation have directly adverse consequences for unemployment. Before turning to these subjects, however, it is necessary to consider the place of the Phillips curve in the debate on the theory of inflation.

The debate on inflation is clouded. The lines of demarcation that are supposed to discriminate between various interpretations of the inflationary process are very inaccurately drawn. In part, this outcome can be traced to an oversimplification of mainstream ideas within standard economic textbooks. But more significant has been the tendency of economists to eschew synthesis and divide up into a number of opposing camps or schools. Each school has tended to exaggerate the difference between itself and the others, even to the point of misrepresentation. Accordingly, much of the debate devolves aridly on issues of what this group or that "really said."

In considering the causes of inflation, there have been said to be two main schools of thought: the Keynesian and the monetarist. There might also be a third school, which takes autonomous increases in costs, possibly brought about by trade unions, as being the root cause of price increases. Some appear to include the Keynesians within this latter group.[2] Others bracket the Keynesians with the monetarists (in this respect) as believing primarily in demand-induced inflation.[3] This provides an example of the kind of basic disagreement to which we have referred. We elect to take the Keynesians as a separate group for the time being, and we shall largely restrict our attention to the Keynesian and monetarist interpretations; chapter 13 considers cost-push notions.

It is convenient to begin with the basic quantity theory of money, which can be expressed as

$$MV = PY \qquad (12.1)$$

where M is a measure of the stock of money;
V is income velocity of circulation;
P is a measure of the general price level; and
Y is a measure of real output.

It can be seen that, if we assume both V and Y to be constant, as did the classicals, then an increase in M must be balanced by an increase in P. Thus,

---

2. See, for example, R. Kahn, "Inflation—A Keynesian View," *Scottish Journal of Political Economy* 23 (1976): 11.

3. See J. A. Trevithick and C. Mulvey, *The Economics of Inflation* (London: Martin Robertson, 1975), p. 37; G. Ackley, *Macroeconomic Theory* (New York: Macmillan, 1961), pp. 421–426.

a quantity theorist can be regarded as viewing increases in the price level as being mainly the outcome of prior increases in the quantity of money in circulation. When the quantity of money increases, an imbalance will emerge between the demand for money ($M_d = kPY$, where $k = 1/V$) and its supply. Individuals will be dissatisfied with the amount of money they are holding, preferring instead to buy commodities with the surplus money balances. But, because the supply of commodities is given by real factors, any attempt to purchase more than is currently being produced will act to bid up the prices of commodities until the demand for and supply of money are again in equilibrium. The levels of output and employment are determined by real forces of supply and demand which operate behind the "veil" of money. Thus, given a stable income velocity of circulation and a fixed real output, it follows that increases in the money supply produce equiproportionate increases in the price level.

Quantity theorists thus regarded the level of real income as being fixed by a set of relations that are independent of the size of the money stock and, hence, of the price level. In addition, they asserted that there would be an automatic tendency for full employment to be established in a competitive economy where prices and wages are free to vary in response to market pressures. The elements of this classical model are given in figure 12.1. In quadrant I are given the classical labor demand and supply schedules with respect to the real wage, W/P. With flexible wages and prices, an equilibrium level of employment, N_F, and an equilibrium real wage rate, $(W/P)_F$, will be established simultaneously. To determine the real level of income corresponding to the equilibrium level of employment, N_F, we introduce the notion of a short-run production function, $Y = f(N)$, in quadrant II. We observe the full employment level of real income to be Y_F. Quadrants III and IV relate to nominal values. Quadrant III illustrates the determination of the absolute price level, given the level of output and the money supply. Thus, with real output equal to Y_F and money supply equal to M_0, the price level will be P_0. The line W_0, in quadrant IV, shows the locus of the real wage–price level combinations for a given money wage W_0. For a full employment real wage, $(W/P)_F$, and with money supply M_0, we must be at point A with money wage W_0.

Now consider an increase in the supply of money. This is indicated by an outward shift of the rectangular hyperbola in quadrant III of figure 12.1 to M_1. For full employment output, Y_F, to continue to prevail, and assuming a given V, the price level must rise to P_1. At this price level, and if the full employment real wage is to hold, we must be at point B in quadrant IV. This implies a higher money wage, as is shown by the new dashed money wage locus, W_1. Figure 12.1 thus illustrates how the money wage level can adjust to the predetermined price level to give a real wage that equates the demand for and supply of labor. It also shows how increases in the quantity of money can serve to increase the money wage and price levels and have no effect on real magnitudes.

Figure 12.1   The Classical Model

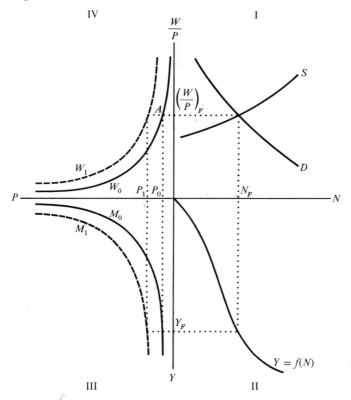

The depressions of the 1920s and 1930s and concurrent developments in economic theory undermined this view of the world. Keynesian theory, employing different behavioral assumptions, predicted instead that the price level and the level of unemployment were determined by an interaction of the monetary and real sectors. In the specific context of inflation, Keynes largely confined his analysis to the goods market. Inflation, he argued, could be traced to an excess of aggregate expenditure over producible real income. Thus, if the equilibrium level of real income exceeded its full employment level, an *inflationary gap* would open up. There is then an excess demand for the output of the economy and it is this excess demand that is the root cause of inflation. From the point of view of policy, it follows that inflation can only be brought under control by a sustained policy of demand restriction.[4]

In terms of the labor market, a central premise of Keynes' theory of employment was the view that expansion in the level of aggregate demand would exert an upward pressure on the price level relative to the money wage whenever there was substantial unemployment. In such circumstances, an

4. J. M. Keynes, *How to Pay for the War* (London: Macmillan, 1940), chap. 3.

increase in the level of aggregate demand would fail to increase the money wage. On this view, the money wage can be taken as a constant at less than full employment.[5] The money wage only starts to creep upward once expenditure increases push the economy toward its full employment level, which is defined as a situation of zero involuntary unemployment. Yet the other component of the real wage, the price level, reacts very differently to increases in expenditure. Far from remaining constant in the face of changes in the pressure of demand, the price level was viewed by Keynes as an increasing function of the level of expenditure, even in positions of considerable capacity underutilization. This is because, as production expands in response to demand stimulation, the marginal costs of production rise, putting upward pressure on the price level. Keynes did not, then, deny that inflation would result from expansionary policies. His concern with inflation was, however, relegated to situations of "true inflation," that is, where inflation was not accompanied by increases in employment.[6]

If this interpretation of Keynes is the correct one, what then are the differences between his view and that of the monetarists, who after all seem to stress a clear excess demand interpretation of the inflationary process? The first difference to which we might point is that Keynes objected to any mechanical connection between M and P, because he saw no reason to take velocity of circulation as constant.[7] He argued that peoples' desire to hold cash and liquid assets such as bank demand deposits (their demand for money), rather than illiquid assets, depended not only on the rather stable factor of the volume of transactions they were expecting to finance but also on unstable precautionary and speculative factors. For example, if individuals believed that prices would fall in the future, it would be sensible for them to postpone their purchasing decisions and to hold more of their wealth in cash for the time being, raising the demand for cash and lowering velocity. Such an expectation has in fact been advanced as one major reason for the marked decline in velocity in the United States during the latter part of World War II.[8] This objection by Keynes has been accepted by monetary theorists, though its empirical relevance remains in dispute. That is to say, over the long run and in ordinary times (excluding periods of war or great depression), it might be worth treating velocity as at least predictable, if not

5. Thus Keynes wrote, ". . . workers will not seek a much greater money wage when employment improves or allow a very great reduction rather than suffer any unemployment at all." See J. M. Keynes, *The General Theory of Employment, Money and Interest* (London: Macmillan, 1936), p. 253.

6. Ibid., p. 304.

7. Keynes's objections to the quantity theory, and the circumstances in which he regarded it as acceptable, are succinctly expressed in chapter 21 of the *General Theory* (ibid.).

8. Velocity, measured as currency plus demand deposits divided by net national product, stood at 1.84 in 1942 but had fallen to only 1.16 by 1946. See M. Friedman and A. Schwartz, *A Monetary History of the United States, 1867–1960*, National Bureau of Economic Research (Princeton, N.J.: Princeton University Press, 1963).

fairly stable.[9] Whether or not this is a useful assumption will depend on the alternatives. For example, it might be that autonomous expenditures bear a more predictable relation to money income, as suggested by the Keynesian consumption function, than does the quantity of money.[10] This is an issue that is still undecided. However, the main point here is for us to get the outlines of the debate correct: for the quantity theory to be useful in analyzing inflation, the demand for money function must be empirically stable so that changes in the velocity of circulation are predictable from the form of this relation.

Keynes' second main criticism related to the assumption that real output should be taken as given. In the *General Theory,* written at the time of the Great Depression, he emphasized the likelihood of unemployed resources so that expansionary monetary policy could increase real output, as well as spilling over into inflation. To explain how such expansionary policies could eat into unused capacity, Keynes introduced his distinctive assumption of sticky money wages. Thus, an increase in the supply of money in the short run is likely to stimulate an increase in real income, and probably prices, to the extent that it lowers interest rates and thereby increases investment expenditures. If investment increases, so too does real income via the multiplier. Given that money wages are sticky, the rise in prices will reduce the real wage. This "validates" the increase in employment brought about initially by the increase in expenditure.[11]

But it appears that Keynes adhered to the simplifying assumption that the full employment level of output and capacity utilization could not be exceeded in physical terms. Keynes defined full employment as a situation of zero involuntary unemployment, a definition that can be linked directly to some notion of the market clearing wage rate. Recent interpretations of the Keynesian scheme have thus argued that the more fundamental distinction between Keynes and monetarism is one of whether the Keynesian full employment rate coincides with the Friedmanite natural unemployment rate.[12] Specifically, the full employment properties of the Friedmanite natural unemployment rate have been questioned. The argument here is that inflation can be fully anticipated over a range of unemployment rates, although workers may nonetheless not demand full compensation for price increases in their nominal wage contracts up to the full employment level of unemployment. The essence of this argument is that workers are prepared to accept cuts in the rate of growth of their real wages but not in the rate of

9. See M. Friedman, ed., *Studies in the Quantity Theory of Money* (Chicago: University of Chicago Press, 1956).
10. See A. Ando and F. Modigliani, "The Relative Stability of Monetary Velocity and the Investment Multiplier," *American Economic Review* 55 (1965): 693–728.
11. See J. A. Trevithick, "Inflation, the Natural Unemployment Rate and the Theory of Economic Policy," *Scottish Journal of Political Economy* 23 (1976): 42.
12. See J. Tobin, "Inflation and Unemployment," *American Economic Review* 62 (1972): 1–18; Trevithick, "Inflation," pp. 44–48.

growth of their nominal wages. We see in this explanation an attempt to erect an inflationary counterpart of the underemployment equilibrium proposition we earlier encountered in chapter 11. The upshot of this particular interpretation is that there is a long-run tradeoff between inflation and unemployment up to the full employment rate of unemployment.

The degree of association of expansionary monetary or fiscal policy with real output increases, rather than with inflation, should be regarded as largely an empirical matter. It depends on how appropriate are the assumptions of underutilized capacity and sticky money wages. In a given period when there is unemployment, there can at any rate be said to be agreement that we do not know how a given change in nominal income will be divided between real output change and inflation in the short run.[13] With respect to empirical work, there seems to be a justification here for including the level of unemployment, as well as money supply, in equations determining the rate of increase in prices,[14] that is, for a Phillips-type relationship between unemployment and wage or price increases. A further, perhaps more basic, justification for the Phillips curve can also be advanced. Keynes, as we have pointed out, focused attention on the *money* and not the real wage. To the extent that this focus is correct, we require a theory of money wage rate determination. The Phillips curve, incorrectly specified though it might have been, is based on such a theory, or theories.[15]

It is likely that the assumption of fully employed resources is more reasonable in the long term. Consequently, the monetarist explanation of inflation has a firm basis in the long term and, equivalently, the Phillips curve less of a role. However, a continually rising price level, unless that increase is fully anticipated, may stimulate investment and therefore real income because of a reduction in the burden of debt. Thus, a slowly rising price level may itself be necessary to promote real output and employment growth. This would suggest the possibility of a long-term and not merely a short-run connection between money supply increases and real output increases.

The monetarist position has also been criticized for its assumption of an exogenous money supply. Is it changes in the supply of money that bring about changes in nominal income, ignoring the question of how this is split into price and output changes, rather than the converse? If we paraphrase the

13. See M. Friedman, "A Theoretical Framework for Monetary Policy," *Journal of Political Economy* 78 (1970): 222.
14. D. E. W. Laider, "The Influence of Money on Real Income and Inflation: A Simple Model with Some Empirical Tests for the United States, 1953–1972," *Manchester School* 41 (1973): 367–395, puts forward such a model.
15. Friedman, "Theoretical Framework," p. 215, and Ackley, *Macroeconomic Theory,* p. 416, would agree. However, Trevithick, "Inflation," p. 45, argues that if unions try to match each other's wage claims, as Keynes believed, then money wages will tend not to be responsive to labor market slack. This latter point is, however, an argument against the particular specification of the money wage determination function in terms of unemployment and is not contrary to the concept itself.

Friedmanite argument by saying that the demand for money depends on money income and the money interest rate, might not the supply of money also depend on these two variables? Thus, if the monetary authorities sought to peg the interest rate at a low level, they would effectively lose control of the supply of money. By the same token, if the authorities allowed the money supply to accommodate itself to the level of money income produced, say, by cost-push factors in the form of union wage demands, then the money supply would itself be a function of the level of money income. These issues have not been settled. For the United States, however, Friedman and Schwartz have cogently argued that the money supply has been exogenous.[16] Also in the American context, it is possible that the lesser strength of trade unions *and* the smaller size of the public sector, compared with the United Kingdom, combine to make the Keynesian assumption of sticky money wages and cost-push pressures less relevant.

12.3   Inflation and Excess Demand

The Phillips Curve.   The original impetus for the Phillips curve literature was Phillips' pioneering study of 1958.[17] Phillips proposed that the proportionate rate of change in money wages, $(\partial W/\partial t)/W$, or $\dot{W}$, would be largely a function of the level of excess demand in the labor market. The labor market was thus taken to be analogous to a commodity market. Excess demand was proxied by the level of unemployment (U). When unemployment was low (excess demand high), wages would rise; when unemployment was high, wages would tend to fall, albeit slowly because of the downward stickiness of wage rates. A curvilinear relation was thus postulated

$$\dot{W} = a + bU^{-c}. \tag{12.2}$$

To eliminate transitory fluctuations, Phillips grouped his observations into class intervals, established mean values for $\dot{W}$ and U for each group, and then fitted the curve to these mean observations. The fitted relation for the period 1851–1913 was

$$\dot{W} + 0.9 = 9.638\ U^{-1.394}$$

or,

$$\log (\dot{W} + 0.9) = 0.984 - 1.394 \log U.$$

16. M. Friedman and A. Schwartz, "Money and Business Cycles," *Review of Economics and Statistics* 45 (1963): S32–S64.
17. A. W. Phillips, "The Relation Between Unemployment and the Rate of Change of Money Wage Rates in the United Kingdom, 1861–1957," *Economica* 25 (1958): 283–299. But see also I. Fisher, "A Statistical Relation Between Unemployment and Price Changes," *International Labor Review* 13 (1926): 785–792.

No standard errors or coefficients of determination were reported, but inspection shows the curve to be a close fit to the observations. Diagrammatically, this curve was of the form PP' shown in figure 12.2.

Phillips also incorporated the rate of change of unemployment, $(\partial U/\partial t)/U$, or $\dot{U}$, and of prices, $(\partial P/\partial t)P$, or $\dot{P}$, into the explanation of money wage increases. The scatter around the fitted curve PP' was to be explained by the former variable. The rate of change in wages thus tended to be higher than predicted during the upswing and lower than predicted during the downswing for a given level of unemployment. This phenomenon is indicated in figure 12.2 in the form of a loop, with arrows indicating the direction of the cycle. Explanation of the loop can run in terms of the conditioning influence imparted by $\dot{U}$ upon the expectations of the parties to the wage bargaining process. At a given level of unemployment, employers might be more willing to agree to a higher wage when employment is rising than when it is falling. Phillips also incorporated an institutional element into the determination of $\dot{W}$, operating via $\dot{P}$. He argued that, when prices rose very strongly, the threatened decline in real wages would lead unions to submit additional wage claims.

In his well-known examination of the Phillips curve, Lipsey began with the assumption that a positively sloped supply curve and a negatively sloped demand curve could be constructed in Marshallian money wage–employment space for a single labor market.[18] He hypothesized an unchanging adjustment function, by which a given excess demand would cause a given

18. R. G. Lipsey, "The Relation Between Unemployment and the Rate of Change of Money Wage Rates in the United Kingdom, 1861–1957: A Further Analysis," *Economica* 27 (1960): 1–31.

Figure 12.2   The Phillips Curve

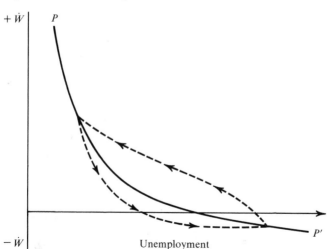

rate of change in money wages. Also, he assumed that there would be some positive and unchanging amount of frictional unemployment whenever excess demand was zero; but, as excess demand increased, this quantity of frictional unemployment would decline at a decreasing rate.

From these two assumptions, the basic Phillips curve can be constructed. Lipsey's adjustment mechanism, or reaction function, is illustrated in quadrant IV of figure 12.3. Line AA', for example, represents the assumption of a proportional relation between the excess demand for labor, $(D_L - S_L)/S_L$, and the rate of change in wages, with $\dot{W}$ zero when excess demand is zero. The frictional unemployment assumption is depicted in quadrant III, which portrays the postulated relation between the excess demand for labor and the level of unemployment. Frictional unemployment equal to U_F is recorded when excess demand for labor is zero. Expansion of demand will reduce the level of unemployment to below U_F. The larger is excess demand, the easier it will be to find jobs and the less will be the time taken in moving between jobs. Thus, unless there is a completely offsetting increase in the numbers of

Figure 12.3   Derivation of a Phillips Curve from Wage Adjustment Function and Unemployment—Excess Demand Relationship

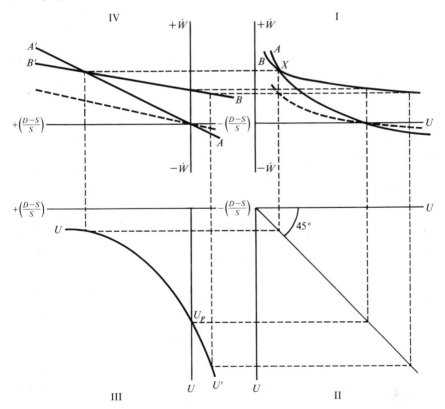

persons moving between jobs,[19] an increase in excess demand will cause a reduction in frictional unemployment. But frictional unemployment cannot be reduced to zero. As a result, the UU' curve will assume a nonlinear form for levels of unemployment below U_F. An emergence of excess supply (negative excess demand) will merely increase unemployment, so that UU' can be given a linear form for levels of unemployment above U_F.

A curve analogous to the Phillips curve is then obtained by collapsing the wage reaction function AA' and the excess demand–unemployment function UU' into one graph. This is shown in quadrant I. Figure 12.3 shows that the Phillips curve thereby obtained is a function of the speed at which money wages adjust to a disequilibrium. More sluggish adjustment, represented by the dashed line in quadrant IV, gives a flatter Phillips curve, namely the dashed line in quadrant I.

Lipsey's fitted relation for the period 1861–1913 was as follows (DW not reported, t-statistics not reported):

$$\dot{W} = -1.21 + 6.54\ U^{-1} + 2.26\ U^{-2} - 0.019\ \dot{U} + 0.21\ \dot{P}. \quad (12.3)$$
$$R^2 = 0.85$$

Equation (12.3) indicates that variations in the variables on the right-hand side explain 85% of the variance in $\dot{W}$. The squared partial correlation coefficients on U, $\dot{U}$, and $\dot{P}$ were 0.78, 0.50, and 0.17, respectively. These show that variations in U explain 78% of the variance in $\dot{W}$, that $\dot{U}$ removes a further 50% of the variance not associated with U, and that $\dot{P}$ removes a further 17% of the variance not associated with U and $\dot{U}$. The implication is, then, that unemployment constitutes the most important determinant of money wage changes over the period in question.

Lipsey argued that the Phillips loops were not caused by an expectations effect, but were instead the result of variation in the distribution of excess demand among sectors of the labor market over the course of the cycle. This is the basis of the *aggregation hypothesis*. On this hypothesis, the aggregate Phillips curve is only the average relationship that emerges from the experience of underlying sectors, each of which possesses its own micro-Phillips curve. Assuming these sectoral Phillips curves are similar, and assuming that all are nonlinear, it follows that, for a given overall fraction unemployed, $\dot{W}$ will be higher when there is greater dispersion in the distribution of unemployment among sectors of the labor market. This is shown in figure 12.4. For expositional convenience, we assume two equally sized markets, A and B, with identical Phillips curves, as illustrated. Unemployment rates are taken to be U_A and U_B, with corresponding rates of wage change of zero and $\dot{W}_B$. In this case, the economywide unemployment rate would be U_T and the average

19. For a discussion of this question, see B. A. Corry and D. E. W. Laidler, "The Phillips Relation: A Theoretical Explanation," *Economica* 34 (1967): 189–197; J. Vandercamp, "Comment," *Economica* 35 (1968): 179–183.

Figure 12.4   The Aggregation Hypothesis

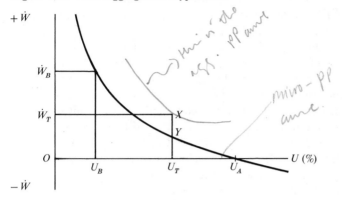

rate of wage change would equal $\dot{W}_T$ ($= \frac{1}{2} \cdot \dot{W}_B$), implying a point X on the aggregate Phillips curve above the micro curve. However, if the dispersion of unemployment were reduced, so that unemployment was U_T percent in both markets, then the average rate of wage change would fall to Y for the same economywide average unemployment rate as before. This reasoning also generates the prediction of an anticlockwise loop around the curve if it is further assumed that, for some reason, the dispersion of unemployment is greater in the upswing of the cycle than in the downswing.

The fundamental criticism of the Phillips curve, although still within the excess demand tradition, comes from Friedman, whose analysis may be said to represent an attempt to revive the classical model of the labor market under which full employment tends to be continually maintained.[20] Friedman argues that it is *real* wages and not money wages which will respond to excess demand. If that is so, money wages will respond both to excess demand and *expected* changes in prices, in the latter case with an adjustment coefficient, Φ, of unity. Thus,

$$\dot{W}_t = f(U)_t + \Phi \dot{P}_t^e \qquad f'(U) < 0 \qquad (12.4)$$

where $\dot{P}_t^e$ is the proportional rate of change in prices that is expected at time t.

Here, the nominal wages that workers are willing to accept depends on the price level that they expect to prevail. If they anticipate an increase in the price level in the future, they will compensate for this factor by enlarging their wage aspirations by the same proportion—conveyed in the equation by the specification that Φ is unity.

20. M. Friedman, "The Role of Monetary Policy," *American Economic Review* 58 (1968): 1–17. See also E. S. Phelps, "Money Wage Dynamics and Labor Market Equilibrium," *Journal of Political Economy* 76 (1969): 687–711.

In the Friedman model, there is a natural rate of unemployment consistent with any of a wide variety of steady rates of inflation or deflation, as determined by the rate of growth of the money supply. This natural rate of unemployment is determined by such factors as the costs of gathering information about job vacancies in a given market (chapter 11). It is possible to reduce unemployment temporarily below the natural rate by expanding aggregate demand. But, by causing prices to rise, this lowers the real wage and induces employers to expand output and employment. At first, workers do not realize that the increase in prices has reduced their real wage. Once this fact is recognized, however, they demand and obtain higher nominal wages and the reduction of real wages below the equilibrium level can be maintained only by a further rise in prices. As prices and wages continue to rise at a steady rate, workers eventually come to anticipate the price increases and to act on their anticipations. Accordingly, in the course of time, real wages and employment fall back to their equilibrium levels and unemployment is restored to the natural rate, which is the rate at which $\dot{P} = \dot{P}^e$. All that is happening is that prices and wages are rising together, with real wages remaining constant. Attempts to maintain a level of unemployment below the natural rate imply an accelerating rise in prices.

The argument can be pursued using figure 12.5, which conforms to the Phelps-Friedman model. Assume an economy initially to be in equilibrium at point A, at which there is wage and price stability, given a zero growth rate of productivity, and at which employment is U_n. If the authorities in the economy were now to decide that U_n was too high a level of unemployment, that U_1 was preferable, they could initially achieve this by increasing aggre-

Figure 12.5   The Phelps-Friedman Model

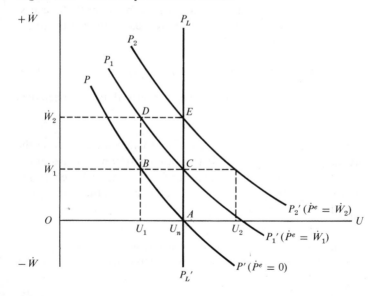

gate demand. This expansion will feed back to the factor markets, create an excess demand for labor (and all other factors of production), and thereby pull the economy up the Phillips curve PP' to point B. A rate of wage inflation of $\dot{W}_1$ will be generated. However, with zero productivity growth—removal of this assumption does not much change the analysis—accompanying these developments, the effect of rising factor prices will be to raise goods prices at a rate of $\dot{W}_1$. This latter experience will feed back into the formation of price expectations. Now, so long as people form their expectations about inflation on the basis of current and past behavior of prices, the price inflation thus induced would begin, after some adjustment lag, to be anticipated. Prior to this adjustment, however, duration of the average spell of unemployment can be expected to fall as individuals tend to overestimate the real value of wage offers made to them; in effect, their real reservation price falls and unemployment declines to U_1. But if the authorities pursued policies to maintain wage inflation at a rate of $\dot{W}_1$, the expected rate of inflation would move closer to the actual. The duration of unemployment spells would creep up again as individuals ceased to overestimate the real value of wage offers. Under these conditions, the short-run Phillips curve would shift closer to its ultimate location at $\dot{P}^e = \dot{W}_1$, and the level of unemployment compatible with the rate of wage inflation, $\dot{W}_1$, would become closer to U_n. In short, as soon as workers recognize that wage increases equivalent to $\dot{W}_1$ are necessary to match current and expected price increases, they will adjust to the real situation and may be envisioned as moving to point C. Wages and prices will now rise in line with expectations and the behavior of all labor market participants is fully adapted to the inflationary environment. Unemployment will tend to return to its original level, U_n, assuming that the period of boom has not itself changed U_n.[21]

Further attempts to reduce the level of unemployment would imply a movement along a new Phillips curve, depicted as P_1P_1' in figure 12.5. Assuming the policy required reduction in unemployment to be the same as before, namely U_1U_n, we move along P_1P_1' from C to D. However, as soon as the new rate of inflation is fully discounted by labor market participants, a move from D to E would result. Then, a new short-run Phillips curve would operate appropriate to the level of expectations ruling at E ($\dot{P}^e = \dot{W}_2$).

It is also important to look at the consequences of attempting to reduce the rate of inflation within this framework. Assume we begin at point E, and the authorities manage to bring down the rate of wage increase to $\dot{W}_1$. Because labor market participants are supposed, for some period, to predicate their

---

21. A period of boom might draw young people into the labor force earlier than might otherwise be the case. Because the young tend to shop around for jobs more than other groups and tend in any case to be less well informed, we would expect this to raise the natural rate of unemployment in the future, for any level of inflation. In this way, an economy's history of inflation might itself affect the natural unemployment rate. This phenomenon has been termed "hysterisis." See E. S. Phelps, *Inflation Policy and Unemployment Theory* (London: Macmillan, 1972), p. 79.

behavior on the expectation of money wage increases of $\dot{P}^e = \dot{W}_2$, unemployment will tend to rise to U_2 as workers underestimate the real value of wage offers made to them. As inflationary expectations are revised downward, however, unemployment is supposed to tend to fall back to U_n. The point to notice is that the longer is the adjustment period (the more stubbornly outdated inflationary expectations are held) the longer will be the period of high unemployment associated with attempts to force inflation downward. The policy implication here is that measures to shorten the adjustment lag, such as incomes restraint or indexation, will lower the unemployment cost of anti-inflation policies.

The long-run Phillips curve or equilibrium relation between $\dot{W}$ and U in the Phelps-Friedman model is shown by the vertical line $P_L P_L'$. Thus, the system is said to tend toward the natural unemployment rate, U_n, and any rate of wage inflation is theoretically compatible with this level of unemployment in long-run equilibrium. The latter occurs when price expectations have fully caught up with, and allowed for, the actual rate of price inflation, that is, when the following condition holds:

$$\dot{W}_t = \dot{P}_t^e = \dot{P}_t$$

where $\dot{P}_t$ is the actual rate of change in prices in period t.

Consequently, in equilibrium,

$$\dot{W}_t - \dot{P}_t = 0 = f(U)_t. \tag{12.5}$$

Thus, in equilibrium, it is suggested there is no Phillips relation between $\dot{W}$ and U because all labor market participants have become adjusted to inflation, which thus has no effect on such real variables as the level of unemployment.

Much controversy has surrounded this extreme version of the expectations hypothesis in which the price expectations variable $\dot{P}^e$ enters equation (12.4) with a coefficient of unity. The debate can most easily be represented by modifying the basic Phillips equation, after Smith,[22] so that $\dot{W}$ is a function not only of the level of unemployment, U, but also of the expected rate of wage inflation, $\dot{W}^e$. The modified equation is

$$\dot{W}_t = f(U) + \Phi \dot{W}_t^e.$$

Assuming that $\dot{W}_t^e$ is equal to the rate of price inflation from the previous period, $\dot{P}_{t-1}$, which would represent static expectations, we have

$$\dot{W}_t = f(U) + \Phi \dot{P}_{t-1}. \tag{12.6}$$

22. W. L. Smith, "On Some Current Issues on Monetary Economics: An Interpretation," *Journal of Economic Literature* 8 (1970): 767–782.

If it is further assumed that $\dot{W}$ exceeds $\dot{P}$ by the rate of change in output per man-hour, $\dot{q}$, then

$$\dot{P}_t = \dot{W}_t - \dot{q}_t.$$

Substitution gives

$$\dot{W}_t = f(U) + \Phi \dot{W}_{t-1} - \Phi \dot{q}_{t-1}.$$

As $\dot{W}_t = \dot{W}_{t-1}$ in long-run equilibrium, we have

$$\dot{W}_t = \Phi \dot{W}_t + f(U) - \Phi \dot{q}_{t-1}. \tag{12.7}$$

From equation (12.6), it can be seen that Friedman's hypothesis requires that the value of coefficient Φ be unity. In this case, equation (12.7) becomes

$$f(U) = \dot{q}_{t-1}.$$

Accordingly, the only way to raise $f(U)$, and reduce unemployment, is to raise $\dot{q}$.

But what if the value of Φ were less than unity? This could be because, as Keynes so strongly argued, unions are not sensitive to real wage changes that come about via movements in the price level, because such movements must affect all workers equally and so leave relativities undisturbed.[23] Then, equation (12.7) becomes

$$\dot{W}_t = \frac{1}{1 - \Phi}[f(U) - \Phi \dot{q}_{t-1}]. \tag{12.8}$$

Now an increase in inflation, given a constant rate of change of output per man-hour, would lead to a decrease in unemployment. In summary, the Friedmanite argument is that an increase in product demand would leave real wages and thus unemployment unaffected. Others argue to the contrary that real wages would fall (that is, $\Phi < 1$), giving employers the incentive to increase employment. In this case, a stable long-run Phillips curve does emerge, albeit of greater slope than the family of short-run, expectations-augmented Phillips curves. Later in this chapter, we consider the results of attempts to measure Φ.

The analyses of Phelps and Friedman are part of a body of theory that has come to be known as the new microeconomics of inflation and employment. Basically this represents an attempt to describe the mechanics of the relationship between excess demand and search or informational unemployment. The new microeconomics dispenses with the Walrasian assump-

23. Keynes, *General Theory*, pp. 14, 264.

tion of complete information. Decisionmaking within the market is assumed to take place against a backdrop of risk, uncertainty, imperfect information, and search costs.

Perhaps the best known micro treatment is that of Holt, in whose model the prospective employer and employee have to estimate the wage that they are prepared to offer and accept in the light of the imperfect information on market conditions that is open to them.[24] The prospective employee, searching the labor market for a job, is seen as formulating his wage aspirations according to the information of market conditions that he has derived from his past experience. Holt argues that these wage aspirations are a declining function of the duration of search because knowledge will be acquired about the universe being sampled and because financial resources will become drained. Consequently, the longer the time spent searching, the lower becomes the aspired wage.

It is possible to generate a Phillips relation from this framework. Let us assume that there is an increase in the aggregate demand for goods. Firms, discovering a reduction in their inventories, will take steps to increase production. In so doing, their vacancies for labor will grow and this will make it easier for those in the current stock of unemployed workers to obtain jobs. The duration of unemployment or search will shorten, while the duration of vacancies lengthens, and wage aspirations will rise. Similarly, currently employed workers, observing these trends, may engage in job search, either on or off the job, for better paying employment. As a result of this process of purposive search and movement to better-paying jobs, firms that are slow to raise their wage offers as aggregate demand increases will gradually find that they are not filling their vacancies successfully and will have to raise wages in line with firms that are quicker off the mark. The effect of an increase in aggregate demand is thus an increase in the average wage level. In this way, a Phillips relation emerges. Hence the Holt model, which incorporates a series of behavioral relations specific to the labor market, suggests that although the orthodox market analysis used by Phillips is oversimplified the end result is similar. Aspects of the Holt model are presented in appendix 12-A.

None of the above studies challenges the basic notion of a short-run tradeoff between inflation and unemployment, though inflationary expectations might remove or at least weaken the tradeoff in the long run. Let us now turn our attention to studies that question the relevance of this association.

Alternative Approaches. Excess demand for labor can be produced either by shifts in the supply curve of labor or in the demand curve and is quite

24. C. C. Holt, "Improving the Labor Market Trade-off Between Inflation and Unemployment," *American Economic Review,* Papers and Proceedings 59 (1969): 135–146.

independent of the sources of these shifts. Thus, Lipsey's theoretical explanation of the Phillips curve makes that analysis neutral as between the demand-pull and cost-push theories of the inflationary process.

The *bargaining power* variant of cost-push theory, while assuming that unions have the power to engineer wage increases, nevertheless argues that the pressure of demand is a determinant of the relevant bargaining power of unions and firms in wage negotiations. The smaller the margin of slack in the economy, it is assumed, the easier it will be for unions to impose wage increases on employers. First, the cost to employers in terms of foregone profits will be larger if they take a strike when the pressure of demand is high. Second, the ability of a union to take a strike depends on the financial resources of the union and its membership, and this ability is also said to increase with the pressure of demand.

Many of the alternative routes to the Phillips curve rely on this bargaining power explanation, in which the pressure of demand, as reflected in the level of profits, acts as the trigger mechanism or stimulus of an inflationary situation and also as a determinant of the speed of wage inflation. For example, Kaldor has suggested that the Phillips relation emerges from a spurious correlation between unemployment rates and profits.[25] For the United Kingdom, however, there is little evidence that profits and money wage rate changes are related.[26] The American evidence, on the face of it, provides more support for the profits variable. Bhatia found profits in American manufacturing to be an excellent explanatory variable for wage change during the postwar period. Eckstein and Wilson, using wage round data (chapter 13), and Perry, using annual time-series data, also for manufacturing, confirmed the significance of profits in American wage equations.[27] However, those studies that have found a close relation between wage changes and a profit variable typically do not include the rate of change of prices as an explanatory variable. The inclusion of a cost-of-living term generally reduces the significance of the profit variable.[28] And although the profits variable was popular in American wage equations prior to 1968, it was quickly discarded when profits failed to track the wage explosion of 1967-70. Recent American wage equations do not even mention ability to pay and liquidity as determinants of short-run wage changes.

25. N. Kaldor, "Economic Growth and the Problems of Inflation, Part II," *Economica* 26 (1959): 287-298.
26. See R. G. Lipsey and M. D. Steuer, "The Relation between Profits and Wage Rates," *Economica* 28 (1961): 137-155.
27. R. J. Bhatia, "Unemployment and the Rate of Change of Money Earnings in the U.S., 1900-1958," *Economica* 28 (1961): 286-296; O. Eckstein and T. Wilson, "The Determinants of Money Wages in American Industry," *Quarterly Journal of Economics* 70 (1962): 379-414; G. L. Perry, "The Determinants of Wage Rate Changes and the Inflation-Unemployment Tradeoff for the U.S.," *Review of Economic Studies* 31 (1964): 287-308.
28. W. G. Bowen and R. A. Berry, "Unemployment Conditions and Movements of the Money Wage Level," *Review of Economics and Statistics* 45 (1963): 163-172.

The tightness of the relation between profits and wage changes, were it demonstrated, might be thought to indicate the importance of cost-push elements in wage inflation. However, demand-pull theory need not preclude profits from influencing the course of W. When sales are increasing and short-run above-normal profits are being earned, the actions of employers to expand their labor forces will affect the excess demand for labor and thereby bid up wages, *ceteris paribus*. This argument posits that both the unemployment and the profits variables should reflect the excess demand for labor, though it is then necessary to explain why there is not always a close association between them.[29] Be this as it may, enough has been said to indicate that, even if we observe a close relation between profits and wage changes, this does not provide us with clear-cut evidence in the demand-pull/cost-push controversy.

Another criticism of the profits variable has been advanced by Kuh, who argues that profits are a proxy for a more fundamental determinant of wages: the marginal revenue product of labor. The argument is that profits are not a causal determinant of wage inflation and that the variable only obtains significance in an empirical sense because it is associated with the movement of labor productivity. If we assume that average and marginal products vary in the same direction—given a Cobb-Douglas production function with neutral technical change, then marginal and average productivity differ only by a multiplicative constant—we can use average revenue product to proxy marginal revenue product.[30] Average revenue product (PX/N, where P is the price index of production) also resembles a profit markup (PX/WN, where W is the hourly wage rate). A profits variable could thus simply be a proxy for average revenue product. When the demand for labor rises, either because P or X rises relatively faster than N, wages will also rise so long as the supply of labor is inelastic with respect to the wage level.

This analysis is helpful in explaining the association between profits and wage changes, but there remain problems. It is true that Kuh's empirical results tend to favor his productivity formulation over the Phillips-plus-profits relation for the United States. However, these results are no better than those obtained for many more orthodox models. The difficulty is that important issues of labor supply are disposed of by the assumption of labor supply inelasticity. Moreover, there is the possibility that labor productivity is not, as Kuh suggests, an alternative to labor excess demand as proxied by unemployment), but additional to it. Vanderkamp has cogently argued that,

---

29. It has also been suggested that profits reflect business expectations about future product demand. See S. J. Turnovsky and M. L. Wachter, "A Test of the Expectations Hypothesis," *Review of Economics and Statistics* 54 (1977): 48.

30. Consider a Cobb-Douglas production function of the form $X = A \cdot N^a \cdot K^b$, where X is total physical product, N is the input of man-hours, and $a + b = 1$. The marginal product of labor is $\partial X/\partial N = a \cdot A \cdot N^{a-1} \cdot K^b$; the average product of labor is $X/N = A \cdot N^{a-1} \cdot K^b$. Thus, $\partial X/\partial N = a \cdot (X/N)$. See E. Kuh, "A Productivity Theory of Wage Levels—An Alternative to the Phillips Curve," *Review of Economic Studies* 34 (1967): 333–370.

because labor is a quasi-fixed factor, only a part of the difference between actual and desired employment in any period is eliminated and reflected in variations in unemployment. Part of this difference will also be reflected in variations in labor productivity, which should thus also be included in the equation.[31]

Phillips' study did not emphasize union influence on the rate of change in wages. It is true that he specifically gave unions a role via the $\dot{P}$ variable. However, he found that the curve derived from 1861–1913 data also fitted the 1948–57 experience quite accurately,[32] despite a doubling in the proportion of the labor force unionized over the period in question.

However, subsequent research has somewhat revised this implication. Lipsey's results, for example, are compatible with a movement of the aggregate Phillips curve in the twentieth century on the lines suggested by the *bureaucratic union* hypothesis.[33] The latter argues that unions' money wage demands are not very sensitive to the level of unemployment. This means that unions create an inflationary bias only over a certain range of unemployment situations, as can be demonstrated by using figure 12.3. Let us assume that the union wage reaction function takes the path BB' in quadrant IV. If we further assume that the relationship between labor market tightness and unemployment is the same for both unionized and nonunionized sectors of the labor market (quadrant III), it then follows that the Phillips curve applicable to the union sector (curve B) will cut across the steeper sloped curve of the nonunion sector (curve A). In quadrant I of figure 12.3, we see that it cuts at point X, indicating unions create an inflationary bias when unemployment is higher than X. A cross-section study for the postwar United States is in fact consistent with this hypothesis.[34] However, other studies have reported that the coefficient on the excess demand proxy is larger for strongly organized groups than for weakly organized groups, such that the former sector's Phillips curve is displaced above that of the latter at all levels of unemployment.[35] Nevertheless, the balance of the evidence favors the interpretation that unions damp down the scale of wage change at low levels of unemployment. Equally clearly, there are a number of inconsistencies in the empirical evidence. For example, how are we to make consistent the finding that unions damp wage reaction to excess demand with the empirical result that they apparently escalate wage reaction to price inflation?[36] One possible explanation is that unionization is

31. J. Vanderkamp, "Wage Adjustment, Productivity and Price Change Expectations," *Review of Economics and Statistics* 39 (1972): 62.
32. Phillips, "Relation Between Unemployment," p. 297.
33. Lipsey, "A Further Analysis," pp. 26–27.
34. K. M. McCaffree, "A Further Consideration of Wages, Unemployment and Prices in the United States, 1948–1958," *Industrial and Labor Relations Review* 17 (1963): 60–74.
35. G. Pierson, "The Effect of Union Strength on the U.S. Phillips Curve," *American Economic Review* 58 (1969): 465–467; J. Vandercamp, "Wages and Price Level Determination: An Empirical Model for Canada," *Economica* 33 (1966): 194–218.
36. Ibid.

perhaps not the real determining variable explaining the observed differences between the wage adjustment functions of weakly and densely organized sectors, but is itself an endogenous variable determined by more fundamental microeconomic factors. Here we return to the distinction made in chapter 5 between open and closed labor markets. Open markets function in an auction fashion, whereas closed markets evince a career labor market structure, in which idiosyncratic jobs present a bilateral monopoly problem for firms and employees and lead to the establishment of rules of wage adjustment that minimize bargaining and turnover costs that may arise from such a situation. The evolution of such rules may damp down wage change response to nonclearing situations, but at the same time make for full and speedy compensation via wage changes for the effects of price inflation, so that the real income growth path of career labor market participants is stabilized closer to its trend value than is the case with the participants of auction labor markets. At the same time, there are good theoretical reasons for hypothesizing that the same factors determining the existence or absence of these rules, large firm-specific human capital investments, high costs of labor turnover, and so on, are determinants of the degree of unionization of a labor market.

Other investigators have attempted to assess the role of trade unions in the wage inflation process by measuring trade union pushfulness more directly. The best known study is that of Hines, whose work challenges the basic notion of a simple short-run tradeoff between inflation and unemployment.[37] Hines postulated that $\dot{W}$ crucially depends upon trade union pushfulness, and that the latter might be proxied by the rate of change in the percentage of the labor force that is unionized, $\dot{T}$, and the level of union density, T. The rationale for adopting this proxy is that, when unions are militant, they will simultaneously go in for union drives and make demands for wage increases. The degree of militancy is greater per unit change in union density when T is high than when it is low, because it is more difficult to secure a given increase in membership when that membership is already nearly complete than when it is not.

The empirical evidence provided by Hines for the period 1893–1961 yields strong support for this hypothesis, especially for the years 1921–38 and 1949–61, when the fitted relation emerged as ($|t|$ are given in parentheses):

$$\dot{W}_t = -7.3570 + 2.9224\ \dot{T}_t + 0.317\ T_t.$$
$$(16.9) \qquad (7.04)$$
$$R^2 = 0.9069$$
$$DW = 1.57$$

37. A. G. Hines, "Trade Unions and Wage Inflation in the United Kingdom, 1893–1961," *Review of Economic Studies* 31 (1964): 221–252. For an earlier study employing impressionistic estimates of union militancy, see L. A. Dicks-Mireaux and J. C. R. Dow, "The Determinants of Wage Inflation: United Kingdom, 1946–1956," *Journal of the Royal Statistical Society*, Series A, 122 (1959): 194–218.

Hines even found that the U variable became insignificant when included with $\dot{T}$ and $\dot{P}$.[38] Similar findings were reported by Hines in a series of subsequent studies.[39] For the United States, Ashenfelter, Johnson, and Pencavel have also found union pushfulness to be important, although the unemployment variable retains significance in their formulation.[40] Their result, using manufacturing wage data for the period 1914 to 1963, is as follows:

$$\dot{W}_t = 3.68 - 0.47\ U + 0.37\ \dot{P}_t + 16.2\ N + 0.43\ \dot{T}_t + 0.60\ S_t$$
$$\quad\ (2.78)\ (2.94)\quad\ (1.61)\qquad (4.12)\qquad (3.07)\qquad (2.22)$$
$$R^2 = 0.83$$
$$DW = 2.26$$

where N takes the value of 1 in 1935 to allow for the National Recovery Act of that year, which legislated a decline in weekly hours with no change in weekly pay;

S is a strikes variable; and

$|t|$ are given in parentheses.

Hines noted that T was uncorrelated with U, using various lags. Instead $\dot{T}$ appeared to be highly dependent on the current rate of change of prices and also, to a small but significant extent, on the level of profits. From these results, there seems to be no evidence that union aggressiveness is conditioned by the tightness of the market. Rather, the relations suggest that a wage-price spiral is at work, whereby price increases generate union militancy, which in turn generates wage increases.

However, the validity of the Hines model has been questioned. It may, for example, be objected that his findings merely reflect the influence of changes in the proportion of the labor force in receipt of union wages. Thus, if the union-nonunion differential is positive, an increase in this proportion will raise the average wage. This aggregation phenomenon is not of itself immediately related to issues of union militancy.[41] Second, the direction of causality is not clear-cut. For example, one might argue that the demand for union membership status will rise before wage negotiation bouts, because the mere fact of a wage negotiation between union and employer raises employee expectations of the probability of a work stoppage. The expected

38. Ibid., p. 228.
39. See, for example, A. G. Hines, "The Determinants of the Rate of Change of Money Wages and the Effectiveness of Incomes Policy," in H. G. Johnson and A. R. Nobay, eds., *The Current Inflation* (London: Macmillan, 1971), pp. 143–175.
40. O. Ashenfelter, G. Johnson, and J. H. Pencavel, "Trade Unions and the Rate of Change of Money Wage Rates in United States Manufacturing Industry," *Review of Economic Studies* 39 (1972): 27–54.
41. D. Metcalf, "Unions, Incomes Policy, and Relative Wages in Britain," *British Journal of Industrial Relations* 15 (1977): 157–175.

income loss entailed will be lower for a union member than for a nonmember because of the strike benefits paid out to the former by their trade union. An observed association between $\dot{T}$ and $\dot{W}$ may thus be a reflection of a passive security motive for minimizing the income loss associated with a stoppage.[42] Alternatively, we might regard it as more plausible to hypothesize that, when trade unions obtain increases in wages, for whatever reason, the union may attract an increase in membership (chapter 7). Third, despite Hines' assertions to the contrary, there does appear to be some association between $\dot{T}$ and the level of economic activity; hence, the former variable may track labor market pressures.[43]

An alternative measure of union pushfulness has taken the form of a strikes variable. A number of studies have recorded a positive correlation between the volume of strike activity, variously defined, and $\dot{W}$. Equally, others have reported that they can discern no robust statistical association between the two variables.[44] However, as we have seen in chapter 7, there is little reason for associating strikes with militancy. They are more likely to be associated with a lack of information. If strikes are the outcome of mismatched expectations held by employers and employees, and if, as would appear plausible, this mismatching is directly associated with the rate of inflation, then any positive association between strikes and $\dot{W}$ is independent of militancy.

What then are we to conclude from this brief review of the role of trade unions in the inflationary process? The ambiguities of the empirical literature bedevil the task of arriving at firm empirical generalizations. It remains to be convincingly demonstrated that the presence and militancy of unions affect $\dot{W}$ independently of underlying economic forces. Pending theoretical and methodological refinement of the union inflation model, it would be unwise to discard Friedman's dictum that "unions are simply the thermometers registering the heat, rather than furnaces producing the heat" of inflation.[45] In any case, the findings reported above are excessively general and tell us little of the mechanics of the inflationary aspect of trade union behavior.

---

42. D. L. Purdy and G. Zis, "On the Concept and Measurement of Trade Union Militancy," in D. E. W. Laidler and D. L. Purdy, eds., *Inflation and Labour Markets* (Manchester: Manchester University Press, 1974), pp. 38–60.

43. O. Ashenfelter and J. H. Pencavel, "American Trade Union Growth: 1900–1960," *Quarterly Journal of Economics* 83 (1969): 434–448; R. Richardson, "Trade Union Growth," *British Journal of Industrial Relations* 15 (1977): 157–175.

44. See respectively L. Godfrey and J. Taylor, "Earnings Changes in the U.K. 1954–1970: Excess Labour Supply, Expected Inflation and Union Influence," *Bulletin of the Oxford University Institute of Economics and Statistics* 35 (1973): 197–216; J. Johnston and M. C. Timbrell, "Empirical Tests of a Bargaining Model of Wage Rate Determination," *Manchester School* 41 (1973): 141–167.

45. M. Friedman, "Some Comments on the Significance of Labor Unions for Economic Policy," in D. M. Wright, ed., *The Impact of the Union* (New York: Harcourt-Brace, 1951), p. 222.

More detailed examination of this particular issue is remitted to chapter 13. Meanwhile, let us turn to recent developments of the excess demand model.

Recent Developments. Apart from the role of expectations within the wage change equations, there arises also the question of which type of statistics should be used to represent a given variable. Compared with the amount of work devoted to methodological and equational innovations, little attention has been given to this point. Hence, before we investigate the role of expectations in the wage change estimating equation, let us first focus our attention upon the specification of data question. We restrict our analysis to refinements of the basic Phillips variables, $\dot{W}$ and U.

Measurement Issues. First, consider the dependent variable. The suggestion has been made that the particular wage rate index chosen by Phillips and numerous other commentators has generated misleading results. For example, it has been argued that the demand price of labor is better measured by earnings, together with other nonwage labor costs. This criticism relates largely, though not exclusively, to countries with two-tier bargaining structures.[46] In the United Kingdom, for example, wage *rates* tend to be established by collective agreements at the industry or national level, whereas wage *earnings* reflect plant-level bargaining, productivity changes, and regrading in addition to wage rate adjustments. Thus, earnings may display more flexibility than rates and the relationship between the two pay series may diverge—as happened in the United Kingdom over the period 1961–65. In such a situation, it has been argued that the pay series to be used depends on the problem at hand. Rothschild, for example, argues that wage rates are the correct series to take if we wish to test the influence of unemployment, that is, the labor market situation, on bargaining; whereas earnings might prove the more appropriate index if demand-pull forces are regarded as being more important.[47] However appealing this suggestion might appear at first blush, the fact remains that the decision as to which series to use as a proxy for the true price of labor cannot be made until the full structure of the wage change model has been specified. We are unable to report any convincing theoretical developments in this area.

A second criticism levelled at the use of the wage rate series is that it has resulted in equation specification errors. Suppose that in any given quarter of a year, we divide workers into two groups, A and B: those who receive

46. M. H. Peston, "The Micro-economics of the Phillips Curve," in Johnson and Nobay, *Current Inflation,* p. 137. For a review of recent American attempts to construct a more sophisticated wage index, see W. Y. Oi, "On Measuring the Impact of Wage-Price Controls: A Critical Appraisal," in *The Economics of Price and Wage Controls,* Carnegie-Rochester Conference Series on Public Policy 2 (1976): 26–28.
47. K. W. Rothschild, "The Phillips Curve and All That," *Scottish Journal of Political Economy* 18 (1971): 261.

adjustments to their wages in that quarter and those who do not. Let λ_t denote the proportion of workers receiving wage rate changes in the tth quarter. If $\dot{W}_{At}$ is the rate of change in wages for workers getting wage changes, which means that $\dot{W}_{Bt} = 0$, the rate of change in the aggregate wage rate will be a weighted average of $\dot{W}_{At}$ and $\dot{W}_{Bt} = 0$; that is,

$$\dot{W}_t = \lambda_t \, \dot{W}_{At}.$$

It is reasonable to suppose that $\dot{W}_{At}$ will be a function of some vector of explanatory variables, X_t, representing, say, unemployment measures and price inflation variables. We then have

$$\dot{W}_{At} = \alpha + \beta X_t + e_t.$$

Substituting, we obtain an equation in which the observed rate of change of an aggregate wage rate index, $\dot{W}_t$, is related to λ_t and the vector of explanatory variables, X_t,

$$\dot{W}_t = \alpha\lambda_t + \beta(\lambda_t X_t) + U_t$$

where $U_t = \lambda_t e_t$ is the random disturbance in the wage equation.

In much of the British literature using quarterly changes in aggregate series, it is assumed that $\lambda_t + \ldots + \lambda_{t-3} = 1$ for all values of t. That is, the sum of the fraction of workers receiving wage adjustments over any four-quarter period is assumed to equal unity and, further, that $\lambda_t = \frac{1}{4}$ for all periods. However, Ashenfelter and Pencavel have pointed out that the proportion of British workers obtaining wage changes varies widely from quarter to quarter.[48] When they included λ_t and the interaction of λ_t and X_t in a Phillips-type wage equation, the explanatory power rose sharply. It might also be conjectured that the proportion of workers receiving increases may well increase during periods of rapidly changing excess demand/ unanticipated cost-of-living changes, so that the frequency of settlements is endogenous. Thus, the omission of the variable λ not only enlarges the size of the unexplained residual variance, but also gives biased estimates of the parameters of the wage change equation.

Let us now turn to the unemployment or excess demand variable. While U, or its reciprocal, has remained the most commonly used measure of excess demand, there has been an increasing tendency to seek alternative measures. This can perhaps largely be attributed to the apparent collapse of the Phillips curve in the late 1960s in both Great Britain and the United States.

Attempts to refine the unemployment variable have largely focused upon vacancy statistics and estimates of hidden unemployment and hoarded labor.

48. O. Ashenfelter and J. H. Pencavel, "Wage Changes and the Frequency of Wage Settlements," *Economica* 42 (1975): 162–170.

Dicks-Mireaux and Dow constructed a measure of excess demand using both vacancy and unemployment data, namely $(V - U)/S_L$. Other studies have used vacancy data instead of unemployment.[49] On theoretical grounds, we might expect vacancies to be related in a nonlinear fashion to unemployment and thus to provide an equally satisfactory excess demand proxy, but the fact is that vacancy data, which are for all practical purposes unavailable in the United States, can be considered much less reliable than unemployment statistics.

The use of unemployment data as the sole excess demand proxy has also been criticized as an unreliable indicator, because it fails to take account of the various types of hidden unemployment and labor hoarding. The issues involved in such measures have been examined in chapter 11, and so here we can simply repeat the argument that excess demand can be approximated by

$$\frac{D_L - S_L}{S_L} = \frac{(E - D) - (E + R + H)}{E + R + H} = \frac{-(D + R + H)}{E + R + H}$$

where R is registered/recorded unemployment;
$\quad D$ is hoarded labor; and
$\quad H$ is hidden unemployment.

The approach taken has been to use an augmented unemployment variable, that is, to supplement R with measures of D, or H, or both. Simler and Tella found that the inclusion of hidden unemployment contributed significantly to the explanation of annual percentage changes in hourly wages in American manufacturing over the period 1948(1)–1964(2).[50] Yet Taylor reports that the inclusion of hidden unemployment had little effect upon the performance of the unemployment variable in a Phillips-type analysis of American wage data over the period 1948(4)–1968(4). Rather, it was hoarded labor that, when included in the numerator of the unemployment rate, significantly improved the performance of the unemployment variable in his wage equation. For the United Kingdom as well, Taylor found that the unemployment variable, when adjusted to allow for hoarded labor, performed better in explaining the rate of change in overtime-adjusted *earnings* than recorded unemployment alone.[51] (However, this was not true

49. L. A. Dicks-Mireaux and J. C. R. Dow, "The Determinants of Wage Inflation: United Kingdom, 1946–56," *Journal of the Royal Statistical Society*, Series A, 122 (1959): 145–174; J. K. Bowers, P. C. Cheshire, and A. E. Webb, "The Change in the Relationship Between Unemployment and Earnings Increases: A Review of Some Possible Explanations," *National Institute Economic Review* 54 (1970): 44–63.
50. N. J. Simler and A. Tella, "Labour Reserves and the Phillips Curve," *Review of Economics and Statistics* 50 (1968): 32–49.
51. See, respectively, J. Taylor, "Hidden Unemployment, Hoarded Labor, and the Phillips Curve," *Southern Economic Journal* 37 (1970): 1–16; idem, "Incomes Policy, the Structure of Unemployment and the Phillips Curve: the United Kingdom Experience, 1953–70," in J. M. Parkin and M. T. Sumner, eds., *Incomes Policy and Inflation* (Manchester and Toronto: Manchester University Press and Toronto University Press, 1972), pp.182–200.

of the wage *rate* equation and, moreover, the good earnings fit depended upon the inclusion of a union militancy variable.)

Given the statistical difficulties of measuring hidden unemployment and hoarded labor, we should perhaps not be surprised at these results. It seems likely that estimates of hidden unemployment have overstated the degree of labor market slack, because of a failure to consider the characteristics of the hidden unemployed: the relatively low skill level and high ratio of part-time to full-time workers within this category. Hoarded labor may well be the firmer variable. Clearly, this concept of internal labor market slack is an important one.

Finally, mention should be made of the attempt by Perry in the United States to measure disequilibrium in the labor market by the reciprocal of an income-weighted unemployment rate.[52] Perry began with the premise that all members of the labor force do not provide equivalent labor flows, although the official unemployment rate attaches the same weight to all unemployed persons, whether they are black teenagers or middle-aged engineers. The suggestion is that the downward pressure on an aggregate wage index will be greater when the pool of unemployed persons contains larger fractions of individuals who, on average, earn higher hourly wages and work longer hours per year. Therefore, Perry weighted both the labor force and the pool of unemployed persons, classified by age and sex, although not color, by their average annual wage earnings relative to the earnings of prime age males, 35–44 years of age. In this adjusted excess demand index, females and young males, who typically experience higher unemployment rates and who represent an increasingly higher proportion of the American labor force, thus receive smaller weights. This analysis is interesting because it offers a suggestion as to why the Phillips curve for the United States, measured in the conventional way, appeared to have shifted to the right in the 1960s. On this reasoning, the upward shift in the conventional curve, linking $\dot{W}$ to the recorded unemployment level, was in practice to be explained by the fact that, relative to prime age males, young people and women had come to make up a higher proportion of the labor force than hitherto.

Specification of the Curve.   Let us now turn to the choice of variables in the augmented Phillips curve approach. We will begin with the variable $\dot{U}$. It will be recalled that $\dot{U}$ was construed by Phillips as an expectational variable, whereas Lipsey interpreted it as a proxy for the dispersion of market unemployment rates around the aggregate value—the aggregation hypothesis. This debate has been clouded, however, because a number of studies have found no statistically significant relationship between $\dot{W}$ and $\dot{U}$ or, for that matter, between $\dot{U}$ and the dispersion of unemployment between micromarkets.[53]

52. G. L. Perry, "Changing Labor Markets and Inflation," *Brookings Papers on Economic Activity* 3 (1970): 411–488.

53. See, for example, G. C. Archibald, "The Phillips Curve and the Distribution of Unem-

A number of studies have substituted a more direct measure of the dispersion of unemployment rates between markets, such as a variance term, for U. For example, Archibald has included a measure of unemployment dispersion as an additional variable. His findings suggest that, for both the United Kingdom and the United States, unemployment dispersion does increase the aggregate rate of change in wages for a given level of unemployment. Work by Perry, using a dispersion index based on the dispersion of age and sex specific unemployment rates from the overall unemployment rate, also supports the structuralist hypothesis in the United States.[54] Similar conclusions have been reached by Thomas and Stoney for the United Kingdom, whose estimates suggest that unemployment dispersion exerted an upward pressure on aggregate rates of wage change of more than two percentage points in the postwar period and of more than four percentage points in the prewar interval.[55]

However, there might be little room for optimism concerning the possibility of improving the overall short-run inflation-unemployment tradeoff by policies designed to reduce regional dispersion in unemployment rates. First, a number of more recent empirical studies have found evidence unfavorable to the aggregation or structuralist hypothesis.[56] Second, even if it could be shown that the aggregate tradeoff is a function of the structure of unemployment, it does not follow that dispersion minimization is the way to achieve the best possible tradeoff. This depends, as we have seen in discussing figure 12.4, on the assumption that the micro-Phillips curves are similar. However, published estimates suggest that slopes of regional Phillips curves, for example, can differ widely. To take the case of Great Britain, the slopes are so different that dispersion minimization could, it seems, actually worsen the aggregate tradeoff.[57] But it is best not to emphasize these counterintuitive results; rather, we shall take the aggregation hypothesis as not proven.

Let us now turn to the price change variable. Lipsey's hypothesis that price changes affect money wage changes continuously, rather than with a threshold effect as Phillips assumed to be the case, has found general

ployment," *American Economic Review,* Papers and Proceedings 59 (1969): 124–134; R. H. Thomas and P. J. M. Stoney, "Unemployment Dispersion as a Determinant of Wage Inflation in the United Kingdom, 1925–1966," *Manchester School* 39 (1971): 83–116.

54. Archibald, "Phillips Curve"; Perry, "Changing Labor Markets."

55. Thomas and Stoney, "Unemployment Dispersion."

56. A. G. Hines, "The Phillips Curve and the Distribution of Unemployment," *American Economic Review* 62 (1972): 155–160; F. P. R. Brechling, "Wage Inflation and the Structure of Regional Unemployment," *Journal of Money, Credit and Banking* 5 (1973): 355–379; D. I. MacKay and R. A. Hart, "Wage Inflation and the Phillips Relationship," *Manchester School* 42 (1974): 136–161.

57. A. P. Thirlwall, "Regional Phillips Curves," *Bulletin of the Oxford University Institute of Economics and Statistics* 32 (1970): 19–32; D. Metcalf, "The Determination of Earnings Changes: A Regional Analysis for the U.K., 1960–1968," *International Economic Review* 12 (1971): 273–282.

empirical support. In the literature of the early 1960s, the significance of the $\dot{P}$ variable was generally rationalized in terms of trade union policies that had as their objective the protection of the real wage. However, we must be careful in making this inference. According to the expectations theory, a steady increase in the price of final output, perhaps because of a steady increase in the money supply, would eventually feed back to the labor market. This would lead to an expected upward shift in money wages demanded and offered (otherwise an excess demand for labor would emerge), and so to an increase in actual money wages. Consequently, a pattern of price increases followed by money wage increases is compatible with the demand-pull hypothesis, once inflation comes to be expected.

It will be recalled that the expectations hypothesis, as developed by Friedman, is that wage earners have a real wage level in mind and will adjust their money wage aspirations in the light of anticipated changes in prices. The absence of money illusion implies that the expectational variables, $\dot{W}^e$ and $\dot{P}^e$, should enter the wage equation with a coefficient equal to unity. The question of whether this coefficient equals unity is important, for this would in turn imply the absence of a long-run money wage–unemployment tradeoff or, equivalently, the existence of a long-run Phillips curve that passes vertically through the natural rate of unemployment—assuming that this natural rate is invariant with respect to the economy's history of inflation.[58]

Unfortunately, direct observations on expectations are not widely available, so a proxy variable needs to be substituted. The initial approach adopted in the literature was simply to regress $\dot{W}_t$ on $\dot{P}_t$. The interpretation was that the expected rate of inflation was approximated by the current rate—the "static expectations" approach. More recently, this has given way to the view that expectations of price changes can *adapt,* and thus depend on price changes in some, perhaps many, periods in the past. A weighted average of past price changes can be constructed in which the weights are made to decline the further back in time are the price changes in question. One commonly used approach is as follows. First, it is necessary to make some assumption as to the way in which price change expectations in the current period depend on actual and expected price changes in the past period. A simple method is to assume

$$\dot{P}_t^e = b\dot{P}_t + (1 - b)\,\dot{P}_{t-1}^e \qquad 0 \leqslant b \leqslant 1 \qquad (12.9)$$

where $\dot{P}_t^e$ is the expected rate of change of prices in period t;
$\quad\ P_t$ is the actual rate of change of prices in period t; and
$\quad\ b$ is a constant.

We see that current price change expectations are a weighted average of current actual price changes and the last period's expected price changes,

58. But see M. Friedman, *Inflation and Unemployment: The New Dimension of Politics,* 1976 Alfred Nobel Memorial Lecture (London: Institute of Economic Affairs, 1977), pp. 23–29.

where b and $(1 - b)$ are the weights. If b is so large as to approach unity, it can be seen that current expectations depend closely on what is currently happening, but little on what has happened in the past; conversely, if b is small (near zero), more weight will be placed on past events. If the periods we are working with are short, say we are using monthly rather than annual data, then we might choose the following, slightly different formulation

$$\dot{P}_t^e = b\dot{P}_{t-1} + (1 - b)\dot{P}_{t-1}^e \qquad 0 \leqslant b \leqslant 1.$$

Here, it can be seen that current price change expectations are not made to depend upon current actual price changes. This is appropriate if the periods in question are so short that we cannot realistically expect the current period's actual price change to have worked its way into current expectations of price changes.

Selecting a scheme such as equation (12.9) above, it follows that the underlying way in which $\dot{P}_t^e$ depends on past actual values $\dot{P}_{t-1}$, $\dot{P}_{t-2}$, $\dot{P}_{t-3}$, $\ldots$ is given by

$$\dot{P}_t^e = b\dot{P}_t + b(1 - b)\dot{P}_{t-1} + b(1 - b)^2\dot{P}_{t-2} + b(1 - b)^3\dot{P}_{t-3} + \cdots$$

$$= b\sum_{j=0}^{\infty} (1 - b)^j \dot{P}_{t-j}. \qquad (12.10)$$

This result follows because if equation (12.10) holds for $\dot{P}_t^e$ it also holds for $\dot{P}_{t-1}^e$, so that

$$\dot{P}_{t-1}^e = b\dot{P}_{t-1} + b(1 - b)\dot{P}_{t-2} + b(1 - b)^2\dot{P}_{t-3} + \cdots.$$

Therefore

$$\begin{aligned}
\dot{P}_t^e - \dot{P}_{t-1}^e &= b[\dot{P}_t + (1 - b)\dot{P}_{t-1} + (1 - b)^2\dot{P}_{t-2} + \cdots] \\
&\quad - b[\dot{P}_{t-1} + (1 - b)\dot{P}_{t-2} + (1 - b)^2\dot{P}_{t-3} + \cdots] \\
&= b[\dot{P}_t - (b\dot{P}_{t-1} + b(1 - b)\dot{P}_{t-2} + b(1 - b)^2\dot{P}_{t-3} + \cdots)] \\
&= b(\dot{P}_t - \dot{P}_{t-1}^e).
\end{aligned}$$

Upon rearranging, we obtain equation (12.9). Thus, equation (12.10) and equation (12.9) are equivalent. From equation (12.10), however, we can better understand the role of the constant b, which measures the speed of adaptation. Let us suppose that $b = .1$, namely a process of slow adaptation. Equation (12.10) now becomes

$$\begin{aligned}
\dot{P}_t^e &= .1\,(\dot{P}_t + .9\,\dot{P}_{t-1} + .81\,\dot{P}_{t-2} + .729\,\dot{P}_{t-3} + \cdots) \\
&= .1\,\dot{P}_t + .09\,\dot{P}_{t-1} + .081\,\dot{P}_{t-2} + .0729\,\dot{P}_{t-3} + \cdots.
\end{aligned}$$

In this case, it can be seen that past periods' inflation rates are given considerable weight in determining current expected rates. On the other hand, if $b = .9$, then

$$\dot{P}_t^e = .9\,(\dot{P}_t + .1\,\dot{P}_{t-2} + .01\,\dot{P}_{t-3} + .001\,\dot{P}_{t-4} + \cdots)$$
$$= .9\,\dot{P}_t + .09\,\dot{P}_{t-2} + .009\,\dot{P}_{t-3} + \cdots.$$

Here we observe swift adaptation, with the current actual rate of inflation having by far the greater weight in determining current expectations. Finally, equation (12.10) shows that, if the actual rate of inflation remains constant, the expected rate of inflation will move toward this constant rate and eventually come to equal it, although this process will take longer if b is small than if b is large.

There are several problems with this approach. To take a relatively minor one first: there is nothing intrinsically correct about the geometrically declining weights in equation (12.10). We could just as well take an arithmetically declining series. For example, the series of weights could be

$$2N/N(N + 1), 2(N - 1)/N(N + 1), \ldots, 2(N - N + 1)/N(N + 1)$$

where N is the number of periods over which the average is assumed to extend. A short N would imply swift adaptation and a long N would indicate slow adaptation. As with b in the geometric case, N has to be estimated.

A more important limitation of the adaptive expectations approach is that it implies that people ignore the trend of inflation. To illustrate this point, let us assume that our sequence of weights is $0.4\,\dot{P}_t + 0.3\,\dot{P}_{t-1}, + 0.2\,\dot{P}_{t-2} + 0.1\,\dot{P}_{t-3}$. Now suppose that the actual inflation rate had been steadily falling, such that $\dot{P}_{t-3} = 3\%$, $\dot{P}_{t-2} = 2\%$, $\dot{P}_{t-1} = 1\%$, and $\dot{P}_t = $ zero. On the adaptive expectations model, this would generate a $\dot{P}_t^e$ of 1%, which is the same value as that predicted by the model had the rate of inflation been held at 1% over the four-year interval in question. This is clearly rather unlikely. It implies that, in a period of continually rising inflation, people would always underestimate the future rise in prices. An alternative approach would be to postulate an *extrapolative* expectations process, whereby $\dot{P}_t^e = \dot{P}_t + c(\dot{P}_t - \dot{P}_{t-1})$, $0 \leqslant c \leqslant 1$. Here, expected price changes are made to depend on the current rate of inflation and adaptively on the trend rate of inflation. But, again, people would systematically make the wrong predictions if there were a sustained rate of increase in the inflation rate. The virtue of the model represented in equation (12.10) lies in its simplicity. There is no neat solution here; rather, the deciding factor must be how well it performs in empirical work.

Economists have also experimented with direct data on the state of price expectations. In the United States, for example, quantitative data on the inflation expectations held by businessmen and business economists have been obtained from survey material.[59] In the United Kingdom, methods have been devised to obtain an estimate of the expected rate of inflation from a time series of qualitative survey data generated by asking people whether they believe certain prices will rise, fall, or remain constant over some specific future period.[60] The chief value of this work at the moment is that we can regress the directly observed expectations variable on its lagged value and actual inflation rates in a regression of the form suggested by equation (12.9). We are then able to gain an insight into the performance of the adaptive expectations assumption. In fact, it appears to perform quite well, which increases our confidence in its use.

The basic empirical questions are: (1) Does the coefficient on $\dot{P}^e$ in the Phillips curve, Φ in equation (12.4), have a value of unity? (2) What is the speed of adaptation of the labor market to new rates of inflation, b in equation (12.9) or equation (12.10) above? These questions are related, because it is necessary to have an estimate of the speed of adaptation, b, in order to estimate Φ. Two methods have been adopted to estimate b. The first is directly to estimate b along with the other parameters. This is done as follows. Repeating equation (12.4), we have

$$\dot{W}_t = f(U) + \Phi \dot{P}_t^e$$

and also

$$\dot{W}_{t-1} = f(U) + \Phi \dot{P}_{t-1}.$$

Assuming equation (12.9), we have

$$\dot{P}_t^e = b\dot{P}_t + (1 - b)\dot{P}_{t-1}^e$$
$$= b\dot{P}_t + \frac{(1 - b)}{\Phi}[\dot{W}_{t-1} - f(U)].$$

Substituting into equation (12.4) gives

$$\dot{W}_t = f(U) + b\Phi \dot{P}_t + (1 - b)[\dot{W}_{t-1} - f(U)]$$
$$= bf(U) + b\Phi \dot{P}_t + (1 - b)\dot{W}_{t-1}.$$

Thus, a regression of $\dot{W}_t$ on $\dot{W}_{t-1}$ would yield an estimate of $(1 - b)$. The value of b, thereby derived, could then be divided into the estimated coefficient on $\dot{P}$ to yield an estimate of Φ. In this manner, Turnovsky and Wachter used biannual data for the United States over the period 1949–69 to obtain

59. S. J. Turnovsky and M. L. Wachter, "A Test of the Expectations Hypothesis Using Directly Observed Wage and Price Expectations," *Review of Economics and Statistics* 54 (1972): 47–54.
60. J. A. Carlson and J. M. Parkin, "Inflation Expectations," *Economica* 42 (1975): 123–128.

$$\dot{W}_t = 1.61 + 21.9 * U_t^{-1} - 10.21\ U_{t-1}^{-2} + 0.493 * \dot{P}_t$$
$$-0.021\ \dot{W}_{t-1} - 2.36 * D_t$$
$$R^2 = 0.716$$
$$DW = 1.47$$

where * denotes significance at the 5% level; and
D_t is a seasonal dummy.

From this, we calculate $b = 1 - (-0.021) \simeq 1$, implying rapid adaptation (within six months), and the value of Φ is estimated as .493, considerably less than unity. Unfortunately, regressing $\dot{W}_t$ on itself gives rise to nasty econometric problems: the estimates of neither the coefficients (and their standard errors) nor the Durbin-Watson statistic can be trusted. Consequently, a second method has been developed.

In this second method, a set of $\dot{P}^e$ series is constructed, one for each of a range of values of b, from $b = .1, b = .2, \ldots, b = 1$. A set of Phillips curves, one for each $\dot{P}^e$, is then estimated. The Phillips curve, with its associated values of Φ and b, is then chosen that has the highest R^2. Thus, Vanderkamp, using quarterly Canadian data for the period 1949-68, found this best-fitting Phillips curve to be based on a $\dot{P}^e$ series constructed with $b = .3$.[61] This implies rather slow adaptation. To illustrate: if the economy switched to a new, steady rate of inflation, it would be about ten quarters before inflationary expectations caught up. The value of Φ in this case was estimated at .91, insignificantly different from unity. Using a similar method with postwar quarterly American data, Solow obtains a similar value for the speed of adaptation, $b = .4$. On the other hand, his estimate of Φ is only .4.[62]

There is thus a wide range of estimates of the speed of adjustment, b, and the extent to which the long-run Phillips curve is or is not vertical, which is given by Φ. It would be dangerous to be dogmatic at this stage. The main requirement is that we understand the issues involved. However, there is one further point to be made that would suggest that estimates of Φ tend to be biased downward. We refer to the issue of simultaneity. A simultaneous system could be expressed thus:

$$\dot{W} = f(\dot{P}, \dot{T}, X)$$
$$\dot{P} = g(\dot{W}, Y)$$
$$\dot{T} = h(\dot{P}, Z)$$

where $\dot{W}$, $\dot{P}$, and $\dot{T}$ are simultaneously determined (or endogenous) variables and
X, Y, and Z are given-from-the-outside (or exogenous) variables.

In this system, we note that $\dot{P}$ has both a direct effect on $\dot{W}$ and an indirect effect—via the third equation—in encouraging $\dot{T}$, which measures increases in union membership and which also pushes up $\dot{W}$. In such a

61. Vanderkamp, "Wage Adjustment," app. B.
62. See R. M. Solow, *Price Expectations and the Behaviour of the Price Level* (Manchester: Manchester University Press, 1969), p. 14.

system, this indirect effect might be quite strong. Thus, Ashenfelter et al. show that taking account of the indirect effect moves their estimate of Φ from 0.37 (see page 435 above) to about 0.75.[63]

12.4 Policy Questions

Assuming for the moment that the Phillips curve does represent a menu for policy choice, what special point on the curve is to be chosen? If we can decide a social preference field for the various combinations of price change and unemployment, the optimal solution follows quite simply. Having transposed the Phillips relation of section 12.3 into one between $\dot{P}$ and U, according to a simple markup pricing assumption, we may superimpose a set of community indifference curves as in figure 12.6. The community indifference curves I_0, I_1, and I_2 are supposed to reflect decreasing levels of collective utility. Both unemployment and inflation have negative marginal utilities and the marginal rate of substitution between the two is negative. The indifference curves are drawn concave to the origin on the assumption that although people are prepared to sacrifice some price stability to reduce unemployment they become progressively less willing to do so as the rate of inflation rises and the level of unemployment falls. Clearly, the highest practicable level of collective utility is attained at point A, yielding the inflation rate $\dot{P}^*$ and the unemployment rate U^*.[64]

63. Ashenfelter, Johnson, and Pencavel, "Trade Unions," p. 49.
64. See R. G. Lipsey, "Structural and Deficient-Demand Unemployment Reconsidered," in A. M. Ross, ed., *Employment Policy and the Labor Market* (Berkeley and Los Angeles: University of California Press, 1965), pp. 210–218.

Figure 12.6   The Optimum Combination of Price Inflation and Unemployment

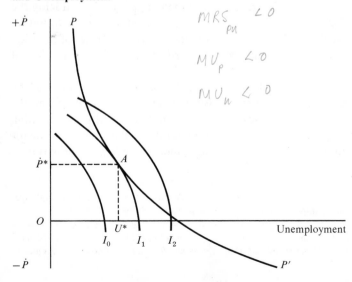

But there are problems with this approach, even if the collective utility function is acceptable.[65] In particular, rather different results are obtained for critical Phillips unemployment levels, depending on the period chosen, the structure of the model, and the additional variables included.[66] Also, given the multivariable explanation in augmented Phillips curve studies, we are faced with a choice not with regard to one point on a more or less stable curve, but with a variety of combinations all of which yield the same rate of wage or price increase. Nevertheless, the approach followed in figure 12.6 illustrates the general principles that must be involved in deciding on policy, given the tradeoff assumption.

If we accept the notion of a long-run Phillips curve, the facts of the tradeoff may nevertheless be unpalatable. For example, full employment may imply the cost of intolerable inflation, and acceptable price stability may require the sacrifice of full employment. The possibility of there being an unsatisfactory tradeoff between $P(W)$ and U has encouraged governments to complement their traditional monetary and fiscal instruments by adding policies designed to shift this tradeoff into more satisfactory politico-economic reaches. These have included wage restraint measures and active manpower policies.

Wage Restraint. Proponents of the monetarist position argue that the inflationary process can be explained mainly in terms of the supply of money. Other policies that may be in operation as part of an anti-inflation package will only have a beneficial effect insofar as they reduce the rate of monetary expansion. On this view, because incomes policies are not institutions of demand management, they can play no role in reducing the rate of inflation. However, it is possible to attribute a useful role to incomes policy on a priori grounds and without resorting to an institutionalist interpretation of the inflationary process. Thus, prices and incomes policy, by reducing the expected rate of inflation, can be an important adjunct to a policy of tighter monetary management. The process of adaptation to lower rates of inflation can therefore be less painful, as was indicated in our earlier discussion of figure 12.4.

There have been numerous forms of wage restraint policy practiced by various governments in recent years.[67] But whatever their specific form, the primary objective of most policies has been the mitigation of price inflation. Given simple wage cost price determination, it follows that prices and factor shares will remain stable when money wages increase in line with the rate of

65. Rothschild, "Phillips Curve and All That," pp. 271–273.
66. See G. L. Reuber, "Comment: The Specification and Stability of Estimated Price-Wage-Unemployment Relationships," *Journal of Political Economy* 75 (1967): 750–754.
67. See L. Ulman, and R. J. Flanagan, *Wage Restraint: A Study of Incomes Policy in Western Europe* (Berkeley and Los Angeles: University of California Press, 1971): D. C. Smith, *Incomes Policies: Some Foreign Experiences and Their Relevance for Canada* (Ottawa: The Queen's Printer, 1966).

growth of average labor productivity within the economy. This suggests a basic rule for wage restraint policy. However, there is the difficulty that, because industries have different rates of productivity growth, a policy of this kind will generally lead to excess demand for labor in some industries and excess supply in others.[68] There is also the problem of implementation. There exist an immense number of individual contracts. Rather than monitor all such settlements, governments have traditionally attempted to reduce what would otherwise be an enormous policing cost by focusing controls on a number of highly visible contracts in the belief that these provide the motive force of an essentially institutional wage transmission process (chapter 13). There is also the problem of exceptions to the productivity guideline, for example, the low paid.

With these considerations in mind, we can now examine whether incomes policy has served to reduce the rate of wage inflation compared to what it otherwise would have been. We will comment upon the British and the American experience in turn.

One of the earliest attempts to take into account the effects of an incomes policy was undertaken by Klein et al.[69] The authors inserted a dummy variable into their wage rate change equations in an attempt to pick up the shift effect resulting from the introduction of the 1948–50 wage restraint interval. The sample period investigated was 1948(1)–1956(4); the shift dummy was assigned the value of zero before January 1952 and unity thereafter. The shift dummy for the incomes policy interval indicated that the annual change in weekly wage rates was 2.9 index number points lower before 1952 than after that year. Phillips, in his original study, also drew attention to the lower-than-predicted value of wage inflation in 1949, which he ascribed to the policy of wage restraint then ruling. Brechling's more recent analysis has also concluded that experimentation with incomes policy over the period 1948–65, applied during the intervals 1948(1)–1950(4), 1961(3)–1962(2), and 1964(4)–1965(4), has had a depressing influence upon the rate of increase of money wages. Specifically, reductions of two, one, and two percentage points, respectively, were estimated.[70]

Lipsey and Parkin have, however, questioned whether the effects of incomes policy can be fully captured by the use of an intercept shift dummy alone.[71] Policies of wage and price restraint might not merely shift the intercept but also change the coefficients (the magnitude of response of $\dot{W}$ to its determinants) and may even substitute new behavior relationships (for example guidepost-following behavior). Indeed, a wage restraint ceiling

68. See K. Lancaster, "Productivity-Geared Wage Policies," *Economica* 25 (1958): 199–212.
69. L. R. Klein, R. J. Ball, A. Hazlewood, and P. Vandome, *An Econometric Model of the United Kingdom* (Oxford: Blackwell, 1961).
70. F. P. R. Brechling, "Some Empirical Evidence on the Effectiveness of Prices and Incomes Policy," in Parkin and Sumner, *Incomes Policy and Inflation*, pp. 30–47.
71. R. G. Lipsey and J. M. Parkin, "Incomes Policy: A Re-appraisal," *Economica* 37 (1970): 115–138.

might tend to become the norm, whatever the circumstances of an industry, with the result that wage change would become much less responsive to market forces. This would be shown by a shift in the wage adjustment function in quadrant IV of figure 12.3 from AA' to, say, BB' during the operation of incomes policy. This change acts to pivot the Phillips curve, as shown in quadrant I.

To test this hypothesis, quarterly data for the period 1948 to 1967 were separated into those quarters when incomes policy had been in operation and those when it had not. Separate regressions were then run for each set of data. The results obtained were as follows ($|t|$ are given in parentheses):

$$\text{Policy off} \quad \dot{W} = 6.672 - 2.372\ U + 0.457\ \dot{P} + 0.136\ \dot{T}$$
$$ (5.79) \quad (3.64) \quad\ \ (6.25) \quad\ \ (0.07)$$
$$R^2 = 0.856$$
$$DW = 1.231$$

$$\text{Policy on} \quad \dot{W} = 3.919 - 0.404\ U + 0.227\ \dot{P} + 3.764\ \dot{T}$$
$$ (2.27) \quad (0.56) \quad\ \ (0.93) \quad\ \ (1.61)$$
$$R^2 = 0.138$$
$$DW = 0.724$$

Looking at the equations, it appears that incomes policy does in fact weaken the relation between $\dot{W}$ and U. We also note that the feedback effect from price changes to wage changes is weakened. But the union aggressiveness variable has its significance increased, which suggests that incomes policy creates a relation between $\dot{W}$ and $\dot{T}$ where none existed before! For the policy on equation, R^2 does not differ significantly from zero. In these periods, therefore, the model does not explain $\dot{W}$. This misspecification is also indicated by the low value of the Durbin-Watson statistic.[72]

Allowing for the feedback effect of wages on prices and assuming a rate of productivity growth of 3% per year, the Phillips curves shown in figure 12.7 can be calculated. The policy off and policy on Phillips curves appear as PP' and YY', respectively. It can be seen that PP' cuts YY' at U_p, which corresponds to 1.8% unemployment. The suggestion is that incomes policy tends to reduce the rate of inflation at levels of unemployment below 1.8%, but to increase it above what it otherwise would have been when unemployment exceeds 1.8%—thereby giving some support to opponents and supporters of incomes policy alike.

This attempt to establish the precise form of the policy-induced shift in the wage equation has generated a series of studies of this problem. Results have been mixed. Hines' results, for example, may be said broadly to resemble those of Lipsey and Parkin. The unemployment effect is, for example, almost

---

72. This means there is a pattern in the residuals, which should be random. The equation is misspecified; there is a missing variable or variables (see chapter 1).

Figure 12.7   The Pivoting Phillips Curve of Lipsey and Parkin

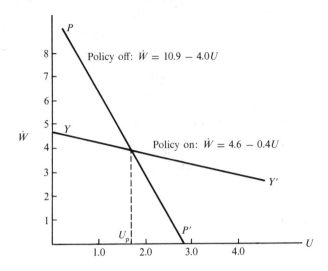

identical. However, his results diverge from Lipsey and Parkin with respect to the unionization effect; Hines finds a significant role for unionization in policy off intervals.[73] On the other hand, Taylor's estimated equations for policy off and policy on intervals do not appear significantly different from the equation for his entire sample period.[74] Thomas and Stoney provide results that mirror those of Taylor, although their analysis does not proceed beyond 1966. On an *F*-test, their policy on and policy off equations can be regarded as the same as those estimated for the entire sample period.[75]

The conclusion then with respect to the British position is that, on the basis of our present knowledge, incomes policy might have had little effect upon either the wage determination process or the average rate of wage inflation. But we cannot conclude that incomes policy has had no significant effects until we have fuller analyses of price formation and the interaction between price and wage formation.

American wage restraint experimentation includes the Kennedy-Johnson guideposts (1963–65) and phases I through IV of wage and price controls instituted by the Nixon administration (1971–74). The guideposts were voluntary in form and set the guide for noninflationary wage behavior as equal to the trend rate of overall productivity increase, namely 3.2%, with no allowance for increases in the cost of living. The second period of incomes restraint was more formal. Phase I of that policy began in August 1971 with a ninety-day freeze of wages, salaries, prices, and rents. At the end of this phase, a more long-range and flexible program was introduced: phase II of

73. Hines, "Determinants of Rate of Change."
74. Taylor, "Incomes Policy."
75. Thomas and Stoney, "Unemployment Dispersion."

the new economic policy allowed for wage and price increases in line with guides that were to be formulated by newly created bodies. With respect to wages, a pay board set the figure of 5.5% as a guideline—the wage criterion adjusted upward to allow for ongoing inflation. In January 1973, the Nixon administration announced phase III of the controls program, which was in effect a switch from mandatory controls to voluntarism. Voluntarism was accompanied by a sharp rise in prices; because of this, there followed another price freeze in June 1973. This lasted one month (for food prices), then a phase IV policy was announced. This represented a return to some of the forms of mandatory controls earlier imposed under phase II; the 5.5% wage increase guideline was, for example, retained.

Let us first examine the impact of the guideposts. Perry has tested the visibility hypothesis.[76] The latter rests on the argument that incomes policy relies heavily on techniques of publicity and censure, so it is likely to have its strongest impact on those wage settlements that are most in the public eye. Classifying a number of American industries into visible and nonvisible categories (according to some criterion of "expert" opinion), Perry found that, for the visible industries, the average annual wage change for the guideposts period of 1963 to 1966 was 2.1 percentage points lower than from 1954 to 1957; for the nonvisible industries, the slowdown between the same two periods was only 0.5 percentage points. Some support for this hypothesis is perhaps also provided by Pierson's results, which show a difference in the behavior of wages between highly unionized and poorly organized industries in the United States during the guidepost era. The slowing of wage inflation was more pronounced in the highly unionized—and therefore more visible(?)—industries.

Other studies conducted during the 1960s again used the dummy variable approach to measure the impact of the guideposts. Sheahan has reported the studies to indicate a downward deflection in the rate of wage inflation of between 0.8% and 1.6% a year.[77] Sheahan's own, essentially case study, approach can be construed as crediting the guideposts with having held wages and prices below what they otherwise would have been. Nevertheless, he offers three factors alternative to the guideposts to account for the relative wage and price stability recorded over the period: a lessening of inflationary expectations following the recessions of 1957–58 and 1960, an increase in competitive pressure from abroad, and a more even pace of expansion, which avoided the inflationary pressure to be associated with differential sectoral growth. More recent quantitative evaluation by Perry also points to a significantly lower intercept term during the guidepost period.[78] On the other hand, as we have noted earlier, there is also the possibility that the slope

76. G. L. Perry, "Wages and the Guideposts," *American Economic Review* 57 (1967): 897–904; Pierson, "Effect of Union Strength."
77. J. Sheahan, *The Wage-Price Guideposts* (Washington, D.C.: The Brookings Institution, 1967), pp. 83–92.
78. Perry, "Changing Labor Markets."

coefficients will vary between periods with and without wage restraint. In fact, it appears that we must reject the assumption of equal slopes in the Perry equation.[79] We might also note that Gordon, using different explanatory variables, has found no significant effect for this shift dummy.[80] In his analysis, disguised unemployment and variations in personal tax rates can explain the modest wage increases of the 1962–65 period without resort to a guidepost shift dummy.

The evidence with respect to the impact of wage-price controls for 1971–74 is also difficult to interpret. Gordon, for example, using equations developed earlier for predicting wages and prices, compares the actual course of wages and prices during the controls period 1971(3) through 1972(2) with the course predicted from the estimating equations. During the controls program, wages increased at the rate of 6.2% per year as compared with the 6.7% predicted by the model. However, prices increased by 2.1% per year, considerably less than the 3.6% which would have occurred according to the estimating equations.[81] Wage restraint is thus estimated to have reduced the rate of wage increase by about .5 percentage points per year, while price controls apparently reduced price increases by much more—1.5 points per year. In a subsequent paper, Gordon extends his time scale to consider post-phase II developments through the third quarter of 1973.[82] His results suggest that controls had no direct effect on wages, given the actual behavior of prices. Here, we might note that positive price effects of the controls program were achieved by constraining prices relative to wages. Restoration of profit margins might be expected to follow, leaving no long-term effects on inflation attributable to that program.

In a wider ranging study of wage restraint, Wachter presents regressions of wage change on the reciprocal of the official unemployment rate and a number of inflation variables.[83] His most successful equation is a regression of $\dot{W}$ upon U^{-1} and the private nonfarm price deflator, entered in distributed lag form. To test for the impact of phases I through IV, the equations estimated for the period 1954(1) to 1972(2) are used to predict the path of wage inflation over the controls period. The results of this exercise suggest that controls did not directly affect the rate of wage change. In fact, the residuals for the period 1971(3) to 1974(2) are positive on average. If controls did affect wages, Wachter thus concludes, they must have worked indirectly by slowing the rate of price inflation.

79. See Oi, "Wage-Price Controls," pp. 23–25.
80. R. J. Gordon, "Wage-Price Controls and the Shifting Phillips Curve," *Brookings Papers on Economic Activity* 2 (1972): 385–421. See also idem, "Inflation in Recession and Recovery," *Brookings Papers on Economic Activity* 1 (1971): 105–166.
81. Gordon, "Shifting Phillips Curve," p. 411.
82. R. J. Gordon, "The Response of Wages and Prices to the First Two Years of Controls," *Brookings Papers on Economic Activity* 3 (1973): 765–778.
83. M. L. Wachter, "The Wage Process: An Analysis of the Early 1970s," *Brookings Papers on Economic Activity* 2 (1974): 507–524.

Research thus points to an insignificant direct impact of incomes policy on wage change in the United States, although the effect on prices is more pronounced. We have suggested that this latter effect might be short-term in nature. Nevertheless, wage and price restraint potentially has an important role to play. Incomes policy, by controlling prices and wages for a period, can reduce not only the current rate of inflation but also the expected rate of inflation. To have this effect, such a policy would have to convince labor market participants that the course of prices while restraint was in force was a good indicator of the likely course of prices when the policy was removed. Expectations might be revised upward again with the dismantling of the controls program, unless this process were accompanied by the introduction of other anti-inflationary measures that the public would expect to moderate the rate of change of prices. But it can still be argued that incomes policy has a significant role to play in speeding up the erosion of inflationary expectations. If incomes policy can succeed in significantly reducing the actual rate of inflation, and if indexation is widely accepted for all nominal contracts, then there is the possibility that appropriate monetary restrictions can be applied without the large-scale dislocations in terms of protracted unemployment that might normally result.

Manpower Policies.   If indeed incomes policy does not form a satisfactory solution in the long run to the problem of achieving low rates of unemployment at tolerable levels of inflation, what alternative instrument is available to policymakers? Many would view manpower policy as providing a realistic basis for a long-run attack on inflation and unemployment by reducing structural unemployment. In other words, manpower policy could favorably affect the position of the Phillips curve. The problem is to distinguish between movements along the curve that will be induced by any increase in the demand for labor and true shifts of the curve. Only the latter permit lower rates of unemployment at a given rate of inflation. Thus, it is important to estimate the impacts of alternative policies that are standardized for the inflationary effects of the policies.

Two main forms of manpower policy may be distinguished. The first accepts the existing characteristics of supply and demand and aims for better matches between workers and jobs by improving placement efforts and by counseling workers looking for jobs and employers looking for workers. Programs of this kind may also include schemes for increasing the mobility of workers. The second attempts to influence the pattern of the supply of labor by upgrading skills and abilities. There is also a third form, which seeks to influence the composition of labor demand by establishing measures to increase the number of employment opportunities, especially by opening up good jobs for disadvantaged groups.

At the outset, we should emphasize that manpower policies are relevant, irrespective of whether or not one believes in the existence of a long-run tradeoff between inflation and unemployment. Those who express a belief in the tradeoff point to manpower policy as an important mechanism to shift that tradeoff favorably. Those who deny the existence of a tradeoff, but believe instead that the economy has a natural rate of unemployment consistent with any steady inflation rate, tie the size of the natural rate to the institutional arrangements of the labor market. The latter evidence union restrictions, minimum-wage legislation, occupational licensing, and unemployment compensation as important institutional barriers that influence the natural unemployment rate; but they would not deny that resources should be allocated to manpower policy up to the point at which that policy yields the ruling social rate of return.

It is clear from the analysis of chapter 11 that the flows through the market are enormous relative to the stocks of unemployment, vacancies, and employment. This would suggest that the efficiency of the public employment service is important if the authorities wish to reduce the level of unemployment for a given level of demand. There are a number of ways in which unemployment could be reduced in this manner, each of which involves either reducing the flow into unemployment or shortening the duration of unemployment. First, the quality of matches between employees and jobs could be improved. This would presumably require a considerable input of counseling, but would also reduce future labor turnover, part of which flows into unemployment, by lowering the probabilities of both quits and layoffs. Second, the search process itself can be made more efficient so that placements are made more easily. One possible solution here concerns the extension of computerization of vacancies or searchers, possibly by liaison with private agencies on a fee-splitting basis.[84] It is not yet clear, however, how the type of information that the employer typically requires about an individual (motivation, discipline, and mental dexterity) can be easily incorporated in a computer file.

Holt et al. have proposed a tripling in the number of counselors and interviewers in the employment service, together with centralization of information about job openings through computerized matching.[85] The overall effect of their proposals would, the authors estimate, reduce by 4% the average time an unemployed worker requires to find a job and would lead to a further 5% decrease in the flow of workers into unemployment through quits and layoffs. These two figures taken together imply a 0.5 percentage point reduction in the level of unemployment, to 4.0%, with the level of inflation held constant.

One problem with this estimate is that the goals of speeding up placements and reducing quits and layoffs are in conflict with one another,

84. For a pessimistic evaluation of the first phase of the American job bank program, see J. C. Ullman and G. P. Huber, "Are Job Banks Improving the Labor Market Information System?" *Industrial and Labor Relations Review* 27 (1973): 171–185.

85. C. C. Holt, C. D. MacRae, S. O. Schweitzer, and R. E. Smith, *The Unemployment Inflation Dilemma: A Manpower Solution* (Washington D.C.: Urban Institute, 1971); idem, "Manpower Proposals for Phase III," *Brookings Papers on Economic Activity* 3 (1971): 703–722.

because the easier it is to find a job, the more likely it is that a worker will quit, and because the easier it is to fill a position, the more likely it is that an employer will lay a worker off. Moreover, we must also consider the fact that many employers may fill jobs without recourse to the external market because of internal labor market structuring, union limitations upon entry, and the phenomenon of queue unemployment. Taking account of these objections, Hall has argued that the scope for improvement along these lines is much reduced; his estimates suggest that faster and improved placement on the lines suggested by Holt et al. would only reduce the aggregate unemployment rate by 0.1 percentage point with the level of inflation held constant.[86]

Differences of interpretation also attach to the second manpower policy instrument, namely the training and retraining of workers. The rationale for these programs is that they raise the employment prospects of workers who otherwise have obsolete skills. The majority of studies relating to training programs have obtained favorable results in the sense that the estimated benefits, predominantly accruing in the form of increased income to the trainee, exceed the estimated costs, comprising the foregone earnings of the trainee and the operating costs of the program.[87] The basic difficulty surrounding such estimates concerns the question of a control group. Thus, to quantify the impact of a training program, it is necessary to compare the earnings and employment experience of those who have received training with those of a control group of similar individuals who have not. Differences between the two groups in education, age, race, and so on are removed by regression analysis. However, it is often the case that the magnitude of the difference is such as to suggest the presence of other differences between the two groups. For example, in a study by Main of a random sample of trainees who had received institutional, as opposed to on-the-job, training under the U.S. Manpower Development and Training Act, no less than 49% of the trainee sample were high school graduates as compared with only 32% of the controls.[88] Thus, motivation, intelligence, and other factors, which the standardizing variables in the regression may not pick up, may have some contribution to make. If differences in motivation, intelligence, and the like are not strongly correlated with observed characteristics, such as education, the impact of training on, say, continuity of employment experience may be seriously overstated.

86. R. E. Hall, "Prospects for Shifting the Phillips Curve Through Manpower Policy," *Brookings Papers on Economic Activity* 3 (1971): 664–668.
87. See, for example, G. G. Somers and W. D. Wood, eds., *Cost-Benefit Analysis of Manpower Policies,* Proceedings of a North American Conference (Kingston, Ont.: Industrial Relations Center, Queen's University, 1969), especially pp. 97–118; A. Ziderman, "Costs and Benefits of Adult Retraining in the U.K.," *Economica* 36 (1969): 363–376.
88. E. Main, "A Nationwide Evaluation of M.D.T.A. Institutional Job Training," *Journal of Human Resources* 3 (1968): 159–170.

However, there is also the question of translating individual effects into aggregate effects. The newly trained worker may displace another worker or, if he was previously employed, another untrained worker may take his place when he moves up the occupational ladder. Hall has attemped to obtain aggregate estimates of the shift in the Phillips curve, with inflation held constant, induced by a training program, using a simple two-sector Phillips curve model and applying estimates of individual effects.[89] He does not find a large improvement in the inflation-unemployment tradeoff as a result.

Finally, let us consider the third manpower policy approach, namely the restructuring of demand for labor under job creation programs. Such schemes have traditionally made little attempt to differentiate between movements along as opposed to shifts in the Phillips curve. A case in point is provided by the 1971 Emergency Employment Act in the United States, under which attention shifted from the disadvantaged to the cyclical problems of rising unemployment. Similarly, despite a substantial redesign of manpower policy in 1973, with the enactment of the Comprehensive Employment and Training Act (CETA), which had as its twin objectives the creation of employment opportunities for the unemployed and for the disadvantaged, the onset of the 1974 recession again shifted the emphasis to countercyclical policy. If a shift in the Phillips curve is to be obtained by a restructuring of demand, then presumably there must be an incentive to provide permanent jobs that are funded by subsidy to close the gap between the wage paid to the unit taking on disadvantaged workers and their productivity. We have earlier argued that subsidies (and taxes) to encourage firms to undertake specific and on-the-job training or to reduce turnover are justified on the ground of the external effects inherent in specific training and the social costs of turnover (chapter 11). The emphasis, therefore, must be upon training. Interestingly, despite its professed goal of increasing the employability of disadvantaged workers, CETA contained little provision for training. Job creation policies geared to this end would be difficult to administer, requiring to be closely tailored to the circumstances of individual placements, and slow to work, because they require the adoption of new production techniques. However, structural problems do not have quick solutions, so that the long time horizon involved should not necessarily deter policymakers.

What then are we to conclude from the foregoing? The strikingly different hopes that Hall and Holt and his colleagues express for future manpower policies illustrate how little hard information is available about the effects of such policies. Their estimates reflect differing views as to how labor markets operate in practice, although there are many sources of agreement. Our own view is that the type of proposals suggested by Holt et al. do have a positive role to play in reducing inflation. But we have little solid evidence to suggest

89. Hall, "Manpower Policy," pp. 679–681.

that recent manpower programs[90] have been effective in shifting the Phillips curve or reducing the natural rate of unemployment.

12.5 Conclusions

There is fairly convincing evidence in favor of the hypothesis that the rate of change of money wages, $\dot{W}$, is related, at least in the short run, to the tightness of the labor market. We have noted that, so long as unemployment is a valid proxy for excess labor demand, the short-run tradeoff can be taken as a valid and independent mechanism in the labor market. Much controversy surrounds the apparent collapse of the Phillips relation in recent years, but the fact remains that the predictive value of the general relation seems fairly acceptable—at least until the mid-1960s. Nevertheless, the explanation of the Phillips relation is less clear-cut. We refer to the bargaining power versus demand-pull controversy. Our objections to the institutional theories of inflation will be documented more fully in chapter 13. Here we simply make the point that much of the evidence supplied by protagonists of the bargaining power hypothesis is consistent with demand-pull. It is true that a number of studies suggest that unions inject a distinct inflationary bias into the system, so that the rate of inflation tends to be higher in the presence of unions for a given level of excess demand. Other studies point to a dampening effect of trade unions. Ordered on a head count, the balance of evidence would favor this latter interpretation. We have attempted to reconcile this predominant view with the findings that unions apparently escalate the reactions of wages to price change by arguing that unionization may well be an endogenous variable determined by more fundamental microeconomic factors. When we turn to consider militancy and strike variables, we have shown that the ambiguities of the empirical literature bedevil the task of arriving at firm empirical generalization. The conclusion is that, pending further theoretical refinement of the union inflation model, it is unwise to discard the view that the traditional union militancy variables are a reflection, rather than a cause, of inflation.

Excess demand theories of inflation provide an entirely plausible explanation of the origins of the inflationary process, provided that the important role of price expectations in determining the actual rate of inflation is explicitly acknowledged. There is little disagreement on the sources of the demand pressure, namely the failure of governments to match higher public expenditure with higher taxes and/or a larger volume of domestic borrowing. Nor should we ignore the international consequences of such behavior in a world of fixed exchange rates, because world excess demand can be transmitted to the domestic economy through both import and domestic prices. Indeed, international inflationary pressures may be sufficient to overcome the deflationary pressure of domestic excess supply.

---

90. For a descriptive treatment of recent manpower programs, see D. Werneke, "Job Creation Programmes: The United States Experience," *International Labour Review* 114 (1976): 43–59.

We note that the Phillips curve is not the most stable of economic relationships. In part, this reflects its widely varying applications. Almost everybody's Phillips curve includes prices and unemployment as determinants of wages. However, beyond these common elements, the various formulations that have been fitted differ substantially with respect to the other explanatory variables included in the estimate, the particular statistics used to represent variables, the mathematical form of the assumed relationships and the form in which the variables are included in the estimated equations, the degree of disaggregation, and the time period to which the models are fitted. Given these differences, it is perhaps more surprising that the differences are not greater than they actually are.

One of the difficult questions to be faced in estimating wage-unemployment relationships is how to allow satisfactorily for the effect of price and wage expectations. There is still a lively debate as to whether the long-run tradeoff between inflation and unemployment is vertical. There are really two empirical questions at issue. First, do wage increases adjust fully in the long run to expectations of price increases? Second, how quickly do price expectations adjust to changes in the actual rate of inflation? The empirical evidence is inconclusive on both questions. Taking the former issue first, it could be argued that a simple head count of study results indicates that wages do not appear to adjust fully to expectations of price increases. But there is a pattern to the empirical findings in that the tendency of studies to obtain a Φ coefficient significantly different from unity appears to diminish the more recent the study. This result has led certain investigators to develop models in which the Φ parameter is allowed to vary in response to changes in the inflationary environment; the argument is that firms and workers might not have paid much attention to the overall expected rate of inflation in setting wages and product prices if the rate of inflation in the past had fluctuated fairly randomly around a mean of zero, but they would have an economic incentive to adjust fully once the price level had developed a noticeable positive trend that was not expected to be reversed. Support for this threshold hypothesis is provided by Eckstein and Brinner and by Gordon,[91] whose results thus permit the natural rate hypothesis to be reconciled with recent American postwar data. Turning next to the speed of adjustment of price expectations to changes in the actual rate of inflation, the balance of the evidence would suggest that the adjustment process is protracted. This result raises somewhat pessimistic implications for the labor market in terms of anti-inflation policy; the less rapidly price expectations are revised downward, the longer will be the period of low capacity utilization and high unemployment consequent upon a reduction in the rate of monetary expansion.

91. O. Eckstein and R. Brinner, "The Inflation Process in the United States," *Joint Economic Committee,* 92nd Congress, 2nd Session, 72-171-0 (Washington, D.C.: U.S. Government Printing Office, 1972), pp. 1–46; Gordon, "Shifting Phillips Curve."

As for the effects of structural changes in the labor market upon the Phillips curve, these have yet to be convincingly demonstrated. The basic problem here is not really one of whether, to take an American example, there has been a changing demographic composition of the labor force toward teenagers and women and away from prime-age men, but whether shifts in the Phillips curve are to be attributed to these developments. If, for example, some expectational mechanism was shifting the Phillips curve adversely during the same period when more women and teenagers were increasing their share of the labor force, the techniques adopted in the literature could attribute to demographics those effects that are actually due to changing expectations.

Some time around the end of 1966, the Phillips curve appeared suddenly to have lost much of its explanatory power. Three main approaches to accounting for the decline in the explanatory power of the model were advanced. First, it was argued that unemployment had ceased to be an adequate indicator of the excess demand for labor. Second, the intensified wage inflation of the 1966–71 period was explained largely in terms of expectations effects, while holding more often than not that unemployment remained the best proxy of excess demand for labor. Third, it was argued that inflation was an international phenomenon such that domestic variables had only the most limited influence. It so happened that fundamental international monetary developments, principally to be associated with the American attempt to finance the Vietnam war by means of budget deficits rather than domestic borrowing, did occur in the mid-1960s. The effects of such developments were held by proponents of the international monetarist model to swamp domestic labor market relations such as the Phillips curve.

The conventional wisdom appears to be that the two latter influences have been dominant, but that the Phillips curve remains viable, even if overshadowed by world inflationary pressures. This interpretation, though comforting, is oversimplistic in our view. Economists of monetarist persuasion have, with the notable exception of Friedman, largely failed to consider their models against the current background of what appears to be a positively sloped Phillips curve. That is to say, one observes situations in recent years of "stagflation" and "slumpflation." These may respectively be defined as a situation in which there is positive inflation for a wide variety of unemployment conditions, and a situation in which an accelerating rate of inflation is accompanied by a rising level of unemployment. Unfortunately, there are no immediate answers available to us in this area. Friedman views the positive association between inflation and unemployment as a transitional phenomenon that will ultimately disappear as market participants adjust both their expectations and their institutional and political arrangements to a new reality.[92] His argument proceeds as follows. A high rate of inflation is unlikely to be steadily maintained during the transition period. Governments

---

92. Friedman, *Inflation and Unemployment*.

do not seek high inflation as a conscious strategy; inflation is a by-product of other policies, such as the pursuit of "over full" employment. However, a burst of inflation produces strong pressures to counteract it. As a result, considerable policy oscillation produces wide variation in the actual and anticipated rate of inflation. A high rate of inflation is therefore a highly variable rate of inflation. Thus, there is great uncertainty within the market, and no one has single-valued expectations. Friedman then argues that an increased variability of actual or anticipated inflation may raise the natural rate of unemployment, thereby tracing out the positively sloped Phillips curve. Increased variability of the actual or expected inflation rate serves to lower economic efficiency and leads to changes in the organization of production—effects that are anyway compounded by the distorting impact of price controls. But the crucial statement in Friedman's treatment is that an increased variability of actual or anticipated inflation may raise the natural rate of unemployment because of heightened uncertainty. However, the link between economic efficiency and the level of unemployment remains a somewhat tenuous one. The question thus arises as to the generality of the monetarist explanation of the inflationary process. Arguably, this controversy could well occupy the forefront of the inflation debate in the years ahead.

Leaving aside this area of the controversy, let us review the discussion of incomes regulation and manpower policy. The debate over whether or not incomes restraint policy is a useful anti-inflation instrument is fraught with difficulty. Those who argue against such policies point to the misallocation of resources that results from restricting variation in relative prices. They argue that a changing economy needs a continually changing set of relative prices in order that the correct signals can be transmitted to the relevant economic agents who then act on the basis of these signals to reallocate resources. The strength of this argument clearly depends on the scale of other disturbances already present in the structure of relative wages and prices. All of us can give examples of the anomalies caused by the introduction of incomes policy. However, those who argue in favor of a prices and incomes policy minimize the misallocation of resources problem, arguing that relative prices are anyway highly stable and that the signals, if they appear at all, are very slow to emerge.

More fundamentally, opponents of incomes policy point out that, because such policies are not instruments of demand management, they can play no role in reducing the rate of monetary expansion and hence in reducing the rate of inflation; they therefore impose welfare costs with no offsetting gain. On the other hand, there are those who argue that incomes policy can short-circuit the relation between $\dot{W}$ and U, thereby enabling the economy to operate at a full level of employment with a lower rate of inflation than would otherwise be the case. There are also more extreme variants of each view. Some would argue that incomes policy, by substituting a new set of behavioral relationships (to be exact, a new adjustment function), may actually increase the rate of inflation over some ranges of demand. Alternatively, there are those of sociological persuasion who would deny the importance of demand in the inflationary process, arguing that wages are determined by social factors and custom (chapter 13), the equivalent of a horizontal Phillips curve. Such observers might attribute an important role to incomes policy by moderating the conventional norm.

Interpretations of the inflationary process that deny the importance of demand are not tenable, but nonetheless a case can still be made for income restraint. In our view, the potential contribution of incomes policy can only be realized within a wider anti-inflation economic package, through which the rate of monetary expansion is brought gradually into line with some tolerable rate of inflation, making sufficient allowance for output growth and secular changes in the velocity of circulation of money. Incomes policy imposed in isolation would, at best, merely lead to pent-up liquidity, the outcome of which, following the termination of that policy, would compound the inflationary problem. Incomes policy may be a useful adjunct to monetary policy, in that it might erode inflationary expectations more rapidly. Thus, if incomes policy can succeed in actively reducing the experienced rate of inflation, and if indexation is widely accepted for all nominal contracts, a policy of reducing the rate of monetary expansion quite substantially, in line with the inflation target, may avoid the excessive search unemployment that would normally result from such a policy.

Less controversy attaches to the principle of manpower policy, although some of the more optimistic results claimed for this instrument require closer scrutiny. For example, the goals of achieving better matches between workers and jobs and of upgrading skills and abilities can be accepted by monetarist and nonmonetarist alike, subject to the standard marginal conditions being satisfied. Perhaps more controversy surrounds the third facet of manpower policy, direct job creation, because of its dualist undertones. The issues involved here have received an airing in chapter 11. But a certain consensus may be reached, once we again recognize that manpower policy is only one component of an anti-inflation package.

APPENDIX 12-A
THE PHILLIPS CURVE AND THE HOLT SEARCH MODEL[1]

Once unemployed, a worker is assumed to have a minimum asking wage. He is seen initially as determining this asking wage by multiplying the wage he had received when he began his previous job, $w(t)$, by his estimate of the rate of growth, over the period of his employment, Tc, of the average money wage rate, $\dot{w}^*$, and by a markup, A, to allow for an initially high aspiration level. Thus, his 'asking wage' would initially be given by

$$w(t + Tc) = w(t)e^{\dot{w}^*(Tc)}A. \tag{12-A.1}$$

As the worker searches without success, he is assumed to reduce his asking wage exponentially at the rate D. Thus, if Tu were the length of time over which he had been unemployed, the worker's asking wage would have become

$$w(t + Tc + Tu) = w(t)e^{\dot{w}^*(Tc+Tu)}Ae^{-DTu}.$$

Dividing through by $w(t)$, we have

$$\frac{w(t + Tc + Tu)}{w(t)} = e^{\dot{w}^*(Tc+Tu)}Ae^{-DTu}. \tag{12-A.2}$$

The resulting term represents the percentage change in the wage rate of the worker in question over the period $Tc + Tu$. If we call the average rate of change of the ith worker's wage $\dot{w}_i$, equation (12-A.2) becomes

$$e^{\dot{w}_i}(Tc + Tu) = e^{\dot{w}^*(Tc+Tu)}Ae^{-DTu},$$
$$\dot{w}_i = \dot{w}^* + \frac{\ln A}{Tc + Tu} - \frac{DTu}{Tc + Tu}. \tag{12-A.3}$$

---

1. C. C. Holt, "Improving the Labor Market Tradeoff Between Inflation and Unemployment," *American Economic Review,* Papers and Proceedings 59 (1969): 144–146.

But Holt assumed that the asking wage was only partially adjusted to $\dot{w}^*$, because some of the worker's work experience might not be transferable and because of the element of uncertainty involved in changing jobs. Thus, introducing a ($0 < a < 1$) to reflect the extent of this adjustment, equation (12-A.3) becomes

$$w_i = aw^* + \frac{\ln A}{Tc + Tu} - \frac{DTu}{Tc + Tu}.$$

Now if $\dot{w}_i$ is aggregated across all workers, ($Tc + Tu$), which is the average turnover period from job to unemployed status back to new job, will be seen to be the inverse of the average turnover rate, H/L (where H is the number of workers hired per period and L is the size of the labor force). Also, the fraction of time unemployed, namely $Tu/(Tc + Tu)$ in the third term, when averaged across all workers, is simply the average unemployment rate, u. Thus, by substitution,

$$\dot{w} = a\dot{w}^* + \frac{H}{L}\ln A - Du.$$

Finally, Holt assumed that $\dot{w}^*$ equalled $\dot{w}_{t-1}$, leaving

$$\dot{w}_t - a\dot{w}_{t-1} = \frac{H}{L}\ln A - Du$$

or, in equilibrium (where $\dot{w}_t = \dot{w}_{t-1}$),

$$\dot{w}_t = \frac{1}{1 - a}\left(\frac{H}{L}\ln A - Du\right). \tag{12-A.4}$$

Thus, we see that equation (12-A.4) closely resembles our modified Phillips curve equation (12.8), particularly if H/L can be assumed to be either a constant or a function of u.

CHAPTER 13
INSTITUTIONAL PROCESSES
IN WAGE INFLATION*

13.1   Introduction

Throughout the postwar period, there has existed a considerable dichotomy of opinion among economists regarding the relative importance of market and nonmarket forces in transmitting inflationary impulses across the labor market. The traditional or orthodox view is that market forces determine both the structure of relative wages and the movement of the general money wage level. Others perceive that the workings of the modern, institutionalized labor market no longer correspond to this orthodox view and that, in particular, *spillover forces* have become the primary transmission mechanism of wage change. Many neoclassical market theorists have responded to this claim with the counter-assertion that the institutionalists have merely diagnosed certain superficial changes in labor market behavior, behind the veil of which the forces of the market operate much as before. For their part, spillover theorists do not believe that this reply gets to the heart of the matter. And so the debate continues.

Let us set the scene for what follows by presenting a formal statement of the opposing hypotheses. We begin with a review of the orthodox market model, which postulates that wage changes for a particular occupation/industry will reflect variations in underlying supply and demand conditions. Assuming that (1) firms are profit maximizers, (2) the labor supply to any sector is a function of its own real wage rate and those obtaining in alternative occupations, and (3) the wage adjustment process is lagged, it can be shown that the market-induced rate of change of wages in sector i will in general be determined according to the following reduced-form equation:[1]

$$\dot{W}_{it}^M = f(\dot{v}_{it}, \dot{w}_{at}, \dot{w}_{it-1}, \dot{P}_t^e)$$
$$f'_{\dot{v}_{it}} > 0, f'_{\dot{w}_{at}} > 0, 0 < f'_{\dot{w}_{it-1}} > 1, f'_{\dot{P}_t^e} = 1 \tag{13.1}$$

---

*This chapter draws on J. Burton and J. T. Addison, "The Institutionalist Analysis of Wage Inflation: A Critical Appraisal," *Research in Labor Economics* 1 (1977): 333–376.

1. See J. T. Addison and J. Burton, "The Identification of Market and Spillover Forces in Wage Inflation: A Cautionary Note," *Applied Economics,* March 1979 (forthcoming).

where $\dot{W}_i^M$ refers to the market induced rate of growth of nominal wages in
   section *i;*
   $\dot{v}_i$ refers to the rate of growth of value-added in sector *i*, measured
   in real terms;
   $\dot{w}_a$ refers to the rate of growth of real wages in alternative sector *a*,
   $a = 1 \cdots m$, $a \neq i;$
   $\dot{w}_i$ refers to the rate of growth of real wages in sector *i;*
   $\dot{P}^e$ refers to the expected rate of growth of the price level; and
$t, t - 1$ are time subscripts.

Institutionalists, arguing that the market explanation ignores the crucial
role of "social factors,"[2] the "force of equitable comparison," and "political
forces,"[3] have proposed an alternative wage transmission process. However,
the terminology used to describe this process has varied widely—spillover,
key bargains, wage leadership, pattern wage adjustment, imitation, and
diffusion—and, not surprisingly, the conceptualization of what we shall term
the spillover transmission process is underdeveloped compared with that
postulated by the market model. Nevertheless, all analyses of this type agree
upon one central issue—that the level of money wages in any sector is
determined by the political comparisons that participants in that sector,
workers, unions, and employers, make with an institutionally given set of
wages in some other reference sector(s). Thus, nominal wage changes are
transmitted across the labor market not by market pressures, but by a
spillover mechanism of the general form:

$$\dot{W}_{it}^S = \sum_{r=1}^{n} \phi_{ir} \dot{W}_{rt} \qquad \phi_{ir} \geqslant 0 \tag{13.2}$$

where $\dot{W}_{it}^S$ is the spillover-induced rate of growth of money wages in sector *i;*
   $\dot{W}_r$ is the rate of growth of money wages in reference sector *r* (W_r,
   $r = 1 \cdots n$, constituting the *reference wage set* for *i*th sector
   participants); and
   ϕ_{ir} is a spillover coefficient, defining the degree of pattern-following
   dependency of *i*th sector wage increases on *r*th sector wage
   increases.

Opinions differed in the 1950s among institutionalists as to the presumed
inflationary effects of their diagnosis. Hicks was led to suggest that the *labor
standard,* as he termed the situation, would not necessarily generate a
continuous rise in the general level of money wages,[4] while Kerr postulated

2. B. Wootton, *The Social Foundations of Wage Policy* (London: Allen and Unwin, 1955).
3. A. M. Ross, *Trade Union Wage Policy* (Berkeley and Los Angeles: University of California Press, 1948).
4. J. R. Hicks, "The Economic Foundations of Wage Policy," *Economic Journal* 66 (1955): 389–404.

that the institutionalization of labor markets muted wage-change reaction to labor market disequilibrium.[5] Others, such as Slichter,[6] were less sanguine, arguing to the contrary that institutional forces imparted an inherent and significant inflationary bias to the workings of the modern labor market. The latter view has come to predominate in the institutionalist discussion of wage inflation. For example, it is claimed that a condition of leapfrogging wage claims generated by institutional pressures has eventuated in a nondamped wage-wage spiral that is a cause, if not a root cause, of the *new inflation* of the contemporary era.[7]

Despite the prominence of institutionalism in the early postwar labor economics literature and the continued prominence of neoinstitutionalist views in many discussions of the contemporary inflation problem, it has failed to dislodge neoclassical economics as the dominant scientific paradigm in the study of wage determination and inflation. We have noted in earlier chapters a neoclassical retaliation to the institutionalist critique, taking the form of human capital theory, labor market search theory, and the new microeconomics. This resurgence has provided neoclassical explanations of many of the empirical phenomena, such as wage dispersion and the skewed distribution of labor market earnings, upon which the institutionalist denigration of the explanatory power of orthodox economics has rested. More particularly, as regards the study of wage inflation, the more widely accepted hypothesis among academic economists has remained the notion that it is market forces that are the root cause of wage inflation (chapter 12).[8]

Why then do we adopt the policy of devoting an entire chapter to institutionalism? In the first place, the institutionalist analysis of wage inflation constitutes a significant and ongoing research tradition in its own right and one, moreover, that has had a profound impact on the discussion of the contemporary inflation problem in political and policymaking circles, as well as in lay discussion of the topic. Second, developments are currently afoot in mainstream economics that are partially conducive to, rather than inconsistent with, spillover hypotheses of wage inflation. We would conjecture that the institutionalist and neoclassical analyses of wage inflation may well become more closely related in the future.

To facilitate exposition, our treatment of institutionalism will first expand upon equation (13.2), which we shall term the *generalized spillover hypothe-*

5. C. Kerr, "Labor Markets: Their Character and Consequences," *American Economic Review,* Papers and Proceedings 40 (1950): 278–291.
6. S. H. Slichter, "Do the Wage-Fixing Arrangements in the American Labor Market have an Inflationary Bias?" *American Economic Review,* Papers and Proceedings 44 (1954): 322–346.
7. See, for example, E. H. Phelps Brown, "The Analysis of Wage Movements under Full Employment," *Scottish Journal of Political Economy* 18 (1971): 233–243; J. Tobin, "Inflation and Unemployment," *American Economic Review* 62 (1972): 1–18; P. Wiles, "Cost Inflation and the State of Economic Theory," *Economic Journal* 83 (1973): 377–398.
8. Initially in the guise of the Phillips curve literature, and more recently in the guise of the new microeconomics-cum-monetarist reinterpretation of that curve as a transient relationship generated by dynamic adjustment processes under conditions of labor market disequilibrium.

sis. Then, in sections 13.3 and 13.4, we shall consider two more-restrictive versions of that hypothesis, namely the *wage leadership* and *wage round* hypotheses. Finally, in section 13.5, we shall summarize the market and institutionalist hypotheses and hint at the outline of a more general framework within which the respective labor market mechanisms appear as but two particular classes of wage adjustment process to be observed in a world of uncertainty and imperfect information.

13.2 The Generalized Spillover Hypothesis

Institutionalists argue that the workings of the spillover process differ fundamentally from those of the market process. What then are the micro-behavioral foundations underlying the sparse formal representation of equation (13.2)? Five principal contenders for this role may be identified: the wage contour hypothesis, the relative deprivation hypothesis, the morale effect hypothesis, the union politics hypothesis, and the threat effect hypothesis. Each hypothesis, and evidence relating to it, is next discussed.

The Wage Contour Hypothesis. According to this interpretation, wages are not set by the interaction of supply and demand, but are instead administered prices. As such, they are determined by the workings of institutional markets, the boundaries of which are set by rules, both formal and informal.[9] While not denying that market forces exert some impact, proponents of this view would argue that these forces work so slowly, and are shut out over such wide ranges of play by the costs of change and the effect of uncertainty, that there is considerable scope for decisionmakers to administer wages according to extramarket criteria, at least within a considerable range that is but loosely constrained by the market. In this view, many companies are visualized as administering their own internal labor markets, the latter being only loosely linked to the external market via certain jobs that fulfill the function of being ports of entry to the internal labor market. The wage rates for these jobs, which are the contact points between internal and external labor markets, have been termed *key rates* and these key rates are hypothesized by Dunlop to lie on one or more *wage contours*.[10] The latter thus constitute a connected locus of key rates. Other rates, specific to the firm, cluster around and follow the movement of key rates, but in a manner that permits considerable discretion because of varying job description and content. Similarly, the key rates are assumed to move together following the pattern set in one or more key bargains (or contracts) negotiated with a leader firm or firms.

A number of studies of intersectoral wage determination processes employing regression techniques have made reference to the origins of their

9. See Kerr, "Labor Markets"; idem, "The Balkanization of Labor Markets," in E. W. Bakke et al., *Labor Mobility and Economic Opportunity* (New York: Wiley, 1954), pp. 92–110.

10. J. T. Dunlop, "The Task of Contemporary Wage Theory," in G. W. Taylor and F. C. Pierson, eds., *New Concepts in Wage Determination* (New York: McGraw-Hill, 1957), pp. 117–139.

postulated model in wage contour concepts.[11] In fact, the wage equations actually estimated in such studies bear only an indirect relationship to the wage contour hypothesis because of their level of aggregation. The hypothesis as formulated relates specifically to the behavior of firms. Studies of *pattern bargaining* in the United States are, however, somewhat more relevant. Detailed case studies of intraindustry behavior relating to the steel and automobile industries, presumed to be the classic cases of the key bargain/ wage contour mechanism in many expositions of the hypothesis, while generally concluding that the evidence favors the existence of key bargains and pattern-following behavior, also find that deviations from the pattern can be considerable, most especially in the case of marginal firms.[12]

As regards the United Kingdom, a recent study of wage interconnections in a local labor market reports clear evidence of key bargain/pattern-following activity in interfirm wage determination.[13] A related study of employer-monitoring activity of wage developments in the external labor market, as revealed by company wage surveys, also provides evidence of key rates.[14] Monitoring activity by firms in the local labor market was concentrated upon the wage rates in other firms for particular classes of potentially mobile employees with general training. However, the identity of firms sampled in wage surveys tended to change through time, sometimes quite radically.

We would conclude that, while evidence certainly exists that may be interpreted as support for the existence of wage contours, the contours that have been delineated by empirical studies do not appear to be immutable. Furthermore, the predictive content of the wage contour hypothesis is by no means clear. Not only is the crucial question of the determination of the key bargain left unclear in treatments of the hypothesis, but also the very nature of a wage contour is ill-defined theoretically. Without further theoretical development, the wage contour hypothesis cannot provide a firm foundation for the institutionalist analysis of wage inflation.

The Relative Deprivation Hypothesis. Relative deprivation is that feeling which is said to arise when individual/group i observes another group r,

11. See O. Eckstein and T. A. Wilson, "The Determination of Money Wages in American Industry," *Quarterly Journal of Economics* 76 (1962): 379–414; M. L. Wachter, "Cyclical Variation in the Interindustry Wage Structure," *American Economic Review* 60 (1970): 75–84; J. D. Sargan, "A Study of Wages and Prices in the U.K. 1949–1968," in H. G. Johnson and A. R. Nobay, eds., *The Current Inflation* (London: Macmillan, 1971), pp. 52–71.

12. See H. M. Levinson, "Pattern Bargaining: A Case Study of the Automobile Workers," *Quarterly Journal of Economics* 74 (1960): 296–317; G. Seltzer, "Pattern Bargaining and the United Steelworkers," *Journal of Political Economy* 59 (1951): 319–331; K. Alexander, "Variations from Pattern Bargaining: A Closer Look," *Industrial Relations* 14 (1959): 211–231.

13. J. T. Addison, "Productivity Bargaining: The Externalities Question," *Scottish Journal of Political Economy* 21 (1974): 123–142.

14. J. T. Addison, "Information Flows: The Employers' View of the Market," *Applied Economics* 8 (1976): 37–57.

$r = 1 \cdots n$ (constituting i's comparative reference group), experiencing something, such as a higher wage than i currently has, which i is also desirous of obtaining.[15] Perception of relative deprivation is intimately related to the process of reference group comparison. The choice of reference groups by i will dictate the magnitude of the relative deprivation experienced by i. This leads Baxter to predict that changes in the selection of reference groups will give rise, via an induced change in the magnitude of relative deprivation, to changes in the level of wage claims.[16] Furthermore, it may be predicted that the larger is $\dot{W}_r$, the greater will be the rate of growth of relative deprivation for i, and hence the larger will be $\dot{W}_i$.

Unfortunately, it is impossible to predict, on the basis of current work in reference group theory, which comparative reference group will be selected by any group of employees. Accordingly, we cannot predict the distribution of relative deprivation or rates of change of relative deprivation.[17]

The Morale Effect Hypothesis. The relative deprivation hypothesis by itself fails to explain how feelings of relative deprivation are translated into wage increases. The morale effect hypothesis provides one such mechanism and is based upon the assumption that labor turnover is costly to the firm, because of hiring costs and firm-specific human capital investments, and also that the cost of policing employee effort is non-zero. If we assume that, when employees become dissatisfied with their job, they react by either quitting the firm altogether or reducing their effort input, it follows that profit maximizing firms have an incentive to avoid deterioration in the morale of their work force. Thus, if wages rise due to expanding demand in one sector of the labor market, the effect on morale in other sectors will lead to a generalization of the wage increase throughout the rest of the economy. Behman found that the quit rate explained 90% of the movement that occurred in the rate of change of straight-time hourly earnings within aggregate American manufacturing over the period 1946–61.[18] This, then, may be one of the mechanisms whereby feelings of relative deprivation induced by wage increases in other employments are brought to bear on the wage determination process, causing sectoral rates of wage inflation to move in line with one another. Although the hypothesis has been termed a "demand-pull plus spillover" model by Rippe,[19] the basis of the analysis is clearly that of a market model

15. See W. G. Runciman, *Relative Deprivation and Social Justice* (London: Routledge and Kegan Paul, 1966). A postscript, "Relative Deprivation and Social Justice: Some Lessons of Hindsight," is appended to the 1972 edition (Harmondsworth, England: Pelican Books).
16. J. L. Baxter, "Inflation in the Context of Relative Deprivation and Social Justice," *Scottish Journal of Political Economy* 20 (1973): 262–282.
17. See J. Burton, "A Critique of the Relative Deprivation Hypothesis of Wage Inflation," *Scottish Journal of Political Economy* 24 (1977): 67–76.
18. S. Behman, "Labor Mobility, Increasing Labor Demand, and Money Wage Rate Increases in United States Manufacturing," *Review of Economic Studies* 31 (1964): 253–266.
19. D. Rippe, "Wages, Prices and Imports in the American Steel Industry," *Review of Economics and Statistics* 52 (1970): 34–46.

of wage determination in which hiring costs and work-effort policing costs are non-zero. As such, the model hardly constitutes a revolutionary challenge to the orthodox tradition in labor economics.

The Union Politics Hypothesis. First proposed by Ross in his seminal study of trade union wage policy,[20] the union politics hypothesis lies firmly within the tradition of the institutionalist analysis of money wage determination. In this treatment of the spillover process, it is assumed that union leaders are concerned with maintaining the size, survival, and growth of the organization they head and upon which their status rests. They are also concerned with the maintenance of their continued tenure in office. Both factors, so the argument runs, will lead union leaderships to attempt to match the wage increases obtained by other leaderships. Failure to match the economic performance of their rivals threatens the prospects of membership loss to more aggressive unions and of growing disaffection among the rank and file, the latter serving to increase the probability of an effective challenge being made to the incumbent leadership from within the union. Thus, wage increases will spill over from union jurisdiction to jurisdiction because of intra- and interunion political factors. Ross furthermore assumes that this process will occur in a manner unconstrained by the employment effects of wage increases, because of the difficulty of estimating the slope and position of the wage-employment tradeoff in a world of uncertainty and the presumed variable and lengthy time lags in the employment effect.

Despite its behavioral insights, the general rate of wage inflation in the unionized sector of the labor market is indeterminate in this model because all spillover coefficients are, by assumption, unity in value and because the wage inflation process is unconstrained by the demand side of the labor market. Indeed, the union politics model does not provide concrete predictions about union wage settlements. Rather, it is to be seen as a theory of the formulation of union wage bargaining goals. With respect to the empirical relevance of the model, it does appear that unionized firms adhere more rigidly to a wage pattern.[21] On the other hand, there is also evidence to suggest that unions do take account of employment effects in formulating their wage policies, often offering downward concessions to marginal firms.[22] Finally, we should note that the union politics hypothesis, by its very nature, can only supply us with a model of the spillover transmission process that is specific to the union sector; it cannot generate any predictions about the be-

20. Ross, *Trade Union Wage Policy.*
21. See M. O. Locks, "The Influence of Pattern Bargaining on Manufacturing Wages in Cleveland, Ohio, Labor Market, 1945–50," *Review of Economics and Statistics* 37 (1955): 70–76; C. Kerr, "Wage Relationships—The Comparative Impact of Market and Power Forces," in J. T. Dunlop, ed., *The Theory of Wage Determination* (London: Macmillan, 1957), pp. 173–193.
22. Shultz and Myers maintain that this response is by no means the exceptional case that Ross would have us believe. See G. P. Shultz and C. A. Myers, "Union Wage Decisions and Unemployment," *American Economic Review* 40 (1950): 362–388.

havior of money wage change in the nonunionized sectors of the labor market.

The Threat Effect Hypothesis. This more promising approach provides a determinate model of spillover wage inflation that embraces the behavior of both union and nonunion sectors, while recognizing the impact of potential employment effects upon the determination of union wage policy.

Assume that the labor market is divisible into a unionized and a non-unionized sector, that the money wage level is uniform within each sector, and that the average money wage level in the two sectors taken jointly ($\overline{W}$) is given as the geometric average of the union wage (W^u) and the nonunion wage (W^n).

The overall rate of inflation within the economy may be approximated by the equation:[23]

$$\dot{\overline{W}}_t = \dot{W}^n_t + m\dot{R}_t + (R_t - 1)\,\Delta m \tag{13.3}$$

where m is the proportion of employees in unions;
  R is the union-nonunion wage ratio, W^u/W^n; and
    the dot and Δ operators refer respectively to the proportional and the absolute rates of growth of the variable to which they are attached.

The conventional procedure adopted in attempting to assess the influence of unions on the movement of money wages has been to compare the movement of W^u with that of W^n, after removing the effect of other variables upon wage changes insofar as this is possible.[24] However, this procedure is only correct if we make the assumption that W^u and W^n are independent of one another. It is the contention of the threat effect hypothesis that this is not the case. To the contrary, it is argued that changes in W^u have a direct and positive spillover effect, a threat effect, on W^n as nonunion employers react to an increase in W^u by increasing their wage offers, in order to reduce the threat of unionization of their work force posed by the initial increase in R.

A formal elaboration of this hypothesis is provided by Rosen,[25] who assumes that nonunion employers will set W^n so as to minimize the expected wage rate $E(W)$ that they face, as given by:

$$E(W) = pW^u + (1 - p)W^n \tag{13.4}$$

23. Given that $\ln R = \ln(1 + d) \simeq d$ for $|d| < 0.3$, where $d = (R - 1)$. As the empirical evidence for the United States would indicate d to be in the order of 0.1 to 0.15 (chap. 8), this approximation is reasonable.

24. Thus A. W. Throop, "The Union-Nonunion Differential and Cost Push Inflation," *American Economic Review* 58 (1968): 79–99, attempts to measure the influence of unions on wage inflation in the United States, 1950–60, by an empirical estimate of the second term in equation (13.3), netting out the influence of R of variations in industry skill mix inter al. Because $\Delta m \simeq 0$ in the 1950s, the last term in equation (13.3) drops out.

25. S. Rosen, "Trade Union Power, Threat Effects and the Extent of Organization," *Review of Economic Studies* 36 (1969): 185–196.

where p is the probability (or threat) of unionization of the firm's work force, and is assumed to be an increasing function of R and m.

It follows that the optimal threat response wage for nonunion employers, W^{n*}, is an increasing function of the union wage rate:

$$W_t^{n*} = x W_t^u \qquad 0 < x \leqslant 1 \qquad (13.5)$$

It is furthermore assumed by Rosen that the union is an optimizing entity.[26] The lower are wages in the nonunionized sector relative to those in the unionized sector, the lower will be the relative costs and selling prices of nonunionized firms and thus the lower will be the demand for the outputs of, and demand for labor in, the unionized sector, and vice versa. Thus, it is predicted that union wages will be positively related to the level of wages in the nonunion sector. Formally, the trade union will adjust to a wage-employment combination in the union sector whereby the union preference function, defined on the wages and employment prospects of its members, is maximized subject to the constraint of the demand curve for unionized labor. The demand curve for union labor will shift to the right if W^n increases. Thus, the optimal union wage, W^{u*}, is an increasing function of W^n, as given by:

$$W_t^{u*} = y W_t^n e^{D^0} \qquad y \geqslant 1 \qquad (13.6)$$

where D^0 is the value of the natural log of the union-nonunion wage ratio that would obtain if y were equal to unity, which makes it a measure of the pure impact effect of unionization; and

e refers to the number e.

From the derived reaction functions (13.5) and (13.6), it follows that the union-nonunion differential will converge on a stable equilibrium R^*, provided $xy < 1$.[27] In the absence of changes over time in x and y, which are the slope parameters of the spillover reaction functions in the nonunion and union sectors, respectively, the equilibrium rates of inflation in the two sectors will be equal. Rosen predicts from the threat model that the slope of the union reaction function varies directly with m, because an increase in m will reduce the elasticity of demand for unionized labor by reducing the possibility of product substitution for unionized sector output (chapter 7). Testing for such a relationship on a cross-section basis for a sample of fifty-nine American industries in 1958 and using union coverage data as a

26. Rosen's approach follows the lines proposed by J. T. Dunlop, *Wage Determination Under Trade Unions* (New York: Kelley, 1950), and is thus sharply delineated from the political model of union behavior espoused by Ross, *Trade Union Wage Policy*.

27. In this situation, the rate of wage inflation will be determined by excess demand factors and price expectations.

proxy for m,[28] Rosen finds strong evidence that the absolute wage level is indeed an increasing function of m. Cross-section and time-series corroboration of the hypothesis is also provided by Ehrenberg and Goldstein[29] and by Ashenfelter, Johnson, and Pencavel,[30] respectively (chapter 8). However, two more recent time-series studies of postwar American data by Flanagan and Johnson are unable to detect a clear spillover effect from the union to the nonunion sector.[31] Rather, their results suggest that the union sector emulates, via the attempt to maintain a desired union differential, the wage movements of the nonunion sector, but not vice versa. Johnson has attempted to reconcile the discrepancies in the time-series findings by arguing in effect that unions were "dominant" over much of the 1914–63 period (the sample period chosen by Ashenfelter et al.) and "relatively stagnant" in the period 1954–75 (the sample period covered in his own study and that of Flanagan). Yet this does not provide an adequate *explanation* of the failure of the threat effect hypothesis in the postwar interval, particularly in view of the fact that Johnson is unable to show that the union to nonunion spillover coefficient is significantly different from zero.

Two further problems attach to the threat effect hypothesis.[32] First, the analysis ignores the supply-side effects of relative wage changes. An increase in W^u will, *ceteris paribus*, reduce employment in the union sector and increase the number of job applications in the nonunion sector. This effect, by creating a downward pressure on W^n, runs counter to the threat effect. Second, the conceptualization of the probability of unionization function is incomplete. If we are to be consistent in our application of rational choice theory, p is not only a function of the returns to union entry but also of the costs of entry, and the costs and returns to the existing membership of admitting further members (chapter 7).

13.3 The Wage Leadership Hypothesis

The wage leadership hypothesis postulates that reference wage sets are neither large nor variable across the labor market. All wage comparisons are

---

28. The Bureau of Labor Statistics classifies an establishment as covered by a union if more than 50% of employees are union members. Union coverage data is thus an imperfect surrogate for m.

29. R. G. Ehrenberg and G. S. Goldstein, "A Model of Public Sector Wage Determination," *Journal of Urban Economics* 2 (1975): 223–245.

30. O. C. Ashenfelter, G. E. Johnson, and J. H. Pencavel, "Trade Unions and the Rate of Change of Money Wages in United States Manufacturing Industry," *Review of Economic Studies* 39 (1972): 27–54.

31. R. J. Flanagan, "Wage Interdependence in Unionized Labor Markets," *Brookings Papers on Economic Activity* 3 (1973): 635–673; G. E. Johnson, "The Determination of Wages in the Union and Nonunion Sectors," *British Journal of Industrial Relations* 15 (1977): 211–225.

32. Ashenfelter, Johnson, and Pencavel, "Trade Unions," assume that the slope parameter of the union wage reaction function is an increasing function of the proportional rate of growth of union membership and the strike rate. The difficulties attaching to such arguments were discussed in chapter 12.

assumed to be made with respect to one singular leading sector in the spillover system, or a select key group of mutual leading sectors. Thus, equation (13.2) simplifies to:

$$\dot{W}_{it}^{s} = \phi_{iL} \, \dot{W}_{Lt} \qquad \phi_{iL} > 0 \qquad\qquad (13.7)$$

where $\dot{W}_L$ refers to the rate of growth of money wages in the leading sector.

There is no single wage leadership hypothesis, but rather a number of competing hypotheses of this nature.[33] Here, we review three such models.

The National Pattern Bargaining Hypothesis. As regards the United States, the wage leadership hypothesis attracting the most work and interest is that which Snodgrass has termed the national pattern bargaining hypothesis (NPBH).[34] It represents an extension to the national level of the key bargain/wage contour hypothesis discussed in section 13.2. The rate of wage inflation is thus said to be set by a key bargain, or bargains, of national significance and diffused to the rest of the labor market from the leading sector along interconnecting wage contours.

Evidence of this process was first presented by Ross, who found that a group of hard goods industries had received virtually identical wage increases in absolute terms over the period 1939–52.[35] Subsequently, Eckstein and Wilson employed a virtually identical list of eight two-digit industries, comprising the durables manufacturing sector, as their assumed key group in an empirical model of manufacturing wage determination.[36] Key group wages were set by a bargaining process in which the relative opportunity costs of concession (chapter 7) to unions and employers in the key group were related to key group profit and unemployment rates. Nonkey wages in the residual sectors of manufacturing were taken to be determined by industry-specific unemployment and profit rates and also by the rate of wage increase in the key group.

Despite the early success of the key group and nonkey group regressions obtained by the authors, the NPBH hypothesis must be regarded as unsatisfactory for a number of reasons. First, while proponents of the hypothesis appear to be closely agreed on the membership of the key group, no rigorous criteria for classifying an industry as within or without the group has been provided. Indeed, the classification procedure is one of ad hoc judgment.

33. For a classification of the available array of wage leadership hypotheses according to the number, intertemporal constancy, and characteristics of the leading sectors, see Burton and Addison, "Institutionalist Analysis." table 1, pp. 345–349.
34. D. R. Snodgrass, "Wage Changes in 24 Manufacturing Industries 1948–1959: A Comparative Analysis," *Yale Economic Essays* 3 (1963): 177–221.
35. A. M. Ross, "The External Wage Structure," in G. W. Taylor and F. C. Pierson, eds., *New Concepts in Wage Determination* (New York: McGraw-Hill, 1957), pp. 173–205.
36. Eckstein and Wilson, "Money Wages in American Industry."

The significance of this is that tests of the NPBH cannot be replicated using data for other countries, because there are no theoretical guidelines as to precisely what to test. Second, it is nowhere clearly established in the NPBH which contract will function as the key bargain in the key group. All we are provided with is a set of arbitrary postulates.[37] Third, the empirical failure of the NPBH has administered a death-blow to the concept. Eckstein, fitting his model to data for the 1960s, was forced to admit that the much vaunted cohesion of wages within the key group had loosened, while a new spillover channel running from construction to durable manufacturing had apparently developed.[38] Thus, the key group was no longer the key group!

The Industrial Structure Hypothesis. A more fruitful wage leadership approach is that advanced by Wachter[39] and Ross and Wachter.[40] Their model visualizes the economy as being divided into two sectors: a competitive or price taking sector, in which wages respond rapidly to market forces, and an administered sector, possessing features of the Eckstein-Wilson key group,[41] in which prices change only infrequently due to the need to minimize the risk of breakdown of implicit price collusion agreements. This in turn requires that cost conditions are stable over the horizon of the prices-planning period, so there is an incentive to settle for long-term wage contracts and also to offer a wage premium over the competitive sector wage. The latter will insulate the large firms from fluctuations in the aggregate demand for labor by the formation of a worker queue for jobs in the administered sector. The analysis predicts that an increase (fall) in aggregate demand, as proxied by a fall (rise) in unemployment, should lead to a decline (increase) in the dispersion of the interindustry wage structure, as the competitive sector responds more quickly to changed market conditions. Wachter finds this hypothesis to be confirmed by the evidence.

We note that this hypothesis reverses the direction of causation implied under the NPBH; now it is the competitive sector that leads in the wage determination process, and it is the administered sector that reacts sluggishly to changes in its wage premium.

The attraction of the wage structure hypothesis is that, unlike the NPBH, it is based on some sort of theoretical foundation as opposed to ad hoc

---

37. For an elaboration of these points see Burton and Addison, "Institutionalist Analysis," pp. 347–350.

38. O. Eckstein, "Money Wage Determination Revisited," *Review of Economic Studies* 35 (1968): 133–143.

39. M. L. Wachter, "Cyclical Variation in the Interindustry Wage Structure," *American Economic Review* 60 (1970): 75–84; idem, "Relative Wage Equations for U.S. Manufacturing Industries, 1947–67," *Review of Economics and Statistics* 52 (1970): 405–410; idem, "Phase II, Cost-Push Inflation and Relative Wages," *American Economic Review* 64 (1974): 482–491.

40. S. A. Ross and M. L. Wachter, "The Pricing and Timing Decision of Oligopoly Industries," *Quarterly Journal of Economics* 89 (1975): 115–137.

41. Namely, high-wage, capital-intensive oligopolistic industries possessing a high union density.

judgments. Thus, the development and replicated testing of the hypothesis is possible. The hypothesis has thus far been restricted to predicting the relative wage structure of the economy; further research is needed before we can derive predictions from the model with respect to the average rate of wage inflation in the economy.[42]

The Productivity Growth Leadership Hypothesis. Another form of wage leadership model is to be discerned in the work of Turner and Jackson[43] and Jackson, Turner, and Wilkinson.[44] The model in question, which we term the "productivity growth leadership hypothesis" (PGLH), argues that money wages will rise in the leading sector at the same rate as real labor productivity is growing in that sector. However, because money wages in other sectors tend to follow the rate of wage increase in the leading sector, money wage inflation is uniform across the economy. Assuming mark-up pricing in all sectors of the economy, and assuming a constant mark-up, then the rate of price inflation is simply the difference between the rate of growth of productivity in the leading sector and the average growth rate of productivity in the economy.

Given the central assumption of the Turner and Jackson analysis—that the leading sector has the highest rate of labor productivity growth within the economy—then the spillover transmission process and the mark-up pricing assumptions imply a continuous inflation of the general price level. The greater the rate of price inflation, the greater is the difference between the rate of productivity growth in the leading sector and the mean rate of labor productivity growth in the economy as a whole.

While the data provided by Turner and Jackson in support of the PGLH are superficially persuasive, it emerges on closer inspection that the data do not contain any direct measurements of labor productivity growth. However, Eatwell, Llewellyn, and Tarling have conducted an intercountry analysis of the hypothesis that does employ productivity growth data directly.[45] Selecting as the key sectors in each country the three industries that experienced the most rapid productivity growth over 1958–67, they found that 83% of the international variation in wage inflation is statistically explained by this proxy variable for the rate of productivity growth in the leading sector. But the authors obtain this result by excluding one country (the Netherlands) from their sample. When the full sample is employed, the explanatory power

42. See Burton and Addison, "Institutionalist Analysis," p. 351.
43. H. A. Turner and D. Jackson, "On the Stability of Wage Differentials and Productivity-Based Wage Policies: An International Analysis," *British Journal of Industrial Relations* 7 (1969): 3–18; "On the Determination of the General Wage Level—A World Analysis: Or Unlimited Labor Forever," *Economic Journal* 80 (1970): 827–849.
44. D. Jackson, H. A. Turner, and F. Wilkinson, *Do Trade Unions Cause Inflation?*, University of Cambridge, Department of Applied Economics, *Occasional Paper No. 36* (Cambridge: Cambridge University Press, 1972).
45. J. Eatwell, J. Llewellyn, and R. Tarling, "Money Wage Inflation in Industrial Countries," *Review of Economic Studies* 41 (1974): 515–523.

of the equation falls. Indeed, it performs scarcely better than an equation in which the rate of money wage inflation is presumed to be a linear function of the *average* rate of productivity growth in the economy!

The assumptions of the PGLH are also open to dispute. Jackson, Turner, and Wilkinson argue that the basis of the equality between changes in wages and in labor productivity within the leading sector is the existence of kinked demand curves in the leading sector, so that firms maintain stable selling prices and compete by means other than competitive price reductions. However, evidence in favor of the kink hypothesis is not very robust.[46] Moreover, the casual evidence that we have from the contemporary behavior of the computer and calculator industries would hardly suggest that price cutting has become an extinct mode of business competition in rapidly growing industries. Finally, the PGLH fails to examine the impact of *relative* price movements predicted by their model and the prospects that such differential productivity growth patterns may pose for output and employment in the slow growth sectors.

Our analysis of productivity growth leadership would be incomplete without mentioning a recent refinement to that model. We refer to the analysis of the Swedish economists Edgren, Faxen, and Odhner.[47] This model, which relates to the Nordic experience, sets wage leadership in the context of constraints on price movements established by competition in international export markets. Thus, international price movements are central to the Swedish model and occupy a position equal in significance to the productivity growth rate of the leading sector in the wage determination system.

The scenario of the Swedish model is that of a small open economy under a regime of fixed exchange rates. The economy is assumed to be divided into two sectors: an exposed sector, comprising the exporting industries and import-competing industries, and a sheltered (or nontrading) sector. The model does not assume a uniform across-sector mark-up, but makes allowance for fluctuations in the latter within the sheltered sector. The equilibrium growth rate of wages in the exposed sector emerges as the sum of the rate of change in international prices and the rate of change of productivity in that sector. It is assumed that the exposed sector acts as the leading sector in the wage determining system. The rate of wage inflation in the sheltered sector adjusts to equality with that of the exposed sector due to a combination of spillover, market, and collective bargaining (solidaristic wage policy) forces. Inflation, imported via the exposed sector, thus ripples through to the rest of the economy because of the wage-following behavior of the sheltered sector.

46. See G. J. Stigler, "The Kinky Oligopoly Demand Curve and Rigid Prices," *Journal of Political Economy* 55 (1947): 432–449.

47. G. Edgren, K. Faxen, and C. Odhner, "Wages, Growth and the Distribution of Income," *Swedish Journal of Economics* 71 (1969): 133–160; idem, *Wage Formation and the Economy* (London: George Allen and Unwin, 1975).

While more refined than the crude PGLH described above, the Swedish model is not without blemish itself. First, it cannot provide us with a general theory of wage leadership, restricted as it is to the experience of small, open economies.[48] Second, under a system of flexible exchange rates, the premises behind wage determination in the exposed sector are no longer necessarily true. Thus, the domestic rate of inflation of goods traded on the world market may be divorced from international price movements via appreciation or depreciation of the currency. Third, recent evidence suggests that there may not be any necessary connection between the identity of the exposed and leading productivity growth sectors.[49] Summarizing these points, we would argue that the Swedish model is not so much a theory of wage leadership as a theory of the international transmission of inflation in a world of fixed exchange rates.

In conclusion, the discussion of wage leadership hypotheses indicates that the industrial structure hypothesis holds most promise of further development. As for other contenders, the NPBH would appear to be defunct, the PGLH to be refuted, and the Swedish model better understood as a hypothesis about the international transmission process of inflation to a small, open economy.

13.4 The Wage Round Hypothesis

Just as the wage leadership hypothesis is a particular hypothesis about the intersectoral patterning of the spillover system, so the wage round hypothesis is a particular hypothesis about its intertemporal patterning. A wage round comprises the bargaining cycle over which, it is assumed, a bunched sequence of similar settlements will occur, thereby generating a wavelike pattern of wage increases over time. An implication of the hypothesis that has suggested itself to some spillover theorists is that the correct observation period to employ in analyzing the behavior of the spillover system is not an arbitrary time unit, such as a quarter or a year, as is utilized in most empirical models of money wage determination, but the wage round periods themselves, which may be variable in terms of calendar time.[50] Formally, the hypothesis postulates that:

$$\dot{W}^s_{iT} = \phi_{iT}\, \overline{\dot{W}} \qquad \phi_{iT} > 0 \tag{13.8}$$

where T refers to the current wage round period; and
$\overline{\dot{W}}$ is some measure of the central tendency of the general rate of money wage inflation over round T.

48. See W. D. Nordhaus, "The Worldwide Wage Explosion," *Brookings Papers on Economic Activity* 2 (1972): 431–463.

49. See G. Bird, "Explaining the Recent International Acceleration in Rates of Inflation," *Economics and Politics Discussion Paper No. 17* (Kingston-upon-Thames, England: School of Economics and Politics, Kingston Polytechnic, 1974).

50. See Eckstein and Wilson, "Money Wages in American Industry."

We should note at the outset that the wage round hypothesis does not necessarily imply the wage leadership hypothesis. Even if wage rounds are well defined empirically, with an invariant entry pattern to the round, to impute wage leadership exclusively upon the basis of temporal initiation would be to indulge in the *post hoc ergo propter hoc* fallacy. Conversely, neither does the wage leadership hypothesis necessarily imply that an intertemporal bunching of settlements will occur. Nevertheless, the two hypotheses are often blended in practice.

Although the concept of the wage round has perhaps been most fully exploited within the British context (where, despite evidence to the contrary, the conduct of wage claims is often alleged to be as rigidly stylized as the classical ballet),[51] we here propose to restrict our attention to the North American experience. This is because British studies have focused exclusively upon a narrow, descriptive account of repetitive wage patterns. While the early American literature follows a similar methodological course, the approach has increasingly become more sophisticated.

In the years following 1945, many American observers became convinced that the pattern of wage determination within the United States followed a systematic course, with wage increases taking place within fairly clearly defined rounds. We have already noted Ross' finding that a group of hard goods industries received virtually identical wage increases over the period 1939–52.[52] The immediate behavioral limitations of the Ross approach—his study used annual earnings data, which concealed the dating of wage contracts and, moreover, related to the industry level rather than the bargaining unit—were corrected by Levinson[53] and Maher.[54] Levinson argued that wage contracts within a thirty-company sample, 1948–58, conformed to three broad rounds of increase, namely 1946–48, 1950–54, and 1955–58.[55] Within each round, a pattern bargaining sequence was observed, pattern bargaining being defined as the process of negotiating a collective bargaining agreement on the basis of the same or very similar provisions to those established in a prior and key bargain. Levinson's fundamental purpose was

51. The general tenor of the British debate is invoked by the following comment of K. G. J. C. Knowles and D. Robinson, "Wage Rounds and Wage Policy," *Bulletin of the Oxford University Institute of Economics and Statistics* 24 (1962): 270: "The wage round is like the flying saucer: many people are led to believe in its existence, although few would claim to have actually seen it and fewer still to have photographed it."

52. Ross, "External Wage Structure."

53. H. M. Levinson, "Postwar Movements of Prices and Wages in Manufacturing Industries," in *Study of Employment, Growth and the Price Level,* Study Paper No. 21, Joint Economic Committee, U.S. Congress (Washington, D.C.: U.S. Government Printing Office, 1960), pp. 7–13; idem, "Pattern Bargaining: A Case Study of the Automobile Workers," *Quarterly Journal of Economics* 74 (1960): 296–317; idem, *Collective Bargaining in the Steel Industry: Pattern Setter or Pattern Follower?* (Ann Arbor: Institute of Industrial Relations, University of Michigan, 1962).

54. J. E. Maher, "Wage Pattern in the United States, 1946–1957," *Industrial and Labor Relations Review* 43 (1961): 277–282.

55. Levinson, *Collective Bargaining.*

to discover whether collective agreements in the steel industry had acted to establish a pattern or had merely conformed to a pattern over each wage round. Key bargains exceeding the general levels previously achieved elsewhere were attributed either to the steel or to the automobile sector. But toward the end of the period, although the wage round retained its general configuration, some significant deviations occurred as a result of changes in wage contract periodicity. Wage contracts within establishments populating a perceived steel industry orbit were, nevertheless, found to be clustered both in time and in similarity of wage contract provision.

Mather's sample of agreements approximates closely that of Levinson, although it is restricted to the hard goods subset of manufacturing industry. Some twenty-three bargaining units, within eleven such industries, are identified; and their wage contract experience over 1946–57 is examined. Maher argues that wage rates within the sample have changed in very similar fashion and that this "striking similarity" cannot be explained by the productivity forces specified by the competitive model.[56] However, as with the Levinson study, we do observe a relatively wide spread of negotiated increases within each (annual) period, although much the same subpatterns emerge. Maher explains this wage change uniformity in basic industry in terms of the following factors: the interrelationship between basic industries that leads to interdependence (the input-output nexus), similar internal technological and economic constitution that will produce similar responses to external change, the geographical clustering of firms, and the similarity of unions involved and their competition for representation of similar workers causing a common type of response to bargaining stimuli. The result of these factors is that one major criterion is established for wage change in basic industry, namely wage changes in comparable employments. This is held to have led to close conformity to a recognized pattern. The percentage of workers included within class intervals representing the basic industry pattern varies from a low of 31% to a high of 71% and most often 50%. This evidence is considered by the author to confirm his hypothesis of pattern diffusion.

Eckstein and Wilson make use of Levinson's wage round construct in erecting their model of money wage determination in American industry.[57] Their central hypothesis is that wages are determined in rounds of increases: a primary round being located in a key group and a secondary round being generated by spillover from the former sector to the nonkey group. The wage round concept of this study was, as we have noted, borrowed from Levinson; yet Eckstein and Wilson observe five such rounds over the period 1946–58.[58] Moreover, in his follow-up study, Eckstein redefines the wage round as a three-year period. It is this redefinition that constitutes a sharp conceptual

56. For a critique of Maher's analysis, see M. Benewitz and A. Spiro, "Comment," *Industrial and Labor Relations Review* 16 (1962): 122–125.
57. Eckstein and Wilson, "Money Wages in American Industry."
58. The fifth was added "to bring the analysis to the latest date for which data was available"!

break with the earlier model.[59] The argument would seem to be that the wage round mechanism weakened after 1960 to the extent that its replacement by a simple three-year cycle was more appropriate. Yet this very procedure yields poor results after 1963.

The slippage of the Eckstein-Wilson model in the 1960s has led other observers to conclude that the use of wage rounds as the observation period is not so attractive as was originally suggested by the proponents. Perry,[60] Howard,[61] and Howard and Tolles[62] have obtained good fits for American durables manufacturing with wage equations employing adjusted quarterly and annual observation periods, respectively. Furthermore, Reuber, in an analysis of wage adjustments in Canadian manufacturing industry, 1953–66, could find no evidence of a wage round from inspection of the data.[63] He also found that, when the Eckstein-Wilson cycle dates for the United States were incorporated into his model, the coefficients on the dummy variables identifying each wage round were mostly statistically insignificant.

There is apparently only one exception to this general pattern of rejection of the wage round concept in the recent empirical literature on wage inflation in North America. In direct contrast to Reuber's earlier study, Smith has found that the grouping of data on the basis of Eckstein-Wilson American wage rounds substantially reduces the proportion of unexplained variance in his empirical model of Canadian wage determination, when used instead of annual observations.[64] However, as Smith's round model is estimated on the basis of American wage round dates, it is difficult to see how it can provide a durable model of Canadian wage determination at a time when researchers south of the border have increasingly found it difficult to detect a clear or coherent wage round in the American data.

We conclude our survey of the wage round literature with the following observations. First, the methodology of much of the research has been of a primitive nature. The early studies largely represent inductive searches for repetitive patterns and have not sought to clearly delineate spillover causation from market causation. Second, although the studies of entry pattern to wage rounds yield some interesting facts and may even hint at some form of coalition behavior, the mere fact of entry stability does not necessarily have any causal significance. Third, it appears difficult from the data to generate precise and generally acceptable empirical specifications of the wage round;

59. Eckstein, "Money Wage Determination Revisited."
60. G. L. Perry, "The Determinants of Wage Rate Changes and Inflation-Unemployment Trade-Off in the United States," *Review of Economic Studies* 31 (1964): 287–308.
61. W. A. Howard, "Wage Determination and Wage Rounds," mimeographed (Clayton, Victoria: Department of Economics, Monash University, 1974).
62. W. A. Howard and N. A. Tolles, "Wage Determination in Key Manufacturing Industries, 1957–70," *Industrial and Labor Relations Review* 27 (1974): 543–559.
63. G. L. Reuber, "Wage Adjustments in Canadian Industry, 1953–66," *Review of Economic Studies* 37 (1970): 449–468.
64. D. A. Smith, "Wage Linkages between Canada and the United States," *Industrial and Labor Relations Review* 29 (1976): 258–268.

and the element of judgment that this inevitably introduces means that different studies come up with quite different measurements of the round. Finally, even if the latter problem did not arise, the apparent variability of wage round phenomena makes it useless as a forecasting device, which, taken with the generally poor performance of wage determination models using rounds as the selected observation period, means that we must conclude with Kuh that the wage round concept cannot be used as the basis of a durable model of wage determination.[65]

But the central issue is that the wage round is essentially an empirical construct and as such can only be applied to the data in a post hoc fashion. Without a *theory* of the wage round, the concept can only be applied in a retrospective fashion.

13.5   Conclusions

A discernible flaw in much of the institutionalist treatment of wage inflation is the failure of its proponents to establish with sufficient care the logical and methodological foundations upon which their theoretical and empirical arguments rest. The concepts invoked by the institutionalists—contours, relative deprivation, rounds, and so on—emerge on closer inspection to be remarkably flimsy constructs. Similarly, the foregoing analysis has called into question the methodological validity of much of the empirical research undertaken by institutionalists.

A second conspicuous flaw in the institutionalist analysis of wage inflation is the failure of many of its followers, with the partial exception of the developers of the Swedish model, to approach the analysis of inflation in the labor market within the wider context of the interaction of this sector with other sectors of the total economic and politico-economic system. This lacuna is most evident with respect to the institutionalist treatment of the role of the monetary sector in the total inflationary process. Hicks, for example, ignored the monetary aspects of his labor standard—merely observing that "it would be simpler to talk as if 'steps have to be taken' to procure the increase in demand (necessary to sustain the spillover process)."[66] It would indeed be simpler. It would not, however, be acceptable. While institutionalists are as fully entitled to make use of "as if" methodology as any monetarist, it is also a requirement of this methodological position that those who make use of it be prepared to spell out precisely their substantive assumptions in order that the predictions implicit in their arguments may be examined and tested. Accordingly, we maintain that the theory is unsatisfactory if it fails to divulge or announce its assumptions about the velocity and supply of money, and other determinants of aggregate demand.

65. E. Kuh, "A Productivity Theory of Wage Levels—An Alternative to the Phillips Curve," *Review of Economic Studies* 34 (1967): 333–360.

66. J. R. Hicks, "The Economic Foundations of Wage Policy," *Economic Journal* 65 (1955): 393.

Despite these criticisms, it is clear that significant progress has occurred in the institutionalist analysis of wage inflation and that the analysis has contributed positively to the understanding of the inflationary process. Much of this progress has taken place only to the extent that spillover theorists have been prepared to borrow the tools and postulates of orthodox economic theory and establish thereby a solid theoretical basis for their analysis, albeit one enriched by the incorporation of specific institutional assumptions as one or more of the foundation stones in the model building process. Here, we would single out the threat effect hypothesis and the industrial structure hypothesis, both of which make use of the postulates of rational choice theory in the derivation of predictions about the behavior of the spillover system. They have also introduced specific assumptions about the institutional environment that have traditionally been ignored in the orthodox analysis of wage inflation.

And what of the market model? The theoretical basis of the market hypothesis of the wage adjustment process, as described in equation (13.1), is implicitly that of neo-Walrasian economics. In such a model, the labor market is assumed to be atomistic, with all labor market participants acting as wage takers and accepting as given the real and relative wages called out by the "market auctioneer" or "secretary of the market." As the well-known story then unfolds, all participants then compute and write down on "tickets" their optimum demands and supplies of labor of different types at the stipulated array of wage rates. This ticket information, collated and aggregated by the auctioneer, in turn allows him to calculate the excess demand for labor vector that would exist at the preannounced wage structure. If the labor market is not fully cleared, the auctioneer then proceeds to apply the Walrasian price adjustment rule: wages are raised (lowered) in those job markets in which positive (negative) excess demand currently exists. Ignoring problems of dynamic instability and multiple equilibria, this tâtonnement process will eventually home the wage structure onto a general equilibrium situation, whereupon the auctioneer allows actual trading to take place.[67]

It is this frictionless, perfect information model of the wage adjustment process that has inspired much of the heat in the market versus spillover forces controversy. Institutionalists have generally been led to argue that the market approach to wage determination is clearly false because labor markets do not typically resemble auction markets and must rather be seen as institutionalized markets, in which wages are administered either unilaterally by firms or bilaterally by firms and unions in a collective bargaining process.

However, the economic and institutionalist analyses of wage determination become potentially comfortable once we relax the confining assumptions of the tâtonnement model and turn to the new microeconomics that has

---

67. See D. A. Walker, "Competitive Tâtonnement Exchange Markets," *Kyklos* 25 (1972): 345–363.

emerged in economic theory over the last decade or so.[68] The point of departure of the new from the old microeconomics is essentially an acceptance of the institutionalist critique that markets—in particular, labor markets—do not typically behave like auction markets. More specifically, it is conceded by the new microeconomics that: labor market participants do not have perfect information of the entire array of wages and prices in the economy, firms can administer wages, and labor market mobility is a costly and uncertain process. The assumption that the auctioneer bears the costs of finding equilibrium prices and wages is replaced in the new microeconomics literature by the assumption that trading takes place at false or disequilibrium prices and that market participants must themselves bear the cost of the price revision and the resource mobility involved in market adjustment processes.

The new microeconomics is not fundamentally inconsistent with certain basic institutionalist postulates. But where the new microeconomics parts company with the institutionalist analysis is that the former remains within the broad traditions of mainstream neoclassical thought, accepting the rational choice postulate as the foundation stone of the model-building process. Meanwhile, the institutionalist analysis has, with the exceptions noted above, been founded on a selective and ad hoc series of propositions about vague sociological or political forces. As we see it, the institutionalists have made the mistake of ejecting the baby with the bathwater.

Supporters of the new microeconomics, on the other hand, have restricted their analysis to the examination of but one class of possible wage adjustment process, focusing on the search-quit paradigm, in a world of frictions and imperfect information. Consequently, they have largely ignored the spillover phenomena to which institutionalist research has drawn so much attention. Yet Alchian demonstrated long ago that imitative economic behavior, as spillover phenomena are widely conceived to be by institutionalists, although inexplicable in a world of maximizing behavior and perfect information, becomes quite comprehensible once we enter a world of purposive behavior under conditions of market uncertainty.[69] The suggestion is, then, that the new microeconomics does not in its present form provide us with a sufficiently general theory of non-tâtonnement wage adjustment processes.

It is our view that the adjustment mechanisms emphasized by the two schools of thought can indeed be fitted into the same general framework and viewed as but two particular types of adjustment process that we may expect to occur in labor markets characterized by positive information and adjustment costs, and by firm-administered disequilibrium wage rates. A formal model along these lines is presented by Addison and Burton, which erects a

68. See, for example, E. S. Phelps et al., *Microeconomic Foundations of Employment and Inflation Theory* (New York: Norton, 1970).
69. A. A. Alchian, "Uncertainty, Evolution and Economic Theory," *Journal of Political Economy* 58 (1950): pp. 211–221.

general typology of wage adjustment processes in terms of the information production and adjustment activities that underpin them.[70]

To illustrate this model let us first assume that the firm has an expected wealth maximizing motive to follow a wage administration policy that involves the stability over time of an expected wage differential. This policy of maintaining customary differentials is not without either difficulty or cost. Thus, firms do not have perfect information about competitors' wages, or the general wage level, costlessly provided them by an omniscient auctioneer; rather, they must themselves undertake resource consuming *information production activities* to obtain estimates of these uncertain variables. Because it is optimal for firms to make such estimates on the basis of less than perfect information (chapter 5), any *i*th firm's estimate of, say, the general money wage level may differ from the true value of that variable. An underestimate (overestimate) will impose a windfall loss (gain) of income on the firm's employees. It follows that workers have an incentive to undertake their own information production activities, in order to cross-check on the adequacy or accuracy of their employer's wage forecasting and wage administration procedures. If the information so produced leads them to believe that their employer has set the money wage differential below its customary value, this will create an incentive for them to engage in *adjustment activities,* so as to eliminate or minimize the resulting windfall drop in their income. Note that such responses impose costs on the firm, but at the same time provide it with information feedback on the probable downward bias of its actual current wage differential.

Let us now examine these two sets of activities—information production and employee adjustment—in more detail. Information production may be defined as any activity that provides labor market participants with a better understanding of the true probability distributions of uncertain economic variables. Now the new microeconomics literature has emphasized a partic-ular form of information production activity, labelled *search activity,* whereby firms and employees produce information about labor market conditions by direct sampling of job applicants and job vacancies, respec-tively. But, as spillover theorists would inform us, there is another form of information production activity available to both parties. This we shall term *monitoring activity,* namely the production of information about wages elsewhere by indirect means. Labor market participants may, for example, monitor the wage signals relayed over informal information networks in the market, conduct their own wage surveys, or engage agents to undertake such activities on their behalf. As regards the latter mode of monitoring, we note that one of the main services provided by trade unions for their members is the detailed monitoring of wage movements in comparable employments and across the market generally.

70. J. T. Addison and J. Burton, "Wage Adjustment Processes: A Synthetic Treatment," *British Journal of Industrial Relations* 16 (1978): pp. 208–223.

Both search and monitoring involve the devotion of time and other resource inputs, but the input mix and output mix of the two activities differ. Thus, search activity tends to generate, for a given volume of inputs, a relatively larger quantity of detailed nonwage information concerning the heterogeneous characteristics of job vacancies and job applicants than does monitoring activity. Conversely, monitoring tends to generate a relatively larger volume of information about alternative wages than does search. As for the input mix, search involves a higher ratio of time to other inputs than does monitoring.

Now consider adjustment activities. We argue that there are two main classes of such activity. First, employees can adjust to the expected mismatch between expected and actual wage differentials by a class of activities that Hirschman has termed "exit behavior" (chapter 9),[71] typically taking the form of voluntary separations but also including reductions in work effort. It is this type of adjustment activity, specifically quits, that has been singled out in the new microeconomic models. But there is another form of adjustment activity open to employees: the perceived disparity may be brought to the attention of the employer directly, and negotiations opened with him on the wage in light thereof. This latter type of adjustment activity (Hirschman's "voice" mechanism) has largely been ignored in the new microeconomics, although it assumes prime importance in the institutionalist explanation. We shall label the former mode of adjustment activity as *quitting activity* and the latter as *bargaining activity*.

In the light of the above classification, we can erect a general typology of non-tâtonnement wage adjustment processes in terms of the information production and adjustment activities that underpin them. This typology is set out schematically in the matrix of figure 13.1. From the figure, we can now see that the new microeconomic and institutionalist analyses of wage adjustment processes are complementary rather than competitive and contradictory theories of the wage adjustment process. Recall that the paradigm cases of the new microeconomic and institutionalist analyses are the SQ and MB combinations, respectively. These are neither mutually exclusive nor inclusive of the full array of possibilities.

71. A. O. Hirschman, *Exit, Voice and Loyalty* (Cambridge, Mass.: Harvard University Press, 1970).

Figure 13.1   A Typology of Information Production and Wage Adjustment Activities

		Adjustment Activity	
		Quitting	Bargaining
Information Production Activity	Search	SQ	SB
	Monitoring	MQ	MB

On the basis of this much simplified model, we would argue that the crude analytical distinction between economic and institutionalist forces is best dropped. In our view, the more fundamental theoretical distinction is that between the various mixes of information production and adjustment activities. This leads to a consideration of the potentially more fruitful questions: what factors determine the mix of search and monitoring, and of quit and bargaining adjustments, chosen by different labor market participants?[72] Having hopefully whetted the reader's appetite, this is perhaps an appropriate note on which to end.

72. See Addison and Burton, "A Synthetic Treatment," pp. 215-220.

AUTHOR INDEX

SUBJECT INDEX

Ability
  birth order and, 341
  mother's education and, 341
  schooling correlated with, 133, 153
  skewed distribution of, 341
  See also Education; Human capital; School
Activities, time intensive, 80
Act
  Civil Rights, 229, 231
  Comprehensive Employment and Training, 457
  Emergency Employment, 457
  Equal Pay, 230
  Fair employment practice, 229–30
  Fair Labor Standards, 88
  Industrial Relations, 263, 312
  Industrial Training, 150–51
  Manpower Development and Training, 456
  National Insurance, 395
  National Labor Relations, 255
  Redundancy Payments, 309, 326, 395
  Sex Discrimination, 231
  Social Security, 94
  Taft-Hartley, 255, 263, 312
  Trade Union and Labor Relations, 308
  Voting Rights, 203
Added worker hypothesis. *See* Participation
Advertising, help-wanted, 176
Age
  decline of earnings with, 122
  participation and, 93–95
  returns to search and, 174
  human capital and, 119
  unemployment and, 320, 402–3
Airline pilots, union effect on wages of, 242
American Medical Association, 236, 342
Anti-pirating agreements, 331
Apprenticeship
  general training related to, 112
  laborforce coverage of, 311
  restriction of supply and, 311
  See also Closed shop
Arbitration
  development in U.S., 305
  final offer, 262
  "splitting the difference" in, 260

Arithmetic progression, used in economics, 25, 161

Barbers, occupational licensing and, 311
"Bargaining power," concept of, 243
Bargaining zone, concept of, 237
Bias, fault of statistical models, 13, 17, 33
"Boulwarism," in wage bargaining, 261
Budget constraint and labor supply, 72–7
Budget constraint of the firm. *See* Cost

Capital transfer tax, 365
Closed shop
  human capital theory underlying, 206, 214–16, 300
  legislation on, 312
  See also Discrimination
Coal mining, strikes in, 251, 257
Cobb-Douglas production function, 61, 290
Coefficient of multiple correlation, explained, 16
Coefficient of variation, 137
Conciliation, 263
Confidence interval, explained, 9
Contract curve, 238
"Corner" solution, 76
Costs, in the theory of the firm, 40, 42–44
Covariance, explained, 10, 30
Craftsmen
  equal pay and, 209
  pay differential of, over the century, 343–49
  pay differential of, over the cycle, 349–52
  unemployment and, 350–51, 401–2
Cramer's rule, explained, 20, 28
Cyclical changes in economic activity
  discouraged workers and, 103
  participation and, 98, 101, 106
  skill margins and, 349–52
  unemployment associated with, 65, 344–50, 376

Death duties, 365
Degrees of freedom, 11, 15

495